THE NEW POLITICS OF THE BUDGETARY PROCESS

THE NEW POLITICS OF THE BUDGETARY PROCESS

Third Edition

Aaron Wildavsky

University of California, Berkeley

Naomi Caiden

California State University, Los Angeles

 **LONGMAN**

An imprint of Addison Wesley Longman, Inc.

New York • Reading, Massachusetts • Menlo Park, California • Harlow, England
Don Mills, Ontario • Sydney • Mexico City • Madrid • Amsterdam

Acquisitions Editor: Margaret Loftus
Project Coordination: Electronic Publishing Services Inc.
Cover Designer: Sandy Watanbe
Electronic Production Manager: Christine Pearson
Manufacturing Manager: Helene G. Landers
Electronic Page Makeup: Americomp
Printer and Binder: R. R. Donnelley & Sons Company
Cover Printer: Phoenix Color Corp.

For permission to use copyrighted material, grateful acknowledgment is made to the copyright holders on pp. 359–360, which are hereby made part of this copyright page.

Library of Congress Cataloging-in-Publication Data

Wildavsky, Aaron B.
    The new politics of the budgetary process / Aaron Wildavsky, Naomi
Caiden. —3rd ed.
      p.   cm.
    Includes bibliographical references and index.
    ISBN 0-673-52462-0
    1. Budget—United States.   I. Caiden, Naomi.   II. Title.
HJ2051.W483   1996
353.0072′2—dc20   96-29439
                                                             CIP

ISBN 0-673-52462-0

12345678910—DOC—99989796

To

Mary Wildavsky

Gerald Caiden

Contents

Chapter Twelve
The Politics of Radical Reversal   299

Biographical Note*

Aaron Wildavsky

Aaron Wildavsky was born in New York City in 1930, the son of Russian Jewish immigrant parents. He grew up in Brooklyn and graduated from Brooklyn College. He wrote his first book on Australian politics and, following a doctorate at Yale and assistant lectureship at Oberlin College, joined the Department of Political Science, University of California, Berkeley. He remained there for the rest of his life, except for two years as President of the Russell Sage Foundation in New York. At Berkeley, he was Chair of the Department of Political Science, the founding Dean of the Graduate School of Public Policy, and he was also President of the American Political Science Association. He died at his home in Oakland in August 1993. . . .

This brief recital of a life's chronology does not communicate the vibrancy and fullness of the life itself. It was a life of accomplishment, reflected in the publication of hundreds of books and articles. It was a life of intellectual endeavor and enjoyment, a continuous reflection on the interplay of ideas and experience. It was a life of collaboration and research, a perpetual voyage of discovery into political behavior, values, and institutions. . . .

Aaron's mind was restless, tackling fresh issues, inventing new concepts, and mapping out and achieving ambitious agendas for research. His findings and conclusions were written in provocative, lucid, and eminently readable prose. Aaron was a master craftsman whose influence stemmed not least from his expressive use of the English language to capture ideas, arguments, perspectives, and realities of political life and change. . . .

Beyond scholarship, Aaron will be remembered for his personal qualities. Many are indebted to him for acts of kindness and consideration. He was honest and unpretentious. He honored his deeply held values and obligations as a Jew, a citizen, and to his family. He was realistic and yet optimistic. . . .

Through his writings, professional activities, and life, Aaron Wildavsky touched and influenced an extraordinary number of friends, collaborators, colleagues, students, researchers, practitioners, and others. He was generous with ideas, time, resources, attributions, and encouragement.

---

*Taken from Naomi Caiden, "Foreword," in Naomi Caiden and Joseph White, eds., *Budgeting, Policy, Politics: An Appreciation of Aaron Wildavsky.* (New Brunswick, N.J.: Transaction Publishers), 1995, 1–3.

Preface to the Third Edition

For over forty years, Aaron Wildavsky researched, wrote, and spoke about public budgeting. His contribution was to transcend the narrow world of budgeting and to transform its study into a central concern for political scientists. Budgeting was not just a technical realm for experts, but a critical manifestation of politics. For Aaron, budgeting *was* politics, writ large in basic questions of how a society organized itself to determine the relative domains of the public and private, who gained and who lost, who benefited and who paid. What would he have made of the great budget revolution of 1995, if indeed it is a revolution? Would he have welcomed it as a vindication of much of what he had written ever since *The Politics of the Budgetary Process* appeared in the mid-sixties—the over-reaching of government, the need for limits, the restoration of balance? Or would his sharp mind, honest logic, and trenchant wit have analyzed critically a phenomenon in which all is not as it appears, decried accelerating dissensus and polarization, and laid bare hypocrisy, opportunism, and ideological politics? Or would he have taken the progression from the old politics of the budgetary process to the new yet one stage further to confront us with a new vision, a different way of looking at reality, a fresh vocabulary, so that readers would immediately recognize his insight to exclaim "yes, that is how things are!"?

We shall never know the answer to these questions, but we do know that had Aaron Wildavsky lived to respond to the events of the last five years since the last edition of *The New Politics of the Budgetary Process*, he would have taken the moral high ground, sifted the significant from the clutter of detail, related the story with accuracy and the highest standards of scholarship, and produced an understandable, readable, and stimulating account of events. I have endeavored to do the same. While I cannot know how Aaron would have felt and thought about all that has transpired, I have tried to be faithful to his general approach. But in the intervening years since the second edition, while much has remained the same, much has also changed, and what has changed requires in some measure reassessment, a fresh perspective on both past and present.

The Politics of the Budgetary Process responded to V. O. Key's famous question "On what basis shall it be decided to allocate X dollars to activity A instead of activity B?"[1] Aaron's answer was framed in political and behavioral terms. The different aspects of incrementalism combined to portray a world in balance, secured through the unwritten rules observed by its participants. This was the world of classical budgeting, whose norms were annualarity, unity, and balanced budgets.

In *The New Politics of the Budgetary Process*, the balance had gone. The rise of entitlements eclipsed the previous norms, which no longer acted to control the budget. Huge budgets overwhelmed the capacity of government. Dissensus about the kind of society we want and the role of government strained political processes and politicized the budget debate. Appropriations—once the very stuff of budgets—were dwarfed by entitlements which grew without restraint. Developments in processes—the Congressional Budget Act, Gramm–Rudman–Hollings, the Budget Enforcement Act—were all attempts to stuff the genie back into the bottle again, and to restore previously unwritten norms through legislative fiat.

This interpretation of budgetary politics has been challenged. An ongoing debate about the existence of incrementalism in different contexts has been a staple of academic research for decades, with inconclusive results.[2] A recent study of federal budgeting by Roy Meyers questioned whether a "classical" period of budgeting really existed, and suggested a more complicated and dynamic set of strategies and tactics than that present in *The Politics*.[3] More trenchant was the charge by Allen Schick that the focus of analysis was narrow and limited, failing to take account of the broader political context against which budgetary politics in Congress was played out.[4] The closed "classical" world of budgeting was a world of insiders, and the notable growth of spending which was already beginning, even as *The Politics* was being written, reflected greater participation in American political life by groups previously excluded. The expansion of entitlements did not take place simply because of a desire to avoid the appropriations process, or to increase government spending, but in response to perceived demands—even if all of these were not equally fulfilled.

In the preface to the second edition of *The New Politics*, Aaron acknowledged the transformation of the budget process to deal with major policy issues, and the expansion of the budgetary arena to include more participants and more complex political divisions. He wrote about the emergence of a politics of ideology; the looking to budgetary reform to solve political questions; and the necessity for agreement on limits to make the budget process workable again. The current budgetary turmoil reflects these themes, though its outcome is uncertain, but also adds a further dimension to them: an attempt to reverse the domestic role of the federal government and at the same time balance the federal budget.

---

[1]V. O. Key Jr., "The Lack of a Budgetary Theory," *American Political Science Review*, Vol. 34 (December 1940), pp. 1137–40. Reproduced in Albert C. Hyde and Jay M. Schafritz, eds., *Governmental Budgeting: Theory, Process, Politics* (Oak Park, Ill.: Moore Publishing Company), p. 20.

[2]See Joseph White, "(Almost) Nothing New Under the Sun: Why the Work of Budgeting Remains Incremental," in Naomi Caiden and Joseph White, eds., *Budgeting, Politics, Policy: An Appreciation of Aaron Wildavsky* (New Brunswick N.J.: Transaction Publishers), 1995, pp 111–132.

[3]Roy T. Meyers, *Strategic Budgeting* (Ann Arbor, Mich.: University of Michigan Press), 1994, pp. 1–14.

[4]Allen Schick, "From the Old Politics of Budgeting to the New," in Naomi Caiden and Joseph White, eds., op. cit., 133–142.

Neither of these aims is new: The Reagan administration had similar objectives, and the last edition of *The New Politics* covered in detail the deficit issue and the politics surrounding the Omnibus Budget Reconciliation Act (OBRA). Now it is time to add new material to cover developments during the Clinton administration, beginning with the deficit reductions of his first budget in 1993 (Chapter 6), and continuing with the efforts of the Republican Congress to reshape the budget in 1995 through unprecedented cuts in taxes, and mandatory and domestic discretionary spending (Chapter 12). But whenever I thought I had completed the manuscript, some new and interesting development would occur. I was able to take the narrative to the end of January 1996, before the new president's budget. In this wonderland of budgeting, who knows what more awaits us? But books, like budgets, demand closure, if only to be reopened.

We live in an era of limits, and even classics have limits if they are to remain alive and relevant. It has therefore been necessary to cut as well as to add, and also to take account of changing emphasis. Details of earlier reforms, such as Gramm–Rudman–Hollings, are now primarily of historical interest. Some of the arguments and speculation in the second edition have been settled or superseded and deserve less space. What appeared new or astonishing only a few years ago is now accepted, or regarded as only one element in a broader trend.

Yet history is still important. Aaron used to ask, "How do we know where we are, if we do not know where we have come from?" Facts and examples do not lose relevance because they occurred a few, or even many, years ago. For this reason I have tried to retain enough of the experience of budgeting as Aaron observed it for the reader to understand and appreciate his insights. While we may have difficulty in interpreting the present, the past record enables perspective, comparison, and deeper appreciation of consequences.

Another issue is that of opinion. Aaron and I did not always agree, but I have not changed his conclusions. I have also left some of his first-person references as they stood. "I" means Wildavsky. "We" is used in the conventional sense of all of us.

Finally, in order to make the text somewhat easier to follow, the earlier chapters relate the chronology of developments up to 1994, and the previous Chapters 5 and 6 have been merged into a single chapter discussing the development of the budget process during the 1980s. The new Chapter 6 picks up the chronological thread where Aaron left it at the Budget Enforcement Act of 1990, to cover the Clinton budget of 1993. The chapters that follow (entitlements, defense, reform, and the deficit) have been updated: they adopt a more analytical approach. This format avoids the moving backward and forward between present and past, which was often confusing for students or those with little or no background in the subject. The final chapter covers the tumultuous developments of 1995. I think that had I been able to explain what I have done, Aaron would have approved.

Naomi Caiden

Preface to the Second Edition: Expanding the Political Meaning of Budgeting

The first edition of this book was considerably more complex than its older sibling, *The Politics of the Budgetary Process.* The reason was that the process itself had grown more complicated, with much being added and nothing being taken away. The new chapters (Chapters 11 and 12) in this second edition seek to draw lessons about budgeting from the maneuvering around the problem of reducing the deficit. It also seeks to explain the new parts of the budgetary process put in place by the Omnibus Budget Reconciliation Act of 1990 (OBRA). True, this time, a little has been taken away or, like Gramm–Rudman, placed in suspended animation. But much more has been added. Now there are three sequestrations, for instance, instead of one. We could pretend that OBRA doesn't exist. The upside would be that there would be less to learn; the downside, however, would be that for the next five years budgeting would be unintelligible. Are we to study the process that exists or the much simpler one of our distraught imaginings?

Through all the maneuvers, and the maneuvers based on other maneuvers, the same political struggles that animated the first edition of *The New Politics of the Budgetary Process* shine through. There is still deep budgetary dissensus. And these ideological differences about the kind of government and society America ought to have are still being played out through the budget. Only now these conflicts are sharper. Therefore, those who wish to understand politics must acquaint themselves with budgeting if they want to know what is going on.

In *The Politics of the Budgetary Process* I sidestepped the problem of defining "the politics" part by saying that the book was "concerned with budgets as political things" and by focusing on the budget as a record of outcomes and a process of decision making:

> Taken as a whole the federal budget is a representation in monetary terms of governmental activity. If politics is regarded in part as conflict over whose preferences shall prevail in the determination of national policy, then the budget records the outcomes

of this struggle. If one asks, "Who gets what the government has to give?" then the answers for a moment in time are recorded in the budget. If one looks at politics as a process by which the government mobilizes resources to meet pressing problems, then the budget is a focus of these efforts. (p 4)

Because what we-the-people decide to politicize is what constitutes "the political" at any one time, this evasion has merit.[1] Enough time has passed and sufficient experience accumulated, however, to begin to put more flesh on the bare bones of politics.

Whether the nation will gain from the political maneuvering that led to the passage of the Omnibus Budget Reconciliation Act of 1990 is an open question. But I have no doubt that the coexistence of a Budget Summit made up of the congressional leaders of both houses of Congress and top officials of the Bush administration and OBRA are good for analysts of political aspects of budgeting. Evaluating the outcomes in these two arenas will enable us to separate those aspects that the national government leadership agreed on in both arenas from those that were altered in OBRA. Thus we can distinguish between the politics that separates elected politicians from the citizenry and the politics of ideology that separates these politicians from each other.

The question of "Who will bear the cost of change?" is of enduring importance. Senior legislators, especially those on appropriations committees, have come to believe that their committees and the agencies for which they are responsible have been getting short shrift. Therefore, they have succeeded in writing into OBRA "hold harmless" provisions that make them more responsible for changes in taxing and spending they initiate but take them off the hook for changes outside of government (war, famine, flood, depression) they feel cannot control. This withdrawal of responsibility is not as foolish as it sounds. As the continuing debate over the savings and loan collapse indicates, it may be that Americans have been disposed to have government insure them against change (by guaranteeing deposits) while no one worries about who is going to uphold government. Nevertheless, the question of whether it is desirable to have government escape responsibility for what presidents choose to call external changes while citizens must cope with them should be more widely debated than it has been, for it has hardly been discussed at all.

The noticeable speeding up of budgetary reform is convincing evidence that a politics of ideological dissensus is on us. From the Budget Act of 1921 to the Budget Act of 1974 took a little over half a century. Then the act of 1974 was substantially modified as the Gramm–Rudman–Hollings Act (GRH, or Gramm–Rudman in short), with significant new elements added, in 1986, a bare twelve years later. Now OBRA has come a mere four years after Gramm–Rudman. This speed-up, I think, is due to heroic but failing efforts to replace the classical norms of balance, annualarity, and comprehensiveness with new procedures that provide by legislative stipulation what used to be done by informal understandings. The Budget

---

[1]For a discussion of this point in the context of political cultures, see Michael Thompson, Richard Ellis, and Aaron Wildavsky, *Cultural Theory* (Boulder, Colo.: Westview Press, 1990).

Resolutions of the 1974 act, the deficit-reduction targets of the 1986 act, and the stipulated agreements of the 1990 act (containing, for two years at least, the equivalent of both resolutions and reductions) give legal directions providing overall ceilings, divisions among major programatic areas (i.e., between defense and domestic, entitlement and appropriation), and provide pathways for adjusting to new circumstances. The more precise these instructions become, the more they straitjacket the budgetary process, however, the more fragile they are. With basic differences over policy left standing, these surface to weaken and then destroy the most carefully wrought paper plans. Even now, as I write in mid-March 1991, Republicans are talking about holding off on previously agreed tax increases due to the recession and Democrats are using loosely worded portions of OBRA dealing with supplemental spending to bring in items that would not count against the totals they previously agreed to support.

The expansion of the political agenda to include social issues such as abortion, with its budgetary implications for whether government ought to help poor women afford this choice, should make us aware of the desirability of conceptualizing political values more broadly. The old divisions between left and right, liberal and conservative, were useful at a time when the major political cleavage was between supporters of somewhat larger or somewhat smaller welfare programs. Since both Democrats and Republicans are now divided as well over questions of abortion, of defense, and of prayer in schools, it is desirable to have a way of conceptualizing policy differences that accommodates a wider range of issues. That is why I have introduced cultural language carving the political scene into three unequal parts, namely, egalitarians who believe in diminishing power and resource differences among people, hierarchists who wish to maintain differences with the understanding that the individual parts ought to sacrifice for the collective whole, and individualists who wish to substitute self-regulation for authority. If individualists agree with egalitarians that government ought not to regulate people's personal lives, but disagree with egalitarians about the extent and desirability of regulation of economic activity, the pattern of political conflict we observe should now make better sense. If individualists desire limited economic regulation and hierarchists agree, because they want every person to fulfill the duties of his or her station, yet they disagree about the hierarchists' willingness to intervene in individuals' personal lives, we can understand both the rationale behind their coalition in the Republican party and the precarious nature of that coalition should attention shift from economic to social issues.

From the Budget Summit we learn that Republicans wanted lower taxes, thereby enabling their constituents to hold on to more income, and Democrats wanted higher taxes on higher-income people so as to achieve the more egalitarian objectives on which their party is agreed. From OBRA, which opened up the Summit agreement to legislative preferences after House Republicans defeated the Summit, we learn that rank-and-file Democratic members of Congress are more egalitarian than their leaders. No one who listened to the congressional debates over whether the United States should use armed force to make war in the Persian Gulf, or whether having begun with an air war it should begin a ground war, can have failed to notice that the disagreements were not only about the Persian Gulf itself but also about whether such a war, however successful on its own terms, was a lesser priority than redressing inequalities in American society.

Individual leaders do not matter. President Bush's popularity plummeted when he abandoned his promise not to raise taxes, arguing, instead, the greater national need to reduce the deficit. Bush's popularity soared to historic heights when the war ended much sooner and with far fewer casualties than pessimistic forebodings suggested. As Bush stumbled by bringing down on himself maximum disapprobation on the budget, he arose tall during the war when his guidance was both sure and successful. It may be that President Bush's enormous war-gained popularity will confer retrospective validation on his budget-balancing choice, wiping out the fatuity of "read my lips" and replacing it with the vision of "our president doing his best for the country." If the political dissensus theory that animates this book is on the right track, however, the president's personal popularity, except on matters rather directly connected to that war, will not extend to agreement with his less-than-wholly egalitarian views.

If there is now less consensus and more dissensus, how is the budgetary process affected? There should be more disputes over larger amounts that take longer to resolve. And so there have been.

The Politics of the Budgetary Process was animated by a quite different vision of budgeting as an incremental process. This understanding is reflected in Chapter 3 on ". . . Classical Budgeting" under the straightforward rubric that "budgeting is incremental." My major purpose in introducing this term to budgeting was to make readers aware that comprehensive consideration of the budget as a whole, each item compared to all the others, went beyond the possibilities of human calculation. Were it tried, comprehensive calculation would also make agreement on the budget much more difficult. And so, at a time of budgetary dissensus, it has done. The need established by the Budget Act of 1974 to relate total spending to total revenues from the top down has indeed exacerbated conflicts. It does matter greatly when many more major matters are disagreed. Why else would the budget process be so stultified, taking up so much more time and room, often to so little effect?

Consensus means that there is agreement on the budgetary base; when that consensus dissipates, so does incrementalism. Just as the notion of incrementalism depended on the prior existence of a fairly fixed base, which depended on historical continuity, which, in turn, depended on political consensus (see Chapter 3), so budgetary dissensus gravely weakens reliance on the past and opens up policy direction as well as amount of money to change. That is why there is now much more attention to budgeting than before, but by no means more agreement. Just as budgeting was incremental because it was consensual, and consensual because incremental, so dissensual budgeting leads to larger and more rapid changes, which increase disagreement.

Aaron Wildavsky

Dead on Arrival?
A Preface to
The New Politics of
the Budgetary Process

*Confronted with the vast array of figures in the Budget of the
United States, one is likely to think of budgeting as an arid subject,
the province of stodgy clerks and dull statisticians. Nothing could be
more mistaken.*

In introducing the old *Politics of the Budgetary Process* in 1964, I began in all innocence by sharing my most important discovery: Budgeting was interesting. Amazing but true; far from being the preserve of mere technicians, budgeting was the lifeblood of government, the medium through which flowed the essential life-support systems of public policy. No one then seemed to object to being told the obvious.

Today, when budgeting has become the major issue of American national politics, admonitions about its importance, like being told to breathe regularly, have a superfluous air about them—essential but unnecessary. For taxing and spending, resource mobilization and resource allocation, now take up as much or more time on the floors of Congress than all other matters put together. How large government will be, the part it will play in our lives, whether more or less will be done for defense or welfare, how much and what sort of people will pay for services, what kind of society, in sum, we Americans want to have—all these are routinely discussed in budget debates. The importance of conflicts over the size and distribution of the budget—failure to pass a budget on time or at all has become a sign of inability to govern—testifies to the overriding importance of budgeting. Nowadays the State of the Union and the state of the budget have become essentially equivalent.

As the sheer volume of budgeting has risen along with increasingly higher stakes and ever-changing procedures, the need grows apace for an up-to-date account of the new process through which spending decisions are made. As I write (April 1987), there is no contemporary account of how budgets are made. Events have outdistanced all books. Yet I believe a description and analysis of the budgetary process that focused solely on what is happening now would be inadequate, even misleading. Indeed, it is possible to convey an adequate understanding of contemporary budgeting only by comparing it with what has gone before. Since my belief in the indispensability of a historical approach accounts for the organization of the "new" Politics and informs its analysis throughout, the reader should know why I have not simply done the best I could with the budget of the day and left it at that.

What is it that no longer exists and is still with us? The substantial changes in budgeting that have taken place in the last twenty years have not really replaced anything; rather, the new has been layered onto the old. There is more of everything—more programs, more money, more debt, more spending devices, more control mechanisms, more participants, more procedures. It is necessary to know about the past because it is still with us. The decentralized, fragmented, legislatively centered budgeting process that stems from its 200-year-old origins still distinguishes the American budgetary process from that of any other democratic nation. The classic dance of the dollars in the appropriations process (memorialized in Richard Fenno's *The Power of the Purse* and my "old" *Politics*) remains: Spending estimates still wend their way from bureaus to departments to the Central Budget Office to the president to the House, Senate, and conference committees, even if some participants have changed roles and new actors are pushing in different directions.

Appreciation of the new depends on distinguishing it from the old. Deciding how much should be spent in toto, how much revenue ought to be raised, and whether a surplus or deficit would be desirable or possible, for instance, seems straightforward. And so it would be anywhere else. But not in America. Not until 1921 did departmental spending estimates go to the Bureau of the Budget (now the Office of Management and Budget) for review before being sent to Congress for consideration. Not until 1974 did Congress commit itself to pass resolutions establishing targets for total spending and revenues. Not until the late 1970s did the president's budget message, which used to set the starting point for congressional action, cease to perform that function; nowadays it is pronounced "dead on arrival."

Here, in the extreme volatility of the budgetary process, we have another reason for taking a historical approach. No one can say whether the Gramm–Rudman–Hollings Emergency Deficit Reduction and Balanced Budget Act of 1985 (GRH) will remain in force (it is now in limbo). It has survived so far not because it is considered desirable but rather because there is no agreement on more sensible alternatives. Whatever happens, GRH's provisions for counting federal credit toward the deficit or, in the Senate, for requiring offsets (new revenues or spending cuts) in order to raise spending beyond the budget resolution, may matter a good deal. It is also possible for the very newest changes to undo the merely new changes; some argue that the 1974 reforms, such as the requirement that Congress make budget resolutions and therefore set up budget committees, make it more difficult to reach agreement. Amid this flux, it seems wise to hold on to a variety of budget procedures, as history has presented them to us, on the chance that practice may well revert back to what it once was.

Whatever form of exposition is adopted, the major omissions of the old *Politics* must be remedied in the new version. Since entitlements (legal obligations on the Treasury to provide people who qualify with stipulated benefits) now amount to just under half of the budget, no book on the subject should neglect it. Yet, aside from an excellent article by Kent Weaver,[1] there is no generic study of entitlements. Nor is there a chapter in a text that can be considered a guide to budgeting for national defense. I shall remedy these lacks here.

This book begins with a discussion of the multiple meanings of budgeting as well as a description of key terms and actors in the process of resource allocation. In order to compare past procedures with contemporary practices, the second chapter surveys the history of budgeting. Here I emphasize the enduring characteristics (from a devotion to budget balance to fragmentation of power) that distinguish America from other nations, and the failing efforts of reformers to provide through the budgetary process the centralized control absent from U.S. politics.

The third chapter on the classical period, roughly 1946 through 1973—now sufficiently remote to wear the patina of time—presents a summary of salient aspects of budgetary calculations and strategies drawn from the old *Politics*. The point made then was that budgeting is so complex—so many items interacting in numerous ways, involving difficult subjects—that budgeters had to simplify by adopting aids to calculation. Certainly the problem of calculation has not gotten any easier; on the contrary, the growth of government (meaning more programs) and the decline of agreement (meaning more closely contested choices) has made figuring out what to do more difficult. The convergence on past agreements that once constituted the base from which calculations proceeded has been eroded; focusing on incremental departures from the base wavers when one cannot agree on where to start: Is it last year's outlays, the president's budget request, the current services budget, the House or Senate budget resolutions, the conference committee recommendation, the continuing resolution, or what? As annual budgeting gives way to continuous revision, agencies cannot be sure of keeping what they were promised nor, given stalemate among the politicians, can they count on getting funds at the stipulated time. Anyone who doubts the increased complexity of the process itself need look only at the Gramm–Rudman–Hollings sequestration procedures (which call for sequential, across-the-board reductions in budget authority when deficit reduction targets are not met) or at the different Senate and House rules for the 302(a) and 302(b) provisions of the 1974 Budget Act, as amended, that, when implemented, shape the rules under which the budget is broken down in Congress. Without such understanding, one cannot tell which subcommittee can handle what items within certain guidelines, or how amendments from the floor can be considered so that it can be known when proposed laws conform to or depart from the agreed spending total—if one exists.

Students of budgeting are safe in studying budgetary calculations, which have merely become more complex; but surely strategies for securing funds must have changed qualitatively. Yes and no. All the old strategies—from the camel's nose to the cultivation of clientele, as the reader will see—are still with us. As is true of

---

[1]Kent Weaver, "Automatic Government: The Politics of Indexation," typescript, 1986.

the budgetary process itself, new strategies have been grafted on to the old. Strategies based on having the House Appropriations Committee assume the role of guardian of the Treasury, with the Senate acting as an appeals court, have to change when those roles reverse and a newcomer, the budget committees, takes over what is left of guardianship. Participants are bound to have more trouble figuring out the "fair share" for their agency or program when the multiplication of spending sources—loans, loan guarantees, tax preferences, provisions for indexing spending to price changes, annual versus multiyear versus permanent appropriations—makes it so hard to determine who is getting how much. Relationships have to change when the Office of Management and Budget reduces its contacts with agencies in order to conduct continuing negotiations directly with congressional committees.

Chapter 4 provides snapshots of contemporary history that reveal how and why budgetary consensus declined. Entitlements threatened to drive out other spending. Federal credit grew astronomically. Agreements on a balance between revenue and expenditure weakened under the impact of strained economic circumstances and under the theoretical guidance of Keynesian economic doctrine. As economic distress made budget conflicts more severe, other standard practices—agreement on a budgetary base, confining conflicts to incremental departure from that base—began to erode. Reaction to President Nixon's impounding and to Watergate gave Congress reformed procedures under the Budget Act of 1974 but not agreement on how to use them. And the election of Ronald Reagan brought to the fore deep differences over taxation and welfare and defense spending that sharpened budgetary conflict.

The institutional manifestations of this budgetary dissensus, described in the fifth chapter, include transformations in the role of OMB and the appropriations committees and the appearance of the new budget committees. Strategic innovation becomes imperative as agencies and their clientele contemplate new rules of the game. No one and nothing are as they were.

Dissensus, as Chapter 6 shows, brings out both the worst and the best in budgetary procedures. Gimmicks, soft appearances substituting for harsh realities, dismay even those who use them. Across-the-board cuts in GRH substitute for intelligence. Yet there is another side to GRH. When faced with the need to recommend cuts in other programs or tax increases (rather than just asking for more), due to Senate offset provisions, interest-group lobbies begin to engage in previously unheard-of behavior; they become interested in cutting other parts of the budget. Thus an objective that reformers were never able to achieve by exhortation—considering and comparing programs as part of a larger budget—has, for the time being in the Senate, been achieved through the offset mechanism. Were agreement ever reached to limit total spending and to choose the most desired programs within that limit, budget reformers have had a real-life lesson in what to do.

In the seventh and eighth chapters on entitlements, changes in strategies begin to be visible. It is better for program advocates to have funds guaranteed until Congress decides to make a change, than to chance the viscissitudes of the annual appropriations process. It is better for recipients to have their benefits tied to a generous index of rising prices, so that cost of living adjustments are automatic, than to have to ask Congress every year to hold constant the purchasing power of retirees or the unemployed. Unfortunately, such stability for beneficiaries is achieved by risking the instability of government. What is strategically rational for program advocates—indexed permanent entitlements with expanding benefits and beneficiaries—is irrational for budget controllers, who find themselves unable to make large cuts in the relatively small remainder of the budget. Since entitlements make up just under half the budget, freeing them from having to be considered for cuts makes budgeting quite a different game. How to be "entitled" rather than "controllable" is of the strategic essence. Yet there is no budgetary safe harbor. Entitlement status is no guarantee either of rapid growth or of protection against cuts. That is why, in addition to high flyers, I also look at entitlements that failed.

Just as being technically listed as "uncontrollable" in the sense of not being subject to the discipline of annual appropriation does not prevent entitlements from being continuously adjusted, the fact that defense spending takes up the lion's share of "controllable" (i.e., annually appropriated) spending need not signify it will bear the brunt of reductions. But it is large, tempting, and, occasionally, vulnerable.

A chapter on defense spending follows entitlements because it is the second largest type of expenditure. Indeed, with social welfare (mostly entitlements) taking up some 46 percent of total spending, defense 28 percent, and interest on the debt 14 percent, only 12 percent is left for the rest of the budget. These figures constitute the indispensable starting place for any intelligent consideration of contemporary budgeting.

I would be surprised if anyone claims to comprehend fully defense budgeting. Huge dollar figures, long lead times for weapons built out of complex technologies, feast and famine in resources, a rapidly changing world scene, all combine to create confusion. Is there too little oversight or too much micro-management? Are defense managers prevented from doing their best, dragged down by the sheer weight of regulation, or are the services preparing to fight their wars alone so they require much more constraint? All of the above are true under some conditions. As with allegations of "waste, fraud, and abuse" in welfare programs, the general modicum of truth does not tell one where to draw the line between harshness and leniency, initiative and control. If all we care about is having what we need when we need it, and expense is no object, duplication is desirable. Since "how much" affects "what for," the cost influencing the amount and kind of troops and weapons, budgeting is crucial to defense. You tell me: Is it better to learn to live with the faults of defense budgeting, like "goldplating" and "stretchouts," because they are a part of real life and therefore likely to be always with us? Or should we try once again to reform the process, because there has to be a better way? What I can do is explain why every administration complains about the sins of its predecessors and then proceeds to do exactly the same.

The tenth chapter is about proposals for reform of the budgetary process—the line-item veto, constitutional spending limits, statutory balanced budget requirements, and more. The difference between the treatment of reform in the old and new books lies in a much wider perspective. The old *Politics* was virtually bereft of history; although I was astonished at the degree of informal coordination achieved under the old process, I did not pursue its roots in the achievement of balance, annualarity, and comprehensiveness. The new chapter on reform begins with the grave weakening of these norms that once had facilitated coordination of spending and revenue, had lent predictability to budgeting behavior, and had enabled budgeters to minimize their disagreements. Whereas the politics of the old process operated under considerable consensus, so that the importance of agreement on substance was played down, the new politics in a time of dissensus is about grand questions: How much, what for, who pays; in sum, what side are you on? Where before reformers were concerned with improving efficiency and effectiveness in the pursuit of agreed-on objectives, these micro-questions (touched on under such designations as performance budgeting, program budgeting, and zero-base budgeting) now have given way to more solemn macro queries: Can we govern? Is there sufficient agreement among the nation's political elites about what kind of society they want in order to do the one thing every government must do—pass its budget? Reforms look quite different if one assumes that changes in political personalities or in budget procedures will produce consensus, rather than fearing that the political visions separating the contestants are too wide to be bridged by anything less than a fundamental change in political alignments. Since I adhere to the latter position, which stresses ideological dissensus, I am less sanguine than others about budgetary cures for political ailments.

Let me put it this way: When there was (mostly) agreement on the base, the old *Politics* stressed conflict over the increments. The new *Politics* stresses the base because it is often disagreed. Conflict is now about fundamentals.

In one respect, neither I nor the budgetary process can go back to where we once were. *The Politics of the Budgetary Process*, circa 1964, has been praised beyond its merits. The budgetary process then was simple; anyone who stumbled on to budgeting could quickly get a grasp of it. Alas, budgeting is no longer so transparent. I have tried to make understandable such previously unheard of subjects as the ability of the federal financing bank to tumble credit off and on the budget, but I cannot guarantee that others will think so. The importance of federal credit is now so manifest—the credit budget, so to speak, being comparable in total to federal spending—that its dimensions cannot fail to impress. After all, credit is money too. So are tax preferences and other forms of resource allocation that do not appear in the budget.

Nearly a quarter of a century ago, budgeting was different, and so was I. Closer to students in age (and far closer to them in understanding than my confident prose might suggest), I faced no serious problem of selection; everything I knew about budgeting is in that book. Everything. But no more than the budgetary process can shrug off the accretions of time, can I recapture the days when budgeting meant appropriations and everyone, myself included, took for granted the understandings that made procedures seem so simple. In the old volume, politics was mostly internal to the budgetary process itself. Outside forces figured only through the operations of interest groups and the perceptions of participants as they assessed the political moods of the day. The new volume (in which all is entirely new except for one chapter and a few pages on the nature of budgeting) is much more concerned with the impact of external political forces on the budgetary process. The interests are still there, but they are now joined by ideologies connecting individual programs to the general purposes of government. When budgeting was a side-show, albeit an important one, political stability could be taken for granted. Indeed, that stability made budgeting less vital. The emergence of budgeting center stage signifies its increased dependence on shifting political alignments.

When budgeting operated under a hidden consensus, the subject was considered too dull to attract readers. Nine publishers, by my recollection, turned the book down; budgeting was easy to describe but hard to sell. Now that budgeting has acquired some of the interested audience it deserves, the subject unfortunately has become difficult to describe. I hope again to show that the effort to understand is worthwhile. Budget, budget, budget, as members of Congress complain, is all we can do unless and until we Americans once again agree on what kind of society and which sort of government we want.

Aaron Wildavsky

Acknowledgments

Without the extraordinarily favorable reception of the old *The Politics of the Budgetary Process* (Little, Brown and Company, 1964, first edition), I would not have been encouraged to undertake the many studies that have led to this new version. Nor would I have had the material for Chapter 3 on the classical period. Without my collaboration with Carolyn Webber on our *A History of Taxation and Expenditure in the Western World* (Simon and Schuster, 1986), it would not have been possible for me to write the second chapter on the historical development of American budgeting. Without my continuing collaboration with Joseph White on "The Battles of the Budget: From the Last Year of Carter through Gramm–Rudman–Hollings, and Tax Reform," I would not have known enough about contemporary budgeting to write the fourth through the sixth chapters. Without the many papers on entitlements prepared by students in my seminars on budgeting, Chapters 7 and 8 could not have been written. Without the research assistance of Ronald D. Pasquariello, Dean Hammer, and John Gilmore, Chapter 9 on defense budgeting would have been much poorer. Blake Edgar read appropriations hearings so as to supply me with up-to-date versions of budgeting strategies. Readers will benefit by his good taste.

Truly this book, even more than most research, is a collective enterprise. As always, I have benefited from continuing conversation with participants in budgeting. Congressional hearings and GAO reports and the works of scholars have proved invaluable. Far more than in earlier times, I have learned a lot from work by reporters who specialize in budgeting and from periodicals, like the *Congressional Quarterly* and *The National Journal,* that cover the subject. Newsletters—*Inside the Administration* and Stanley Collender's *Federal Budget Report*—and periodic reports from Carol Cox's Committee on a Responsible Federal Budget have helped me understand what is happening as it happens.

After a draft of the manuscript had been completed, I asked Dean Hammer to stand in for all those who did not know about budgeting but wanted to learn. As my lay reader, he helped me simplify my presentation, add material where it was missing, and generally reorganize the manuscript. If I have achieved a level of exposition appropriate to a beginner in the study of budgeting, I owe that to Dean's unremitting efforts to set me straight.

The award for help above and beyond the call of duty goes to colleagues who read the entire manuscript—Naomi Caiden, Mark Kamlet, David Mowery, Jonathan Rauch, James Savage, and Joseph White. They have saved me from many errors and their criticisms have sharpened my perceptions. All of them will have an opportunity in their own work to set the world straight on matters budgetary.

John Ellwood provided a critique of my use of budgetary terms, and Gordon Adams helped improve the chapter on defense. I am grateful to these immensely knowledgeable students of budgeting.

Marie-Ann Seabury edited this book for me with her usual eye for my infelicities. Doris Patton, my secretary, not only typed several drafts of the manuscript impeccably but also prepared research material. No doubt she wondered whether the mountains of note cards would ever diminish. Neither the budget nor budgeting shows any sign of diminishing, so why should studies of the subject decline?

For the first time I am fortunate in having colleagues on the Berkeley campus who are themselves students of budgeting. I am grateful for conversations on the current trends with David Mowery in the Haas School of Business and for a variety of source materials and detailed comments on the last two chapters by John Ellwood in the Graduate School of Public Policy.

Stanley Collender of Price Waterhouse; Robert W. Hartman, Senior Analyst for the Budget Process of the Congressional Budget Office; and Joseph White of the Brookings Institution provided me with detailed comments on Chapters 11 and 12. I am especially grateful to Joe White, who helped me organize these chapters in a more coherent manner. Truly, he has learned more than he was taught. Other reviewers who offered helpful suggestions include: James W. Fossett, State University of New York, Albany; Mark S. Kamlet, Carnegie Mellon University; Alfreda J. Mc-Collough, College of Charleston; Kevin V. Mulcahy, Louisiana State University; David J. Olson, University of Washington; and R. D. Sloan, Jr., University of Colorado, Boulder.

A.W.

I should like to acknowledge the support of California State University Los Angeles in granting sabbatical leave to enable the writing of the third edition, and of Margaret Loftus and her colleagues at Addison Wesley Longman for their encouragement and expertise. I would also like to thank the following individuals, who took the time to review the draft manuscript: John A. Hamman, Southern Illinois University; L. R. Jones, Naval Post-Graduate School; Andree Reeves, University of Alabama; Diane E. Schmidt, Southern Illinois University; Fred Thompson, Willamette University; and Jacqueline Vaughn Switzer, Southern Oregon State College. Their comments and suggestions were greatly appreciated. Finally, I should like to thank Mary Wildavsky for suggesting that I undertake this revision.

N.C.

Chapter
1

Budgeting as Conflicting Promises

*T*he word that originally meant a leather bag or pouch used for carrying money has, through the years, taken on a larger meaning. Today we still find etymological traces of the word "budget" when we hear, for example, about the "budget package" put together by Congress and the president. We have come a long way since the days of carrying the budget by hand, though we may regret it. Not only has the pouch expanded considerably, but it has become rather amorphous. No single document represents "the United States budget." The only document that resembles a formal budget is a book representing the president's preferences—his asking price, so to speak. When we hear that this budget is "unrealistic," we learn that many of these preferences are unlikely to be realized. The same can be said of House and Senate budget resolutions specifying how much should be spent in total, and on major programs, as well as how much revenue should be raised. These, too, may be only pious hopes. In the end, we are left with a variety of pieces of legislation—spending through appropriations, entitlements, credit, tax preferences, and more—that taken together constitute the budget.

What do we mean when we speak about the budget? At one level a budget is a prediction. A budget contains words and figures that propose expenditures for certain objects and purposes. The words describe types of expenditures (salaries, equipment, travel) or purposes (preventing war, improving mental health, providing low-income housing), and the figures are attached to each item. Presumably, those who make a budget intend there to be a direct connection between what is written in it and future events. If requests for funds are granted, if they are spent in accordance with instructions, and if the actions involved lead to the desired consequences, then the purposes stated in the document will be achieved. Budgets thus become links between financial resources and human behavior in order to accomplish policy objectives. Only through observation, however, is it possible to determine the degree to which the predictions postulated in budget documents turn out to be correct.

In the most general definition, budgeting is concerned with translating financial resources into human purposes. A budget, therefore, may also be characterized as a series of goals with price tags attached. Since funds are limited and have to be divided in one way or another, the budget becomes a mechanism for making choices among alternative expenditures. When the choices are related to one another so as to achieve desired goals, a budget may be called coordinated. Should it include a detailed specification of how objectives are to be achieved, a budget also may serve as a plan of work for those who assume the task of implementation. If emphasis is placed on achieving the most policy returns for a given sum of money, or on obtaining the desired objectives at the lowest cost, a budget may become an instrument for ensuring efficiency.

There may be a wide gap, however, between the intentions of those who make up a budget and their accomplishments. Although the language of a budget calls for achieving certain goals, through planned expenditures, investigation may reveal that no funds have been spent for these purposes, that the money has been used for other purposes, that quite different goals have been achieved, or that the same goals have been reached in different ways.

Viewed in another light, a budget may be regarded as a contract. Congress and the president promise to supply funds under specified conditions, and the agencies agree to spend the money in ways that have been agreed upon. (When an agency apportions funds to its subunits, it may be said to be making an internal contract.) Whether or not the contract is enforceable, or whether or not the parties actually agree about what the contract purportedly stipulates, is a matter for inquiry. To the extent that a budget is carried out, however, it imposes a set of mutual obligations and controls upon the contracting parties. The word *mutual* should be stressed because it is so easy to assume that control is exercised in a unilateral direction by superiors (congressmen, department heads, and so on) over those formally subordinate to them. But when an appropriations committee approves some expenditures and not others, when it sets down conditions for the expenditure of funds, the committee is also obligating itself to keep its part of the bargain. A department head (to choose another example) who hopes to control the actions of her subordinates must ordinarily follow through on a promise to support some of their requests or else find them trying to undermine her. A budget thus becomes a web of social as well as of legal relationships in which commitments are made by all parties, and where sanctions may be invoked (though not necessarily equally) by all.

The web of interactions involved in allocating resources suggests the manifold difficulties that may arise during the budgetary process. Agreement is difficult because people want different things (or different amounts of the same things). People may also judge the future differently, partly because they prefer different futures, and this will lead them to disagree about what limits (and opportunities) the group faces. In the household, different guesses about next year's food prices and income will justify buying more or less expensive furniture; in government, different guesses and desires about the next year's inflation and revenues will justify buying more or less expensive battleships. Even people who can agree on what to buy may disagree on who should pay for it. The two incomes in a household could contribute equally to the rent, or the rent could be divided proportionately to the incomes. Each person may attempt to pay less by getting others to pay more. But preferences for different ways of life—for more competition, order, or equality—also play a part. Whether one prefers equality of condition or equality of opportunity—the richer subsidizing the poorer or the poorer trying to work their way up, or some combination of the two to maintain social stability—makes a great difference to one's view of desirable public and, therefore, budget policy.

Budgeting in any group is a process in which various people express different desires and make different judgments. In order to construct agreement on a range of items, group members resort to arguments about what is right and just. Now no one makes these values up; they come out of a worldview, an array of preferences about how people ought to live with other people. When these values are not merely ethereal (e.g., brotherhood) but lead to action—more for them, less for us—we see that budgeting is really about opposing and reconciling different ways of life. Sometimes peoples' preferences are dictated by principles (for example, that each should pay according to his ability; or that she who makes the largest contribution should have the most influence). It is hard to tell when people are sincere in invoking principles, for sometimes a principle is just a convenient excuse for a preference that has some other ground. In either case, ideals are invoked in order to persuade others; we have all been involved in arguments where the "principles" seemed to cause more furor than the action (Who will wash the dishes tonight?) would seem to justify. It is one thing, for instance, to argue that defense or social welfare spending is too high; it is another to contend that it would be morally wrong to provide the funds. More or less is easier to compromise than right or wrong. Because it raises questions about how people should relate to each other, budgeting can encompass disputes larger than their seeming subjects.

The desire not to disappoint or anger others makes planning to ensure that promises are kept important. Agreement in advance on spending (the promises in budget legislation) has two advantages: It bypasses continuing negotiation about each purchase, and it allows each member of the group to plan activities with assurance that the others will cooperate. Budgeting is part of the process of cooperative action in which commitments to contribute resources are joined to commitments as to their use. When promises cannot be kept for a year or more, budgeting breaks down.

Always, in the background, questions of authority—Who has the right to decide for whom?—and legitimacy—Do we trust our institutions to act for us?—overlay each choice. "Papa knows best" is different than majority rule or each person making the best deal. The greater the legitimacy accorded institutions, the more disposed are participants to accept outcomes as authoritative. When consent as well as content have to be hammered out on each and every matter, decision making becomes onerous. The process slows down both because many more choices are likely to be contested and because their significance has been enlarged from "how much" and "what for" to "who has the right to decide."

The budgetary process is further complicated by the many different implications for policy in the budget. There is a fiscal policy implication in which the total amount of spending and its deficit or surplus relationship to revenue are designed to stimulate or restrain the economy—to fight unemployment or inflation. The budget is indicative of the role of government; the budget summarizes the balance between public and private sectors of the economy—that is, what proportion of gross national product (GNP) consists of federal government spending—in short, "how much" federal government we have. The distribution of spending in very broad categories describes the kind of government we want: one that emphasizes military might, or protects the middle class, or helps the poor, or builds for the future. The assumptions in budget resolutions, and action on appropriations or entitlements or tax expenditures, also mean that the budget is a package of thousands of specific programs: how much to invest in airport safety; which people, if any, should receive special nutrition benefits; how many F-16s the air force needs.

All these policies are controversial. Some—unemployment versus inflation, the size of government, emphasis on military or social spending—are those that best distinguish Democrats from Republicans, liberals from conservatives. Yet budget politics need not cleave on these lines alone. Not all Republicans are conservatives; many Democrats are not liberals. The choices in budgeting pose tradeoffs that make it hard to predict all choices from party or ideology. Greater military expenditure, without corresponding cuts in social spending, means bigger government and larger deficits; being a conservative or Republican will not tell a member of Congress whether he or she should prefer budget balance to defense. Party lines will also be blurred by contradictions between different preferences: Liberals usually like defense contracts for their districts; budget balancers can nevertheless like mortgage subsidies; conservatives can see good in social security or food stamps. Nevertheless, knowing a politician's party is a better guide than any other single factor to predict whether he or she is likely to vote for larger welfare and less defense.[1]

Just as it is made up of many policies, the budget also has many meanings according to one's institutional position in the government. To the ordinary citizen, budgeting is both mysterious and simple. It is so hard to understand that its complexity may be ignored in resorting to a simple test of virtue: Can the government balance its books or not? Is it in control of itself? For a federal agency—and for the state, local, and semiprivate organizations largely funded by the federal government—the budget is the irrigation system that provides the water without which an agency and its products would parch and wither. Interest groups may see the many steps of budgeting as opportunities or obstacles and budgeting institutions as allies or enemies. Some parts—an appropriations or authorizing subcommittee—may be "captured," but there are too many centers of decision to capture them all. If interest groups can simply try to get more for their favored programs, their strategies may be straightforward; if the budgetary process is arranged so that desires of various groups conflict—more for one of them means less for others—it is harder for each group to figure out what to do.

For the budget and appropriations committees, budgeting is their purpose and their power; their members must work to preserve that power. Since budgeting often encroaches on the turf of authorizing committees, they may view the budgetary process as a threat and an intrusion. For members of Congress with strong issue preferences that have been stymied by the relevant authorizing com-

---

[1]See James L. Payne, "Voters Aren't So Greedy After All," *Fortune* (August 18, 1986), pp. 91–92.

mittees (committees whose domain is to recommend programs and activities for congressional approval), budgetary action may provide power. The budget resolutions, appropriations, and occasional debt-ceiling increases are trains that must run, and there may not be time to kick off the stowaways. Appropriations especially become targets of opportunity for "riders"—opposition to abortion and military aid to Central American forces, for example. Budget resolutions provide chances for votes on issues that might not otherwise reach the floor (e.g., public works funding or increases in veterans' benefits). For partisans, particularly leaders, of the Democratic and Republican parties, the totals for big programs in the budget resolutions measure their party's influence on the course of American government; short of the actual organization of the two houses (election of the Speaker, committee assignments), no other action is potentially of as great moment to the party leadership. The battle of the budget is the test of generalship. The ability of the parties to stay together in the final encounter (apart from the vote to organize the houses along partisan lines) is now their ultimate test of cohesion.

To those members of Congress who identify with the institution—and this, depending upon the issue and challenge, ranges from a few to all of them—budgeting is a test of Congress. Can Congress choose, can it enforce its will? In short, can Congress govern? The president asks the same questions, slightly changed: "Can I govern the agencies? Can I govern Congress? Can I govern responsibly and maintain public support?" Both president and Congress must ask, "Do we make policy or do the policies control us?" And, "Can any of us control events?"

The complexity of the federal budgetary process—the large numbers of wide-ranging yet uncertain consequences—reveals that the purposes of budgets are as varied as the purposes of the people who make them. One budget may be designed to coordinate diverse activities so that they complement one another in the achievement of common goals. Another budget may be put together primarily to discipline subordinate officials within a government agency by reducing amounts for their salaries and pet projects. And a third budget may be directed essentially to mobilizing the support of clientele groups who benefit by the services the agency provides. Nothing is gained, therefore, by insisting that a budget is only one of these things when it might be any or all of them or many other kinds of things as well.[2] One may, however, adopt a particular view of the budget as most useful for the purposes one has in mind. Without claiming to have found the only right perspective, or to have exhausted the subject in any way, I would like to propose a conception that seems useful in talking about the budgetary process as a phenomenon of human behavior in a governmental setting.

Taken as a whole, the federal budget is a representation in monetary terms of governmental activity. If politics is regarded in part as conflict over whose preferences shall prevail in the determination of national policy, then the budget records the outcomes of this struggle. If one asks, "Who gets what the government has to

---

[2]A good discussion of the nature and variety of budgets may be found throughout Jesse Burkhead's *Government Budgeting* (New York: Wiley, 1956). See also the illuminating comments in Frederick C. Mosher, *Program Budgeting: Theory and Practice, with Particular Reference to the U.S. Department of the Army* (Chicago: Public Administration Service, 1954), pp. 1–18.

give?" then the answers for a moment in time are recorded in the budget. If one looks at politics as a process by which the government mobilizes resources to meet pressing problems, then the budget is a focus of these efforts.

The size and shape of the budget is a matter of serious contention in our political life. Presidents, political parties, administrators, members of Congress, interest groups, and interested citizens vie with one another to have their preferences recorded in the budget. The victories and defeats, the compromises and the bargains, the realms of agreement and the spheres of conflict in regard to the role of national government in our society all appear in the budget. In the most integral sense, budgeting—that is, attempts to allocate scarce financial resources through political processes in order to realize disparate visions of the good life—lies at the heart of the political process. That there are visions of the good life enables people to make commitments to one another through the budget; that these visions conflict means that not all such promises can be kept.

BUDGETS ARE CONFLICTING COMMITMENTS

Our government makes different commitments to people and to other units of government, and these commitments take varied forms. All the commitments ultimately are shaped by law (and therefore by Congress, the president, and the courts). Some of these laws, *appropriations acts,* constitute permission for agencies of the government (e.g., the FBI or National Institutes of Health) to either spend or contract to spend specific amounts of money during the coming year or years. Other laws, such as the 1935 Social Security Act with its numerous amendments, contain promises to individuals that the government will pay specific sums to those who meet certain criteria. These laws, frequently called *entitlements,* differ from appropriations acts in four crucial ways:

1. Entitlements do not specify spending totals. Total spending under these programs, such as unemployment compensation, is simply the sum of the legislatively mandated payments to individuals. Administering agencies may withdraw from the Treasury whatever funds the law and the situation require.
2. Since totals are not legally mandated, they can be "guesstimated" but cannot be known in advance. Actual figures will depend on the number of people who qualify for the program and the amounts to which they are entitled. Payments for unemployment compensation, for example, depend upon both the number of unemployed and their previous base earnings, neither of which can be known exactly in advance. Not only are totals not directly chosen, they can only be known in retrospect.
3. The authority to spend is not limited in time. Rather than being authorized for use in the coming fiscal year, funding is available so long as a program exists; no ending date is established.
4. Unlike the relationship of other agencies to the budget process, the process for creating and amending these programs does not, in any meaningful way, involve House and Senate appropriations committees.

"Once enacted," a Government Accounting Office report summarizes the differences, "entitlement legislation may automatically authorize an administrative agency to spend the funds for making the prescribed payments without advance appropriations from the Congress, thereby effectively relinquishing congressional control through the normal appropriations process."[3] The differences between appropriated and entitlement spending mean that legal authority for spending is the product of decisions taken by different kinds of committees at different times. Entitlements proposed by legislative committees have been adopted and amended separately over the years. The appropriations acts themselves, recommended by a separate set of committees, moreover, are not all considered at the same time. Every year there are at least thirteen of them, each considered by a different subcommittee of the appropriations committees in the House and Senate, often at somewhat different times.

There is also a combination of these two commitments: the *appropriated entitlement*. As in the case of Aid to Families with Dependent Children, authority to make payments is enacted in the authorizing statute, but Congress must also make an annual grant of spending authority in an appropriations bill.

Among the most important misunderstandings about federal government appropriations is the belief that they ordinarily enumerate the specific projects on which money will be spent. They may, but they often do not. Instead, money is appropriated in lump sums for general purposes with particular projects listed in conference committee reports or the reports of House or Senate appropriations subcommittees.

The nomenclature of budgeting adds to the difficulty in understanding the process. Laws that commit the government to spend money create budget authority. Budget authority (BA) is just what it sounds like: authority granted to some agent of the government to spend money. When the money is spent, it is called an outlay. Outlays cannot be made without budget authority.

The federal government cannot provide money to individuals or other units of government unless Congress gives legal authority to do so. This authority is defined in most cases (although not in all cases, as with loans and loan guarantees) as budget authority. The statutes that grant budget authority are of two general types: appropriations bills and "backdoor authority," which occurs outside the normal appropriations process. The most common forms of backdoor authority are borrowing authority, contract authority, and entitlements.

Appropriated funds are not necessarily all spent in a given year; the acts provide budget authority, but each year's outlays (i.e., actual spending) result from a combination of this year's and previous years' authority. For example, an appropriation may allow the Urban Mass Transit Administration (UMTA) to commit $200 million for a rapid transit extension in Chicago. This budget authority allows UMTA to enter into an obligation (i.e., contract) to spend that money. The money will, however, actually be outlaid (spent) over a period of years as the extension is built and material, labor, and design paid for.

In retrospect, outlays or actual expenditure for a given fiscal year are known. In prospect, they can only be estimated. Jonathan Rauch says it well: "Where

---

[3]Report to the Congress by the Comptroller General of the United States, "What Can Be Done to Check the Growth of Federal Entitlement and Indexed Spending," March 3, 1981, PAD-81-21, p. 10.

Congress is concerned, budget authority is law, and therefore solid; outlays are staff estimates of the probable effect of the law, and thus are slippery."[4]

This difference between budget authority and outlays is a primary source of confusion for people who follow federal budgeting. Congress votes on BA, but each year's spending, and thus fiscal policy and the deficit, depends on outlays. Members of Congress have some idea about the size of outlays that will result from their votes on BA, but, as we will see, the estimates can be controversial. What they vote on—authority—therefore, is not quite what they fight about— outlays. The distinction between budget authority and outlays allows all sorts of tricks, traps, and maneuvers, some of them inadvertent. Why, then, does it exist?

This situation results from the nature of many federal programs and the problems in administering them because of the size of the federal government. In our early history, the size that mattered was geography. Before the telegraph and the locomotive, communications were much slower. The federal government did not do very much, but what it did often took place a long way from Washington. Federal agents—customs officials from Boston to New Orleans; postmasters or army units spread from the Northwest territories to Florida—could not possibly be directed closely from the center. Slow communications meant that in the War of 1812 the Battle of New Orleans was fought weeks after peace had been made. In those days the government had to let its agents incur costs as they came along; then auditors would check the records in slow and excruciating detail. Congress provided authority to spend and under the Treasury Department chiefly controlled the honesty and frugality of actual outlays through its accounting system. Smaller local governments could vote on annual outlays directly because their work was closer at hand, and errors could be corrected if necessary by getting the legislature, say, a city council, together for a special meeting. Gathering Congress was more difficult. The kind of annual focus on outlays that concerns us now was impractical, at least for much of the nineteenth century.[5]

Later, change from a focus on budget authority to one on outlays was inhibited by established congressional routine and the nature of many federal activities. The organizational structure of federalism had become important. An organization that does its own work, like an individual spending only on himself, can change spending plans more easily than can one that works through obligations to others. The federal government has always done a lot of its work through others; contractors carried mail through Panama or built dams; in later years, state and local governments received federal funds for everything from law enforcement to caring for the poor. Working through third parties meant that federal planners had less idea of how work would be scheduled, while recipients of money needed some guarantees about federal action for their own planning. The organizational

[4]"Senate Budget Panel Leaders Wage War on 'Budget-Busting' Appropriations Bills," *National Journal* (November 30, 1985), p. 2706.

[5]See Leonard D. White's histories, *The Federalists* (New York: Macmillan, 1961), *The Jeffersonians* (New York: Macmillan, 1951), and *The Jacksonians* (New York: Macmillan, 1956). See also Frederick C. Mosher, *The GAO: The Quest for Accountability in American Government* (Boulder, Colo.: Westview Press, 1979); and James Sterling Young, *The Washington Community, 1802–1828* (New York: Columbia University Press, 1966).

complexity, the layers of federal administration, therefore, encouraged a system in which funds were committed annually but their use was not restricted to a strict annual schedule.

In short, Congress's focus on budget authority rather than outlays arises chiefly from the difficulties of managing federal activities. Those difficulties in turn inhibit control of the deficit. The annual balance sheet—the outlays—is not the same as commitments—the budget authority.

Among outlays based on entitlements, outlays based on previous years' appropriations, and outlays voted and spent that year, each year's spending is based on commitments made at different times. In fiscal 1980, according to the Office of Management and Budget, only 27.3 percent of outlays were determined by the appropriations process for that year. In addition to interest on the debt and prior year's authority, most of the rest was made up of entitlements, and these in turn were largely composed of payments to individuals. Government has gotten good at writing checks.

TAX PREFERENCES

What is true of spending is more true of taxing: Tax law is an accretion of years of decisions. Like entitlements, tax law is open-ended in that individuals are obligated to contribute according to various criteria, rather than the government's being guaranteed some sum of revenue. Revenue may be influenced and estimated but, in these circumstances, not decreed. When economic or demographic conditions change—how many people at which incomes fit into certain categories—revenues rise or fall accordingly.

Tax legislation is handled by the House Committee on Ways and Means and the Senate Committee on Finance. These committees also have jurisdiction over many entitlement programs, such as unemployment compensation and the massive Old Age, Survivors, Disability and Health Insurance (OASDHI) system. OASDHI includes the old age pensions we normally call social security, disability pensions, and medicare, the largest programs in the budget. The tax committees have jurisdiction over these entitlements because, by their design, these programs directly relate taxes to benefits. People earn the right to benefits by contributing to the system, thereby making the program look like insurance (you pay premiums to insure against the risk of being old, sick, or unemployed). The contributions are earmarked for trust funds, and benefits are paid out of each program's fund.

Such contributions are taxes: If you meet the criteria for paying them, but fail to do so and are caught, you may go to jail. While payments to individuals in some of these programs, like medicare, have little to do with the amounts contributed (and the Treasury is obligated to make up any shortfall through its general revenues), the trust-fund financing device requires that decisions about benefits be linked to financing. That link is accomplished institutionally by giving the revenue committees jurisdiction over benefit levels as well. The insurance (real or hypothetical) mechanism of these programs also deepens their character as obligations that may not be changed: People have paid for their benefits. Of course, people also have paid for appropriated programs, but in the social insurance programs, recipients can argue that they individually contributed for the specific purpose of personal insurance.

The committees have another type of spending jurisdiction—"tax preferences." These provisions of the law reduce taxpayers' liability to the government so long as they are engaged in some activity that the government wishes to encourage. Tax preferences are used to encourage certain industries or to promote widely desired individual goods (the tax deduction for mortgage interest encourages the construction industry as well as home ownership). Also they may be justified in terms of the wider national interest (credits for energy exploration serving to reduce dependence on foreign oil). Those who do not like tax preferences call them "loopholes," "gimmicks," or "tax expenditures." The metaphor suggests money escaping, or being diverted from its intended use, and is misleading. Such loopholes are passed by Congress and are as intended as any other legislation (although, as with other legislation, there may be unintended consequences, so that a group that was not originally supposed to receive tax preferences is able to qualify). The mortgage interest deduction and the nontaxation of employee health benefits (which, after all, are equivalent to income) are examples of tax decisions that involve many billions of dollars and major social policies. Because tax preferences affect many groups, the tax committees are petitioned for aid by a huge array of constituencies, all trying to get something out of a given tax bill.

Tax preferences and entitlements are similar in that it is hard to imagine either of them being subject to substantial annual review. In each case, large numbers of people make commitments on the basis of government policy—to invest under certain depreciation rules; to save at a certain rate because social security exists. Entitlements in particular involve commitments that politicians view as substantially different from those made by appropriations; the consequences will come up in Chapter 7. Our discussion so far should establish that taxing may look like spending, and spending may be many different things.

For most of American history, as in the old *Politics*, appropriations were what people meant when they spoke about the budget. We can understand this if we review some of the power stakes in appropriations.

APPROPRIATIONS: THE POWER OF CONGRESS AND POWER WITHIN CONGRESS

Americans have long feared oppression by the political executive. Members of Congress have long seen themselves as the bulwark against such oppression. The public, judging from opinion polls, trusts Congress no more than the presidency; but members of Congress still see themselves in a protective role. Their major weapon is the "power of the purse"—the fact that, as the Constitution states, "No money shall be drawn from the Treasury, but in consequence of Appropriations made by law." The power of the purse is, then, a legislative power in that no money may be spent without the granting of budget authority by Congress.

The process of annually appropriating funds for federal agencies is intended to enforce dependence upon Congress of those agencies' officers. Unless an agency justifies itself each year, it risks losing funding. If the agency behaves in ways that upset Congress, it has an annual opportunity to bring the agency into line through threats or actual changes in appropriations. The agency does not have the advantage of delay, as it would if Congress needed to legislate a change because funding was permanent or multiyear unless otherwise altered. Unlike entitlement funding, annual appropriations mean that delay will cause funding to run out and the agency's activities to cease. Appropriations acts are privileged in floor consideration because members of Congress do not ordinarily want maneuvering or logjams to shut down programs.

The House Appropriations Committee, being larger in number but with fewer duties (and therefore more specialized), has always paid more attention to detail than has its Senate counterpart. Not all details are incorporated into the annual act or report, but intensive review enables members and staff of the appropriate House subcommittee to judge whether an agency is using the money as Congress intended, or as its members intend, rather than in the political interests of the current administration or the desires of administrators.

The appropriations process is in part a response to the very problem of designing expenditure controls in a system full of advocates. We may ask why budget oversight, just like the rest of oversight, is not left to the authorizing committees—those, such as Armed Services or House Energy and Commerce, which write the legislation that creates, and gives power to, the agencies. The answer is that they do not have budget powers because Congress does not trust them to control themselves. Other members of Congress believe that the authorizing committees have very strong incentives to ally with the agencies they authorize. By looking at their job, we can understand both this belief and why members of Congress act on it by regulating themselves.

Members of Congress, as Richard Fenno emphasizes in his *Congressmen in Committees,* have multiple goals: They want to make good policy, have personal power, keep Congress strong (their power depends on the institution's), make voters happy, and please people who can influence voters (by giving money or publicity or other campaign help). The congressional committee system helps members pursue all of these goals, but with some drawbacks for budgeting.[6]

The committee system divides the labor—of attending to the facts, and of assessing the group preferences involved in hundreds of policy issues—because most members can develop expertise only in a tiny portion of policy matters. But they can look to the committees for guidance on other legislation; and they expect others to look to them for guidance in their own fields, where they have power and the attendant chance to make policy.

Committees do not always get their way. They cannot push through Congress legislation that a majority finds obnoxious; committees that persist in trying (e.g., House Education and Labor in recent years) risk losing the benefits of deference from their colleagues. Other members, however, rarely are familiar with the details of legislation in a committee's jurisdiction and therefore may not even know that they do not like it. There is a large gray area in which a committee will have discretion.

---

[6]See Richard F. Fenno, Jr., *Congressmen in Committees* (Boston: Little, Brown and Company, 1973).

Further, legislation needs committee approval to reach the floor. Therefore, the committees have a virtual veto over, and largely shape, policy initiatives in their areas. While it is possible to bypass committees through such devices as a discharge petition, the immense effort, as well as hard feelings, discourage most efforts. Hence those concerned—farmers and the USDA for agriculture, the Federal Communications Commission and broadcasters for Energy and Commerce, for example—greatly value influence on those committee members.

Often members sit on a committee because they bring to Congress a special interest in that subject. Sometimes the clientele served can provide helpful support (or damaging opposition) for reelection. Members may seek to do the most good, however conceived, and that may well mean doing good for those people and in that policy area over which, as committee members, they have the greatest influence. Interest groups encourage such attention, whatever its origin, with campaign assistance; agencies respond to policy suggestions even if not incorporated in legislation; and over time there develops a mutually supportive, three-point relationship among committee members, interest groups, and agencies. These alliances have been called iron triangles, and critical observers hold that these bonds cannot be broken by outsiders. Actually these triangles are of widely varying strength (as a study of entitlements will show).

When the House Ways and Means Committee and the Senate Finance Committee report legislation on social security and unemployment compensation, they may simultaneously be spending and supporting that spending with revenues. When legislative committees authorize spending without specific revenues, as in entitlements such as kidney dialysis, other members fear this spending may be excessive. Since members of individual legislative and appropriations committees do not know the needs of other committees as well, and since they are particularly aware of and concerned by needs in their own areas, members of Congress fear that each of their committees will ask for more funding than they, as a body, are willing to support. The total requested may be more than Congress is willing to vote in taxes.

All members of Congress care about the relation of spending to taxing, and so do voters; they fear the consequences, both for their own reelection and for the institution, if they continually spend more than they can raise. For that reason the appropriations committees were constituted with extensive powers. Members of authorizing committees have delegated to members of appropriations committees the power (subject to floor votes) to limit spending. Thus the appropriations committees are in an inherently adversarial relation with the rest of Congress. They are protected by confidence in their discretion; when they are believed to have overstepped their bounds, they might lose their power (as happened in both House and Senate in the last quarter of the nineteenth century). The late-nineteenth-century experience, however, was not deemed a success, and since 1921 the appropriations committees have been among the more powerful in Congress.

Budgetary policy is determined by both authorizing and appropriating legislation. Louis Fisher has described the standard model of the relationship:

As a general principle, authorizing committees are responsible for recommending programs and activities to be approved by Congress. The committees establish program objectives and frequently set dollar ceilings on the amounts that can be appropriated. Once this authorization stage is complete, the Appropriations Committees recommend the actual level of "budget authority," allowing federal agencies to enter into obligations. This, of course, is an idealized model. Actual congressional operation is substantially different.[7]

And it is different because appropriations now fund substantially less than half the budget.

The old authorizing-appropriating dichotomy no longer works so neatly. The old relationship does not apply, mostly because presidents and Congresses have wanted to spend more by guaranteeing payments to individuals. Appropriations acts are so complicated, moreover, that the appropriations subcommittees develop substantial independence from the parent committee, thus limiting the potential to trade off spending among the activities funded by the acts. The authorizing committees, unsurprisingly, sometimes resist and try to reverse appropriations committee action on the floor. Almost always this is done to increase spending.

The boundaries between authorizing and appropriating decisions are hard to maintain in practice. A decision not to fund an activity, or to fund it under certain conditions (e.g., abortions allowed only in case of rape or serious threat to the life of the mother), looks much like a policy decision. Unfortunately, the many possibilities for undermining appropriations and authorizations exacerbate power struggles among committees. They also create incentives to complicate appropriations legislation with floor amendments ("riders" that the authorizing committees would disapprove); appropriations, which must pass, thus may be held hostage.

Yet the appropriations process has been and is meaningful: Appropriations committees derived power from the special advantages granted to legislation on the floor; placement on the committee, for many years, of members from fairly safe districts; and the influence of powerful chairmen, in the years when chairmen had great formal powers over committees (which lasted until the mid-1970s). Most important, the role of the committee was accepted both by its own members and by other members of each house. Since anybody could spend, committee members for many years found both virtue and power in limiting expenditure.

The appropriations committees exemplify the American practice of opposing ambition with ambition, of functioning under the checks and balances so eloquently justified in *The Federalist*. The ambition of those committees to restrain spending counters that of the authorizers to increase it; the results vary. In a wider sense, House, Senate, and president all check each other. When they were thought not to check each other enough, a new layer of committees, called budget committees, was added to help safeguard the treasury. Once that happened, something obvious, yet unexpected, occurred: The appropriations committees withdrew from their previous positions as guardians of the treasury. Support for committee norms gave way in part to self-expression by members. For some members, program advocacy became the main purpose. For others, still adhering

---

[7]Louis Fisher, "The Authorization-Appropriation Process in Congress: Formal Rules and Informal Practices," *Catholic University Law Review*, Vol. 29, No. 5 (1979), pp. 52–105.

to notions of helping improve the management of federal program efficiency remained important but holding down spending did not.

Despite these changes in ideology and perceived self-interest, the appropriations committees remain important. For one thing, the growth of government to over a trillion dollars a year means that the two-fifths going through the appropriations committees represents big money. Put another way, although the proportion of the whole passing through the appropriations process has declined, the absolute amount is still far larger than the total budget for all but the last two decades. For another thing, as social security has been placed politically out of reach, and other entitlements get harder to decrease, appropriations become a large part of what is up for grabs in the short term. But we run ahead of our story.

The mutual checking of House and Senate is easily overlooked, but hard to overemphasize. These bodies represent people in different ways; their members deal with different political facts (campaigning every six years instead of every two changes members' perspectives immensely); their budget committees are of different sizes (causing different patterns of division of labor, the Senate being less detail- and more debate-oriented). The leadership and members of the two bodies depend on each other very little, and neither will accept leadership from the other. Independent and different, the two houses frequently support different policies. In appropriations or tax bills, as on any other, disagreement must be resolved by bargaining on conference committees, in which delegates from each house work out a package of provisions that can be supported by both. What emerges from conference, if anything, may be quite different from what either house wanted. Members of the House, anticipating conference, build coalitions and take positions with one eye always on the Senate. Senators may vote for more defense spending than they really want, establishing a bargaining position to take to conference. House members may vote for a program that wins constituency support, even if they dislike it, calculating that Senate nonsupport will allow dropping the proposal in conference. An interest group, defeated in the House, will work to prevail in the Senate and then in conference. So does the president.

The bicameral system complicates legislation, assuring that many votes will be taken before a final decision is made. It provides numerous opportunities for bargaining. Until a bill emerges from conference and gains final approval, not only its fate but its provisions may be uncertain. Because it is hard to distinguish between maneuver and preference, interpretation of congressional action is difficult. Even after a bill is passed, the president might veto it. Of course, if all the president gets a crack at is a single omnibus bill for the whole government, a continuing resolution, it is not easy to veto that.

THE PRESIDENT IS BOTH RIVAL OF AND PARTNER OF CONGRESS

The president has the first and last moves in the budget process. He can both check and use Congress, and it can both check and use him.

The last move is the veto—a bludgeon where a scalpel might be more apt. Rarely will a president dislike more than a small part of an appropriations bill, the bulk of which funds relatively uncontroversial and long-standing activities. There-fore, the veto of an appropriation act becomes part of a game of chicken; neither the president nor the act's supporters in Congress want to be blamed for shutting down federal activities in a dispute over details. The president—if only because members of his own party do not want to see him lose—usually can find enough support in at least one house to sustain the veto. He also holds the high ground in a public mudslinging contest with Congress: The president commands more me-dia attention; as the only nationally elected official, he can claim to represent the national interest better than any set of congressional leaders; and Congress is less popular with voters than even the most unpopular president. For these reasons the president is likely to win a veto battle, with Congress having to pass a new bill that suits the chief executive.

Yet the relationship has its own dynamic. Members of Congress do not like a pattern of vetoes and may unite to defend their institutional power against a president who overdoes it. Presidents do not like to lose, especially because losses reduce the White House's credibility. Anticipated reaction—the side that expects to lose giving in—is the usual rule. When the president fails to heed the signals, as with the Women's, Infants, and Children's program, he can ask for less and end up having to spend more (see Chapter 8). In essence, both president and Congress have good reason to avoid a public veto fight, in which one or the other may be embarrassed, programs that each values be hurt, and much time be wasted. The veto, therefore, gives the president a loud voice in the bargaining over spending and tax legislation; its threat is more important than its use.

The Constitution, through the veto, gave the president a voice in bargaining; Congress gave the president the right to set many of the terms. The Budget and Accounting Act of 1921 created the Bureau of the Budget. The Bureau, in a cou-ple of steps, became the Office of Management and Budget (OMB), located in the Executive Office of the president. OMB prepares, and the president submits to Congress, a budget for each fiscal year. (Each fiscal year runs from October 1 of the previous calendar year to September 30 of the same numbered calendar year; thus fiscal 1995 began October 1, 1994, and ended September 30, 1995.) The president's budget is submitted at the beginning of the congressional session at which appropriations for that fiscal year must be made (e.g., January of 1995 for fiscal 1996).

The president's budget is a combination of proposals for legislation and predic-tions of events. It suggests amounts of budget authority for various line items (e.g., salaries and expenses) for each agency, which will be considered by the appropria-tions committees. The president's budget estimates outlays both from last year's ac-tual spending and from the combination of old and new budget authority. It predicts the performance of the economy and, from that, the revenues and expen-ditures that will be produced by current tax and entitlement law. Estimated inter-est rates (which, at times, are difficult to predict) determine estimates of the government's debt-service costs. These proposals and estimates are summed to a bottom line: surplus (quite unlikely) or deficit (now quite large). The deficit, total spending, and revenues are the most publicized aspects of the president's proposal and must be justified both to himself and to others as good policy and good politics.

In the past the only way to affect the totals was to affect the components. The budgetary process worked by adding together spending and revenues as they emerged in separate actions, though with informal understanding of what the totals would be. Recent formal and informal deficit reduction processes work the other way—from totals to parts. Outlays have to fit within prespecified deficit reduction targets.

In preparing his budget, the president faces the problem of matching preferences over programs with preferences about overall spending, taxing, and borrowing. In the past, since agencies limited their spending bids, the first step was to ask them what they needed or wanted. Budget examiners at OMB analyzed detailed agency submissions, searching for the best places to make cuts, if needed. Their judgments were based both on rules of thumb (cut new elements or reduce ineffective programs) and on a sense of the administration's attitude toward each program. While OMB was examining, the president's economic advisors—the Secretary of the Treasury, Chairman of the Council of Economic Advisers, Director of OMB, and others—prepared estimates of economic performance and arguments in support of particular tax and spending levels. But that was then. Nowadays, with presidential preferences starting out at much lower totals, the OMB sends out advice on the level of permissible spending. Sometimes this advice includes "give backs," that is, previously allowed funds that must be returned. This is not to say that the OMB previously existed only as a passive repository of departmental requests. The OMB did provide spending guidelines in the past, but the extent and focus of this involvement has changed dramatically.

Normally the totals suggested mean spending at a lower level than the total of the agency submissions to OMB. How the president resolves that mismatch depends on the economic situation, the president's own policy preferences and management style, and how other political actors, such as commentators, Congress, and interest groups, are expected to respond. Whatever politico-economic judgments are made, decisions on individual programs may be reconciled with preferred totals by:

1. Changing appropriations requests for the agencies either by presidential command through OMB or by placing supporters in charge of agencies. This method has a distinct advantage; Congress has to enact some appropriation and therefore must confront the president's proposal and justify different action.

2. Recommending changes in the laws governing entitlements. Congress need not act at all. Thus the president cannot force the Committee on Ways and Means to report out medicare changes. But Congress may choose to act by limiting eligibility, reducing payments, or limiting cost of living increases.

3. Recommending tax changes. Tax hikes are usually political poison; politicians do not want to be seen sponsoring them. Hikes, therefore, tend to be disguised as loophole closing, reform, "revenue enhancement," or are called "temporary" surcharges.

4. Changing the economic projections to make the tax and spending estimates come closer together. In the past, economic projections were made only by the White House. Now the House and Senate budget committees and the Congressional Budget Office join in the act. Former

budget director David Stockman's admitted juggling of the numbers is unusual only in its notoriety. This tactic if done too often or too blatantly, however, may cause Congress to ignore the president's budget altogether. But it has an advantage: The administration need not propose to hurt anyone. Since economic forecasting is a highly uncertain art, the economists in any event are quite probably wrong. Use of this tactic requires that the president care more about fiscal appearances than consequences. After all, the budget and the economy will be there again next year.

5. Deciding that the totals are not so bad after all. Ronald Reagan did that with his deficits, but so did Jimmy Carter and many other presidents. When Congress decided that the appearance of meeting the Gramm–Rudman–Hollings deficit reduction targets was better than the havoc caused by the necessary cuts, it was doing the same sort of thing. Problems are bad only if their solutions are not worse.

However the president defines his problem, his budget is issued with great fanfare. The budget documents include detailed justifications of his choices. Agency heads are expected to argue for the president's proposals even if they had requested larger funds.

The obvious questions are: Why did Congress establish this procedure? How much effect does it have on what Congress does? The main advantage to Congress is that this procedure gives the president primary responsibility for proposing cuts. The president can impose his priorities on the executive branch in a way that is impossible for any part of Congress, since the executive is in principle (and, in part, in fact) a hierarchy; Congress is anything but. A president can create a package that the noncentralized appropriations committees would have a hard time doing. Congress can then respond to his package of programs, changing it where it differs too much from congressional priorities or where constituency pressures are great, and letting the president take the blame for other decisions. But in 1995 the primary benchmark for budget cutting was the program of the Republican majority, and the critical questions were whether the leadership could maintain its majority to achieve that program, and how the president would react to that initiative.

Often the price of power is blame; this gives both president and Congress reason to duck responsibility in budget politics. The process was once flexible enough for members of Congress to act if they felt it necessary. They could beat up on agencies in hearings, showing these agencies did not deserve increases. They could ask leading questions at appropriation hearings, enabling agency heads to establish for the record why higher spending might be justified. They could pick and choose among presidential requests, raising popular ones (the National Institutes of Health) and cutting unpopular ones (foreign aid). By cutting here and increasing there, appropriations committees could expand some programs while staying below the president's total. Members of Congress who disliked the committees' actions could blame them or fight for changes on the floor.

These partly cooperative and partly conflicting relationships existed within a general framework of informal understandings: The budget would be balanced, the level of taxing and spending would not grow rapidly, and agreements on the amount and distribution of public monies would be maintained. The understandings and agreements that underlay the old budgetary order, however, have been undermined, as I shall show, thus raising in a more acute form the question of which of the many promises that make up the budget will be maintained.

CONFLICTING PROMISES: THE MULTIPLE MEANINGS OF BUDGETARY CONTROL

Thus far I have sought to describe what is meant by the budget and to depict the various actors and procedures involved. Underlying the discussion has been the question of who is in control. As might be expected, the question of control raises a host of difficult issues.

The word "control" may usefully be considered a synonym for "cause" or "power": One controls events by making them come out as intended, against opposition. Budgetary control involves conflict among people who want different outcomes and who attempt to exert power in order to make the size and distribution of spending different than it might otherwise have been. To say that "the budget is out of control," therefore (to invoke the most common public statement), implies a whole series of failed relationships among participants that relate to intentions and outcomes. Inability to specify these relationships makes control (over what, by whom, under which circumstances) a murky subject. Consequently, the information content of most statements about budgetary control is near zero or even negative. Before readers delve into the history of budgeting, they may wish to consider various useful ways of thinking about common questions of control.

Who is to do the controlling? Is it the general population, interest groups, Congress as a whole, appropriations committees alone, the president, agency heads, political parties, or some combination of the above? If it is the general public one has in mind, then certain considerations—well-known to students of democracy but rarely applied to the process of budgeting—must be taken into account. There may well be no general opinion on most matters of budgeting. Politics in general, let alone expenditure in particular, is far from being at the forefront of citizen consciousness; that is one good reason for electing representatives. Indeed, whatever opinion the citizenry holds may be but a shallow reflection of what they have learned from their politicians and parties. Even supposing there are definite opinions, these cannot be directly applied to the budget. For, in the absence of referenda, people vote for or try to influence their representatives. Now, since these representatives deal with many nonbudgetary matters, voting against a candidate solely on budgetary grounds may be unwise. Hence it is possible that citizens may actually vote for people whose budgetary preferences they oppose.[8]

The advent of public-opinion polling, however, has made it possible to ask whether citizen preferences do or do not generally accord with those expressed in

---

[8]See, by inference, Robert A. Dahl, *A Preface to Democratic Theory* (Chicago: The University of Chicago Press, 1956).

consecutive budgets. In a rough and ready way, government does not appear to hae departed too far from the people. A good illustration would be the presidency of Ronald Reagan. The best evidence[9] suggests that most people thought welfare spending was too high and defense spending too low in 1980. Opinion on the level of taxation was mixed, but there was widespread sentiment that the tax code was biased in favor of those already well-off. The Reagan administration moved spending in the direction desired by the electorate and then some. By 1984, polls revealed that the general public wanted more welfare and less defense spending than Reagan. Congress followed these wishes. In the discussion of clever maneuvering around the budget, it is well to note that shifting political alignments, which come from elections, remain by far the largest determinant of outcomes. The ultimate power remains with the people. But if the people are divided, as we often are, and are too far away to exert direct control, that task belongs to officeholders.

Who has power over the budget does not tell us whether or not the budget is under control. That is to say, we need to develop criteria to judge the prospect of budget control or, for that matter, of knowing what it would mean to be in or out of control. Actually, two approaches are commonly proposed. The first of these is to look at the apparent agreement on, but failure to achieve, budget balance. Surely, it is said, the government budget must be out of control if Congress cannot keep its continuously reiterated commitment to budget balance. It is true that huge majorities in Congress say they want balance. It is probably true that they mean what they say. But that truth is not the only truth because reducing the deficit is not the only goal that is important to members of Congress. Some want to reduce welfare spending while others wish to raise taxes. Only a minority cares more about balance than about other policies. The majority supports balance but not to the extent of giving up other preferences.

A second criterion for viewing the budget as out of control is that appropriations committees no longer make annual decisions on anything like most of the budget. These "relatively uncontrollable" expenditures, to use government parlance, essentially are estimates of spending that cannot be changed without altering the statute that authorized the expenditure. As the General Accounting Office puts it:

> From the perspective of the Office of Management and Budget (OMB), the spending in any 1 year for a program that is determined by existing statute, contract, or other obligation is considered relatively uncontrollable and is so classified. OMB also treats the legislative and judicial budgets as uncontrollable; the Congress, on the other hand, regards these budgets as alterable. Under OMB's general rules, the President's budget, submitted on January 15, 1981, reported that about 76 percent of the budget is now relatively uncontrollable.[10]

Thus, relatively uncontrollable spending includes not only entitlements but also obligations incurred and contracts signed in prior years. There are also im-

---

[9]See J. Merrill Shanks and Warren Miller, "Policy Direction and Performance Evaluation: Complementary Explanations of the Reagan Elections." Presented to the Annual Meeting of the American Political Science Association, New Orleans, Aug. 29–Sept 1, 1985.

[10]Report to the Congress by the Comptroller General of the United States, "What Can Be Done to Check the Growth of Federal Entitlement and Indexed Spending?" p. 10.

mutable or fixed costs, such as interest on the debt or a variety of loans to which the credit of the United States is pledged. Only an unthinkable default can alter these expenditures. Looked at another way, much of the rest of the budget is tied up in salaries for soldiers and civilians, operating expenses, data collection, and other items not easy or desirable to change at a moment's notice.

Is it true, then, that the budget becomes uncontrollable because the appropriations committees cannot cover most of it every year? I think not. Taxes generally continue in force until changed, yet few claim they are out of control; this is because, at any time, Congress can alter them. The same is true of entitlements.

There is some utility to the relatively controllable and relatively uncontrollable dichotomy. The observer is sensitized to certain important facts: The relative uncontrollables are growing; the portion passing through the appropriations committees is declining; most controllables are in the defense budget; and it may be more difficult to change a law than to alter an appropriation.

Yet to identify controllability with appropriations and uncontrollability with entitlements also can be misleading. The distinction between controllable and uncontrollable expenditures "indicates *how* budget items may be changed."[11] Appropriations are seen as easier targets for change because Congress must act on them annually, but they are not necessarily more flexible. Congress can cut the Coast Guard, the Bureau of Labor Statistics, and the Federal Aviation Administration somewhat but not a great deal; after all, people need to be rescued, unemployment statistics are vital, and safety in the air is a legitimate concern. Since entitlements occupy a large budgetary space, moreover, they can actually offer more tempting targets—and these targets are hit every year, albeit not every one or to the same extent. The Omnibus Reconciliation Act of 1981, for instance, raised the level at which the states would start paying extended benefits for Unemployment Compensation. And states toughened eligibility requirements.[12] Further, since many appropriations are sacrosanct while most entitlements are frequently adjusted—through changes in eligibility, indexing against inflation, taxation of benefits, and a host of other devices—to speak of the former as controllable and the latter as uncontrollable is somewhat inaccurate.[13]

The truth of the matter is that the 75 percent figure for uncontrollables significantly underestimates the proportion of the budget that is politically subject to change at any one time.[14] As discussion of classical budgeting will make clear, a good 90 to 95 percent of total spending is locked in as a consequence of past commitments and present promises. Here, in commitments to others, lies the insight we have been seeking into the apparent decline of controllability.

Congress wants to keep more expensive promises to a more extensive body of people (a phenomenon that sometimes goes under the name of the welfare state)

[11]Lance LeLoup, "Discretion in National Budgeting: Controlling the Controllables," *Policy Analysis*, Vol. 4, No. 4 (Fall 1978), pp. 455–75; quote on p. 456, italics in original.

[12]Kent Weaver, "Controlling Entitlements," in John E. Chubb and Paul E. Peterson, eds., *The New Direction in American Politics* (Washington, D.C.: The Brookings Institute, 1985), p. 321.

[13]For an excellent discussion, see LeLoup, "Discretion in National Budgeting."

[14]Martha Derthick, *Uncontrollable Spending for Social Services Grants* (Washington, D.C.: The Brookings Institute, 1975).

than it did in the past. Consequently, though Congress could renege on its promises all at once, it does not want to do so. Whether this reluctance stems from fear of retribution at the polls from those who lose a portion of social security payments, or from abandoning a moral commitment, as with kidney dialysis, or, more likely, from some combination of motives, Congress is torn between two kinds of contradictory promises: to certain beneficiaries in particular, or to people in general, in regard to budget balance. This conflict is resolved in the usual way by backing and filling, that is, by doing something that seems to satisfy each promise. With rare exceptions, such as revenue sharing, Congress keeps most commitments while making marginal moves toward budget balance. Just as political parties under pressure from rival factions move first "left" and then "right," and just as appropriations members used to satisfy committee norms by cutting the president's budget and constituency demands, by granting more money than in the previous year, Congress keeps its promises by modifying them.

For good reasons, this policy flexibility has been rendered more difficult in recent years. Automatic protection of entitlement against price rises makes sense in many ways. Needy beneficiaries no longer have to chase declining purchasing power. Politicians are no longer tempted to make up for inflation by election year benefit increases. Promises to the sick and elderly are kept with a minimum of fuss. Idyllic, isn't it? Well, the trouble is that as government absorbs the shock of price increases, it also loses the flexibility to respond to other changes—such as huge deficits that themselves stem in part from another set of promises, to provide tax cuts and to protect people against facing higher tax brackets because of inflation. It is neither right for people to pay more taxes while their purchasing power remains the same and government collects more from inflation, nor for government to have to spend more through indexing entitlements while simultaneously collecting less from income taxes. A "right" for one side obviously makes a "wrong" for the other.

Promises today conflict in other ways unknown to practitioners of budgeting until after the Second World War. The Employment Act of 1946 made the federal government responsible for keeping people at work. That promise, in keeping with the principles of Keynesian economics, was deemed to require varying the deficit or (rarely) surplus to suit the needs of the economy. While fiscal policy called for varying the rate of spending, however, the promise of entitlement policy was to keep the value of benefits constant. If government often resembles a contortionist, this is because it promises, in effect, to move simultaneously in two opposite directions.

Thus far we have looked at conflicting promises as residing between governmental actors and between government and citizens. But there is a different dilemma that occurs in budgeting—the conflict between individual and collective rationality. What makes sense to pursue individually may appear undesirable when these individual actions are viewed from a more general perspective. We see this conflict in budgeting: A desire for more programs conflicts with spending control.

Often, it is revealed with a certain amount of cynicism that members of Congress will vote for spending increases for specific programs and then turn around and vote for deficit reduction measures. But to focus solely on Congress is to investigate only part of the issue. Polling data, for example, suggest that the public is similarly ambivalent. While a large majority of citizens favor a balanced budget, they do not want higher taxes and they support most programs most of the time.

In trying to understand this dilemma, it is important to examine both attitudes and the structure of opportunity. There is little doubt that increasing program expenditures is compelling for congressional participants and the electorate alike. Each of us has particular programs that benefit us or aid someone we know, or we may view particular governmental activities as essential to the community or the nation. But the structure of the political system does not permit us to choose which programs we want and discard the rest; rather the political system works toward the exchange of benefits. To get what we want necessitates our acceptance of programs other people want, programs to which we may be either indifferent or averse. Within Congress, this is exemplified by the bill that becomes laden with a multiplicity of programs designed to muster widespread support.

What we desire in particular (more programs) turns out not to be what we desire in general—less total spending and lower taxes. The trouble is that while incentives exist to expand programs, few incentives exist to control the totals. The voter is rarely presented with the choices spelled out and usually does not have the opportunity to place limits on totals (whether that be taxes or program expenditures). Members of Congress, while having the opportunity to see budget totals, do not have a corresponding incentive to control these totals. Whether because of a perception by members of Congress that cuts will alienate voters or because of an inability to agree on what programs should be cut, the fact remains that even with the new focus on totals (brought about by the Congressional Budget and Impoundment Control Act of 1974), the incentives to cut remain weak.

For government to keep its promises requires not only a will but a way. Agreement on budget policy satisfies only governmental actors; no internal agreements can guarantee that external forces—wars, the weather, what have you— won't interfere with the best-laid plans. Resilient response is made more difficult, however, because governmental resources are now dedicated in advance to so many good causes. Alice Rivlin, former head of the Congressional Budget Office, observed that

> Spending is no longer growing for the old pork barrel, log-rolling reasons. Prospective spending growth is concentrated in a small number of programs with very broad popular support (primarily defense, pensions, and medical benefits), and revenues after the tax changes in 1981 and 1982 are simply not growing fast enough to close the gap, even if the economy continues to improve. This is not a procedural problem, it is simply a question of wanting more government services than there are revenues to pay for them and having to make some hard choices to bring the two sides of the budget closer together.[15]

I am not suggesting that controlling the budget implies that it must be balanced or that domestic and/or defense spending must be held down. Rather, control goes more to the roots of governmental will. For there to be control, there must be a conjuncture of purposes; the promises government makes to others must coincide with its own budgetary plans. As it now stands, the promise of bal-

---

[15]Alice M. Rivlin, "Reform of the Budget Process," *The American Economic Review*, Vol. 74, No. 2 (May 1984), pp. 133–37; quote on p. 137.

ancing the budget conflicts with all the other commitments government makes and would like to keep.

We are more likely than our predecessors to suspect that "the budget is out of control" because there are so many more knowledgeable people around to tell us so. In olden times, reaching back through the 1950s, public officials and a few politicians on appropriations committees were the only budget experts. And they rarely quit their jobs or were removed from office. The monopoly of expertise and security of tenure that Max Weber listed as defining characteristics of modern bureaucracy applied to this tiny cadre of political administrators. No longer. Every area of public policy has layers of experts who once served in office or who soon expect to do so. They are in the think-tanks, the universities, state and local governments, foundations, research centers, and the big consulting and accounting firms. In effect, there are rival teams out there in the hinterlands. Second-guessing becomes a sophisticated art when there are so many informed people to do it. With the loss of their former near-monopoly of information, public officials find it increasingly difficult to keep deficits from being publicized. Whether we are talking about welfare or defense, super-fund or the trade deficit, very little can be kept from public scrutiny. More and more people now know where the dollars are buried.

The existence of a loyal opposition in parliamentary democracies guarantees a string of criticism against existing governmental policy. But such criticism tends to be quite general. The only people who know much are civil servants who now work for the other side or who are silenced by official secrets acts. The existence of rival teams of policy analysts in the United States, with no commitment to governing but with superior sources of information, by contrast, guarantees that there will be numerous and quite specific allegations of unwise or improper budgeting. Too much is being spent for X, not enough for Y. Error rates (the wrong people receiving welfare payments) or cost overruns (the wrong people profiting from defense) are exposed. Needy populations, the emergence of children as the largest category of poor people, or unmet technological needs that, if neglected, promise to ruin American competitiveness are heard of every day. Criticism has been institutionalized, but support has not. The remarkable devices used in the Omnibus Budget Reconciliation Act of 1990 to leave congressional appropriators free of fault if external circumstances make their budget plans go awry, as we will see in Chapter 6, have their roots in a criticism so constant that legislators despair of being thought to have acted wisely no matter what they do. The task of control, of coordinating commitments, is so difficult because of the many different meanings the budget has for different people, hence the conflicting criticisms leveled against a particular budget. In the past these variegated desires were held together by certain common concerns: a balanced budget, avoidance of rapidly rising spending or taxing, and a broad agreement on the distribution of expenditures. The collapse of these premises of the old budgetary order, has loosened the strictures that constrained these many desires. Because the new order is being built on the scaffolding of the old—not so much replacing as adding to it—the next chapter begins with the historical origins of American budgeting, origins that still affect what is done today.

Chapter
2

Budgets as Struggles for Power: The Evolution of Classical Budgeting

*F*ew truisms of American political thought are more hoary than this: The power of the purse is the heart of legislative authority and thus an essential check on the executive branch. An executive establishment freed from dependence for funds upon the legislature (and hence the public) would be a law unto itself and ultimately a despotism. Those who made the American Revolution concluded from experience in Britain and the colonies that a free people had to keep its governors on a tight fiscal leash. From the earliest days of American government, budget decisions were treated as a struggle for power.

The evolution of federal budgeting thus reflects the political struggles of the nation, translated into the institutions of government. The early strictures of the colonists against the powers of the colonial government were quickly adapted to efforts by the Congress to constrain the president.[1] Various turning points—wars, the income tax, the executive budget process, and the depression—cumulatively tilted the balance toward the executive branch. This development did not take place in a vacuum: between the late eighteenth century and the mid-twentieth century, the United States moved from an agrarian to an industrial economy; its citizenry diversified to include former slaves and immigrants from totally different backgrounds; urban growth and revolutions in transportation transformed the lives of every person; and the nation assumed the powers and burdens of an international power. Governments acknowledged newer responsibilities, and federal budgets grew, but with the exception of wars, expenditures were constrained. Until the beginning of the great budget battles of the 1960s, the politics of the federal budget process seemed oddly untouched by the developments around it, a reflection of the political system as a whole. The compromises, balances, and under-

---

[1]For a more detailed study, see Carolyn Webber and Aaron Wildavsky, "Balanced Regimes, Balanced Budgets: Why America Was So Different," Chapter 7 in *A History of Taxation and Expenditure in the Western World* (New York: Simon and Schuster, 1986).

standings of the early years of the Republic, which restricted participants in the budget process and stamped institutions and budgets with a conservative view of the world, continued to hold fast, and to maintain a "classical" dance of dollars.

COLONIAL ORIGINS

Colonial expenditures were simple in nature. Care of the poor, insane, sick, or otherwise indigent was a local responsibility. Public works were few and scattered. Highways were short and rough, and courthouses, though sometimes gilded with a handsome facade, were small. Judges were few and did not require many helpers. No colonial navy existed and the army—except in the period of the great Indian wars, or during the war with France for control of the North American continent—was composed of local militia. Legislatures met only for short periods, and payment, if received, was small. Colonial executive departments were tiny, and officials were often paid by fees rather than from general revenues. Royal governors alone received substantial salaries.

The extraordinary effort of colonial legislatures to control executives by limiting their expenditures, the duration for which they could be paid, and the objects for which the money could be spent, gives this period its peculiar stamp. If the colonies belonged to England, and if the colonists were English subjects, then it was their duty to support royal governors. Since the colonists wanted British protection but not British rule, however, they freely used the English tradition of denying supply in order to force compliance with the legislative will.[2]

It was common colonial practice to vote salaries annually. Indirect taxes, excises, and import duties were often reenacted yearly. Royal governors were allowed no permanent sources of revenue that might make them "uppity."[3] And that was only the beginning: Appropriations were specified for object and amount; extremely long appropriation clauses prescribed exactly what could and what could not be done and for how much. The requirement that all unexpected balances revert immediately to the treasury added insult to injury.

Even so, it might be thought that once an appropriation was voted, a royal executive could proceed to spend the money for the purpose stipulated. Several colonies, however, went so far as to elect independent treasurers that precluded the governors from managing their own finances. Other legislatures insisted that no payment might be made without their specific consent, thus giving colonists control over the disbursement of public funds. And when an emergency arose that everyone felt should justify a special appropriation, colonial assemblies might well appoint special commissioners accountable to them rather than to the governor. Should such measures prove too loose, there were still others: Revenues were segregated by voting taxes for exceedingly narrow purposes (such as the building of a

---

[2]See Robert C. Tucker and David C. Hendrickson, *The Fall of the First British Empire: Origins of the War of American Independence* (Baltimore/London: Johns Hopkins University Press, 1982), pp. 152–59, 174–75, 406–10.

[3]Charles Bullock, "The Finances of the United States from 1775–1789 with Special Reference to the Budget," *Bulletin of the University of Wisconsin,* Vol. 1, 1894–1896, Frederick Turner, ed. (Madison: University of Wisconsin Press, 1897), pp. 217, 225.

fort or of a lighthouse or the salary of a governor), always with the added clause that once the purpose had been accomplished, that money could be spent for "no other use or purpose whatsoever."[4] Colonial assemblies also reduced the salaries of royal officials; they stipulated the precise name of the person who was to do the work and made these officials legally accountable for all funds expended.[5]

When it came to doing sums, everyone understood what was at stake: Royal governors and their supporters desperately wanted a civil list of appointments and perquisites independent of the funds supplied by legislatures; the colonists wanted to create uncertainty, parsimony, and narrowness so as to bend royal governors to their will. To the English, it seemed only reasonable for the colonists to pay for the support of the royal government. The Stamp Act, duties on tea, and other impositions on colonists were a parliamentary effort to provide independent sources of income for English officials in America. Power, not money, was the issue.

After the Revolution, Americans found that it was hard to run a government that lacked authority. If they wanted action, they had to give the executive leeway. The Constitutional Convention was called into being by those attempting to create a more energetic government than existed under the Articles of Confederation—one with direct coercive power over individuals. Nevertheless, the influence of supporters of legislative power helped weaken the executive. For Roger Sherman, as for many others, an independent executive was "the very essence of tyranny. . . ." The legislature was "the depository of the supreme will of the society."[6]

Alexander Hamilton also saw political power behind financial power. He believed it necessary to fund state debts incurred during the Revolutionary War not only to establish strong credit, but also as a means of attaching the people who would be paid to the purposes of government.[7] From the outset of his term as Secretary of the Treasury, he wrote Congress that Americans had to learn "to distinguish between oppression and the necessary exercise of lawful authority."[8] Hamilton's interest in levying taxes other than tariffs and in enforcing the exercise of the taxing power in the case of an excise tax on whiskey had as much to do with his desire to strengthen government as it did with the need to raise money.

Immediately upon Hamilton's appointment there arose a clamor, unfathomable outside the United States, that a powerful Secretary of the Treasury, by giving his opinion to Congress, might overawe or otherwise influence that body in an undesirable manner.[9] The law establishing the Treasury Department merely said that the Secretary was supposed to send departmental estimates to Congress;

---

[4]Ibid., pp. 216–19.

[5]Ibid., pp. 219–21.

[6]Leonard D. White, *The Federalists: A Study in Administrative History* (New York: Macmillan, 1961), p. 14.

[7]William J. Schultz and M. R. Caine, *Financial Development of the United States* (New York: Prentice-Hall, 1937), p. 100.

[8]Dall W. Forsythe, *Taxation and Political Change in the Young Nation 1781–1883* (New York: Columbia University Press, 1977), pp. 44–45.

[9]Schultz and Caine, *Financial Development*, pp. 93–94.

the law did not say that the Secretary was to revise these estimates or, if he did, whether anybody had to pay attention. Over time, an informal understanding developed that though the Secretary might interest himself in estimates, his sole duty was to collect them, and send them, without comment, to Congress. Though there is evidence of a secretary questioning this or that estimate and of occasional intervention by a president, the trend was to make appropriations without participation of the president or the Secretary of the Treasury.

Since the strong executive was part of their platform, the Federalist Party preferred "lump-sum" appropriations for each specified purpose—say, customs collection or a navy—which would give administrators as much leeway as possible. Favoring economic stringency and distrusting the executive—the one reinforcing the other—the Republican party sought specific, line-item appropriations—for personnel, maintenance, supplies, on and on—that would limit departmental heads to exactly what Congress had commanded.[10]

What could Congress do? Plenty. It could itemize appropriations in excruciating detail; it could seek to apportion funds by the month or quarter so that agencies did not run out of money before the end of the fiscal year—potential deficiencies that might lead to requests for supplementary funds to carry out essential functions; it could limit transfers from one line-item to another and recapture unexpended funds, or at least it could try. Congress could and did specify the number of employees, their exact remuneration, and sometimes their names. One of the many budget reform acts forbade all departments, except State, to spend more than $100 on newspapers; denied funds for commissions of inquiry, except courts-martial; refused extra allowances and additional clerks; insisted upon detailed reporting about the expenditure of contingency funds; prohibited the purchase of engravings, pictures, books, or periodicals other than by written order of head of department; and set the maximum amount that could be paid to the Dragoman of Constantinople.[11]

Despite continuous legislative effort to narrow administrative leeway, Congress could not control everything. The army and the navy, insisting they could not be held to specific line-items, did get their way.[12] The legislated sanctions against executive offices for overspending, unauthorized transfers, or other violations of the innumerable prohibitions were not invoked; no doubt enforcement was not possible.[13] Most departmental appropriations soon became regular and customary as to both content and amount. Whether or not a new annual appropriations bill was passed, Congress did renew allocations in more or less the same manner year after year; social stability had produced agreement on a budgetary base.

An easy way around specific appropriations was to transfer sums from one purpose to another. The Act of 1820 allowed the president to make only certain

---

[10]Ibid., p. 324.

[11]Leonard D. White, *The Jacksonians: A Study in Administrative History 1829–1861* (New York: Macmillan, 1954), pp. 126–27.

[12]Ibid., p. 131.

[13]Ibid., p. 141; and Albert S. Bolles, *A Financial History of the United States, 1774–89* (New York: Appleton, 1879), pp. 539–40.

transfers; all others were forbidden. But when Congress became overburdened with requests for change and discovered it could not monitor even a small proportion of transactions, it tried to legalize prevailing practices. Funds for forts could be moved from one stockade to another, as could appropriations for naval forces from branch to branch, and postal funds from here to there. Departments kept appropriated funds from lapsing by finding ways to spend at the end of the fiscal year. When, in 1842, department heads received authority to transfer surplus funds from one item to some other (always excepting, of course, funds for newspapers, which in those days were party organs), the battle against transfers had been lost.[14]

Even at this point, the great financial issues of the times—the tariff, federal public works, and the debt—reflected ideological divisions among those contending for power. The Federalists and their successors sought to promote social order through deficit finance, first by making internal improvements and second by the financial arrangements arising out of the resulting debt. They were supported by growing commercial interests, advocating high tariffs and expanded debt. Besides encouraging the growth of industry, the tariff provided surplus revenues to expand roads, canals, and other facilities.[15] The debt also increased money in circulation, thus aiding industry as well as tying its holders to the central government.

But these allied interests had to contend with supporters of Jeffersonian Democratic Republican thought, reflecting fear of strong centralized government.[16] Small agricultural communities with an educated electorate, not far from one another in economic status and geographical distance, could handle their affairs on a face-to-face basis. If government were to grow too large, and if substantial inequality of resources were to develop, Jeffersonians believed, then personal liberties would be endangered. The Jacksonians, two decades after them, continued and embroidered on their distrust of government and debt.

Interests supporting social order, economic individualism, and the Jeffersonian-Jacksonian Democrats disagreed about the potential and purposes of government, and the nature and dangers of rule. But they found common ground in the belief that liberty and equality could be made compatible and in consensus on the small size of the federal government.[17]

The era before the Civil War remained a time of tiny government. Between 1800 and 1860, as Table 2.1 shows, federal expenditures rose from about $11 million to $63 million in total. More than half were military expenditures. The general category of "Civil & Miscellaneous" included a substantial amount for the postal deficit, thus covering everything except defense, pensions, Indians, and interest on the debt. Kimmel is correct in concluding "that federal expenditures

---

[14]White, *The Jacksonians*, pp. 133–34.

[15]Leonard D. White, *The Jeffersonians: A Study in Administrative History 1801–1829* (New York: Macmillan, 1951), p. 483.

[16]Adrienne Koch and William Peder, *The Life and Selected Writings of Thomas Jefferson* (New York: Modern Library, 1944), p. 123.

[17]Lewis H. Kimmel, *Federal Budget and Fiscal Policy 1789–1958* (Washington, D.C.: The Brookings Institution, 1959), p.19; and White, *The Jeffersonians*, p. 483.

Table 2.1   FEDERAL EXPENDITURES, FISCAL YEARS 1800, 1825, 1850, AND 1860

	(in million of dollars)			
	1800	1825	1850	1860
Civil & miscellaneous	1.3	2.7	14.9	28.0*
War Department	2.6	3.7	9.4	16.4
Navy Department	3.4	3.1	7.9	11.5
Indians	—	0.7	1.6	2.9
Pensions	0.1	1.3	1.9	1.1
Interest	3.4	4.4	3.8	3.2

*Includes postal deficit of $9.9 million.

made little or no contribution to the level of living. Only a minor portion of Civil and miscellaneous expenditures were for developmental purposes. . . ."[18]

TURNING POINTS: CIVIL WAR THROUGH WORLD WAR I

The written law often follows from the law of necessity. Public officials who believe an act to be essential may undertake it without legislative warrant, appealing to Congress to approve their conduct retroactively. The strongest proponent of this view was undoubtedly Abraham Lincoln. As the nation split into irreconcilable factions, Lincoln took the position that whatever was required for national defense had to be approved. On grounds that there was then "no adequate and effective organization for the public defense," he justified ordering the Treasury to advance $2 million to a variety of private agents to provide requisitions for the military:

> Congress had indefinitely adjourned. There was not time to convene them. It became necessary for me to choose, whether, using only the existing means, agencies, and processes which Congress had provided, I should let the Government fall at once into ruin or whether availing myself on the broader powers conferred by the Constitution in cases of insurrection, I would make an effort to save it, with all its blessings, for the present age and for posterity. . . . The several Departments of the Government at that time contained so large a number of disloyal persons that it would have been impossible to provide safely through official agents only for the performance of the duties thus confided to citizens favorably known for their ability, loyalty, and patriotism.[19]

The higher law was one thing and low-down behavior another; investigations provided ample evidence of abuse of contract power during the war.[20]

---

[18]Kimmel, *Federal Budget and Fiscal Policy,* p. 57.

[19]Lucius W. Wilmerding, Jr., *The Spending Power: A History of the Efforts of Congress to Central Expenditures* (New Haven, Conn.: Yale University Press, 1943), p. 14.

[20]Albert S. Bolles, *The Financial History of the United States from 1861 to 1885* (New York: Appleton, 1886), p. 231.

Performance being more important than protocol during the war, Congress legally authorized all that it had been denying for the past century: lump-sum appropriations, spending in excess of authorizations and appropriations, transfers, revolving funds perpetuated by reimbursements, and more.[21]

When, because funds were inadequate, transfers failed to produce necessary moneys, departments could and did resort to the tactic of the coercive deficiency. What could Congress do if the money for an essential service were to run out before the end of the fiscal year, other than to pass a supplemental appropriation? Deficiencies before the Civil War rose to something like 10 percent of total spending. Congress did demand to be informed of an emergency leading to a waiver of required apportionments, but by the time the waiver was reported there was no effective remedy.[22] From time to time, departments also used unexpended balances for purposes not previously contemplated in congressional statutes, following earlier instances of administrative discretion, particularly involving the building up of naval forces.

The Civil War thus acted as a catalyst for the president to wrest from Congress some discretion over spending. The war also resulted in a structural transformation of the congressional budgetary process. For the first 75 years of the republic (from 1789 to 1864), revenue and expenditure matters in the House of Representatives were handled by its Committee on Ways and Means (and in the Senate by the Finance Committee). Largely in response to the Ways and Means Committee being overworked, the House in 1865 and the Senate in 1867 carved a Committee on Appropriations out of the old single committee. This dual committee system—one for taxes, the other for spending—lasted until 1885.[23]

The new Appropriations Committee "embodied a balance between the need for some financial expertise with the aversion to placing too many institutional resources in the hands of one individual."[24] The arrangement allowed for unified control of spending in one committee. Yet, it did not have authority to control all spending—the size of pensions and other permanent appropriations (together constituting over half the budget) were determined by other committees.[25]

By and large, members of Congress appeared content with the new arrangement. Collaboration occurred between the Ways and Means and the Appropriations Committees and there was consensus in Congress that Civil War spending and waste needed to be curtailed and that war profiteering had been widespread. Additionally, Congress was too preoccupied with Reconstruction to get caught up in other domestic issues.[26]

In the succeeding years, the House Appropriations Committee came under attack for amassing too much control over other committees' programs, primarily

---

[21]Wilmerding, *Spending Power,* p. 154.

[22]Ibid., pp. 137–47.

[23]E. E. Naylor, *The Federal Budget System in Operation* (Washington: Hayworth Printing, 1941), pp. 20–21.

[24]Charles Haines Stewart III, *The Politics of Structural Reform: Reforming Budgetary Structure in the House, 1865–1921,* Dissertation, Stanford University, August 1985, p. 139.

[25]Ibid., pp. 139–40.

[26]Ibid., p. 140.

through Appropriations control over reporting bills out. As the smooth flow of patronage was threatened by the Appropriations Committee, members of Congress reacted in 1885 by giving a number of spending bills to the substantive legislative committees made up of spending advocates. Congress first stripped Appropriations of constituency-oriented legislation (rivers and harbors spending, agriculture) and then moved to more general items (army, navy, diplomacy, post office, and Indian affairs). By these acts, more than half of the total appropriations, including the most controversial items, were effectively removed from the Appropriations Committee's jurisdiction.[27]

These changes became "a symbol of dysfunctional fragmentation in Congress and of waste and mismanagement, and would serve as a rallying point in the creation of an executive budget focused around presidential leadership."[28] Actually, the escalation of spending after 1885 was less the result of decentralization (spending rates increased at fairly equal rates for bills outside Appropriations control compared to bills under Appropriations jurisdiction) and more the consequence of an acceleration of visible spending, including army and navy reform and the rebuilding of southern productive centers destroyed during the war, in response to two decades of neglect.[29]

The leading budget reformer before World War I, Frederick A. Cleveland, excoriated the chairmen of these spending committees as

> functionalized, bureaucratic, feudal lords [who] did not look to their titular superior, the leader chosen by and responsible to the nation, for powers and policies. They looked to irresponsible committees. And because of the independence that was thus given, each chief built around himself a bureaucratic wall that even the constitutional Chief Executive himself could not get over. . . .[30]

Cleveland's theme, bureaucratic feudalism, reveals the emergent pattern of budgeting. Close relationships were developing among chiefs of governmental bureaus, their clientele, and the chairmen and ranking members of the congressional appropriations committees.

It appears that administrative bureaus would advocate higher spending; their estimates would be cut by the House Appropriations Committee, but the Senate would then act as an appeals court to give the money back. The Appropriations Committee was slowly assuming its role as "watchdog of the Treasury" or defender of the public purse. "You may think my business is to make appropriations," said Joseph Cannon, a powerful former Speaker of the House and Chairman of the Appropriations Committee, "but it is not. It is to prevent their being made."[31]

---

[27]Richard F. Fenno, *The Power of the Purse: Appropriations Politics in Congress* (Boston: Little, Brown, 1966), p. 43.

[28]Stewart, *Politics of Structural Reform*, p. 211.

[29]Ibid., p. 215.

[30]Frederick A. Cleveland, "Leadership and Criticism," *Proceedings of the Academy of Political Science*, Vol. 8 (1918–20), p. 31.

[31]Fenno, *Power of the Purse*, p. 99.

A further turning point came in 1894 when Congress passed and President Cleveland signed the first income tax bill. Its strongest proponents argued that this tax would be paid for by "wealth, not want"; the time had come to "put more tax upon what men have, less on what they need."[32] Opponents argued that the income tax was a tax on "mind and energy," taking from the "thrifty and enterprising" to give to "the shiftless and the sluggard."[33] In the political conditions of the 1890s, the kind of taxation and its incidence were far more important than the amount.

The Supreme Court ruled the progressive aspects of income tax unconstitutional in *Pollock v. Farmers Loan and Trust Co.* (157 U.S., 429) in 1895. The federal government was in deficit 11 of the 21 years from 1894 through 1914. What to do? Faced with revenue shortfalls, Presidents Roosevelt (in his 1906 annual message) and Taft (accepting the Republican nomination in 1908) both endorsed the idea of an income tax. But the Supreme Court was a large barrier. In 1908 the Democrats called for a constitutional amendment to allow the tax, and in 1909, under substantial pressure, Taft agreed. The amendment sped through Congress with little debate in 1909[34] and was ratified in 1913. The income tax subsequently enacted was, however, extremely small. And any prospect that it could handle budget shortfalls was eliminated when America entered World War I. Income-tax revenues were greatly expanded, but failed by a large amount to match wartime spending. In the three years from 1917 through 1919, federal debt grew from $1.2 billion to $25.5 billion.[35]

Coping with that massive debt, retrenching from wartime to peacetime expenditures, and responding to the new public awareness of budgetary issues resulting from a direct tax (rather than hidden taxes such as tariffs) posed a major challenge. As usually happens when problems arise, people were waiting with pet solutions. The appropriations committees wanted their power back. The president and a group of Progressive reformers wanted an executive budget. Congress moved to create an executive budget, but also to strengthen itself.

THE EXECUTIVE BUDGET MOVEMENT

Reformers are not radicals; those who left their imprint upon American budgeting between the Civil War and 1920 were not opposed to American social structure or to competitive markets, nor were they proponents of income redistribution. A political force unique in this most unusual of nations, reformers were the establishment's antiestablishment—critical of the fragmented way politicians did things—and also the anti-anti-market, who opposed threats by corporate trusts to limit competition. To lessen the "irresponsible power" of party bosses and chairmen of congressional standing committees, the budgetary reformers wanted a vis-

---

[32]Edwin R. A. Seligman, *The Income Tax* (New York: Macmillan, 1921), p. 497.

[33]Ibid., p. 500.

[34]Ibid., p. 590–96.

[35]Historical Statistics of the United States, Colonial Times to 1970, Part 2; U.S. Department of Commerce, Bureau of the Census, pp. 1104, 07–08, 14–15, 21–22, 24–25, 49.

ible and democratically accountable Chief Executive served by experts dedicated to the public interest. The experts, whose ideas and attitudes matched the reformers', would be the instruments of change.

The people of the United States had a deep attachment to the Constitution and to the separation between executive and legislative branches it embodied. Yet it was precisely this separation (or at least the form it took in America) that the reformers opposed.[36]

The budgetary practice to which the reformers most objected was the time-worn one of itemization of spending, known today as the line-item budget. Itemization was wasteful and, worst of all, did not allow for executive discretion. President Taft's Commission on Economy and Efficiency argued that because government did not trust its officers, "judgments which can be made wisely only at the time that a specific thing is to be done are attempted to be made by a Congress composed of hundreds of Members from six months to a year and a half beforehand on the recommendation of a committee which at most can have but a limited experience or fund of information as a basis for their thinking."[37] The principle of deference to expertise was thus twice denied by Congress, once to the Chief Executive and then again to his subordinates.

The piecemeal process by which budgets were put together—each committee recommending appropriations for the agencies and purposes under its control and the houses of Congress acting on them one at a time—was singled out for special condemnation. Because of this fragmentation, no formal attention was given to total spending.[38]

Reformers had no concept of informal coordination and never thought to ask whether all concerned might not have had a pretty good idea of where they were, and were likely to end up. It was chiefly the form of the budget, and what it represented, to which they objected: "no standard classifications . . . of expenditures according to their character and object . . . no uniform scheme of expenditure documents calling for the recording of expenditure data in accordance with any general information plan . . . no budgetary message, no proper scheme of summary, analytical and comparative tables. . . ." In short, nothing in the United States appropriations process remotely resembled budgeting in the executive-centered governments of Europe.[39]

So much for what the reformers were against; what were they for? Hierarchy, known to them as "executive leadership," is the best short answer. Leadership would purify politics. This was Woodrow Wilson's theory, and his practice as president.[40] Wilson was ready with both diagnosis and remedy: "This feature of disinte-

---

[36]Nicholas M. Butler, "Executive Responsibility and a National Budget," *Proceedings of the Academy of Political Science*, Vol. 8 (1918–20), p. 46; Wilson, *Congressional Government*, p. 284.

[37]Quoted in Wilmerding, *Spending Power*, p. 150.

[38]Charles Wallace Collins, *The National Budget System* (New York: Macmillan, 1917), p. 3.

[39]William Franklin Willoughby, *The Problem of a National Budget* (New York: Appleton, 1918), pp. 56–57.

[40]Arthur Macmahon, "Woodrow Wilson: Political Leader and Administrator," in Earl Latham, ed., *The Philosophy and Policies of Woodrow Wilson* (Chicago: University of Chicago Press, 1958), pp. 100–22; reference is to page 113.

gration of leadership runs ... through all our legislation; but it is manifestly of much more serious consequence in financial administration than in the direction of other concerns of government." Budgets must be "under the management of a single body; only when all financial arrangements are based upon schemes prepared by a few men of trained minds and accordant principles, who can act with easy agreement and with perfect confidence in each other" will budgets make sense.[41] The major premise of executive leadership led also to its important corollary: executive discretion by reliance on experts. It is important to understand that the reformers believed their recommendations derived from scientific principles. Often they referred to "the science of budgetmaking,"[42] or said they were subjecting budgetary problems "to scientific analysis."[43] Their assumption was that the goals or objectives of budgeting were agreed so that only the details of administrative execution were left to be considered.

The policy-administration dichotomy—in which political choices are made through general legislative enactments, and administrative choices are limited to technical implementation of these larger and prior decisions—was an essential postulate of budget reformers. They held that if administrators also were to make large and therefore political choices, the principle of neutral competence—which justified civil-service reform and the important role reformers wished to give to experts—would be undermined. Their text was Frank J. Goodnow's *Politics and Administration*. Goodnow believed that the two primary functions of government were to determine the will of the people and to execute that will. Though, as Dwight Waldo observes, Goodnow was far from making the distinction exclusive (seeing better than his followers the interpretation of the two functions), when taken up by less sophisticated acolytes Goodnow's ideas generated the doctrine of a strict separation between the two.[44] This dichotomy legitimizes taking power from the legislature and giving it to the executive—and, ultimately, to the executive's expert administrators, the reformers themselves.

The reformers' recommendation to adopt business practices manifestly did not mean approval of bidding and bargaining among legislature and executive. Rather, they adopted from big business its internal organization, that is, its hierarchical structure, which served to solidify the distinction between policy and administration that the reformers wished to make.

The reformers' budgetary principle of principles was reiterated like a litany: "There must be established a national budget prepared and recommended by the Chief Executive."[45]

If the proposals were adopted, how did the reformers picture themselves (or people like them) as participants in the budgetary process? They had already been instrumental in staffing commissions to recommend the proposed reforms. These

---

[41]Wilson, *Congressional Government*, pp. 180–81.

[42]Charles Beard, "Prefatory Note," *Municipal Research,* No. 88 (August 1917) (New York: Bureau of Municipal Research), p. iii.

[43]Willoughby, *Problem of a National Budget*, p. 55.

[44]Dwight Waldo, *The Administrative State* (New York: Ronald Press, 1948), pp. 105–107.

[45]Butler, "Executive Responsibility," p. 49.

same men aimed to become part of the expert staff of the executive—mayor, governor, or president—whose task would be formulating the budget. As A. E. Buck said so succinctly, "budget-making requires special staff assistance . . . to . . . assist the executive. . . ."[46] By extending this function to other governmental purposes, budget experts could easily become a general administrative staff supporting the executive. When one recognizes that presidents of the United States up to Franklin D. Roosevelt's time were assisted at most by a few clerks, these were far-reaching proposals.

A simile—be like Britain—justified recommendations for budget hierarchy in the United States. The only way Parliament could alter the budget was to change the government. "If one looks for the secret of . . . the English system," Willoughby comments, "it must be found in . . . the clear distinction . . . between legislative and administrative powers. . . . No proposals for . . . expenditure . . . shall be made . . . except . . . by the cabinet acting as the custodian of the administrative powers of government. . . ."[47]

Because the British Chancellor of the Exchequer and Department of the Treasury were responsible for both expenditure and revenue, the reformers believed that these would be taken up at the same time and that, therefore, comprehensive and simultaneous consideration would be given to the relative desirability of spending versus taxing.[48] Whether this formal unity would make any difference, either to the totals or to the division of expenditures among departments, was not a subject for discussion by reformers who already knew the answer.

Agency personnel were to be completely subservient to budgetary decisions of the president. If agency heads could not support estimates changed by the president, they should be fired.[49] Apparently it never occurred to the reformers that heads of spending departments might speak privately with legislators or, if wide-ranging differences arose, that presidents might not be able to maintain dominance over the cabinet. In those days cabinet members represented party factions; asking a cabinet member to step down therefore had significant political costs.

The reformers insisted that, having gained executive approval, every spending proposal would ipso facto represent the national view, allowing no room for "log-rolling" in Congress.[50] In Lewis Carroll's *Through the Looking Glass,* the Red Queen tells Alice, in the same manner, that anything she says three times is true.

At the time, the reformers' position was effectively criticized by Edward A. Fitzpatrick in his *Budget Making in a Democracy* (1918). His views are interesting because they embody the stance of the expert administrator who does not aspire to be a staff assistant to the Chief Executive. Fitzpatrick looked at the political im-

---

[46]A. E. Buck, "The Development of the Budget Idea in the United States," *Annals of the American Academy of Political and Social Science,* Vol. LXIII (May 1924), p. 36.

[47]Willoughby, *Problem of a National Budget,* pp. 59–60.

[48]Ibid., p. 405.

[49]Frederick A. Cleveland and Arthur E. Buck, *The Budget and Responsible Government* (New York: Macmillan, 1920), pp. xviii–xix.

[50]Collins, *National Budget System,* p. 41.

plications of the president amassing such budgetary power. "Are we to have a one-man government? That," Fitzpatrick told his readers, "is the fundamental question in back of the executive budget propaganda."[51]

As for the much-vaunted British example, cabinet government, he said, was not government by one person, but by a committee of the legislature, a parliament with the ultimate right to dismiss its cabinet.[52] "*Do those who are proposing the executive budget also propose the legislative recall of the executive?*"[53] This is what the British Parliament does and that is what a business board of directors does when it loses confidence in management. Fitzpatrick, however, insisted such action is impossible under presidential government with its fixed terms.[54] Reformers, Fitzpatrick contended acidly, should tell the people they want to make a fundamental change in the American form of government, and not camouflage the issues "under the name of 'executive budget.'"[55]

To promote the idea of a federal executive budget, President William Howard Taft set up a Commission on Economy and Efficiency. The commission's tone was set by its chairman, Frederick A. Cleveland, then director of the New York Bureau of Municipal Research, and by other noted budget reformers appointed with him, including Frank J. Goodnow and W. F. Willoughby.[56] The commission's basic task, accepted by Taft in its entirety, was that the president would submit spending estimates to Congress and would assume responsibility for them.[57] The commission's major report, "The Need for a National Budget," completed in 1912, was followed by "A Budget for the Fiscal Year 1914," in which President Taft, at the commission's instigation, submitted the kind of budget document he thought appropriate for the Chief Executive as top administrator.[58] It rejected the prevailing narrow view of economy—of spending merely the minimum. Instead, the President (like earlier advocates of internal improvements) stated that he wanted the government to operate economically in order to do more for the people with available resources.[59] Power for presidents and their advisors was sublimated under a rubric with which it was difficult to argue: efficiency.

Congress was of a different mind altogether. Expressing fear of the executive's usurpation of power (in language harking back to the early days of the republic), Congress passed a law requiring department heads charged with preparing estimates to do what they had always done: to send estimates directly to congressional appropriations committees.[60] And department heads responded to these contra-

[51]Edward Augustus Fitzpatrick, *Budget Making in a Democracy* (New York: Macmillan, 1918), p. 55.

[52]Ibid., pp. 50–51, 59.

[53]Ibid., p. 54.

[54]Ibid., p. 5.

[55]Ibid., p. 292.

[56]Naylor, *Federal Budget System in Operation*, pp. 23–24.

[57]Cleveland, "Leadership and Criticism," p. 33.

[58]Naylor, *Federal Budget System in Operation*, p. 24.

[59]Wilmerding, *Spending Power*, p. 151; and Jesse Burkhead, *Government Budgeting* (New York: Wiley, 1956), p. 119.

[60]Naylor, *Federal Budget System in Operation*, pp. 24–25.

dictory directives by preparing one set as Congress specified, and another as directed by the president. As business conditions improved and passage of the Sixteenth Amendment in 1913 permitted a graduated income tax, thus raising revenue, pressures for change in the budget system diminished.

Nothing was done to establish an executive budget until after the First World War,[61] when the desire for fiscal prudence, both against the growing debt and for a balanced budget, reasserted itself with a vengeance. World War I had been fought largely on borrowed money. From 1914 to 1918, the government's role in directing economic activity expanded enormously. There was a new public concern that the profligate habits of wartime would carry over into peacetime civilian life,[62] and renewed interest in a national executive budget; between 1918 and 1921, the reformers presented proposals to congressional committees. Once again reformers criticized the federal expenditure process: There was overlap among substantive committees, and hence duplication of effort; there was no comprehensive consideration of revenues and expenditures; the consequence of bureaucratic rivalry was waste.

In the name of managing the huge national debt, the Budget and Accounting Act of 1921 made the major changes budget reformers had long supported. Departments sent spending estimates to the president through a new institution, the Bureau of the Budget, and the Chief Executive had total control over the Bureau of the Budget.[63] Henceforth no appropriation could be considered unless first reviewed by the president and the two appropriations committees. "Review," however, was a far cry from the near-absolute control exercised by European cabinets.

No stronger statement of the spirit of legislative supremacy, or of its practical consequences, can be found than in the House report commenting on the Budget and Accounting Act of 1921. The only executive aspect of that act, the House insisted, was that the president would henceforth be held responsible for the agency estimates he submitted. After that, the budget was still legislative all the way. Members of Congress could still move his proposed numbers up, down, or sideways by ignoring them entirely. If anyone doubted that the president's budget was just his set of recommendations, the Committee Report sought to disabuse them:

> The President's responsibility ends when he has prepared the budget and transmitted it to Congress. . . . the proposed law does not change in the slightest degree the duty of Congress to make the minutest examination of the budget and to adopt the budget only to the extent that it is found to be economical. If the estimates contained in the President's budget are too large, it will be the duty of Congress to reduce them. If in the opinion of Congress the estimates of expenditures are not sufficient, it will be within the power of Congress to increase them. The bill does not in the slightest degree give the Executive any greater power than he now has over the consideration of appropriations by Congress.[64]

---

[61] Burkhead, *Government Budgeting*, pp. 20–21.

[62] Kimmel, *Federal Budget and Fiscal Policy*, p. 88.

[63] Fritz Morstein Marx, "The Bureau of the Budget: Its Evolution and Present Role," *American Political Science Review*, Vol. 39, No. 4 (August 1945), pp. 653–84.

[64] House Report No. 14, 67th Congress, 1st Session, 6–7 (1921), cited in Louis Fisher, "The Item Veto: The Risks of Emulating the States." Prepared for delivery at the Annual Meeting of the American Political Science Association, New Orleans, August 29–31, 1985, p. 6.

If Congress were to give the president the power to propose, it wanted also to ensure its power to dispose, and then to oversee the execution of its decisions. It created the Bureau of the Budget and the Executive Budget process, but checked the president in two ways. In 1920 the House, and the Senate in 1922, restored their former powers to the appropriations committees, thus providing an institutional counterweight to the centralized executive process. In addition, Congress removed from the Treasury the power to audit and account for expenditures (where it had resided since 1789) and lodged it in a General Accounting Office (GAO) outside of the president's control. The Comptroller of the Treasury was replaced by a new official, the Comptroller General of the United States. He had a single, 15-year term and could be replaced only by a joint resolution of both houses of Congress, signed by the president.

What remained to be decided was the function of the newly created Budget Bureau within the executive branch. Its first head, General Charles G. Dawes, a student and practitioner of administration, insisted that the offices not be in the Treasury Building, but outside it, and near the White House (Dawes wanted to insulate the Bureau from interdepartmental squabbles).[65] He insisted on his right to call department heads into conference; President Warren Harding wisely suggested that such conferences be held in the White House Cabinet Room (instead of in the Budget Director's office), to emphasize the Chief Executive's commanding role in budget decisions.[66]

The 1920s witnessed a major assault on federal spending. Led by General Dawes, his successors, and businessmen whom Dawes brought into government (often working for "a dollar a year"), the Bureau zealously pursued efficiency. Its accomplishments provoked panegyrics. Martin Madden, chairman of the House Committee on Appropriations, wrote as if the promised land had been reached: "One noticeable feature has been the . . . self-sacrificing of local interests in favor of the common good. When one recalls the former days when appropriations were sought with avidity for local projects . . . it is appropriate to commend the change from local to national attitude."[67]

An economy mood prevailed. The reconstitution of the appropriations committees and the Budget and Accounting Act of 1921 reflected overwhelming agreement on a balanced budget at a restricted level of spending. That consensus enabled the system to work with little friction. Far from exceeding revenues, spending had to fit within them, and then some, to permit deficit reduction. Through the 1920s, conveniently a time of plenty when Congress was receiving few petitions for help anyway, the debt was steadily reduced.

Then came the market crash of 1929, followed by the Great Depression of the 1930s. Federal revenues were cut in half (1930: $4.06 billion; 1932: $1.92 billion); state and local revenues plummeted; demands for relief soared. State and local funds ran out; people turned to Washington.

---

[65]See Charles G. Dawes, *The First Year of the Budget of the United States* (New York: Harper, 1923).

[66]Ibid., p. 29.

[67]Quoted in William Franklin Willoughby, *The National Budget System with Suggestions for Its Improvement* (Baltimore: Johns Hopkins, 1927), pp. 287–88.

DISLOCATION AND CONTINUITY: DEPRESSION, WAR, AND THE POST-WAR INTERLUDE

At the beginning of the depression, consensus on balancing the federal budget continued. Both Presidents Hoover and Roosevelt stressed its priority. By the early 1930s, a number of Americans in the Democratic party began to seek a rationale for encouraging the government to expand public works and thus increase employment. They found it in the work of economist John Maynard Keynes and introduced his thought to key figures, including President Roosevelt.[68] Keynes argued that it was appropriate, in a deflationary period when vast economic resources went unused, for the government to create deficits as a means of expanding demand. When economic activity was slow, government should step in to speed it up; when the economy overheated and inflation resulted, government could decrease spending. In short, raising and lowering the deficit would become a prime means of economic control.

The New Deal in the United States was never a coherent set of measures. Rather it comprised ad hoc answers to immediate crises.[69] Accordingly, Roosevelt's program (presented to Congress in the famous first Hundred Days) aimed at relief, recovery, and reform: proposals to reestablish public confidence in the banking system, to achieve a balanced budget by cutting government spending, to revive agriculture through an increase in farm incomes, to assist industry by creating a system of price codes, and to institute a program of public works.

In response, the House of Representatives passed the Economy Bill, which halved the pensions of disabled war veterans, reduced congressional salaries as well as those of all federal employees, and curtailed other federal expenditures. The Economy Bill was designed to balance spending with revenue, which, since two-thirds of it was based on individual and corporate income taxes, had declined by nearly a half between 1930 and 1933. This bill increased hardships among pensioners and, by curtailing government expenditure, reduced individual purchasing power.

Clearly, Roosevelt was no believer in the desirability of deficits. Indeed, when Keynes conferred with Roosevelt in Washington in 1935, the two apparently did not agree. Roosevelt maintained his balanced budget preferences; throughout the 1930s, he viewed current spending as pump priming. After an overwhelming victory in the 1936 election, Roosevelt tried to cut spending in 1937 to balance the budget, but a sharp upturn in unemployment in 1938 forced him to abandon this effort.[70]

A look at federal income and expenditure between 1929 and 1939 gives some sense of government's growth and its expanded role in the economy. In 1929, federal expenditure was $3.3 billion; in 1939, $8.9 billion. While federal spending increased by 170 percent, there was only a 25 percent increase in fed-

---

[68]For Felix Frankfurter's efforts in this direction, see H. N. Hirsch, *The Enigma of Felix Frankfurter* (New York: Basic Books, 1981), p. 113.

[69]Jim Potter, *The American Economy between the World Wars* (New York: Wiley, 1974), p. 113.

[70]Robert Lekachman, *The Age of Keynes* (New York: McGraw-Hill, 1966), pp. 122–23.

eral revenues (from $4.0 billion in 1929 to $5.0 billion in 1939). Federal expenditure as a percentage of gross national product (GNP), moreover, tripled (from 3.2 percent in 1929 to 9.7 percent in 1939) whereas federal revenue as a percent of GNP during the same period did not even double (from 3.9 to 5.5 percent).

The enduring legacy of the New Deal was acceptance by the American public of the doctrine that the federal government has ultimate responsibility for the economy. The struggle for power that marked the budget process since colonial times took on a new dimension: As government faced outward toward society—to alleviate poverty—its budgetary procedures, previously reflecting an orientation toward internal control, became more concerned with relating spending to revenue than with the substance of spending itself. Consensus as to governmental responsibility was joined to a decline of the balanced-budget norm.

Under Keynesian doctrine, as understood and practiced at the time, the idea was to balance the economy at full employment (accepting between 3 and 5 percent of "frictional" unemployment), not necessarily to balance the budget. To the extent that relationships between participants in budgeting depended on belief in balance—since revenue limits expenditure, no spending agency can grow faster than the economy without taking unfair advantage of the others—the pillars of spending control were severely shaken. So long as there was more for everyone, so good. If (or, rather, when, in view of historical experience) the rate of economic growth declined, however, the participants in budgeting would have to agree on their fair share of a more limited pie. Before we can understand how operating under conditions of ideological dissensus affects budgeting, we need to understand how ideological consensus, when it existed, moved budgeting along a more incremental path.

Chapter
3

The Dance of
the Dollars:
Classical Budgeting*

*W*ars are catalysts of change. The United States emerged from the Second World War determined not to reexperience the depression of the 1930s. Its federal government, being victorious, enjoyed an enhanced respect. The task assigned was to maintain prosperity by managing the economy, institutionalized in the Full Employment Act of 1946, which created the Council of Economic Advisers. How far government should go was a matter of controversy, but that it should act was accepted. Along with that consensus came an expanded importance for the Executive Office of the President, including the Bureau of the Budget (BOB).

Although there was a lot of doubt and soul searching about the place of the United States as a (perhaps the) major international power after the war, internationalism won out over isolationism. There was no turning back.

The budgetary consequences for postwar America were profound. War had accustomed the nation to hitherto unheard of levels of taxation; while these went down considerably, they never fell to prewar levels. Domestic spending rose not only for veterans (the G.I. Bill put many through school) but also to some degree for social purposes. After the roller-coaster of rapid demobilization was followed by the buildup after the Korean War, the defense budget had stabilized at levels much higher than the prewar period. By 1955 defense constituted over two-fifths of total spending while social welfare programs, including social security, were about one-fifth. The economy began to grow. Keeping defense stable in constant dollars (adjusted for inflation and without raising tax rates) allowed domestic spending to rise in the late 1960s and early 1970s with the advent of new and expanded welfare programs, such as medicare for the elderly and medicaid for the poor. Government grew painlessly. Though President Kennedy cut taxes to stimulate the economy in the early 1960s and President Johnson rejected the advice of

---

*This chapter is largely a summary of the sections on "Strategies and Calculation" in the 1964 edition of *The Politics of the Budgetary Process*.

the Council of Economic Advisers to raise them during the Vietnam War in the mid-1960s, revenue and expenditures remained close, with small, albeit growing, deficits. No great sacrifices—substantial tax increases or large spending cuts— were seen to be necessary. Incremental advance was the order of these times.

Yet the inherited practices and understandings of the budgetary process continued to be accepted. The Truman and Eisenhower administrations saw a balanced budget as economically desirable. Their position was supported by a conservative coalition in Congress: an alliance between conservative Republicans and conservative Democrats, mostly from the South. The coalition was held together by basic policy agreement on limited government and was facilitated by joint meetings among leaders. Throughout the 1940s and into the late 1950s, the conservative coalition was able to win at least 70 percent of the votes in both Houses.[1]

A growing economy and increasing federal revenues, however, made it simultaneously possible to accommodate advocates of defense spending, social spending, limited government, and balanced budgets. Adequate revenues within a framework of mutual expectations maintained the formal institutions of the budget process, and created a "classical" world of budgeting. It was a world bounded by its own horizons, in Allen Schick's words,

> shut off from the outside world. Its participants knew one another, maintained ongoing contact, fought repeatedly, and always came to terms. They were budget and program officials in federal agencies, finance experts in the old Bureau of the Budget, and members and clerks of the appropriations committees. Many of these bonded together at annual retreats, swigging beer and trading war stories. Theirs was "the private government of public money" . . . It was a world in which the budget was a tightly guarded secret during months of preparation in the executive branch and a bewildering book of numbers after it was released to Congress. The insiders had a monopoly on budget information, and they did not share much with outsiders. In that world, budgets were made by government talking to itself; agencies to the bureau, the bureau back to the agencies, agencies to the appropriations committees, the committees to the agencies.[2]

Classical budgeting, we see in retrospect, was premised upon agreement on the size, scope, and distribution of expenditure. Conflict was confined to the margins, a little more here, a little less there.

Should we look at this period as an exception, a situation resulting from a peculiar set of circumstances at a particular time? Was classical budgeting simply the manifestation of a disappearing era, in which an elite played out dying rituals even as it was undermined by the currents of history? Did those years in fact represent lost opportunities for forging more viable solutions for critical problems of American society, instead stretching the fabric of inherited institutions and accompanying compromises, deals and evasions, until it tore and collapsed? Was classical

[1]John F. Manley, "The Conservative Coalition in Congress," *American Behavioral Scientist*, Vol. 17, No. 2 (November/December 1973), p. 239.

[2]Allen Schick, "From the Old Politics of Budgeting to the New," in Naomi Caiden and Joseph White, eds., *Budgeting, Politicy, Politics: An Appreciation of Aaron Wildavsky* (New Brunswick, N.J.: Transaction Publishers, 1995) p. 134.

budgeting merely an interlude, a pause before the storm to come, and a respite following the traumas of war and depression? In stressing the static elements of the postwar world to, say, the end of the 1960s, are we ignoring its more dynamic movements, which ultimately overwhelmed what might have been previously taken for granted as normal political life in a prosperous, stable, superpower?

However legitimate these questions, and whatever their answers, it is worth pausing to examine the characteristics of classical budgeting. It provides a base, a point of contrast, for later transformations. Since reform of budget institutions is typically cumulative, much remains in place. While calculations and strategies may have changed to adapt to new constraints and opportunities, their necessity continues.

What follows is therefore often written in the present tense so as to retain a sense of immediacy. The Bureau of the Budget became the Office of Management and Budget in 1970, but in discussing classical budgeting it is referred to as the Budget Bureau for reasons of clarity. The reader should be aware, however, as the following chapters attest, that much of what follows belongs to a bygone era. Calculations remain complex but the roles and strategies of the participants and the budgetary process itself have been markedly altered.

CALCULATIONS

Participants in budgeting operate in an environment that imposes severe constraints on what they can do. Neither the opportunities they seize upon nor the disabilities they suffer are wholly, perhaps not even largely, within their control. Though perceptions of reality differ somewhat, and views of what is desirable differ more, budgetary actors accept certain elementary facts of life to which they must adjust.

Everyone is aware of the structural conditions of political life—such as the separation of powers, the division of labor within appropriations committees, and the customary separation between appropriations and substantive legislative committees. All participants face the usual overt political factors involving group pressures, relationships between members of Congress and their constituents, political party conflicts, executive-legislative cooperation and rivalry, interagency disputes, and the like. Participants soon come to know the rules of the budgetary game, which specify the roles they must play and the kinds of moves that are more or less permissible. It would be hard indeed to ignore the contemporary climate of opinion—a spending or cutting mood—as when a rise in defense spending becomes obvious after a provocation, or when a rise in unemployment demands creating jobs. Trends in the growth of national-welfare programs and increasing federal responsibility for a host of services are unlikely to be reversed. The participants take these conditions as "given" to a considerable extent and make calculations based on the way they perceive their environment. By "calculation" is meant the series of related factors (manifestly including perceptions of power relationships) that budgetary actors take into account in determining the choice of competing alternatives. Calculation involves a study of how problems arise and are identified; how they are broken down into manageable dimensions; how they relate to one another; how determinations are made of what is relevant; and how the actions of others are given consideration.

Complexity

One cannot hope to understand why people behave as they do unless one has some idea about how they make their calculations, and calculations are far from neutral. "Who gets what and how much" in politics depends on how calculations are made. Different methods of calculation often result in different decisions.

Budgeting is complex, both because there are many interrelated items and because these often pose technical difficulties. Suppose that you were interested in the leukemia research program and you wondered how the money was being spent. By looking at the National Cancer Institute's budgetary presentation you would discover that X amount is being spent on a project studying "factors and mechanics concerned in hemopoiesis," but that much less is being put into "a study of the relationship of neutralizing antibodies for the Rouse sarcoma virus to resistance and susceptibility for visceral lymphomatosis." Could you tell whether too much is being spent on one as compared to the other, or whether either project serves any useful purpose? It is not surprising, therefore, that members of congress express dismay at the difficulties of understanding technical subjects. Representative Jensen has a granddaughter who is reputed by him to have read "all the stuff she can get on nuclear science. . . . And . . . she just stumps me. I say, 'Jennifer, for Heaven's sake. I can't answer that.' 'Well,' she says, 'You are on the Atomic Energy Commission Committee, Grandpa.' 'Yes,' he replies, 'but I am not schooled in the art.'"

Endless time and unlimited ability to calculate might help. But time is in short supply, the human mind can encompass just so much, and the number of budgetary items may be huge. "We might as well be frank," stated the chairman of the Defense Appropriations Subcommittee, Representative George Mahon (D-Tex.), "no human being regardless of his position and . . . capacity could possibly be completely familiar with all the items of appropriations contained in this defense bill. . . ."

Aside from the complexity of individual budgetary programs, there remains the imposing problem of making comparisons among different programs—how much highways are worth as compared to recreation facilities, national defense, and schools—that have different values for different people. No common denominator among these functions has been developed. No matter how hard they try, therefore, officials discover that they cannot find an objective method of judging priorities among programs. How, then, do budget officials go about meeting their staggering burden of calculation?

Aids to Calculation

The ways in which the appropriations committees go about making budgetary calculations are affected by their central position in the congressional system. Their power to make budgetary decisions is in a sense rooted in their ability to help keep the system going by meeting the needs of other members of Congress. Appropriations must be voted each year if the government is to continue to function. To put together budgets running into the billions of dollars and involving innumerable different activities is a gargantuan task. But sheer effort is not enough. The committees must reduce the enormous burden of calculation involved in budgeting, in order to reach the necessary decisions. Otherwise, the necessity for decision might propel them into making random or wholly capricious choices that would throw governmental operations out of kilter. Nor could Congress as a whole shoulder the burden. Most members are busy with other things; they can hardly hope to become knowledgeable in more than a few areas of budgeting, if that. Unless they are to abdicate their powers, some way of reducing their information costs must be found. The way they have adapted is to accept the verdict of the appropriations committees most of the time and to intervene just often enough to keep the committees (roughly) in line.

Their mode of decision making might be characterized as incremental, enabling management of calculations and resolution of conflicts within the timeframe of the budget. The various aspects of incrementalism reinforce each other in an informal system of coordination based on mutual expectations of participants pursuing their own agendas in a fragmented institution.

INCREMENTAL BUDGETING

The largest determining factor of this year's budget is last year's. Most of each budget is a product of previous decisions. The budget may be conceived of as an iceberg; by far the largest part lies below the surface, outside the control of anyone. Many items are standard, simply reenacted every year unless there is a special reason to challenge them. Long-range commitments have been made, and this year's share is scooped out of the total and included as part of the annual budget. The expenses of mandatory programs (entitlements), such as price supports or veterans' pensions, must be met. Some ongoing programs that appear to be satisfactory are no longer challenged. Agencies are going concerns and a minimum must be spent on housekeeping (though this item is particularly vulnerable to attack because it does not appear to involve a reduction in services or benefits). Powerful political support makes including other activities inevitable. At any one time, after past commitments are paid for, a rather small percentage—seldom larger than 30 percent, often smaller than 5—is within the realm of anybody's (including congressional and Budget Bureau) discretion as a practical matter.

Budgeting is incremental, not comprehensive. The beginning of wisdom about an agency budget is that it is almost never actively reviewed as a whole every year, in the sense of reconsidering the value of all existing programs as compared to all possible alternatives. Instead, it is based on last year's budget with special attention given to a narrow range of increases or decreases. General agreement on past budgetary decisions combined with years of accumulated experience and specialization allows those who make the budget to be concerned with relatively small increments to an existing base. Their attention is focused on a small number of items over which the budgetary battle is fought. Political reality, budget officials say, restricts attention to items they can do something about—a few new programs and possible cuts in old ones.

Budgeting Is Linked to Base and Fair Shares   Central to incrementalism is the concept of the base. The base is the general expectation that programs will be carried on at close to the going level of expenditures. Having a project included in the agency's base thus means more than just getting it in the budget for a particular year. It means the expectation that the expenditure will continue, that it is accepted as part of what will be done, and, therefore, that it will normally not be subjected to intensive scrutiny. (The word *base,* incidentally, is part of the common parlance of officials engaged in budgeting, and it would make no sense if experience led them to expect wide fluctuations from year to year, rather than additions to or subtractions from some relatively steady point.)

Linked to the concept of the base is the idea of "fair share." Fair share means not only the base an agency has established but also the expectation that the agency will receive some proportion of funds, if any, which are to be increased over or decreased below the base of the other governmental agencies. Fair share, then, reflects a convergence of expectations on roughly how much an agency is to receive in comparison to others.

The absence of a base, or an agreement on fair shares, makes it much harder to calculate what the agency or program should get. That happens when an agency or program is new or when rapid shifts of sentiment toward it take place. When times are tough, the base is subject to debate and adjustment. The base may be defined either as the "current estimate" (existing spending level of an agency) or next year's anticipated cost of maintaining programs at current levels of service (particularly important in inflationary times). In any case there will be disagreement on what constitutes the base.

Budgeting Is Consensual   There must be agreement on the general direction of public policy, at least on most past policies, or Congress would be swamped with difficult choices. Past policies would have to be renegotiated every year, a time-consuming and enervating process. Simultaneously, new programs are sure to engender controversy; without agreement that keeps the past mostly out of contention, it becomes harder to deal with the present. Consensus on policies need not be total; conflict is ever-present. Yet if disagreement encompasses too many policies, aids to calculation will not work well.

Budgeting Is Historical   One way of dealing with a problem of huge magnitude is to make rough guesses while letting experience accumulate. When the consequences of various actions become apparent, it is then possible to make modifications to avoid the difficulties. Since members of Congress usually serve for several years before getting on appropriations committees, and since they are expected to serve an apprenticeship before making themselves heard, the more influential among them typically have long years of experience in dealing with their specialties. They have absorbed the meaning of many past moves and are prepared to apply the results of previous calculations to present circumstances. In this way the magnitude of any one decision at any one time is reduced, and with it the burden of calculation.

A line-item budgetary form facilitates this historical approach. Instead of focusing on various programs as a whole, the committees usually can concentrate on changes in various items—personnel, equipment, maintenance, specific activities—which make up the program. By keeping categories constant over a number of years, and by requiring that the previous and present year's figures be placed in adjacent columns, calculations made in the past need not be gone over again completely. And though members know that the agency is involved in various programs, the line-item form enables them to concentrate on the less divisive issue of how much for each item.

Yet the past is not a foolproof guide to the future. Because so many actions are being undertaken at the same time, it is hard to disentangle the effects of one particular action compared to others. Consequently, disputes may arise about the benefits of continued support for an item. Ultimately, reliance on a theory of cause and effect to provide guidance as to what is expected to happen becomes necessary.

Budgeting Is Fragmented   Budgets are made in fragments. Agencies develop budgetary requests based on their specialized needs. These requests are then channeled to any number of the multiple levels of specialization within Congress—the House and Senate appropriations committees, their subcommittees, the subject areas within these subcommittees, the Senate Appropriations Committee appeals procedure, the Conference Committee, and the authorizations functions of the substantive committees and their specialized subcommittees. Even the subcommittees do not deal with all items in the budget but will pay special attention to instances of increases or decreases over the previous year. In this way, it might be said, subcommittees deal with a fragment of a fragment of the whole.

Budgeting Is Simplified   Another way of handling complexity is to see how actions on simpler items can be indices for more complicated ones. Instead of dealing directly with the cost of a huge new installation, for example, decision-makers may look at how personnel and administrative costs, or real estate transactions with which they have some familiarity, are handled. If these items are treated properly, then they may feel better able to trust administrators with the larger ones. Unable to handle the more complex problems, decision makers may retreat to the simpler ones.

Budgeting Is Social   Participants take clues from how others behave. They try to read character to reach programs. This method calls for looking at the administrative officials responsible rather than at the subject matter. To see if they are competent and reliable, officials can be questioned on a point here and there, a difficulty in this or that. One senior congressman reported that he followed an administrator's testimony to probe for weaknesses, looking for "strain in voice or manner," "covert glances," and so on.[3] Also, if an official can get people to go along, and if too many others do not complain too long and loud, then he may take the fact of agreement on something as his measure of success.

---

[3]L. Dwaine Marvick, *Congressional Appropriation Politics,* Ph.D. Dissertation, Columbia University, 1952, p. 297.

Budgeting Is "Satisficing"   Calculations may be simplified by lowering one's sights. Although they do not use Herbert Simon's vocabulary, budget officials do not try to maximize but, instead, they "satisfice" (satisfy and suffice).[4] Which is to say that the budgeters do not try for the best of all possible worlds (whatever that might be) but, in their own words, try to "get by," to "come out all right," to "avoid trouble," to "avoid the worst." And since the budget comes up every year, and deals largely with piecemeal adjustment, this is one way to correct glaring weaknesses as they arise.

Budgeting Is Treated as if It Were Nonprogrammatic   This statement does not mean that people do not care about programs; they do. Nor does it mean that they do not fight for or against some programs; they do. What it does mean is that, given considerable agreement on policy, decision makers may see most of their work as marginal monetary adjustments to existing programs so that the question of the ultimate desirability of most programs arises only once in a while. "A disagreement on money isn't like a legislative program . . . ," one appropriations committee member said in a typical statement, "it's a matter of money rather than a difference in philosophy." An appropriations committee member explains how disagreements are handled in the markup session when members retire behind closed doors to work out their recommendations. (Nowadays many such sessions are open.) "If there's agreement, we go right along. If there's a lot of controversy we put the item aside and go on. Then, after a day or two, we may have a list of ten controversial items. We give and take and pound them down till we get agreement."[5] Obviously, they did not feel too strongly about each item or they could not agree so readily.

Budgeting Is Repetitive   Decision making in budgeting is carried on with the knowledge that few problems have to be "solved" once and for all. Everyone knows that a problem may be dealt with over and over again. Hence considerations that a member of Congress neglects one year may be taken up another year, or in a supplementary action during the same year. Problems are not so much solved as they are worn down by repeated attacks until they are no longer pressing or have been superseded by other problems. Problem-succession, not problem solving, best describes what happens.

Budgeting Is Sequential   The appropriations committees do not try to handle every problem at once. On the contrary, they do not deal with many problems in a particular year, and those they do encounter are dealt with mostly in different places and at different times. Many decisions made in previous years are allowed to stand or to vary slightly without question. Then committees divide up subjects for more intensive inquiry among subcommittees and their specialists. Over the years, subcommittees center now on one and then on another problem. When

---

[4]Herbert, Simon, *Models of Man* (New York: Wiley, 1957); see also Jerome S. Bruner, Jacqueline J. Goodnow, and George A. Austin, *A Study of Thinking* (New York: Wiley, 1956), for a fascinating discussion of strategies of concept attainment useful for dealing with the problem of complexity.

[5]Simon, *Models of Man.*

budgetary decisions made by one subcommittee adversely affect those of another, the difficulty is handled by "fire-truck tactics," that is, by dealing with each problem in turn in whatever jurisdiction it appears. Difficulties are overcome not so much by central coordination or planning as by a cybernetic approach—attacking each manifestation in the different centers of decision in sequence.[6]

These aids ease the burden of calculations that are necessary for the development of a budget. Because attention is focused on the increment rather than on the relative value of a particular program compared to others, aids to calculation also serve to moderate conflict. The specialized and apparently nonprogrammatic character of decisions enhances the appearance of the budgetary process as technical. Since decisions are simplified and are made in different arenas at different times, the chance that severe conflict will converge is reduced. In such a situation, the role of participants—agencies, appropriations committees, and the Bureau of the Budget—were clearly defined.

ROLES AND PERSPECTIVES

The Agency

Agency people are expected to be advocates of increased appropriations. A classic statement of this role was made in 1939 by William A. Jump, a celebrated budget officer for the Department of Agriculture, who wrote that in budgeting

> . . . there inevitably are severe differences of judgment as to whether funds should be provided for a given purpose and, if so, in what amount. . . .
>
> It is at this stage that the departmental budget officer becomes an advocate or special pleader of the cause he represents. His position in representing the department then is analogous to that of an attorney for his client. In such circumstances, departmental budget officers put up the strongest and most effective fight of which they are capable to obtain . . . funds. . . . No apologies are offered for a vigorous position, or even an occasional showing of teeth, if circumstances seem to require it.[7]

Jump justified playing the advocate's role partly on the grounds that other participants had counterroles that necessitate a strong push from the departmental side.

Appropriations committee members tend to view budget officials as people with vested interests in raising appropriations. This position is generally accepted as natural and inevitable for administrators. As Assistant Chief Thayer of the Forest Service put it, "Mr. Chairman, you would not think that it would be proper for me to be in charge of this work and not be enthusiastic about it and not think that I ought to have a lot more money, would you? I have been in it for thirty years,

---

[6] The methods of calculation described here are similar to those attributed to social scientists by David Braybrooke and Charles E. Lindblom in their *A Strategy of Decision* (New York: Free Press, 1963), and the private firms by Richard Cyert and James March in their *A Behavioral Theory of the Firm* (Englewood Cliffs, N.J.: Prentice-Hall, 1963).

[7] W. A. Jump, "Budgetary and Financial Administration in an Operating Department of the Federal Government." Paper delivered at the conference of the Governmental Research Association, September 8, 1939, p. 5. See also the psychological portrait in Robert Walker, "William A. Jump: The Staff Officer as a Personality," *Public Administration Review*, Vol. 14 (Autumn 1954), pp. 233–46.

and I believe in it." At times this attitude may lead to cynicism and perhaps annoyance on the part of House Appropriations Committee members. Yet if agencies did not advocate, Congress would have a harder time figuring out what they needed and wanted.

Deciding How Much to Ask For   With appropriations always falling short of desires, how much of what they would like to get do agencies ask for? The simplest approach would be to add up the costs of all worthwhile projects and submit the total. This simple addition rarely is done, partly because everyone knows there would not be enough resources to go around. With revenues fixed in the short run, asking for a lot more would mean taking these sums from other agencies and programs; this would not be popular. Largely, however, the reason is strategic. If an agency continually submits requests far above what it actually gets, the Budget Bureau and the appropriations committees lose confidence in it and automatically cut large chunks before looking at the budget in detail.

It becomes much harder to justify even items with top priority because no one trusts an agency that repeatedly comes in too high. Yet it is unrealistic for an administrator not to make some allowance for the inevitable cut that others will make. Administrators realize that in predicting needs there is a reasonable range within which a decision can fall, and they just follow ordinary prudence in coming out with an estimate near the top.

Budgeting goes on in a world of reciprocal expectations that lead to self-fulfilling prophecies; agencies are expected to pad their requests to guard against cuts. As Representative Jamie Whitten (D-Miss.), Chairman of the Appropriations Subcommittee on Agriculture put it, "If you deal with the Department [of Agriculture] long enough and learn that they scale down each time, the bureau or agency can take that into consideration and build up the original figures." The Budget Bureau is expected to cut, partly because of its interest in protecting the president's program, and partly because it believes that agencies are likely to pad. Appropriations committees are expected to cut to fulfill their roles, and because they know that the agency has already allowed for just this action. Cuts may be made in the House in the expectation that the Senate will replace them. Members of Congress get headlines for suggesting large cuts, but they often do not follow through for they know that the amounts will have to be restored by supplemental appropriations. Things may get to the point where members of the appropriations committees talk to agency officials off the record and ask where they can make a cut that will have to be restored later.

Whether disposed to pad or not, the agency finds that it must allow for cuts, and the cycle begins again as the prophecies confirm themselves. We have seen that an agency's budget is chiefly a product of past decisions. Beyond this is an area of discretion in which budget people want to get all they can, but cannot get all they want. Asking for too much may prejudice their chances, so it soon becomes apparent that the ability to estimate "what will go" (a phrase of budget officials) is a crucial aspect of budgeting.

Participants look out for, and receive, signals from the Executive Branch, Congress, clientele groups, and also their own organizations; in this way they arrive at a composite estimate of how much to ask for in the light of what they can expect to get. After an administration has been in office for a while, agency personnel have a background of actions and informal contacts to tell them how its various programs are regarded, especially for the preceding year. They also keep up with public announcements and private reports about how tough the president is going to be in regard to new expenditures. Formal word comes in the shape of a policy letter from the Budget Bureau, which usually has some statement on how closely this year's budget should resemble the last one. The impression made by this letter may be strengthened or weakened by reports or remarks made in cabinet meetings or by statements from those high up in the administration. If the president's science advisor speaks favorably of a particular program, his comments may offset tough remarks by the Director of the Budget. And, together, all these are seen in the light of the agency's experience in day-to-day dealings with the Budget Bureau staff, whose attitudes and nuances of behavior may speak more eloquently than any public statements as to administration intentions.

A major factor for agencies to consider is the interest of specialized publics in particular programs. Periodic reports from the field on the demand for services may serve as a general indicator. Top officials may travel and see at firsthand just how enthusiastic the field personnel are about new programs. How detailed and concrete are their examples of public reaction? Agencies also may have advisory committees and use newspaper clipping services to provide information on the intentions of the interests concerned. The affected interests ordinarily lose no time in beating a path to the agency's door and presenting data about public support. When the agency begins to notice connections between the activities of supporting interests and calls from people in Congress, it has a pretty good idea of the support for a program.

Since there is much continuity of both agency and personnel and the committees and staffs in Congress, there is a rich history on which to base predictions. Agency officials are continuously engaged in "feeling the pulse" of Congress; likes and dislikes of influential members are well charted. Hearings on last year's budget are perused for indications of attitudes on specific programs, particularly on items that may get the agency into trouble. If the committee chair lets it be known that not enough is being done in a certain area, the agency knows that a program there will meet with sympathetic consideration. Overall congressional support may be indicated by debates on votes or amendments or new legislation. Finally, continuous contacts with appropriations committee staff leave agency people with definite feelings about what is likely to go over with the committee.

Last—but certainly not least—agencies also study the national political situation in deciding how much to try to get. Are there political reasons for increasing or decreasing spending? Is control over the national government split between the parties, with the result that there will be competition for support of particular programs or for holding the line? Do certain elements in Congress want to force presidential vetoes, or will the threat of veto result in program changes more favorable to the president?

From time to time agencies are affected by emergent problems, current events that no one could have predicted but that will radically alter budgetary prospects for particular programs. A change in missile technology, a drought, a new plant disease, a social problem may drastically improve the prospects for some programs. The agency or interest group that can exploit the recognized needs arising from these events or generate such recognition is in an excellent position to expand support for its budget.

Deciding How Much to Spend   Deciding how much to ask for may be a big problem; but sometimes it is equally hard for an agency to figure out precisely how much to spend. If an agency has a substantial carryover, this may be taken as a sign that the agency does not need as much as it received and may cut off that amount in the future. The practice of penalizing carryovers leads to a last-minute flurry of spending in the fourth quarter of the year despite apportionment of quarterly allotments. But you can't win. The agency that comes out exactly even is likely to be suspected of spending its limit without considering the need for economy. Coming out even seems just too neat to be true. The hapless agency that runs out of funds, on the other hand, may well be accused of using the tactic of coercive deficiency, or trying to compel Congress to appropriate more funds on the grounds that a vital activity will otherwise suffer. Most agency budget people try to end up with a little amount in reserve for most programs, but with an occasional deficit permitted in programs to which they are certain the funds will have to be restored.

Where agencies are likely to lose funds they carry over, however, their incentive is to spend up to the limit. Agencies are acutely aware that the reputation they have built up can help or hinder them greatly in matters of this kind. The agency with a reputation for economy may be praised for turning funds back and not get them cut the following year, whereas the agency deemed to be prodigal may get slashed on the grounds it must not have needed the money in the first place.

Department versus Bureau   The term *agency* has been used thus far to signify either a bureau or a department, and most of the considerations do apply with equal force to departments and bureaus. Now it will be useful to make a distinction between departments and their component units, the bureaus, in discussing the special problems that departments face in deciding how much to try to get for bureaus under their jurisdiction. Let us assume that the department secretary and her staff have managed to work out some notion of the secretary's policy preferences, and it so happens that these preferences run counter to those of a bureau. Problems of influence immediately arise. The most obvious is that some bureaus may have considerable support in Congress and can thus override departments. Still, the secretary and her staff might well decide to push their own preferences anyway, if that were all that had to be considered. One difficulty, however, is that a record of a department recommending far less than Congress appropriates (and a bureau wants) may lead to a general disregard of what the secretary proposed. Why pay attention if she is obviously a loser? Another difficulty is that if department officials need bureau support in other matters, they may find that hostility over deep cuts can interfere with the necessary good relations. So the department often finds it wise to temper its preferences with a strong dose of calculations as to what would be acceptable to the other participants.

Considerations such as these involve the various departments (whether they know it or not) in resolving a basic question of political theory: Shall each bureau ask for what it wants or shall priority go to the total departmental situation in making requests? (Put in a different way, the question might be phrased: Is it best for each interest to pursue its own advantage or shall each seek a solution it believes is in the interest of all?) Of course, if every bureau just shoots for the moon, the total reaches an astronomical figure and that is not much help. Except in years when there are exceedingly powerful reasons for keeping budget totals down, the approach preferred by most department officials is a modified version of "tell us what you really want."

The usual practice is for a high department official to lay the whole budget before the bureau heads to show them why they cannot get any more than their limited share, despite the fact that the programs are eminently deserving. Some budget officials are extremely talented at cutting without getting the blame.

The Bureau of the Budget

The dominant role of the Bureau of the Budget, in form and in fact, is to help the president carry out his purpose,[8] and its orientation, therefore, depends on that of the Chief Executive. His concerns about the relative priorities of domestic and foreign policy programs, his beliefs about the desirability of a balanced budget, and his preferences in various other areas determine a good deal of what the Bureau tries to do. Ideally, a meeting of the various executive policy decision streams—domestic and defense budgeting, and fiscal policy, represented by the president with advisors from the White House, National Security Council, Defense Department, Council of Economic Advisers, Treasury, and Budget Bureau—will produce a "target total" for outlays and promote a rough indication of domestic and military priorities. A decision on target total outlays serves as the basis for the Budget Bureau to develop agency ceilings. Thus the Bureau finds itself trying to get appropriations from Congress for presidential programs and, at times, prodding agencies to come in with new or enlarged programs to meet the president's desires. Yet the BOB is also responsible for establishing agency ceilings based on the target total outlays. Thus BOB ordinarily gives less weight to advocating presidential programs than to keeping them within bounds, particularly since everyone already expects the agencies to perform the functions of advocacy.

This top-down approach to budgeting (i.e, the establishment of boundaries by setting budgetary totals) contrasts with the bottom-up incremental development of budgetary totals reflected in congressional decision making.

There are, of course, always some people in the Budget Bureau who identify more closely with an agency or program than do others, or who develop policy preferences independent of the president. They have a creative urge. ("I don't like

---

[8]See Fritz Morstein Marx, "The Bureau of the Budget: Its Evolution and Present Role, II," *American Political Science Review,* Vol. 39 (October 1945), pp. 869–98; Richard Neustadt, "Presidency and Legislation: The Growth of Central Clearance," *American Political Science Review,* Vol. 48 (September 1954) pp. 641–71; Arthur Maas, "In Accord with the Program of the President?" in Carl Friedrich and Kenneth Galbraith, eds., *Public Policy,* Vol. 4 (Cambridge, Mass.: Graduate School of Public Administration, 1954), pp. 77–93; Frederick J. Lawton, "Legislative-Executive Relationships in Budgeting as Viewed by the Executive," *Public Administration Review,* Vol. 13 (Summer 1953), pp. 169–76; and Aaron Wildavsky, *Dixon–Yates: A Study in Power Politics* (New Haven: Yale University Press, 1962), p. 64.

to think of myself as a red-pencil man.") They see themselves as doing the right thing by pursuing policies in the public interest, and they may convince themselves that the president would support them if only he had the time and inclination to go into the matter as deeply as they had. They would rarely resist a direct presidential command, but these are few at any one time and ordinarily leave much room for interpretation. The role adopted by its budget examiners is important to an agency even if the general orientation of the Budget Bureau is different.

Even within the same administration, different budget directors can have an impact of their own on Budget Bureau decisions. Some directors have much better relationships with the president than others; they get in to see him more often and without going through subordinates; he backs them up more frequently on appeals from the agencies. In bargaining on recommendations, a budget director who is close to the president has an important advantage since he knows how much leeway he has within the Chief Executive's desires. Should the president turn down an appeal, the agency and its supporters may seek to discover how much of an increase they can get from Congress without risking a presidential veto, or strong opposition.

Members of Congress are ambivalent about the Bureau of the Budget; essentially they regard it as a necessary evil. The ambivalence comes through, for example, when a member of the House Appropriations Committee, at one time, with a trace of contempt calls Bureau officials a bunch of bureaucrats who think they are making the budget, but on another occasion reviles them for not having done enough. Or, further, the Bureau may be regarded as a rival for control of appropriations. Representative Flood (talking as a member of the Defense Appropriations Subcommittee) dramatized this feeling when he said, "Mr. Secretary [of Defense] . . . you are a very important man in the Government . . . but you are a minor deity, believe me, compared to the Director of the Budget. He is the Poo-Bah of this town. . . . I feel so strongly about it and many members of the committee and Congress, that we think the Bureau of the Budget as it is now set up should be ripped out altogether."

Every agency, and its officials, has to decide what kind of relationship to maintain with the Budget Bureau and particularly with its examiners. Since no examiner can know everything, the agency may decide to provide only the data specifically requested. More and more, however, one sees a tendency actually to heap data on the examiners all the time, not merely when they ask. Why? First, abundant information helps the examiners to defend the agency's viewpoint competently at Budget Bureau meetings when agency personnel is not represented. Second, well-informed examiners may become converted into advocates of particular programs. Third, the examiners' knowledge can be turned to advantage by getting them to secure administration assistance in clearing up some difficulty. The associated disadvantage, of course, is that examiners "get to know where the bodies are buried this way," as one budget officer put it. "But," he continued in words echoed by many others, "you can't hide serious weaknesses for very long anyway, and so the advantages far outweigh the disadvantages."

Agency people agree that Budget Bureau support is worth having if you can get it without sacrificing too much in Congress. Given the congressional propensity to cut, what the Budget Bureau proposes for an agency is likely to be the upper limit. (What was true in the classical period, I remind the reader, is not necessarily true now.) In addition, there are multitudes of small items that Congress would not ordinarily investigate but that might have trouble getting funded if Bureau approval were lacking.

Agencies recognize two basic limitations on Budget Bureau influence. The most serious handicap under which the Budget Bureau labors is not so much that Congress may raise its proposed spending (though this is obviously important) but that the BOB cannot guarantee a cooperating agency will receive the amount it has recommended.[9] Agencies that could depend on receiving what the Budget Bureau recommended would have much greater incentive to cooperate.

A second limitation of the Bureau is that its actions are often constrained by its perceptions of how Congress will view agency requests. Everyone knows that agencies make end runs around the Bureau to gain support from Congress. Yet if agencies do so too often, the Budget Bureau finds that its own prestige has declined. Hence, the Bureau frequently accepts consistent congressional action as a guide. A close eye is kept on congressional action for the preceding year before the Bureau sets an agency's total for the next one. The Bureau must also be wary of particular programs favored by Congress. Suppose an agency must choose between two alternatives, one favored by Congress, another by the Budget Bureau. The strategy probably would be to side with Congress because its record with Congress determines how an agency is viewed and treated both by the Budget Bureau and the department.

The Appropriations Committees

One of the prevailing roles played by members of the House Appropriations Committee is guardian of the public purse. Committee members are expected to cast a skeptical eye on the blandishments of a bureaucracy ever anxious to increase its dominion by increasing its appropriations. The role of guardianship is reinforced by the House leadership, which deliberately chooses committee members from safe districts who can therefore afford to say "no."

This role, of course, is not the only one that guides all committee members in all situations. Some members identify completely with an agency or its programs. "To me forestry has become a religion . . . ," said Representative Walter Horan. In a profound violation of House Committee norms, he took his protest against his own appropriations subcommittee to the Senate hearings, declaring that "The items are totally inadequate and I do not care particularly which way *we* get them, but we do need funds" (emphasis supplied). At times, then, the feeling of having served a great cause may create a sense of identification with an agency or program that overwhelms other considerations. To get credit for cutting, by contrast, requires an institutional milieu in which people are honored for being negative.

In the case of local constituency interests, the deviation from guardianship of the budget is exceedingly powerful because it touches on the most basic relationship members of Congress may have—that with the people who elect them and might conceivably defeat them—and because representatives are prone to take on faith another of their roles as defender of constituency interests. Where their constituencies are affected, appropriations committee members use all the vast lever-

---

[9]See the first edition, *The Politics of the Budgetary Process* (Boston: Little, Brown, 1964), p. 41.

age over men and money their positions give them to secure favorable outcomes. Representative John Rooney engaged in a battle royal to keep a Department of Commerce office in New York City so that his constituents would not lose their jobs. Then there was Representative Ivor Fenton's tenacious campaign to have an anthracite laboratory located in Schuylkill Haven instead of Hazleton, Pennsylvania. Fenton said that he got no action until he got on the Appropriations Committee. In another skirmish, a little armtwisting was applied by Senator Lyndon Johnson in order to make certain that a prison was built in the right place. "I sure would hate to put in this money to build a prison in Congressman Grey's district and Senator Dirksen's state in Illinois and find out that they got it in X, Y, Z, somewhere."

Tough as they may be when cutting the budgets of their agencies, appropriations committee members, once having made a decision, generally defend the agencies against further cuts on the floor. In an exchange with a member of the Appropriations Committee, Representative Clarence Brown (R-Ohio) complained that when an amendment is offered "to reduce an appropriations item, the Appropriations Committee stands like a stone wall most of the time, saying 'No, you mustn't touch this.'"[10] This kind of action is in part self-interest. The power of appropriations subcommittees would be diminished if their recommendations were successfully challenged very often. Members believe that the House would "run wild" if "orderly procedure"—that is, acceptance of committee recommendations—were not followed. But the role of defender also has its roots in the respect for expertise and specialization in Congress, and in the ensuing belief that members who have not studied the subject should not exercise a deciding voice without the presence of overriding considerations. An appeal to the norm of specialization is usually sufficient to block an attempt to reduce appropriations.

A member of the Senate Appropriations Committee is likely to view himself as the responsible legislator who sees to it that the irrepressible lower House does not do too much damage either to constituency or to national interests. And though members of the House Appropriations Committee tend to view their opposite members in the Senate as frivolous spendthrifts of the public purse, senators reverse the compliment by regarding their brethren in the other chamber as niggardly and jealous types who do not care what happens to "essential" programs so long as they can show that they have made cuts.

The senators are rather painfully aware of the House committee's preeminence in the field of appropriations; they know that they cannot hope to match the time and thoroughness that the House body devotes to screening requests. For this reason, Senate members put a high value on having agencies carry appeals to it. "We all know," said Senator Richard Russell (D-Ga.), Chairman of the Agriculture Appropriations Subcommittee, "that almost since the inception of the Government, the Senate Appropriations Committee has served as an appeal body and has heard requests . . . that deal principally with items that have been changed or reduced or eliminated by the House of Representatives." Senators value their ability to disagree on disputed items as a means of maintaining influence in crucial

---

[10]House Government Operations Subcommittee, *Improving Federal Budgeting and Appropriations*, 85th Congress, 1st Session, 1957, p. 139.

areas, while experiencing the least possible strain on their time and energy. This dominant Senate function as responsible appeals court depends upon agency advocacy and House committee guardianship.

STRATEGIES

Budgetary strategies are actions by governmental agencies intended to maintain or increase their available funds. Strategies are the links between the intentions and perceptions of budget officials, and the political system that both imposes restraints and creates opportunities for them.

Strategic moves take place in a rapidly changing environment in which no one is quite certain how things will turn out and in which new goals constantly emerge. In this context of uncertainty, choice among existing strategies must be based on intuition and hunch—on an "educated guess"—as well as on firm knowledge. Assuming a normal capacity to learn, however, experience should eventually provide a more reliable guide than sheer guesswork. While the strategies recounted here relate to a bygone era of Congress—one without budget committees, budget resolutions, and vastly changed rules—many are timeless and form part of participants' repertoires in a variety of situations.

Be a Good Politician

What really counts in helping an agency get the appropriations it desires? Long service in Washington has convinced many high agency officials that some things count a great deal and others only a little. Although they are well aware that it is desirable to have technical data to support requests, budget officials commonly derogate the importance of the formal aspects of their work. As several informants put it in almost identical words, "It's not what's in your estimates but how good a politician you are that matters."

Being a good politician, these officials say, requires essentially three things: cultivation of an active clientele, the development of confidence among other governmental officials, and skill in following strategies that exploit one's opportunities to the maximum. Doing good work is viewed as part of being a good politician.

Clientele

Find a Clientele For most agencies, locating a clientele is no problem at all; the groups interested in their activities are all too present. But some agencies find this a difficult problem, demanding extraordinary measures to solve. Men and women incarcerated in federal prisons, for instance, are hardly an ideal clientele. And the rest of society cares only to the extent of keeping these people locked up. So the Bureau of Prisons tries to create special interest in its activities by inviting members of Congress to see what is going on. "I wish, Mr. Bow, you would come and visit us at one of these prison places when you have the time. . . . I am sure you would enjoy it." The United States Information Agency faced a similar problem—partly explaining its mendicant status—because its work is all abroad rather than directly benefiting people at home. Things got so bad that the USIA sought to organize our country's ambassadors to foreign nations into an interest group, to vouch for the good job USIA said it was doing.

Serve Your Clientele   For an agency that has a large and strategically placed clientele, the most effective strategy is to serve those who are in a position to help the agency. "If we deliver this kind of service," an administrator declared, "other things are secondary and automatic." His agency made a point of organizing clientele groups in various locations, priming them to engage in approved projects, serving them well, and encouraging them to inform their representatives of their reaction. Informing one's clientele of the full extent of the benefits they receive may increase the intensity with which they support the agency's request.

Expand Your Clientele   In order to secure substantial funds from Congress for domestic purposes, it is ordinarily necessary to develop fairly wide interest in the program. This is what Representative Whitten did when he became a member of the Appropriations Committee and discovered that soil conservation in various watersheds had been authorized, but that little money had been forthcoming: "Living in the watersheds . . . I began to check . . . and I found that all these watersheds were in a particular region, which meant there was no general interest in the Congress in this type of program. . . . It led me to go before the Democratic platform committee in 1952 and urge them to write into the platform a plank on watershed protection. And they did." As a result, Whitten was able to call on more general support from Democrats as well as to increase appropriations for Soil Conservation Service watersheds.

Concentrate on Individual Constituencies   After the Census Bureau had made an unsuccessful bid to establish a national housing survey, Representative Sidney Yates (D-Ill.) gave the bureau a useful hint. The proposed survey "is so general," Yates said, "as to be almost useless to the people of a particular community. . . . This would help someone like Armstrong Cork, who can sell its product anywhere in the country . . . but will it help the construction industry in a particular area to know whether or not it faces a shortage of customers?" Later, the Bureau submitted a new program that called for a detailed enumeration of metropolitan districts with a sample survey of other areas to get a national total. In another case, the National Science Foundation made headway with a program of summer mathematics institutes not only because the idea was excellent but also because the institutes were spread around the country, where they became part of a constituency interest members of congress are supposed to protect.

Secure Feedback   Almost everybody claims that their projects are immensely popular and benefit lots of people. But how can elected officials find this out? Only by hearing from constituents. The agency can do a lot to ensure that its clientele responds by informing them that it is vital to contact their representatives and by telling them, if necessary, how to go about it. In fact, the agency may organize its clientele in the first place, and then offer to fulfill the demand it has helped to create. Policies create clients just as clients can create policies. Indeed, members of Congress often urge administrators to make a show of their clientele:

Senator Wherry: "Do you have letters or evidence from small operators . . . that need your service that you can introduce into the record. . . . Is that not the test on how much demand there is for your services?" When feedback is absent or limited, members of Congress tend to assume no one cares and they need not bother with the appropriation.

End-runs   When political considerations attach to the idea of a balanced budget, an administration may seek appropriations policies that minimize the short-run impact on the budget, even though total expense may be greater over a period of years. In the Dixon–Yates case (1954–1956) a proposed TVA power plant was rejected partly because it involved large immediate capital outlays. The private power plant that was accepted was to involve much larger expenditures over a 25-year period, but this spending, spread out over time, would have had comparatively little impact.[11]

When clientele are absent or weak there are some techniques for making expenditures so that they either do not appear in the budget or appear much later on. The International Monetary Fund may be given a Treasury note to be used at some future date when IMF needs money. Buildings for public use may be constructed by private organizations so that the rent paid is, in the short run, much lower than an initial capital expenditure would have appeared. (In the 1980s the military tried to take that approach to its housing.) An agency and its supporters who fear hostile appropriations committee action may seek authorization to spend directly from the Treasury to avoid direct encounter with the normal budgetary process. This action is bitterly opposed as backdoor spending, especially in the House Appropriations Committee.

Confidence

The sheer mass of budgetary matters means that some people have got to trust others because only rarely can they check up on things. "It is impossible for any person to understand in detail the purposes for which $70 billion are requested," Senator Thomas declared in regard to the defense budget. "The committee [recall this is way back when] must take some things on faith." If we add to this the idea of budgeting by increments (where large areas of the budget are exempt from serious questions each year), committee members will treat an agency much better if they feel that its officials will not deceive them.

Administrative officials unanimously agree that they must, as a bare minimum, enjoy the confidence of appropriations committee members and their staff. "If you have the confidence of your subcommittee your life is much easier and you can do your department good; if you don't have confidence you can't accomplish much and you are always in trouble." How do agency personnel seek to establish this confidence?

Be What They Think They Are   Confidence is achieved by gearing one's behavior to fit the expectations of committee people. Essentially, the desired quali-

---

[11]See the author's *Dixon–Yates: A Study in Power Politics.*

ties will appear to be projections of the committee members' images of themselves. Bureaucrats are expected to be masters of detail—hard-working, frank, self-effacing people devoted to their work, who are tight with the taxpayer's money, recognize a political necessity when they see one, and keep Congress informed. To be considered aboveboard, a fair and square shooter, a frank person is highly desirable.

But if and when a subcommittee drops the most customary role and becomes an outright advocate of a program, as with the Polaris missile system, the budget official is expected to shoot for the moon; he will be criticized if he emphasizes petty economies instead of pushing his projects. It is not so much what administrators do but how they meet the particular subcommittee's or chairman's expectations that counts.

Play It Straight! Everyone agrees that the most important requirement for confidence, at least in a negative sense, is to be aboveboard. A lie, a blatant attempt to cover up some misdeed, a tricky move of any kind, can lead to an irreparable loss of confidence. A typical comment by an administrator states, "It doesn't pay to try to put something over on them [committee members] because if you get caught, you might as well pack your bags and leave Washington." And the chances of getting caught are considerable because interested committees and their staffs have much experience and many sources of information.

A committee that feels that it has been misled can take endless punitive actions. Senator Carl Hayden (D-Ariz.), Chairman of the Senate Appropriations Committee, spoke at one time when a bureau received a lump-sum appropriation as an experiment. "Next year . . . the committee felt outraged that certain actions had been taken, not indicated in the hearings before them. Then we proceeded to earmark the bill from one end to the other. We just tied it up in knots to show that it was the Congress, after all, that dictated policy."

Integrity The positive side of the confidence relationship is to make it known that the agency official is a person of high integrity who can be trusted. He must not only give but must also appear to give reliable information. Agency people must keep confidences and not get members of Congress into trouble by what they say or do—willing to take blame (but never credit). Like a brand name, a budget official's reputation comes to be worth a good deal in negotiation.

An agency that enjoys good relations with subcommittee staff has an easier time in Congress than it might otherwise. The agency finds that more reliance is placed on its figures, more credence is given to its claims, and more opportunities are provided to secure its demands. Thus one budget officer who received information that a million-dollar item had been casually dropped from a bill was able to arrange with his source of information on the staff to have the item put back for reconsideration. On the other hand, asked if they would consider refusing to talk to committee staff, agency officials uniformly declared that such a stance would be tantamount to cutting their own throats. A staff person whose nose is out of joint can do harm to an agency by expressing distrust of its competence or integrity.

I'd Love to Help You But . . .   Where the administrator's notion of what is proper conflicts with that of a member of Congress with whom he or she needs to maintain friendly relations, there is no perfect way out of the difficulty. Most officials try to turn the member down by suggesting that their hands are tied, that something may be done in the future, or by stressing some other project on which they are agreed. After Representative William Natcher (D-Ky.) spoke for the second time of his desire for a project in his district, Don Williams of the Soil Conservation Service complimented him for his interest in watershed activity in Kentucky but was "sorry that some of the projects that were proposed would not qualify under the law . . . but . . . they are highly desirable."

Congressional Committee Hearings

Play the Game   The Bureau of the Budget lays down the rule that members of the Executive Branch are not to challenge the Executive Budget. But everyone knows that administrative officials want more for their agencies and—in league with supporting members of Congress—sometimes are in a position to get it. On such occasions the result is a ritual that any reader of appropriations hearings will recognize. The agency official is asked whether or not he supports the amounts in the president's budget and he says "yes" in such a way that it sounds like yes but that everyone realizes means "no." His manner may communicate a marked lack of enthusiasm or he may be just too enthusiastic to be true. A committee member will then ask how much the agency originally requested from the Budget Bureau. There follows an apparent refusal to answer, in the form of a protestation of loyalty to the Chief Executive. Under duress, however, and amidst reminders of congressional prerogatives, the agency official will cite the figures. Could he usefully spend the money? he is asked. Of course he could. The presumption that the agency would not have asked for more money if it did not need it is made explicit. Then comes another defense of the administration's position by the agency, which, however, puts up feeble opposition to congressional demands for increases.

It Works: The Problem of Effectiveness   Apart from overwhelming public support, there is nothing that succeeds better than tangible accomplishment. The Polaris does fire and hit a target with reasonable accuracy; a range-reseeding project does make the grass grow again. Congressional interpretation of accomplishments as being worthwhile depends on what criteria of effectiveness agencies use and on how tough Congress permits them to be. There is great temptation for agencies to devise a criterion that will enable a project's supporters to say that it works. At the same time, opponents of a project may unfairly propose criteria that cannot be met. And there are times when reasonable people disagree over criteria. We hope and pray to avoid nuclear war. But if it comes, what criteria should a civil-defense program have to meet? If one argues that it must save everyone, then no program can show results. Suppose, however, that one is willing to accept much less—say half or a third or a fifth of the population. Then everything would depend on estimates that surely could be improved upon, but which nobody can really claim to be reliable—as to likely levels of attack, patterns of wind and radiation, and a multitude of other factors.

Strategies Designed to Capitalize on the Fragmentation of Power in National Politics

The separation of powers and the internal divisions of labor within Congress and the Executive Branch present numerous opportunities for program advocates (including both agency personnel and congressmen) to play one center of power off against another.

Compensation Program supporters who have superior access to one house of Congress may seek to raise the program's grant in one house to allow for bargaining with the other. If they can get their way or arrange to split the difference in the Conference Committee, they are that much ahead. A member of Congress may ask the agency for the lowest addition that would make a project possible so as to know how far to go in conference. Thus Senator Pat McCarran (D-Nev.) told the Census Bureau that he "just wanted to see . . . how much we could lose in the conference, and still give some assistance to be of value." Although the presence of differing interests and degrees of confidence in House and Senate may give an agency room to maneuver, this may also subject it to a withering cross fire from which there is no immediate escape.

Both Ends against the Middle The separation between appropriations and substantive committees creates another opportunity to exploit differences between dual authorities. Appropriations committees often refuse funds for projects authorized by substantive committees. And substantive committees, with or without agency backing, sometimes seek to exert influence over appropriations committees. As the classical period ebbed, substantive committees greatly increased their use of annual rather than multiyear or permanent authorizations. A familiar tactic is the calling of hearings by substantive committees to dramatize the contention that an authorized program is being underfinanced or not financed at all. Knowing that the appropriations committees have the final say, substantive committees can afford to authorize any project they deem good without too much concern for its financial implications. Also, appropriations committees sometimes seek to write legislation into appropriations bills; this effort may lead to a conflict with the substantive committee that spills over onto the floor of the houses of Congress.

Agencies stand to gain by exploiting such conflicts to their advantage. They can try to use an authorization as a club over the head of the appropriations committees by pointing to a substantive committee as their source of commitment for funds. In seeking an increase for fishery research, for example, the Fish and Wildlife Service declared that it "came about through direction of a Congressional Committee. . . . The [substantive] committee directed that hereafter the department should include this item for their appropriations." This strategy does not create much difficulty in the Senate, where some members of the substantive committees are likely also to sit on the Appropriations Committee. But House members do not like it at all—though a member may from time to time brag about how he got through a pet appropriation without a real authorization—and they are quick to remind administrators of their prerogatives.

Cut Less-visible Items   Counterstrategies are available to legislators. Many members of Congress feel a need to cut an agency's requests somewhere. Yet the same member may be sympathetic to the agency's program or feel obliged to support it because people in his or her constituency are believed to want it. Where, then, can cuts be made? In those places that do not appear to directly involve program activities: The department office or general administrative expenses for example, may be cut without appearing to affect any specific desirable program. This fits in well with a general suspicion current in society that bureaucrats are wasteful. Housekeeping activities may also suffer since it often appears that they can be put off another year and they do not seem directly connected with programs. Yet deferred maintenance may turn out to cost more in the end. But cutting here enables a representative to meet conflicting pressures for the time being.

All or Nothing   This tactic is to assert that if a cut is made the entire program will have to be scrapped. "Reducing the fund to $50,000 would reduce it too much for us to carry forward the work. We have to request the restoration . . . ," said the Bureau of Mines. The danger is that Congress may take the hint and cut out the whole program. So this strategy must be employed with care, and only in connection with a program that is most unlikely to be abolished.

Shift the Blame   A widespread strategy is to get the other party to make the difficult decisions of cutting down on requests, thus shifting the onus for the cuts. He who must take the blame may not be willing to make the cut. Everyone knows that many agencies raise their budgetary requests (among other reasons) in order to show their supporting interests that they are working hard but are being thwarted by the president. So the Budget Bureau is disposed to cut. The most frustrating aspect of this activity is that when an agency's budget is squeezed it is often not the "wasteful" things that come out; priorities within the agency and Congress vary greatly and some legendary, obsolete facility may survive long after more essential activities have disappeared. Thus the Budget Bureau may be caught between a desire to make the agency responsible for a cut and the need to insist that cuts be made in certain places rather than others.

They Made Me   Members of Congress have developed their own strategies for making cuts without taking full responsibility. Just as budget officials say that "circumstances" have compelled them to ask for increases, so do people in Congress assert that "outside forces"—a climate of opinion against spending strong views of influential colleagues, presidential opposition, attempts by the other party to make spending an issue, an overriding need to balance the budget—leave them with little choice. This strategy has a corollary: If a subcommittee is not sure what to cut but feels pressure, it may make the cut and let the agency's protests reveal what the agency is really unwilling to give up.

The Transfer   One way of moving ahead while appearing to stand still is to keep appropriations for particular categories constant so that no change seems to be made although various past expenditures, no longer being made, have been replaced with others. Items may be transferred from one category to another so that no particular one stands out as being too far out of line. If a committee or the Budget Bureau is concerned over increases in administrative expenses, ways may be found of transferring these expenditures to other items by including them as part of less suspect costs. Some agencies include administrative expenses under each program instead of under the administrative category.

The Camel's Nose   A large program may be started by an apparently insignificant sum. The agency then claims that (1) this has not become part of its base and that (2) it would be terrible to lose the money already spent by not going ahead and finishing the job. As Representative Rooney observed, "This may be only $250 but this is the camel's nose. These things never get out of a budget. They manage to stay and grow." Congress has tried to counter this strategy by passing legislation requiring a total estimate for a project before any part can be authorized. But estimates are subject to change and a small sum one year rarely seems imposing even if a large amount is postulated for the future.

In arguing against a change in accounting procedures, Representative Mahon sketched the strategic implications:

> I believe it was last year that we appropriated $1 million, just a little $1 million to start a public works project of the Army Engineers which is to cost $1 billion. Why, if I go to Congressman Kilgore and say, "Listen, Joe, we have been colleagues for a long time, can't you vote for this little $1 million for my area to help me and my people?"

> Well Joe, I am sure he would do whatever was right and proper, but it might be something tempting, particularly if I had voted for a million-dollar project for Joe on a former occasion to vote for my proposal. But what if I got up to Joe and I say, "Listen, Joe, I want you to vote for this project, it costs a billion dollars over a period of years, and if you start it, it is going to be completed."[12]

A Foot in the Door   The desire of budget officials to keep items in the budget, even if they are small and underfinanced, is readily explained once it is understood that they may one day serve to launch full-blown programs when conditions are more favorable. Research projects are often not terminated when they have either proven successful or have failed; a small item concerning applicability of the research is retained in the budget so that if the agency wishes to resume it has a foot in the door.

Just for Now   "Is there anything more permanent than a temporary agency of the Government?" Representative John Phillips (R-Calif.) wanted to know. His colleague, Mr. Thomas, spoke with some asperity of a temporary activity that had begun four years ago. "Of course, [the agency] said it would take them about two years to clear it up and then they would be off the payroll. Since then I think you

---

[12]*Improving Federal Budget and Appropriations,* House Subcommittee on Government Operations, 85th Congress, 1st Session, pp. 132–33.

have added 30 [people] to this group." A temporary adjustment to a passing situation results in an emergency appropriation for a fixed period, which then turns out to be a permanent expenditure.

The Commitment   Although expenditures may rise and requests for money may increase, an agency can hardly be blamed if it had no choice. As one official put it, "The increases are in every case presented as either related to commitments . . . or other uncontrollable factors."

A favorite strategy is to lay down long-range goals for an existing program, which the agency can use to show that its requirements are not being met. The very statement that there are X acres not yet under soil conservation practices or so many Indian children who need schooling may serve to create an implied commitment to meet the demand. The NIH and its congressional allies go one step further by speaking of "moral obligations" for continuing projects mounting up to tens of millions of dollars.

It Pays for Itself; It Makes a Profit   An increase may not seem like one if it can be shown that the increase brings in revenue equal to or greater than the cost. Although government is presumably not conducted for profit, the delight members of Congress take in finding an activity that returns money to the Treasury is indicated by the frequency with which they use this fact to praise administrators and to support programs they prefer. Senator Dworshak told the Fish and Wildlife Service that "when you return money like that [$1 million from seal furs] back in, you should be proud of it and have the record show it." Not to be outdone, J. Edgar Hoover pointed out that the FBI had recovered $73 million more through its investigation activities over a ten-year period than it had received in appropriations.

The Crisis   There comes a time, however, when it is necessary to admit that a new program is in the offing or that substantial increases in existing ones are desired. This situation calls for a special campaign in which three techniques—the crisis, salesmanship, and advertising—are often called into play. The purpose is to generate extraordinary support so that the agency or program does not merely inch ahead but secures sizable new appropriations.

Events do not have meaning in themselves; they are given meaning by observers. The agency in a position to meet a crisis, as TVA was by supplying huge amounts of power to nuclear-energy installations, can greatly increase its appropriations. And, soon after a jet plane had crashed because of contact with a flock of starlings, the Fish and Wildlife Service was able to obtain funds for research into the habits of these birds. There is also a borderline area of discretion in which crisis may be made to appear more critical. A number of agency officials are famous in budgetary circles for their ability to embellish or make use of crisis. By publicizing a situation, dramatizing it effectively, and perhaps asking for emergency appropriations, an agency may maneuver itself into a position of responsibility for large new programs.

Salesmanship runs the gamut from a cops-and-robbers' appeal—"agents of our [Narcotics Bureau] . . . engaged in a 45-minute gun battle with Mexican smugglers"—to the "agony sessions" at NIH hearings. Who could resist Senator Hill's plea:

> As we begin today's hearings on appropriations . . . we take notice of the passing of . . . John Foster Dulles [who] fell victim to the most dreaded killer of our time, cancer.
>
> Cancer, that most ancient and accursed scourge of mankind, has . . . robbed the U.S. Senate of some of its greatest leaders: Robert A. Taft, Arthur Vandenberg, Kenneth Wherry, Brian McMahon, and Matthew Neely. What more fitting . . . memorial . . . could there be than a high resolve . . . to redouble our research efforts against the monstrous killer which . . . will claim the lives of 250,000 more Americans before this year has ended? . . . We are very happy to have with us our colleague, Senator Neuberger. . . . [then dying of cancer]

Who would vote against appropriations for medical research after being subjected to this treatment?

In the classical era of American national budgeting, that quarter century between the end of World War II and the early 1970s, there was a recognizable budgetary process, almost a budgetary minuet. Conflict was routinized and confined by informal understandings. These understandings, supported by the arm of balance, reinforced by agreement on the general lines of public policy and an ex-pansive economic climate, led to budgetary incrementalism. Since there was agreement on most programs, these constituted a base that was generally considered untouchable. For the most part, differences centered upon small departures from the base, rather than the program itself. By focusing upon remedial measures, by usually dealing with difficulties as they revealed themselves, and by making repeated attacks upon problems in different forums—within agencies, between agencies and the OMB, in House and Senate subcommittees—those problems could be factored down into small and manageable components. Calculation was improved and conflict limited by this incremental, remedial, and serial approach.

Just enough central control had been grafted on to historical budgeting—the process remained focused on the legislature and fragmented within that—to create a semblance of order. Indeed, my first reaction to classical budgeting was a sense of wonder of how much coordination actually was achieved without a central coordinator. Revenue and expenditure were approximately equivalent. Decisions were made on time. Deference was shown to informed judgment. Evident political self-interest was both accommodated—representatives were expected to vote their district—and limited. The leadership populated appropriations committees with people from safe districts; the president could be expected to impound overspending by prearrangement; spending considered unwise could be voted for and then allowed to die. Though there were complaints about insufficient analysis, followed by efforts to introduce more systematic intelligence, moderation remained the order of the day. Improving analysis of choices on individual programs was the great hope; no one thought of directly deciding total revenue and expenditure. All this came to an end with the collapse of the underlying political consensus, and opening of the budget process to the hurricanes of change.

Chapter
4

The Collapse
of Consensus:
The 1970s

*We're a very divided committee, with some very conservative
Republicans and very liberal Democrats. I always had to find different
members for each coalition.*

—A Congressman

*Any book that says the appropriations committee sees its job as to cut
the President's budget would just be wrong. They may see their job as
to rearrange priorities but to stay within the total. But on this
subcommittee the pressure's all upward.*

—A Committee Staffer

Shortly after the standard accounts of classical budgeting were published in
the early 1960s—Richard Fenno's *The Power of the Purse* and the first edition of
Politics of the Budgetary Process—that process began to collapse. What Allen
Schick in *Congress and Money* calls the "Seven Year Budget War" lasted from
1966 to 1973. It ended with what he calls "The Congressional Budget Treaty of
1974," which Congress called the Congressional Budget and Impoundment Control Act of 1974 (the Budget Act). The new act did not abolish the old process; it
heaped new relationships and institutions atop, and also layered them among, the
old ones.

In retrospect, the pattern is clear; Congress and presidents had trouble agreeing. More time was being spent on budgeting to less effect. The difficulties were
attributed variously to recalcitrant personalities, hard economic times, or defects
in the process. The personalities, the time, and the process changed but to no
avail. What caused the budgetary process to become so unsatisfactory?

It is not always easy to separate cause from effect, reality from symptoms. The
actors in the budgetary minuet—president, congressional committees, adminis-

trators—could not indefinitely insulate their own politics from those of the real world. The ferment of the 1960s reflected long-standing dissatisfactions of groups previously excluded from the political process: denial of voting rights and racial discrimination in a democracy, hunger in the midst of plenty, poverty in prosperity. No less divisive issues of war and environment also took their place on the political agenda.

Legislature, executive, and judiciary changed in response, and social and environmental policies were rapidly enacted during the 1960s and early 1970s. The implications for budgetary politics were far-reaching. As long as the economy yielded an adequate increment and mutual understandings prevented too rapid a rise of expenditures, the budget could accommodate the powerful new trends. It had in fact gradually been doing so for some time. Keynesian economics also permitted and even encouraged deficit financing, which could act as a kind of safety valve, allowing the fragmented self-balancing budget process to continue to operate even if it were out of balance.

But the simultaneous pressures on expenditures of social programs and the Vietnam War strained the budget. Faltering economic growth ended the fiscal dividend, and with it the politics of accommodation among advocates of social spending, defense spending, more or less balanced budgets, and tax reductions. The legacy of earlier policies—entitlements, indexing, tax cuts, Keynesian economics, federal credit—was now visible in the changed composition and dynamics of the federal budget. This budget was much less flexible, far more difficult to control, and extraordinarily vulnerable to breakdown as the consensus underlying the old order collapsed.

THE GROWTH OF ENTITLEMENTS

Entitlement spending grew swiftly from 1960 to 1974. In part, entitlements grew from the need to keep old promises; as more and more people reached retirement age, the promised social security or civil service retirement pensions cost the government more. Entitlements grew also from the making of new promises— medical care to the aged (medicare), nutrition to the impoverished (food stamps)—and by the increasing costs of big, old programs (social security).

New efforts to preserve old promises were particularly important. Benefits promised in specific dollar amounts, such as pensions based on earnings, lost as inflation devalued their dollar worth. As a result Congress had to raise pension benefits frequently. By the early 1970s—in part to keep the promises solid, and in part to prevent members from voting over-adjustments on highly popular programs—Congress began indexing major benefit systems.

Entitlement spending grew faster than did other spending. Thus an increasing portion of federal spending could not be determined by the appropriations process. By "uncontrollable," of course, OMB did not mean beyond human control. Congress could, at any time, reduce spending or cancel the entire program. It is just that entitlement spending could not be controlled through the appropriations process.

A lot more could (and should) be said about entitlements (see Chapters 7 and 8). They grew partly at the expense of defense, which remained relatively stable in constant dollars but declined greatly as a proportion of total spending (see Chapter 9). With defense and economic growth used up as a means of funding social welfare programs, one question was, Where else might the money come from? More was going on to raise spending in ways that did not appear directly or fully in the budget. One way was through loans and loan guarantees, which we will discuss later in the chapter. Meanwhile, as agreement about priorities diminished, attitudes toward budget totals also changed. Total revenue and expenditure became both more controversial and more important. To the old conflicts over marginally "how much?" was added the potentially more divisive question of "what for?"

ECONOMIC ACTIVISM

Until the mid-1960s, attitudes toward total spending could be summarized in a few simple statements:

1. Deficits are bad. Borrowing has to be paid for later, gives financiers too much power (if you are liberal), and diverts money from productive use in the private economy (if you are conservative). The public views debt as bad for the government in the same way as for the household: a burden for the future, an indicator of poor management, and a sign that the country is in trouble.
2. Spending helps people in need and is therefore good, except that it must be paid for. Of course, some spending is better than others.
3. Taxes are necessary but unpalatable. Responsibility for tax hikes is dangerous. Avoid across-the-board tax increases by the "silent tax" of bracket creep or by selective, marginal changes that are difficult to oppose. Hope that economic growth will create a dividend in enhanced revenues so that part can fund higher spending, and part can keep income tax rates stable or even reduced.

These rather contradictory premises fit with a set of decision rules for Congress designed to make calculations simple, conflicts manageable, and public policy predictable:

1. Do what you did last year if that worked out OK. Change only at the margins so you can easily change back again.
2. Budgets should be balanced, or if not, as close as possible, and should look like they are getting closer.
3. If you have room to increase spending, do not increase it to an extent that would require tax increases or borrowing.
4. If none of the above is possible, something unpleasant must be done. To minimize political cost, make the president propose a solution first. If his solution is tolerable, adopt it and blame him for what unhappiness does result (representatives with different constituencies will blame him for different consequences). If a seemingly more popular solution can be found, adopt it and take the credit. Reaction to the president's proposal can be used to gauge the political pressures.

These premises and decision rules were challenged by the Keynesian revolution in macroeconomics. The simplified Keynesian premise is:

The goal of policy should be to balance not the budget, but the economy. The government should adopt the levels of spending, taxing, and borrowing that will produce acceptable levels of GNP, inflation, and unemployment.

Keynesianism was as much a political as an economic revolution. Keynes pointed to a theoretical way out of the strictures of classical economics (although through actual experimentation several European countries had arrived at Keynesian solutions without benefit of Keynes). No longer did government have to raise taxes and cut spending in times of recession. Politicians could finally justify what they had long desired to do, namely, do something (spend) to help people (and, in turn, benefit the economy) in a time of crisis. Thus Keynesianism destroys old premise 1, that deficits are bad. Sometimes deficits are necessary to stimulate the economy. In an obvious way, this makes budgeting much easier. Constraints are loosened, especially when the economy declines, which automatically reduces revenues and increases both entitlement costs and thus the deficit. Keynesian theory says that deficits are desired precisely when unemployment rises, which is certainly convenient, if not largely unavoidable. There are, however, hidden costs to the Keynesian perspective.

In most of Europe and the United States, after the initial fear of postwar depression proved unfounded, rapid economic growth in stable economies was expected to continue indefinitely. The Keynesian doctrine of economic stabilization by means of counter-cyclical spending triumphed everywhere. So powerful was this faith in the feasibility of economic fine-tuning and of its potential for sustaining economic stability that few if any mainstream advisors to governments in those days considered the possibility of having to make cuts in spending. The political difficulty of cutting was still recognized, but, expecting the expansion to go on indefinitely, no one worried much about reductions or how to implement them.

As Keynesianism developed through years of political use, old premises 2 and 3 also were revised. When times are good, according to Keynes, spending should be limited and taxation increased to keep the economy from overheating. Put in terms of political appearance, "Times are good so we should do less because citizens can afford to pay (their real income is rising) and they won't notice." Instructions to reduce benefits people are already enjoying, however, are not attractive. Consequently, in both good times and bad, despite Keynesian doctrine, spending kept going up.

Less obviously, the Keynesian perspective calls the first decision rule into question. What "worked," which means what was politically acceptable last year, cannot be assumed to work this year, since the perceived needs of the economy may have changed. When politicians assume responsibility for managing the economy, and the economy changes faster than party coalitions, the political task becomes complicated.

The president's role also becomes more troublesome to Congress, for budget totals become more important. Keynesian economics would see a tradeoff between unemployment and inflation; a healthy economy is defined in terms of some balance of the two evils (hopefully both at low levels). Unfortunately, politicians may not see eye to eye on the proper balance; some politicians (usually Democratic) are more worried by unemployment, others (usually Republican) are more fearful of inflation. The choice depends on whether one's constituents are labor unions (which can defend in their contracts against inflation but have trouble defending against unemployment) or stock or bond holders (who worry less about unemployment but can be clobbered by inflation). The tradeoff therefore hits at the fundamental difference between Democratic and Republican constituencies. When a Republican president must deal with a Democratic Congress, members of Congress, in allowing the president the first move, do not necessarily succeed in getting him to take the blame for going in the direction that Congress wishes; instead, the president could push them in a direction—say, choosing unemployment over inflation—where they would not choose to go. And at that particular time, before the Congressional Budget and Impoundment Control Act of 1974, the appropriations process gave Congress no way to articulate a coherent alternative.

When budget totals become a tool of economic policy, then those totals, not just the spending programs within them, become a subject of major constituency conflict. Politicians can be blamed if the economy runs into trouble, for proper fiscal policy would presumably have kept the economy healthy. This responsibility is dangerous enough if politicians are actually able to direct the economy. In the last half of the 1970s, acceptance of Keynesian premises did establish political responsibilities while the policy theory it represented turned out to be less useful than expected.

The stagflation of the 1970s, when unemployment and inflation rose together, could not be solved within the Keynesian framework. Perhaps the causes were outside of the framework, or perhaps the fiscal tools available were too blunt for the job. Possibly, as Robert Eisner argues, failure to measure the proper level of deficits, due to inflation and the lack of a capital budget, gave the wrong signals.[1] The community of economists, business executives, and labor leaders, however, persisted in demanding the "proper" macroeconomic adjustments. Even the revolt against Keynesianism in the form of supply-side economics (basically, much lower marginal tax rates to increase incentives for economic activism) presumed that there was a proper economic policy that would save the country if misguided politicians would only see the light.

Yet the public never abandoned the old premises. Deficits remained unpopular, spending for programs appreciated, and taxes difficult to justify. Macroeconomic activism added a new layer of expectations and responsibilities to budgeting without eliminating the old concerns.

PRIORITIES

The division of roles among the president and Congress, OMB, and the appropriations committees was weakening simultaneously with the growth of entitlements. The system could work only so long as conflict about both totals and relative prior-

---

[1]See Robert Eisner, *How Real Is the Federal Deficit?* (New York: Free Press, 1986).

ities was kept within negotiable bounds. In 1960 most government programs had either been around long enough for their existence and scope to be taken for granted (the New Deal ended 20 years earlier) or, if recent, had been endorsed by both Democratic and Republican administrations in the course of passage. Even though Congress was Democratic and the administration Republican, or vice versa, there was broad agreement about the existence or size of programs: Government was to limit itself to the existing tax take. During the 1960s, however, and especially after the 1964 landslide election, Congress became more Democratic and northern liberals dominated the Democratic party. Lyndon Johnson's Great Society created many new programs and agencies. These changes in priorities reflected the opening up of Congress and changes in its procedures.

During the early 1970s, the norms of participatory democracy had their way in Congress. Power was dispersed from committee chairs (no longer guaranteed by seniority) to a proliferation of subcommittees (all committees had to have them) and new staff. Democrats did the most; under a subcommittee "bill of rights," the prerogative of determining the number, budget, size, and jurisdiction of subcommittees was transferred from the chairs of standing committees to the caucus of the majority party. The Democratic caucus also had the right to elect subcommittee chairs. From 1967 to 1980 the personal staffs of representatives rose from 4051 to 7376, an 82 percent increase, while in the Senate the increase was 114 percent (1749 to 3746). During the decade of the 1970s, Senate standing committee staff rose 88 percent (635 to 1917).[2]

Whereas in earlier times, subcommittee members might be chosen with an eye toward countering constituency influences, now they mostly selected themselves. "What we find," a staff member told Allen Schick, "is that the city and inner-city guys are all on Labor-HEW, all of the hawkish guys go to Defense, and the big (full) committee chairman no longer has the power to take a guy who has a defense interest and say, 'you serve on the Agriculture subcommittee and do the public some good.' "[3]

No wonder individual legislators had more clout. No longer under the thumb of seniority, loaded with staff, they could express many more preferences with less personal expertise than in the past. The tendency to behave as individual political entrepreneurs, often running against Congress as an institution, was strengthened by a greater ability to intervene in more areas of policy, and thus serve larger numbers of constituencies or by their own visions of desirable public policy. While Democratic chairs had more reason to stand close to their party cohorts, it was not just the Speaker and the whips but the entire caucus (which could not be expected to act very often) to whom they were beholden. Members could act with impunity on individual programs, providing their overall voting record was roughly in line.

With increasing rapidity, from the 1950s until the present time, permanent or multiyear spending authorizations gave way to the annual kind. (Before 1950, there were only two; three were passed in the 1950s, seven in the 1960s, sixteen in

---

[2]John W. Ellwood, "The Great Exception: The Congressional Budget Process in an Age of Decentralization," in Lawrence Dodd and Bruce Oppenheimer, eds., *Congress Reconsidered*, 3rd ed. (Washington, D.C.: CQ Press, 1985), pp. 4–5 of typescript.

[3]Allen Schick, *Congress and Money* (Washington, D.C.: Urban Institute Press, 1980), p. 432.

the 1970s, several more in the 1980s.)[4] One reason for this trend toward annual authorization was to exert better or more frequent control over administrative agencies; another was to increase influence over appropriations subcommittees. By and large authorizing committees want higher spending. While reducing authorizations is an effective way of cutting spending over the next few years, raising authorizations may be ineffective if the appropriations committees refuse to recommend the necessary budget authority. By repeating those requests on an annual basis, authorizing committees create more numerous opportunities to lobby for them; this lobbying also serves as a means of influencing the actions of agencies. On the one hand, annual authorizations are a pain to administrators who have to keep testifying. On the other hand, since the result is more likely to be higher than lower future spending, there is some recompense for this inconvenience.

With two sets of hearings—appropriations and authorizations—scheduled each year in each house, the opportunities for interaction on spending between administrators and legislators, as well as among legislators, expand greatly. So do the opportunities for delay. The complexity of the joint authorizing-appropriations process, moreover, lends itself to further maneuver.[5]

Presidents, too, responded to change. Republican Richard Nixon was nothing if not flexible. In his first term (1968–1972) he approved or allowed large spending increases, especially, as in housing, where the costs did not show up immediately. When spending was popular, despite contrary rhetoric, he spent. Faced with the consequences of past commitments, including those of his own administration, buoyed by a large electoral victory in 1973, Nixon returned to his long-standing convictions, determined in his second term to rein in spending.

Northern liberals had created many new programs and agencies to heal social ills that ranged from inadequate medical care for the aged to poverty in the mountains of West Virginia. To most Democrats these programs, many of which included implicit promises of more to come, were the new base. To Richard Nixon, most Republicans, and many southern Democrats, these programs were bad ideas at worst or, at best, nice sentiments that could not be afforded. These attitudes toward spending commitments were reversed when the spending was for the military. Particularly after Nixon took office and they were no longer constrained by loyalty to their Democratic president, congressional liberals thought the levels of spending generated by what they considered a stupid and immoral war in Vietnam could hardly be claimed as an inviolable "base." Conservatives thought new domestic welfare programs were equally illegitimate. The result was a series of debilitating battles over budget priorities. Richard Nixon used his budget powers to challenge congressional priorities. He proposed some funding levels far below what majorities in Congress expected. Then when the appropriations committees responded by raising the allocations, Nixon refused to spend the money. He impounded the funds.

---

[4]See Louis Fischer, "Annual Authorizations: Durable Roadblocks to Biennial Budgeting," typescript, n.d.

[5]Mark S. Kamlet and David C. Mowery, "Contradictions of Congressional Budget Reform: Problem of Congressional Emulation of Executive Branch," *Journal of Policy Analysis and Management*, Vol. 6, No. 3 (1987), pp. 365–84.

IMPOUNDMENT

It had always been understood that if money were appropriated for a purpose that turned out to be unnecessary, or if the funds could not be spent usefully and immediately, the executive did not have to spend it, so long as most concerned members of Congress concurred. Indeed, they might want the president to do what was necessary when it was nonpolitic for members to do so. Thus impounding based on tacit consent was an informal safety valve for keeping spending under control. Congress would not have to vote to repeal the funding (since that was troublesome); the president, through OMB and the Treasury, would merely refuse to release the funds to the affected agency. And of course the decision would come too late for the agency to protest effectively. Nixon tried to change this tradition of informal understandings in special cases to a general presidential prerogative: He would spend only what he chose to. After other efforts to shape appropriations through vetoes and lobbying had failed, and after the 1972 election had, he claimed, given him a mandate, Nixon resorted to impoundment en masse. As Allen Schick wrote,

> Far from administrative routine, Nixon's impoundments in late 1972 and 1973 were designed to rewrite national policy at the expense of congressional power and intent. Rather than the deferment of expenses, Nixon's aim was the cancellation of unwanted programs. . . . When Nixon impounded for policy reasons, he in effect told Congress, "I don't care what you appropriate; I will decide what will be spent."[6]

The policy stakes in Nixon's impoundments may have been striking enough, but the political stakes were decisive. Save during a major war, no president had ever asserted his primacy over Congress so bluntly. If Nixon could get away with massive impoundments, what could he not do? If the power of the purse could be defied, what was left for Congress?

The power of the purse had to be protected in 1974 as in 1774—but in 1974 for the opposite reason. The world had been stood on its head. For two centuries Congress had defined the threat as an executive that wanted to spend too much. Since the days of royal governors and their civil lists, the legislature's problem had been to restrain the executive by limiting its funds. Now it faced a chief executive who wanted to spend too little, and who defied the legislature (or, as Congress saw it, the people) by refusing funds for the bureaucracy. The challenge to Congress was as great, but its meaning to the public and the possible remedies now had to be very different.

A division of labor and sharing of power in budgeting requires shared notions of what is accepted, and thus not subject to dispute—that is, controversy must be limited to the margins, and battles once settled must not be continually refought, lest the system collapse. Much of the legitimacy of OMB and the president depends on a belief that they too concur in Congress's base, that they merely adjust it by judging the technical aspects of programs and the management needs of agencies. If, instead, the president's preferences differ and if his budget becomes mainly an attack on programs he does not like, its use to Congress is drastically re-

---

[6]Schick, *Congress and Money*, pp. 46, 48.

duced. The appropriations committees' power similarly depends on their not going overboard and using that power to change policy beyond the will of Congress. If they overstep their bounds, Congress will revolt. If the appropriations committees had gone along with Nixon, they would have been overridden in their parent houses. When, instead, they conformed to congressional intent, Nixon, by impounding, tried to short-circuit the entire appropriations process. Congress had to respond and attempted to reassert its role in the Congressional Budget and Impoundment Act.

THE BUDGET ACT: MORE CHECKS, MORE BALANCES, BUT NOT MORE CONTROL

Another word is in order about that elusive concept called control. By itself it is a synonym for power. But power over people is not necessarily the same as power over events. Controlling the president is not necessarily the equivalent of control over the budget, and neither necessarily adds up to control over the economy. While Congress in general did want more power over presidents and did wish to relate expenditure more closely to revenue, it was not in agreement about whether expenditures per se were too high, or revenues were too low, or, if so, which parts should be raised or lowered. The question of whether Congress could achieve self-control, at least making the budget come out as it wished, was solved at a formal level: It could command itself to do right. Whether Congress was sufficiently in agreement to obey its own command was the question. If Congress was agreed on the desirability of making big choices on total spending and taxing but disagreed about the content of these decisions—both "how much" and "what for"—Congress would get not control but stultification.

The old procedures were controlling neither spending nor the president. Yet new procedures would shift power within Congress and therefore would meet resistance. Decisions about totals would need to be converted into decisions on programs. The taxing and spending committees would have to be both coordinated and coerced. Any procedure that could do all that, however, would put great power in someone's hands. Historically members of Congress have been unwilling to give that power to any of their number.

The solution, of course, was compromise. Nothing was taken away (hence the need for chapters on historical, classical, and entitlement budgeting). Following the traditions of the American political system, Congress created new committees above and beside the appropriations and tax committees, adding to the system of checks and balances.

Impoundment Again

A new procedure was created that formalized the impoundment process. If the president wishes not to spend appropriated funds, he can propose a rescission; if he wishes only to delay spending, he must propose a deferral. Since 1983 the president may not use a deferral for policy purposes. For a rescission to take effect, both houses must pass a bill approving the change within 45 legislative days of its proposal. If they do not do so, the money must be spent as originally appropriated. A deferral takes effect automatically but cannot last longer than through the end of the fiscal year. Either house can reject the deferral with a vote specifically disapproving it. This procedure exploits the difficulty of congressional action. By requiring positive action in both houses, the more serious policy change (rescission) is made unlikely. The lesser change (deferral) is allowed to occur, but either house can choose by majority vote to enforce the appropriation legislation.

If the president fails to spend the money but does not report to Congress, the Comptroller General (who, as head of the General Accounting Office, monitors the executive for Congress) reports the action himself. His report has the same legal effect as the president's proposal of a rescission or deferral. If presidents ignore congressional disapproval, the Comptroller General can bring a civil action in the courts. Presidents can, of course, choose to provoke a constitutional crisis. Because they must live with Congress, they are unlikely to do so. Because they are increasingly at odds with Congress, presidents are tempted to take back with one hand (impoundment) what they cannot gain with the other (the congressional budget process).

CBO

The 1974 Act also created a new staff institution, the Congressional Budget Office (CBO), budget committees in each house, and new budget procedures.

The CBO was set up to provide a congressional counterpart to the OMB and the president's economic staff, the Council of Economic Advisers (CEA). Much of budgeting, such as projection of entitlement costs, involves technical analysis. It is fairly easy to rig the numbers, and congressmen did not believe that the presidential staff would be above such activity. In fact, they did not even believe that congressional committee staffs would be much more reliable. The CBO was to provide a bastion of neutral analysis, loyal to the institution of Congress, rather than to committees or to parties. Its director, with extensive authority over the office, is appointed jointly by the Speaker of the House and Senate President Pro Tem for a four-year term.

In a development that reminds us that our institutions can work well, the CBO, under its first director, Dr. Alice Rivlin, won a reputation for both competence and neutrality. While its reports have not always been popular, its technical work has been credible. CBO became a modest actor in budgeting, greatly reducing congressional dependence upon the president's experts.

Because estimates of future spending cannot be made with certainty, there are bound to be errors. CBO, no more immune than anyone else, also may make overoptimistic or overpessimistic assumptions about economic growth, inflation, unemployment, and other matters—such as the value of the dollar or the price of oil or interest rates—that confound expectations. In its first few years, especially, CBO's estimates proved more accurate and OMB and agency estimators moved closer to CBO by prior consultation. In short, the existence of competition in estimation has led to modest improvements in accuracy. Evidence suggests that executive long-range economic forecasts tend to be more optimistic than CBO projections, though the accuracy of both forecasts is similar.[7]

CBO and impoundment control easily found their places in the congressional process. Budget committees, and the new budgeting schedule, however, were more problematic.

SBC and HBC

The Senate Budget Committee (SBC) was established in 1974 with sixteen members, to be chosen by the party caucuses and to serve indefinitely. The House Budget Committee (HBC) was structured in an unusual manner. Five of its members were to come from the Appropriations Committee and five from Ways and Means. One was a member of the Democratic leadership and one from the Republican leadership. The other thirteen members were appointed through the usual House procedures (this discussion is in the past tense because of changes in details, but not in the basic design, in later years). The committee is a mixture, therefore, of regular members and representatives of power centers within the House. In addition, membership is rotating, rather than permanent; no member could then serve on the Budget Committee for more than four years (now six) out of every ten. Rotation decreases the chance that budget members will become isolated or parochial in their viewpoints, and helps the committee to gain information from other committees. Rotation also ensures that power will not be hoarded by a small group of representatives.

Scheduling

The new schedule both added new steps and changed the timing of old ones. Previously, Congress convened in early January, the president submitted his budget in late January, and Congress had to adopt appropriations acts by July 1, when the next fiscal year began. Appropriation and authorization legislation created logjams; often an appropriation could not be made because some part of the act was annually authorized and the authorization had not yet passed (e.g., as in military procurement). Frequently, appropriations were delayed past July 1, forcing Congress to pass a continuing resolution (CR). A CR provides funding for agencies lacking appropriations for some short period of time at the rates authorized during the previous year. Its need was minimized for a short while, however, by changing the fiscal year's start to October 1. The calendar change gave Congress three extra months to perform all its old tasks and to pass the new budget resolutions.

Resolutions

These budget resolutions were the centerpiece of the new process. The first resolution, originally to be passed by May 15 (now April 15), was intended to set tar-

---

[7]Mark S. Kamlet and David C. Mowery, "Contradictions of Congressional Budget Reform: Problem of Congressional Emulation of Executive Branch," *Journal of Policy Analysis and Management*, Vol. 6, No. 3 (1987), pp. 365–84.

gets for other committees, and Congress as a whole, to meet. It included recommended levels for budget authority, outlays, revenues, that year's deficit or surplus, and the resulting total public debt. The first resolution also recommended totals for spending divided into a small number of budget functions. These were the same categories of programs into which the president's budget is divided—such as Function 150, "International Affairs," or Function 350, "Agriculture." The resolution is a formal reply to the president's proposal. Budget committee staff and members tend to have rather detailed ideas of how the functional totals translate into committee jurisdictions and report those to the committees as required by Section 302 and since 1990 602 of the Budget Act. For much of this time there were nineteen functions. These divisions match the president's budget, but not Congress's committee structure. Consequently, there arose the need to "crosswalk" between the nineteen categories in the president's budget and those used by the thirteen congressional subcommittees.

The first resolution was assembled on the basis of a wide range of information. HBC and SBC were to have available a Current Services Budget prepared by OMB to show the cost of continuing services at the current level (including changes in prices). The president's budget provided another basis for comparison, analysis, and argument. CBO analyzes the president's budget and its deviations from current policy. After submission of the president's budget, committees with jurisdiction over spending and/or taxing legislation were to submit to the budget committees views and estimates that told the budget committees what members on other committees would like to do.

The budget committees, meanwhile, would hold hearings to discuss the president's economic policy and projections, as well as other aspects of his budget. With the president's proposal, their colleagues' views and estimates, and much technical analysis in hand, HBC and SBC then craft their versions of the resolution. Procedures in passing that resolution are much like those for any other bill except that since the resolution is a rule for Congress, it does not need the president's signature. Neither does it have the force of law or appropriated funds. Disagreements between House and Senate must be resolved in conference.

As designed by the Budget Act, this resolution is more than, less than, but much like the president's budget. It resembles the president's budget in being only a recommendation, something to which action will be compared. It is less than the president's budget because it is less detailed; aggregated only at the functional level, it usually contains only very general guidance and standards for comparison. The resolution is more than the president's budget because it is the product of a lengthy process of discussion and accommodation within Congress; it is therefore more likely to reflect what Congress will actually do. And it is, again, much like the president's budget in being, in its estimates of revenue and debt and entitlement spending, dependent upon predictions of the future course of economy.

After passing the resolution, Congress is to go about its business of authorizing and appropriating. By the Monday after Labor Day, the regular authorizing and appropriating legislation—the laws that actually commit funds—should have passed. The budget committees in late summer would have held hearings to review the latest data about the economy and the actions taken or expected to be taken by the rest of Congress. In the original act this information was to be used to decide whether the targets from this first resolution needed adjustment. HBC and SBC then reported out versions of a second concurrent resolution on the budget. The second resolution had the same components as the first, except that the second resolution's total was supposed to be binding. Thus any legislation considered after passage of the second resolution, which would cause limits in that resolution to be breached, could be objected to and ruled out of order.

Reconciliation

If the limits in the first resolution could not be met, due to unforeseen changes or new legislation, reconciliation instructions could be included in the second resolution. These instructions could direct one or more committees to report legislation in order to bring revenues or spending into conformity with that resolution. This process could apply to authorizations as well as appropriations. Reconciliation was to be packaged by the budget committees without change and enacted by September 25.

In fact, reconciliation was not used in this form: until 1979 appropriations were simply packaged into the second resolution without conscious efforts to make them fit into preassigned (or any other) totals. The reasons were simple. At the very end of the process, after all the deals were made and the bargains struck, participants were in no mood to reopen the whole budget debate again. The potential of reconciliation was not discovered until the last year of the Carter presidency, or fully exploited until the Reagan administration used it as a unprecedented weapon of budgetary policy. It was then used in conjunction with the first resolution, which became the only resolution.

Complexity

The budget resolutions added a new layer of activity to what was already a complicated process. Appropriations already were conditioned by authorizations. Now both were to be based on budget resolutions, which in turn were derived from estimated authorizations and appropriations. All this instruction and advice among different parts of Congress were to be coordinated by provisions of the Budget Act. Authorization bills were to be reported by May 15, enabling the appropriations committees to work with both the reports and the First Resolution as guidelines. No act making budgetary commitments—appropriating funds, creating a new entitlement, or changing taxes—could be considered on the floor before adoption of that resolution. Special procedures expanded both the appropriations committees' ability to question entitlement growth, and their control over various other types of "backdoor" spending. CBO reports, required by the act, provided information for decision making at specified times. These assorted provisions were meant to relate action on programs to action on the totals. The budget committees, presumably, were to do the coordinating. But could they?

A Congressional Budget, or Merely More Budgeting?

In form, therefore, the 1974 act created a budget: Congress would look at programs, think about totals, choose a relationship between spending and revenue, and bring the two together. Entitlement spending would be confronted while considering the totals. New entitlement spending would be analyzed by CBO and delayed by provisions in the schedule, thus getting a longer, harder look than it had before. Established entitlements might be adjusted during reconciliation. The budget resolutions would enable congressional majorities to respond directly to the president's budget, asserting their own functional priorities and fiscal goals. The process of adopting resolutions would focus attention on these questions—the relative sizes of revenue and expenditures and their effects on the economy—far more explicitly than had been done in the past; and voting would force members of Congress to take stands in a way not previously required. Hearings and CBO analyses would generate information; resolutions would occasion debate; debate would inform Congress and the public about the choices made. The procedures relating taxing and spending to the size of the budget would force members to take the totals seriously.

All that was possible; yet, instead of creating a budget, the new procedures might merely create more budgeting. Members would follow the budget act's rules only if they wanted to do so; they would want to do so only if they valued the process itself more than they valued what they would lose if they obeyed the act.

THE BUDGET PROCESS, 1975–1979: THE STRUGGLE TO RELATE TOTALS TO DETAIL

At stake was power and policy: power within Congress, the power of Congress in regard to the executive branch, and congressional power over programs. If Congress disagreed over policy, however, its members would find that power over one another had a different institutional significance than power vis-à-vis the presidency.

Members of the budget committees had a power stake in making the process work. Unless budget resolutions influenced taxing and spending action, HBC and SBC members would gain nothing from membership. Appropriations committee members objected to their loss of power, of course, but they also had reason to go along with the process. Before 1974, deficits were blamed on them; the new process made it possible to direct attention toward the authorizing, in particular the tax, committees. Members of these other committees were threatened by the Budget Act, which could undermine their committee's independence and ability to serve constituents. Because only a minority of representatives serve on budget and appropriations committees, enforcement of budget totals required either that they be satisfactory to other members of Congress and their roles as committee members, or that other roles and allegiances (to party, to a president, to a constituency, or to an ideology) override loyalties as committee members. The budget committees therefore tried both to create resolutions that stepped on very few toes and to mobilize those other loyalties to pass and enforce resolutions on the floor of their respective houses.

In the Senate, budget committee chairman Edmund Muskie (D-Maine) and ranking minority member Henry Bellmon (R-Okla.) worked to develop resolutions that could command substantial bipartisan support. They then united in defense of the recommendations on the floor. In the House, the resolutions became partisan documents. Republicans continually opposed them on the ground that taxing and spending were too high. Democrats were forced to seek resolutions that could carry without Republican votes. In mobilizing Democratic majorities, party leaders became key actors in that process. Only the Speaker and his lieutenants could (sometimes) muster the Democratic troops. The Democratic House resolutions and bipartisan Senate plans were often difficult to compromise in conference.

By 1980 budget process observers and participants were engaged in a running debate as to whether these resolutions, and the entire process, were having any, and if so what, effect on spending and taxing policy. The views and estimates submitted by the committees to HBC and SBC on March 15 tended to turn into wish lists. Requests averaged about 10 percent higher for spending than actually were approved. Because the budget committees had so many alternative sources of information, they fortunately did not have to depend on the March 15 reports for technical data. Instead, both the formal reports and informal contacts among committee staffs made budget drafters aware of how much conflict might be expected in considering alternative spending levels. HBC and SBC therefore had enough information for their purposes. They had estimates of the program base— what was spent last year, which obligations existed, and how the expected performance of the economy would influence program costs. This information might not be accurate, for some of it was unknowable, but members would be as informed as anyone else. They also knew, normally, what kinds of changes would be proposed by various participants, such as the president and the authorizing committees, and could judge the political force of those proposals.

A far greater difficulty was the potential that the First Resolution, however nicely calibrated, would be ignored at other steps of the process. First Resolution totals for the functions—spending, taxing, etc.—were only targets, but, as it turned out, they were moving targets open to challenge.

The stakes, and difficulty, of such challenges were highlighted in the first year of the process (1975 for fiscal 1976). Senator Muskie, whose chairmanship of the Senate Budget Committee gave him the incentive to keep spending within the limits of his committee's resolution, challenged authorization legislation for both military procurement and the school lunch program, thereby showing he had no policy axe to grind. In each case he was able to force changes in the legislation, but in doing so he risked a backlash, which materialized a year later, from members whose policies were threatened by reduced spending.

Within this context of mutual uncertainty, HBC and SBC worked to accommodate other congressional actors, who also tried to avoid direct confrontations with budget committees. The terms of accommodation depended in part upon who was trying to change the status quo. The budgeters could more easily resist new legislation, by publicizing its cost or nonconformance to the resolution, than they could force the passage of a change that would cut spending or increase revenue. It is easier to stop people from acting than to make them do something, especially if the action is complicated, requires cooperation, and involves members of Congress. Proponents of legislation, who had strong incentives to avoid complications on the floor (delay can be deadly), tried to adapt bills to satisfy the budget committees. But the budget committees could do little to urge, say, Ways and Means to report out medicare reforms. In between these two extremes were legislative changes that seemed so pressing to so many members that, if budget committees got in the way of passage, they might be regarded as pests and brushed aside—as happened whenever they tried to reduce the rate of increase in social security. In general, if the first resolution assumed either legislative changes to programs or funding below what had been Congress's habit, the first resolution had to be adjusted upward.

ECONOMIC MANAGEMENT

One of the major aims of budget reform was to connect more closely attempts to manage the economy with the expenditure process. And it does appear that members of budget committees took the trouble to learn more about the relationship between levels of spending and the condition of the economy. One difficulty is that not much is known; another is that ability to apply what little is known is strictly limited.

Economic management (or fiscal policy, as it is called) requires a notion of what level of expenditure is appropriate either to stimulate or depress economic activity. Commitments of the past make up the largest part of the budget, however, and it is difficult, either legally or politically, to alter them drastically. Considerations of desirable defense and domestic expenditures compete of necessity with optimal fiscal policy, assuming anyone knows what that should be. Among the many constraints within which the makers of fiscal policy operate, the least understood are those imposed by time and by targeting.

Take time: There is a fallacy that assumes that fiscal policy goes into effect at the time it is made. If we are talking about expenditures, that assumption cannot be correct. The most important time, usually, for bringing fiscal considerations to bear on budgetary totals is during the spring preview conducted by OMB in April. Suppose this is done in April. The fiscal policy total is considered along with other matters, and OMB establishes and passes down a budgetary target to the spending agencies. For the moment, suppose that this total is not challenged by agencies nor revised by the president but goes directly into his budget in the winter. Even if these contrary-to-fact conditions are met, Congress will not finish acting on appropriations bills until almost a year later in the fall of the next calendar year. Spending agencies will take several months to act on this legislation; the impact of these expenditures, then, will not begin to be felt until the winter of the following year. Thus about two years elapse before the thoughts that went into fiscal policy are reflected in real budgetary behavior. By that time, to be sure, conditions may have markedly changed so that what seemed appropriate then is now inappropriate.

The two years can be shortened to eighteen months by postponing or modifying fiscal policy decisions until November or December. This alternative, however, sacrifices the benefit of considering fiscal policy in the ceilings initially set by OMB. Renegotiating all the bargains of the prior six months in a few weeks in late November and December is an experience that most participants will try to avoid. By late fall, fiscal policy can be adjusted but the entire orchestral arrangement (insofar as budgetary totals are concerned) is likely to have been settled earlier or not at all. Fall fiscal policy is even tighter than what was already an extremely constrained situation the previous spring.

The existence of unprecedented rates of inflation in the mid-1970s, followed by extraordinarily high interest rates in the late 1970s, coming together with multi-hundred-billion-dollar deficits in the early 1980s, and topped off by the largest unemployment rate since the Great Depression highlighted congressional responsibilities for economic management. But no budget committee could do this alone. Reducing the deficit, for instance, would have required a package deal about taxation and domestic and defense spending that could have been achieved only by concerted action among congressional committees, backed up or led by the formal leadership, and supported by the president. Without such agreement, the members of Congress would only end up fooling themselves: There are any number of innovative ways that Congress can circumvent its own will. Congressional efforts at economic management were stymied both because of doubt over effective policy and inability to act together to enforce whatever set of actions is deemed desirable.

DID THE BUDGETARY PROCESS HAVE A PRO-SPENDING BIAS?

The Budget Act of 1974 expressed Congress's desire to enhance its own power of the purse by granting it the ability to visibly relate revenue and expenditure. Since the broad coalition supporting the Act included both high and low spenders, however, the new process was not designed to favor either side. On the one hand, the mere existence of budget committees raised another possible impediment to higher spending; on the other hand, the need for these committees to maintain collegial relations with tax and spending committees, as well as to remain subject to the will of Congress, meant that budget committees had to subordinate themselves to the widespread desires for higher spending. The evidence from Allen Schick's *Congress and Money* is conclusive:

> In almost a hundred interviews with Members of Congress and staffers, no one expressed the view that the allocations in budget resolution had been knowingly set below legislative expectations. "We got all that we needed," one committee staff director exulted. The chief clerk of an Appropriations subcommittee complained, however, that the target figure in the resolution was too high: "We were faced with pressure to spend up to the full budget allocation. It's almost as if the Budget Committee bent over backwards to give Appropriations all that it wanted and then some."[8]

All internal incentives worked to raise expenditures. Who, for instance, would take the lead in reducing expenditures? Each sector of policy, including the people in Congress who cared most about it, naturally was concerned with its own internal development. Those who favored radical restructuring of programs soon discovered that this was exceeding difficult to do without sweetening the pot. More money made it easier to settle internal quarrels. The price of policy change

---

[8]Schick, *Congress and Money*, p. 313.

was program expansion.[9] Like all others who wish to be influential, budget committees could afford to lose only a few times, for if it becomes obvious that budget committees are likely to lose, no one need pay attention to them.

The HBC's difficulties in enforcing reductions, to no one's surprise, came from advocates of increased spending. But it was in the Senate that the clash between the Budget and Finance committees was most severe. Chairman Muskie of SBC was interested in the big picture. As he told the Senate, the Budget Committee "is not a line-item committee."[10] Tax preferences cause so much loss of revenue and, indeed, are so much an alternative form of accomplishing the same purpose as expenditures, Muskie felt, that to ignore them would be to nullify efforts at budget control. In colorful language, he raised and answered the rhetorical question:

> Are we supposed to meet each March to propose a congressional budget and then retire to the cloakroom until the fall, when it is too late to advise the Senate of the implications of its tax and spending decisions? And then pop back out like some unwelcome jack-in-the-box each fall to shout, "Surprise! You've blown the budget."? Hardly.[11]

Not to be outdone, Senator Russell Long, chairman of the Committee on Finance, retorted, "The chairman of the Budget Committee cannot find anything small enough for the Finance Committee to decide anything about."[12] Back at the House, an HBC staff member expressed dismay at such direct confrontation, saying, "We're aware that we'll get killed if we take on other committees head to head. All we have to work with is the good will of other committees."[13]

The budget reform was designed to help Congress relate obligations to income by setting targets for total expenditures. Senator Muskie said of legislators' simultaneously voting for more spending and lower budget deficits, "We just can't make the system work with that kind of philosophy."[14] Yet Joel Havemann reported several instances of representatives engaging in this sort of behavior on the grounds, as one put it, "That's the beauty of the budget process. You can vote for all your favorite programs, and then vote against the deficit."[15] What, then happened to congressional efforts to engage in economic management?

To increase spending, no coordination is necessary; program advocates already want to do that. To decrease spending, coordination is essential. Without

---

[9]For example, see Aaron Wildavsky, *Speaking Truth to Power* (Boston: Little, Brown, 1979), Chapter 4, "Coordination Without a Coordinator," pp. 186–107.

[10]*National Journal*, September 25, 1976, pp. 1348–49.

[11]Ibid., p. 1347.

[12]Ibid., p. 1348.

[13]Ibid.

[14]See Aaron Wildavsky, "Ask Not What Budgeting Does to Society but What Society Does to Budgeting." Introduction to the second edition of *National Journal Reprints* (Washington, D.C., 1977), p. 4.

[15]Ibid. See Mark S. Kamlet, David Mowery, and Gregory Fischer, "Modelling Budgetary Tradeoffs: An Analysis of Congressional Macrobudgetary Priorities, the Impact of the Congressional Budget Act, and the Reagan Counterrevolution." Paper prepared for the Midwest Political Science Association Meetings, Chicago, Illinois, April 22, 1983; and Louis Fisher, "In Dubious Battle? Congress and the Budget," *The Brookings Bulletin*, Vol. 17 (Spring 1981), pp. 6–10.

spending ceilings that require choice among programs, budgeting by addition rather than subtraction remains common practice, and participants will look for creative ways to evade attempts at control.

On Again, Off Again: Federal Credit

Without doubt, credit is an important way to increase federal spending; it vastly expands the scope and extent of federal influence. Credit is also a flexible instrument that helps implement diverse public policies—from rural electrification to student loans to increasing the volume of exports. Given the desire to subsidize certain activities, the instruments used—loans, guarantees—may be an efficient mode of accomplishing that result.

Subsidization of such favored borrowers, however, may well decrease the growth of the economy by diverting resources from more to less productive uses. These debt instruments also make the desired activities budgetarily more attractive; either they do not show up in the budget at all or they appear at a much lower amount than they would if they came in the form of appropriations. By the same token, credit instrumentalities raise federal spending and its reach far beyond what would take place in their absence, partly by obfuscating accountability. Credit instruments make it difficult to determine how much is being spent by whom for what purpose and with what consequences. Though the formal responsibility of the federal government for increasing national debt seems diminished, because much of this debt does not show up in the budget as proposed by the president or enacted by Congress—since the resources are provided directly by the federal treasury—the debt itself does go up. Though the actual operations of federally assisted credit are hard to believe (especially the shell games through which debt on budget was passed through the Federal Financing Bank so that, voila! it goes off-budget), a tour through the interstices of these operations does help explain why credit is an important mechanism for funding public policy.

Big changes often come from small beginnings. The authority of federal agencies to borrow money through the Treasury is not an ancient practice; it dates back only to 1932 when, after bills to create a Reconstruction Finance Corporation (RFC) were on the way to passage, the Treasury Department recommended that in addition to being able to borrow from the general public, RFC should also be able to borrow from the Treasury so as to avoid interfering with its own debt issues.[16] In the next few years, once the precedent had been set at a time when anti-depression measures were paramount, borrowing from the Treasury was extended to housing authorities, the Tennessee Valley Authority, and the Commodity Credit Corporation.

From this beginning in 1932 to mid-1965, funds going through the then-normal appropriations committee amounted to nearly $2 trillion while authorization to borrow amounted to $106.6 billion or 5.4 percent of spending by appropriations, a small proportion. Of this borrowing authorization, the appropriations committees provided $12.7 billion while $93.9 billion came directly from the

---

[16]Sun Kil Kim, "The Politics of a Congressional Budgetary Process 'Backdoor Spending,'" *Western Political Quarterly,* Vol. 21 (December 1968), pp. 606–23; especially pp. 607–609.

Treasury. These direct drafts came to be called treasury budgeting or, more popularly, backdoor financing, on the grounds that these sums had been obtained by bypassing the appropriations process.[17]

Gradually five types of borrowing authority came into being—or, as the Treasury Department called it, "the authority to expand from public debt receipts." The amounts could be definite, that is, have a ceiling, or indefinite, that is, of unlimited duration, limited to one specified fiscal year or to no fiscal year. By contrast, borrowing through the appropriations process was far more constrained, nonrevolving, available only in specified fiscal years, and with fixed ceilings.[18] Revolving funds could use repayments to sponsor still more borrowing ad infinitum.

From an institutional and partisan point of view, the backdoor method was favored by the more liberal Senate in the 1950s and early 1960s while the more conservative House, fearing invasion of its prized power of the purse, unsuccessfully resisted the device. Appropriations committee members disliked most the fact that the Senate would pass additional credit authorizations in what Appropriations considered violation of the constitutional provision requiring that money bills originate in the House. The granting of such "special favors," Chairman Clarence Cannon thundered, had made the Senate into "the dominant body of Congress."[19] Supporters would argue that programs would be more effective if funded by loans available over the long term, while opponents responded that all such matters should go through the appropriations process where, of course, requests were certain to be treated less generously. "The debate over 'backdoor spending,'" Sun Kim concluded, "is a contingent battle over the programs themselves."[20]

During the 1960s and early 1970s, federal credit offerings increased. By 1972 such issues appeared in financial markets three out of every five days, and by 1973 there were $43.9 billion outstanding in direct loans and $174.1 billion in loan guarantees.[21] By the time the Budget Act was passed, there was considerable concern about the efficiency of federal credit operations. Coming from everywhere, without order or expertise, federal credit offerings were often badly placed, wrongly sized, and poorly publicized, so that rates of interest were considerably higher than ordinary treasury securities. In order, it said, to reduce costs of administration and of interest, the Treasury Department proposed in 1973 (and in 1975 the government began) the Federal Financing Bank (FFB), a small unit within the Treasury that would centralize the issuance of federal securities, thereby eliminating underwriting fees and securing other such economies. That did happen. But Paul Volcker, the Undersecretary for Monetary Affairs, promised that the FFB would not be "a device to remove programs from the federal budget. . . . The

---

[17]Ibid., p. 609.

[18]Ibid., p. 607.

[19]Ibid., pp. 617–18.

[20]Ibid., p. 622.

[21]See Dennis S. Ippolito, *Hidden Spending: The Politics of Federal Credit Programs* (Chapel Hill: University of N. Carolina Press).

Bank would in no way affect the existing budget treatment of federal credit pro-grams."[22] But that promise was not kept.

It has been well said in ecology that no act does only one thing. Nowhere is that more true than of the FFB. It did indeed cut the micro-costs of borrowing. Despite its small one-eighth of a percent loan fee, FFB brought in far more than it spent. Loan costs to agencies went down considerably. But as James Bickley put it, "The very success of the FFB's operation may have also contributed to the rapid growth of federal credit assistance."[23]

At the outset, it is important to understand that the size of the Bank's holdings were not limited by statute nor were its disbursements and receipts included within budget total nor was there any limit on its outlays (that is, the excess of loans over receipts).

There were four basic types of FFB operations whose effects on the federal budget need to be distinguished. In what might be called "replacement borrow-ing," agencies that were "on-budget," that is, in the budget, borrowed from FFB as a substitute for the public financial markets. No change there except easier ac-cess and lower cost of funds. In "operational borrowing," agencies already "off-budget" used the Bank to finance their activities. Since this borrowing would not otherwise have appeared in the budget, the only change was again lower cost and easier access. There were, however, two methods of changing on-budget to off-budget loans that deserve scrutiny.

When a loan was sold by an on-budget agency to the FFB, which was off-budget, the same status was conferred on that loan. The agency retained title to the loan, continued to service it, and remained responsible for defaults. This meant the loan no longer was added to the deficit attributable to the federal bud-get though it did, until repaid, add to total government borrowing. Since these "loan assets," as they were conventionally called, belonged to the Bank while the sponsoring agency still had the title, the agency could use these presumed assets as, in effect, collateral for additional loans. Easy as pie.

The fourth category, which might be termed a "second party loan," occurred when a federal agency, providing a guarantee, directed the FFB to issue a loan to a nonfederal borrower. Though the agency was responsible for any defaults, the loan was, with the speed of a single transaction, converted into off-budget status.[24]

It should come as no surprise, therefore, that FFB on-budget agency debt from 1975 to 1984 declined from 41.2 to 20.2 percent while loan assets went from 0.3 to 43.7 percent and its second party guaranteed debt rose from 16.6 to 35.3 percent.[25] Between 1974 and 1981, direct on-budget loans doubled from $46.1 bil-lion to $91.3 billion; off-budget direct loans increased sixfold from $151.4 billion

[22]James M. Bickley, "The Federal Financing Bank: Assessments of Its Effectiveness and Budgetary Status," *Public Budgeting and Finance*, Vol. 5, No. 4 (Winter 1985), pp. 51–63; quote on p. 51.

[23]Ibid., p. 57.

[24]Ibid., pp. 54–55.

[25]Ibid., p. 55.

Table 4.1   SUMMARY OF OUTSTANDING FEDERAL AND FEDERALLY ASSISTED CREDIT*

| | | (in billions of current dollars) | | |
Year	Direct loans on-budget	Direct loans off-budget	Guaranteed loans	Government sponsored enterprise loans	Total
1974	$46.1	$15.4	$180.4	$ 43.8	$ 285.7
1975	49.8	24.4	189.0	43.5	306.7
1976	64.2	21.6	200.7	54.0	340.5
1977	68.2	32.7	214.5	71.8	387.2
1978	76.5	43.9	226.1	93.8	440.3
1979	83.0	57.5	264.6	123.0	528.1
1980	91.7	72.3	299.2	151.0	614.2
1981	91.3	93.7	309.1	182.3	676.4
1982	100.2	107.6	331.2	225.6	764.6
1983	105.0	118.0	363.8	261.2	848.0
1984 (est.)	103.7	128.8	393.6	301.0	927.1
1985 (est.)	101.5	139.3	428.1	343.9	1,012.8

*Table from Clifford M. Hardin and Arthur T. Denzau, "Closing the Back Door on Federal Spending: Better Management of Federal Credit," Formal Publication #64, September 1984, Center for the Study of American Business, Washington University, St. Louis, Missouri. Table 10.1 provides additional information on federal credit in the 1990s.

Source: Special Analysis F., *Budget of the United States Government, FY1985*, and earlier special analyses; and *Mid-Session Review of the 1985 Budget.*

to $93.7 billion; and guaranteed loans rose from $180.4 billion to $309.1 billion. Meanwhile government sponsored enterprise loans grew from $43.8 billion to over $182 billion (see Table 4.1). While this debt did count toward whatever overall debt limit Congress established, it did not count in the federal deficit. And that—enabling agencies to borrow more on behalf of their clients while keeping the formal deficit down—was apparently the purpose of these transactions.

How much, we may ask, following the medieval philosophers, is a loan guarantee worth? Defaults are counted as outlays. But the difference between the cost in private markets and the rate at which the FFB-cum-Treasury could borrow was not. And that difference was real money amounting to billions over a large volume of transactions. Guaranteed loans get priority, which is also worth something. In 1982, for example, new direct loans of $44 billion and loan guarantees amounting to $78 billion were given by the federal government. Total cash disbursements were $15.3 billion, but only $4.8 billion was noted in budget accounts. It would not be excessive, though there was no agreement, to estimate the cost of the subsidy at over $20 billion, albeit not in one year.[26] Thus the size of the deficit was distorted in two ways, one by moving nearly 80 percent of loan transactions off-budget and the other by providing a substantial but unaccounted-for interest rate subsidy. Whatever opportunity there might be, moreover, for comparing the

---

[26]Marvin Phaup, "Accounting for Federal Credit: A Better Way," *Public Budgeting and Finance*, Vol. 5, No. 3 (Autumn 1985), pp. 29–39; figures from p. 30.

relative desirability of different loans—say, Rural Electrification Administration versus Farmers' Home Administration versus the Foreign Military Sales Program, to mention three of the largest—or to evaluate them in the context of on-budget spending programs was lost or made more difficult.[27]

Why were not all FFB loans placed on-budget? "Right now we deal with Congress and FFB to finance our programs," the president of the National Rural Electric Cooperatives said. "If we are put on budget, we will also have to deal with OMB."[28] The Rural Electrification and Telephone Revolving Fund (RETRF) needed all the help it could get. Created in 1973 under a Republican administration, the funds provided loans for 35 years at 5 percent interest, 2 percent for hardship cases. Its $7.9 billion endowment funds were mostly composed of old loans bearing a 2 percent interest rate whose repayment (interest only until 1993, principal thereafter) was to go to the Treasury until the entire amount had been paid off. Since these payments amounted merely to $314 million while new disbursements were twice that sum, the rural fund made up the difference by reducing its cash on hand, borrowing short-term notes from the Treasury, and issuing Certificates of Beneficial Ownership to FFB, for which the rate was one-eighth percent plus the rate of long-term treasury debt, then around 13 percent. Clearly, with defaults on the rise, repayment would be difficult. So refinancing legislation was introduced that would, according to a CBO estimate, increase costs to the federal government by $10.4 billion over a quarter century.[29]

What was the Tennessee Valley Authority to do when it accumulated excess inventories of nuclear fuel due to a slowdown in plant construction? I won't go into the leaseback arrangement to "sell" the fuel and buy it back as needed; presumably that made TVA's balance sheet look better. First TVA thought of borrowing $1 billion from private lenders, through a subsidiary, to buy back the fuel. The Treasury suggested FFB. So TVA arranged a $2 billion line of credit, thereby saving over $20 million a year in interest costs without having to pay the usual substantial commitment fee for the right to use the remaining balance. This loan was larger than the New York City and Chrysler loans without the attendant publicity and with much less security.[30]

The 1980s saw several attempts by the federal government to control credit. OMB regularly provided an appendix to the president's budget that tried to account for all governmental credit. In fiscal year 1981, for the first time nonbinding targets for federal credit were made part of congressional budget resolutions. In the following two years these targets were disaggregated to functional levels, tied to the same appropriations subcommittees that consider regular spending. Where

---

[27]Thomas J. DiLorenzo, "Putting Off-Budget Federal Spending Back on the Books," *The Backgrounder,* No. 406, Heritage Foundation, January 30, 1985, p. 3.

[28]Darwin G. Johnson, "Comments" on Robert Hartman, "Issues in Budget Accounting," in Gregory B. Mills and John L. Palmer, *Federal Budget Policy in the 1980s* (Washington, D.C.: Urban Institute Press, 1984), pp. 448–56; quote on p. 451.

[29]Phaup, "Accounting for Federal Credit," p. 33.

[30]Clifford M. Hardin and Arthur T. Denzau, "The Unrestrained Growth of Federal Credit Programs," Formal Publication 45, December 1981, Center for the Study of American Business, Washington University, St. Louis, p. 14.

formerly the Defense Department used FFB to place guaranteed loans for arms purchases off-budget, Congress decided in 1984 that in the future such loans would appear on-budget. The Gramm–Rudman–Hollings bill of 1985 (GRH) included a section placing the FFB on-budget. Further comprehensive reform took place in 1990 (see Chapter 10).

POLARIZATION: CLASSICAL BUDGETING WITHERS WITHOUT QUITE DISAPPEARING

By the beginning of the 1980s, the practices of classical budgeting had been seriously undermined. Compromise more frequently gave way to confrontation that threatened the budget process altogether. Both Presidents Nixon and Reagan stepped beyond the conventional power of their office in pursuing their own policy agendas. Increasingly it became clear that compromise on the budget would be difficult to obtain. The president wanted higher defense spending, much lower domestic spending, and no tax increases. The opposition wanted higher taxes, lower defense spending, and higher domestic spending than did the president. Each insisted that their preferred programs were not up for negotiation. The result was stalemate. From 1982 on, the budgetary process slowed down. Individual appropriations were delayed. Continuing resolutions came to replace the ordinary budget process. Dissensus was the order of the day.

The budget was no longer elastic. More for one meant less for someone else. In a sense the budget had been preempted, as entitlements and entrenched programs left less and less margin for new initiatives or even expansion of older programs. Budget management on Keynesian principles seemed less viable: While the theory came under attack, its practice seemed discredited by persistent (even if in retrospect not very large) deficits.

The major effort to regain control, the 1974 Congressional Budget Act, had mixed reviews. The legislation itself had been weakened by compromises, notably the inability of the budget committees to enforce ceilings on the other committees of Congress. Their attempts to assert authority ran counter to the committees' assumed prerogatives, and their own cautious sense of self-preservation. The proliferation of credit programs during the 1970s, and also later in the 1980s, attested to the upward pressures on spending.

Meanwhile the major players of the old budget process, the appropriations committees, no longer appeared capable of performing their old role. In the 1970s the appropriations committees had moved away from their role as guardians of the Treasury. A combination of appointing advocates to appropriations and the existence of budget committees did the trick. With more liberal Democratic members and more conservative Republicans, the policy distance among members grew, thereby reducing internal cohesion. And as budget committees were placed over appropriations committees, the spending committees tended to regard their recommendations not as likely to be final but rather as opening bids in a sequence of negotiations. Like the executive spending agencies, therefore, appropriations subcommittees tended to pad their favorite programs so as to leave room for cutting by budget committees and by action on the floor.

New patterns began to emerge. Neither the guardian norm nor spending control had totally disappeared. Indeed, spending control was what made appropriations decisions worth contesting. But appropriations politics became vastly more centralized—a contest not only among committees and agencies, but also among OMB and congressional leaders, whose differences were not so much about individual programs as about spending totals or about the largest possible divisions, domestic versus defense, within them.

Little in Congress is completely original; heirs to old practices tend to bear some resemblance to their parents. So it was with appropriations. Committees continued to write bills and party leaders within the committees still had important roles in bargaining and in floor maneuvers. Many programmatic differences (especially on defense) were worked out in committee. In small matters, the attention to district interests, which critics of all political persuasions find so unseemly, remained. So did the unusual nonpartisanship of House appropriations staff, especially compared to the partisan rancor in the House budget committee. Most important, the appropriations committees still held the role of translating program preferences into the line-item language of appropriations acts. Therefore, they maintained a crucial position in the process of program funding.

But while much was still familiar in the 1980s, the relationship among all the parts of the process changed drastically as the broad sweep of partisan budget politics, reflecting deep division over public policy took primacy over the management of agencies and distribution of benefits through appropriations oversight. The new policy partisanship did not so much displace the old as subsume it.

Chapter
5

The Politics of
Dissensus: The 1980s

*T*he battles over the budget that have been waged from the end of the 1970s until today are remarkable. Neither in American history nor in contemporary budgeting in other industrial democracies do we see their like. Disagreement over the size or scope or content of budgets has been a frequent occurrence before and after the founding of the American republic, but not all of these at once. Never have budget battles been pursued for so long.

While the sources and manifestations of dissensus had been apparent for over a decade, the beginning of the Reagan administration in 1981 not only intensified polarization over policies, but also accelerated the search to find solutions for a budget process allegedly gone awry. In addition to deliberate reform, both institutions and procedures adapted to the new situation. Although congressional committees and executive agencies continued to operate according to the Congressional Budget Act and within traditional frameworks, their roles and patterns of mutual expectations had been disrupted. Dissensus was reflected in budget processes, whose turmoil in turn intensified it.

WHY BUDGET DECISIONS BECAME SO DIFFICULT

From the end of the Second World War until the late 1960s, the budgetary process was stable. Though there were efforts to alter its form, such as program and performance budgeting, these were largely concerned with improving the efficiency and effectiveness of existing programs. Hence we can conclude that there was general agreement on ends, give or take a few percent and a few programs, but some dissatisfaction with the means of achieving them.

While efforts to improve efficiency continued, the Budget Reform Act of 1974 focused attention on the substance of the budget—how much in total, how divided among major programs, who should pay. From the mid-1970s onward, the reformed process worked in a manner of speaking—decisions were made—but the procedures did not work in quite the same way in any two consecutive years. Sometimes the president's budget message provided the starting point, sometimes it didn't. Sometimes there was a first, second, and third budget resolution, sometimes two, other times only one. The relative power of appropriations, finance, and budget committees varied markedly. And the coalitions in Congress that eventually made the crucial choices—so much for defense and domestic, so much in total, reallocation of tax burdens—could not have been predicted from one year to the next. Nor could anyone say who (by position, role, or ideology) would take the lead in putting together the winning coalition. Uncertainty, delay, disarray, crisis, even fatalism (Why bother if each heroic effort had to be followed by another, or if interest rate increases wiped out the effects of months of struggle?) became hallmarks of budgeting. There was increasing complexity (the old appropriations and tax processes still operated but they were overlaid with the new resolutions, reconciliation procedures, presidential sequester orders, let alone credit and tax expenditure budgets) but there was not clarity. What did all this mean?

I recall hearing it said about a father of eleven children that he was always one child over being adequate. Perhaps the simplest explanation is that the demands made on Congress, together with its self-imposed requirements, always remained one step above congressional capacity to manage. In the dramatic rise of government spending from the mid-1960s through the 1970s, there was nothing intrinsic that had to lead to overloading the budgetary process. Even the decline in economic growth, though it undoubtedly made decisions more difficult (there being less to go around), was no insuperable obstacle. Indeed, the Budget Reform Act enabled Congress, were it so inclined, to relate revenue to expenditure—either raising taxes or reducing expenditures so as to arrive at totals it thought appropriate. And Congress did try. The rate of increase in spending did slow down. New entitlements, and other forms of spending that had hitherto escaped the appropriations process, were made more difficult to achieve. If rates were not raised, "bracket creep" increased the tax take in an inflationary period. While deficits continued, they did not represent as large a proportion of national product.

At the same time, however, Congress had placed itself in the position of having to take global positions unique in American budgetary history. It did have to establish total spending and revenue and divide these totals by major substantive categories. Whereas before such choices were best described as outcomes or resultants—known only by adding up choices made on an item-by-item or program-by-program basis through a maze of semi-independent committees and subcommittees—now Congress had to operate as a collective body.

A notable accompaniment of the concentration on budget resolutions—total taxing and spending—was an increase in partisanship. After 1975, as Schick reminds us, "the two parties have been polarized on budget policy. Twenty resolutions [not every one passed] have wended their way through the House over the past decade; on every one of these, a majority of Democrats have been on one side and a majority of Republicans on the other."[1]

Why has partisanship over the budget increased so sharply? Ellwood suggests that

---

[1]Allen Schick, "The Evolution of Congressional Budgeting," in Allen Schick, ed., *Crisis in the Budget Process* (Washington, D.C.: American Enterprise Institute, 1986), p. 35.

the movement toward a coordinated, top-down decision making process is one explanation. In the appropriations process members are cross-pressured. They have an individual and party commitment to increases or decreases in expenditures, revenues
and deficits; but they also want to serve their constituencies and interest groups. In
such a situation they are more likely to abandon their ideological and party position.[2]

The difference in the type of issue—parts versus the whole budget—may well account for the higher scores on global issues but it does not serve to explain the
general rise in partisanship.

Louis Fisher of the Congressional Research Service, an astute observer of
budgeting, argues that changes in the form of budgeting were responsible for the
rise not only in partisanship but also in the intensity of conflict. According to
Fisher:

> Increasing the size of a legislative vehicle—from an appropriations bill to a budget res-
> olution—magnifies the scope of legislative conflict and creates the need for additional
> concessions to Members. The likelihood is that it will cost more to build a majority. . . .

> Paradoxically, it appears that Members could redistribute budgetary priorities more
> easily under a fragmented system. They could trim the defense appropriations bill and
> add to the Labor-HEW appropriations bill, without ever taking money explicitly from
> one department and giving it to another. The budget process of 1974, Schick explains,
> may have complicated the congressional process because it focuses attention on bud-
> get priorities, especially by moving money from one functional category to another.
> Yet Members are reluctant to vote on amendments that transfer funds between cate-
> gories. They prefer to do this implicitly and by indirection. The ironic result is that
> congress did more reordering of budgetary priorities "before it had a budget process
> than it has since."[3]

In this view, inserting centralized procedures into a decentralized institution had
diminished Congress's capacity to cope with conflict.

Another sign (and further cause) of polarization is what Robert Reischauer
has called "the fiscalization of the public policy debate." Few programs are considered solely on their substantive or political merits. Rather, it is asked, to what degree do programs contribute to the deficit? Do they fit within the latest
congressional budget resolution or the president's budget? How fast would defense or welfare grow? The substantive question, however—What is being bought
with the money?—increasingly is shunted aside.

Fiscalization of the policy debate is a crude but effective way of accounting
for wins, losses, and ties. To the extent that bigger is deemed better for some and
worse for others, more for welfare or less for defense, higher or lower tax rates,
these sum up the political struggle. Where observers once thought that confining
conflict to amounts would make it easier to reconcile differences as a matter of a
little more or a little less, fiscalization has come to have the opposite effect. By ag-

---

[2]John W. Ellwood, "The Great Exception: The Congressional Budget Process in an Age of Decentralization," in Lawrence Dodd and Bruce Oppenheimer, eds., *Congress Reconsidered,* 3rd ed. (Washington, D.C.: CQ Press, 1985).

[3]Louis Fisher, "The Congressional Budget Act: Does It Have a Spending Bias?" Paper delivered at
Conference on the Congressional Budget Process, Carl Albert Congressional Research and Studies
Center, University of Oklahoma, Norman, February 12–13, 1982, pp. 21–22.

gregating totals and converting them into signs of who is ahead or behind, budgeting becomes a conflict of principles that is difficult to resolve.

The End of Economic Management

One reason for emphasizing the aggregate amounts was that these are what matter for purposes of macro-economic management. Efforts at economic management by the federal government, however, largely disappeared in fact, though not in form. The villainous "stagflation," that hitherto unheard-of, simultaneous occurrence of inflation plus unemployment undermined congressional confidence in Keynesian methods of managing the economy. "Fine-tuning" was out. Instead of the widespread consensus based on positive postwar economic performance, doubt grew not only about whether deficits were desirable but also about whether there was any right way to proceed.

The broad agreement on economic management had not been total. Always there were market individualists—supporters of a smaller government that would intervene less in economic activity. What was new in the 1970s was that they had developed ideas—monetarism, supply-side economics—at variance with the by-then conventional Keynesian wisdom. For a time it was hard for individualists to argue with economic success. Stagflation brought them to the fore. At the same time, the Democratic party was demoralized as the Carter administration sought to fight inflation through recession. Consequently, when there was disagreement over the causal relationships, the general public and political elites were disposed to try something new.

The doctrinal basis had gone. Automatic stabilizers, such as Unemployment Compensation, still operated. But President Reagan's policy was simply to reduce income tax rates as low as possible. When the economy did well, rates would be cut because they could be; and when the economy did badly, rates would be cut as a necessary stimulus. Presumably, tax cuts were good for all seasons.

Despite hard times, however, Democrats would like to increase taxes in order to reduce the deficit and prevent the compounding of interest on the debt that will force out future spending. In good times, taxes should be increased because the extra can be used to fund more programs. With the major parties committed politically to tax decreases or increases irrespective of economic circumstances, there was not much room for adjustment. Ideology replaced economic "fine-tuning" with Johnny one-note. And the reconversion of Democrats to budget balance made it even more difficult for them to use the Keynesian approach to the size of deficits in order to manage the economy.

Dominance of the Deficit

When Congress was better at resolving differences, it was also true that those differences were narrower. Conflict resolution took place in a climate of informal understandings about the tolerable limits of taxation and the extent of permissible spending; budget balance, that is, provided strong guidelines. Once that agreement collapsed, Congress and the president were left with the shell—balance the budget—but not with agreement to do it through higher taxes or lower spending, nor whether domestic or defense programs should bear the brunt.

"In the current environment," Robert Reischauer comes closer to the problem, "the nation and its budget process may be capable of handling a fight over the relative distribution of spending benefits and tax burdens but they are not capable of taking on both fights at once."[4] The difficulty of reaching agreement is certainly multiplied by the intersection of these two global issues. But why are they considered part and parcel of the same conflict? Spending issues might be ameliorated, no doubt, if there were more ample revenues. And tax questions would be easier to answer if more revenue were not necessary. Yet how can revenue and expenditure ever be kept separate when each depends to vitally on the other? Only in America, as the saying goes, have the two sides of the budgetary coin historically been kept separate. The overriding reason revenue and expenditure did not meet up at the same time and the same place with the same set of officials is not that they could not have agreed but rather that they would have agreed only too well. Revenue was limited by common consent which, except in wartime, changed only gradually. Expenditure was expected to (and mostly did) fit within that revenue. No formal instructions were needed. Now we need such formal instructions because agreement is lacking—has not Congress voted any number of times to balance the budget? But rules in the midst of disagreement are very hard to enforce.

To the extent that taxing and spending are viewed as essentially the same, or as similar issues, disagreement is intensified. One set of issues then cannot be resolved while the other remains open. The more comprehensive the agreement required (not only because there are global resolutions but because the issues are linked in the minds and hearts of participants), the harder it is to achieve.

Conservative Republicans insist that the budget be moved toward balance by sharp reductions in domestic spending while defense is increased—and all without new taxes. Liberal Democrats agree on balance but only by cutting defense while maintaining domestic programs, preferably aided by new taxes on business or high-income individuals. Conservative Democrats and moderate Republicans together insist first and foremost on balance, the sooner the better, however it is arrived at; they contemplate defense and domestic cuts as well as tax increases. Everyone, it seems, is for balance but not on the same terms. No perspective commands a majority. What to do?

The prospects for agreement would be better if balance were regarded as a prudential virtue, to be achieved or approximated over time, with no strict timetable so long as it was increasing. Lower interest rates might reduce the cost of refinancing the debt, and sustained economic growth might bring in higher revenues. Combined with somewhat lower expectations (Would not a deficit of only $100 billion be supportable as the economy expands?), the deficit becomes manageable. Reasonable, yes; politic, no.

For the deficit has become both an obsession and a weapon. Controlling the deficit has become a "metaphor for governing."[5] On the political extremes, the deficit is a stick with which (take your pick) to beat liberals for excessive domestic

[4]Robert Reischauer, "Mickey Mouse or Superman? The Congressional Budget Process during the Reagan Administration." Paper presented to APPAM, October 20–22, 1983, Philadelphia, p. 3.

[5]Symposium on Budget Balance: Do Deficits Matter? New York City, January 9–11, 1986, p. 161.

spending or conservatives for excessive defense spending. Precisely because those at the extreme poles correctly suspect each other of insincerity and know each other to be vulnerable, both types speak as if possessed of the one true religion. How better to beat the other side than by spewing forth what former Supreme Court Justice Thomas Reed Powell called a "parade of horribles" about the catastrophic consequences of deficits? In this, extremists are gladly joined by the party of responsibility because this is the one belief (and weapon) that they genuinely share. So the fiscal responsibles trot out streams of the nation's economists who swear that (even without actual hard evidence) it is in the nature of things, or plain common sense, that awful events—depression, inflation, higher interest rates, the fall of civilization as we know it—are just over the horizon. This may or may not be true in the long run. Short-run cries of catastrophe, such as those contained in David Stockman's *The Triumph of Politics,* have not yet been borne out. But it is certain that any adverse economic circumstances will be blamed on deficits, so, whatever else happens, it is necessary to disassociate oneself from their contaminating influence. In sum, the deficit became a means of holding adversaries accountable for adversity without oneself being responsible, and polarized the parties.

Polarization of the Parties

A general rule is that to cross-cut cleavages is to reduce the intensity of conflict. Legislators who oppose each other on some issues know that they will need one another's support on a different type of issue. Therefore, they moderate their positions. Budgetary polarization may be explained (or, at least, described) by exactly the opposite phenomenon: self-reinforcing, hence ever-deepening, cleavages. The same people who oppose each other on one kind of issue now tend, more than before, to oppose each other on other issues as well.

Most of those who wish to maintain or add to welfare spending wish to decrease spending on defense—and vice versa. Nor is that all. The social issues—school prayer, abortion, women's rights, affirmative action, parental versus children's rights—tend to move in the same direction, with conservatives and liberals taking opposite positions. Of course, there are issues—the social safety net, equal pay for equal work—on which widespread agreement does exist. But those still leave plenty of room for these three major cleavages (welfare, defense, and social issues) to reinforce one another.

At least on domestic issues, Republicans vote for less and Democrats for more.[6] My guess is that the movement of Republicans to the south and of southern conservatives to the Republican party has made the major parties more internally cohesive. By the same token, however, this development has driven the parties further apart on the budget. While everyone will say, with self-satisfaction, that they favor a balanced budget, the parties differ dramatically on how this should be done. Balance at lower levels is quite different than balance of taxing and spending at high levels. The mix between defense and domestic, even the distribution between welfare and infrastructure are matters of controversy.

---

[6]James L. Payne, "Why They Spend," typescript, 1986.

Enter Ronald Reagan. Attention has been focused on his efforts to reduce domestic spending. He and his administration tried in their first term but they were only modestly successful. Had they cut more, however, nothing would have prevented Democrats from raising spending later. Too little attention has been devoted to the important ways in which Reagan made it harder to budget in the old ways. The Kemp–Roth income-tax cuts wiped out several years of resources otherwise available for incremental program increases and deficit reductions. Indexation of tax brackets took away revenue increases that would otherwise have come about without requiring legislative action. Increases in defense spending left less room for maintenance of domestic programs or deficit reduction. Taken together, these Reagan-inspired changes made hard choices by Congress more necessary but also more difficult. For such changes foreclosed the most important actions—quiet revenue and spending increases—that participants in budgeting might, in earlier times, have used to come to an accommodation.

The visible presence of Ronald Reagan brought to the surface a phenomenon that had been going on for at least two decades—an increasing polarization of elites. The conservative majority of the Republican party and the liberal majority of the Democratic party were further from each other in the 1980s than they had been in earlier decades. The main cleavage was over how far government should go in reducing social and economic inequalities. It was easy to draw such a conclusion in a time of diminishing fiscal resources, sizable defense increases, and cuts in many social programs.

Let us suppose that there was general agreement on budget balance. One way to proceed would be to raise revenues and/or reduce expenditures. But Democrats want to maintain or increase domestic spending while Republicans wish to cut taxes and increase defense spending. No room there. Another way would be to cut all spending (except interest on the debt) across the board, thus avoiding disputes over distributive issues. But if Democrats insist on not cutting welfare programs and Republicans refuse to touch defense, the scope for cuts would be small. When there are big things neither side will give up, the scope for compromise is much diminished.

Thus disagreement over the desired levels of spending and taxing became intertwined with differences over how benefits and burdens should be distributed. If decisions on taxing and spending could be disaggregated, it might be possible to find shifting majorities on this or that alternative. That is exactly how things were done from the mid-1970s through the early 1980s. But Congress increasingly denied itself that option. The result, consequently, of having to confront the issues—the size and composition of taxing and spending—all at once was the creeping stalemate that characterized budgeting in the 1980s and influenced the working of the Congressional Budget Act.

EVOLUTION OF THE CONGRESSIONAL BUDGET ACT

In form (and, occasionally, in fact) the budget process as reformed in 1974 does (or could) work. Congress could attack deficits and any other problem or priorities through its resolution and reconciliation procedures. Given a determined majority in favor of a particular policy, Congress has all the necessary tools to implement its desires. The trouble was the lack of majorities. Individual appropriations might pass with substantial majorities, but these majorities differed among the thirteen appropriations bills, and the budget reductions that were designed to tie them together had even less support. Indeed, the fact that budget resolutions require a majority of majorities—a majority comprehensive enough to integrate all other majorities—stultified the process.

The lack of support for a central comprehensive approach to budgeting did not come from lack of opportunity. Budget resolutions operating through budget committees gave Congress an opportunity to work out a central solution. Party leadership and party caucuses were now routinely involved in budget negotiation. So was the president. What was missing was an agreement at the center on a solution that would be validated by legislative majorities, or even on an agreed starting point. The procedures of the 1974 Act evolved to accommodate the pressures of the conflicts, without being able to resolve them.

R and R: Resolution and Reconciliation

It used to be said of Latin America that what was needed was a law stating that all the other laws be enforced. In this respect, budget resolutions may be said to represent the Latin Americanization of federal budgeting. For these resolutions do indeed resolve to enforce all the other actions that Congress claims it is undertaking to balance the budget or control spending or achieve some other worthy purpose.

The first victim of the pressures was the second resolution. The second resolution, as contemplated in the act of 1974, was the one that was supposed to be binding. The first resolution, to be passed in May, was to be tentative, setting the process in motion with a general sense of revenue and spending goals. The work of the tax and spending committees was to proceed until September when the Second Resolution would, if necessary, reconcile the whole to the parts. "The idea of waiting until September to make strategic budget decisions and still have time to translate them into detailed appropriations and tax laws before the first of October," Alice Rivlin insisted, "is patently absurd."[7] But why? Why couldn't Congress either ratify committee decisions or shape them at the margins during the month of September before the fiscal year begins on October 1st? Were there informal understandings about the size and shape of the budget, codified in the form of a First Resolution, committee recommendations would bear a family resemblance to that resolution. Only modest adjustments would then be required to arrive at the second and final resolution. In the early years after 1974, something like this did happen as the budget committees, by anticipation, made room for spending desires. Spending discipline was not evident but then neither had it been before.

Two things happened to make the second resolution unsatisfactory. One was that it exerted too little control, the other that it exerted too much. Control was insufficient in that even when economic conditions changed and ideas about public

---

[7]Alice M. Rivlin, "The Political Economy of Budget Choices: A View from Congress." Paper presented at AEA meeting, December 29, 1981.

policy moved toward lesser spending, such views were difficult to translate into practice. The concentration of benefits made potential losers far more aware and better organized than taxpayers whose costs were widely dispersed. Nor, since the First Resolution was not binding, was it possible to apportion sacrifices, for reductions on the First Resolution might well be made up on the Second. By giving in advance, congressional program advocates got nothing except to watch others spend what had once been their money. As everyone learned quickly to open with higher bids, without being able to accommodate the totals to which the bids added up, the new budget process proved flawed. From 1979 on, the second resolution required either big cuts (in the $30 billion range) if it were to live up to the first, or admitting large deficits. After neglect for years, the Second Resolution fell into disuse.

The solution in essence was to strengthen the First Resolution with the reconciliation procedure and other protection.

Reconciliation procedures did not feature prominently in the Budget Act of 1974. Originally, reconciliation was to be applied to spending bills after they had passed in order to bring them within the budget resolution's totals. While under fire in fiscal 1981 for tolerating a deficit during rampaging inflation, the budget committees rediscovered their "elastic clause," a hitherto obscure provision of the budget act permitting them to install "any other procedure which is considered appropriate." By then, the necessity of using third Resolutions to accommodate excesses in the second (necessary because of overages on the first) had persuaded budget committee members that they needed a device to make the first resolution stick. For this reason reconciliation was made part of the first resolution in the Carter administration.[8] A 1981 rule provided that if the second resolution had not been passed by October, the first resolution would become final, and the initiative of the Reagan administration made reconciliation the central machinery for unprecedented budget cuts, which included entitlements as well as budget authority and appropriations. The reconciliation acts, while less in amount, continued as an intrinsic part of the budget process and as a vehicle for critical legislation.

With their elastic clauses in hand, the budget committees, led by the Senate, expanded into trying multiyear controls. Spending targets, beginning in 1978, were to be made for five years at a time. Containing allotments for both revenue and spending, these budget resolutions propounded targets not only for the next fiscal year but for the two succeeding ones. The budget committees were willing, but it turned out that congressional flesh was weak. So new devices to assist self-control were added.

The enrollment of bills, that is, putting bills into official form so as to be in shape to send to the president for consideration, was subject to deferral if subcommittees' spending threatened to exceed their functional allocations. The original bulwark against exceeding budget limits—the point of order raised against legislation that went over the budget resolution—formerly had been available only after the Second (binding) Resolution, including its ceiling on outlays and total

---

[8]Jean Peters, "Reconciliation 1982: What Happened?" *PS*, Vol. 14, No. 4 (Fall 1981), pp. 732–36. See also Allen Schick, *Reconciliation and the Congressional Budget Process* (Washington D.C.: American Enterprise Institute, 1981).

budget authority as well as its floor on revenues, had been passed. And there was no way of compelling committees or subcommittees to keep to those mandated limits. Scorekeeping and early-warning reports only emphasized the helplessness of budget committees. So they invented deferred enrollment. No legislation that reduced revenues by more than $100 million or exceeded the functional Section 302 totals specified in the resolutions could be "enrolled."

The threat of deferral proved stronger than its use. A minor reason is that some committees, knowing they are over their allotments, would choose to wait until the start of the next fiscal year on October 1st when deferral lapses. This sort of hide-and-seek suggests the major reason: Congress has been deferring many bills until after the fiscal year.

Deferral and Rescission Redux

Even as Congress modified its procedures for reconciliation and resolutions in an effort to impose centralization on its decentralized processes, the deep dissensus between president and Congress led the president to impose his will unilaterally. The struggle over the impoundment of funds reveals presidential efforts to gain by executive action what Congress will not give through its budgetary process.

Presidents can try to act on their own. They can try to forbid agencies from making requests for programs presidents want eliminated or reduced. They can reorganize units and categories so as to make it more difficult for affected interests to figure out where their money is and, therefore, how much they are being cut.[9] Presidents can impose hiring freezes and otherwise try to reduce what they consider unnecessary personnel. Their most direct approach, however, is to refuse to spend funds Congress has appropriated.

In the past, impounding was based on tacit consent; either the president's staff persuaded the committees involved, or committees indicated they would not mind too much if the money were not spent. When the Reagan administration found itself unable to persuade Congress, and as it failed to get approval for an item veto, it tried to achieve similar results by a delay or a refusal to spend. Then the courts entered the fray by calling the impounding procedure into question.

Under the act of 1974, designed to limit the president's powers, presidents can stop spending, provided that within 45 days *both* houses of Congress give their consent to this rescission. Alternatively, president can delay spending to the end of the fiscal year, unless the Senate *or* the House voted to override the deferral. In 1983, however (*Immigration and Naturalization Service v. Chadha*), the Supreme Court declared a legislative veto by one house an unconstitutional violation of the separation of powers thus negating the provision. In response, Congress disallowed presidential deferrals for policy reasons. They could only be employed to provide for contingencies or to achieve efficiency or other savings through changes in requirements.[10] The president could use impounding as a de

---

[9]See Irene Rubin, *Shrinking the Federal Government: The Effect of Cutbacks on Five Federal Agencies* (New York: Longman, 1985), inter alia.

[10]Allen Schick, *The Federal Budget: Politics, Policy, Process* (Washington D.C.: Brookings Institution, 1995), p. 173.

facto item veto. He could wait, thus delaying spending; he could postpone until the end of the fiscal year when it might be too late for Congress to act; he could attempt to straddle the fiscal years, combining a future cut with a past deferral. "What's at stake," Democratic Representative Bruce A. Morrison explained in regard to the struggle over appropriations with a deferral, "is how many bites of the apple the President gets in the appropriations process."[11] The other view, expressed by Budget Director Miller, in testifying before Congress, was that "You took a risk in utilizing the one-house veto. Well, you rolled the dice and the President won."[12] However, as life would have it, other courts temporarily took the president's deferral power away.

Miller's talk was hardly the stuff to smooth already ruffled feathers in an era of budgetary dissensus. Miller cast away an agreement reached between former OMB Director David Stockman and the Appropriations Committee chairmen that OMB would not consider amendments disapproving individual deferrals to appropriations bills as grounds for a presidential veto. When Reagan used deferrals in several programs that Congress had explicitly told him to continue, Congress responded with outrage. Although the administration suggested that the deferrals were no different than deferrals in prior years, Congress felt Reagan was attempting "to an unprecedented extent . . . to implement his controversial policy goals" through this method.[13]

Efforts to distinguish between deferring spending for management efficiency and for policy impoundments foundered in a spate of accusations. Unless there is agreement on the frame of reference, technical (or management) deferrals cannot be distinguished from changes in policy. The only real distinction is between programs you approve of and the ones you don't.

There's the rub: Agreement on the broad outlines of the budget—how much, what for—facilitates compromise on the details. Knowing they are headed in the same direction, participants can talk about better ways to get there. Divided as they stand, however, disagreement over policy turns in on itself in two directions: Technical management questions become policy disputes, and policy differences become converted into disputes about who has the authority to decide. While it is true that there can be no fast line between means and ends, techniques and objectives, converting every question of fact into one of value expands the scope and intensity of conflict. The same is true of the old policy-administration dichotomy. It is quite wrong to imagine that Congress makes only broad policy choices while the executive branch merely implemented the legislative will. If there is no difference between policy and administration at all, however—that an administrative regulation is equivalent to a congressional statute—relationships between the branches of government would become chaotic. And that, just that, as the controversy over impoundment reveals, was beginning to happen to budgeting.

---

[11]Jonathan Rauch, "Power of the Purse," *National Journal,* May 24, 1986, p. 1261.

[12]Ibid., p. 1259.

[13]*National Journal,* May 24, 1986, p. 1060.

The Shifting Budgetary Base

There was dissensus at every stage of the budgetary process, disagreement over policy compounded by differences over process. Deals on appropriations totals had to stretch across a variety of bills and stages of the process. Each stage's agreement required trust that all parties would perform as promised at the next stage. Of course if everybody really were reliable, they would have delivered on the spot. In fact, agreements on defense between the administration and parts of Congress kept unraveling, while at the same time antagonists ceaselessly looked for ways to make up lost ground on domestic spending. Every agreement between the Republican administration and the Democratic House eventually collapsed under charges that the legislators had not provided sufficient cuts in social programs or that the executive branch had spent too much on defense or that both had distorted the budgetary base.

In days of old, budgeting had far fewer participants. Though the rule was sometimes honored in the breach, the president's budget was the acknowledged starting point for congressional considerations. Most disputes about initial requests were resolved within the executive branch—albeit in anticipation of congressional action. Now differences that would have been resolved within the executive spilled over into Congress. Why?

It is easy to forget the obvious. The power of the purse belongs to Congress. Presidents have previously acknowledged that fact by the ancient rule of anticipated reactions; the presidential role was to both acknowledge and alter incrementally the prior year's congressional action. By this act of acquiescence, presidents provided a convenient starting point, not far from last year's congressional action, so as to maintain continuity in budgeting. When in President Reagan's time, however, the president's desires were far from congressional majorities on taxes, defense, and welfare, his budgets were routinely pronounced "dead on arrival." The president's base had become his own preferences.

On the congressional side also, the base, and the agreements which underlay it, were undermined. Reconciliation had introduced an important new dimension. It was now attached to the First Resolution, and required separate negotiation of its own majority. Budget negotiations moved from the budget committees to extra-committee groups. "Members do not defer to the decisions of autonomous, well-integrated committees, as they would in a committee-centered budget system," John Ellwood informs us. "Instead, the policy decisions conveyed by budget resolutions are the result of direct negotiations among large numbers of members that produce a majority coalition in favor of a single budget policy."[14] Reconciliation had been transformed, Allen Schick informs us, "from a means of reviewing decisions made during the current year into a process of revising legislation (mostly entitlements and revenue laws) enacted in previous years."[15] Reconcilia-

---

[14]John W. Ellwood, "Providing Policy Analysis to U.S. Congress: The Case of the Congressional Budget Office." Paper prepared for 1984 Annual Meeting of the Association for Public Policy Analysis and Management, New Orleans, October 18–22, 1984.

[15]Allen Schick, "The Evolution of Congressional Budgeting," in Allen Schick, ed., *Crisis in the Budget Process* (Washington, D.C.: American Enterprise Institute, 1986), p. 13.

tion, therefore, especially reconciliation of budget authority, represents a permanent institutional attack on the budgetary base.

The budget both reflects and justifies the existing political order. Its boundaries guard that order. This is the social significance of the budgetary base, the bulk of which is protected from serious scrutiny, so it will remain unchallenged.[16] Inside the base, except for small additions or subtractions, all is protected; outside that base, everything is up for grabs. On the stability of the budgetary base, therefore, rests the stability of ongoing government programs. An across-the-board attack on the budgetary base is equivalent to a radical restructuring of spending priorities. Governments, therefore, seek to invest major items of expenditures with some sort of sanctity; "entitlement" is but a stronger method of guarding one's borders. Breaching the base is equivalent to opening up to renegotiation the boundaries of past political contracts. The fundamental priorities of the regime—who will receive how much for which purposes—are in danger of being turned upside down.

Way back then, the budgetary base—the residue of past agreements not normally opened up for reconsideration—was approximated by the amounts in the prior year's budget. Recommending small changes, depending on presidential desires for economic management as well as preferences on a few programs, the president's proposed budget was an acceptable further approximation of the base. Not now. Kamlet and Mowery pronounce the last rites:

> . . . agreement within Congress on the definition of the budgetary base no longer exists. Both the House and Senate Budget Committees frequently have employed a definition of the budgetary base that differs from the one utilized in the Appropriations Committees. This practice has created severe problems in the compatibility of budget resolutions and appropriations actions. Moreover, the House and Senate Budget Committees themselves frequently use different definitions of the budgetary base, with disastrous consequences for the conference committees charged with the development of a joint budget resolution.[17]

Whether or not the president's budget is pronounced unsuitable, unworthy of further use, a mere historical curiosity, or even if it is closer to certain congressional desires, it no longer served as the base. Instead, Congress, through its budget committees, used either the CBO's current-services budget or the House or Senate budget resolutions, or some combination thereof, depending on the programs in question.

Since playing the budgetary game in Congress now requires a respectable deficit-reduction number—deficit cuts, not the total deficit, are the focus of attention—obfuscation of the base might be a deliberate move to overestimate how much will be cut. Manipulating baselines enables legislators to meet the twin imperatives of helping clients by saving programs and helping the economy by cutting deficits. "The baselines have an important political advantage," Schick tells

---

[16]See Aaron Wildavsky, *The Politics of the Budgetary Process*, 4th ed. (Boston: Little, Brown, 1984), pp. 16–18, 102–108, 231–33, for discussion of the budgetary base.

[17]Mark S. Kamlet and David C. Mowery, "The First Decade of the Congressional Budget Act: Legislative Imitation and Adaptation in Budgeting," *Policy Sciences*, Vol. 18, No. 4 (December 1985), p. 320.

us. "They depict rising expenditures as budget cutbacks. Between fiscal 1981 (when reconciliation was first applied) and fiscal 1986, medicare has climbed from $39 billion to an estimated $67 billion. Yet Congress has taken credit for almost $25 billion in medicare cutbacks during these years."[18] Like the youngster in my childhood experience who would save the candy store from being robbed by deciding not to do it, "savings" are not calculated as reductions from last year's outlay but from a hypothetical baseline—an estimation of what future spending would have been without the action in question. Baselines, therefore, are man-made, depending on predictions of price changes and participation rates. Suppose a $100 billion increase is projected; would a mere $80 billion increase lead to a $20 billion "saving"? Like the man who "saves" $50 by buying the $100 hat (that he didn't have to have) at a half-off sale?

The disappearance of an agreed base is both a symptom and a cause of disagreement over the amount and distribution of expenditures and revenues. It is a symptom because disagreement must be running deep if participants cannot agree where to begin, no less than where to end. It is a cause of further disagreement because policy differences are exacerbated by quarreling over the proper place to start.

The Fazio Rule

Another problem blurs the operation of the Congressional Budget Act in enforcing resolutions and clarifying budget figures. The budget committees report out and their members vote on budget resolutions containing two numbers, a total for budget authority and a total for outlays. Moving between the two numbers creates possibilities for strategic interplay. The budget committees generally wish to come out with the highest possible deficit reduction number. Therefore they tend to estimate less in outlays than is likely to be obtained from a given amount of authority. This conversion factor going from authority to outlays creates difficulties for the appropriations committees. Before I can show why this difficulty occurs, and how the two chambers differ in handling it, we must consider how the appropriations committees divide the totals given to them in budget resolutions among their subcommittees.

In the Senate, totals for outlays and authority are handed down to the Senate Appropriations Committee under Section 302(a) of the Budget Act of 1974. In the House, by contrast, a further distinction is made between mandatory and discretionary accounts. The definitions are to some extent arbitrary, but in the main they distinguish between entitlements, like provision for civil service retirement, that go up or down by a preset formula, and annual appropriations.

The question arose as to what should happen if entitlement spending within a subcommittee's jurisdiction went up. Should the total ceiling be enforced, thus cutting discretionary spending, or should the mandatory increase be accommodated? The Senate follows the low-spending rule: Spending control is subject to a point of order to enforce the 302(b) provisions of the 1974 budget act, which are

---

[18]Allen Schick, "Controlling the 'Uncontrollables': Budgeting for Health Care in an Age of Mega-Deficits." Paper prepared for AEI Pew Fellows Conference, November 1985, pp. 25–26.

enforceable at the subcommittee level for budget authority, credit authority, entitlement authority, and outlays. Each subcommittee can be kept within its own allocation of outlays or authority by a point of order. This is a vital difference.

But in the House, the Fazio rule means that subcommittees cannot be subject to points of order if their discretionary proposals are within the total spending allowed under the 302(b) allocations for discretionary budget authority. Therefore, if an appropriations subcommittee spends beyond the amount allocated to it by the House budget resolution, there is no procedure for stopping it until total approved spending goes beyond the ceiling specified. The Fazio rule enables the House Appropriations Committee and its subcommittees to ignore the effects of misestimation of mandatory spending on overall allocations. The bill is still in compliance with House rules if discretionary spending is within the limits set out in the House budget resolution.[19]

Continuing Omnibus Resolutions

Continuing Resolutions, which provide interim funding, are old hat. Where in the past they were exceptional, during the 1980s they became routine. What is more, CRs have become longer; between 1975 and 1984 they grew from five pages to an average of 100 pages. Length grows with function. Where before CRs were applied only to a few programs or agencies, now they may cover most of them. Where before simple language would do—merely stating the agency would be funded at the lowest level passed by House or Senate, or a committee thereof—now entire appropriations bills were included.

"[T]he growth of continuing resolutions," Robert Keith and Edward Davis correctly conclude, "appears to be directly related to the growing inability to enact some regular appropriations bills on time or at all."[20] True, but not true enough. If time were the major difficulty, pushing back the fiscal year, together with abandoning the second resolution, should have alleviated it. If time mattered most, CRs would be shorter, not longer. On the contrary, the complexity of CRs is a strong indicator of dissensus; CRs carry on the struggle over spending in another guise. The overwhelming detail can only be meant to commit the parties to specified spending. Thus we learn that by incorporation CRs now commonly include references to authorizing legislation whose sponsors were otherwise unable to have them passed on their own merits. The more continuous Continuing Resolutions become, the more they testify to a breakdown of what had been ordinary modes of accommodation.

The culmination of the Continuing Resolution occurred in 1986. Instead of using a CR for only a few appropriations bills, the CR packaged all 13 bills in an Omnibus Appropriations Act. No, Congress wasn't kidding; the act included all regular appropriations bills and a lot more (from Pentagon procurement rules to transferring Washington's airports to local control). To vote "no" or to veto meant

---

[19]See Allen Schick, *The Federal Budget*, p. 88.

[20]Robert Keith and Edward Davis, "Congress and Continuing Appropriations: New Variations on an Old Theme," *Public Budgeting and Finance*, Vol. 5, No. 1 (Spring 1985).

closing down government. To vote "yes" meant voting in ignorance. "Either vote is irresponsible," Representative Henry Hyde (R-Ill.) expostulated.

When conflicts are of long standing, the CR is the ultimate weapon. It is now possible for the entire texts of appropriations bills that would otherwise face special difficulties on the floor to be folded into an omnibus CR. In this way foreign aid has been partially protected from members of Congress who want to shift funds to domestic spending.

Although a CR gives committee chairs power over subcommittees, because the chair is in charge, it is hard to see why so few members protest unless they are seeking leverage against the president. Continuing Resolutions do vitiate the veto power. While the president, through OMB, has ample opportunity to express his preferences, it is not easy for him, in effect, to veto the government. For instance, President Reagan vetoed a bill for several executive agencies in 1985 because it contained $900 million more spending than he wanted, but he signed a CR for only $115 million less.

Representative Neal Smith (D-Iowa) summed up the main advantage: "It [the CR] permits both sides to be forced to compromise."[21] But at the beginning of the 1990s, Congress was passing appropriations bills on time, and it seemed that omnibus continuing resolutions were becoming a thing of the past, until the great budget conflict of 1995. Meanwhile, the executive branch was also feeling the effects of change.

OMB IN AN ERA OF PERENNIAL BUDGETING

As governing and budgeting became equivalent in the late 1970s and the 1980s, the part played by the Office of Management and Budget (OMB) was bound to be more important than it had been. No matter who was (or is) the director of the budget, the rise of budget resolutions, continuous resolutions, reconciliation, the deficit, the strategic centrality of negotiations over the size and composition of taxing and spending, the ensuing stalemate (and hence the extraordinary degree to which budgeting crowds out other issues)—any, or all, of these would have made OMB more pivotal. David Stockman, a man of exceptional force and talent, and President Reagan's Director of the Budget from 1981 to 1985, speeded up the transformation of OMB from an agency-centered to a congressionally centered presidential adviser-cum-negotiator. Stockman also gave this change an enhanced centralized slant. But under circumstances in which the budget dominated policy making, no one could have prevented OMB from being a key player.

Since its establishment in 1921, when it was cutting small sums, to its revitalization in the late 1930s—and again after the Second World War as presidential staff agency with a cutting bias—OMB (then the Bureau of the Budget) has counted itself (and has been considered by others) to be powerful. Without money of its own, without authority except what the president lends it, and without a large staff (around 200 examiners being the norm), OMB has long been an

---

[21]Stephen Gettinger, "Congress Returns to Tackle Biggest-Ever 'CR'," *Congressional Quarterly,* September 6, 1986, pp. 2059–63.

elite unit. It is one of the best places to be. Service there counts high for promotion elsewhere. The sense of service to the president, upon whose backing all depends, coupled with a belief that this central staff has a national (rather than parochial) viewpoint, has long created a strong esprit de corps.

Up to the 1980s, OMB worked both from below and above. The usual practice was for OMB to conduct a Spring Preview in which likely spending demands (estimated by OMB staff) were compared to expected revenues; then both were manipulated to achieve desired effects on the economy. Agency spending bids, therefore, were made in a controlled context. Because agencies were told how high they could go, they could accurately translate administration intentions into a loose (ask for more) or tight (keep what you've got) budget request. Agencies could appeal to the president or make an end-run to Congress. But such attempts had to be limited not only because they might fail but also because, given limited time and attention, extra political efforts were better reserved for the most important issues. On run-of-the-mill stuff, the guts of agency activities, OMB recommendations were likely to be final.

There was now a pronounced difference. During the 1980s, in Allen Schick's words, the formal Spring Preview "withered away, possibly because of OMB and White House preoccupation with congressional budget activity and possibly because they did not want to risk premature leaks of budget cuts."[22] Working largely top down was not the same as working largely bottom up. Once budget examiners used to examine; they went into detail on programs, made final visits, and otherwise kept track of agency programs. Some still did; many did not. Now most examiners dealt with aggregates, with total agency spending. Within that total, agencies were freer to spend as they wished (subject, of course, to congressional constraints and clientele demands). The price of this enhanced discretion was increased uncertainty. There might be not only less money but its flow also might be interrupted by delay, deferrals, rescissions, the latest continuous round of negotiations, stalemate followed by continuing resolutions, on and on. Budgetary planning is not easy. The decline of the annual budget, early decisions good for a year, is but the other side of the coin of continuous budgeting.

Differences in quantity, if they are large enough, may become differences in quality. BOB–OMB always had relations with Congress. There were always appropriations committees. Since these committees were even more important then than they are today (taking up a larger share of the budget), the director and his chief aides, including top civil servants specializing in public works and other matters of interest to these legislators, had frequent contact with appropriations committees. Failure to pass appropriations on time or the need for supplementals or raising the debt ceiling required OMB to arrange a policy position for the Executive Branch. The difference now lay in the increased frequency of contacts, the institutional arrangements facilitating them, and the character of the interactions.

Totals dominated all discussion. How much, not what for, was the first question. Escaping from macro-choices over total taxing and spending, moreover, was hardly possible when the Budget Act of 1974 required an annual resolution to do

---

[22]Allen Schick, *The Federal Budget Process,* p. 54.

just that, a requirement reinforced by the establishment of congressional budget committees whose main assignment this was.

"The creation of the budget committees," Bruce Johnson writes, "gave the OMB its own committees to work through. OMB became a client of the budget committees—perhaps their chief client—like the Veterans Administration is a client of the Veterans committees. A similarity of purpose grew, and staff-to-staff contacts developed. The budget committees became a window through which the OMB could view and influence Congress."[23] The assumed role of the Senate Budget Committee as spokesman for responsible finance—that is, deficit reduction through increased control over budget authority—made it a natural ally of OMB. OMB also became a window through which SBC could obtain information about executive office discussion, and thus leverage in trying to influence executive policies. When the Executive Office of the President reached out to external constituencies, by the same token, SBC reached in. For what was going on in Congress then became a part of White House deliberation.

Partisanship and ideology also influence executive-legislative relationships. The informal cooperation between SBC and OMB depended in part on the fact that from 1981 to 1986 the Senate was Republican while the House was Democratic. As policy differences between moderate Senate Republicans and the more conservative Reagan administration deepened, moreover, it became more difficult for OMB and SBC to maintain informal cooperation. OMB and SBC became antagonists, but the early reasons for their cooperation remained.

The existence of the Congressional Budget Office (CBO) was the scene for another mixed-motive game. Unlike the old days, OMB no longer had carte blanche in manipulating agency estimates. Should events prove CBO's spending estimates more accurate in too many instances, OMB's reputation would suffer. Over time, therefore, the staffs of the two agencies came closer together. This regard was furthered by the substantial presence in both organizations of economists (the four heads of CBO have been economists) with similar perspectives about how to value governmental programs. This does not mean that the two organizations harmoniously coexisted. Much of President Reagan's first term was marked by strenuous disagreement between the OMB and CBO over economic assumptions and deficit projections.

Changes in attention (the financial markets, other governments, and congressional budget committees observe total spending) and in process (continuous budgeting) have made the central budget agency more important. Bruce Johnson had it just right:

> To respond immediately to changing financial market reactions to the Federal budget, the Executive branch has to be able to change the budget quickly. Only the OMB can

---

[23]Bruce Johnson, "The Increasing Role of the Office of Management and Budget in the Congressional Budget Process." Paper prepared for the Fifth Annual Research Conference of Association for Public Policy Analysis and Management, Philadelphia, October 21–22, 1983, p. 6. See also Bruce Johnson, "OMB and the Budget Examiner: Changes in the Reagan Era," *Public Budgeting and Finance,* Vol. 8 (Winter 1988), pp. 3–21; and Bruce Johnson, "The OMB Budget Examiner and the Congressional Budget Process, *Public Budgeting and Finance,* Vol. 9 (Spring 1989), pp. 5–14.

perform this function for the Executive branch. The fine-tuning of fiscal policy is now occurring every 3 to 6 months when it used to be an annual affair.

Not only is the Executive branch, under the guidance of the OMB, formally changing its budget requests to Congress more frequently, but implicit Administration budget policy is changing almost every month as a result of compromises struck with Congress. . . . Each time a new "bipartisan compromise" is announced by the President, the Administration's internal budget estimates change (although for public consumption they may just receive an asterisk to show they are out of date). Various deals are also struck with Congress as the appropriations bills wind their way through committee floor and conference action. OMB is the only Executive branch agency able to sum the totals of all the give and take of the Congressional process to see where the budget estimates are going. The importance of budget "scorekeeping"—keeping track of all these deals—has been increased by the emphasis on budget projections and their importance to the financial community. For this reason alone, the OMB has assumed a leading role in negotiating budget and fiscal policy adjustments with Congress.[24]

Had total spending not become all-important, neither would OMB. It was the concentration on totals, combined with the requirement for annual budget resolutions, together with the possibility of invoking reconciliation, and later the necessity of avoiding or following Gramm–Rudman–Hollings sequestration procedure, that made the central budget agency so central. When one budgets all the time, budgeters may indeed get more tired, but also they become more important.

Though any specific starting point must be arbitrary, the entry of OMB into congressional negotiations may be traced to the time of James T. McIntyre, Jr., President Carter's budget director, who gradually recognized the need for stronger contact with Congress. He increased his liaison staff from two to six.[25] When Carter submitted his last fall budget, the fact that it had a (what, in retrospect, looks like a tiny) $16 billion deficit so discomfited the financial markets and congressional leaders, already down on the president, that it was withdrawn. After a week of negotiation with Democratic party leaders, McIntyre helped resubmit a new budget. In order to implement the deficit-reduction package (the first of many to follow), McIntyre made novel use of then-dormant reconciliation procedure. Given the short time available, McIntyre, instead of going through the authorizations, appropriations, and finance committees, dealt only with top party and committee leaders.

As Carter began to squeeze the budget in FY80, OMB took a more active role in lobbying Congress for the president's preferences. The budget negotiations of March 1980 and subsequent continuing resolution difficulties increased the relative influence of OMB. David Mathiasen, deputy assistant director for budget review at OMB, has noted that more important than the package of cuts in 1980 was "the way in which this revision took place. Traditionally the American budget has been developed by the executive and presented to the Congress and the public without formal discussions or negotiations. . . . In contrast, the 1981 budget revi-

---

[24]Ibid. pp. 7–8.

[25]Jonathan Rauch, "Stockman's Quiet Revolution at OMB May Leave Indelible Mark on Agency," *National Journal*, Vol. 7, No. 21 (May 25, 1985), p. 1213.

sions were literally negotiated between executive branch representatives (primarily the Office of Management and Budget and the White House) and the leadership in both houses of the Congress."[26]

The 1980 (fiscal 1981) budget battles therefore foreshadowed a situation in which detailed examination of agency performance and estimates by appropriations committee members would have less influence on spending decisions. When "how much" matters more than "what for," agencies and appropriations subcommittees matter less than the actors (presidents and congressional leaders) who negotiate about totals. When these legislative leaders vary from time to time, however, according to who can craft the necessary compromise, the process becomes less predictable. The combination of more intractable problems with more numerous and diverse participants spells trouble.

Stockman institutionalized the ad hoc developments of 1980 and took them a giant step further. He sent a list of proposals for cuts, with accompanying explanations, to Capitol Hill, following them up with personal visits to assess reaction. Earlier, under the Ford administration in the mid-1970s, Director James Lynn had used similar advocacy papers, and Carter's director, McIntyre, had sometimes utilized the requirement under the Budget Impoundment and Control Act for narrative statements explaining how actions met "national needs" to sell the budget. Stockman provided the all-time hard sell. He was able to gauge support from reactions to his proposals, all the while making program supporters feel lucky to get by with cuts that, though modest by Stockman's standards, were considerably larger than agencies otherwise would have contemplated.[27]

Stockman changed OMB's focus from the examining and assembling of agency requests to that of lobbying the administration budget through Congress. Budget examiners spent far less time in the field getting to know their agencies. Instead, staff was dedicated to tracking budget action through the multiple stages of the congressional process—resolutions were tracked from budget committees to the floor and into conference, out again into appropriations subcommittee and full committee markups, to reappearance on the floor in a continuing resolution, then again in a regular appropriations bill, seemingly settled only to pop up again in markup on a supplemental. To facilitate this tracking, Stockman ordered the development of a computer system that aggregated budget items by both budget function categories and committee jurisdictions, allowing him to trace the spending implications of action at all levels. He also increased the size of the OMB unit that was tracking spending legislation through Congress. Stockman could afford to take this course because there was nothing that he really needed to know about the agencies. For at least a few years he could get by on previous analysis by OMB, the extensive literature produced by GAO, CBO, and the think tanks, and his own preferences about what government should and should not do. Ideology provided a substitute for information. The new OMB approach, Hale Champion

---

[26]"Recent Developments in the Composition and Formulation of the United States Federal Budget," *Public Budgeting and Finance* (Autumn 1983), p. 107.

[27]Bruce Johnson, "From Analyst to Negotiator: The OMB's New Role," *Journal of Policy Analysis and Management*, Vol. 3, No. 4 (1984), p. 507.

commented, therefore "almost excluded cabinet departments and agencies from the formulation of the budget."[28]

Since Stockman (and the president) were interested in achieving a preferred set of cuts, not in using the budget to finance agencies, OMB also moved away from the norm of annual budgeting. The annual budget served many needs, but its primary purpose was to regularize the funding, and therefore functioning, of government agencies. Funded for a year in advance, an agency would be able to plan and coordinate its activities. Since in many cases the administration either did not care about these agency functions or was convinced it knew a better (and, not coincidentally, cheaper) way to do the job, in 1981 and 1982 Stockman discarded the norm of annual budgeting, proposing instead large rescissions—administratively imposed cuts of previously approved appropriations. Basically the budget was under continuous negotiation so that even a place in the formal budget did not guarantee funding at the once-agreed level. Federal agencies, therefore, were whipsawed back and forth, torn between hope and fear that their allocations would be changed during the year. Predictability of spending flows, and whatever short-term planning went with it, were lost.

OMB also gave up its role as protector of agencies against sudden and unreasonable reductions. The place of agencies in the new appropriations process was both precarious and peculiar. Both their budget authority and staffing levels (also partially controlled through that process) were unpredictable. Many agencies were running reduction-in-force (RIF) operations, which were designed to reduce employment while maintaining civil service preferences and protection against political bias. RIFs and a twist called RIF exercises—in which procedures were war-gamed in a drill to determine who would land where in the game of civil-service musical chairs—were spreading fear and chaos in agencies far out of proportion to actual layoffs.

After the congressional elections of 1982 increased Democratic majorities in the House and discomfited the Republican majority in the Senate, reconciliation no longer seemed a viable option to the administration. Nor—considering the liberal Democratic majority in the House and the moderate Republican party Senate majority, which wanted higher taxes and lower defense spending—was Reagan likely to get acceptable budget resolutions. Therefore, Bruce Johnson explains,

> in the absence of a budget resolution acceptable to the president, the director of the OMB attempted to impose presidential budget targets on the various appropriation bills. Because of the implicit and sometimes explicit threat of a presidential veto, the OMB was successful in exerting such influence in an area of decision normally reserved for an agency and its appropriation subcommittees. Thus, although the process of budget resolution and reconciliation was near collapse in 1983, the OMB continued to be active in the appropriation process, attempting to sell pieces of the president's budget to Congress in that forum.[29]

---

[28]*Federal Budget Policy in the 1980s* (Washington D.C.: Urban Institute Press, 1984), p. 292. Also see Hugh Heclo, "Executive Budget Making," in Gregory B. Mills and John L. Palmer, eds., *Federal Budget Policy in the 1980s* (Washington, D.C.: Urban Institute Press, 1984).

[29]Johnson, "From Analyst to Negotiator," p. 504.

One might well say that OMB became the president's lobbyist in Congress.

Within OMB, the realization was growing that the budgetary game had undergone decisive changes. Resolutions did not carry enforcement powers; they could not be counted on to pass; if they did, they often were not enforced. Failing to agree meant only that the real play was in a continuing resolution. Besides, appropriations committees could work without a resolution. Authorizations matter for entitlements but big ones were unbudgeable and little ones didn't move much. Not much point in talking to authorizers when there are no new programs.

Discovering by 1984 that it could not get authorizations down far enough to bite, OMB concentrated almost entirely on discretionary appropriations and, within that, on the 302(b) allocations under which appropriations committees divided the amount they received from budget committees. Like the old joke about the man who looks for his collar button under the street lamp rather than where he lost it—because the light is better there—OMB concentrated on the pieces of budget it could do something about. This focus on appropriations accounted for the bulk of time Director Stockman spent negotiating with committee members as well as tracking bills. Before deals could be struck on appropriations, it was necessary to estimate how much they were worth and where the bill was located in the process.

OMB expanded its handful of bill trackers to thirteen, one for each of the major committees. Trackers infiltrated hearings, got data whenever they could, and immediately prepared letters to all concerned on Capitol Hill about whether they thought savings were real or illusory. Keeping score is serious business, but why was it necessary?[30]

The appropriations committee can transfer funds from an entitlement to a discretionary account. This maneuver has the effect of increasing discretionary spending while often creating a shortfall in the entitlement, a shortfall that has to be made good in the future. Two examples are transfers of $39 million to the Agriculture Extension Service from food stamps and $66 million from the CCC (Commodity Credit Corporation) reimbursement for prior year losses to the Conservation Service. OMB's bill trackers would not treat such transfers as savings, but the appropriations committees may use them to fit within the budget resolution.[31]

OMB wanted to show the amounts authorized in a fiscal year even if they were not spent in that year. Advance appropriations, to be spent in future years (no further action required) and appropriations deferred because they lack authorization (although funds are likely to be provided in a supplemental or continuing resolution) were not scored in that year by Appropriations but they were scored by OMB. Reasonable people might disagree. Similarly, where supplements were routinely provided, as for fire fighting, or discretionary activities were purposely underfunded in OMB's opinion, it would score the funds as if they had been fully appropriated. There were also occasional adjustments, such as provisions for sav-

[30]For more on scorekeeping see Roy Meyers, *Strategic Budgeting* (Ann Arbor: University of Michigan Press, 1994), pp. 123–24.

[31]OMB, "OMB's Scoring of Appropriations Bills," March 4, 1986.

ings—pay reductions or delayed repayments of loans—that never materialized, which OMB scored as spending.

Among the most important and most controversial scoring choices was the distinction OMB made (and would like appropriations committees to make) between discretionary and entitlement programs. A cut in appropriations for a discretionary program was indeed a cut. But an apparent reduction in spending for an entitlement "not accompanied," in OMB's words, "by language in appropriations bills to reduce the statutory spending requirements are not scored by OMB as reductions."

This emphasis on scoring, reinforced by a cadre of OMB bill trackers, testified to the importance of the deficit, hence the significance of progress toward reduction and the temptation to appear to be saving more or less depending on the political needs of the moment. For their part, appropriations people figured OMB was cheating when it told them to cut entitlements that were outside their jurisdiction.

As OMB improved its congressional intelligence, thus being able to intervene in the right subcommittees at the right time, it sought further to streamline its task by combining consideration of appropriations hitherto dealt with separately. The development of continuing resolutions, from stopgap funding to program changes with future spending implications, provided OMB with another point of entry.[32] OMB was monitoring spending not only in agencies but also in Congress. Would the role of salesman to Congress of spending cuts, the OMB staff wondered, interfere with its tradition of neutral competence and general repository of wisdom about the value of programs?

The director's use of budget examiners as personal staff or, better still, as research assistants, became well known. According to a civil servant, "It's not uncommon to be called over there—boom, boom—and have him say, 'OK, I've prepared this presentation, I want you to check it and fill in the numbers.' And he'll say, bring it back tomorrow."[33] Not everyone cared for this kind of spot-research role. Observers worried that OMB's stature as an institution to serve presidents and the Executive branch over the long term might decline while its political clout temporarily increases. Hugh Heclo, for instance, was troubled "that the capacity for loyal independence . . . may have diminished over time."[34] Heclo quoted an OMB division director: "He [Stockman] bangs on you for information on the day that he needs it. He doesn't think about how to strengthen the agency's general ability to provide what is wanted. He gets what he wants when he wants it and wherever he can. He doesn't say to himself, I'd better get an organization and process in motion to be able to supply what is needed."[35]

There are, as usual, two sides to this story. OMB had become somewhat demoralized due to low morale in the Carter administration in general, and to disre-

[32]Johnson, "From Analyst to Negotiator," and "Increasing Role of the Office of Management and Budget."

[33]Rauch, "Stockman's Quiet Revolution," p. 1215.

[34]Interview quoted in Rauch, "Stockman's Quiet Revolution."

[35]Hugh Heclo, "Executive Budget Making," in Gregory B. Mills and John L. Palmer, eds., *Federal Budget Policy in the 1980s* (Washington, D.C.: Urban Institute Press, 1984), pp. 255–91.

gard of administration recommendations in particular. There is nothing better for restoring high spirits than having a respected director who is on the winning side. OMB under Stockman was an important and exciting place for those staff members to be.

So far as loss of agency supervision was concerned, it was compensated for by greater OMB influence with Congress. True, examiners whose predecessors had once spent the slow summer months nosing around agencies could no longer do so. Yet, if they were honest with themselves, they knew that the old ways had started to crumble with the new requirements of the 1974 budget reform. Phenomena like budget resolutions, running totals, even reconciliation, had not been invented, only intensified, by David Stockman. The Central Budget Management System, which records existing spending-decision and projects alternatives, was inevitable in that era of conflict over totals and panic over deficits.

Depending on one's political philosophy, the politicization of OMB began either with its predecessors (BOB as linchpin of big government under Franklin Roosevelt) or with the Reorganization Plan Number 2 in 1970 under President Nixon, which established a new strata of four Program Associate Directors who were political appointees. President Carter's creation of a new Executive Associate Director for Budget to supervise the earlier four only intensified this practice. Politicization is bipartisan. Heclo is rightly interested in maintaining the ethos of OMB, that "It was not a place to be just another bureaucrat. It was a place to work for the presidency broadly understood."[36] But if the presidency is no longer "broadly understood" in the sense of presidential preferences being widely agreed, the politicization of those who serve presidents may be unavoidable.

In a polarized political environment the significance of significance, as it were, also changes. Is it significant to understand the effects on programs of changes in funding? Surely. But it may be deemed more significant to understand the implications of different programs for the size of government. If the Budget Review Division, where the big budget totals are put together, has become the place in OMB where bright young people try to go, as Heclo informs us,[37] that may be because they know where the action is. Unless and until there is consensus rather than dissensus over the size and composition of government, the division that deals with totals is where the action will continue to be. The counterpart to OMB's activity was in Congress, which was trying to work out its own adjustments.

DISSENSUS IN CONGRESS

The stable relationships of the past had been disrupted. Instead of their usual role as advocates, agencies found themselves defending the cuts mandated by the Republican administration. While something of the old relationships remained, appropriations committees and subcommittees in a Democratic House (and later Democratic Senate) took on a role of program advocate. Their hearings became a forum for policy disagreements, and a three-way conflict among authorizing and

---

[36]Ibid.

[37]Ibid., p. 283.

appropriations committees and the administration. The appropriations committees lost authority on the floor of the House, as budgeting grew both to displace
and include other legislative activities. It was fertile ground for proliferation of
budgetary gimmicks.

Role Reversal

With agencies under repeated attacks, appropriations committees had to come to
their defense. Committee members of both parties objected to the repeated cuts
on programmatic grounds but also, and more important, because rescissions were
presidential challenges to the power of Congress and to its appropriations committees. Yet the politically appointed heads of the agencies, and their immediate
civil service subordinates, formally supported most of these OMB decisions. In
appropriations hearings, agency heads continually cited the need for budget restraint, or the administration's philosophy, as the reason for cuts. There were some
cases in which the positions taken probably did reflect the views of the senior civil
servants involved. But, generally, civil servants were testifying in obedience to the
desires of their political superiors; they had to worry about the consequences for
their careers of defying those superiors. This hierarchical control, as well as placement of ideological Reaganauts in policy-making positions, left agencies in the peculiar position of publicly endorsing their own suffering. The peculiarity was not
that agencies had never been in such a position before—they surely had—but that
saying "yes" and meaning "no" had become the standard position.

Although thus formally neutralized, civil servants could, of course, feed information secretly to the appropriations staffs. Then, in hearings, committee members would try to establish for the record that the justifications for many
reductions were, in their view, insupportable. Members of Congress also used
hearings to inform the administration that it was stirring up hornets' nests that
were best left undisturbed. A good example of a number of these themes—skepticism about agency justifications; agency leaders squirming to justify reductions;
members furious about the short life span of agreements with the administration;
the adverse effects on agency operations; and the disregard for Congress—is provided by a Senate hearing on compensatory education and programs for special
populations. Ms. Harrison, for the Department of Education, claimed that state
and local governments could, and would, find cheaper ways to do things, or pick
up the slack, in response to reductions in federal aid. In the circumstances of 1982
this argument won little support, since state and local governments themselves
were slashing programs because of their own recessionary fiscal crisis. Mark Andrews (R-N. Dak.) was skeptical on principle:

> You know the impression you give us on the other side of the bench when you come
> up with a statement like that is that somehow or another you have found a magic way
> of doing exactly the same thing that has been done years ago for two-thirds of the cost.
> Have your people somehow or another found a way to spend in essence two-thirds of
> the money and have exactly the same amount of success?[38]

---

[38]Hearings before a Subcommittee of the Committee on Appropriations of the U.S. Senate on Departments of Labor, Health and Human Services, Education, and Related Agencies, Appropriations for
FY1983, Part IV, pp. 100, 105.

Clearly, Senator Andrews and his committee were not convinced. Shortly there-after the majority whip, Senator Stevens (R-Alaska), and department representa-tives crossed swords over the use of rescissions. The agency argument that entitlement overruns required discretionary reductions did not win praise.

SENATOR STEVENS: I'm greatly concerned with the 1982 rescission concept. It seems to me that [the grant recipients] have been led to believe they had money for 1982, and now you come and say there is no money for 1982. . . .

MS. HARRISON: I can only respond that this is consistent with our position in Septem-ber 1981 relating to those programs. In fact, if you look at a program like the Follow Through program, that program has been proposed for phaseout and abolishment by successive administrations. These grantees are well aware of the fact that there has never been any guar-antee of the money.

SENATOR STEVENS: But successive Congresses have disagreed. So it looks like what you are telling us is that this year you are not going to spend the money in spite of the action of Congress last year. The President signed that bill last year.

MS. HARRISON: That's why we are proposing a rescission. . . .

SENATOR STEVENS: I think the Department is just buying itself a fight. . . . There is a de facto breaking of a commitment as far as the government is concerned to those people, because you are putting us in a position of fighting the fiscal year 1982 battle again, the battle that you lost last year.

MR. JONEᶜ: . . . In order to stay within our budget mark, we needed to stay with the President's budget request because of the nearly $1 billion supple-mental request for the guaranteed student loan. So, if you subtract the supplemental from the rescission—

SENATOR STEVENS: . . . What you are saying is that you are going to take the increasing en-titlements out of discretionary funding, which you can't. You people are not reading Congress correctly if you think you are going to get away with this.[39]

No, they would not. Far more important, the principle followed—the president's budgetary base was what he recommended last year, not what Congress voted and he signed—signalled a radical change in the president's role.

The Reagan administration's proposals were likely to put agency heads in a tough spot because people in Congress expected agencies to defend their own missions. Responses of bureaucrats and political appointees varied with their in-clinations and their circumstances. But the observer of budgeting who overslept the 1970s, though possibly surprised by the intransigence, nevertheless would still recognize the classic motives. The voice might be the voice of Republican Senator Norris Cotton ("You will forgive me, but you will not forget the Norris Cotton Cancer Center up in Hanover, will you? That will be the only memorial I will leave after 28 years in Congress"[40]) but the body might be any one of a legion of legislators. An official of the National Cancer Institute, anxious like his predeces-sors to follow the strategy of "spend to save," contends that ". . . each annual co-hort of patients brings into the national economy about $3 billion. Federal

---

[39]Ibid., pp. 142—43.

[40]Quoted in Scott Stofel, student paper on "Budgetary Strategies."

revenues from their earnings is in the range of $500 million a year. So in just a cost effectiveness consideration, the program has been very productive."[41]

The "all or nothing" strategy was also alive and well. While the head of the Federal Aviation Administration (FAA) joined the Reagan administration in rallying "around to help reduce the deficit" in 1985, he was careful to point out that his agency was "a carefully woven organization designed to function as a whole."[42] Everyone knows that seamless garments should not be cut.

Voices calling for "fair shares" could still be heard. Amtrak, the government-owned and -operated railroad, had its reputation damaged by studies showing that every passenger cost the government $35. Without quite denying the allegation, Amtrak insisted it was "misleading and unfair" because, taking into account tax expenditures, airline passengers were subsidized even more heavily.[43]

Though our Rip-Van-budgeter might not see many differences in kind, he could not help but observe considerable differences in degree. There were many more programs whose futures were threatened criticisms ranging from fraud and abuse to lack of evidence of performance.

Unusual in the extreme in classical budgeting, but common during the Reagan administration, was to present cuts that looked less severe than they actually were. The Environmental Protection Agency's (EPA) press release stated that "When comparing EPA's 1981 operating and superfund budget of $1.43 billion and 10,621 work years, the President's proposal for next year represents a 2% reduction in spending." While the statement was true as far as it went, the EPA budget included $200 million for the superfund, an item that did not exist when the 1981 budget was adopted. If superfund spending was excluded, EPA's operating budget would have represented a cut of 12 percent in 1982.[44]

There were many more instances of appropriations committee members acting as program advocates than there used to be. Most often administrators showed quiet appreciation. If legislators insisted that the National Park Service acquire new space, using that to justify more money for maintenance, officials would play along with the "squeezed to the wall" strategy. Explaining why NPS could not "take a cut," an NPS official gave his "personal feeling . . . that the Park Service is stretched about as thin as it can be manpowerwise and financially, given the new areas and responsibilities that have been added in the last several years."[45]

So far, so much the same. As legislators rushed to protect programs, however, their administrators began to fear being crushed by a too-loving embrace. Asked in 1984 what was the biggest obstacle to the improvement of Amtrak's financial position, its chairman, Graham Claytor, Jr., claimed that "the single biggest threat

[41]Ibid.

[42]Clifton Von Kann, Testifying in Hearings before a Subcommittee on the Committee on Appropriations, Subcommittee on the Department of Transportation and Related Agencies, Appropriations, for FY1986, House of Representatives, 99th Congress, 1st Session, Part 5, April 3, 1985, p. 322.

[43]W. Graham Clayton, Jr., ibid., Part 8, May 2, 1985, pp. 284–85.

[44]Lawrence Mosher, "Will EPA's Budget Cuts Make It More Efficient or Less Efficient?" *National Journal*, No. 33 (August 15, 1981), p. 1468.

[45]House, Hearings Before the Appropriations Subcommittee for the Department of Interior and Related Agencies, 96th Congress, 2nd Session, p. 599.

is that Congress will legislate reversals of management decisions that we make not to run trains that are going to cost a lot of money, or not to do cost saving things that we have undertaken to do, or not to do re-routes because there's local opposition."[46] Between those who liked them too little and those who loved them too much, federal administrators were caught between a rock and a hard place.

Hearings turned into forums for attacks on the administration that had little to do with budgets, but a lot to do with disagreement over policy. Observers witnessed the strange spectacle of agency representatives and members of Congress trading barbs—hardly a model for how to get funds from guardians of the public purse. Appropriations hearings became the site of policy wars between the administration and House Democrats. Often members elicited information they could use to justify their positions. In one case—personnel levels for the National Park Service—Representative Sidney Yates (D-Ill.) established that what was really at stake was an administration preference for "contracting out" federal personnel needs, thereby reducing direct federal employment:

MR. YATES: It is almost like a yo-yo, because last year you added 300 employees. What is it, the Secretary giveth and the Secretary taketh away, blessed be the name of the Secretary? [Secretary of the Interior Watt was known for his religiosity.] . . . Your figures . . . do show that rather than paying $5,732,400 in employee salaries, you are going to contract that work out. . . . Let me ask somebody who operates a park. What is the advantage: Is it better to have your employees on hand, or to contract the work out? Which would you rather do?

MR. DICKENSON: [Russell Dickenson, Director of the National Park Service]: I have to tell you in all candor that as an experienced manager there really is no substitute to having the flexibility that comes from Federal employees. But the thrust of the Administration right now is to move into the contractor field. Therefore, we are adhering to that instruction.

The defense subcommittees on appropriations and the substantive Armed Services Committees had self-selected members with a bias toward the military. But the full Appropriations Committee in the House was more liberal than its authorizing counterpart; hence it was concerned about leaving room for social programs. The late House subcommittee chairman Joseph Addabbo was a solid liberal whose committee staff was far more suspicious of the military than was its counterpart at Armed Services. As a result, House Appropriations and Addabbo were the military's most dangerous domestic adversaries, and their exchanges reflected that relationship. This excerpt from testimony on the FY82 supplemental captures the flavor of that antagonism:

MR. ADDABBO: My spies got a copy of a memorandum to the chief of Naval Operations written by the Chief of Navy Legislature Affairs dated July 9, 1981. It was stated that: "Appropriation members and their staffs are not as thoroughly briefed and informed as their authorization counterparts." How did the Navy arrive at that conclusion? [The Navy's man made a properly deferential denial.] . . . I think they meant our staff and the

---

[46]J61, A6, 98th Congress, #23, Part 5, House, AMTRAK, 3/29/84, p. 871.

> members of the Appropriations Committee are not [as] brainwashed as the authorizing committee members.

If liberals were watching defense to create room for domestic spending, the conservative Reagan administration, to be sure, was attempting its own end-runs around authorizing committees in the domestic policy arena. Thus the administration's FY82 education rescissions included legislation that changed the rules on guaranteed student loans. Though such legislation was clearly out of order in an appropriations bill, that route was still more promising than going through the House Education and Labor Committee. This zeroing out of programs was a slightly more formally acceptable way to legislate through appropriations, but only slightly.

> MR. YATES: Tell me about the historic preservation fund. Has Congress repealed the basic legislation for which you are eliminating all funds?
> MR. DICKENSON: No, sir, the Congress has not.
> MR. YATES: Why are you eliminating the funds then?

Budget fights took so much time that little was left for floor action on authorizations. Since the widely different positions of the administration and the authorizing committees made agreement on legislation difficult, the committees tried to hitch rides on the appropriations process, particularly the continuing resolutions, as well as to exploit reconciliation. Representative Silvio Conte expressed the appropriators' discomfort with the result. "Personally," he told the House, "I am not at all comfortable dealing with issues such as steel import licenses and the International Coffee Agreement. But," he added, "the facts of life are that when the legislative committees are not able, for whatever reason to resolve highly controversial issues, Congress will find some other way, which is usually appropriations bills."[47]

Rolled on the Floor

During the heyday of the House Appropriations Committee, its members prided themselves on the high (over 95 percent) proportion of recommendations that were accepted by the House. Being "rolled on the floor" was a mark of ineptitude or disgrace. It meant that members were out of touch, that they had not performed their political function of anticipating and, therefore, failed to ward off opposition before it occurred. Why, if they were to get rolled often, the most knowledgeable and (more important) the most responsible members might lose control so that budgeting and chaos became equivalent terms.[48]

In the twenty years following 1963, the number of amendments offered annually to appropriations acts rose continuously, from 120 to 433. The average number of amendments per bill went up from 2.5 to 9.2. Where the number of amendments approved by the House (more accurately, the Committee of the Whole) remained at roughly 25 percent until the mid-1970s, by the end of the

---

[47]cf. Richard F. Fenno, *The Power of the Purse: Appropriations Politics in Congress* (Boston: Little, Brown, 1966).

[48]*Congressional Record*, October 1, 1982, p. H8360.

decade it had gone to 43.3, after 1980 rising to over 50 percent. Looking more precisely at the success rate of contested amendments, these went from a high of 30 percent in the 1960s to the 1980s average of just under half.[49] Evidently, as Stanley Bach concludes,

> Increases in the number of amendments proposed in recent years, and increases in the percentage of winning amendments, suggest that the Committee has had increasing difficulty in accommodating to the preferences of the House and in anticipating and settling potential controversies in advance. In turn, this may reflect decreasing sensitivity and acumen among Committee and subcommittee leaders, a decline in adherence to such norms as reciprocity and comity, or the increasing divisiveness and controversy within the House as a whole over spending policies and priorities.[50]

Incomplete explanations for the growth of victorious amendments to appropriation bills are easy to find. There were more subcommittees with more members. Access to meetings was far more open while interest in activities was more widely spread. After all, government had grown larger, programs had broader impacts (defense, housing, and unemployment programs occur almost everywhere), legislators had more staff, and they were more interested in making a name for themselves in a number of areas rather than just in one. Congressional centers of expertise, such as CRS and CBO, offered help in tracking the status and effects of appropriations, as did a generation of informed legislators. All this is persuasive. Members of Congress offered more amendments because there was more to amend, more interest in amending it, and more of a chance to be successful.

There were now fewer sanctions than in the past for stepping out of line by challenging committee recommendations. Chairmen were no longer powerful enough to control the outcomes. The growing partisanship over budgetary matters increased the likelihood that subcommittee members would visibly disagree; choosing among various majority and minority reports, consequently, was less a violation of the norms of reciprocity than it once would have been. Party leaders and committee chairs could do little to invoke sanctions. Assignments were difficult to deny, since now there were many more to go around. Staff was plentiful; so were subcommittee positions. Indeed, because members served on more subcommittees, they were less liable to assign overriding importance to a single amendment or to be challenged on one of their recommendations. Short of the ultimate sanction—reading a legislator out of the party, which is only a last resort—the publicity and perhaps even the power went to those who act and speak up.

Consideration of the merits might also lead legislators to try to overturn subcommittee judgments. Because there were many more programs and expertise was more widely shared, there was less reason to believe that subcommittees knew more than other members. Since turnover on subcommittees also had risen, there was less reason to defer to expertise.

---

[49] The data come from Stanley Bach, "Representatives and Committees on the Floor: Amendments to Appropriations Bills in the House of Representatives, 1963–1982." Paper prepared for 1985 Annual Meeting of the American Political Science Association, New Orleans, August 29–September 1, 1985.

[50] Ibid., pp. 24–25.

Budgeting Penetrates Congress

Votes on budget resolutions and major spending items became more partisan even though members of appropriations and budget committees were not more partisan than the House as a whole.[51] The basic reason for this is that differences over the budget had increasingly come to define differences between the parties.

A good indicator of this noteworthy development was the growing importance of votes on budgeting in Congress. Before the Budget Act of 1974, votes on budgeting—taxes, appropriations, debt ceilings—represented less than one-third of votes on all matters. To add in votes on authorizations—including entitlements, the fastest growing portion of the budget, as well as the new budget resolutions and reconciliation—produces a startling result: Ellwood's account shows that from 1982 to 1984, half of floor votes in the House and two-thirds (!) in the Senate were concerned with budgeting.[52] It took some thirty-odd roll calls for the Senate to pass its resolution in 1985. If one saw budgetary matters as irrelevant to political parties, there would be little left about which parties would be relevant.

An indirect indicator of the ever-growing importance of budgeting is the workload of the Congressional Budget Office. CBO produces estimates of the likely cost of almost every bill that requires expenditure. As the markup of legislation proceeds, it gives informal input on estimates. But that is not all. CBO is also required to issue periodic scorekeeping reports on the degree to which outlays and authorizations stay within the budget resolutions. So far, so simple—until it turned out that the Senate and House committees wanted different scores.[53]

All along the way, CBO alters its estimates to keep up with the president's budget, committee changes, budget resolutions, floor votes. The important consequence is not that CBO succeeds in keeping all this straight, which it does, but that Congress, as it decomposes itself into subcommittees, is dealing with different budgetary bases.

Because it takes so much time in so many places, the budget displaces whatever else Congress would be doing. Not only are there are more actors but each has to, in effect, negotiate with the others and with the president. In addition to more participants, there are also larger choices—annual budget resolutions, continuing resolutions, and reconciliations—that either were not made before or, if they were, were made far less frequently.

Whether one says "It is Congress, therefore it budgets," or, "It budgets, therefore it must be Congress," the conclusion is the same: Congress and budgeting are becoming synonymous.

One might think that with so much time and effort devoted to budgeting Congress would get better at it. In a sense, this is true. There is much more understanding of spending, taxing, and the relationship between them in Congress.

---

[51]On the House Budget Committee, see John W. Ellwood and James A. Thurber, "The New Congressional Budget Process: The Hows and Why of House-Senate Differences," in Lawrence Dodd and Bruce Oppenheimer, eds., *Congress Reconsidered* (New York: Praeger, 1977), pp. 163–92.

[52]John W. Ellwood, "Providing Policy Analysis to U.S. Congress: The Case of the Congressional Budget Office." Paper prepared for 1984 Annual Meetings of the Association for Public Policy Analysis and Management, New Orleans, October 18–22, 1984, pp. 35–36.

[53]Ibid., p. 10.

But understanding does not agreement make. Indeed, the more that people fundamentally in disagreement know about the consequences of their actions, the better become their reasons for opposing one another. Disagreement has spread not only to present policies but also to past policies; from an agreed base to what that base ought to be; from where the budget should go, to where it is.

Gimmicks

When relations among participants in budgeting are relatively stable and trustworthy, based on long-term convergence over objectives, the use of gimmicks—appearances costumed as realities—have their amusing aspects. Taking a cut that is actually an increase because an inappropriate base has been used, or because lost funds will have to be restored, the ancient Washington Monument ploy (named after impossible proposals to close down this American shrine) may be treated with wry amusement. Large-scale and repeated efforts to deceive would be treated by dismissal or demotion as the participants depend on trust to get their work done, it being impossible, even in those days, up through the 1950s, to study most claims firsthand. Now that budgetary stringency became severe, as a consequence of deficits and a general attack on spending, however, the use of gimmicks reached major proportions. The difference was that gimmicks were now used by participants who once opposed them. As gimmickry became more the rule and less like the exception, it was no longer funny.

Cuts might be used as sanctions against legislators opposed to spending programs. Senator Pete Domenici, chair of the Senate Budget Committee until 1987, was compelled to vote for certain projects in his district so as to show that in this respect he was "one of the boys." When Senator James Buckley attempted to remove 44 public works projects at the committee stage, members of the Public Works Committee ostentatiously voted for 43, all except the one in his state.[54]

Congress might appear to meet targets in budget resolutions by voting only eleven months of funds, knowing the rest would have to be restored. The food stamp program received this treatment several times. Paydays might be moved forward or back so they don't count toward the deficit for the fiscal year in question. A similar feat might be accomplished by failing to provide essential spending authority. The Commodity Credit Corporation is financed by authority to borrow in order to provide farm price supports. By refusing some hundreds of millions of CCC's request, thereby seemingly cutting the budget, Congress would fail to provide funds that would have to be restored later.[55]

Gimmicks chosen for a purpose. Congress needed to meet a certain figure for reducing the deficit. One way to help accomplish this purpose, while still not savaging programs, was to do what consumers do, that is, "buy now and pay later." The deficit figure might be met by choosing the House outlay number for defense, which is lower, and the Senate authority, which is higher but can be paid out over a number of years.

---

[54]Reported in David Mayhew, *Congress: The Electoral Connection* (New Haven: Yale University Press, 1974), pp. 91–92, footnote 32.

[55]Jerome A. Miles, "The Congressional Budget and Impoundment Control Act: A Departmental Budget Officer's View," *The Bureaucrat,* Vol. 5, No. 4 (January 1977).

"Hypocrisy," La Rochefoucauld observed, "is an homage vice pays to virtue." This maxim came to life in light of the budget quandary. There would be no reason to vote for a lower budget resolution and for higher individual expenditures if the appearance were not seen as serving virtue. "In effect," Senator Hatfield complained, "we're talking out of both sides of our mouth. We want everyone else's project reduced." No one wanted to make what have come to be mostly painful choices, although occasionally Congress resisted.

Fiddling with the fiscal year—either to put expenditure in an earlier or later accounting period, depending on which will help the most—is a pure (if that word may be used) gimmick. Defense salaries may be paid a day earlier or later, thus "saving" billions for the next fiscal year. Medicare miraculously lived an eleven-month year in 1980 and a thirteen-month year in 1981.[56] In order to make the 1986 deficit look smaller than it was so as to meet Gramm–Rudman–Hollings targets, Congress moved a big $680 million revenue-sharing payment forward by five days so the Balanced Budget and Deficit Reduction Act would not officially take notice of it. Noting that the advance payment would entail borrowing costs, Representative Jack Brooks said "Isn't it ironic that we are wasting a half a million dollars trying to fool the taxpayer into believing that we are getting the deficit down, when in fact we are actually increasing it?"[57]

There are other unacceptable reasons for the use of gimmicks. One is the reverse gimmick, a real spending cut, but one that actually reduces quality while increasing future costs. In making across-the-board cuts, for example, the first things to go are such "nonessential" items as travel and staff training. These may be false economies, however, when the lack of necessary information or training produces poor performance, more expensive medical treatment, and the like. After the closing of public health hospitals, to take another example, the Indian Health Service had to dismiss a number of its lower-paid professionals in order to make room for higher-paid people from public health who had more seniority.[58]

What is gained by making genuine economies if the result is only further reductions? Padding the budget to leave room for OMB and Congress to cut makes sense in the face of formula cuts. Donna Shalala, a political scientist (then assistant Secretary of the Department of Housing and Urban Development, now Secretary of the Department of Health and Human Services) tells a familiar tale:

> If you want to maintain your budget in an agency at a certain level, there's no incentive for coming and suggesting ways of delivering those precise services in different ways. Cost-conscious budget managers for the President will take advantage of your initiative, and they'll simply take the rest of the money off to someone else who didn't show that ingenuity.
>
> I went to the Hill this year without an increase in my budget. . . . And I told the Secretary I didn't want an increase, and everybody yelled and screamed and jumped

[56]See Allen Schick, "Controlling the 'Uncontrollables': Budgeting for Health Care in an Age of Mega-Deficits." Paper prepared for AEI Pew Fellows Conference, November 1985, pp. 25–26.

[57]*National Journal,* October 11, 1986, p. 2415.

[58]An article by Joseph S. Wholey contains examples of both true and false economies: "Executive Agency Retrenchment," in Mills and Palmer, *Federal Budget Policy in the 1980s* (Washington D.C.: Urban Institute Press, 1984), pp. 295–332.

up and down and said, "You've got to take an increase the way everybody does, 'cause when you get to the Hill you've got to take a cut." The Hill paid no attention to the fact that I went up without an increase; they just gave me the same cut they gave everybody else. And I went up and I argued that I hadn't asked for an increase. And they said that was just dumb.[59]

Padding in the expectation of cuts is part of playing the game. As Senator James Abdnor argued, "While this figure [the 7.5 percent figure for real growth in defense spending] is entirely responsible and defensible in its own right, the truth of the matter, as we all realize, is that whatever numbers we settle on will be our starting point when we go to conference with the House. The House approved only a 2.3 percent increase." Similarly, Representative David Obey, desiring to ameliorate cuts in social programs, suggested that "I simply don't think you should lead with your bottom line. It's like selling your soul to the devil before you're tempted."[60] Later, Representative Obey let it all hang out: "The only kind of budget resolution," said he sadly, "that can pass this place is a dishonest one. I think that degrades the entire congressional process."[61]

Gimmickry has spawned criticism of the post-1974 process inside and outside of Congress. Citing evidence that "the reconciliation process has run amok," for instance, Richard Cohen of the *National Journal* noted that the 1985 bill ran to 198 pages in small print and required 30 subconferences to negotiate Senate-House differences. Among a long list of matters, it included

- a requirement that the Transportation Secretary withhold 10 percent of highway funds starting in fiscal 1989 from states that have not set their minimum drinking age at 21;
- an instruction to build three highway bridges over the Ohio River between designated points in Ohio and Kentucky;
- a plan to allocate to Gulf Coast states billions of dollars from oil and gas drilling on the Outer Continental Shelf;
- extensive overhaul of medicare, including changes in the 1983 law that set up a new prospective reimbursement system for hospital fees to limit costs;
- extension of the right to social security benefits to children adopted by and living with their great-grandparents;
- eligibility of Connecticut state police for social security.[62]

Cohen concluded that "members would do well to stop criticizing his [President Reagan's] shortcomings and take their own role more seriously."[63]

Members of Congress themselves realized that gimmickry was institutionally destructive. Members could now ring all the changes on devices to make spending

---

[59]Quoted in David Broder, *Changing of the Guard: Power and Leadership in America* (New York: Simon and Schuster, 1980), p. 434.

[60]Reischauer, "Mickey Mouse," p. 33.

[61]Quoted in Richard E. Cohen, "House Braces for Showdown Over How It Should Package Its Annual Budget," *National Journal*, November 27, 1982, pp. 2024–26.

[62]Richard E. Cohen, "Unreconciled," *National Journal*, January 11, 1986, p. 110.

[63]Ibid.

fit within resolutions or to have them appear lower than they actually were. Committees reported savings that actually were only temporary. Votes were forced on cuts so as to make it difficult to approve them. Payments for medicare were pushed into the next fiscal year. That is why SBC and OMB tried to get multiyear reconciliations for appropriations and authorizations.[64] The lack of connection between appearance in the resolution and reality in spending fooled no one but did contribute to low morale and self-doubt in Congress.

If, then, Congress was so out of control, if it was in disrepute with its own members, then maybe they could not trust themselves. Why not, then, force themselves to do the right thing, namely, balance the budget in such a fashion that they could not reverse the process by playing the usual games?

GRAMM–RUDMAN–HOLLINGS

Why GRH Passed

The Gramm–Rudman–Hollings bill (formally known as the Balanced Budget and Deficit Reduction Act of 1985), which essentially required five yearly sequential across-the-board reductions in federal spending until the deficit had been reduced to zero, was proof positive of mistrust. (Of course, these sequential reductions were required only if prior agreement on reductions was not forthcoming; but it was the sequences that were normal, the hoped-for agreement, abnormal.) Here we have a procedure that almost every member of Congress believed was foolish, if not stupid; that everyone who knew anything about it thought could be improved upon in five minutes; yet it received majority support in both houses of Congress and was signed by the president. The act, which dramatically affected the future of numerous government programs and congressional budget procedures, was passed without public hearings, without debate by any House or Senate standing committee, and without any substantive debate on the House floor. When everyone says that something is not right, and yet they keep doing it, there is a puzzle that should excite our interest.

Year after year Congress advertised its disabilities by taking longer and longer to reach agreement; few could remember the last year all appropriations bills were passed on time. Congress was tired of budgeting to no purpose, tired of budgeting, budgeting, and nothing but budgeting. Its members despaired sufficiently of accommodation to wish to cover their disagreements by a formula, all the while expecting, even hoping, that the balancing mechanism had been made so onerous (After all, who wants to reduce the number of aircraft controllers?) that it would collapse of its own weight. Crash! This is no way to run a ship, especially not the ship of state, unless you regard the wreckage the lesser evil compared to giving in to the other side.

Gramm–Rudman–Hollings was as (or more) important for what it symbolized as for what it did. The imposition of a formula for replacing the power of the purse, the most important congressional power, was an abdication of power. Congress was saying that it is out of control. It cannot help itself. Faced with difficult

---

[64]Robert D. Reischauer, "The Congressional Budget Process," in Mills and Palmer, *Federal Budget Policy*, pp. 385–413, especially pp. 397–98.

decisions, the one thing Congress knows is that it won't be able to decide wisely. Therefore, guarding against its own worst tendencies in advance, Congress anticipates its collective unwisdom by taking away its discretion.

Binding oneself against one's worst inclinations may appear strange, but it has precedent. Fearing continual scandal, Congress took away its power to appoint local postmasters. Observing as well the unfortunate consequences of the Smoot–Hawley Tariff, Congress also created a buffer, a tariff commission between it and temptation so that it could no longer, as an ordinary matter, set tariff rates on individual items. At least since Ulysses and the Sirens, attempting to protect oneself against self-destructive tendencies has been a well-known strategy. Why did Congress agree to limit its most important power, the power that humbled tyrants and brought about representative government, a power, moreover, on which other legislative powers depend?

The rise of the Gramm–Rudman–Hollings Act took place in an environment of disarray, dismay at the ever-rising deficits, and concern by legislators with their own inability to govern. The opportunity was ripe for an outsider, Phil Gramm of Texas (who, upon being read out of the Democratic party in the House, won a seat as a Republican senator), to ally himself with a Democratic outsider, Senator Fritz Hollings of South Carolina, and with a dedicated budget balancer, Republican Warren Rudman of New Hampshire. The three offered the radical proposal as a rider to the annual misery of raising the debt ceiling, this time to a previously unheard of level of $2 trillion. They believed, as did many other legislators, that unless Congress was faced with something much worse than business as usual, it would continue to avoid balancing the budget.

Ronald Reagan felt (partly rightly, partly wrongly, but with conviction) that every time he compromised by raising taxes, he did not get in return promised cuts in domestic spending. Though he preferred tax reductions to lower deficits, he did want balance if (and only if) it could be achieved solely by spending cuts. The GRH formula looked like it might make that possible. The president did not want to cut defense, but that was happening anyway.[65] So he supported GRH.

But why did Democratic liberals, Republican moderates, and otherwise sane and sensible legislators (there were a few, such as Republican Senator Nancy Kassebaum and Democrat Pat Moynihan, who opposed GRH to the end) go along? Fearful of rising deficits, frustrated by inability to get agreement on taxing and spending, unwilling to say "no" to any plan for balance, realizing that they could change their minds later when the crunch came, they went along.

Liberals have another story to tell. They wanted to pin the deficit tag on Reagan and not allow him to do that to them. Led by Speaker O'Neill, they insisted on changes in the original conception, where everything, except possibly social security, was subject to proportional cuts, and succeeded in getting the most important entitlements for low-income and elderly people either excluded or subject only to modest reductions of 1 to 2 percent. By doing this, congressional liberals hoped not only to protect the poor and elderly but also, by making defense bear a dispro-

---

[65]This summary is taken from a book by Joseph White and Aaron Wildavsky entitled *The Deficit and the Public Interest: The Search for Responsible Budgeting in the 1980s* (Berkeley: University of California Press, 1990).

Table 5.1   THE GRAMM–RUDMAN–HOLLINGS RECORD

	Original deficit limits	Revised deficit limits	Actual deficits
		(in billions of dollars)	
1986	171.9		221.2
1987	144.0		149.8
1988	108.0	144.0	155.2
1989	72.0	136.0	152.5
1990	36.0	100.0	221.4
1991	0	64.0	269.2
1992		28.0	290.4
1993		0	255.1

Source: Compiled from data released to the public record.

portionate share, encourage the president to compromise with them so as not to invoke the dreaded sequestration procedure.

Opinions understandably vary as to whether the Balanced Budget and Emergency Deficit Control Act of 1985 (Public Law 99-172) was meant to be workable. If (as in the phrase Senator Rudman made famous, "it's so bad it's good") the idea was to scare legislators into reducing the deficit, the consequences would have to be horrendous. And, if followed for the full course, so they would be, wiping out half of general government. Anticipating this havoc, legislators might be motivated to settle on a more variegated and hence more sensible deficit-reduction package than across-the-board cuts. Unfortunately, being sensible requires being able to choose among the entire panoply of governmental programs. But the act exempted 48 percent of these (mostly entitlements and debt interest) from across-the-board cuts, with an additional 24 percent available only for very limited reductions. Only 27 percent of the budget, mostly in defense, was fully available for sequestration—that is, the withholding of budget authority up to the amount required to be cut to meet the deficit target. You cannot get 100 percent of the deficit reduction you need from 27 percent of the budget.

In this game of budgetary chicken, one side assumed that as automatic cuts were triggered, the Republicans would blink by raising taxes while the other hoped that as meat-ax cuts in domestic spending grew near, Democrats would blink by making the policy decisions needed for domestic reductions. Each side hoped to prevail by making the budgetary process unworkable. This political Ludditism did not bode well for the ability to govern.

How GRH Was Supposed to Work

The Gramm–Rudman–Hollings process was invoked if (and only if) the preexisting process failed to meet the annual deficit reduction targets—from $171.9 billion in 1986 to $144.0 billion in 1987 to zero in 1991. (See Table 5.1.) Except in the first and last years, a $10 billion cushion was allowed above the target figure before the sequestration procedure was invoked.

Table 5.2 REVISED BUDGET AND DEFICIT REDUCTION PROCESS UNDER
GRAMM–RUDMAN–HOLLINGS

Action	To be completed by
President submits budget	Monday after January 3
CBO report to Congress	February 15
Committees submit views and estimates to budget committees	February 25
Senate Budget Committee reports budget resolution	April 1
Congress passes budget resolution	April 15
House Appropriation Committee reports appropriations bills	June 10
Congress passes reconciliation bill	June 15
House passes all appropriations bills	June 30
Initial economic, revenue, outlay and deficit projections made by OMB and CBO	August 15
OMB and CBO report tentative contents of sequester order to GAO	August 20
GAO issues deficit and sequester report to the president	August 25
President issues sequester order	September 1
Fiscal year begins and sequester order takes effect	October 1
OMB and CBO issue revised projections based on subsequent congressional action	October 5
GAO issues revised sequester report to president	October 10
Final sequester order becomes effective	October 15
GAO issues compliance report on sequester order	November 15

Source: Balanced Budget and Emergency Deficit Control Act of 1985.

The president was required to submit a budget that did not exceed the annual target figure. Congressional budget resolutions also had to conform to the targets for cutting the deficit. Snapshot day was August 15. (See Table 5.2 for timetable.) OMB and CBO were to issue a joint report estimating revenue, expenditures, and, therefore, the gap between them at that moment in time for the fiscal year beginning October 1. This early warning was designed to alert all players to the fact that the rules of the budget game were about to be altered. The month that followed was supposed to be budgetary show-and-tell time. I say "supposed" because no piece of paper, even a law, can make Congress do what it doesn't want to do. Congress could still ignore GRH or make believe, by various gimmicks, that it had done what was required.

On the 20th of August, according to the original legislation, the directors of OMB and CBO had to submit a joint report, not to Congress or the president but to the Comptroller General. This CBO-OMB report estimated revenues and expenditures (income and outlays) for the fiscal year. After comparing the two figures, the report stated for the record whether the difference plus the allowable $10 billion was larger than the allowed deficit. If the amount was smaller, and the Comptroller General concurred, the GRH process stopped there. If the target figure had been breached, the joint report specified the reductions necessary to reach that level.

On the 15th of August, in addition to estimating the size of the deficit, GRH required OMB and CBO to estimate economic growth for each quarter of the existing year as well as the last two quarters of the preceding year. The purpose was to tell Congress whether there had been two consecutive quarters of negative growth, in which case sequestration procedures were suspended. Depression, though obviously undesirable, was one way out of the deficit-reduction process.

At this point, CBO and OMB recommended, and GAO was supposed to decide upon, a base from which sequestration was to occur. The calculation of this base was no simple matter. The spending budget itself is complex. Specific priorities were embedded within GRH, requiring numerous exceptions and adjustments. And congressional desire to limit presidential discretion, especially on defense, led to extraordinary arrangements. The president was not to achieve by sleight-of-calculation what he had not won by legislative majorities.

Step one reduced the base for sequestration by the total of exempt programs. Step two deducted from the base the cost of living increases in the rest of government. These available COLAs were divided in half and then subtracted from domestic and defense programs, respectively. The reason for this rather strange 50-50 split was that defense and domestic programs had come to be seen as competitors. Where defense lost out in step one (because it was eligible for sequestration while the bulk of domestic spending was not), it gained a bit back in the second stage: Though defense represented more than half of the cutable base, some 60 percent, it took just half the hit. By strict proportionality, on the other hand, defense should have had credit for 60 percent of the sequestered COLAs. Such are the odd outcomes of political bargaining.

The defense sequestration was designed not merely to lower spending but to make sure that, after the first year, the president has as little discretion as possible.

The president issued an initial sequestration report on September 1 telling Congress he has followed the rules (the 50-50 defense-domestic split, the exempt and partially exempt categories, the deficit reduction). At the same time, the president was allowed to suggest an alternative budget quite outside these rules, providing it met the MDA. Presidential sequestration had to be by uniform percentage reductions in defense and domestic categories.

The immediate significance of this uniformity was that the president could not, on his own, eliminate programs or make transfers among categories. He could not move to protect programs he deemed vital or to advantage new ones, with small bases, compared to large ones with large bases that could better withstand cuts.

On September 5th the president submitted a list of proposed changes in contracts to the Armed Services and Appropriations committees. At the end of that month, GAO certified that the savings stemming from sequestration of contracts were correct. Starting in mid-August, Congress and the president had the chance to come up with an alternative to sequestration. If they did not, sequestration took place automatically on October 15th.

In 1986, a lawsuit was brought by Representative Michael L. Synar (D-Okla.) and other members of Congress, joined by the Public Citizen Litigation Group affiliated with activist Ralph Nader. They argued that "Gramm–Rudman tried to insulate congress from the hard choices our Founding Fathers gave us and expected us to make."[66]

Under a backup provision, the procedure was changed. The CBO–OMB joint report of the budget snapshot was now sent to a Temporary Joint Committee on Deficit Reduction, made up of the entire membership of the House and Senate Budget Committees. Within five days the Temporary Joint Committee was supposed to report to both houses a joint resolution of sequester based on the arithmetic average of the OMB and CBO reports. The full House and Senate had five days to act on the Joint Resolution. Debate was limited to two hours—easily done by special rule in the House, but requiring unanimous consent in the Senate.

Yet the institutional problem was not the major impediment to achieving its objectives. Within two years, it was clear the original targets were impractical. There were three sets of sequestrations, but even these failed to bring actual spending in line with actual revenues. Though deficits dropped between 1986 and 1989, by 1990, the deficit was again approaching the $200 billion mark.

While it might be possible year by year to meet GRH's formal conditions, compliance was achieved by gimmicks. Revenues could be estimated higher and expenditures lower than realistic; payments could be changed from one fiscal year to another; asset sales could make up gaps. Overlooking gimmicks was widely believed preferable to damaging many desirable programs. Between the rock of sequestration and the hard place of reductions in the deficit, all that was left was appearances.

The most acute comment came from Representative Leon Panetta (later to become director of OMB and then White House Chief of Staff under President Clinton): "This place is reflective of the American people: they don't want taxes, they don't want cuts, and they don't want a deficit."[67]

The best that congressional leaders could do was to use humor to ward off depression. Among the kindest was Senator William Armstrong's (R-Colo.) "A package of golden gimmicks, a package of smoke and mirrors." Harsher was Senator James Exon's (D-Nebr.) characterization of the measure as "perverted, phony, unrealistic." Responding to Senate consideration of this purported deficit reduction, Senator Lawton Chiles (D-Fla.) bespoke the common understanding: "It's midway between the best we could do and the worst that could happen." Others, like Representative Martin Leath (D-Tex.), a member of the House Budget Committee, felt that "We're about to pull the ultimate scam, and everybody's included."[68] The main lesson of the Gramm–Rudman–Hollings process may well be that while total trust is hard to come by, total mistrust makes budgeting impossible.

Why Didn't GRH Work?

Following regular budget procedure, failure to make changes merely sustains the status quo. The deficit might rise or fall because of external events, such as the

---

[66]*Congressional Quarterly*, July 12, 1986, p. 1559.

[67]*New York Times*, September 23, 1986, p. B8.

[68]*New York Times*, September 20, 1986, pp. 1 and 50; *Oakland Tribune*, September 10, 1986.

condition of the economy, but not by deliberate governmental action. In order to bring the deficit center stage, the Gramm–Rudman–Hollings Act transformed inaction into a form of action: When Congress and the president did not work together to reach annual deficit reduction targets, GRH would mandate spending cuts.

While GRH established a fast track for the regular budget decisions, no one had reason to play along with them unless and until they knew whether their favorite programs would do better or worse in negotiation than in sequestration.

The incentives all worked to promote delay. The speeded-up schedule provided in the act was not adhered to because no one wanted to bargain without knowing what the terms were. Would you?

The very same severity of GRH that was supposed to spur negotiation is bound to raise doubts about its workability. If all the consequences are so catastrophic, maybe no one will want to play. Each year the amount needed to meet the deficit reduction level became greater and greater, until, finally, in 1990 the whole effort was abandoned.

Despite its apparently mindless across-the-board cuts, GRH reflected a very strong sense of national policy priorities. That which could not be touched was holy—social security, Unemployment Compensation, WIC (Women, Infants and Children), child nutrition, medicaid, veterans' pensions and compensation, food stamps, AFDC (Aid to Families with Dependent Children). Programs from which large numbers of people receive cash or equivalent value were exempt from cuts. Children, pregnant women, and veterans were favored. And programs, such as payments to doctors and other providers under medicare, under sequestration could be cut no more than 1 percent the first year or 2 percent over the remaining four years.

The trouble was that negative agreement on what cannot be cut overwhelmed positive agreement on what could be cut. Getting all cuts essentially out of defense and general government (a category that goes by the bloodless title of "nondefense discretionary") was too tough and too foolhardy. Given the technical difference between fast-spending and slow-spending accounts of budget authority, moreover, a difference that has nothing to do with the desirability of programs, an awful lot of budget authority would have had to be sequestered to meet GRH's outlay targets. Reduction is one thing; destruction is another.

Apparent agreement on Gramm–Rudman–Hollings obscured the built-in disagreement that it embodied. What had happened, was that growing polarization among political elites had produced agreement on extremism, that is, that Congress should make fundamental choices on total spending and revenues every year. But these self-same elites disagreed over what these levels should be, or how burdens and benefits should be divided. On the one hand, there was agreement that we should stand up like men and women and say our piece: "Yes, this is what the size of the budget should be, this is what the level of taxes should be, this is how spending and taxing burdens and benefits should be divided." The only problem was that while each of us could make a wonderful budget alone, together we cannot agree on how to make a budget for the rest of us. Thus, there is agreement over the desirability of having budget resolutions, but disagreement about their contents. The ability to govern depends ultimately on the capacity to agree; if

Gramm–Rudman–Hollings has taught us anything, it is that no formula can substitute for political consensus. But a formula might help enforce consensus if there is one.

THE IMPORTANCE OF CONSIDERING OTHERS: ENFORCING LIMITS THROUGH OFFSETS

Lost in fascination with Gramm–Rudman–Holling's budgetary formulas were procedural changes of potential importance. Representatives Obey, Beilenson, and others sought to make the economic principle of opportunity costs—the value of a good is what one has to give up to get it[69]—effective in the politics of budgeting by writing procedural changes into the law. Each decision—a giving to someone requires a taking from someone else—is made painful.

Spending control in the Senate is subject to a point of order to enforce the 302(b) provisions of the 1974 budget act, which are enforceable at the subcommittee level for budget authority, credit authority, and entitlement authority. In the House, following the Fazio Rule, subcommittees cannot be subject to points of order if their proposals lie within the total spending for the entire Appropriations Committee under the 302(a) allocations of new budget authority. Therefore, if an appropriation subcommittee spends beyond the amount allocated to it by the House Budget resolution, there is no way of stopping it until total approved spending goes beyond the ceiling specified. Control comes too late.[70]

In the Senate, each subcommittee can be kept within its own allocation by a point of order. This is a vital difference. Section 302(d) limits amendments to reconciliation bills and resolutions by requiring "reduction in other . . . outlays [and/or increases in] . . . revenues equivalent to . . ." the amount of spending being added or the amount of revenue being decreased. According to this "Byrd rule" spending or revenue measures may not be passed that would increase future deficits.[71] Spending cannot go beyond the resolution without offsets at the crucial time, when spending is being approved in the committee or on the floor—not after the process is almost over. While an offset provision existed in the 1974 Budget Act, Gramm–Rudman–Hollings gave the rule some teeth: Three-fifths (rather than majority) must vote to waive the offset rules.

Expenditure does not involve choice unless those resources are in competition for alternative uses. If one good cause does not take from another, there is resource addition, not resource allocation. Here we have the great desideratum of budgeting: More of one good means less of another. If only two-fifths of the Senate is willing to live by the law, by upholding a single member's point of order, it can enforce budget discipline. No process can be stronger than this: To require offsets for increases.

---

[69]See Bruce Wallin and Aaron Wildavsky, "Opportunity Costs and Merit Wants," in *Speaking Truth to Power* (Boston: Little, Brown, 1979), pp. 155–83.

[70]Schick, *The Federal Budget*, p. 88.

[71]Ibid., p. 85.

Enforcing the notion of opportunity costs in budgeting—more for one program means less for another—calls for the intervention of those who stand to lose. In this way, a true conflict of priorities takes place. The entire budget, not just parts of special interest, has become relevant to all the participants. And while not everyone would like what happens to their prized part of the budget, the concept of tradeoffs has removed from a forlorn hope to an everyday reality.

Now we know what it takes to make agencies and interest groups care about the entire budget, not just their small corner. We also know how to arrange a political process in which the values of disparate expenditures are related each to the other. All that is necessary is a firm ceiling on total spending and a rule requiring offsets. Given the willingness to abide by these two conditions, implementation of budget reform becomes easier because the participants will enforce it upon one another. Because spending interests will call attention to any perceived weakness in program or political support for competing programs, there is less reason for controllers to be ever-present. Mutual dependence leads to mutual control. The idea of offsets found more general expression in the spending caps and PAYGO provisions of the Budget Enforcement Act of 1990.

Chapter
6

Changing:
1990–1994

*T*he path of budgetary change in a democratic society is usually tortuous. By change we mean changes in spending priorities, levels of revenues and expenditures, the balance between them, processes and institutions, or the budgetary norms which govern expectations and behavior. Often the budgetary scene seems static, moved only through the weight of its own inertia. Changes in direction are limited by lack of agreement, fickle majorities, decentralized processes, constitutional provisions, and in-built drag derived from past commitments.

But over a longer run, budgets are responsive. Priorities and levels of spending change through incrementalism, the accumulation of numerous small decisions. Automatic mechanisms, such as indexed entitlements, exercise a vast influence on budget totals. Various devices—tax expenditures, availability of credit, public corporations, and trust funds—provide incentives and opportunities to expand spending in some areas, even as it is cut in others.

Sometimes, however, changes in direction may be more abrupt and deliberate. Recent examples are the use of reconciliation and the decision to enhance defense spending by the Reagan government in the 1980s; the Tax Reform Act of 1986; and the 1985 social security reform. During the 1990s there have been further significant shifts in budget direction. These changes have come about in different ways: Through bipartisan agreement in a budgetary summit in 1990; through process reform in the 1990 Budget Enforcement Act; and through executive initiative to gain a sufficient congressional majority for President Clinton's first budget in 1993. The results of these changes were not always the ones intended, but their direction was unmistakable. All were concerned with realigning revenues and expenditures, and taken together they crystallized thinking about the budget, preparing the ground for the radical developments of 1995.

THE BUDGET SUMMIT OF 1990

The hope was that if the prospect of a balanced budget were dangled before the American electorate by an agreement from on-high, the bane of tax increases and spending cuts would be overawed by the glow of a leadership willing to sacrifice itself for the public interest. How could the president and his advisers believe this fairy tale? How could they not when every source of responsible opinion kept telling them that all that was required to make big dents in the deficit was political courage.

The journey from GRH to the Budget Summit to OBRA evokes the grand themes of budgeting in our time—ideological dissensus so deep the opposing sides make minute measurements of outcomes, a deficit octopus so entangling that its grip can be loosened but not cut through, and a temporary truce based on the common desire of politicians to create a process that will not automatically stigmatize them as failures. Thus they moved from budget balance, which they could not achieve, to expenditure control, which they had a fighting chance to attain. But the deadlock over the budgetary base—the levels of revenue and expenditure and, within them, different proportions for different programs and tax-payers—remained.

The Budget Summit of 1990 held between representatives of President Bush and top party leaders in both houses of Congress agreed on an approximately $500 billion deficit-reduction package over a five-year period, only to have it defeated by a bipartisan majority in the House of Representatives. From the start of the Summit, indeed from the beginning of the Bush administration, the question of how to reduce the deficit was complicated by an argument over taxation. President Reagan had followed the strategy of across-the-board reductions in tax rates. In the 1986 tax reform, he accepted capital gains rates equal to those of wage income, reversing historic Republican policy because his free-market principles and advisers argued that all sources of revenue should be treated the same. Moreover, as long as attention was focused on flat, across-the-board tax rate reductions, it was difficult for liberals to raise the question of class conflict. While it was true that the major tax reform of 1986 lowered taxes for higher-income individuals, for instance, it also took some six or seven million of the poorest taxpayers off the tax rolls. Most everyone could see a stake in this reduction for themselves.[1]

By contrast, President Bush sought to lower capital gains rates, and unhinged the implicit social contract in which lower rates were traded for fewer and/or lower tax preferences, the famous "loopholes" or "gimmicks" that enabled some taxpayers greatly to reduce their burdens. Since Bush's proposal mostly favored the better off, the Democrats were able to raise the rich-versus-poor issue of tax equity. The sanctity of the 1986 agreement having been broken by the president, Democrats could attack the rates themselves, especially the infamous "bubble," which reduced deductions and exemptions so that upper-middle-income people would effectively pay 33 percent at the margin of their incomes, until their overall

[1]An account of this story can be found in White and Wildavsky, *The Deficit and the Public Interest.* For the fuller account, see Jeffrey H. Birnbaum and Alan S. Murray, *Showdown at Gucci Gulch: Lawmakers, Lobbyists, and the Unlikely Triumph of Tax Reform* (New York: Random House, 1987).

rate reached 28 percent. Actual tax rates, therefore, rose through the income brackets from zero to 28 percent. But the very richest people were paying a lower marginal rate (28 percent) than the merely quite comfortable (33 percent) below them. To the tax technician that was treating all income the same; to the politicians that 33 percent "bubble" was very difficult to explain.

There was also new reason for hope that budget balance was within reach. Those who argue against the more excitable that tough issues should be postponed have one thing in their favor; sometimes conditions actually change. The incredibly swift collapse of communism in Eastern Europe and the Soviet Union, together with the latter's widely believed more peaceable intent, opened up possibilities of greater reductions in the defense budget. At the same time, there was less need for the Republican administration to defend as sacrosanct the previous pattern of spending. The election of George Bush as president signified the replacement of a hard-nosed ideologue, Ronald Reagan, with a flexible and more moderate conservative. Bush had a history of conveniently changing his mind; unfortunately, to gain an agreement on deficit reduction, he would have to switch on the major promise of his election campaign and a paramount concern of many of his constituents—his pledge not to raise taxes.

The administration finessed the deficit with optimistic economic assumptions in its 1991 budget. By the spring, those assumptions looked even less plausible. Meanwhile, back in the rarified atmosphere of international negotiations, President Bush had been asking all sorts of leaders of all sorts of countries—China, Japan, Germany—to make sacrifices for the common international good. After a while, they naturally turned to him and said when are you going to deal with your problems, especially the deficit. So the president attempted to show his bonafides by negotiating substantial deficit reduction. As so often in the past decade, a key move was technical. Putting pressure, he hoped, on both Congress and his own administration, Budget Director Richard Darman drastically revised his forecast, predicting a deficit so large as to require a $100 billion Gramm–Rudman sequester, enough to devastate the government. Once Darman did that, the president was committed to the high-risk strategy of a deal or a huge sequester.

Democrats, in turn, insisted that the president publicly rescind his no-tax pledge. After much negotiation, the president's men tried to do so with as little fanfare as possible. Richard Darman wrote a short announcement in which the president agreed to support revenue increases provided they were accompanied by expenditure reductions and reform of the entitlement expenditure processes.

The president's backsliding had immediate political consequences. Even some who liked the policy change attacked the president on moral grounds. His reversal was seen as proof of deceit, and thus brought the political process into exactly the kind of disrepute his actions were designed to protect against.[2]

In consultation with the president and the other important summit figures, Chief of Staff John Sununu, Secretary of the Treasury Nicholas Brady, and Budget Director Darman set the strategy. They proposed extreme budget process reforms, such as an item veto, knowing the Democrats would never accept them, so

---

[2]This paragraph is based on large numbers of news stories in *The New York Times, The Los Angeles Times,* the *Washington Post,* the *Washington Times,* and the *Oakland Tribune.*

the White House could blame Congress if the negotiations collapsed. They also used these proposals as a palliative for their right wing, as a promise that the hated tax increases would not simply give more money to the liberal spenders. The Bush administration's priorities were very different from the Democrats' but, unlike President Reagan and his wing of their party, it did not simply identify the deficit with spending.

The leading members of the Bush administration believed that the deficit was a great blight on the country because it showed that government could not control itself. Responsibility, to them, meant supporting governmental institutions by showing that they worked. Part of their view of the deficit problem, shared by any number of business people and editorialists, was that the American people were consuming too much and producing too little. They bought the economic argument that, other things not intervening too much, a lesser rate of savings would mean a lower rate of investment. If the people's representatives were unwilling to reduce expenditure to the lower level desired by the Bush administration, the people would have to support their government at the level to which it had, for better or worse, become accustomed: with new taxes.

The Republican negotiators also knew that there were other problems of great magnitude just beneath the surface. In addition to increasing national savings, therefore, they wanted to use the deficit problem to avoid a crisis everyone could see coming in the financing of medicare. Their ideal agreement would be one that taxed consumption most heavily, especially consumption of undesirable commodities such as liquor and tobacco. They wanted to charge the elderly more for consumption of health services. In return for the unpalatability of taxes in general, the Bush administration wanted to reduce the taxes on business by cutting capital gains substantially and subsidizing small businesses. Their hope was that a large increase in consumption taxes would pave the way for easier credit, higher exports, and capital spending, and thus not dampen economic activity, a position in accord with that of many economists.

Early on, Ways and Means Committee staff devised a format for the Budget Summit, and CBO and Joint Committee on Taxation staff provided support, so congressional participants could cost out, overnight, any proposals and, for the Democratic party members at least, the distributional consequences of revenue measures among richer, poorer, and middle-class individuals. Quickly, as faxes arrived from Andrews Air Force Base, where the later stages of the Summit were held (to avoid, so they said, the distractions of Washington and to keep the meetings down to size) estimates came back. This was a gain in calculating ability but not necessarily in agreement. Allegations that certain parts of proposed packages were unfair (i.e., inegalitarian) brought heated denials on the Republican side. Nevertheless, equality was an important value from beginning to end, institutionalized, as it was, in Democratic demand and available formulas.

The most obvious decision was the target: How much deficit reduction was enough? Virtually all players agreed that they should focus on a long-term package. Four years of Gramm–Rudman created near-consensus that attention to just one year guarantees fraud.[3] Recall the wonderworking devices: shifting a month's heavy payroll to the previous year or not counting spending after the formal Gramm–Rudman deadline, to make the deficit look technically smaller so as to avoid the ultimate ignominy of sequestration. Nobody wanted to allow such dishonest devices to color their proceedings. Well, mostly not! For the short term, the extreme-moderate view that $100 billion was the only deficit reduction worth making quickly went out the window. Very early on, CBO was asked how much of a hit in higher taxes and lower spending the economy could take in 1991 without going into recession; the organization came up with a ballpark figure that would have been agreed to by most economists, namely, around $50 billion, roughly 1 percent of GNP. If one could achieve this in FY1990 (actually 1991) the total amount of cumulative reduction for the five-year planning period the Summit adopted would be more than five times $50 billion or $250 billion, but there could be some further savings in later years, plus savings on interest payments that otherwise would have been paid to finance the previously anticipated higher deficits. The total was about $450 billion. However, Democrats pushed for a $600 billion total and Republicans for $400 billion. Their agreement in the spring of 1990 on $500 billion, which sounded euphonious at least ("50/500"), helped force Bush's hand.

But what were the participants to do about the midsummer outbreak of aggression as Iraq conquered Kuwait? The price of oil began to skyrocket and the costs of military assistance, which would undoubtedly be large, were incalculable. Aside from lowering the first year's deficit-reduction target from $50 to $40 billion, the conferees, decided to ignore the whole thing. Rather than stultify the enterprise by bringing in a variable that could not be calculated, or artificially raising the military budget for future years, they decided to see what happened and to proceed as if the Persian Gulf weren't there.

Now we come to a subject of great intrinsic interest for budget aficionados: The more detailed the instructions of the Budget Summit, the greater the potential for conflict with congressional committees. If programs were to be grouped, the obvious place to start was with the thirteen appropriations subcommittees and then the authorizing committees with substantial authority over entitlements. But this is exactly what experience shows must be avoided. For one thing, save for the chairs of the full appropriations and tax committees, committee chairs were not at the Summit and would not look kindly on being told what they must do. For another, the negotiators would be more likely to make mistakes the more they engaged the details. For a third, smaller categories left less room for change while still adhering to the deal. Fortunately, David Stockman had originated and CBO had developed for another high-level negotiating enterprise just five categories— taxes, entitlements and mandatory items, offsetting receipts and net interest, national defense, and nondefense discretionary. These were small in number and,

---

[3]Robert W. Hartman, "Budget Summit 1990: The Role of Economic and Budget Analysis," paper prepared for the Association of Schools of Public Policy and Management Research Conference, October 18–20, 1990.

except for defense, did not appear to be concerned with substance, yet matched mechanisms of control (nondefense discretionary and defense, for instance, were annual appropriations, while changes in entitlements and other mandatory programs were covered in the reconciliation process). Moreover, given the ideological policy differences between largely egalitarian Democrats and the economically and socially conservative Republicans, the divide between defense, thought of as taking money otherwise available for welfare payments, and nondefense discretionary, which basically covered what we think of as the entire domestic government outside of entitlements, facilitated large scale negotiations. The Democratic party idea was to cut defense as much as possible while keeping domestic cuts down.

How much would each category contribute to the deal? The easiest category was the savings to be achieved by compounding the interest that otherwise would be necessary to service the high level of debt that would be incurred if there were no deficit reduction. To get $500 billion total, they could expect $70 billion in interest savings and thus need "only" $430 billion from everything else. Next there were discretionary programs, both defense and nondefense. (The reader is reminded that the term "discretionary" means the item is within the annual control of the appropriations committees in Congress while "entitlement" or "mandatory" signifies that the expenditure is required by prior legislation, not that it must last forever or that Congress and the president could not cut or eliminate the program were they so inclined.)

Not usually thought of as the budget-cutting party, the Democratic representatives initially came up with a target of nearly $200 billion in discretionary programs, while the Republicans wanted a lower amount, approximately $160 billion. Both numbers were large by historical standards; both parties were assuming the big cuts in defense made possible by the end of the cold war. The Republicans wanted to do less cutting on defense, so their total was lower.

Rather early it was agreed to split the difference so total discretionary spending would be cut—from the baseline—about $180 billion. But thereby hangs a tale.

Some Republican negotiators wanted cuts in discretionary domestic spending. The Democrats, especially the appropriators, wanted increases. They argued that the domestic sector under the appropriations process had been paying for deficit reduction for years; that vital national needs had been neglected; and that small increases for them were diddly-squat compared to getting a fair contribution from entitlements. In this they had a quiet ally in Budget Director Darman. The administration had lots of initiatives, such as space exploration and other scientific research—all of them discretionary. The appropriators' goal could be viewed as paying for those initiatives (which the committees might otherwise deep-six) by cuts in entitlements. That doesn't sound so bad. Darman told the appropriators he would give them their increases, but in order to avoid flack from his right, they would have to let him manipulate the baseline so it would look as if there were no growth, which he did. In fact, the Summit deal allowed at least a 4 percent and perhaps as much as 6 percent real increase in outlays from FY1991–1993. The bulk of the increase was in FY1992, the first year to be fully debated after the Summit.

The real disagreement was whether the Democrats could try for bigger domestic increases by cutting defense even more. Democrats wanted "caps" for discretionary spending in total; to protect its priorities, the administration wanted separate figures for defense, international affairs, and domestic spending. In the Summit agreement, as well as the final package, they compromised on separate caps for 1990–1992 and combined caps for 1993–1994. The reason for this division was to give whoever won the 1992 presidential election a chance to make changes.

There would be lots of little disputes, but the basic framework on discretionary spending was clear in mid-September: Cuts that would be called $180 billion and were likely to be $10 to $20 billion less. That left the hard cases, entitlements, which Democrats wanted to protect, and taxes, where Republicans hoped to hold down the damage.

What would be a "fair" or "acceptable" outcome? Presumably $125 billion in new taxes and $125 billion in entitlements cuts would split the differences down the middle. Almost. At the last moment the summiteers, reduced to the three main Democratic leaders and the Bush administration, came up with a $134 billion increase in revenues and $119 billion reduction in entitlements.

Here, as everywhere, however, there were technical questions that quickly became strategic. Consider the question of user fees. These fees covered such things as a $25 sticker required on boats (that presumably benefited from Coast Guard services), animal inspection, and a lot more. Negotiators agreed to try to raise some $14 billion in additional revenues from fees. Not easy, but also only part of the story: Where should these revenues be counted? Republicans wanted them counted toward revenues, thus reducing the total hit with relatively noncontroversial items. By contrast, Democrats wanted fees to count toward domestic programs so as to hold down the amount they would have to cut. In the end, fees were counted under "Entitlements and Mandatory," which helped the Democrats but not the Republicans.

Then there were taxes on capital gains. The president had made cutting capital gains a major priority. The Democrats, presenting the bubble as a self-evident example of unfairness (why should the rich be taxed at a lower rate, 28 percent, than the upper-middle class, 33 percent?), responded by proposing to eliminate the bubble through eliminating the fourth marginal tax bracket, so brackets would just go 15/28/33 instead of 15/28/33/28. As the negotiations neared their end, congressional Republicans, namely minority leaders Dole and Michel, decided they would be better off if both issues were taken off the table, and so ended the capital gains fight.

Was there nothing on which both parties agreed? Yes, there was: excise (essentially sales) taxes on tobacco, alcohol, gasoline, and what they considered luxuries. This widespread agreement, however, hid a disagreement: Yes, these excise taxes should be substantially increased, but, the Democrats countered, if poorer and middle-income people paid more of their income proportionately that would have to be offset by hitting richer people harder. In the end, Democrats won a covert increase in income taxes on the better-off in terms of a reduction in allowed itemized deductions (one solution to disagreement is complexity and confusion). But their leaders also accepted a series of subsidies for small-business investment, which Bush could call "growth oriented" tax provisions, but were greeted with scorn by tax professionals.[4]

Therefore, the final deal, agreed to by Speaker Foley and majority leaders Mitchell and Gephardt early on September 30, was, by Democratic lights, regressive. And that quickly became evident as Congress members scanned the distributional tables, conveniently prepared by Ways and Means Committee staff on the basis of calculations provided by CBO and the Joint Committee on Taxation, showing how the income of each fifth of the population would be affected by the total agreement. This calculation included the efforts of generally regressive consumption taxes but did not include the effects of large reductions in defense spending. In the midst of much argument, the tables showed that the top 20 percent of high-income individuals had their taxes increase by 0.9 percent, while the lowest 20 percent had theirs increased by 2 percent. To a budgeteer, such as Robert Hartman of CBO, imagining a conversation with a wavering Congress member, such regressivity was small:

> I'd have to tell my undecided Congressman that he does have to apply a sense of proportion to these numbers. If the average family in the lowest quintile's tax burden could have been reduced by about $60 a year, there would have been no grounds to proclaim this as a regressive change. Is this a sufficient sum to cause you to fall on your sword? (To the sharp Congressman's rebuttal—"OK, then put the $60 in the package and I'll be happy" or "$60 is a lot of money if you don't have it"—I confess to having little to say!)[5]

But many liberals who believed that the time had come for progressive changes were not convinced by such arguments. Nor did they much like the cuts in entitlements.

The one that raised the most anger would have made recipients wait two weeks for unemployment benefits.[6] By far the two largest cuts were $13 billion in farm support and $60 billion in medicare over five years, the reductions being divided between lower fees to hospitals and providers and higher fees and deductibles for medicare recipients. Location of these cuts tells us that budgeters were looking both for big cuts and for programs that were vulnerable for specific reasons (because farm supports were to be negotiated down in international agreements and because medicare was running out of money). So far, so sensible; but how it was done, in the case of medicare, turned out to be crucial.

When the agreed-on deficit-reduction plan was presented in the House of Representatives early in October 1990, the unexpected result—at least unexpected to the Bush administration—was instantaneous and total defeat. Democratic party liberals might have gone along with their leadership—angrily!—providing the Republicans had supplied the necessary minimum, to wit, more than half their mem-

---

[4]Richard Kasten and Frank Sammartino, "Who Pays for Federal Deficit Reduction?" CBO, paper presented at the APPAM research conference, October 18–20, 1990.

[5]Hartman, "Budget Summit 1990 . . . ," p. 15.

[6]It could be justified as inhibiting people going on and off the rolls systematically. Construction workers are accused of doing so; some policy analysts argue that being able to go on unemployment enables them to demand higher wages, which in turn reduces construction activity, all partly subsidized by the government.

bers supporting the package. But the Democrats got lucky. Economically conservative Republicans vehemently rejected the plan. Led by Minority Whip Newt Gingrich of Georgia (who became Speaker of the House in 1995), they felt left out of the whole process, alone and set adrift to face likely defeat in the midterm elections. They had not yet reconciled themselves to the president's abandonment of his no-new-tax pledge. Besides, a lot of Republicans had no more interest than Democrats in a plan that would get $30 billion in medicare savings (around half of the total) from the pockets of the most powerful group in America, the elderly. Their reaction makes it easier to understand that one lawmaker's budget savings may be a lot of citizens' higher spending.

Once Republicans would not provide the minimum level of support, Democrats felt free to vote against the plan as well. Since all concerned recognized that deficit reduction, or at least Gramm–Rudman avoidance, still remained a task to be accomplished, negotiations continued.

Defeat of the Summit agreement was a double disaster for the president. Not only was it embarrassing, it also put him on the defensive in the next round of negotiations. And it put the conservative (mostly House) Republicans on the outside looking in. Consequently, he would have to rely mostly on Democratic votes to get it passed. As a result, the package would be more "Democratic" than the defeated agreement.

On the theories that anything was better than Gramm–Rudman and that some agreement was necessary to show they could govern, Speaker Foley and majority leaders Mitchell and Gephardt had accepted a package far less progressive, particularly due to gasoline taxes, than their troops could buy. When they did so, it made some sense. If the talks broke down, and Democrats had to offer their own plan, it would be progressive—at least by raising the top rate. They could hope voters understood that the increase hit only a very small percentage of households. But class jealousy on taxes rarely works in a vacuum. Middle-class voters think they might be rich themselves one day—or the politicians might tax them next. A Democratic package without the Summit would have given the Republicans a chance to exploit these suspicions, while themselves being vague about alternatives.

Instead, the president went on television to endorse the Summit package, identifying himself with its provisions. Once House Republicans torpedoed the deal, Democrats could sell their package as an alternative to the Summit, particularly to its fuel taxes and medicare costs. That option made more egalitarian taxes a much more attractive proposition. From the moment the Summit package was defeated, the issue was not whether, but how and by how much the next package would be more progressive. When pain is to be distributed, it doesn't pay to go first.

Unfortunately for the Democrats, they could not be sure of support in the Senate, where their own troops were more conservative. Further, they had no more interest than the president in allowing a sequester; if he played chicken, they could not just wait him out. They needed to get home to campaign. Finally, political advantage was in the battle, not the peace treaty. They therefore stretched out the fight as long as they could and, when Bush had taken a heavy pounding for such politically dubious but budgetarily insignificant positions as resisting a surtax on millionaires, settled for a moderately progressive settlement.

THE SUMMIT VERSUS OBRA

At 1 A.M. on October 27, 1990, the staff of The Committee of Conference issued a "Summary of Reconciliation Conference Report" on what was to become the Omnibus Budget Reconciliation Act of 1990. It increased the top rate from 28 to 31 percent, began taxing the top rate at $82,000, and increased the alternative minimum tax rate (what a person pays despite the value of deductions) from 21 to 24 percent. It also increased excise taxes on luxuries. So far, so simple. Then came the complications. Raising the top rate to 31 percent replaced the old 33 percent as well. But that reduced revenue and gave a tax cut to families with incomes in the $80,000 to $150,000 range. So other measures increased income taxes by raising taxable payroll on medicare to $125,000 or phasing out personal exemptions or limiting itemized deductions.

Amidst the revenue-raising measures were others deliberately designed to reduce governmental income in the substantial amount of $27.5 billion. Other revenue-losing propositions, which were hardly known to the general public, such as credits for orphan drugs, added up to over $9 billion. The credits for children were part of an unannounced, children-oriented family policy, as was the credit for health insurance for people of low income, insurance that includes children.

The seemingly straightforward income tax rate increase would bring in only $8.2 billion—partly because for some people it was a cut. That was small compared to the $18.2 billion reduction in allowable deductions, almost equal to the phasing out of benefits in personal exemptions for people of high income, and tiny compared to raising wages taxable for medicare, which weighed in at a hefty $26.9 billion. The moral of the story is to pay attention not only to what is affected but by how much.

There were little, itty-bitty changes, barely noticeable except to those directly involved, and so-called "other changes" that sum to over $24 billion, by altering what was taxable (the unemployment insurance surtax) or who was taxable (extending social security taxes to state and local employees without other pension coverage) or how much was taxable (upping interest rates for late corporate tax payments) or changing the rules (viz. insurance company amortization) so that more income was taxable. Amid a very simple political battle over distribution, tax policy remains as complicated as ever.

"Saving" is a nice term because it fudges the difference between an actual reduction in prior years' outlays and money projected to be spent but that wasn't. This strategy, which Allen Schick calls "Cutting Back and Spending More," is known in the trade as "baseline budgeting." As Schick explains,

> The baseline assumes that existing programs will continue without policy change. It adjusts projected expenditures for estimated inflation and mandated workload changes. A simple example will show how a baseline is constructed and used. A program spending $100 million a year and projected to have an annual 5 percent increase in participants and a 5 percent inflation rate would have approximately a $110 million baseline for the next year, a $121 million baseline for the second year, and a $133 million baseline for the third. . . . Suppose that a . . . program with the spending profile outlined above receives a $105 million appropriation for the next year. Using their "old math," the appropriations committees would record this as a $5 million increase.

When the baseline is used, the same $105 million appropriation is scored as a cutback even though it is above the previous level.[7]

There can be good reasons for baseline budgeting: If inputs do cost more and are related to outputs, as they usually are, the unadjusted figures hide the program impacts of the budget. Put differently, as in Britain, a practice of assuming increases in efficiency, thereby reducing the amount of the budgetary base, places the onus on the spending departments. But baseline adjustments also let the players hide their actions, which disguises increased domestic discretionary spending.[8]

As a consequence of mutual accommodation on budgetary baselines, Schick comments, "Anything goes in federal budgeting these days, as long as it is agreed to by the White House and congressional leaders."[9] In regard to estimating the size of expenditure cuts or additions, Schick believes, honesty requires rules for keeping score that count only reductions in outlays.[10] The basic fault of the baseline approach, Schick says and I agree, is that it concedes what must be fought for if there is to be expenditure control. By giving program advocates protection against inflation, they start from a protected base when it is that base they should have to defend.[11]

The biggest difference from Summit to OBRA was in medicare, for which the Summit's $60 billion saving became $42.46 billion over five years, $32.4 billion in reductions to providers of medical care and $10.7 billion in increases that beneficiaries would have to pay. The differences all came by reducing the Summit's planned charges to beneficiaries.

Congress kept looking for ways to cut without hurting anyone. In medicare they simply added $1.25 billion for mammography screening (which in the long run might save money). Savings on medicaid, which is designed to help people of low incomes afford medical care, comprised $2.9 billion over five years and were made up by getting discounts on pharmaceutical items and by using private insurance where that costs less. Again, it appears that the providers would do the saving, not the beneficiaries. Given the proven ability of providers to shift costs to beneficiaries or to withhold services, however, one could question whether this was a costless saving. There was also an expansion of coverage for the most vulnerable elements in the population—children, the mentally ill, and the frail elderly.

Did Congress write a more equitable set of tax increases than did the Budget Summit? That depends on how you look at it. If you adopt the usual definition of

---

[7]Allen Schick, *The Capacity to Budget* (Washington, D.C.: Urban Institute, 1990), p. 96.

[8]Reality is a little more complicated than this. For discretionary programs, the CBO baseline adjusts only for inflation, so the $105 million would be scored as no gain/no loss from baseline. Liberals can argue that more participants mean a real cut. Conservatives can say $105 million is bigger than $100 million.

[9]Ibid., p. 204.

[10]Ibid.

[11]Ibid., p. 210. For a more substantial discussion of just this point under earlier British circumstances, see Hugh Heclo and Aaron Wildavsky, *The Private Government of Public Money*, 2nd ed. (New York: Macmillan, 1981). See especially "The Politics of Projection or Rashomon Revisited," pp. 216–26.

Table 6.1   PROPOSED SPENDING CUTS BASED ON FOUR PLANS*

	Summit	Senate	House Democrats	Compromise
Medicare				
Cost to beneficiaries	$ 27.8	$ 17.1	$ 10.0	$ 10.0
Cost to providers	32.2	32.1	33.0	33.0
Total Medicare Savings	60.0	49.2	43.0	43.0
Agriculture Savings	13.0	15.1	16.3	13.4
Medicaid Savings	1.6	0.9	0.3	—
Military Savings	$182.4	$182.4	$182.4	$182.4

*Amounts are in billions of dollars for cuts over a five-year period beginning October 1, 1990.

Source: Adapted from The New York Times, October 26, 1990, p. A10.

progressive taxation in which individuals with higher income have to pay not only larger absolute amounts, which they would anyway, but a larger proportion of their income, then the Omnibus Budget Reconciliation Act of 1990 (OBRA) was far more progressive. But if you focus not on who pays proportionately more or less of their income but rather on who pays what proportion of total taxes paid, then you come to a diametrically different conclusion.

As the House Budget Committee explained it to House Democrats:

When *all* tax changes are considered, the increases for the middle class are less than 2½ percent, while the average increase for those with over $200,00 incomes is about 6 percent. The poor are shielded from tax increases by expanding the earned-income and other tax credits; on average, their taxes are reduced.[12]

Conservatives claimed this calculation was unfair because the rich were already paying a larger share of the total tax take than they had in 1981. This was true but their share of the income had increased even more. Which is it, then, paying a larger share of total taxes or a smaller share of income that was more just? The two sides differ not only on how much each income class should pay but also about which criterion to apply.

Table 6.1, adapted from a chart by *The New York Times*, contrasts spending cuts from four plans—the Summit, the Senate, and House (with its big Democratic majority), and the compromise (OBRA) that became law. The largest by far was medicare. The Summit wanted $60 billion shared between providers and beneficiaries with providers paying somewhat more. The Senate reduced that by $10 billion while creating the opposite disparity in which providers pay the bulk of the cost. House Democrats cut $6 billion from the size of the total plan while making the cost to providers more than three times larger than that of the beneficiaries, whereas in the Senate plan the difference had been somewhat less than two to one. And the House won. In short, with each stage in the development of OBRA there was stronger egalitarian sentiment. But would the agreement hold? Enter the Budget Enforcement Act (BEA) of 1990, Title XIII of OBRA.

---

[12]U.S. House of Representatives, Committee on the Budget, "Fiscal Year 1991 Budget Agreement Summary Materials," October 27, 1990, p. 24.

THE BUDGET ENFORCEMENT ACT OF 1990

Before new procedures can take place, it is necessary to do something about the old way. The first thing done by the BEA, therefore, was to raise the fiscal year 1991 GRH deficit target (actual 1990) way up to $327 billion (and these figures were adjusted upward in fiscal 1991 by the Bush administration, as the law allows). Why were these targets so large? The short answer is (a) recession, (b) the savings and loan bailout, and (c) surpluses in the social security trust funds would no longer count toward reducing the deficit. That recessions increase deficits by lowering revenues and increasing spending we know, but why do something voluntarily to make the deficit look much larger?

Proponents of balance believe that Congress and the president (the politicians) will not do enough unless they feel threatened. The larger the deficit, presumably, the greater the threat. This antipolitician sentiment also explains why they refuse to publicize the deficit in terms of proportions of GNP but insist on absolute numbers. Some $200+ billion is enough to frighten anyone, whereas under 3 percent of GNP sounds (and, in my opinion, is) a modest amount. The politicians also wanted to reassure retirees that social security was safe from budget cuts.

As a matter of economics, there are two currently popular ways to analyze the budget. The first economic approach emphasizes aggregate demand. By borrowing and spending the proceeds, the government increases demand for goods, thereby raising employment (good) or prices (bad). The second approach emphasizes savings: Government borrowing reduces total national savings, leaving less money to be invested; if we borrowed less we could invest more, the theory is, and hence the economy would grow more.

Neither approach would count the savings and loan bailout, which would supposedly cost more than $100 billion in 1991.[13] The bailout, much as we may resent it, is necessary to preserve our financial system. Not spending the money would hardly increase savings, because bank failures don't increase investment. Spending the money doesn't increase demand; instead it preserves the values people already have in their accounts. The S&L bailout, prayerfully, is a one-time thing. According to figures in the FY 1996 budget, deposit insurance cost $2.4 billion in 1992, $28 billion in 1993, and $7.6 billion in 1994.[14] Usual accounting practice, as followed in regard to sending forces into the Persian Gulf, is to keep these off-budget. Since money is to be returned in part to the federal government in later years, deficits would be artificially diminished in return for making deficits artificially larger in the first few years. Why was this done?

Over the next five years, it was estimated that social security would spend $1.5 trillion and collect $300 billion in surplus taxes. Demand managers say the social security surplus has an immediate economic effect, and should not be ignored. Those who focus on savings, however, want to increase the social security surplus. They say we should treat the surplus not as income this year, but as savings for later social security expenses, when the baby-boom generation retires.

---

[13]House Budget Committee Summary, October 27, 1990, p. 52.

[14]*United States Budget FY 1996*, Analytical Perspectives, Table 1.6: Adjusted Structural Deficit, p. 7.

If Congress and the president had adopted the demand managers' perspective, they would have kept savings and loans out and social security surpluses in the totals. Then, even with a more plausible (lower) economic forecast, the deficit would fall to around 1 percent of GNP, comparable to that of Germany or Japan, by 1994. It would indeed balance by 1996 if not before. But they adopted the savers' perspective on social security, taking its surpluses out, while keeping the S&L bailout in the deficit calculation. The S&L costs ballooned immediate deficits, on top of which the social security decision raised the 1994 deficit by $87 billion.[15] At baseball games, the hawkers say you can't tell the players without a scorecard. How much more true this is for the deficit!

This paroxysm of accounting "responsibility" created two problems. First, opponents of removing social security from the deficit feared that it would create an inviting target for those who wish to appropriate social security surpluses for their own preferred policy purposes. The House and Senate, therefore, adopted an array of provisions to try to prevent such raids.

As things worked out the S&L costs became relatively small and their impact on the deficit was slight. As for the social security issue, Allen Schick comments:

> Because social security is so large, excluding it from the deficit impairs the budget's utility as a measure of fiscal impact. How can the budget impact on the economy be assessed when one-fifth of the government's revenues and outlays are excluded? In fact, social security is almost always included in both government and news references to the budget. By law, social security is excluded; in practice, it is included.[16]

More important, they had to find some way around the optimistic economic forecast, which they had adopted to make up for their social security scorekeeping but which, by not coming true, would put them right back in sequester land. For both Bush and congressional leaders, 1990's pain would be worthless if it did not at least result in peace through the 1992 election.

Therefore the president was legally required to alter the hoped-for deficit target each year in order to account for changes in the economy, changes in budgetary terms, and changes in estimates of the cost of federal credit programs. That is, the deficit reduction targets were not really targets—thereby abolishing, at least for 1990–1992, the deficit sequester.

In reality, the old Gramm–Rudman sequester, designed to force action to reduce the deficit, was replaced by two much more sensible sequesters designed (a) to keep Congress from increasing the deficit, thereby enforcing the new package, and (b) to maintain the status quo by making proposers pay for spending increases and revenue decreases. Separate limits were set out for budget authority and outlays for discretionary, defense, the international arena, and for domestic purposes for the years between 1990 and 1992, after which these merged to a single category called total discretionary spending. Should expenditures within the relevant category be deemed, after the end of session, to exceed their target, the accounts

---

[15]These comments are adapted from Joseph White, "Better News Than They Think," published in the *San Diego Union* on October 7, 1990.

[16]Allen Schick, *The Federal Budget: Politics, Policy, Process,* (Washington, D.C.: Brookings Institution, 1995), p. 28.

for that category in the following fiscal year would be reduced across-the-board to make up the difference. There were further complications, but that was the basic idea: The offending category pays the fine.

The second new sequester applied to decreases in revenue or increases in entitlement expenditure enacted into law. This PAYASYOUGO sequestration had to occur within fifteen calendar days of congressional adjournment and on the same day as enforcement of limits on discretionary spending and overall deficit targets. Thus there was one sequestration for deficit targets, another for discretionary spending, and a third for new entitlement spending or revenue reduction. All of these provisions were further buttressed by elaborating on previous Gramm–Rudman points of order, designed to prevent offending legislation from being passed in the first place. It should also be noted that the entitlement sequester followed the GRH pattern in that the exemptions from sequestration for poor people's programs were still in place. The "cap" on medicare reductions, however, was raised from 2 percent to 4 percent.

As part of a long process of change, the Budget Enforcement Act contained provisions on federal credit reform. It not only called on the federal government to state the cost of loans and loan guarantees but required that, except for entitlements and the credit programs of agricultural price supports, there had to be appropriations to cover outlays defined as "the long-term costs . . . on the net present value basis. . . ."[17] This required calculating the cost to the federal government of borrowing to acquire the funds that were being lent in guaranteed loans in relation to the amount the borrower pays back. This is a positive and important change.[18]

Government sponsored enterprises (GSEs), which are established by the federal government but operated and owned by private individuals, have long been the object of suspicion. Such entities include the Federal Home Loan Bank system, the Student Loan Marketing Association, the Farm Credit System, the Federal National Mortgage Association, and the Federal Home Loan Mortgage Corporation. By the end of April 1991, the Treasury Department and CBO were required to report to Congress on the GSEs' financial soundness. The savings and loan debacle had made everyone more cautious, thus giving force to concern over the last several decades about the exposure of federal finances to failures of GSEs. The BEA required reports on GSEs and federal credit activities in the president's budget.

These substantial changes in the budgetary process, partially eliminating but mostly adding new procedures on top of old, as has become customary, were the product of experience under GRH. This experience had made its impact on observers as well as on members of the executive and legislative branches. Believing that general sequesters do not work, both because these tend to be too large and because the penalty does not fit the crime, they had made them more numerous, more precise, and more responsible.

---

[17]Joseph White, "Better News Than They Think," p. 8.

[18]In the general spirit of protecting the appropriators from things they don't control, the discretionary targets are "held harmless" by being adjusted for the calculations that will be made to translate previous loan levels into BA levels for fiscal 1994–1995.

The BEA restored budgeting's long-term focus and substituted real policy change for Gramm–Rudman's hostage game. It used, rather than fought against, our political system's designed difficulty of action. It tried to limit scorekeeping games, and extended oversight to areas such as credit and GSEs.

What the BEA did not do is prevent the economy from destabilizing the budget. Entitlement spending that rises because of changes in the economy, or because of aging of the population or other demographic reasons, or for anything and everything outside of legislative enactment was not covered. Subjecting any change in entitlements to PAYASYOUGO principles would be much more powerful. But this would mean that entitlements would not be total entitlements but only quasi-entitlements, in that full payment could not be guaranteed. And it might be economically perverse. On the one hand, new benefits would be more difficult to establish; on the other hand, the growth of costs under existing guidelines would not be touched at all. And there you have the essential compromise.

On the political level there was not so much compromise as unspoken agreement to resolve the main charge against all politicians—that they cannot govern because they cannot balance the budget—in the two ways intractable problems are usually solved: (1) by doing something about them, that is, reducing the deficit and (2) by redefining them so they become solvable. Essentially the politicians moved away from a deficit reduction enforcement process to a spending control enforcement process. Inasmuch as objectives may be inferred from legislation, the goal of the budgetary process was to keep spending down to current policy, liberally defined, rather than to specific dollar limits. OBRA switched from deficit to expenditure control.

Perhaps the BEA should be called the revenge of the appropriators. It gave them at least in the short term fairly generous spending caps, and protected these against all comers, whether external (e.g., the economy) or internal (e.g., direct spending). As much of the budget total as possible was put under preset, automatic controls. Like the economic stabilizers that kick in when unemployment grows large, these protections for appropriations were designed to create lulls in the budget battles so that the appropriators would not have to refight the same battles over and over and over again. The onus was against changing priorities by saying so through direct legislation.

Other informed observers expressed amazement that a Democratic Congress allowed OMB to gain so much power over the budget by deciding such seemingly arcane but vital matters as what item of expenditure fitted under which spending cap, or how much program costs had risen due to factors out of Congress's control.[19] As we know, this power was granted because it is essential to budgetary control and the courts have ruled that only an executive agency can perform this function. And the Democratic budget professionals were not, in private, concerned.[20]

Both the House and Senate Budget Committees issued long descriptions and analyses of the process changes. The rules had changed so much and so often that

[19]Susan F. Rasky, "Substantial Power on Spending Is Shifted from Congress to Bush," *The New York Times,* National Edition, October 30, 1990, pp. 1A, 13.

[20]Joe White, conversations with Appropriations, Ways and Means, and Budget staff.

making them had become part of budgeting. To get the feeling, here is one such process change.

> *Estimating adjustments.* There is a very small BA allowance and a larger outlay al-
> lowance provided on an "as used" basis. They differ from the other "as used" adjust-
> ments in that they are not intended to be used under congressional scorekeeping. . . .
> Imagine that appropriation bills meet their caps using congressional scorekeeping but
> breach them using OMB scorekeeping; if the breach is within the allowance, there
> would be no sequester.[21]

Technicalities include a series of "estimating adjustments" to bridge the inevitable small differences between congressional and OMB scorekeeping. Note also that while Senate and House do not follow precisely the same rules, the thrust of the major proposals in the BEA, especially the three sequesters, was expected to compel similar behavior.

THE PARTS VERSUS THE WHOLE

Through the thicket of budget provisions, piled helter-skelter atop one another, there comes the recognizable outline of disputes that have pitted institutions in the budgetary process against each other as far back as anyone can remember. If one were to ask the members and chairs of the House and Senate appropriations committees how they felt about their part in the budgetary process, they would undoubtedly answer "Hard done by." Why? Because, they would reply in classical tones, their authority was not commensurate with their responsibility, especially because presidents had gone too far away to share responsibility and budget committees had come too close for the appropriators to exercise what they felt is their rightful autonomy, the budgetary process had come into deserved disrepute. In the classical process of the 1950s and earlier decades, presidents submitted budgets that accorded with their policy preferences, adding a gaming factor to allow the House Appropriations Committee, through its subcommittees, to cut at the margins, knowing full well the Senate Appropriations Committee would act as an appeals court, making selective additions so that in the end almost all the players got most of what they wanted. That is, the appropriators were second-guessers, marking up or down the bids proposed by the president and the authorizing committees. However, this budget minuet depended on the participants being close enough to begin with so they could play their appointed roles: There cannot be a second guess without a first.

In an age of budgetary dissensus, by contrast, presidents have maintained responsibility to their party and their own preferences but have behaved irresponsibly, as appropriators in both parties see it, by presenting budgets so far from what is likely to pass muster in Congress that they are pronounced (as we know) dead on arrival. Understanding as well the sense of the medieval dictum that one prince

---

[21]Richard Kogan, "The Budget Enforcement Act of 1990: A Technical Explanation," November 1, 1990, typescript, pp. 6–7. Senate Budget's typescript on the "Budget Enforcement Act of 1990" is supplemented by CRS Report 90-520 GOV: "Budget Enforcement Act of 1990: Brief Summary," by Edward Davis and Robert Keith, November 5, 1990.

nearby is worse than many princes far away, the appropriators have not taken kindly to the efforts of budget committees to control their operations. Members of appropriations committees would rather be constrained, if they must, by a president concerned mostly with the size of spending than by many representatives and senators with detailed changes they wish to enforce. Little as the appropriators liked to observe the outlays of entitlement programs grow ever larger ("Look ma, no hands!"), they liked even less being told by budget committees through reconciliation orders (yes, instructions are orders) that they must make up for entitlements out of control by cutting their own appropriations authority far more than they thought desirable. Nor were the appropriators enthralled to observe deeply divisive ideological debates over budget resolutions, which may have sounded fine to those who like abstract discussions, but which, in their view, brought Congress into disrepute by forbidding the bargains and compromises that might have added up to the appearance of responsible budgeting.

The BEA tried to change all of this. While it could not create ideological and policy agreement where it did not exist, it did take away the necessity of making believe there is such agreement, thereby demonstrating once more that Congress is not what it was never supposed to be, a unified body. To begin with, presidents were now required to submit a budget within the ball park of existing past agreements as memorialized in multiyear instructions about levels of taxing and spending. Therefore, for the subsequent five years the appropriators could look forward to the ancient pleasure of working off presidential budgets, marking them up here, marking them down there, as they used to do in what they think of as better days. Moreover, the appropriators succeeded in getting an additional $37 billion to spread around their part of the budget so as to lubricate the joints and ease the pain of making adjustments as they were wont to do in days of old. Nor could budget committees tell appropriators what to do. For one thing, the appropriators themselves had worked out agreements on what they are supposed to do, thus usurping the place taken in the bad old days by budget resolutions. For another, problems that arise from shortfalls in revenue or overages in entitlements would be dealt with where they occurred; only where appropriations themselves departed from agreed-on guidelines would there be points of order and sequestration provisions to restrain them by passing out the pain within their bailiwick, a principle they could accept provided it is accepted by others. Oh yes, this nonsense about meeting some artificial deficit target regardless of whether the world is at war or at peace and the economy is booming or busting has been done away with. In the future, the appropriators devoutly hoped, each part of the process would be held responsible for what it does or does not do and the rest of the world will have to take care of itself.

In order to make them play their assigned parts, presidents, through the OMB, were given stronger procedural powers. It is they who must submit a certain kind of budget according to their own calculations; who must alter their budget proposals according to the state of the economy; and whose findings must or must not trigger sequestrations of various kinds. This is a lot of procedural clout. It could be that some far-seeing budget director will attempt to use these procedural powers to bargain with the appropriations committees at every stage of the process, not just the stage of formulating the budget or of certifying sequestration. But Congress has the means, namely, the power of the purse, to compel OMB and through it the president to back down. In following the thrust and maneuver of budgeting, it is all too easy to imagine that skill is all (or most) that matters. Skill counts but votes count more, especially in an age of ideological dissensus. That is why OBRA and not the Budget Summit is now the law of the land.

The BEA also relieved the president and Congress of the necessity of responding to external events that cause downward perturbations in revenue or upward alterations in expenditure, thus bringing the budget way out of balance. Held more tightly responsible for the effects they cause directly, the appropriators were relieved from responsibility for what they could not help immediately. If we assume that the balance of political responsibility has been shifted too far toward government and not enough toward the citizenry, holding government harmless is a good idea. If we think that government should bear its burden of the cost of change, or that everyone has to deal with forces they cannot control, then these hold-harmless provisions are a bad idea.

THE BUDGET EQUATION AND THE CLINTON BUDGET OF 1993

The BEA provided the terms of reference for the first half of the 1990s. The discretionary spending caps and the mandatory PAYGO provisions were adhered to and set out the variables of an accepted budget equation derived from the five categories used in negotiating the 1990 budget summit (see p. 139). It was composed of a number of dynamic and continually augmenting relationships, which governed the budget discourse. Each budget represented a renegotiation of those relationships, whose changes were measured against the baselines of what would otherwise have happened. Anyone wishing to influence the course of the budget had to take account of the balances between the budget and the economy, between revenues and expenditures, between mandatory and discretionary spending, between defense and domestic discretionary spending, and among the categories of domestic discretionary spending.

These balances were not static: They adjusted over time both gradually and sometimes more abruptly. Adjustments were limited by the provisions of the Budget Enforcement Act; shifting party and coalition relationships in and outside Congress; and the accumulated commitments represented in the budget. The outlines of the equation were also blurred and uncertain, because budgets deal less with the present than the future, with the playing out of the implications of current policies in a world of shifting economic forecasts and assessments, and disputed assumptions or methods of calculation. The first budget of President Clinton in 1993 exemplifies the constraints and possibilities of the budget equation.

The election of Bill Clinton in 1992 meant that both executive and legislature were in Democratic hands. It might be thought that since a Democratic president was working with a Democratic majority in Congress, there would no longer be an adversarial relationship, and the president would be able to count on support for his choices. Not so. The Democratic party is by no means cohesive. It is split between those who hold to a fiscally conservative philosophy, whose primary agenda is to cut spending to bring down the deficit, and those supporting a socially liberal philosophy to roll back the Reagan revolution and increase public spending to deal with the country's social ills.[22] Even within this group there is a split between "old style" Democrats, primarily concerned with social equity, and "new " Democrats, who put priority on a stronger economy, greater efficiency, and reform of public programs. In addition, members of Congress have their own interests stemming from their constituencies, running the gamut from the unabashed pork of public works projects to protection and promotion of state and local economies.

Support for the president, even by his own party, is by no means automatic, especially as his own relationship to the electorate is not a strong one. He won the election with only 43 percent of the vote, not in itself such a weak position. But one reason for his victory was the split vote between his Republican opponent, Bush, and the maverick independent Perot, who had gained 19 percent of the vote. It appears any future election victory might depend on garnering at least some proportion of those voters—a group disillusioned with politics as usual, fixated on the deficit, and hostile to government. Superimposed on these concerns is Clinton's own agenda which includes an industrial policy of sorts, scientific and educational investment, and health care reform.

The first problem is the first balance in the budget equation—between the budget and the economy, expressed in fiscal policy. Whereas once, fiscal policy, implemented through annual decisions on taxation and expenditures was seen as guiding the economy, emphasis is now on the impact of the economy on the budget.[23] The summit year of 1990 was also the beginning of a period of slow real economic growth. By mid-1991 the economy was in the trough of a recession, from which recovery was slow and uncertain. At the beginning of 1993, CBO was predicting the beginning of a period of "self-sustained growth," but noted that the rate of expansion appeared sluggish, making "the normal fits and starts of the growth process seem more daunting than usual."[24]

Today's budgets are extraordinarily sensitive to economic trends and fluctuations. The introduction to every budget has a section on "Sensitivity of the Budget" which documents the effects of changes in assumptions key economic indicators—unemployment, inflation, interest rates—on the budget. Allen Schick has commented "The president and Congress are thus hostage to the performance of the economy."[25] The effect of the recession of the early 1990s was to disrupt the predictions of the 1990 agreement, as the half a trillion or so of expected deficit reduction evaporated in unprecedented deficits.

[22]John Brummett, *Highwire: The Education of Bill Clinton* (New York: Hyperion, 1994), pp. 92–93.

[23]See Congressional Budget Office, *The Economic and Budget Outlook: Fiscal Years 1993–1997*, January 1992, p. xii; Congressional Budget Office, *The Economic and Budget Outlook: Fiscal Years 1994–1998*, January 1993, p. xiii; Congressional Budget Office, *The Economic and Budget Outlook: Fiscal Years 1995–1999*, p. xiii; Congressional Budget Office, *The Economic and Budget Outlook: Fiscal Years 1996–2000*, p. xi.

[24]Congressional Budget Office, *Economic and Budget Outlook, Fiscal Years 1994–1998*, January 1993, p. 1.

[25]Schick, *The Federal Budget*, p. 25.

Table 6.2   CONGRESSIONAL BUDGET OFFICE DEFICIT PROJECTIONS

					(in billions of dollars)						
	1990	1991	1992	1993	1994	1995	1996	1997	1998	1999	2000
January 1992	220	269	352	327	260	194	178	226			
Summer 1992				331	268	244	254	290			
January 1993		270	290	310	291	284	287	319	357		
September 1993					253	196	190	198	200		
January 1994			290	255	223	171	166	182	180	204	
August 1994					202	162	176	193	197	231	
January 1995					203	176	207	224	222	253	
April 1995						177	211	232	231	256	276

Source: Congressional Budget Office, *The Economic and Budget Outlook*, 1992 to 1995, and Update for April 1995. The actual deficit for FY1995 was later assessed at $164 billion.

On taking office President Clinton was keen to rekindle economic growth, as a necessity to achieve his agenda for human investment. He therefore proposed as a supplementary to the FY 1993 budget an economic stimulus package. But the package was defeated in Congress. The prospect of huge deficits could not be ignored. In January 1993, CBO was predicting a current year deficit of $310 billion and the administration forecast was even higher (see Table 6.2). The second balance in the budget equation—between revenues and expenditures—had to take priority.

A gap between revenues and expenditures may be filled either by increasing revenues or cutting expenditures, or both. Revenues cannot be expected to rise sufficiently to meet the expenditure levels of the 1990s due to the cyclical adjustments in the economy. Clinton inherited a structural gap dating back to the beginning of the 1980s and the Reagan cut in taxes and increase in defense expenditures. According to both Schick and Wildavsky, however, these decisions reflect a generally observed norm in United States politics that keeps tax revenues down to below 19 percent of GDP.[26] (See Table 6.3.) What was the president to do?

The budget had not been a central element in his campaign, which had emphasized change, political reform, economic growth and job creation, investment in human resources, and health care reform.[27] In his State of the Union address, Clinton declared there was nothing intrinsically good about deficit reduction alone, though it was necessary to reverse the trend toward a government which was unable to act because the burden of debt servicing prevented development of programs to help people. But he could not ignore the deficit. As Allen Schick explains

> With the budget awash in red ink, Clinton was barred by both the politics and the rules of budgeting from proposing actions that would add to the deficit. It was not tenable for him to insist that coveted initiatives be funded despite the budget's dire condi-

---

[26]Ibid., p. 4.

[27]*Congressional Quarterly Weekly Reports*, November 14, 1992, p. 3631.

Table 6.3   THE GAP BETWEEN REVENUES AND EXPENDITURES, 1985–2000

	Receipts	Percentage GDP	Outlays	Percentage GDP	Deficit	Percentage GDP
		(in billions of dollars)				
1985	734.1	18.5	946.4	23.9	212.3	5.4
1990	1,031.3	18.8	1,252.7	22.9	221.4	4.0
1991	1,054.3	18.6	1,323.4	23.3	269.2	4.7
1992	1,090.5	18.4	1,380.9	23.3	290.4	4.9
1993	1,153.5	18.4	1,408.7	22.5	255.1	4.1
1994	1,257.7	19.0	1,460.9	22.0	203.2	3.1
1995 (est.)	1,346.4	19.2	1,538.9	21.9	192.5	2.7
2000 (est.)	1,710.9	18.6	1,905.3	20.7	194.4	2.1

Source: United Stated Budget, FY1996, Historical Tables: Table 1.4, *Receipts, Outlays and Surpluses or Deficits by Fund Group, 1934–2000*, pp. 19–20. Numbers have been rounded.

tion. Nor could he wish away the deficit the way Ronald Reagan did—with rosy economic forecasts that overestimated future revenue and underestimated the program cuts or tax increases needed to close the budget gap. . . .

He could not risk discrediting his new administration by pretending that the deficit would go away by itself. And he could not assume that journalists who had become increasingly skeptical about budget promises and more knowledgeable about the budget's arithmetic than they had been when Reagan came to Washington, would ignore bad news.[28]

The immediate outlook for the deficit was gloomy. For FY 1992 the deficit had set a record at $290 billion, although this was far below the January 1992 projections of the Bush administration ($400 billion) and CBO ($357 billion). On going out of office Bush had predicted a deficit of $327 billion for FY 1993, and while CBO's estimate was less at $310 billion, the figure was still daunting. For FY 1994, CBO estimated only a slight fall, to $291 billion, and believed that forecast improvements in the economy would reduce this figure only marginally.[29]

Clinton responded first by trying to raise revenues. Top tax rates (for couples with gross adjusted incomes over $140, and individuals over $115,000 a year) would rise from 31 percent to 36 percent. Incomes over $250,000 would pay a 10 percent surcharge. There were also increases in corporate taxes and increased taxes on high income social security recipients. According to Allen Schick, increased taxes on business and high income recipients would account for more than five-sixths of additional revenues sought by the president, whose election campaign had ruled out increased taxes for the middle classes.[30] Taken together, these tax increases would amount to $185 billion in deficit reduction for the next five years. In addition, the president proposed a broad based energy tax (BTU),

---

[28]Schick, *The Federal Budget,* p. 3.

[29]Congressional Budget Office, January 1993.

[30]Schick, *The Federal Budget,* p. 6.

Table 6.4   DISCRETIONARY AND MANDATORY EXPENDITURES, 1985–2000

	(in billions of dollars)					
	Discretionary			Mandatory		
	Total Outlays	Percentage Budget	Percentage GDP	Total Outlays	Percentage Budget	Percentage GDP
1985	416.2	44.0	10.5	433.4	45.8	10.9
1990	501.7	40.1	9.2	603.5	48.2	11.0
1991	534.8	40.4	9.4	633.5	47.9	11.2
1992	535.9	38.8	9.1	684.8	49.6	11.6
1993	542.5	38.5	8.7	704.8	50.0	11.3
1994	545.6	37.3	8.2	750.2	51.3	11.3
1995 (est.)	553.8	36.0	7.9	792.2	51.5	11.3
2000 (est.)	549.6	28.8	6.0	1,085.9	57.0	11.8

Source: United States Budget, FY1996, Historical Tables: Table 8.1, *Outlays by Budget Enforcement Act Category, 1962–2000*, p. 95; Table 8.3, *Percentage Distribution of Outlays by Budget Enforcement Act Category, 1962–2000*; and Table 8.4, *Outlays by Budget Enforcement Act Category as Percentages of GDP, 1962–2000*, p. 98.

initially estimated to bring in $80.6 billion.[31] But to bring down the budget deficit from an estimated 4.1 percent of GDP in FY 1993 to about 3.2 percent in FY 1998, against a baseline taking into account inflation and expected growth in entitlements, would require $447 billion in deficit reduction. Leaving aside assumptions about the behavior of the economy (balance 1) it would be necessary to make adjustments in the other balances of the budgetary equation.

The BEA had divided expenditures into discretionary and mandatory. Discretionary expenditures were subject to caps, but if there were no new policy initiatives mandatory spending could increase without constraint. And increase it had, shifting the third balance between mandatory and discretionary spending.

In 1985, mandatory and discretionary spending were almost even as proportions of the federal budget (see Table 6.4). By 1990, mandatory programs had drawn ahead, representing over 48 percent of the budget against the discretionary spending share of just over 40 percent. By 1993, mandatory spending took up half the budget, while discretionary spending had dropped to 38.5 percent. The trend was unmistakable: By the year 2000, it was estimated that entitlements would take up 57 percent of the budget, while discretionary expenditures would be less than 29 percent. Entitlements, it seemed, were eating up the budget.

Why were entitlement programs growing so rapidly? The fastest growth was occurring in three of the largest programs: social security, medicare, and medicaid (see Table 6.5). Between 1985 and 1993, social security grew from about $186 billion to $302 billion. In the same period, medicare doubled and medicaid more than tripled.[32] When Bill Clinton took office, he was facing, according to CBO

---

[31]Karl O'Lessker, "The Clinton Budget for FY 1994: Taking Aim at the Deficit," *Public Budgeting and Finance*, Vol. 13, no. 2, Summer 1993, p. 13.

[32]Congressional Budget Office, January 1993, Table 8.3, *Outlays for Mandatory and Related Programs 1962–2000*, pp. 102–3.

Table 6.5   FASTEST GROWING MANDATORY EXPENDITURES, 1985–2000

		(in billions of dollars)			
	Social Security	Medicare	Medicaid	Income Security	Veterans
1985	186.4	64.1	22.7	109.1	15.9
1990	246.5	95.8	41.1	123.6	15.9
1991	266.8	102.0	52.5	144.6	17.3
1992	285.2	116.2	67.8	168.8	18.5
1993	302.0	127.8	75.8	176.0	19.3
1994	316.9	141.8	82.0	178.4	20.3
1995 (est.)	333.7	154.4	88.4	183.9	20.2
2000 (est.)	430.7	174.7	136.5	239.9	24.0

Source: United Stated Budget, FY1996, Historical Tables: Table 8.5, *Outlays for Mandatory and Related Programs, 1962–2000,* pp. 99–103.

baselines, mandatory outlays of $816 billion, of which $319 were for social security, $167 billion for medicare, and $92 billion for medicaid.[33] In the medium term baseline budget projections, these figures swelled to a total of over $1 trillion, of which social security would be $385 billion, medicare $259 billion, and medicaid $146 billion. To accommodate such expenditures, even while keeping discretionary expenditures below the caps, would result in a deficit of nearly $300 billion in FY 1994, which would increase to over $350 billion in 1998.

The Clinton budget for FY 1994 lowered the mandatory portion of the budget through both revenue and expenditure measures. By repealing the medicare tax cap and increasing the taxable portion of social security benefits, he gained nearly $45 billion in deficit reduction; reductions in medicare growth would amount to nearly $56 billion, and in other entitlements to a further $35 or so billion. Altogether the mandatory portion of the budget would have yielded $136 billion or nearly one third of the deficit reduction over five years.

Discretionary expenditures continued to be constrained within the BEA caps (see Table 6.6). For the first three years, there were separate caps for defense, international, and discretionary expenditures. These caps were adhered to, although some adjustments were made in accordance with the provisions of the BEA.[34] In 1993, the three caps were replaced by a single cap on discretionary expenditures and were extended a further three years (from 1995 to 1998). The caps affected the fourth balance between defense and domestic discretionary expenditures.

By 1990, total discretionary expenditures were just over $500 billion, representing about 40 percent of total outlays. The outlay cap for 1991 had been set at about $514 billion (later adjusted for Operation Desert Storm to about $552 billion). At this time defense expenditures stood at just over $300 billion and domestic discretionary at $183 billion. Defense expenditures made up 24 percent of the

---

[33]Ibid., pp. 46, 49.

[34]See Dale Oak, "An Overview of Adjustments to the Budget Enforcement Act Discretionary Spending Caps, *Public Budgeting and Finance,* Vol. 15 (Fall 1995), pp. 35–37, for an overview of the caps and explanation of the adjustment provisions.

Table 6.6 DISCRETIONARY SPENDING LIMITS AS ORIGINALLY ENACTED

		(in millions of dollars)							
		Budget Enforcement Act of 1990					Omnibus Budget Reconciliation Act of 1993		
		Fiscal Year							
		1991	1992	1993	1994	1995	1996	1997	1998
Total discretionary	BA	491,718	503,443	511,485	510,800	517,700	519,142	528,079	530,639
	Outlays	514,360	524,944	533,986	534,800	540,800	547,263	547,346	547,870
Discretionary categories									
Domestic	BA	182,700	191,300	198,300					
	Outlays	198,100	210,100	221,700					
International	BA	20,100	20,500	21,400					
	Outlays	18,600	19,100	19,600					
Defense	BA	288,918	291,643	291,785					
	Outlays	297,660	295,744	292,686					

Sources: Section 13111 of the Budget Enforcement Act of 1990, and section 12(b)(1) of House Concurrent Resolution 64 (One Hundred Third Congress). Reproduced in Dale P. Oak, *An Overview of Adjustment to the Budget Enforcement Act Discretionary Spending Caps, Public Budgeting and Finance*, Vol. 15, Summer 1995, pp. 35–37.

Table 6.7   OUTLAYS FOR DISCRETIONARY PROGRAMS, 1985–2000

| | (in billions of dollars) | | | | | |
| | Defense | | International | | Domestic | |
	Current	Constant	Current	Constant	Current	Constant
1985	253.1	261.5	17.4	18.2	145.7	154.1
1990	300.1	273.3	19.1	16.9	182.5	161.8
1991	319.7	281.4	19.7	16.8	195.4	166.2
1992	302.6	253.3	19.2	16.0	214.2	178.4
1993	292.4	238.2	21.6	17.6	228.5	185.5
1994	282.2	221.1	20.8	16.3	242.6	191.1
1995 (est.)	272.1	207.0	22.1	17.0	259.6	199.7
2000 (est.)	268.3	175.8	20.1	13.4	261.1	173.2

Source: United Stated Budget, FY1996, Historical Statistics: Table 8.7, *Outlays for Discretionary Programs, 1962–2000,* pp. 109–113; *Outlays for Discretionary Programs in Constant (FY1987) Dollars, 1962–2000,* pp. 114–118.

budget, while domestic discretionary took up 4.6 percent. These figures do not tell the whole story. Defense expenditures had steadily grown until 1989, and 1990 was the first year their outlay figure had dropped, while their share in the budget had also dropped from its peak of about 28 percent in 1987. So defense spending was actually declining in terms of its share in the budget by the time of passage of the BEA, but its total was still very high. Domestic expenditures too had grown steadily through the 1980s, although their share in the budget had also dropped steadily from the peak in 1984 at 26.8 percent (see Table 6.7).

Between 1990 and 1993, these trends continued. After a brief increase in 1991, defense spending continued to drop in nominal terms, as did its share of the budget. In 1993, defense stood at $292.4 billion, about one-fifth of the budget. Domestic expenditures on the other hand increased, and by 1993 had reached $228.5 billion or 16.2 percent of the budget. For Clinton's first budget, the unadjusted discretionary outlay cap was about $534 billion. Once again, he opted to cut defense, resulting in 1994 defense outlays of $282 billion or 19.3 percent of the budget. Once again, domestic discretionary spending increased, to $243 billion, and its share of the budget actually grew slightly to 16.9 percent. The five-year figures showed that by 1998, defense and domestic discretionary spending would be about even.

From 1993, the single discretionary spending cap meant that defense and domestic discretionary expenditures were in direct competition with each other (and international spending). Only so much could be taken from defense, and in any case the president had his own priorities which he wished to forward. It would, therefore, be necessary to make adjustments within domestic discretionary spending, the fifth balance. The president was working within a zero sum game.[35] CBO analyses had shown that if full adjustment of programs were made for inflation,

[35]Lance LeLoup and Patrick Taylor, "The Policy Constraints of Deficit Reduction: President Clinton's 1995 Budget," *Public Budgeting and Finance,* Vol. 14 (Summer 1994), p. 6.

the caps would be exceeded.[36] The administration had initiated a wide-ranging survey of federal expenditures, "Re-inventing Government" or "The National Performance Review," and one result was a decision to eliminate over a quarter of a million federal employees. Accordingly, Clinton's FY 1994 budget made room for program additions in the areas of crime prevention and education and training through off-setting cuts in over one hundred domestic programs.

The initial Clinton budget represented an amalgam of competing proposals that nonetheless added up to a fairly moderate program. The deficit would be reduced as a percentage of GDP, though not eliminated; taxes would be increased but primarily for high income taxpayers; the rates of the fastest growing entitlements would be slowed; the spending caps would be extended and tightened to freeze the rate of discretionary spending; defense cuts would once again pay for expansions in certain domestic programs; the president would gain at least some of his own human investment agenda; and the environmentalists would support conservation through a broad-based energy tax. Even if some of the assumptions and projections turned out to be doubtful (e.g., revenue estimates, health cost savings, lower debt costs) the president's budget for FY 1994 was a coherent proposal, based on credible assumptions.

But the test of a budget is not in its reasonableness in the eyes of its framers, but whether it can be passed. There was little possibility of Republican support. What about the Democrats? The critical measure was the reconciliation bill, which incorporated the tax increases and entitlement reductions. The bill passed the House of Representatives by a vote of 219–213, but only because last minute promises of more spending cuts were made to moderate and conservative Southern Democrats.[37] Even so, 38 Democrats voted with the Republicans. In the Senate, the bill passed only by a hair's breadth, 50–49, on the vote of Vice-President Gore. Finally in the conference committee vote to reconcile differences between House and Senate, Gore once again had to cast a tie breaking vote, 50–49.[38] During the process it had been necessary for the president to woo individual members of Congress for their votes, to replace the BTU tax with a small energy tax; to make the income tax increase retroactive to the beginning of the year, to expand the earned income tax credit, and to include empowerment zones. As for appropriations, the president was able to gain only about 70 percent of his requests.

As might be expected, the following year's budget (FY 1995) was not dramatic, overshadowed by the debate on health care. The deficit had dropped to about 2.5 percent of GDP, well down from the 4 percent of 1993, although CBO credited the phasing out of deposit insurance and a more buoyant economy rather than the 1993 legislation (whose impact would be much greater in the out years than in the immediate future) for most of the improvement.[39] The rate of spending was projected to slow significantly, with outlays anticipated to drop from the previous

---

[36]See Congressional Budget Office, January 1993.

[37]Brummett, p. 136.

[38]Ibid., p. 185.

[39]See Congressional Budget Office, *The Economic and Budget Outlook: Fiscal Years 1996–2000,* January 1995.

Table 6.8   NET INTEREST PAYMENTS, 1995–2000

	$ billion	% share of budget	% share of GDP
1985	129.5	13.7	3.3
1990	184.2	14.7	3.4
1991	194.5	14.7	3.4
1992	199.4	14.4	3.4
1993	198.8	14.1	3.2
1994	203.0	13.9	3.1
1995 (est.)	234.2	15.2	3.3
2000 (est.)	309.9	16.3	3.4

Source: United States Budget, FY1996, Historical Statistics: Table 8.1, *Outlays by Budget Enforcement Act Category, 1962–2000*, p. 95; Table 8.3, *Percentage Distribution of Outlays by Budget Enforcement Act Category, 1962–2000*, p. 97; and Table 8.4, *Outlays by Budget Enforcement Act Category as Percentage of GDP*, p. 98.

year's level of 22.4 percent to 21 percent of GDP. Discretionary spending was expected to drop slightly, and the rate of growth of mandatory spending to increase at only 4 percent compared with an average increase of over 7 percent annually between 1991 and 1993. Revenues were projected to increase 7.4 percent, mostly from income taxes and increased social security contributions. The policy of gradually readjusting priorities continued. There was no further action on entitlements. Over half the projected reductions came from defense. Efforts were made to boost spending for education, research, anticrime measures, and infrastructure, as well as to help the poor through homeless programs, housing vouchers, and empowerment zones. To balance these increases, there were proposals to eliminate 115 programs and reduce 106 others. But the President again only received 60 percent of his requests.[40] It almost seemed that following the exhausting budget cliffhangers of 1993, budgeting had once again become an incremental affair.

The budget equation seemed for the moment settled. The economy would remain fairly stable with modest growth kept in check by the monetary policies of the Federal Reserve which would maintain low inflation by keeping unemployment at around 6 percent. Future baselines for revenues and expenditures would be based on these projections, and the deficit would be kept somewhere in the 2 percent of GDP range. Mandatory expenditures would be allowed to rise with occasional readjustments as crises were perceived (i.e., trust funds were seen to be running out of money). To keep the deficit within the tolerable range, taxes would gradually rise. Discretionary expenditures would be squeezed, and priorities readjusted, at first to diminish and later stabilize defense spending, and to satisfy certain domestic agendas while cutting others. Interest payments (which in 1995 had grown approximately to equal those for social security) would be allowed to take their own course, and where deficits were diminished, savings in interest could help alleviate the budget position (see Table 6.8). All this would be upset by the Republican 1994 congressional victory.

---

[40]LeLoup and Taylor, p. 21; Naomi Caiden, "After the Earthquake: the President's Budget for FY 1996," *Public Budgeting and Finance*, Vol. 15 (Summer 1995), pp. 3–17.

Chapter
7

The Politics of the Entitlement Process

*T*he old politics remains a good description of 18 percent of the budget. Aside from defense (which now makes up less than 20 percent of the total) and the 14 percent devoted to interest on the debt, some 52 percent—more than half the budget—is devoted to entitlements, mostly payments to individuals, leaving that catchall category—nondefense discretionary—to cover most of what we think of as domestic government—the Weather Bureau, the Forest Service, the State Department, the Labor and Commerce departments, and the rest.

Entitlements are legal obligations created through legislation that require the payment of benefits to any person or unit of government that meets the eligibility requirements established by law. Budget authority for such payments may be, but is not necessarily, provided in advance. Thus some entitlement legislation, such as food stamps, requires the subsequent enactment of appropriations. Examples of entitlements are social security, revenue sharing (now abolished), and Unemployment Compensation. Entitlements comprise the largest single part of the budget. Obviously any contemporary account of budgeting cannot only be about the appropriations process, but must also cover the politics of the entitlement process.[1]

GRAND POLITICS

Before we go into description and analysis, we want to know why it is worthwhile making an effort to understand entitlements, and why their larger significance should be appraised first as a phenomenon radically altering the character of budgeting and thereby, second, changing its political significance.

---

[1]R. Kent Weaver, "Controlling Entitlements," in John E. Chubb and Paul E. Peterson, eds., *The New Direction in American Politics* (Washington, D.C.: Brookings, 1985). For general discussion of entitlements, see John C. Weicher, *Entitlement Issues in the Domestic Budget* (Washington, D.C.: American Enterprise Institute, 1985).

Budgeting and entitlement are incompatible concepts. Budgeting refers (or used to refer) to the allocation of limited resources for financing competing purposes. But if budgeting is supposed to be resource allocation, then entitlement is mandatory resource segregation. Nothing can be taken away; every person or entity who qualifies for payment—by meeting conditions for Unemployment Compensation, for agricultural subsidies, and so on—is entitled to receive the amount stipulated by the formulas in the authorizing statutes, no matter what is happening elsewhere or to other people. Basically, entitlements are about budgeting by addition—each sum for every program added to the others—not budgeting by subtraction, in which programs are eliminated or reduced, or where more for one means less for another.

Entitlement is, well, entitlement; these programs shall not be moved. For if the sums provided are seen to be not merely a matter of judgment of comparative merits, but also of singular moral virtue (this must be provided because a class of people is entitled to receive it), then allocation, priorities, and similarly relative terms are inappropriate when absolute judgments must be made. So where budgets are understood to be integrative, relating one part to another, entitlements forbid comparisons, allowing consideration only of the program, or activity in and of itself. Budgeting is about balancing commitments; if something is an "entitlement" then it is not to be compared to anything else. While it is true, of course, that relating parts of the budget to the whole was an aspiration not an accomplishment, it was universally considered proper conduct.

Entitlements completely change the direction of budgeting. Classical budgeting was concerned largely with internal relationships between central recommenders and allocators (president and Congress), and spenders (the executive agencies). To control spending, the central units sought to control agencies. Nowadays that control apparatus is obsolete because agencies (bureaus and departments) no longer do most of the spending. In the past, most government spending activity was composed of its own purchases of goods and performance of services; now, the era of entitlements has changed all that. Today government spends most of its money by writing checks to individuals. Whereas in earlier times government faced inward, doing and controlling its own programs, in our time government faces outward to the people it must support. Aiding pregnant women to eat nutritious foods, or the elderly to put aside money for retirement, or the poor to use medical services are but a few examples of governmental efforts to alter citizen behavior.

If one asks a grand question about political life—Who will bear the costs of change?—entitlements provide a markedly new answer. The old one—"we the people"—has been changed to "all of us except the entitled." When the entitled are few in number and their entitlements are relatively small, the vast majority pays for a small minority. But when entitlements grow large (covering not only poor but rich, not only the elderly but the young), the budgetary system becomes loaded with many constants and few variables. Put plainly, the prevalence of entitlements means that but a minority of programs and agencies remain to absorb the vast majority of cuts. Resource allocation becomes a lot harder when you have to take three-fifths of total spending (entitlements plus interest) off the table. Bottom-up budgeting (by adding programs together) works just fine for entitlements; but it does not suit budgeting from above (trying to fit spending within a given total) because the cuts that have to be apportioned over the remainder of the budget are necessarily severe. It is obviously difficult, if not nearly impossible, for example, to apportion tens of billions of cuts on 40 percent of the budget, as required by the Gramm–Rudman–Hollings procedure. Where classical budgeting is mostly about modifications of the budgetary base (increments up or down), entitlements guarantee a permanent base, thus foregoing flexibility. The entitlement is the base, and a base that can go only one way—up—unless a deliberate and difficult decision is made to alter the natural course of spending. Moreover, entitlements hold the size of the base hostage to external events—to price increases (if payments are indexed to inflation, to demographic changes (if the entitled group increases in size, to the weather, to the economy, and more.

The external focus that entitlements have imparted to budgeting has profound implications for the political lives of participants in the budgetary process. The lives of the beneficiaries may become more stable but relationships among budgeters become more hostile as agreement on what constitutes "fair shares" breaks down. Once the program base is guaranteed, with additions to it coming from formulas tied to external events, no one can say how much is too much. Internal conflict over budgeting rises. Bad enough, but there is worse to come.

As entitlements grew, members of Congress grew nervous; more and more spending was uncontrolled by appropriations committees. And if spending was out of control, so were legislators and the Congress from which their authority stemmed.

Now if higher spending on entitlements was so desirable that sacrifices could be justified in the form of higher taxes, well and good. But if taxes were not to be raised, and if spending increases came under question, what would Congress's answer be? If the norm of balance were totally gone, the answer could be further deficits. But as that norm has survived, albeit in weakened form, there was no answer. Entitlements posed the grim possibility that Congress would not be deemed responsible enough to hold the purse strings, the main fact and symbol of its power.

Congressional control of public policy was thus under challenge. In pursuing entitlement programs, Congress subjected itself and the budget to great uncertainty. With other programs, legislators would give an agency some money for a project and, if it cost a little more than expected, Congress had a real choice about what to do next: build a smaller building, change some schedules, allocate more money, or just tell the agency to do its best with the funds it had. If the agency incorrectly estimated a project, it could be forced to give up some other part of its budget (e.g., travel expenses). Relations were largely between members of Congress and the agency, and Congress could displace a lot of the burden of error onto bureaucrats. If Congress misestimated entitlement costs, by contrast, it had no opportunity for second thoughts; the money just poured out from the Treasury.

Arguments about uncontrollability or fiscal policy were also weapons, wielded in a battle royal over the size and purposes of the American government. They were used by one side or the other to appeal to neutrals. Conservatives argued that liberal programs created deficits, or inflation (i.e., bad things), so as to upset people who thought the programs were good. When they were not stressing social justice, liberals would invoke Congress's right to make fiscal policy—to counter the president's claim that his program preferences served a higher purpose of economic management.

Who would solve the problem? The budget system laid that burden on the president and the appropriations committees. But neither could touch entitlements. Authorizing committees alone could change entitlement law; neither appropriation bills nor presidential vetoes could change that. If the president and appropriations committees focused on what they were able to do, all the burden of deficit reduction would fall on one part of the budget; interests funded by entitlements would escape scot-free. The appropriations committees naturally did not like that.

With the adoption by Congress of a unified budget in 1969, whereby trust funds were included in the same budget as non-trust fund entitlements and annual appropriations, the tensions between entitlements and appropriations were exacerbated. The new form of the budget structured tradeoffs in a more direct and, hence, conflictive way. Entitlements and appropriations were increasingly forced to fight over the same pie, often to the detriment of the more controllable expenditures—appropriations.[2]

With the arrival of budget committees in 1974, a new alternative presented itself; these super budget committees (see Chapters 4 and 5) could require the legislative committees to cut entitlements by such measures as reducing eligibility or increasing payments by individuals. Procedural possibility did not, however, mean political ease. As long as the principle of entitlement remained and the big ones had overwhelming political support, they had the effect outlined.

The growth of entitlements heightened long-standing tensions between appropriations and tax-writing committees. There had always been jealousies because Ways and Means and Finance were the chief beneficiaries of Appropriations' efforts: If the latter cut spending, taking blame, the former could cut taxes, taking credit. Or it could work in reverse: If Appropriations was lax, the tax committees got the bill. Now as entitlements burgeoned, Ways and Means could take credit for expanding programs, but Appropriations took the blame for the deficit. When Appropriations blamed Ways and Means or Finance, the tax writers replied that entitlements were fully funded by their own taxes; that is, since social security itself was in balance, it could not be blamed for the deficit; true as far as it went, but a bit of the story had been left out. Since social insurance taxes were going up, but the public did not want to pay more in taxes (and half of these taxes were charged to business), Congress had to keep reducing other taxes, particularly the corporate income tax; thus the total tax burden remained a nearly constant proportion of the economy. In other words, entitlements "paid for themselves" by the reduced taxes paid for everything else; the appropriations committees indeed had a legitimate gripe. If revenues remained, say, at 18 percent of GNP but an ever-larger proportion went to social security, much less was left to fund the rest of government.

Thus entitlements squeezed the old budget process (1) directly by increasing spending, (2) indirectly by siphoning off revenues from other programs, and (3) institutionally by pitting appropriations committees against tax committees. The

---

[2]Allen Schick, *Congress and Money* (Washington, D.C.: The Urban Institute, 1980).

Table 7.1   SURPLUSES OR DEFICITS IN THE SOCIAL SECURITY
TRUST FUNDS, 1985–1994

	(in millions of dollars)					
	1985	**1990**	**1991**	**1992**	**1993**	**1994**
OASI	10,673	55,125	51,972	50,862	49,364	60,691
DI	−1,310	3,091	1,543	−116	−2,576	−3,935

Source: United States Budget, FY1996, Historical Tables: Table 13.1, *Cash Income, Outgo and Balance of the Social Security and Medicare Trust Funds, 1936–2000*, pp. 220–229.

guaranteed certainty of entitlement funding creates so much uncertainty for budgeters that it reduces the capacity of public officials to govern. Entitlements place a sizable burden on budgetary actors: They must find a way to support large numbers of individuals while still helping manage the economy and control the deficit, all this with most of the budget "committed" or essential. Government must be simultaneously firm (for entitlements) and flexible (for appropriations) while still trying to govern. It is as if government were a giant centipede on its back in space with innumerable little feet holding up innumerable little people, with scant attention being paid to what holds up the creature who holds everyone else up. More tax money or fewer entitlements—either would solve the problem. But our legislators and presidents so far have not been able to see eye to eye. They agree that entitlements make a big difference, but not on what to do about them.

But the squeeze of entitlements on the budget was not the end of the story. A new player entered the game in the name of trust fund surpluses. After 1985 social security, which is supported by the self-financing old age and survivors insurance trust fund, began to generate large surpluses (although the disability insurance trust fund continued to run deficits or small surpluses). (See Table 7.1.) The inclusion of social security trust funds in the calculation of the deficit makes the deficit appear smaller than it would be without them. (See Table 7.2.) The Gramm–Rudman–Hollings Act explicitly allowed the counting of social security surpluses against the deficit.[3] Since then, social security has been explicitly placed off-budget, but in fact it is almost always included. As Allen Schick explains, "by law, social security is excluded; in practice it is included."[4]

Is there anything wrong with this sort of action? Critics hold there is a danger that we will be deluding ourselves into believing that actual deficit reductions are being made by counting money in one pocket that will later have to be paid out to another. They contend that surpluses in the social security trust fund are there for a purpose: To pay for future costs.

But as Schick argues, the sheer size of social security would mean that excluding it from the deficit would provide a misleading picture of the impact of the budget on the economy. He explains that although offsetting some of the deficit

---

[3]Jonathan Rauch, *National Journal*, February 14, 1987, p. 365.

[4]Allen Schick, *The Federal Budget: Politics, Policy, Process* (Washington, D.C.: Brookings Institution, 1995), p. 28.

Table 7.2   MEASURES OF THE DEFICIT AND SURPLUS, 1985–1994

			(in millions of dollars)			
	1985	1990	1991	1992	1993	1994
On-budget	−221,698	−227,974	−321,367	−340,490	−300,487	−258,823
Off-budget	9,363	56,590	52,198	50,087	45,347	55,654
Total	−212,334	−221,384	−269,169	−290,403	−255,140	−203,169

Source: United States Budget, FY1996. Historical Tables: Table 1.1, *Summary of Receipts, Outlays and Surpluses or Deficits, 1789–2000.*

from the surpluses in social security and other trust funds makes it appear that these funds "are being invaded to finance the current expenses of government and they therefore will not be available to pay future benefits," the situation is more complicated: "The government does borrow trust fund balances but it pays prevailing interest rates on the money," thereby adding billions to the trust funds.[5] The more pressing problem, he considers, is that the security trust funds surplus is projected to disappear early in the next century, a prediction also made regarding medicare. The issue of entitlements, then is central to the problem of the budget as a whole.

ENTITLEMENTS: LEGAL, MORAL, AND BUDGETARY

Entitlements stand somewhere between a privilege—which need not be given or, once granted, may be withdrawn—and a right that cannot be denied. Because entitlements have not been held to comprise fundamental rights, the Supreme Court so far has not expanded its interpretation of the due-process clause of the Fourteenth Amendment to include constitutional guarantees to a specified level of food, clothing, shelter, education, or income. As yet, Congress has not been deemed by the Constitution to be required to provide funds for a variety of welfare programs. By statute, applicants for benefits that Congress has chosen to provide are guaranteed an appeal for review of denial of their applications. And recipients of benefits are held to be constitutionally guaranteed a hearing before benefits authorized by statute are reduced.[6] Procedural guarantees, however, are

---

[5]Ibid., p. 28. For a general discussion of the part played in the deficit by federal funds and trust funds, see *United States Budget FY 1996, Analytical Perspectives*, pp. 252–59. See also General Accounting Office, *Social Security: The Trust Fund Reserve Accumulation, the Economy, and the Federal Budget*, January 1989, GAO/HRD–89–44.

[6]Relevant cases include *Goldberg v. Kelly*, holding that a person receiving welfare benefits under statutory and administrative standards defining eligibility for them has an interest in continued receipt of those benefits that is safeguarded by procedural due process (397 U.S. 254, 90 S. Ct. 1011, 25 L. Ed. 2d 287, 1970); *Board of Regents v. Roth*, holding that a professor hired by annual renewable contract was not entitled to a hearing before dismissal under Fourteenth Amendment due process, absent a showing of sufficient cause for reasonable expectation of renewal (408 U.S. 566, 92 S. Ct. 2701, 1972); *Shapiro v. Thompson*, holding unconstitutional state and federal provision denying welfare benefits to individuals who had resided in administering jurisdictions less than one year as violative of the constitutional guarantee of all citizens to be free to travel throughout the U.S. (394 U.S. 618, 1969); *Rodriguez v. San Antonio Independent School District*, sustaining against equal protection attack on

not substantive rights. A welfare applicant may be denied, or a recipient's payments cut, providing the courts find that the relevant administrative agency acted in a reasonable manner. Thus at present there is no constitutional barrier to diminishing or eliminating entitlements.[7] To do this, of course, is an entirely different matter.[8]

"Entitled to" may suggest "deserving of." Without touching on questions the courts have sought to avoid—namely, whether entitlements constitute what Charles Reich called "the new property"[9]—one's picture of the just society may include a view of what individuals are entitled to, of what they should give to others, and of what part government should play in making such provisions. Who should give or take how much from whom is a fundamental political question. For entitlements are not only benefits to some people, but also represent costs to others. Transfers of income from taxpayers to recipients require moral justification as well as political clout. Should poverty be the criterion? What about the well-off elderly? Should the criterion be financial loss? If there is an entitlement for beekeepers (yes, there was, read on), why not for anyone else in danger of losing income or going out of business? Why are certain farmers who raise particular crops given price supports, but not others? Should anyone who is already a farmer or anyone who wishes to become one be entitled? Actually, it is not so much who is entitled, important though this question is, but rather the priority given to entitlement over nearly all other claims that has occasioned the most controversy.

The status of entitlements is both accepted (no one expects much change in the largest ones) and disputed, due to the budgetary bind into which their cumulative impact has led government. Because entitlements stand as prior claims that must be paid before others, they achieve certainty at the expense of all other residual claimants on government. It is the "non-entitled" who must change. When revenues rise as fast or faster than expenditures, this conflict among classes of claimants—the entitled versus general government programs (justice, information, regulation, etc.) and defense—is muted. When deficits rise, however, and spending levels are considered too high while entitlements have risen to half or more of the total, the desirability of entitlements does come into question. One sign of this questioning is the Budget Act of 1974, subsequently strengthened, that requires special notice of and procedures for new entitlements—which may help explain why there haven't been any. Another is the provision of the Budget

---

public school finance schemes using local property taxation as a base and thereby forcing districts with lower property values to make more effort than others in order to raise the same amount of money per pupil for educational purposes (411 U.S. 1, 1973); and *Mathews v. Eldrige* (424 U.S. 319, 1976) denying the need for an evidentiary hearing prior to termination of social security disability benefit payments.

[7] I am indebted to Maureen Young for an illuminating paper on the legal status of housing entitlements.

[8] For a critique of entitlements as vitiating "the distinction essential to liberal constitutionalism, between the rights the government exists to protect and the exercise of those rights by private individuals, or between state and society. For an entitlement is a right whose exercise is guaranteed to a certain degree by the government—a right that is therefore exercised to that degree by the government," see Harvey C. Mansfield, Jr., "The American Election: Entitlements Versus Opportunity," *Government and Opposition*, Vol. 20, No. 1 (Winter 1985), pp. 3–17, quote on pp. 13–14.

[9] Charles Reich, "The New Property," *Yale Law Journal*, Vol. 73 (April 1964), pp. 733–87.

Enforcement Act of 1990 requiring offsetting cuts against policy increases in exist-ing entitlements.

Entitlements represent a protean subject: At the edges, it is not easy to say ex-actly what is in or out; and one can say virtually nothing that is true of everything. The reason is that entitlements are a product of history, not logic—of evolution, not design. The features one wishes to stress depend on the kind of analysis one wishes to make. Some entitlements, like social security, are permanent (sometimes called "no-year") and run on in perpetuity unless changed. Others, like commodity credit-price supports and food stamps, receive annual appropriations, though, in effect, they are treated as full entitlements because shortfalls are made up by sup-plemental appropriations. Some entitlements, such as medicaid for the poor, are means-tested; that is, eligibility depends on income and other assets. By contrast, unemployment compensation has no means test at the entry stage, but benefits are subject to taxation above a specified level of income. Retirement programs (for civilian and military federal employees but also for others) are financed in part by trust funds based on employer and employee contributions. Some entitlements serve narrow clienteles (e.g., black lung, student loans) and others (e.g., medicare) are broadly based. Railroad retirement and veterans' pensions are tied (or in-dexed) to the consumer price index (so as to protect recipients against inflation), while the kidney dialysis entitlement is not. Merely to describe the characteristics of these programs would be like reading the telephone directory—helpful when you need a bit of data, but not recommended reading. As students of budgeting, what we want to know is how entitlements grow compared to one another and to appropriations and why. How does the struggle over entitlements differ, if at all, from the conflict over appropriations? And what does the rise of entitlements por-tend for the ability of our political institutions to make effective budgets?

THE TREND IS UP

Why is there concern over entitlements? Because (see Table 7.3) entitlements are not merely growing twice as fast as the rest of the budget (outside of interest on the debt) but also faster than Gross Domestic Product; consequently, all sides of the political spectrum are troubled. Conservatives fear much higher taxes and/or deficits; liberals fear that entitlements will squeeze out other programs and, if they keep growing, use up future revenue increases. Taking only those composed of payments to individuals, entitlements went from 33.5 percent in 1970 to 49.9 percent (leaving out interest) of the budget in 1985.[10] From 1985, entitlements grew from 48.2 percent of outlays (excluding interest) to 51.3 percent, and spend-ing doubled. Which programs accounted for most of the increase?

Taken together, social security and medicare amounted to $242.2 billion in 1984, making up 60.6 percent of all entitlement outlays and 28.4 percent of total government spending. A decade later, outlays for social security and medicare had almost doubled, reaching $458.7 billion or nearly one third of total federal spend-ing. Social security ranks first, followed by health (medicare and medicaid), fed-

---

[10]See Weaver, "Controlling Entitlements," Table 11.1 on p. 319.

Table 7.3 GROWTH IN ENTITLEMENT SPENDING 1975–1994

(in billions of dollars)

	1975				1985				1990				1994			
	Current	Constant	% Outlays	% GDP	Current	Constant	% Outlays	% GDP	Current	Constant	% Outlays	% GDP	Current	Constant	% Outlays	% GDP
Entitlement Outlays	160.2	335.8	48.2	10.6	433.4	464.4	45.8	10.9	603.5	527.6	48.2	11.0	750.2	529.5	51.3	11.3
Non-entitlement Outlays	162.5	341.8	48.9	10.8	416.2	433.9	44.0	10.5	501.7	452.1	40.1	9.2	545.6	428.5	37.3	8.2
Net Interest	23.2	48.9	7.0	1.5	129.5	137.3	13.7	3.3	184.2	163.1	14.7	3.4	203.0	160.5	13.9	3.1
Federal Budget Outlays	332.3	698.5	1.00.0	22.0	946.4	1,001.2	100.0	23.9	1,252.7	1,110.3	100.0	22.9	1,460.9	1,140.3	100.0	22.0

Source: United States Budget, FY1996, Historical Tables: Tables 8.1 to 8.4. Constant dollars are 1987 dollars.

Table 7.4 GROWTH IN ENTITLEMENT SPENDING, 1975–1994: SELECTED PROGRAMS

	(in billions of dollars)			
	1975	1985	1990	1994
Social security and related programs	68.3	191.6	246.5	322.2
Health (medicare and medicaid)	19.3	88.0	138.7	228.4
Federal employee retirement	13.2	38.5	51.9	62.4
Food & nutrition assistance	6.6	16.7	21.3	33.0
Unemployment	12.8	15.8	17.1	26.4
Public assistance	9.3	32.9	28.5	51.2
Veterans benefits	12.5	15.9	15.9	20.3
Education, training, etc.	3.1	7.6	11.1	9.0
Agriculture	1.9	23.4	9.3	10.7

Source: United States Budget, FY1996, Historical Statistics: Table 8.5, *Outlays for Mandatory and Related Programs*, pp. 85–103.

eral employee retirement, and food and nutrition assistance. Entitlements are driven by a few programs concerned with retirement, health, and welfare. Thus whatever drives these programs (see Chapter 8) propels the largest part of the budget.

There are legitimate policy reasons—of efficiency, or the political difficulty of alternatives, or the desire to keep promises that are made—for entitlement funding. Entitlements increase stability and security, and represent community provision for the routine hazards of life in a volatile market economy. There are also good policy reasons for protecting government from adversity by enabling it to limit demands on its resources. When good reasons conflict, difficult choices among policies become necessary.

Do all entitlement programs grow at the same pace or do some leap ahead while others lag behind? Table 7.4 masks some variations in year to year spending, but shows the fastest growth is in the largest programs, particularly social security and health. Why?

The political climate of the late 1970s and the first half of the 1980s, running from the decline of the Carter administration to the ascendancy of President Reagan, was less favorable to domestic spending in general and to certain (but not all) entitlement programs in particular. In an incisive analysis of entitlements in 1985, Kent Weaver concludes that

> (1) Income maintenance programs have continued to increase their share of GNP, but their share of the federal budget has ended its secular growth and now responds primarily to swings of the business cycle. (2) Health care entitlements have continued to increase their budget share, although at a reduced pace. (3) Statutory changes in individual programs (policy choices) have been largely in the form of cutbacks, with most of those cuts occurring under the Reagan administration. (4) Means-tested programs have been cut more than social insurance programs, especially for beneficiaries at the higher end of eligibility scales (the "working poor"). (5) Program changes have generally been marginal, rather than comprehensive reforms.[11]

---

[11]Weaver, "Controlling Entitlements," p. 318.

In the 1990s, the entitlements picture has been dominated by the growth in the health care programs. Medicaid payments exploded, jumping by 20 to 30 percent a year from 1990 through 1992, but after that growth slowed to 12 percent in 1993 and 8 percent in 1994. Between 1984 and 1994, medicare grew by an average of 10 percent a year, while social security was increasing at 6 percent annually, still above the rate of growth of GDP or of inflation. Other programs that grew rapidly were food stamps, supplementary security income for the aged, blind and disabled, and the earned income tax credit. Outlays for unemployment compensation peaked in 1992 (a recession year) and then fell steeply.[12]

There is no particular mystery why entitlements grow. One reason is that more people beome eligible to participate. Mounting caseloads are expected to account for about a quarter of the growth in entitlement programs over the next five years, primarily in medicaid, social security, medicare, and supplemental security income, reflecting the growing numbers of elderly, disabled, and poor. Another third of the growth occurs because of automatic increases in benefits, which applies to all the major retirement programs, as well as food stamps, medicare, and the earned income tax credit. A further third of the expenditure growth may be traced to rising costs, particularly in the health areas, due to greater intensity of use, more sophisticated technology and probably, fraud. Other factors—for example, the higher earnings base for calculation of social security benefits—account for the rest.[13] But none of this explains how entitlements got there in the first place, and why some gain ground through policy changes while others lose. To understand these fluctuations in fortunes we need a more detailed knowledge of their history.

THE IMPORTANCE OF BEING ENTITLED

The place to begin is with the protection given to a program by virtue of the fact that it stands as an entitlement and, therefore, is not subject to the pressures of the annual appropriations process. It is not easy for Congress to consider reneging on obligations it already has incurred, or intervening to deprive beneficiaries of something to which the law says they are entitled. Entitlement means not having to say you're sorry, the money has run out.

Like other decision-making bodies, Congress does not necessarily spend its time on what is most important but rather on what it can change. Often this means neglecting the much larger entitlements in favor of the much smaller but more readily changeable appropriations. A typical debate occurred over the fiscal consequences of a $25 million supplemental for the Head Start program after the House of Representatives had left unscathed a 40-times larger increase for Aid to Families with Dependent Children. In seeking to silence protest over this disparity, Representative Holland explained that "We thought this $1,150 million required for welfare funds for the States, and the $28 million required to pay

---

[12]Congressional Budget Office, *The Economic and Budget Outlook: Fiscal Years 1996–2000,* January 1995, pp. 39–43.

[13]Ibid., p. 44.

veterans' and unemployment compensation for Federal employees, were important enough items that we should not permit them to go into default any longer."[14]

Entitlements alter the prevailing conception of the budgetary base. From a concept formerly tied to individual programs, the base emerges here as a function of the type of financing: Entitlements become the base that is expected to continue much as before while appropriations become the increments that are subject to dispute and negotiation. While the expansion of entitlements has not eliminated legislators' interest in distributing projects geographically, the public-works pork barrel has nonetheless been dwarfed by payments to individuals.

As entitlements come to dominate much of public spending, they act so as to place the budget on automatic pilot. Far more than before, the budget is determined by prior authorizations. And, as what might be termed "maximal entitlements" (universal, no-year, fully indexed, financed in part by their own trust funds) come to take up a larger share of the total, the scope for change is reduced still further.

In recognition of the necessary tradeoff between collective and individual security, Congress began to challenge the notion of entitlement as total or forever. Beginning in 1980 and continuing sporadically thereafter, Congress, through its budget committees, began to use the reconciliation procedure to chip away at some entitlements. What happens is that in issuing reconciliation instructions under a budget resolution approved by each house, the budget committees direct other committees to reduce budget authority and outlays by set amounts. While not specifically stating where cuts should be made, the selection of committees to make changes (what else does Ways and Means have?) and a strong norm (violated only in 1981) against changing authorizations on programs the appropriations committees can control serve to focus reconciliation reductions on entitlements. The committees are half compelled and half given political cover to modify promises by such things as delaying or diminishing COLAs (cost of living adjustments), restricting access, or reducing the scope of the service offered.

In 1990 and again in 1993, the reconciliation bill was a key mechanism for reducing the deficit by raising taxes and reducing entitlements, particularly medicare. Now, in 1995, the reconciliation bill is an omnibus measure including huge tax cuts and unprecedented entitlement reductions, particularly aimed at medicare, medicaid, and welfare programs. With the exception of social security (a very large exception), entitlement status no longer seems as sacrosanct as it was, though the political feasibility of reneging on previous commitments remains to be seen.

TRUST FUNDS

Reliance on trust funds deserves further comment because this device has become part of new budgetary strategies. By no mere chance do the two fastest growing types of entitlements, social insurance and federal retirement, share trust-fund financing. Obviously, the large number of beneficiaries and the accepted position that recipients are paying their way help these entitlements pros-

---

[14]*Congressional Record,* 1968, Vol. 114, Part 8, p. 9483.

per. Slightly less obvious is the tendency of trust-fund financing to create vast un- or under-financed liabilities by sweeping costs under the rug of the future. "Over the years," Andrew Ruddock of the Civil Service Commission observed, "all efforts to strengthen retirement financing have been tempered by concurrent searches for ways to postpone the budgetary burden to some future Administration."[15] On the one hand, trust-fund managers (backed up as they are by the credit of the United States), knowing they will not be allowed to default, need only keep funds sufficient to pay for the current year plus a small margin for error. This is quite different from the usual insurance practice of trying to retain enough to pay also for future benefits. On the other hand, accumulations of surplus in the early years, while people are paying in but not taking out, does tempt presidents and congresses to increase benefits. Surpluses may also be artificially created, as was true of social security, by unrealistic assumptions about the level of earnings or the life span of affected individuals. Eventually, of course, these benefits have to be paid for by increased payroll taxes, now the largest tax many people pay.[16]

In the entitlement business there are many ways of making present spending appear less than it is likely to be later on. Underestimating costs is epidemic. So is the strategy of the receding increment. Small increases to beneficiaries, which also cumulate into large future sums, may be obtained because their full future impact is not evident. Thus a pension benefit to be obtained in five years, or slowly phased in, may seem almost as good as one obtained right now, since most recipients will not retire until then. The present cost is at or close to zero, though future costs may be large. In 1966, for instance, the 5 percent annuity reduction for retiring at age 55 (with 30 years of federal service) was eliminated. A colloquy at a 1965 hearing tells the story:

MR. DANIELS: Can you give the Committee any cost figures as to the Government if such a recommendation was enacted?

MR. McCART: . . . Let me simply point out, Mr. Chairman, that the cost is not going to be very high, because what this represents at the most is a 5 percent increase in the annuity that an individual can secure if he retires.[17]

At each step, the costs look small; the overall change since 1942, however, was a 50 percent increase in the annuity of 55/30 retirees. The liberalizations also encourage greater use of early retirement, further increasing costs. Given the vast size of the largest entitlements, the logic of incrementalism is inexorable: A tiny proportion of a huge number, compounding over time, gets to be pretty big itself.

Another strategy is to create a deficit artificially, which has to be repaid. Every year, for example, the president's budget request includes an amount to reimburse the Commodity Credit Corporation (CCC) for losses on price supports so it can

[15]Andrew E. Ruddock, "A Critique of Various Study Documents," in Dan McGill, ed., *Financing the Civil Service Retirement System* (Homewood, Ill.: Richard D. Irwin, 1979), p. 134.

[16]See Martha Derthick, *Policymaking for Social Security* (Washington, D.C.: The Brookings Institution, 1979); and James Tobin, "The Future of Social Security: One Economist's Assessment," Working Paper #4, Project on the Federal Social Role, National Conference on Social Welfare, Washington, D.C., 1985.

[17]Joseph White, "The Budgeting of the Civil Service Retirement 'Entitlement,'" typescript, 1983, p. 19.

retain its full borrowing authority. This is an example of appropriations chasing entitlement spending. Congress can estimate that the entire borrowing authority will not be needed, thereby shifting elsewhere some funds needed to pay for prior years' losses. This strategy helps Congress get out from under its own spending ceilings. In the fiscal 1984 budget, for example, the Reagan administration requested $10.2 billion for the CCC while Congress, led by Representative Jamie Whitten, the wily chairman of the House Appropriations Committee and an advocate of agricultural interests, appropriated $9.7 billion. The $500 million difference was used to fund soil conservation programs that had been cut out by the administration.[18]

THE ECONOMY, DEMOGRAPHY, AND UPTAKE

The size of entitlements depends on how many qualify and how much they are paid. Both eligibility and payment depend in turn on the state of the economy, trends in population dynamics, and provisions for protection against inflation. These three variables are considered together because they show how the size of entitlements may be influenced by external forces. However, I do not want to leave the impression that Congress is helpless in the face of forces it cannot control. Congress could limit expenditures by eliminating or reducing indexing, changing eligibility rules, or even eliminating programs.

Changes in the economy reverberate throughout the realm of entitlements. A decline in employment increases unemployment compensation. If prolonged, it may well encourage more people to retire, thereby raising pension costs. As people drop below the poverty line, they become eligible for medicaid, food stamps, and other programs. For those programs linked to the price level through COLAs, inflation can dramatically increase expenditure. A 1 percent decrease in unemployment, for instance, can lead to a $600 million reduction in food stamp costs. Even in the midst of general prosperity, a decline in farm income, spurred, perhaps, by increased foreign competition or a debt crisis, will increase payments by the Commodity Credit Corporation (CCC).

Demography defeats policy, at least some of the time. Different age distributions have large effects not only on pensions but also on medical care and poverty. Often, demographic trends work in contrary directions. People are healthier than they have been, thus decreasing costs at comparable ages, but they live longer, thereby increasing them. Through the end of the 1940s, early retirement was virtually unknown; almost all men worked to age 64; and half of those over 65 still worked. Therefore they did not receive pensions. Nowadays, retirement by age 65 is the rule, and one-third of men 55–64 retire early.

Sometimes demographic change works in tandem with changes in entitlements. Much improved social security income in the 1970s and 1980s facilitated early retirement, but then total payments grew accordingly.

Levels of entitlement spending were sometimes unintended. Costs were underestimated. Costs of health-care programs in particular—whether well known (as medicare) or less familiar, such as end-stage renal disease (dialysis) support—were

---

[18]From Michael Sieverts, a student paper on agricultural price supports.

far greater than anticipated. In part the underestimates were failures of calculation, but they resulted also from failures to calculate at all—the committees of jurisdiction having little reason to make costs visible, and no other institution picking up the slack. Let me put it this way: If you are worried about spending too much, you take measures against that possibility; but if your main concern is not to do too little, you don't worry about the total cost. The fast growth of entitlement spending would not have been possible without the prevailing view that government's task was to use public money to alleviate private distress, the more the better.

While demographic and program changes may offset each other—the rise in working wives increases equality while the rise in female-headed households decreases it—occasionally programs do what they are supposed to. Whereas 35 percent of the elderly were below the poverty line in 1959 (compared to 21 percent for the rest of the population) by the mid-1980s elderly income, thanks to social security, had risen considerably faster than that of younger people; 14.1 percent of the elderly were deemed poor, a percentage point below the general population. Naturally, this increase in cost led to concern about government's ability to pay social security in the future.[19] There is also concern with intergenerational equity; fewer younger people will be paying to support more older people. But the program did work.

The "uptake," the degree to which eligible people take advantage of entitlements, depends in part on how morally acceptable this use becomes and in part on how advantageous it is. As Aid to Families with Dependent Children declined by a quarter in real terms from 1976 to 1983, for example, the proportion of eligible families who chose to participate declined.[20]

Controlling the costs of entitlements has proven to be quite difficult. In medical care, for example, once the decision is made to reimburse patients for costs as incurred in the private sector, it becomes impossible to limit spending in advance. Every administration has looked for ways to control medicare costs, but the focus has been on regulating use or prices, while praying for an effect on totals.

In food stamps, the government under Carter did submit the program to the appropriations process and a total expense is mandated each year in the agriculture appropriation. But since the law sets rules for payment of benefits and the USDA follows those rules, when the money is nearly used up the USDA just asks Congress for more. Rather than kill the program in June, Congress obliges. The alternative approach, holding to a cap (or ceiling), has two disadvantages: It would not assure nutritional aid adjusted to financial need, and it would require giving administrators massive discretion as to who gets what benefits.

INDEXING: TRYING TO TRANSFER UNCERTAINTY

When the dollars individuals receive from entitlements are tied to a measure of price changes, such as the Consumer Price Index (CPI), the benefit is said to be "indexed." At set intervals, a change in the price index beyond a specified degree

[19]See Frank Levy, "Families, Households and the Government," in *Dollars and Dreams: The Changing American Income Distribution*, Russell Sage Foundation, transcript, 1987.

[20]Ibid., p. 175.

triggers a change in the dollars received by beneficiaries. About 30 percent of federal spending now is indexed, as are nearly 90 percent of payments received by individuals.[21] And the cost is high. The GAO estimates that provisions for indexing accounted for half of the rapid increase of social security in the 1970s and 42 percent of Medicare spending.[22]

More is indexed than meets the eye. Since government pay is linked to private sector pay, for instance, and since wages in the private sector are related to inflation, "... this may be thought of," the GAO correctly informs us, "as an implicit form of indexing."[23] (The linkage is weak, however, because government did not follow recommendations to assure comparability.) Although medicaid and medicare are not indexed to price changes, they do promise to provide a fixed volume of services, so that as these increase in price, so does the cost of programs. When high levels of inflation coincide with high levels of unemployment, programs not indexed for price changes may nevertheless rise, because they are triggered by economic changes. The GAO calls this "indexed eligibility."[24] When federal payments respond to a certain level of state funding, increases by states operate as indexing mechanisms to generate federal spending increases. It is hard to isolate major programs from economic developments. Indexed entitlements offer a fertile field for the interconnection of spending programs.

Hard as it may be to believe, indexation was once adopted as a way to save the government money. In 1972, buoyed by false predictions of future surpluses and perhaps by hopes of electoral rewards, Congress voted to raise social security benefits by 20 percent while raising taxes hardly at all. In 1973, to prevent a recurrence of this episode, Congress, in an act designed to "take Social Security out of politics," adopted automatic indexation. Retirees would not have to wait to catch up with inflation and politicians would have less reason to provide their regular election-time increase. Tax rates were set on the assumption that wages would grow at the rate for the Consumer Price Index (CPI) plus an additional amount of productivity. The plan backfired; although in the past price increases had lagged behind wage growth, starting in the 1970s, inflation began to outstrip wages.[25]

But it is hard to outguess the future. A friend of social security, economist James Tobin, tells us what went wrong.

> In retrospect it is easy to see that indexation by the CPI is not a good idea, even in less turbulent economic times than the 1970s. Such indexation immunizes the favored

---

[21]General Accounting Office, Report to the Congress by the Comptroller General of the United States, "What Can Be Done to Check the Growth of Federal Entitlement and Indexed Spending?" PAD-81-21, March 3, 1981.

[22]GAO, "An Analysis of the Effects of Indexing for Inflation on Federal Expenditures," PAD-79-22, August 15, 1979.

[23]Report to Congress, "What Can Be Done?" p. 13.

[24]Ibid.

[25]Social security, veterans' compensation and pensions, supplemental security income, railroad retirement, food stamps, and benefits for disabled miners are indexed annually to the Consumer Price Index, and federal employees' retirement semi-annually. Other programs vary. For example, Aid to Families with Dependent Children is an open-ended federal commitment to pay a fixed percentage of state costs, so that increases in payment levels by states affect the federal budget in a manner similar to automatic indexing. Unemployment compensation is not indexed.

group from inescapable national losses—in 1973/74 and 1979/80 the big rise in the cost of imported oil—and throws their costs onto unprotected fellow-citizens. Likewise indexation in effect exempts its beneficiaries from paying increased taxes embodied in the prices that compose the index; others must bear the burdens of the public programs financed by those taxes.[26]

When only a favored few are indexed, little harm is done. The selected few may well need more protection than the rest of us. But when indexation covers tens of millions of people, the few begin to protect the many and the social contract of mutual support in society is weakened.

Pity the poor taxpayer. Maybe not. In 1981, as part of the Kemp–Roth across-the-board tax cuts, tax brackets were indexed to inflation. Thus ended the infamous "bracket creep," under which taxpayers were pushed into higher brackets by inflation even though they had no more real purchasing power. The government that under a progressive rate structure used to get 1.6 times the revenue for each percentage point increase in the price level now gets no inflation bonus.

Taking the two forms of indexing together—continuance of expenditure indexing, which pushes spending up, and discontinuance of tax indexing, which keeps revenue down—adds up to a foolproof formula for producing deficits. Unless taxes are raised, or spending is cut, or economic growth rises way beyond prior levels, maintaining the status quo results in deficits.

There is no end of suggestions for diminishing or eliminating the effects of indexing. OMB, CBO, and GAO variously referred to the possibility of abolishing indexing altogether, making the index less generous, delaying COLAs or adjusting them less frequently, and giving the president the right to propose changes in the formula unless Congress chooses to override. Were the law changed, say, to limit indexing to 85 percent of the expected rise in the CPI in social security, CBO under one inflation assumption calculated a cumulative savings of $43.9 billion over five years.[27] For recipients, of course, the income would be lost not saved.

The difficulty lies not in devising measures to limit the effects of indexing but in doing so while (1) maintaining the objectives of the program involved and (2) gaining the necessary political support. After all, if retirees are meant to receive financial protection or poor people to gain access to medical care or farmers to get more income, it is not helpful to have these gains eroded by inflation. Security is not aided by economic uncertainty. The same, however, may be said of those who must pay taxes to provide these entitlements or compete with the federal government for credit. Whether the security of parts of the population can be improved through the insecurity of other parts is the question.

POLITICS: THE "OUGHT" AND "IS" OF ENTITLEMENTS

Moral power—the shared beliefs about who is entitled to what in society—is a necessary though not a sufficient condition for an entitlement program not only to exist on a minimal level but to grow. In the beginning of the American republic,

---

[26]Tobin, "The Future of Social Security," p. 10.

[27]Report to Congress, "What Can Be Done?" p. 29.

the concept of entitlement did not exist and there were no such programs. After the Civil War, pensions were provided for veterans and their widows. The era of modern entitlements begins with railroad retirement in 1934, a combination of influence and of grievance no more easy to disentangle than the general question of where moral norms begin and political power ends.

Suffice it to say now that at one level, individuals appear to be more deserving of entitlements than do governments (viz. the demise of revenue sharing). Affirmative action in regard to employment has not yet been matched by entitlements based on race or gender (except for women's roles as mothers). The elderly, especially, the poor, children, the sick are now favored, but inconsistencies in the categories—some sick, say, black lung sufferers, but not others, say, lung cancer victims—suggest special historical considerations.

The moral force of entitlements has varied with the degree to which beneficiaries are deemed responsible for their condition. The more the individual is considered responsible for poverty, for instance, the less likely is governmental provision. The more government or society is held responsible, the more appropriate an entitlement would be. Two views on civil service retirement illustrate the difference. The conservative position, emphasizing individual responsibility and fearful of government "handouts," was expressed in a 1956 hearing by Tom Murray, chairman of the House Committee on Post Office and Civil Service:

> In this day and time you never hear of the philosophy of saving for a rainy day, or practicing thrift; it looks like everybody wants to depend, or so many want to be dependent, on the Government to keep on supporting them for the rest of their lives after they retire. I cannot go along with that philosophy. I am interested in getting a retirement bill, but I want a sound actuarial fund.[28]

The liberal position, emphasizing adequacy, won out, as is expressed in a House report in 1969:

> Federal staff retirement systems represent a mixture of insurance and humanitarian principles. In the matter of adjusting annuities after retirement, insurance practice would guarantee that whatever annuity an employee had earned at the time of retirement should be preserved without change. On the other hand, humanitarian considerations would argue that the welfare of the retired person is the major concern, and that annuities should be adjusted to changing needs. The latter theory has prevailed through congressional action.[29]

Differences of opinion on who is responsible for poverty, and therefore entitled to what, remain great.[30] As entitlements rose, the balance swung away from individual and toward social (i.e., governmental) responsibility.

In John Mortimer's television series "Rumpole of the Bailey," the irascible Rumpole refers to his long-suffering wife as "she who must be obeyed." Appar-

---

[28]House Committee on Post Office and Civil Service, *Hearings on S.2875 and Related Matters,* June 18, 19, 21, 26 and July 3, 10, 12, 1956, p. 78.

[29]House Committee on Post Office and Civil Service, U.S. House of Representatives Report 91-158, *Civil Service Retirement Financing and Benefits,* p. 14.

[30]See Sidney Verba and Gary R. Orren, *Equality in America: The View from the Top* (Cambridge, Mass.: Harvard University Press, 1985), p..74.

ently, she has acquired entitlement status. The importance of moral force may be seen by returning to the classical notion of a budgetary base—that which ought not be moved. As a policy claim, entitlement is a way of guaranteeing a base. The program may go up but not down; she shall not be cut. This resistance is not only a matter of keeping old conflicts closed, but of a shared sense of justice. The base thus becomes the politically shared belief about "who is entitled to what" and is therefore bolstered and contested by arguments about equity and fairness.

A crucial factor in arguments about entitlements, therefore, is the socially constructed definition of equity or fairness. Should employees get what they paid for? Get what (somehow comparable) employees get? Not lose (to inflation)? Keep pace with society (retiree gets increases in line with increases in the standard of living)? Be guaranteed some "adequate" level of benefit? Any of these may legitimate an increase, but a package that reduces benefits overall can be justified on the ground that beneficiaries are already doing better than they should.

Even the prevailing sense of fairness—people should not be deprived of benefits—has variations. Is it fair to change the benefits for someone already retired, that is, reduce benefits currently received? If that is unfair, what about a change in benefits promised to those already working? Is it more fair to change the promise to younger employees than to older? The notion is that certain obligations are more obligating than others, in part because the ability of recipients to compensate for changes, and the degree to which they may have relied on the old system, varies.

Comparisons are crucial, but they cut both ways. In fiscal 1981, federal outlays for affordable housing came to some $7.5 billion, yet only a small proportion of those eligible were served. In fiscal 1982, however, tax preferences for mostly middle-class homeowners amounted to some $35.5 billion. These, too, can be considered entitlements. Is it that these politically untouchable but indirect tax expenditures should be reduced (they escaped the 1986 tax reform unscathed) or that the housing entitlements be increased?

Only the naive think that political power plays no role in entitlements; only the foolish think that politicians' perceptions of who is deserving play no part in determining who receives entitlements. Indeed, the two conceptions are related; perception that a clientele is powerful makes it easier to think they are deserving and belief that a clientele is worthy makes it easier to justify mobilizing resources on their behalf. Widespread belief that a class of citizens ought to be helped makes it harder to deny them entitlements just as the opposite belief in their unworthiness makes it harder to keep giving them this priority claim on our collective resources. In the nature of human affairs where mixed motives prevail, it is difficult to disentangle them; yet we can still recognize reciprocal influence between the "is" and "ought" of entitlements.

Anyone affected by a program may be among its clientele. This clientele includes not only the direct beneficiaries—wheat growers or schoolchildren who also eat subsidized lunches—but also the service providers—fertilizer and tractor companies, cooks and bottle washers, administrators, and interest groups—who live off of the recipients. Also included are the politicians and publicists who claim credit or bask in the glow of having not only done well but good. Clients comprise, to use Hugh Heclo's term, the issue networks of people not only in the federal but at all levels of government who are regularly concerned with operating, defending, criticizing, and altering entitlements.

The conditions for constituency influence are well known: The broader-based the group, the larger its numbers, the wider its geographic spread, the more intense its feelings (a joint product of the perceived importance of the benefits and beliefs about their rightness—I have fought for my country or worked all my life), the better its organization, the more resources (votes, money, intelligence, ability to appeal to shared values) it can mobilize, the more politically powerful it will be. So far so obvious. The size of a constituency depends not only on those affected now but those who expect to be affected later, not only on those directly involved but on those who care about them. The political potency of social security depends, to be sure, on the many millions of retired people. But it also is a consequence of those who contribute now and hope to benefit later, their families who will have to provide less support, and providers, like nursing homes, who service them.

The size of the direct beneficiaries is not a given factor, out there in nature like a fruit waiting to be plucked, but rather is socially and politically constructed. Who is or is not physically or mentally handicapped to what degree, requiring what sort of assistance, as in the Supplemental Security Income Program (SSI), changes with the standards of the time.[31] While the extremes are usually clear enough, programs can be altered to allow in more or fewer people. Major efforts may be made, as with food stamps, to actively encourage more people to apply. Here social mores figure prominently: Whether programs are seen as stigmatizing or whether recipients are exercising a too-long delayed right makes a considerable difference in "take-up" rates and hence in costs. Potential recipients have both to know about the availability of benefits and to feel the moral desirability of applying before their numbers will rise.

Similarly, a combination of a change in statutes, together with the rise of judicial activism in an egalitarian direction, have led to much greater court intervention on behalf of program expansion than in the past. When the Department of Agriculture failed to comply fully with the 1971 outreach amendment of the food stamp act to inform poor families of the benefits available to them, class-action suits compelled much greater compliance. Even more striking, the department's slowness in implementing the Special Supplemental Food Program for Women, Infants, and Children led to a class-action suit in 1976 requiring it to spend all the budget authority for the program accumulated since 1972.[32] The courts substituted their judgment for that of the Executive branch as to the pace and sum of spending. Thus changes in values among elites, in the judiciary, the media, and sources of opinion formation have their effect on entitlements.

While it is true that political forces create and alter entitlements, it is also true that entitlements help create political forces. Whether or not interest groups are influential in creating entitlements—often they are not—[33] the very existence of these benefits creates incentives for interest groups to organize.[34]

---

[31]See Deborah Stone, *The Disabled State* (Philadelphia: Temple University Press, 1984).

[32]Report to Congress, "What Can Be Done?" p. 24.

[33]See Aaron Wildavsky, *Speaking Truth to Power* (Boston: Little, Brown, 1979), Chapter 3, "Policy as Its Own Cause," pp. 62–85.

[34]Ibid.

Since size is such an important resource in obtaining political support, strong clients with weak claims, to use David Stockman's apt phrase,[35] or with insufficient influence are motivated to form coalitions. The survival of price supports in Congress is largely due to coalition building: Representatives from farm states, already advantaged by the rule that gives states with sparse population equal representation in the Senate, trade votes with each other; cotton is added to wheat and other commodities, farm and urban representatives trade votes on price supports in return for food stamps, nutrition programs, and so on. "It was the height of cynicism," so Robert Bauman, Republican from Maryland, felt, "to marry the food stamp program to the agricultural bill . . . it was done for purposes of political logrolling to gain votes for both bills."[36]

Logrolling may be limited by imposing a limit under which spending must fit, thereby trying to force tradeoffs among programs. Budget Director Stockman hoped to break the practice of budgeting by addition by coming "in with a plan that's unacceptable to the farm guys so that the whole thing begins to splinter."[37] At that time he succeeded; as a farm lobbyist said "It used to be that everybody could get their piece of the pie, and if the pie was too small [Congress] would just make it bigger."[38] An acute observer pictured the situation as a pond where "the water level is going down and the fish are flopping and sticking each other and biting."[39] But the story was not over. By disregarding its own advice not to outguess markets, a combination of external factors—good weather with bad international markets—and internal misjudgment—target prices went up much faster than inflation—spending on price supports soared far more under Reagan and Stockman than under the allegedly profligate Carter administration.

But how, if changing values matter, the reader may wonder, have tobacco supports survived? By compromise and by craft. The bad name given to smoking by the massive evidence of its connection to lung cancer, emphysema, heart disease, and other health dangers has naturally raised questions about why government should subsidize the production of the noxious weed. Then, again, counterbalancing this concern is the plight of the family farmer in the South. On one side, this clash of values led to compromise: Without going into the very technical details, a complex scheme was devised through which it could be said that tobacco farmers were paying for their own support. On the other side, strategies were followed making it difficult to single out tobacco for special (and, therefore, hostile) treatment. At various times, under the aegis of Senator Jesse Helms, Republican of North Carolina, tobacco supports have been combined with wheat and dairy programs or held hostage by southern senators to other dearly desired programs. By reducing the visible budgetary cost and by making opposition politically expensive, tobacco support has been maintained, albeit at a reduced level.

---

[35]David Stockman, "The Social Pork Barrel," *The Public Interest,* No. 39 (Spring 1975), pp. 3–30.

[36]John A. Ferejohn, "Logrolling in an Institutional Context: A Case Study of Food Stamps Legislation," *Working Papers in Political Science,* P-5-85 (Palo Alto, Calif.: Hoover Institute, October 1985), p. 19.

[37]William Greider, "The Education of David Stockman," *The Atlantic,* December 1981, p. 35.

[38]From Sieverts, on agricultural price supports.

[39]Ibid.

BEEKEEPERS AND (PUBLIC) PURSE SNATCHERS: GIVING ENTITLEMENTS A BAD NAME

Though there are good reasons for entitlements (government may wish to keep promises and provide income and services regardless of its own circumstances), their rapid growth began to give them a bad name. Entitlements as a class were held to blame for deficits. Entitlements were balls and chains that kept Congress from running to the rescue of an economy in distress. (Actually, some of them, by going up while the economy went down, may have helped.) While hardly anyone dared to oppose the programs that made up the bulk of entitlements, or that spoke to important values, such as alleviating hunger and providing pensions for the elderly, abuses in less-favored ones were regularly cited. The message was that entitlements were being misused, that charitable impulses had turned into commercial ventures with only government sure to lose. The beekeepers' entitlement is far from typical; but it raises the question of who is getting stung by entitlements in an extreme form. Seeing the worst will help us appreciate the moral force behind other entitlement programs.

Why is the United States federal government the sweetest touch in the world? The answer—because it stores and subsidizes the most honey—tells us something about why entitlements have become suspect. It may be small but the honey entitlement carries a big message.

The rationing of sugar and the need for beeswax to waterproof ammunition in World War II led to an increase in the production of honey. Prices dropped after the war, so the industry requested assistance. The Agricultural Act of 1949 required the Secretary of Agriculture to support the price of honey. The rationale given was that bees are essential in pollinating a number of crops and that this service either would be insufficient due to a shortage of bees or, in any event, farmers could not afford to pay. Naturally, like the World War II buildings that still dot our college campuses, the honey price support was supposed to be temporary. As usual, it was the government that got stung.

A price support level for honey is set. Beekeepers then obtain loans using honey stored with the government as collateral. If the market price rises, the keepers sell the honey and pay the government the principal plus a low rate of interest. If the market price declines, producers may default on their loans (without paying interest), leaving the government holding bags of honey.

Sweet stuff can lull you to sleep. From 1970 to 1979, no loans were in default. Then the usual combination of life (external forces) and government (internal legislation specifying conditions for entitlements) took hold. The inflation of the mid-70s, tied to an index for farm products, doubled the support price from 32.7 cents per pound in 1977 to 65.8 cents in 1984. Around the same time, foreign suppliers increased production and the world price of honey dropped. The rising value of the dollar, which made foreign goods cheaper, led imports to double between 1979 and 1984.

The combination of high support and low market prices had the expected results: Honey loans increased almost three times, honey left to the government increased twenty times (from 5.3 to 106 million pounds); the defaults cost Uncle Sam $133 million, and administrative costs for managing the honey rose from very little to $33 million. Essentially, honey was being produced to serve as collateral on which beekeepers could default. In the 1983 crop year, for example, 113.6 million pounds of honey were used as loan collateral but only about 7 million pounds were redeemed. A little more than half (52 percent) of all honey produced in the United States was defaulted to its government.

Nor is that all. Investigation by the General Accounting Office revealed that it is easy to adulterate bee honey with much cheaper corn syrup; even experts would have difficulty distinguishing by taste or appearance as much as 40 percent corn syrup mixed with honey. Yet the Department of Agriculture does not require tests of honey stored as collateral to see if it has been adulterated. "Some beekeepers told us," the GAO reports, "that they feed corn syrup to their bees during the winter or off-season. One of the beekeepers we talked with was installing a 30,000-gallon tank to store corn syrup at the time of our visit."[40]

Among the population of beekeepers—hobbyists, part-timers, and business— only 1 percent were classified as commercial, yet they operated around half of the honeybee colonies and made 60 percent of the honey. For some reason, only 1 percent of the nation's beekeepers take part in the price support program. It may well be that the entire commercial industry produces essentially for government storage. Departing from its usual staid and cautious approach, GAO leads its report with the headline "Federal Price Supports for Honey Should Be Phased Out."[41] In 1993, the honey support program was finally discontinued.

Funny-honey no more justifies condemnation of all entitlements than evidence of fraud is sufficient to reject welfare programs or "goldplating" (see Chapter 9) should lead us to abandon national defense. Like GAO, I suspect most of us would choose to satisfy our sweet tooth another way. It is not that any single entitlement broke the bank. It is, rather, that entitlements, taken together, without a corresponding willingness to raise taxes, broke the back of classical budgeting.

America, it is said, is promises. In that case, entitlements are very American. But it is also said that promises are made to be broken. Insofar as an old promise is a good promise, because of its long acceptance, we might expect new ones to be more readily subject to cutbacks. Insofar as notions of "fair shares" guide decision makers, those programs that have done well in the past or that have increased rapidly would be subject to cuts. Unfortunately, the record contains examples of "all of the above" without guidelines as to when they are applicable.

Consider the most common explanation: members of Congress cut in the most politically vulnerable areas. According to Kent Weaver

> Policymakers obviously wish to minimize political costs to themselves [in the distribution of cutbacks]. This gives clientele groups that are large (social security recipients), well-organized to mobilize recipients (veterans), and have a wide geographic base an advantage over those that are poorly organized and have a low voter turnout (AFDC recipients). Programs with a narrow geographic base (black lung disability) are also likely to fare poorly unless they can form logrolling coalitions with other programs, or

---

[40]Report to the Congress by the Comptroller General, "Federal Price Support for Honey Should Be Phased Out," GAO/RCED-85-107, August 19, 1985, p. 36.

[41]Ibid., p. 1.

policy control is monopolized by program supporters. Many of the program cuts were indeed directed at groups least able to resist them.[42]

It is true that in 1981 and 1982, the first two years of the Reagan administration, means-tested entitlements were hit hardest. The near-poor lost the most. In 1986, approximately $120 billion in tax preferences were shifted from individuals, with a decided emphasis on the near-poor, to corporations. And in 1984, 1985, and 1986, very large amounts were cut from the defense budget, not everyone's idea of a bastion of budgetary vulnerability. It does appear, if only by definition, that the groups and functions that had benefits reduced must have been weak, for if they had been strong this could not have happened to them. Since these targets of opportunity varied considerably over a short time, however, we are no wiser.

Much has been written that attempts to link the size and distribution of expenditures with such factors as party composition of Congress and party affiliation of the president. Hibbs and Dennis, for example, have sought to identify how shifts in party control of the presidency and Congress have affected the distribution of government spending. They suggest that "the strength of the Democrats in Congress is the main political source of increases in the share of transfers in gross personal income," whereas "shifts in party control of the presidency had negligible direct influence."[43] There is evidence, however, that party control may be rivaled in importance by economic factors (inflation, unemployment) and program-specific spending desires, such as coal mine disasters.[44]

Toward the end of the twentieth century, though, pressures to balance the budget and cut taxes seemed finally to put entitlements in the spotlight, and we do not know at this point which will continue to flourish, and which will wither. As things now stand, it seems likely that social security will remain untouched (although there have been proposals to privatize it); that the rates of growth of medicare and medicaid will be slowed sharply; and that welfare and food stamp and similar means-tested entitlements will be the subject of prolonged wrangling. The distinction between budgeting and entitlements, referred to at the beginning of this chapter, may be becoming less sharp, as entitlements too enter into the politics of subtraction. To obtain a better understanding of why some entitlements have flourished and may continue to do so, while others are vulnerable to reduction or even elimination, it will be informative to take a closer look at the budgetary history of specific entitlements. They are selected to show rapid, moderate, and slow growth. The perceptive reader, who begins to wonder whether scholars are asking for too much—a key to political change—may be on the right track.

---

[42]Weaver, "Controlling Entitlements," pp. 328–29.

[43]Douglas A Hibbs, Jr., and Christopher Dennis, "The Politics and Economics of Income Distribution Outcomes in the Postwar United States," transcript, 1986, p. 16.

[44]See Mark S. Kamlet and David C. Mowery, "Influences on Executive and Congressional Budgetary Priorities, 1953–1981," *American Political Science Review*, Vol. 81, No. 1 (March 1987), pp. 155–78.

Chapter
8

The Rise and Fall
of Entitlements

*E*very human society makes some provision for those who cannot look after themselves: the old, the sick, the disabled, the destitute, and children. Usually this role has been undertaken by the family, predominantly by women, supplemented by charity. In the twentieth century, with the development of modern industrial economies, governments have increasingly stepped in to shoulder the risks arising from economic uncertainties, provide security in old age and illness, and ensure at least a minimum standard of living to those unable to cope on their own. In communist countries where no private sector existed, these benefits were related to the workplace.[1] In Western Europe, with considerable variations, they formed a comprehensive system of rights and guarantees enshrined in the cradle-to-grave policy of the welfare state.[2] In the United States, a patchwork of entitlements grew up, conveying benefits through subsidies, grants, loans, pensions and federal-state payments to differing groups of eligible beneficiaries. By 1990 nearly half of all families in the United States received benefits from one or more of 11 major entitlement programs, averaging over $10,000 annually.[3]

Approaching the end of the twentieth century, all these arrangements are showing strain: The collapse of communism has also disrupted the system of rights and benefits tied to it; the welfare state is in disarray; and in the United States entitlements which have seemed an impregnable and permanent part of the budgetary landscape are being seriously questioned.

The perception—by no means universally held—that entitlements have become too expensive or a drain on the economy may be traced to a number of possible sources. Entitlements have been blamed for the persistent large budget

---

[1]Naomi Caiden, "The Roads to Transformation: Budgeting Issues in the Czech and Slovak Federal Republic 1989–1992," *Public Budgeting and Finance*, Vol. 13, No. 4, Winter 1993, pp. 57–71.

[2]Gerald Caiden and Naomi Caiden, "Brothers' Keepers," *Society*, Vol. 32, No. 6, September/October 1995, pp. 16–22.

[3]Congressional Budget Office, *Reducing Entitlement Spending* (Washington D.C.: Congressional Budget Office, September 1994), p. xi.

deficits. The slower rates of economic growth in the 1980s and 1990s, punctuated by recessions, have pinched middle- and working-class incomes and have intensified resentment of taxation. If the federal budget is to be balanced, entitlements can no longer be allowed to float free, so to speak, but must be constrained within the budget equation. Some entitlements appear contrary to principles of economic theory: Individuals should be free to make their own economic choices without government interference or subsidy which merely impeded the efficient working of markets. Others go across the moral grain: People should take responsibility for their lives and not look to governments to subsidize their own irresponsibility. As the apparent size of the pie becomes smaller, the politics have become sharper, pitting one group against another, old against young, middle class against working class, and ethnicities against each other.

Since 1980, spending for individual entitlements has been limited by reducing cost of living adjustments, holding down payments to medical care providers, and restricting eligibility for benefits. A Bipartisan Commission on Entitlement and Tax Reform, reporting at the end of 1994, proclaimed a crisis in entitlement spending and the need for drastic action *now* to curb the growth of social security, the health programs and other entitlements through such means as limited privatization, cuts in payments, and increasing the retirement age. But not much notice was taken.

The Republican program of 1995 with its determination to balance the budget and reverse social provision confronted the entitlements head on. The eventual resolution is uncertain, but just as the entitlements grew untidily, it is unlikely that the choices to reduce them will be made systematically, that a stable disposition will be achieved, or that outcomes will result from a coherent or universally agreed set of criteria. While certain themes may be common or recurring in each debate—the feasibility or desirability of caps, federal or state provision, block grants versus entitlements, individual versus social responsibility—other issues are specific to each case. The continuation, modification, or elimination of each entitlement will depend on the specific politics surrounding it.

Table 8.1   SELECTED ENTITLEMENT PROGRAMS

	(in constant FY86 billions of dollars)		
	Actual 1977 outlays	Estimated 1986 outlays	Annual growth 1977–1986
Medicare	37.8	66.7	6.86
Medicaid	17.3	24.7	4.02
Social security	147.1	200.1	3.48
Food stamps	9.5	12.6	3.18
Military retirements	14.4	17.4	2.15
Supplemental security income	9.3	10.2	1.00
Veterans compensation	10.0	10.5	0.47
Black Lung	1.7	1.7	−0.41
AFDC	11.1	9.7	−1.48
Social services	4.5	2.6	−5.84
General revenue sharing	11.9	4.4	−10.34
G.I. Bill	6.5	0.9	−19.63

Table 8.2   GROWTH OF SELECTED MANDATORY PROGRAMS
IN CONSTANT (FY1987) DOLLARS, 1987–1994

	1987	1993	1994
Education, training, employment, social services	7.3	11.2	7.3
Medicaid	27.4	59.6	63.5
Medicare	73.4	99.9	109.3
Federal employee retirement and disability	43.7	47.1	48.2
Food & nutrition assistance	16.9	24.9	25.5
Supplemental security Income	9.9	16.6	18.9
Family support assistance	10.5	12.3	12.8
Social security	205.1	237.2	244.6
Veterans benefits & services	15.7	15.7	15.1
Agriculture	24.5	13.3	8.4

Source: United States Budget, Fiscal Year 1996, Historical Tables: Table 8.6, *Outlays for Mandatory and Related Programs in Constant (FY1987) Dollars, 1962–2000,* pp. 107–108.

Why did entitlements grow, and which are likely to decline? As we have seen, entitlements escape annual review through the appropriations process. Entitlements with strong constituency influence and moral power fare better than programs lacking these attributes. Entitlements grow also because of external factors, such as changes in population, inflation, or unemployment. If that were all there was to it, however, programs with entitlement status would keep growing; none would become smaller; and all would fare better than programs in similar policy areas funded by appropriations. But the facts belie such easy generalizations. Appropriations sometimes grow faster than entitlements, which, in turn, do actually decline, or even are abolished. (See Tables 8.1 and 8.2.) As we move into a period in which many entitlements are under attack, understanding the growth or decline of an entitlement calls for a closer examination of the history of particular programs.

All entitlements are not created equal. Some have grown quickly, some have stayed about the same (adjusting for inflation), and some have been terminated or have declined significantly. Obviously, entitlements are not an automatic ticket to financial paradise (although entitlement status greatly helps) and being funded through annual appropriations is not necessarily a death knell.

HIGH RISERS

Medicare

Medicare for the elderly has been one of the fastest growing entitlements. In 1967, medicare enrolled 19 million eligible beneficiaries and had expenditures of $4 billion.[4] By 1982, medicare had 29 million eligible beneficiaries and almost $50 billion in expenditures. By 1994, there were 36 million medicare recipients, and the program cost between $142 billion and $160 billion each year. Medicare pay-

---

[4]This account is drawn from student papers by Walter Wong and Marc de la Vergne.

ments have been increasing about 10 percent annually over the past decade, out-pacing such stiff competition as the rise in the Consumer Price Index and expansion of the federal budget.

The medicare program has two components: Part A provides hospital insurance, and Part B, the supplementary Medical Insurance Program (SMI), covers physician services and other health care services. Under Part A, funds (raised by a 2.9 percent tax on payrolls) are placed in the Hospital Insurance Trust Fund. Anyone over the age of 65 who has contributed wages to social security may have part of their medical costs paid for through Part A. Part A therefore represents a genuine entitlement. Part B, however, is voluntary and requires participants (96 percent of eligibles are enrolled) to pay a monthly premium ($46.10 monthly).

Together, these two eligibility criteria create a strong political base for the medicare program. Aside from the 36 million people currently eligible for payments, medicare also draws support from family members who are protected against possible financial responsibility for the illness of a parent or relative, and of active members of the work force who are current contributors and future beneficiaries of the trust fund. Since medical care for the elderly has come to be recognized by society as the morally correct course to follow, politicians talk about cutting medicare only at the risk of sounding uncaring toward the aged.

The age and social security criteria have served to define the boundaries for expansion of the beneficiary base. In 1972, for instance, disabled individuals younger than 65 became entitled to monthly disability benefits under the social security retirement program; and individuals under 65 suffering from kidney failure were made eligible for the social security or retirement program. Each of these groups was in some way a contributor to the trust fund and, accordingly, had some type of claim to payments from the trust. Yet other groups, such as the unemployed, have been unable thus far to work their way onto the medicare rolls.

Growth in medicare was also sustained by incremental changes. Part A of medicare has been shielded through its relationship with social security, which takes a much larger share of the payroll tax. Individuals are often unaware of the portion being taken to finance medicare and increases in the medicare tax. The changes in a single year may be small, but the cumulative growth rate over, say, five years that they represent is not. The Part B premium also allowed costs to grow without much notice: Originally it was expected that enrollees and the government would pay equally into the fund, but in 1972, Congress limited increases in premiums to the rate of increase in social security cash benefits, and made the federal treasury responsible for any funding gap between premiums and benefits. At the beginning of the 1980s, there were warnings that the Hospital Insurance Fund was running out of money, and starting with the reconciliation bill in 1981, a series of reforms were launched to try to bring down costs, including fixed prospective reimbursements,[5] but medicare continued to grow as much as 10 percent a year.

Why have cost-sharing rules been unable to control demand? One reason is that medicare's primary goal is to improve access. Consequently, rather than de-

---

[5]Congressional Budget Office, *Reducing Entitlement Spending*, p. xi.

signing cost-sharing schedules to ensure that beneficiaries don't overuse services, schedules have been designed to ensure that no one who needs services hesitates to seek help merely because of cost-sharing arrangements. Another is that both providers and intermediaries have strong incentives not to control costs. For providers, like hospitals, lower costs would mean lower revenues. For intermediaries, such as insurance companies, the interest is to promote good relationships with providers, for insurers have to deal with providers to process their own claims. They have no incentive to lower costs, since the government is paying the bills.

Medicare reform is a prickly issue, which critics such as Allen Schick, charge that Congress has been perennially unwilling to grasp.[6]

In the 1990s, medicare, simply because of its size became a prime target for budget cutting. In 1993, President Clinton made savings in medicare of $56 billion over five years. "How" asked Allen Schick, "did the president manage to pare so much without cutting benefits? Medicare proved the job is not as difficult as one might think." Most cuts came from a high baseline which had incorporated a very large allowance for inflation.[7] But this maneuver was only the precursor for far more serious and wide-ranging reforms that may presage the end of the medicare entitlement.

Despite its political base, founded in the large constituency of the elderly and their claims based on contributions and premiums, medicare is vulnerable. Since social security appeared untouchable, medicare, because of its size and rapid growth seemed a logical second best. The case was supported, somewhat disingenuously, by the discovery that the medicare Part A trust fund would run out of money in the year 2002 if nothing were done.[8]

Is there really a crisis in medicare? Theodore Marmur, author of *The Politics of Medicare*, has pointed out that the Part A trust fund will cease to balance early in the next century, but this should not be a cause for panic, or for precipitate or desperate action at this time. The trust fund, he says, is essentially an accounting device, and like social security in 1983, policy adjustments can be made at any time to bring income and outgo into whatever relationship is desired. The Republican agenda, he believes, is reminiscent of the Vietnam War My Lai syndrome: In order to save the program, it is necessary to destroy it.[9] Donna Shalala, secretary of the Department of Health and Human Services, declared "There is no new Medicare crisis," and noted that the trustees had warned nine times of bankruptcy in the past seven years and adjustments had been made to forestall it.[10]

Cuts of the magnitude proposed in the 1995 reconciliation bill require more than incremental tampering. The "health industry," despite consuming about 14

---

[6]Allen Schick, "Controlling the 'Uncontrollables': Budgeting for Health Care in an Age of Mega-Deficits." Paper prepared for AEI Pew Fellows Conference, November 1985, pp. 1–2.

[7]Allen Schick, *The Federal Budget: Politics, Policy, Process* (Washington D.C.: Brookings Institution, 1995), p. 23.

[8]*Congressional Quarterly Weekly Report*, May 29 1995, p. 1166.

[9]Theodore Marmur, PBS radio interview, September 13, 1995.

[10]Colette Fraley, "Democrats Say GOP Surgery on Medicare Goes Too Far," *Congressional Quarterly Weekly Report*, October 7, 1995, p. 3069.

percent of GDP annually, is itself not in good shape. Hospitals had been adversely affected by the growth of managed care, the increasing inability to shift costs to full-paying patients, and the failure of reimbursement rates to keep up with service costs.[11] The inability to pass general health care reform in 1994 had left the situation more or less as it was: a large number of people without any health care at all, and high and rising medical and hospital care costs. Growing medicare payments, which threatened to outrun current sources of funding in the next few years, were a prominent part of this picture.

It was only to be expected that presumably nonsuicidal political leaders, targeting a program with a large constituency of well-organized beneficiaries (for the sake of an abstract goal such as budget balance) would move cautiously. But the size of the reduction they proposed in 1995 was a red flag for the opposition. Why, they demanded (conceding the valuable ground that medicare was sinking and had to be rescued), was it necessary to cut $270 billion, when experts believed the funding gap was less than $100 billion? The president came up with a plan for $100 billion net savings (as well as some increases), and the Democrats with one for $90 billion. Their charge was that excess savings in medicare were being used to finance the Republican tax cut; Republicans countered they were saving medicare from bankruptcy.

The Republican proposal that emerged from Congress and was folded into the reconciliation bill was a complex piece of legislation. It illustrates a number of issues relating to entitlements, replacement of government provision with quasi-markets, and the problematic nature of budget projections in highly uncertain areas. Only the major issues are covered here and negotiations have really only just begun.

The most fundamental change proposed was the setting of a cap on medicare expenditures, thereby ending the open-ended entitlement. If expenditures threatened to exceed the cap, payments to providers would be cut. While the House Ways and Means Committee Chairman William Archer said "We said we would save Medicare and we did," the president vowed to veto the bill, declaring that he had to "protect the people of the United States and protect the integrity of this program."[12] The change was far more than one of financing, as the details of the plan showed.

At the heart of the plan was the proposal to set up a quasi-market in health care for the elderly. In theory, the change would provide more choice—between privately run HMOs, medical savings accounts, and the traditional fee for service. Two issues were foremost. Would the structural changes bring about the anticipated savings? How would they affect groups with differing health and income?

The financing mechanism would first provide fixed payments, based on annual average medicare recipient payments, for each individual enrolled in a health maintenance organization (HMO), which would then look after that person's health needs. If individuals chose to do so, they might instead open medical savings accounts (MSAs), in which the government would place a similar amount, part of which

[11]*National Journal,* July 29 1995, p. 1936.

[12]Laurie McGinley, "Medicare Bill Passed by the House Would End Egalitarian Approach," *Wall Street Journal,* October 20, 1995, p. A1.

would be used to purchase a high-deductible insurance policy, and part of which could be withdrawn for medical needs as the individual thought fit, or allowed to roll over in the account. When these needs were satisfied, the remainder of the funds would be used for fee-for-service, where, if they were not adequate, payments to providers would be cut.

The capability of the plan to achieve savings depended on people's behavior. The CBO confirmed that nearly three-quarters of the savings would come from cuts in provider payments and the minority of beneficiaries already enrolled in HMOs.[13] Only a small amount could be expected from new HMO enrollees, while the MSAs would actually cost the government up to $4 billion. The HMOs and particularly the MSAs, it was charged, would attract the younger, healthier population (one-third of beneficiaries cost less than $1000 each from 1990–1993, and 17 percent of the elderly do not file a single claim). On these, therefore, the government would make a "loss," as their costs were below the average medicare recipients's payments, which were skewed by the very sick.

The equity issue was also important, for the choices were not even for all. While the traditional fee-for-service was an option for everyone, as payments for medicare patients were lowered, providers would have less and less incentive to treat them, unless they were able to pay higher fees than the medicare schedule. The MSAs would not be a viable option for the sicker part of the population, who could not afford to finance the high deductible for medical treatment. In other words, poor people would not be able to afford these options. In Robert Reischauer's words, the plan would operate as a "stealth mechanism to move people into managed care."[14]

There were numerous other details—the doubling of Part B premiums (although it was allegedly Part A of the medicare trust fund that was in trouble), the lifting of antitrust regulations to allow doctors to form their own private schemes, a trust fund for teaching hospitals, a cap on medical malpractice awards. Some of these were incentives for the forthcoming backing of the powerful American Medical Association for the plan, which the American Association of Retired Persons vehemently opposed. Others were added to facilitate the bill's passage; even though it passed on partisan lines, within the Republican party many had reservations, Senate and House versions had to be reconciled, and a variety of interests had to be satisfied. The president also agreed to cuts in medicare, including increase in premiums, but not to the plan itself (see Chapter 12).

Apart from the question of whether the plan will ever be signed into law, it raised a number of questions that would apply to any similar reform or compromise. Is it likely that expenditure growth rates in medicare can be almost halved without either cutting services or quality of care or increasing payments? Would managed care, primarily oriented to younger, healthier working members, be able to achieve the same economies and efficiencies with an older, frailer clientele? Does it make sense to reform medicare without reference to the health care system as a whole? Would the public support changes?

---

[13]*New York Times,* September 28, 1995, pp. A1, A10.

[14]*Wall Street Journal,* September 25, 1995, A16.

More fundamental questions relate to the nature of entitlements, government provision, and equity in markets. "Is every elderly American entitled to the same access to health care? Or should health care be no different from food, clothing and housing—more available to people with money?"[15] And should one section of the population be insulated from the choices, good and bad, that confront the rest of the population?

Medicaid

Medicaid's enactment was an outgrowth of a slow but orderly involvement of government in health care spanning decades. As early as 1798, the federal government funded the delivery of medical services to merchant seamen in special hospitals.[16] Later, the federal government provided hospitalization and other types of medical care for members of the armed forces, veterans, Indians, and certain other groups. The Federal Emergency Relief Act of 1933 constituted the first federal legislation to provide health care for the needy. Under this act, the Federal Emergency Relief Administration (FERA) was set up to make funds available to states for paying medical-care costs of the unemployed needy.

The FERA program lasted only two-and-a-half years. Although it was not uniform throughout all the states, did not cover some essential services, and had many serious shortcomings,[17] the program did exercise great influence on subsequent medical-care programs. FERA, for example, emphasized the role of governmental agencies as purchasers of medical care in contrast with previous reliance on volunteer services of physicians and hospitals, and set a precedent for increased participation of the federal and state governments in financing medical care for the indigent.[18]

Medicaid is one of several federal-state social welfare programs in which benefits are made available to eligible groups of citizens. The benefits are medical services; the eligibles are welfare recipients and poor people; the mechanism is public payments to vendors of services. This vendor-payment mechanism operates as third-party coverage. In other words, state programs pay bills for services rendered to recipients by health providers. Payment is made directly to providers rather than to eligibles. Once eligible, recipients are entitled to receive services for which they are covered.

Like Aid to Families with Dependent Children, medicaid is a means-tested, residual welfare program. As a residual program, it is intended to pick up the slack when the market and the family do not meet the need. Medicaid requires individual applicants for benefits to demonstrate not only that they are poor but also that they meet certain other requirements (which vary with the state).

Medicaid also can be characterized as a grant-in-aid program by which the federal government pays a portion of the cost incurred by states in providing medical

---

[15]McGinley, "Medicare Bill Passed by House Would End Egalitarian Approach," A8.

[16]Anthony Jong, *Dental Public Health and Community Dentistry* (St. Louis: C.V. Mosby, 1981).

[17]See Margaret Greenfield, *Medicare and Medicaid: The 1965 and 1967 Social Security Amendments* (Westport, Conn.: Greenwood, 1968).

[18]Ibid.

care to the poor, the aged, the blind, and the disabled. The program is financed by payroll taxes and general revenues. Medicaid is a bifurcated program; that is, the federal government pays half or more of the money but leaves development and administration of the program to the states. In actuality, medicaid is not a single program but fifty, since the decisions that states make within the federally established framework of laws and regulations determine the character of the program.

Because of the open-ended nature of medicaid, new fiscal controls cannot be applied through budget limits. States can assert fiscal control only by changing their programs—eligibility standards, services covered, and the like. The federal government asserts fiscal control indirectly by enacting laws and promulgating regulations that increase or restrict states' options in designing and administering their programs. How have states reduced medicaid spending?

In general, taking direct action affecting existing beneficiaries was less popular than relying on inflation to effect cuts, though a few states did change eligibility standards. The most important argument against eligibility reductions was the fact that many of the medically needy are aged and institutionalized. Consequently, elimination of eligibility was extremely unpopular. The cost of treating such individuals (at least under medicaid the "feds" pay their half) would have been shifted to county-run hospitals and facilities and ultimately to local taxpayers.

States have an incentive to obtain federal matching dollars. If they choose not to, there is an increased financial burden on states, counties, and cities. The need for government assistance in providing or paying for medical care for the poor would not disappear if medicaid eligibility were constrained. Experience showed that broad medicaid eligibility standards (and higher federal assistance) actually reduced overall medical spending by states, counties, and cities instead of increasing it.[19]

Between 1970 and 1980, medicaid spending by both federal and state governments grew on average over 17 percent a year. In 1981 President Reagan proposed ending medicaid's status as an entitlement program, capping federal expenditures on it. The proposal was defeated, opposed by Congress and most state governors. Instead, Congress gave states more flexibility over their programs to change eligibility and make cuts. During the 1980s spending growth slowed, but still remained at an average of over 8 percent a year.[20] Allen Schick argued that incentives for spending containment were weak because federal savings from cutbacks would gain less than those from medicare, medicaid was seen as a vital part of the safety net for the poor, it was financed out of general revenues (not a trust fund), and states had an incentive to maintain the federal share.[21]

Between 1985 and 1990 federal medicaid outlays almost doubled (from $22.7 billion to $41.1 billion), and had doubled again by 1994 to $82 billion. In 1996, combined federal-state spending was expected to reach $170 billion, with 37 million people participating in the program. Annual growth of the federal share

---

[19]Randall R. Bovbjerg and John Holahan, *Medicaid in the Reagan Era: Federal Policy and State Choices* (Washington, D.C.: Urban Institute, 1982).

[20]Colette Fraley, "The Blossoming of Medicaid," *Congressional Quarterly Weekly Report,* June 10, 1995, p. 1638.

[21]Schick, "Controlling the 'Uncontrollables,'" pp. 27–28.

of medicaid over the next five years has been projected to be 11 percent, making medicaid the fastest growing federal program. By the year 2000, outlays are expected to double again.[22]

Why did medicaid grow so fast? We may cite the lack of universal health care, the ever-rising cost of health care premiums, and the growing gap between rich and poor. Medicaid was now the chief provider of health care for about 25 million poor adults and children, and helped support 5 million disabled people.[23] To a growing extent it also had become a key support for the elderly. Medicaid covered over half the cost of nursing homes and part of medicare coverage for the elderly.[24] In 1993, 35 percent of total medicaid payments went to nursing homes and home health care.[25] While the largest single group of beneficiaries is children from low income families (over 16 million) and welfare recipients and low income pregnant women are another large group, these consume less than half of expenditures. Seventy percent of nursing home residents rely on medicaid to cover their costs.[26] In 1995, over 60 percent of medicaid's $157 billion was spent on the 30 percent of clients who were frail elderly, or disabled: "These are not the stereotypical recipients of welfare," said Stephen O'Connell of the Alzheimer's Association. "They are middle class working families who have spent all their money [on care] and now turn to Medicaid."[27] By this time, medicaid expenditures were estimated to account for 20 percent of the average state's expenditures.

In 1995 the size and growth of medicaid made it an obvious target for Republicans in Congress. Like Reagan, they planned to end the program's entitlement status, and to give states grants instead. The aim was to produce $182 billion in savings over seven years. States would be free to design their own programs and determine eligibility. The Republicans argued that program growth was out of control, and states would be able better to control spending by curbing fraud and abuse and moving to greater use of managed care. Democrats countered that the cuts would eliminate coverage for 4.4 million children by 2002.[28] But unlike earlier experiences, state governors did not uniformly oppose the reforms, though it took considerable time to negotiate an acceptable formula which satisfied states with fast growing populations (in West and South) as well as those with slow growing or declining populations (in mid-West and East).

The consequences of the proposal remain hazy. A 1983 analysis suggested that unless states were required to make specified state contributions, average

---

[22]General Accounting Office, *Medicare: Spending Pressures Drive States to Reinvention,* April 1995, p. 3.

[23]"Attack of the Killer Blockheads," *The Economist,* September 2, 1995, pp. 21–22.

[24]General Accounting Office, "Medicaid: Restructuring Approaches Leave Many Questions," April 1995 (GAO/HEHS-95-103).

[25]Marylin Werber Serafini, "Plugging a Big Drain on Medicare," *National Journal,* March 18, 1995, p. 687.

[26]Elizabeth Shogren, "GOP Nursing Home Plan Holds Perils, Democrats Say," *Los Angeles Times,* October 13 1995, p. A16.

[27]Jonathan Peterson, "Given Facts, Cause to Slash Medicaid Not So Clear-Cut," *Los Angeles Times,* May 16 1995, p. A13.

[28]*New York Times,* October 23, 1995.

state spending levels would be substantially reduced.[29] Studies also suggest that the savings gained by moving groups such as the elderly into health maintenance organizations and other managed care arrangements yield relatively small savings.[30] Currently, nearly a quarter of medicaid recipients are in HMOs and similar plans.[31]

The fate of medicaid is, at the time of writing, still unresolved. At the beginning of February 1996, the conference of the National Governors' Association unanimously adopted a plan that would replace the federal commitment with a block grant. While it would continue health care coverage for certain groups, it would allow states considerable flexibility in determining eligibility for coverage, and also eliminate existing benefits, such as those for children over 12 in families below the federal poverty line.

HOLDING THEIR OWN

Not all entitlements have large groups of beneficiaries, or grow at exponential rates. The history of the Black Lung and End-Stage Renal Disease programs illustrate how the federal government sometimes gets into the business of helping select groups of individuals. Why people with these health problems rather than many others? And what factors explain the budgetary histories of these programs?

Black Lung[32]

On November 20, 1968, a coal mine explosion at Farmington, West Virginia, killed seventy-eight miners and sparked a nationwide outcry over working conditions in the mines. The television pictures of smoke, rescuers, and weeping families made such a powerful impression that the federal government was called to redress the miners' plight with regulation and compensation. It was intended, however, that federal participation would be temporary and limited in scope so as to function while the states and the coal mining industry were negotiating a compensatory mechanism for on-the-job disability and coal-dust pneumoconiosis. Once these arrangements were settled, it was thought, the federal government would withdraw its administrative and financial involvement. Twenty-five years later, the government was still supporting disability payments to miners.[33]

Black lung disease (or pneumoconiosis) refers to the pathological process of inhaled coal dust lining the airways of the lung. The disease, to a very significant degree, increasingly restricts the person's activities. In extreme cases, fibrotic changes can be so overwhelming as to inhibit blood flow from the heart to the

---

[29]See Thomas W. Grammerman and Mark V. Pauly, *Controlling Medicaid Costs: Federalism, Competition and Choice* (Washington, D.C.: American Enterprise Institute for Public Policy Research, 1983).

[30]Marylin Werber Serafini, "Managed Medicare," *National Journal,* March 15, 1995, p. 923.

[31]*Wall Street Journal,* May 12, 1995, p. A1.

[32]This section is based on a paper by Jack Chow.

[33]Budget of the United States Government, FY 1983 (Appendix), Executive Office of the President: Office of Management and Budget, I-014-15.

lungs, resulting in heart failure and eventual death. For the great majority of pneumoconiosis cases, even in coal miners, the result is dust retention with no visible pathology. These "category 1" people may or may not progress to the disabling manifestations of the disease. Since other factors (smoking, lifestyle, and the gender of the individual) may be involved, there is no predictive correlation between the presence of category 1 pneumoconiosis and disability.

The black lung issue became a passion when, by early 1969, spontaneous walkouts at various mines exploded into a series of "black lung strikes" involving over 45,000 miners in West Virginia, Pennsylvania, and Ohio. In West Virginia, a bill was passed that established black lung as a compensable occupational illness with liberal criteria for disability.[34]

The West Virginia law established a black lung entitlement framework that miners took to be a central tenet of their health care interests. As federal policy on the black lung issue evolved, this definition of black lung became a lever by which miners could establish and increase their federal benefits. The fervent demonstration of militancy by the miners, furthermore, instilled a popular notion of moral obligation by the federal government to ensure safety and compensation. The public image of the miner as an economic instrument of the coal companies put that industry, and the expenditure-control groups in Congress, on the defensive for the coming decade.

Soon Congress crafted the landmark Federal Coal Mine Health and Safety Act of 1969, the forerunner to the Occupational Safety and Health Act (OSHA) of 1970. Title IV of the act, entitled "Black Lung Benefits," mandated that the disease be compensable with general revenue funds. The black lung provisions entitled two main groups of people: coal miners totally disabled from pneumoconiosis derived from underground mines, and widows of underground coal miners who died from pneumoconiosis. Basic benefit amounts were linked to Federal Civil Service disability benefit levels that increase as federal salaries rose with adjustments.[35]

It was expected that by mid-1970 over 165,000 applications would be filed. In reality, over 183,000 were filed by June and 250,000 by the beginning of 1971.[36]

Overall, several aspects of the entitlement made for future growth. First, the clauses of irrefutability (the cause of pneumoconiosis is defined by law as related to the amount of time spent in the mine), and the assumption of total disability upon demonstration of "complicated" pneumoconiosis made it hard for government to deny claims. Second, unlike most workmen's compensation programs (where there is an inherent adversarial relationship between worker and company), the black lung entitlement neutralized antagonism by forcing the government to pay out benefits without assessing responsibility upon the coal-mine operators. Although government reserved the right to recover from the operator

---

[34]Alan Derickson, "The Origins of the Black Lung Insurgency," *Journal of Public Health Policy*, Vol. 4, No. 1 (March 1983), pp. 32–33.

[35]Bernard Popick, "The Social Security Disability Program. III. The Black Lung Benefits—an Administrative Case Study," *Journal of Occupational Medicine*, Vol. 13, No. 7 (July 1971), p. 335.

[36]Ibid.

responsible monies paid to workers, the lengthy and costly appeals process available to the operators made such recovery a very expensive enterprise. Third, the appeals process available to unsuccessful applicants incurred additional legal and administrative expenses. Backlogs of cases added to the frustration of both worthy miners and claims adjusters and fueled political pressure to simplify the process by liberalizing eligibility criteria. Fourth, the very specificity of the entitlement—pneumoconiosis and disability derived from underground coal mining—entailed substantial effort to document, review, and assess medical criteria (often incomplete) relevant to the benefit.[37]

In 1972, the entitlement was expanded by liberalizing the medical criteria for eligibility and strengthening the responsibility of mine operators.[38] The amendment effectively expanded the definition of "black lung" to include dust-induced bronchitis and emphysema.[39] Expanding the number of compensable diseases under a generic category not only added financial responsibility for the government, but—through looser standards of medical criteria and administrative review—also greatly enhanced applicants' accessibility to the entitlement. How did this change take place?

Action on eligibility standards by House and Senate authorization committees effectively bypassed the more conservative Appropriations Committee. In the Senate, eligibility provisions fell under the aegis of the Human Resources Committee while trust fund details were the responsibility of the Finance Committee. Splitting the two key elements of the entitlement proposal among separate committees allowed for little leverage by expenditure control groups to limit fiscal obligations. Limitations imposed in one committee could be negated by the liberalizations passed by another.

Congress dropped automatic eligibility, but in 1978 passed more lenient standards of disability and restricted governmental review of x-rays. A new Black Lung Disability Trust Fund was to be financed through a federal excise tax on coal—50 cents a ton on underground coal and 25 cents a ton on surface coal. Congress also gave tax preferences to companies that established their own fund to cover obligations toward miners. The industrywide trust fund was to pay miners for whom the government could not find an individual operator responsible.[40]

Another key provision committed the Treasury to cover deficits produced by the trust fund. Unfortunately, the trust fund began to bleed almost immediately, committing the government to pay nearly $420 million after 1979, $1 billion after 1980,[41] and $1.5 billion after 1981.[42] Lagging coal sales reduced income for the fund as operators continued to contest a high percentage of claims, thus transfer-

---

[37]L. E. Kerr, "Black Lung," *Journal of Public Health Policy,* Vol. 1, No. 1 (March 1980), p. 50.

[38]*1975 Congressional Quarterly Almanac,* p. 494.

[39]Kerr, "Black Lung," p. 57.

[40]*1977 Congressional Quarterly Almanac,* p. 267.

[41]Richard Corrigan, "Miners Rally to Block Black Lung Benefit Cuts," *National Journal,* March 28, 1981.

[42]*1981 Congressional Quarterly Almanac,* p. 115.

ring more cases to the trust fund's responsibility. The number of cases financed by the trust fund nearly doubled: from 69,500 in 1979 to 138,000 in 1980.[43]

With the advent of the Reagan administration, the focus changed from one of increased federal participation to a desire to shift costs to other parties. Reagan's 1982 budget proposals called for restricting benefits to the "truly medically disabled" and increasing the coal tax for the trust fund. In exchange for a sharp reversal in benefit and eligibility standards, Congress transferred 10,200 unresolved cases to the fund, more than offsetting savings from benefits changes for the next five years. The bill doubled the coal tax until such time as the trust fund had fully repaid the government for monies paid from general revenues. The change in eligibility standards was even more striking: It ended the presumption that miners with 15 years in the mines and totally disabled due to respiratory impairment were indeed disabled from black lung disease; and it allowed the Labor Department to seek a second opinion in determining whether an x-ray showed pneumoconiosis.[44] Survivor benefits were limited to cases in which the miner died specifically from black lung disease, and black lung benefits were reduced for those who had earnings above the social security limit.[45]

The entry of black lung disease on the roster of federal entitlements is partly explained by the mood of the time. It felt so good to help those in need in the late 1960s; money appeared not to be an object. The wish was father to the thought. The usual financial myopia led legislators to believe the initial cost would be small and, anyway, that it would be paid by the coal companies. Nevertheless, Congress pledged its general revenues. In the first decade, attention to black lung came from interested parties—the miners and their relatives who wanted to get on the rolls, and the owners who were happy to support their workers provided the federal government paid. Talk of medical procedures introduced notions of bureaucracy and miserliness into what many legislators thought should be concern for human suffering. Only with evidence of cascading costs and the appearance of a new administration did a question, sidestepped in the past, rise to the fore— namely, why the federal government was operating essentially another retirement program. From the joy-through-giving that dominated the early days of the black lung program, the mood by the mid-1980s had changed to one of "How do we get out of this?"

By 1994, the program was paying claims to about 70,000 claimants, and another 10,530 claims were received that year, but claims were projected to fall gradually. Benefits amounted to about $547 million, again scheduled to drop slightly over the next two years. However, interest on advances to the trust fund amounted to nearly $388 million, projected to rise to $448 million in 1996. In other words, an amount almost equivalent to benefits is being paid annually to cover the past indebtedness ($5,091 million in 1996) of the fund, requiring advances from the Treasury.[46]

---

[43]Kerr, "Black Lung," p. 59.

[44]"Plan to Wipe Out Deficit in Black Lung Trust Fund Is Approved by Congress," *Congressional Quarterly,* December 26, 1981, p. 2569.

[45]Ibid.

[46]United States Budget FY 1996, Appendix, pp. 678–79.

End-Stage Renal Disease

End-stage renal disease (ESRD) describes the kidney as it is in its dying moments, unable to filter and process the body's metabolic wastes and allowing the waste to accumulate to fatal levels in the blood. Only medical and surgical intervention can save the person's life. Two methods prevail today—hemodialysis and transplantation. Hemodialysis filters the patient's blood after it has been diverted from the body to an outside machine. The process takes six to eight hours per session and requires the patient's return to the machine three or four times a week. Transplantation is the surgical grafting of a new kidney from a volunteer or cadaver. The successful transplant often results in permanent restoration of kidney function, but the patient must face all of the attendant risks of such surgery—infection, immunological rejection, and other physiological complications.

As early as 1963, the federal government had established a small ESRD entitlement program for veterans eligible for medical benefits. The Veterans Administration had provided for ESRD treatment with the concurrence of the Bureau of the Budget (BOB). By 1972, dialysis units were established in 30 VA hospitals and maintained nearly 15 percent of all dialysis patients in the United States.[47]

In 1967 a group of experts set up by BOB and the Office of Science and Technology endorsed the VA use of dialysis and transplantation, urged use of home dialysis (a much cheaper mode of treatment), and recommended patient care financing for renal disease through medicare.[48]

The appropriations committees moved cautiously by providing only limited support to the first 14 community dialysis centers administered by the Public Health Service (PHS). The Senate Appropriations Committee in 1964 explicitly limited the PHS's use of appropriated monies in renal treatment to "demonstration and training programs" and not toward patient care financing. The overriding concern was costs:

> The Federal Government has borne the cost of treatment for its legal beneficiaries and shared these treatment costs when it has been in connection with research investigation or demonstration. Traditionally, payment for illness has been the responsibility of the patient or the local community. If the Federal Government were to share the full costs of lifetime treatment for all who suffer from these chronic diseases and conditions, the financial burden would be excessive.[49]

If this was the voice of the classic budgeter, new budgeters were more concerned with alleviating individual suffering and less with collective financial burdens.

The general discussion of federal support for medical care rested upon the quality-of-life and inability-to-pay issues. Each of these issues influenced the chairs of key congressional authorization committees to favor ESRD as an entitlement. Senator Russell Long, chairman of the Senate Finance Committee and long-time advocate of health insurance for financially catastrophic illnesses,

---

[47]The ensuing discussion is taken from R. A. Rettig, "The Policy Debate on Patient Care Financing for Victims of End-Stage Renal Disease," *Law and Contemporary Problems,* Vol. 40, No. 4 (Autumn 1976), p. 217.

[48]Ibid., pp. 217–18.

[49]Ibid., pp. 203–204.

viewed kidney disease not only as a disability but also as a disease whose cure or amelioration few people could finance on their own. He favored including kidney benefits under medicare not only to protect people financially from kidney-engendered disability but also to serve as a forerunner of catastrophic health insurance to be funded by medicare.

The plight of people who must undergo dialysis became highly publicized and introduced an emotional element to the issue. A demonstration of dialysis before a hearing of the House Ways and Means Committee apparently convinced the chairman, Wilbur Mills, to favor inclusion of benefits under medicare.

In 1970 community-based dialysis centers, threatened with termination by the Health Services and Mental Health Administration, were transferred through legislation from the Public Health Service (PHS) to the Regional Medical Programs Service (RMPS). This transfer separated the dialysis and transplantation program from the restrictive, research orientation of the PHS and the appropriations committees, to locate it instead within the capacity-building, patient-oriented RMPS. This transfer allowed decentralized funding through the established regions of the service, though patient-care financing continued to be excluded.

Another significant factor favoring ESRD entitlement benefits was the growing number of clinically oriented renal physicians. As opposed to research physicians, the clinicians' primary concern was the advancement of therapy for their patients. As the efficacy of renal therapy improved, the clinicians advocated a stronger federal role in ESRD[50] and became increasingly frustrated by what they considered the denial of patient-care financing.

An existing entitlement framework (VA benefits), a growing cohort of clinically oriented renal physicians, and expanded capacity for dialysis and transplantation brought federal kidney programs to the brink of entitlement. As Allen Schick tells the story:

> On the next to last day of its 1972 session, Congress completed action on an omnibus social security bill that (among its many provisions) entitled victims of kidney failure to medicare benefits. The provision was added to the bill by a Senate floor amendment, without prior committee hearings or review and without any consideration of the issue in the House. When it adopted the amendment by an overwhelming margin, the Senate had no reliable cost estimates and only a fuzzy notion of how expanded medicare coverage would affect future budgets. During brief floor debate, Senator Vance Hartke, the amendment's sponsor, implored the Senate to put health care ahead of budgetary concerns: "How do we explain," he asked, "that the difference between life and death is a matter of dollars." Hartke estimated that the new benefits would cost $75 million in the first year and perhaps $250 million in the fourth. Annual expenditures turned out to be much higher—about one billion dollars by the end of the 1970s. By then, however, the entitlement of kidney patients to medicare was inscribed in law and the budget routinely labeled these expenditures as "uncontrollable."[51]

---

[50]Ibid., pp. 210–11.

[51]Schick, "Controlling the 'Uncontrollables,'" p 1.

Financing for ESRD was derived from the medicare drawing account that is built up by payroll taxes, premiums, and other federal funds.[52] To be eligible for ESRD benefits, a person had to be over 65, disabled, have worked under the social security or railroad retirement system, or be the spouse or dependent child of an employee with enough social security or railroad retirement work credits. This covered nearly 93 percent of all patients needing kidney treatment. The others were covered by the Veterans Administration, Department of Defense, and other agencies, as well as medicare.[53]

ESRD enrollment grew from 11,000 at the start of the program to 63,200 at the end of 1980. More spectacularly, the total cost of ESRD rose from $283 million in fiscal 1974 to $1.8 billion in fiscal 1982.[54] In 1986 the federal government paid over $3 billion for 87,000 kidney patients. How did this happen?

While entitlements are generally thought of as benefits conferred upon individuals or families who meet certain eligibility criteria, the reimbursement mechanism of payment to enterprises and institutions that secure the promised benefit becomes a form of entitlement for the providers. In ESRD, as long as they deliver treatment to the designated beneficiaries, the providers are guaranteed reimbursement for their service. Often more vocal in promoting the entitlement than the beneficiaries, providers themselves then become a vested interest group.

The National Medical Care Corporation (NMC) grew phenomenally after the 1972 enactment of ESRD. By keeping its costs low and opening centers in populous areas, NMC was able to reap substantial profits with government reimbursements. By 1980, NMC earned over $20 million on revenues of $245.5 million, while its 120 dialysis centers treated nearly a fifth of the nation's dialysis patients.[55] It also became a potent lobbying force, able to call upon the most prestigious names in nephrology (the study of kidney disease) to testify about ESRD.[56]

Entitlements that are enacted on the coattails of a larger initiative and that have not been subjected to legislative scrutiny often can generate unanticipated costs in later years.[57] Then again, vast cost underestimation is a feature of almost all entitlements.

The sharp drop of patients using home dialysis, a much cheaper mode of treatment than dialysis at a hospital or proprietary clinic, raised costs to the government. The ESRD amendment, while liberalizing provisions for care in a hospital or outpatient dialysis, did not provide economic incentives, such as full coverage for medical supplies, supportive services, and reimbursement to facilities providing equipment and supervision for home dialysis. As a result, many pa-

---

[52]R. T. Ney, "The ESRD Medicare Program—A Clarification," *Dialysis and Transplantation*, Vol. 10, No. 3 (March 1981), p. 227.

[53]C. L. Fortnier-Frazier, *Social Work and Dialysis* (University of California Press, 1981), pp. 120–23.

[54]J. K. Iglehart, "Funding the End-Stage Renal Disease Program," *The New England Journal of Medicine*, Vol. 306, No. 8 (February 25, 1982), p. 492.

[55]G. B. Kolata, "NMC Thrives Selling Dialysis," *Science*, Vol. 208 (April 25, 1980), p. 380.

[56]Ibid., p. 381.

[57]Aaron Wildavsky, *Speaking Truth to Power* (Boston: Little, Brown, 1979), pp. 101–102.

tients who might otherwise have considered home dialysis continued to depend on hospital or proprietary-center dialysis.

In order to stem the tide of rising costs, in 1978, a bill was introduced to provide incentives for home self-dialysis, additional support for transplantation, and a national quota for patients in renal disease networks to be on home dialysis or in self-dialysis training. All major groups who testified on behalf of eliminating disincentives, however, opposed the establishment of quotas,[58] particularly the National Medical Care Corporation, which contended that home dialysis patients' survival rates were lower than those of center dialysis patients, a controversial medical point at that time. The final bill only contained a statement on the desirability of home dialysis or transplantation.[59] Hospitals and centers also gained differential reimbursement rates which boosted their profits.[60]

When costs rose very quickly after the ESRD entitlement was enacted, the two main authorization committees (House Ways and Means and Senate Finance) used the strategy of liberalizing the provisions surrounding the cheapest mode of therapy to encourage higher demand from home-dialysis patients. Administrative agencies such as HCFA and HHS preferred the strategy of enticing providers of care to have their patients use home dialysis by offering prepayment for services. Spending slowed but was still high.

Kidney patients themselves were never a particularly active or powerful force in the ESRD debate. This may be because eligibility was never questioned by politicians and policymakers, and entitlement seemed assured. Or perhaps there were not enough patients to be a potent force.

RIDING FOR A FALL

Since it is so commonly believed that entitlement status favors programs, it is especially useful to examine programs that belie this common understanding. In this way we can seek to discover conditions that limit the advantages that entitlement status usually confers on programs.

First, a word about a program from which I personally benefited, the G.I. (or government issue, as soldiers' equipment, and then soldiers, in the Second World War, were known) Bill that provided education and offered benefits to facilitate adjustment to civilian life. Annual outlays fell rapidly. The reasons are demographic (the number of World War II and Korean War veterans declined) and legislative (in 1976 Congress limited eligibility to ten years after separation from the service). Following Sherlock Holmes's dictum to search for the dog that didn't bark, the exceptional thing about the G.I. Bill is that it followed the

[58]R. A. Rettig, "The Politics of Health Cost Containment: ESRD," *Bulletin of New York Academy of Medicine,* Vol. 56, No. 1 (January/February 1980), p. 131.

[59]D. Greenberg, "Renal Politics," *New England Journal of Medicine,* Vol. 298, No. 25 (June 22, 1978), p. 1428.

[60]L. E. Demkovich, "Kidney Dialysis Payments May Be Test of Reagan's Commitment to Competition," *National Journal* (December 5, 1981), p. 2162–63.

path specified: It came, blossomed, and faded away just as old soldiers are supposed to do.

Social Services Grants[61]

Title XX of the Social Security Act gives the federal government authority to mete out grants to states for the provision of social services. For each dollar spent on certain social services, as defined by the legislation and in subsequent regulations, the federal government would provide $3 in matching funds to the state. The states give money to local governments, which give money to agencies that provide services to individuals. Many things can happen along this road.

Through 1969, there were no great increases in spending from year to year. Suddenly, expenditures grew rapidly from 1969 to 1972. How come? A few participants learned that certain provisions of the Social Security Act permitted the federal government to pay up to 75 percent of various services that heretofore had been borne by state and local governments. A few federal departments and administrators actually encouraged states to exploit the program.

States were in financial difficulty. Welfare provision was being cut. After Illinois, which had a $100 million overrun on welfare programs, was able to gain federal funding of various social programs, other states followed suit.[62] Creative financing was in order: "An example of how the states took advantage of the program would be an alcohol or drug abuse prevention program that the state had previously financed itself. By purchasing the same services from a private agency, the state would qualify for 75 percent Federal financing."[63] In this manner, the federal government was asked to "buy" Mississippi; in 1972 that state submitted claims for social services grants totaling over half of its state budget.[64]

When the cost of the program was estimated to skyrocket to $4.7 billion in 1973, Congress took action. Media attention made social services into a case of government ineffectiveness in controlling spending. Budget deficits of $20 to $30 billion (that seemed large at the time) caused worry about a program that was out of control. The states were seen as greedy for expecting such huge expenditure growth under such dubious legal conditions. Politics entered as well: "As more Republican governors successfully pressured a Republican administration into granting more funds, more Democrats developed an interest in limiting the volume of funds."[65]

HEW in 1973 proposed restrictive regulations. This upset many of the traditional social services interest groups. Within two months after the proposed regulations were published, HEW received 200,000 letters of protest from private agencies and supporters. In the face of such public outcry, HEW softened the reg-

---

[61]This section is based on a paper by David Gamson.

[62]Allen Schick, "Budgetary Adaptations to Resource Scarcity," in Charles H. Levine and Irene Ruben, eds., *Fiscal Stress and Public Policy* (Beverly Hills: Sage Publications, 1980).

[63]"'67 Law Is Giving States Windfall in Federal Funds," *New York Times*, August 7, 1972, p. 1.

[64]"How the Government 'Bought' Mississippi," *Washington Post*, June 8, 1972, p. 1.

[65]Martha Derthick, *Uncontrollable Spending for Social Services Grants* (Washington, D.C.: Brookings Institution, 1975), p. 7.

ulations to some extent, and Congress kept postponing the new regulations. Provisions were added that required a "maintenance of effort" on the part of states. This meant that federal matching funds could be used only to supplement but not to supplant existing state programs. Finding that out, however, would not be easy.

A consensus had developed that limits were necessary. Ultimately, the State and Local Fiscal Assistance Act of 1972 placed a $2.5 billion annual ceiling on social services grants and limited states' shares to their percentage of the national population.

Revenue Sharing[66]

In 1972, President Nixon signed into law the State and Local Fiscal Assistance Act of 1972 (better known as general revenue sharing). Basically, the General Revenue Sharing (GRS) program consisted of federal grants to state and local (city and county) governments with virtually no strings attached to the funds.[67] Each year a fixed amount was allotted for this purpose, so that unlike most entitlements there was a cap on expenditures. In total, approximately 39,000 state and local governments received GRS funds.[68]

Unlike most entitlements, the GRS program did not grow. After eight years of a slightly declining budget in real terms, the GRS program suffered a severe cutback in 1980; it was terminated in 1986. For GRS, entitlement status did not lead to budget increases, or even budget maintenance. The question, of course, is why?

When GRS was enacted in 1972, different people assigned different purposes to it. The Nixon administration claimed its primary aim to be the return of power to state and local governments.[69] While many Republicans agreed with this goal, they hoped GRS would also bring about the consolidation of other federal grant programs, thus reducing their cost.[70] Still others felt that GRS would allow citizens more opportunities to affect the way their tax money was spent.[71] Many Democrats hoped that GRS would be a particular help to financially strapped cities.

Originally, there were virtually no restrictions on use of GRS funds.[72] Amendments in 1976 strengthened the civil-rights and citizen-participation provisions of GRS, while removing all other restrictions on both state and local governments.[73]

---

[66]This section is based on student papers by Carol Lazzarotto and Ron Mester.

[67]David T. Irwin, "Evaluating Municipal Revenue Sources," *Government Finance,* Vol. 5 (February 1976), p. 11.

[68]Joel Havemann, "Last Minute Extension of Revenue Sharing Expected," *National Journal Reports,* Vol. 7 (August 9, 1975), p. 1141.

[69]Joel Havemann, "Revenue Sharing Plan Likely to Be Extended, Changed," *National Journal Reports,* Vol. 6 (July 20, 1974), p. 1074.

[70]Irwin, "Evaluating Municipal Revenue Sources," p. 13.

[71]Havemann, "Revenue Sharing Plan," p. 1080.

[72]Havemann, "Revenue Sharing Plan," p. 1075.

[73]"Controversy over Federal Revenue Sharing," p. 164.

The biggest changes in the program, however, occurred in 1980, when the state-grant portion of the GRS program was eliminated. From 1980 until GRS expired, only local governments received funds.[74]

The program started to lose support when Nixon proposed substitution of special revenue sharing for a large number of categorical programs. Economist Walter Heller claimed that "the birth of general revenue sharing is being used to justify the homicide of selected social programs."[75] Liberal support began to wane in Congress. As the date for renewal approached and opposition grew, supporters (namely, state and local government organizations) increased their lobbying efforts.

If GRS could be had only as a replacement for, rather than a complement of, categorical grants, then liberals wanted no part of it. Democrats were also disappointed with "the allegedly poor record of the program in the civil rights and citizen participation areas."[76] GRS became an even better candidate for cutting once Congress discovered that states were enjoying fiscal surpluses. Many agreed with the House Government Operations chairman, Jack Brooks (D-Tex.) when he stated, "It [GRS] is a wasteful, illogical giveaway to the states when they're rolling in money."

When the GRS program was enacted in 1972, Representative George Mahon predicted that "the passage of the revenue sharing bill will organize and galvanize the most powerful lobby group this country has ever known." Yet, in 1975, just a year before the program would come up for extension, Senator Edmund Muskie commented, "For the life of me, I can't understand how any program that is supported by thirty-eight thousand state and local governments could conceivably be in trouble in the Congress."[77] But the state and local organizations supporting GRS were a fragile coalition. In any case, as fiscal constraints became stronger there was more competition for funds, and House members would find it difficult to claim credit for revenue sharing compared with the more specific categorical programs. Further, by the 1980s many Republicans believed that GRS was actually strengthening the federal government relative to state and local governments, rather than increasing the independence of these governments. It became clear that many local governments had become dependent on GRS funds for their basic programs.

Social services and general revenue sharing spending slowed way down or were abolished: Their progress, limited by caps, then was whittled down even further. The two programs suffered both from moral doubts and inability to identify constituents—the one flaw compounding the other.

---

[74]Jerry Hagstron and Neal R. Peirce, "The Cities, not the States, May Bear the Brunt of Revenue Sharing Cutbacks," *National Journal Reports*, Vol. 12 (April 19, 1980), p. 637.

[75]Quoted in Carol Lazzarotto, student paper on "Revenue Sharing."

[76]"Congress Clears Revenue Sharing Extension," *Congressional Quarterly Almanac*, Vol. 32 (1976), p. 75.

[77]Joel Havemann, "'Most Powerful' Lobby Faces First Test—Revenue Sharing," *National Journal Reports*, Vol. 7 (December 27, 1975), pp. 1718–20.

ENTITLEMENTS VERSUS APPROPRIATIONS

While the view that entitlement programs always expand faster than appropriations is simplistic, it is true more often than not. Would you prefer to have programs you favor funded through entitlements or through appropriations? This is the same as asking whether you would like more or less. Once we decide not to argue with the obvious, we can concentrate on the special conditions that might lead appropriations to do as well as if not better than entitlements. Since a comparison of entitlements with appropriations would require a separate volume, we must be content with a couple of comparisons—deliberately designed to point in opposite directions so as to make it hard to draw easy conclusions. Relating the popular Head Start Program (HSP) to the less popular Aid to Families with Dependent Children (AFDC) entitlement primes us to ask why, despite its difficulties, AFDC has grown faster. If the entitlement wins out over the appropriation in that pairing, the appropriation for Women, Infants and Children (WIC) has done better budgetarily than the food stamp entitlement. For sure, there is a lot of explaining to do.

Head Start and Aid to Families with Dependent Children

A striking difference between Head Start and AFDC is that while Head Start's allocation formula is used to determine what share of already established program funds a state will receive, the AFDC formula determines how much of a state's benefits the federal government must pay. Head Start allocation is a top-down process, while AFDC allocation proceeds from the bottom up.

Prior to 1965, the most important federal program to help children was AFDC, which sought to alleviate the poverty of fatherless children by providing them and their mothers with cash grants. In the 1960s, however, a new analysis of the problem of poverty suggested that the way to eradicate poverty was to treat its causes rather than its symptoms. The idea of a self-perpetuating culture of poverty was gaining currency among intellectuals. In response to these new ideas, the Johnson administration inaugurated a War on Poverty that would seek to compensate for the social disadvantages of those trapped in what came to be called the culture of poverty.

Project Head Start was the component of the War on Poverty that provided a comprehensive preschool development program. Head Start targeted a subset of the population served by AFDC, and, like AFDC, it is federally funded but locally administered. Yet Head Start provides services rather than cash benefits. Thus, even though both programs address the problem of childhood poverty, they differ in the solutions proposed. This difference has been responsible for very different attitudes toward the two programs. Since the Johnson administration, every president has attempted to reform the welfare system. Liberals and conservatives have united in unrelenting criticism of both the premises and the outcomes of AFDC. Head Start, by contrast, has been deemed a success by both Democrats and Republicans.

A glance at the budgetary history of the two programs shows that the AFDC program has served a much larger proportion of those entitled to its benefits. Neither program has seen much real growth in spending, but over the years Head Start has served less than 20 percent of the eligible children.[78] Given that Head Start has enjoyed bipartisan support while AFDC has received bipartisan condemnation, this budgetary pattern suggests that it is not politics alone that determines the success of a program.

AFDC grew at an annual compound rate of 3.8 percent from 1978 to 1984; but in terms of constant dollars, the program experienced an annual decrease in outlays of 3.5 percent during this period. Thus, rather than an entitlement, Angela Browne calls AFDC the children's "disentitlement."[79] Nevertheless, operating under similar conditions of fiscal stringency, AFDC outperformed Head Start. Benefit levels for AFDC declined by 15 percent from 1973 to 1985, while Head Start expenditures per child declined by over 33 percent.[80]

When Sargent Shriver took his proposal for Head Start to President Johnson, Johnson responded, "That's such a magnificent idea, triple it."[81] Shriver did not need to make much effort in order to expand the program. In March, OEO requested funding proposals from local communities and received such a massive response that it decided to fund 2,500 applications which proposed to serve 530,000 children. By the end of the summer, Head Start had in fact served 561,000.

"In our society," Shriver explained, "there is a bias against helping adults . . . but there's a contrary bias in favor of helping children."[82] So he decided to launch a nationwide program of OEO-sponsored preschool education as a way to "overcome a lot of hostility in our society against the poor in general and against black people who are poor in particular, by going at the children."[83] Community Action Program (CAP) organizers considered Head Start an opportunity to receive favorable publicity. They recruited Lady Bird Johnson to spearhead the publicity drive in hopes that by receiving favorable coverage on the society pages CAP would seem more respectable.[84]

The program began so rapidly because OEO had a major incentive to spend money. In the spring of 1965, OEO officials realized they had several hundred million dollars to spend before the end of the fiscal year on June 30th. They could

---

[78]Hearings before the Subcommittee on the Departments of Labor, HHS, and Education of the House Appropriations Committee, 98th Congress, 1st Session, No. 4, Part 5, p. 24.

[79]From Angela Browne, student paper on AFDC.

[80]Data are the result of calculations based on information provided in Appendix to the Budget of the U.S. Government, FY67-84; Administration for Children, Youth and Families, Department of Health and Human Services Statistical Fact Sheet, 1985; Committee on Ways and Means, U.S. House of Representatives, Background Material and Data on Program's within the Jurisdiction of the Committee on Ways and Means, 1985, House Committee on Ways and Means, 99th Congress, 1st Session, pp. 329–80.

[81]Quoted in Edward Zigler and Jeanette Valentine, eds., *Project Head Start: A Legacy of the War on Poverty* (New York: Free Press, 1979), p. 90.

[82]Interview with Sargent Shriver by Jeanette Valentine in Zigler and Valentine, *Project Head Start*, p. 52.

[83]Ibid.

[84]Jule M. Sugarman, in Zigler and Valentine, *Project Head Start*, p. 117.

hardly expect much support for further appropriations in Congress if they had failed to spend their 1965 appropriation. Head Start provided an opportunity to spend money and at the same time win favor in the nation's communities.[85] As Shriver gleefully explained his use of those funds previously designated for other purposes,

> That illustrates one of the fantastic aspects of OEO. I increased the funding by myself! I didn't have to go to Congress; I didn't have to go to the president; I didn't have to go to the Bureau of the Budget. Congress had appropriated the money, and if I wanted to spend it on Head Start, I could spend it on Head Start. . . . I felt we had a gigantic breakthrough, so I pumped in the money as fast as we could intelligently use it. It was really quite spectacular.[86]

By initiating such a program as part of OEO, Shriver set a precedent that prevented Head Start from achieving the entitlement status implicit in its rationale. Head Start was conceived of as a compensatory education program that, like an entitlement, had both social utility and moral legitimacy. Head Start regulations required that 90 percent of its participants be children of families who were below the official poverty line; it therefore shared the eligibility criteria of entitlement programs. Yet despite concerted efforts during the late 1960s and early 1970s to establish an entitlement for child development services, Head Start was never able to overcome its origins.

Now AFDC began, as Daniel P. Moynihan writes, "almost as an afterthought."[87] It was tacked onto higher priority components of the Social Security Act and the need for it was expected to fade out. As with many depression era programs, AFDC was not designed for the poorest of the poor but rather for the temporarily submerged working and middle classes, such as the wife and children of a factory worker killed on the job. The legislative record indicates Congress's expectation that the program would wither away as the economy improved and as such programs as social security (which was a contributory social insurance program rather than a poverty program) became established.[88]

By the early 1960s, it was clear that AFDC was serving a different constituency—the broken families of blacks and whites who had migrated out of agriculture into urban areas. And despite the fact that the economy was steadily improving, the AFDC rolls were steadily growing—from 803,000 families in 1960 to 1.1 million families in 1965. Though this growth was disturbing,[89] it paled against what came next: Between 1967 and 1971, the number of AFDC cases literally doubled, reaching 3.2 million families by 1974. State and local officials (who had to pay much of the bill) were shaken and angry.

Between the mid-1960s and 1976, the cost of all antipoverty programs tripled to $81 billion (in 1983 dollars) and then grew more slowly, reaching $102 billion in

[85]Ibid., p 116.

[86]Shriver interview, in Zigler and Valentine, *Project Head Start*, p. 56.

[87]Daniel P. Moynihan, *The Politics of Guaranteed Income* (New York: Random House, 1973), p 42.

[88]Ibid., p. 197.

[89]See Frank Levy, *Dollars and Dreams: The Changing American Income Distribution, Russell Sage Foundation,* typescript, 1987, Chapter 8, "Households, Families, and the Government."

1984.[90] The proportion of the population in poverty traced a less optimistic path. Over the 1960s and early 1970s, it fell more or less steadily, reaching 11.1 percent in 1973. It then remained constant through 1979 when it began rising again, and by 1983 it exceeded 15 percent. This contradiction—a rising poverty rate in the face of rising antipoverty expenditures—led to the argument that the expenditures themselves had caused poverty by fostering dependence.[91] As chairman of the Ways and Means Committee, Wilbur Mills (D-Ark.) asked, "Is it in the public interest for welfare to become a way of life?"[92]

Why, despite substantial reductions in its funding, was AFDC maintained at a steady if reduced rate? AFDC is a "matching" program; costs are shared with state and local governments, which have considerable flexibility in establishing eligibility and benefit guidelines. Cutting AFDC is not so attractive as it otherwise might be because the states and the federal government would pay in other program categories, such as general welfare and food stamps, for further reductions.

Head Start's funding tripled between 1989 and 1994, growing from $1.2 billion to $3.3 billion, and the 1995 appropriation added roughly another quarter of a billion. In 1995 Head Start served 740,000 low income preschoolers, representing only 40 percent of eligible children.[93] President Clinton's request for 1996 would have brought Head Start spending almost to the four billion dollar mark.[94] But the House sharply scaled back the appropriation almost to the 1994 spending level, allowing virtually no increase for inflation or for any program expansion. Amendments proposed by Democrats to restore funding were defeated, but this would be to reckon without Head Start's constituencies. Tactics were traditional. "Our focus is on mobilizing parents and other supporters of Head Start to get them to write letters, and [send] faxes, and [make] calls to Members of Congress to let them know that they are really hurting children and families."[95]

Head Start remained uncontroversial. Not so AFDC, which was under serious attack, as it had been for some time. Neither party was comfortable with the program. In 1988, in recognition of the change in its clientele from widows whose needs would eventually be met from social security to "a new class of dependent families," the Family Support Act redefined AFDC as "a form of temporary assistance, with a wholly new emphasis on getting a job and becoming self-supporting." The states were encouraged to experiment, innovate, evaluate.[96] The Act loosened eligibility, included two-parent families, and required states to provide welfare recipients with work, remedial education, and training. Further

[90]Gary Burtless, "Public Spending for the Poor: Trends, Prospects, and Economic Limits." Paper presented at the Institute for Research on Poverty Conference on Poverty and Politics: Retrospect and Prospects, Williamsburg, VA, December 6–8, 1984. In Levy, *Dollars and Dreams.*

[91]Charles Murray, *Losing Ground: American Social Policy, 1950–1980* (New York: Basic Books, 1984).

[92]Cited in Angela Browne, "Welfare Legislation," *Congress and the Nation, 1965–1968,* p. 772.

[93]Rochelle Stanfield, "Jump Start," *National Journal,* February 12, p. 364.

[94]*Congressional Quarterly Weekly Report,* July 15, 1995, p. 2071.

[95]Sarah M. Greene, head of National Head Start Association, quoted in *National Journal,* May 20, 1995, p. 1236.

[96]Daniel Patrick Moynihan, "The Devolution Revolution," *New York Times,* May 6, 1995, p. E15.

efforts continued to try to push welfare recipients into the workforce, particularly through the use of training and provision of child care, but sufficient agreement to "end welfare as we know it" was not forthcoming to restructure the program on the initiative of the Clinton administration in 1994.

Welfare reform was high on the Republican agenda in 1995, but the consensus that something had to be done went little beyond the hoped for contribution of expenditure reductions to budget balance. The welfare debate illustrates the complexity of the issues in reforming an entitlement, even an unpopular one. While a welfare bill passed the House with little difficulty, the Senate debate dragged on throughout the summer of 1995. At one point the bill was withdrawn altogether, but by the time the reconciliation bill was crafted, there was a plan for welfare reform, which was shortly afterward passed by Congress as a separate bill.

As the debate swirled around the reform, it was clear that there were serious divisions on ideology, funding, state autonomy, and conception of the welfare problem. To follow every step of the debate as clauses were added or subtracted from the bill would take more space than is available in this book. The issues, though, may be briefly summarized.

In some sense welfare reform was not really about money. The AFDC program cost only $17 billion a year, despite growth in AFDC recipients from nearly 11 million in 1989 to over 14 million in 1994, and it was sensitive to economic fluctuations. The welfare debate was a debate about morals. Its budgetary aspect was about the influence of federal expenditures on behavior, i.e., the behavior of the poor or the "underclass," rather than the actual dollars themselves. The ideological issues were up front. Should teenage unwed mothers be denied welfare payments? Should mothers already on welfare be denied welfare payments for additional children? It was argued that welfare payments to unwed teenage mothers and mothers already on welfare were incentives to family disintegration, dependency, and out-of-wedlock births, and that their denial would reverse these trends. Evidence on both these propositions was scanty and ambiguous, and questions were raised whether the denial of benefits would encourage a higher abortion rate. In fact, only 8 percent of welfare mothers were teenagers, and less than 3 percent of poor families were headed by women younger than 19.[97]

The funding issue was also critical to the issue of federal–state relations and the nature of entitlement. Properly speaking, welfare was not an individual entitlement but a federal guarantee of assistance to all eligible low-income mothers and children to match state spending. Central to the reform was the end of this guarantee and its replacement with a federal block grant. States would have authority to determine spending levels, conditions, and eligibility. (In fact, states could already make changes in their programs on application under a federal waiver program.)

Which programs should be returned to the states? What should be the level of federal funding be, and how should it be distributed? What about states with rising populations or those with high unemployment rates? What would happen in a prolonged recession? What classes of persons should be eligible for welfare? What

---

[97]Eliza Newlin Corney, "Taking Over," *National Journal,* June 10, 1995, p. 1382–1387.

conditions should be mandated on the states, e.g., work requirements, or provision of child care?

The complications of the debates were reflected in over 200 amendments offered to the revised Senate leadership bill. "Family values" determined one set of votes, but still divided Congress on the abortion issue. Regional issues had to be worked out. There were divisions between those who took a punitive attitude toward the work issue, while others favored an enabling approach. Those supporting state autonomy were not necessarily prepared to leave the states to their own devices when it came to their own concerns.

Nevertheless, the Senate plan received bipartisan support (87–12), despite an administration report which contended that it would push an additional 1.1 million children into poverty. It was estimated that the bill, which cut spending $38 billion from the current law baseline over the next five years, would increase the poverty rate for children under 18 from 14.5 to 16 percent and also make life harder for those already in poverty.[98] While some saw the issue as reform of a flawed system, others were appalled at the ending of the federal guarantee to low-income women and children. Senator Daniel Moynihan declared, "Those involved will take this disgrace to their graves," and predicted children sleeping—and freezing—on sidewalk gratings in the future. As a full-page advertisement in *The New York Times* put it, the proposed legislation "would allow the richest society on Earth to break its most fundamental pledge to women: That if the worst happens, a woman can keep her children with her, with food on the table and a roof over their heads."[99]

When the final welfare reform bill emerged from conference, it retained many of the features of the Senate bill, but rapidly lost Democratic support. The measure would save $58 billion on programs for the poor over seven years, and replace the federal commitment with a block grant to the states. The funding formula would be related to previous AFDC federal funding for each state. States would have to spend at least 75 percent of the state funds they spent on AFDC in 1994. There would also be some additional funding available for states with growing populations or high unemployment, and bonuses for states reducing out-of-wedlock births. A revolving loan fund for emergencies would be set up, but its adequacy was in doubt in light of experience of the recent recession.

The bill would require adult welfare recipients to work after two years and restrict lifetime cash benefits to five years for any adult. Families on welfare would no longer receive larger grants if they had more children. States would have the option of denying benefits to teenage mothers. There would no longer be a guarantee of medicaid benefits to welfare recipients.

Other antipoverty programs, such as food stamps, school lunches, and child welfare programs, would be turned back to the states and funded through block grants. Supplemental security income (SSI) for disabled children would be limited, and denied to substance abusers. New legal immigrants would be denied

---

[98] Bob Herbert, "Asleep at the Revolution," November 6, 1995.

[99] "Why Every Woman in America Should Be Aware of Welfare Cuts," *New York Times,* August 8, 1995, p. B7.

benefits for five years, and existing legal immigrants would be ineligible to claim food stamps or SSI.

President Clinton's veto of the welfare bill did not end the debate. At the beginning of February 1996, the conference of the National Governors' Association voted unanimously in favor of a welfare reform "compromise" plan. (See p. 197 for their medicaid proposals.) This plan retained the central features of the Republican plan, replacing the federal guarantee with a block grant to the states, which would have flexibility to design their own welfare programs. The measure somewhat softened the original by adding (inter alia) more child-care funding and recession assistance, and greater flexibility for states to exempt individuals from the five-year limit and work requirements for parents with young children. While Republicans in Congress expressed general support for the proposal, the administration declared it unacceptable, because it allowed states too much leeway to decrease state contributions to welfare programs, provided inadequate protection for children, would not allow sufficient federal oversight, and did not guarantee equal treatment for all recipients.[100] But in August 1996 the president agreed to support the welfare reform bill.

WIC Program Versus Food Stamp Program

Over the past 25 years, the United States government has greatly increased its investment in attacking domestic hunger. New programs have been added and old programs significantly expanded. Expenditures for food and nutrition programs have increased multifold as the number of benefits, value of benefits, and number of recipients have risen. Today federal antihunger programs are offered in all jurisdictions in every state, and benefits also are available in U.S. territories. There is widespread agreement that the United States has committed itself to putting "an end to hunger in America for all time," in the words of President Nixon in 1969.[101] The food stamp program (FSP) and the special supplemental food programs for women, infants and children, more commonly referred to as the women, infants and children program (WIC), share some important characteristics. Both are specifically intended to help prevent the occurrence of problems associated with undernutrition and malnutrition by helping low-income people obtain an adequate diet. Both programs are administered at the federal level by the Office of Food and Nutrition Services within the USDA. Both provide 100 percent federal funding of actual benefits provided to recipients (in the FSP, however, states share in the cost of administration). Both provide benefits in the form of vouchers that are exchanged for food. These similarities reduce the number of factors that might be expected to result in differences in growth rates, such as differences in state funding commitments.

FSP is the largest federal food program, with a total outlay of about $27 billion in fiscal year 1995. It is intended to fill the gap between the amount of money low-income households are expected to use for buying food, based on a standard

---

[100]Elizabeth Shogrun, "Clinton Demands Changes in Welfare, Medicaid Proposals," *Los Angeles Times,* February 29, 1996, p. A12.

[101]Maurice MacDonald, *Food Stamps and Income Maintenance* (New York: 1977), p. 10.

share of total income (currently 30 percent), and the amount of funds USDA determines is necessary to purchase an adequate diet.[102] Food stamp benefits and eligibility are principally determined by household size, countable monthly income, assets such as real property, and the cost of the USDA Thrifty Food Plan. Food stamp benefits are generally not restricted on the basis of demographic characteristics, such as people's ages, though certain people are deemed ineligible (e.g., illegal aliens). Households may receive benefits from other federal programs; approximately 34 percent of recipients, for example, also receive AFDC. The current national caseload is about 27 million.

In the early 1970s, the provisions of FSP were liberalized and it was made an open-ended entitlement, expanding the number of beneficiaries and program expenditures.[103] In 1977, with the support of President Carter, legislation was enacted that eliminated the purchase requirement and effectively terminated eligibility for some relatively high-income recipients. The aim of these changes was to better target benefits to those most in need, since the purchase requirement was thought to be especially burdensome for those with very low incomes who are unlikely to be able to accumulate the cash necessary to obtain the coupons. The administration claimed that the costs of the proposed changes would offset each other. Congress remained concerned about the program's rising costs, however, and included yearly authorization ceilings.[104] Two years later, the Carter administration acknowledged that eliminating the purchase requirement had resulted in a bigger caseload and indicated that large increases in food costs were driving the program over the authorization limits. The administration asked for and received an increase in these limits.[105]

In 1981 and 1982, as part of a general effort to reduce domestic expenditures, President Reagan requested major cutbacks in the FSP. The Congressional Budget Office estimated the cumulative impact of the 1981–1982 legislation to be a 13 percent cut in FSP expenditures relative to the projected "base," and a 4 percent decline in the number of recipients (representing about a million people).[106]

A smaller ($3.5 billion in total expenditures in fiscal 1995) and more narrowly targeted program than the FSP, WIC is designed to provide both supplemental food and nutrition information for low-income pregnant, postpartum, and breastfeeding women, and for children up to the age of five who are determined to be at special health risk because of inadequate nutrition. The determination of nutritional risk is made by a health official such as a nutritionist or public health nurse.

---

[102]U.S. House of Representatives, Committee on Ways and Means, "Background Material and Data on Major Programs within the Jurisdiction of the Committee on Ways and Means," February 18, 1982, p. 309.

[103]See MacDonald, *Food Stamps and Income Maintenance*, pp. 10–12; and U.S. Congressional Budget Office, "The Food Stamp Program: Income or Food Supplementation?" January 1977, pp. 4–11, 17–18, 31, and 34.

[104]Kathryn Waters Gest, "Major Food Stamp Overhaul Near Approval," *Congressional Quarterly Weekly Report*, Vol. 34 (August 6, 1977), pp. 1642–47.

[105]"The Food Stamp Controversy," *The Congressional Digest*, Vol. 60 (January 1981).

[106]U.S. Congressional Budget Office, "Major Legislative Changes in Human Resources Programs Since January 1981," August 1983, p. 41.

The program is administered regionally by state and health departments that distribute funds to local public and private, nonprofit agencies (e.g., clinics, local health departments), which in turn supply the actual benefits to recipients. These benefits consist of food vouchers for items tailored to the particular family's needs, such as infant formula, as well as nutritional counseling and pamphlets.[107] The total national caseload is about 7.3 million.[108]

WIC grew out of a special commodity distribution effort begun in 1968. The program was first authorized for two years in 1972 with an annual ceiling of $20 million. No funds were actually expended until 1974 when USDA was forced to do so by court action. Then the program took off.

During the Reagan years, several unsuccessful efforts were made to reduce WIC expenditures. In 1982 Reagan proposed combining WIC with an existing maternal and child health block grant, and reducing the total level of funding by $356 million. Congress rejected this proposal, actually adding $100 million in extra funds for WIC as part of the 1983 employment and emergency poverty relief legislation. As a result, WIC grew during the Reagan administration. Indeed, the Congressional Budget Office noted (in its study of the effects of 1981 and 1982 legislation on 26 domestic programs) that WIC was one of only two such programs to have increased expenditures as the result of laws enacted over this time.[109]

WIC has benefited from very strong general congressional support. In conversations with legislative staff members, program administrators, and interest group activists, it was clear that all emphasized the program's "great popularity" with members "on both sides of the aisle." Why was WIC not merely popular but expanding in a restrictive environment?

Favorable implementation reports apparently have been important in congressional support for WIC. Based on analysis of WIC recipients vis-à-vis a control group consisting of a similar population not receiving program benefits, these reports have concluded that WIC leads to such desirable results as increases in childbirth weight, fewer problematic pregnancies, and reduced health care costs. One study showed $3 in health care savings for every $1 invested in WIC. Some of the claims made on behalf of WIC have been challenged, but the bulk of literature and professional opinions available to policymakers remain highly supportive of the program.[110] Interest group activity has been instrumental in the growth of FSP and WIC. Support for both programs has been led by a few nonprofit organizations dedicated to antipoverty advocacy, such as the Food Research and Action Center; liberal church organizations, such as Bread for the World; and also by recipient organizations.

Contrary to common opinion, there is little evidence that farm organizations have played an important role in advancing the cause of either FSP or WIC. In

[107]U.S. Senate, Committee on Agriculture, Nutrition, and Forestry, "Child Nutrition Programs: Description, History, Issues and Options," January 1983, pp. 60–65.

[108]*Congressional Quarterly Weekly Report,* June 17, 1995, p. 1734.

[109]U.S. Congressional Budget Office, "Major Legislative Changes," pp. vii–viii.

[110]U.S. Senate, Hearing before the Subcommittee on Nutrition of the Committee on Agriculture, Nutrition, and Forestry, February 23, 1982.

the early 1960s, farmers were divided in support for FSP, with the National Farmers Union favoring FSP, while the American Farm Bureau Federation and some other agricultural producers supporting the then-existing system of direct distribution of surplus commodities.[111] An advantage of WIC, according to Marc Bendick of the Urban Institute, is that "You're linked into two very powerful communities: the food manufacturing community and the health community. . . . You can believe that the infant formula manufacturers, the milk producers and the cereal manufacturers like it." Producers of sugary cereals and chocolate flavored milk, however, were unable to get their products included in WIC food packages.[112]

Does it make a difference that FSP has generally been treated as an entitlement and WIC as a traditional appropriation? The answer appears to be "no." Although WIC is not an entitlement, its benefits do go directly to people who are eligible if they meet certain qualifications. From the outside, the entitlement to food stamps and WIC vouchers must look very much alike.

In 1995, the strong position of WIC was illustrated by both House and Senate agreeing to a slight increase over the previous year's funding (although below the president's request), allowing maintenance of the current caseload. An attempt to limit the number of participants was defeated in the House.

Food stamps came under stronger attack, and the debates swung backwards and forwards. Finally, as part of the proposed sweeping welfare reform measure, food stamps would cease to be a federal entitlement. States could replace the federal food stamp program with their own nutrition program and could qualify for block grants if they replaced the stamps with an electronic system. Savings were projected at $16 billion over five years.

WIC shows that if commanding majorities treat a program like an entitlement, it will, in effect, become one. AFDC shows that if shifting majorities believe people are not entirely entitled, they will treat the program as more variable. Though some may think Head Start is in some way better, deep down they believe that AFDC is more important. Put another way, public officials do not have to come up with an immediate substitute for Head Start but they could not leave so many AFDC families destitute, especially since they would have to be dumped onto other programs or levels of government.

There are many factors other than size or political organization that contribute to the fate of entitlements. The ways in which entitlements are connected to other programs help determine how public officials will regard them. It is not only the merits of the entitlement itself but which level of government has to pay for it that matters. Comparisons made at certain times—poor states, rich federal government—may be invalid at other times—huge federal deficits, state surpluses. Developments in knowledge may make some programs more and others less expensive. Taken together with economic and demographic changes, entitlements as a class are buffeted by so large a variety of factors that it is vain to search for a common denominator.

Yet despite their image of being inviolable, entitlements are modified all the time. Another, not quite contradictory thing is that despite the fact that entitle-

[111]U.S. House of Representatives, Hearings before the Committee on Agriculture, June 10–12, 1963.

[112]Ibid., p. 2198.

ments as a class are continuously being modified, the people through their government mean to keep these promises. Consequently, control mostly means preventing entitlements from rising too fast, not abolishing or severely diminishing them. Since the largest entitlements, especially the family of programs under social security, are the most sacrosanct, their growth overwhelms efforts to control their poorer cousins.

THE FATE OF ENTITLEMENTS

The outcome of the entitlement debates of 1995 is unknown at the time of writing. The prospective reforms in medicare, medicaid, welfare, and food stamps were folded into an omnibus reconciliation bill which the president vetoed. The issues may still be unresolved by the 1996 election. Alternatively, there may be compromise, given that the president has proposed cuts in medicare and medicaid of his own, and has signed a welfare reform bill. Has the center moved?

The entitlement debate took place in a context of pressure to balance the federal budget. But the context was not one of a poor country, whose citizens, staggering under massive taxation, could no longer afford to support the weaker members of society. At the end of the twentieth century, the United States is a rich country whose burden of taxation compares favorably with that of most Western industrialized countries.[113] But over the past two decades, the gap between rich and poor has grown, and the rebound of productivity growth in the early 1990s, while it has cut unemployment, fails to reverse wage stagnation.[114] Although a recent report found the number of Americans living in poverty in 1994 fell for the first time in five years, nearly 22 percent of children are growing up in poverty, and poverty rates among blacks and Latinos are nearly double those for whites.[115] The policy of the Federal Reserve to maintain 6 percent unemployment rate, the massive redistribution of income from taxpayer to bondholder resulting from the quadrupling of the national debt, the crisis in the health care system, and the despair of inner city populations, were the somber background to the effort to scale back and terminate the major federal entitlements, which form (however patchy) a social safety net for the most vulnerable elements of the population. Half the program reductions in the 1995 budget package would fall on the poorest fifth of families and another quarter on the next poorest fifth. At the same time, the richest 5 percent of the population would benefit from tax breaks almost as large as the reductions in income and health benefits facing families with children.[116] Moreover, the decision to balance the budget by cutting entitlements and domestic appropriations was accompanied by others to cut taxes and "restore" defense expenditures.

---

[113]See Sven Steinmo, *Taxation and Democracy: Swedish, British and American Approaches to Financing the Modern State* (New Haven, Conn. and London: Yale University Press, 1993), pp. 32–34.

[114]Louis Uchitelle, "Flat Wages Seen as Issue in '96 Vote," *New York Times*, August 13 1995, p. A26.

[115]Jonathan Peterson, "Number of Poor Americans Declines, U.S. Report Says" *Los Angeles Times*, October 6 1995, p. A4.

[116] Analyses of the Joint Economic Committee of Congress and OMB, cited in Elizabeth Shogrun, "GOP Budget Plans Would Put Burden on Poor," *Los Angeles Times*, October 29, 1995, p. A20.

Chapter
9

Budgeting for Defense

Understanding defense budgeting, even at a relatively simple level, is a lot like finding your way through a maze blindfolded. Defense is huge; its procurement alone could qualify as the largest business in the world. It plans and funds the largest organization in the free world. The Department of Defense (DOD) employs more than one and a half million active uniformed-service personnel, and nearly another 1 million civilian employees.[1] More than 80 percent of federal employees work for DOD or on defense projects. At least 1.2 million private sector jobs (some say over 2 million) are created directly by DOD procurement, contract projects, and overseas military bases.[2]

The defense budget represents an enormous amount of resources. In fiscal 1985, outlays for defense were $253 billion; in 1989, they passed the $300 billion mark. Ten years later, they were estimated at $271 billion, and the United States was still spending almost as much on defense as the rest of the world combined. Despite the end of the Cold War, defense expenditures remained at about 85 percent of the average level of those years, and actually higher in real terms than under Eisenhower or Nixon.[3]

But in fact the amount budgeted for defense peaked in 1985, and the 1995 figure was 35 percent less in real terms than it had been ten years earlier.[4] (See Table 9.1.) Defense spending had slipped both as a percentage of gross domestic product (from 6.7 percent to 4.1 percent) and as a proportion of total federal spending (26.7 percent to 19.3 percent). As compared with 1955, defense and payments to individuals (entitlements) had almost completely changed places in

---

[1]William W. Kaufmann, *A Reasonable Defense* (Washington, D.C.: The Brookings Institution, 1986), p. 42.

[2]Lawrence J. Korb, "The Process and Problems of Linking Policy and Force Structure through the Defense Budget Process," in Robert Harkavy and Edward Kolodziej, eds., *American Security Policy and Policy Making* (Lexington: Lexington Books, 1980), p. 186.

[3]Lawrence W. Korb, "The Republicans Up in Arms," *Washington Post,* January 31, 1995.

[4]General Accounting Office, *Defense Sector: Trends in Employment and Spending,* April 1995, p. 10 (GAO/NSIAD-95-105BR).

Table 9.1   NATIONAL DEFENSE OUTLAYS COMPARED TO PAYMENTS TO INDIVIDUALS

| | Defense | | Percentage GDP | | Percentage Outlays | |
	Current Outlays ($billion)	Constant Outlays ($1987)	Defense	Payments to Individuals	Defense	Payments to Individuals
1950	13.7	101.1	5.2	5.1	32.2	32.1
1955	42.7	261.8	11.1	3.7	62.4	20.9
1960	48.1	220.1	9.5	4.8	52.2	26.2
1965	50.6	203.9	7.5	4.9	42.8	28.0
1970	81.7	262.9	8.3	6.6	41.8	33.1
1975	86.5	183.9	5.7	10.2	26.0	46.3
1980	134.0	187.1	5.1	10.5	22.7	47.1
1985	252.7	261.2	6.4	10.8	26.7	45.2
1990	299.3	272.6	5.5	10.7	23.9	46.6
1991	273.3	240.5	4.8	11.5	20.7	49.1
1992	298.3	249.7	5.0	12.3	21.6	52.7
1993	291.1	237.2	4.7	12.5	20.7	55.6
1994	281.6	220.6	4.2	12.4	19.3	56.3

Source: United States Budget, FY1996, Historical Tables: Table 6.1, *Composition of Outlays 1940–2000,* pp. 87–88.

their share of the federal budget. Defense related employment also declined, from an estimated seven million workers in 1987 to 4.8 million in 1995, a 32 percent decrease. In 1994, military personnel were down to about 1.7 million.[5]

The defense budget exemplifies the budgetary problems of a world in transformation. Predominant was the question of the objectives and the role of the United States military in the post–Cold War era. Even if agreement were reached on its mission, issues of appropriate level and mix of personnel, weapons, and deployment had to be resolved. Such decisions could not be taken in isolation, as the defense budget was so huge and its ramifications so pervasive, that it affected the economic well-being of whole regions, companies, and individuals all over the United States and overseas. The lines of dissensus on the mission, size, and nature of today's military forces were complicated and fractured by considerations of local and industry interests, arising from the intricacies and dependencies of the military-industrial complex. Disputes over changes in priorities brought into question existing decision-making processes, which typically favored the status quo. It is an old truism that the military is always preparing for the last war. Before attempting, then, to understand the relationship between defense and other governmental actors, most notably Congress, it will be helpful to examine the internal workings of the Department of Defense.

---

[5]Ibid, p. 13.

THE INTERNAL BUDGETING PROCESS

Formal preparation of the defense budget is divided into three phases.[6] The *planning phase,* which begins more than two years before the fiscal year in which funds will be spent initially, establishes defense objectives and indicates the resources needed to meet these objectives. The *programming phase* centers on the development of programs to meet these goals. In the *budgeting phase,* program cost and efficacy are reviewed, and defense spending is combined with the rest of the federal budget for submission to Congress.

The planning phase begins with the drafting of the defense guidance by the Secretary of Defense. This defense guidance outlines the Secretary's perceptions of threats to American security, assesses the ability of U.S. forces to counter threats, and suggests actions in response to a changing environment. Each service is given goals to meet and preliminary levels of spending. These goals and spending levels are planned for the five following years. The defense guidance is preceded by submission to the Secretary of the Joint Services Planning Document (JSPD), which is drafted by the Joint Chiefs of Staff (JCS) and assesses threats to national security and the optimal military response, with no regard given to budgetary considerations. Review of the previous year's guidance is also undertaken by the Undersecretary of Defense for policy, Office of the Secretary of Defense (OSD) officials, the services, JCS, and various military commanders. Major changes in strategy and the global situation, as well as congressional action to date on the previous submitted budget, are discussed.

The JSPD is passed on by the Secretary of Defense to an executive budget committee, the Defense Resources Board (DRB). (Everybody talks about Defense in initials because there are so many organizations dealing with each other, if they didn't use initials, all the time would be spent by naming the participants.) The DRB consists of the top DOD civilian staff, the service secretaries, the chair of the Joint Chiefs, and a representative from OMB. The DRB circulates drafts of the defense guidance to various DOD offices and integrates the feedback it receives. Major decisions on defense policy and spending are made and the JSPD's pie-in-the-sky estimates are brought into line with spending limits.

In the programming phase, the services and defense agencies develop and propose programs designed to meet the five-year objectives of the defense guidance and the fiscal objectives of the projected DOD budget. These proposed programs, presented as program objective memoranda (POMs), are reviewed by the OSD, JCS, and service staffs in a group led by the comptroller and the program analysis and evaluation directorate. The focus of the review is on the relationship of proposed programs to overall goods and fiscal guidelines. Attempts are made to examine the programs across service categories to avoid duplication and to locate efficiencies. The key issues in the POMs are discussed by the DRB and final decisions are relayed through program decision memoranda (PDMs).

---

[6]See also Fred Thompson and L. R. Jones, *Reinventing the Pentagon: How the New Public Management Can Bring Institutional Renewal* (San Francisco: Jossey Bass, 1994).

In the budgeting phase, PDMs serve as the basis for cost estimates to be submitted by DOD elements to the DOD comptroller. The comptroller, with other OSD staffs and the OMB, review the budget for accuracy in cost estimates, feasibility, scheduling, and consistency with established priorities.

The comptroller then develops a "final" budget. Unresolved issues between the OSD and the OMB are discussed, and the latest economic assumptions are incorporated into the budget estimates (usually causing adjustments in hundreds of budget items). The budget is submitted to the president for approval. After this, the OMB incorporates the defense budget with the rest of the federal budget for submission to Congress. In total, 27 months of planning and debating occur before the defense budget is finally adopted. This includes an 18-months planning process within the Defense Department and 9 months of congressional review.

Does the Department of Defense actually use a Planning Programming Budgeting System (PPBS) as it claims? In the sense that DOD provides a breakdown of its spending proposals by broad strategic functions (see Table 9.2), this is true. But does DOD make spending decisions by comparing alternatives for achieving strategic objectives?

A joint DOD–GAO Study Group came up with the same conclusions as past studies of PPBS.[7] A mission-oriented budget, which is what program budgeting is supposed to be, requires corresponding organizational framework procedures. "However, the current organization of DOD is not along strictly combat mission lines."[8] A whole host of essential activities are difficult to accommodate within PPBS—recruiting, medical care, housing, food, repairs, provisions, on and on. They amount to more than 30 percent of service budgets. "It is not clear how those support activities could be related to missions."[9]

Even those programs that could be related to missions suffer from inadequate linkages between funding and outcomes. In a separate study, the GAO "found no accountability systems linking military capability and rising or falling program funding levels. . . . Since funding is not linked to intermediate outputs, such as increased proficiency or mission capable weapon systems, or to ultimate outputs, such as increased readiness, there is no way of determining if the services could achieve the same goals with fewer dollars."[10] In the end as at the beginning, the joint study group was preoccupied with the same subject: "This theme is the difficulty in relating the output orientation of decision making, so necessary for broad

---

[7]See Aaron Wildavsky, "Rescuing Policy Analysis from PPBS," *Public Administration Review*, Vol. 29, No. 2 (March/April 1969), pp. 189–202; and "The Political Economy of Efficiency: Cost-Benefit Analysis, Systems Analysis, and Program Budgeting," *Public Administration Review*, Vol. 26, No. 4 (December 1966), pp. 292–310.

[8]Joint DOD-GAO Working Group, "The Department of Defense's Planning, Programming and Budgeting System." GAO/DOD-84-5, September 1983, pp. 119–20.

[9]Ibid., p. 121. For more on mission budgeting, see Thompson and Jones, *Reinventing the Pentagon*, pp. 320–21, and L. R. Jones and Glenn C. Bixler, *Mission Budgeting to Realign National Defense* (Greenwich, Conn.: JAI Press, 1992).

[10]*Report to the Congress by the Comptroller General of the United States,* "The Defense Budget: A Look at Budgetary Resources, Accomplishments, and Problems," GAO/PLRD-83-62, April 21, 1983, p. 24.

Table 9.2   PRINCIPAL DEFENSE BUDGET FORMATS, FISCAL YEAR 1985

(in billions of dollars)

Item	Budget Authority
Appropriation title	
Military personnel*	68.9
Operation and maintenance	78.2
Procurement	96.8
Research, development, test & evaluation	31.5
Military construction	5.5
Military family housing	2.9
Revolving and management funds	1.7
Receipts and deductions	−0.6
Total	284.7
Component	
Department of the Army	74.4
Department of the Navy	96.5
Department of the Air Force	99.9
Defense agencies, OSD, JCS	13.0
Defense–wide	1.0
Total	284.7
Program	
Strategic forces	27.8
General purpose forces	120.6
Intelligence and communications	25.1
Airlift and sealift	7.0
National Guard and Reserve	15.7
Research and development	24.6
Central supply and maintenance	24.4
Training, medical, and other general personnel activities	33.1
Administration and associated activities	5.9
Support of other nations	0.5
Total	284.7

*This category now includes funds for the military retired pay actual account.

Source: Budget of the United States Government, Fiscal Year 1986, pp. 5–5, 5–6; and Department of Defense Annual Report to the Congress, Fiscal Year 1986, p. 294. Numbers are rounded. Table in William W. Kaufmann, A Reasonable Defense (Washington, D.C.: The Brookings Institution, 1986), p. 13.

policy making at the national level, to the input orientation used for purposes of management and control at the budget level."[11]

Yet a recent observer suggests that PPBS is actually used for decision making in DOD. He contends that it provides the framework for decisions and analysis for making the marginal choices which ultimately determine defense budget decisions (except for the obvious "pork" considerations). While it may be clumsy, it

---

[11]Ibid., p. 113.

also provides the primary opportunity for the military to participate in defense budgeting, aside from the JCS level.[12]

The combination of secrecy and complexity surrounding weapons systems, the immense detail involved, the networks of relationships within the services and between the branches and their contractors and the communities in which they are located make defense budgeting exceedingly difficult to comprehend. Distinguishing between self-serving arguments and defense achievements is difficult for civilian and military defense personnel alike. No one can be certain of the threats that will be faced, or how their choices of weapons and personnel policies will turn out. Mix vast uncertainty with immense complexity and it is not clear that anyone, no matter what position is taken, can have but a small grip on the future.

The combination of huge size and long lead times for weapons systems makes the defense budget prey to all sorts of accounting manipulation. In the late 1960s and the 1970s, defense spending was hurt by low estimates of inflation. In the first half of the 1980s, DOD estimated inflation too high (to the tune of $35 billion for FY82 to FY85).[13] What should happen to this money—a rainy day reserve, compensation for past insufficiency, return to the Treasury—has been subject to much dispute that did not help build trust between DOD and the appropriations committees. Other matters only aficionados would think of, from foreign currency fluctuations to what year should be the basis of comparison for long-lived projects, can amount to hundreds of millions of dollars and more. Let us just say that this chapter is defense budgeting for beginners, not the advanced course.[14]

Rivalry

Competition between agencies within a department for resources and prestige is a commonplace event in all bureaucratic institutions. No other federal department has the intensity of competition or the stakes as high as in the DOD budget. Former Chairman of the JCS General David Jones described the defense budget as an "intramural scramble for resources."[15] The primary level of conflict is between the services: army versus navy versus air force.

Each service is a separate organizational entity. There is no such thing as a "military officer." An officer is a member of either the army, air force, navy, or marines. The services maintain separate facilities, training programs, and budgets. Each service has its own distinct traditions, service academies, and uniforms. Organizational boundaries are clearly marked and well understood by all participants. A particular service is the source of individual identification and serves

---

[12]See L. R. Jones, "Policy Development, Planning, and Resource Allocation in the Department of Defense," *Public Budgeting and Finance*, Vol. 11 (Fall 1991), pp. 15–27.

[13]Gordon Adams and Jeffrey Colman, "Gramm–Rudman–Hollings and the FY 1986 Defense Budget," *Center on Budget and Policy Priorities*, January 6, 1986, p. 2.

[14]See David Morrison, "Defense Focus," *National Journal*, March 29, 1986, p. 794; GAO, "DOD Financial Management—Improper Use of Foreign Currency Fluctuations Account." Report to Senator David H. Pryor, July 1986.

[15]Glenn Pascall, *The Trillion Dollar Budget* (Seattle: University of Washington Press, 1985), p. 6.

"as the predominant source of sanctions, rewards, and focus of organizational loyalty."[16]

Competition is a mixed bag; on the downside, there is plenty of evidence for lack of essential battlefield coordination, even in such a tiny place as Grenada. Services may seek programs because the programs are beneficial to the particular branch—its size, importance, promotions—while claiming (or believing) the programs are good for the nation.[17] The navy fought the Polaris missile submarine program because it believed Polaris was "not a traditional navy mission and therefore should not be financed out of the navy's share of the defense budget."[18] The air force was not enthusiastic about the A-10 ground attack aircraft. The A-10 was designed specifically to destroy tanks and other ground targets while flying above the battlefield at the slow speeds necessary for accurate aiming. Destroying tanks, in the air force mindset, is a job for the army. Air force officers like supersonic aircraft with state-of-the-art technology. One of the few programs the air force voluntarily cut, the simple, slow A-10 was just not their idea of what the air force was about. Defense analyst William W. Kaufmann lays it on the line:

> . . . all three services are trying simultaneously to expand their capabilities, upgrade older weapons, and replace them as rapidly as possible with new and more costly models. Furthermore, [each service] is investing in weapons that will enable it to operate independently of the others. The Army is buying expensive attack helicopters and air defense weapons because it does not expect to be given the necessary support by the Air Force. The Air Force, which could acquire more close air support aircraft and short-range air defense interceptors, prefers to invest in long-range fighter-attack aircraft that can attack targets deep in the enemy's rear and conduct an interdiction campaign in the hope of winning the war regardless of what happens to the Army. The Navy, asserting its independence of everyone else, prepares to fight its own small wars with amphibious forces and carrier-based tactical aircraft, more than half the cost of which goes into protecting this power-projection capability.[19]

On the upside of service independence, all innovation requires advocates. A fine study of naval aviation, for instance, shows that the success of the United States and Japan and the failure of Britain before the Second World War were due to the institutionalization of advocacy. Britain turned naval aviation over to central command, which always had other priorities. It never came up with enough money or promotions to create a cadre of people able to push the cause against other competitors.[20]

President Eisenhower made creative use of interservice rivalry. By setting down a spending ceiling in advance, he encouraged the service chiefs to come to

[16]Arnold Kanter, *Defense Politics* (Chicago: University of Chicago Press, 1975), p. 17.

[17]See Mark Rovner, *Defense Dollars and Sense* (Washington, D.C.: Common Cause, 1983), p. 36.

[18]Alain C. Enthoven and Wayne K. Smith, *How Much Is Enough?* (New York: Harper & Row, 1971), p. 17.

[19]Kaufmann, *A Reasonable Defense*, pp. 101–102.

[20]Thomas C. Hove and Mark D. Mandeles, "Interwar Innovation in Three Navies: USN, RN, IJN," sponsored by the Office of Net Assessment, DOD, 1982.

him when they could not agree on how to divide that sum.[21] The Packard Commission believed that reinstituting this practice—"the President would issue provisional five-year budget levels to the Secretary of Defense reflecting competing demands on the federal budget"[22]—would create incentives for the services to resolve their differences earlier and would diminish the practice of putting in wish lists while waiting until the last minute to engage in serious negotiations.[23]

In 1986, in an effort to improve coordination among the services, Congress passed the Goldwater-Nichols Reorganization Act. The act, according to Thompson and Jones, "corrected some of the more pathological administrative shortcomings of the defense department." In particular it clarified the role of the Joint Chiefs of Staff and strengthened the position of its chair.[24]

Better Weapons

The services constantly strive for greater performance from military hardware. The search for superior performance requires expensive research into new fields at the cutting edge of science and engineering. The services promote the production of sophisticated, and therefore costly, weapons systems. The air force paid $7 billion (1983 dollars) for 6,300 airplanes in 1951. In 1983, for $11 billion, the air force bought 322 fighter aircraft.[25]

The drive to acquire the most sophisticated weaponry available is dramatically revealed in cost differences for weapons between the Carter and Reagan administrations. According to a Congressional Budget Office study, in his first term, Reagan bought 6.4 percent more missiles than Carter, but it cost 91.2 percent more in constant dollars. Reagan funded 30 percent more tanks, but paid 147.4 percent more for them;[26] 8.8 percent more aircraft cost 75.4 percent more; and 36.1 percent more ships were acquired at a cost that was 53 percent higher.[27] By 1995, costs had escalated further: A single Sea Wolf submarine would cost $1.5 billion, while a C17 long-range cargo jet aircraft had a tab of $2.4 billion and a single LHD helicopter cost $1.3 billion.[28]

All soldiers understandably want the best weapons they can get. As General Tooey Spatz said, "A second-best airplane is like a second-best poker hand. No

[21]Kanter, *Defense Politics*.

[22]President's Blue Ribbon Commission, "National Security," p. 4.

[23]President's Blue Ribbon Commission on Defense Management, "A Formula for Action." A Report to the President on Defense Acquisition, April 1986.

[24]Thompson and Jones, *Reinventing the Pentagon*, p. 78.

[25]J. Ronald Fox, "Revamping the Business of National Defense," *Harvard Business Review*, Vol. 62, No. 5 (September/October 1985), p. 63.

[26]Jacques S. Gansler, "How to Improve the Acquisition of Weapons," in Robert J. Art et al., eds., *Reorganizing America's Defense* (Washington, D.C.: Pergamon Brassey, 1985), p. 384.

[27]Kaufmann, *A Reasonable Defense*, p. 43.

[28]*Congressional Quarterly Weekly Review*, June 29 1995, p. 2288.

damn good."[29] The services know that expensive equipment will lead to fewer units being purchased, but they are willing to accept fewer weapons in order to have the highest possible quality. Weapons development takes years and cannot easily be quickened. Since each service only gets a new generation of weapons every ten years or so, moreover, each seeks to incorporate all conceivable capabilities in every upgrade. The services know from experience that in times of war or heightened tension Congress will make available the funds to expand forces and increase production of weapons. However, congressional action cannot instantly create the advanced technology the services believe will be needed. It takes a long time so they try to stick everything on each weapon, so it takes longer, so a vicious cycle ensues.

Some observers believe that the desire for enhanced performance goes beyond reason and is derided as "goldplating." In recent years, a chorus of voices has called for a larger number of simpler weapons. Others rely on the adage of fewer but better. In this war of the proverbs—many heads are better than one but too many cooks spoil the broth—where no one specifies conditions of applicability, it is not easy to discern where wisdom lies.

Cost Overruns

The history of weapons procurement cost overruns is long and inglorious. On March 27, 1794, Congress approved the creation of a sea-going navy by appropriating funds to build six frigates. The work was contracted to six private shipyards geographically spread in order to distribute the benefits of federal spending and to garner political support for the program. War in Europe prevented the purchase of necessary supplies and the keels were not laid until the end of 1795. Shortly thereafter, due to mismanagement, delays, and cost overruns, the number of frigates to be purchased was cut to three.[30]

On average, weapons systems' costs (including inflation) increase 100 percent over the initial cost estimate given to Congress by the services for the first appropriation.[31] An example of this problem occurred with the B-1 bomber. The initial cost for 100 aircraft was estimated by Rockwell International, the prime contractor, as $11.9 billion in 1981 dollars. This estimate was given to the House Appropriations Subcommittee in January of 1981. Fifteen months later the air force estimated the cost at $25 billion (excluding inflation.)[32] No doubt there are reasons (redesign, reductions in quantities, etc.), but the result is the same. Roy Meyers reports that underreporting total expected costs for weapons was "a way of life in the Defense Department for decades."[33]

---

[29]Robert J. Art, "Restructuring the Military-Industrial Complex: Arms Control in an Institutional Perspective," *Public Policy,* Vol. 30, No. 4 (Fall 1974), pp. 429–30.

[30]Charles Hitch, *Decision-Making for Defense* (Berkeley: University of California Press, 1970), p. 6.

[31]Rovner, *Defense Dollars and Sense,* p. 42.

[32]Ibid., p. 44.

[33]Roy Meyers, *Strategic Budgeting* (Ann Arbor: University of Michigan Press, 1994), p. 95.

At the end of 1992, the General Accounting Office reported that "Despite the laws and regulations, overpricing of defense contracts remains significant and widespread, costing the taxpayer billions of dollars more than necessary for the goods and services purchased."[34] Three years later, the situation did not seem to have changed much. A GAO official testified before Congress:

> DOD weapons acquisitions frequently experience cost overruns, schedule delays, and performance shortfalls. For example, we have reported that cost increases of 20 to 40 percent have been common for major weapons programs and that numerous programs have experienced increases greater than that.

> Despite past and current efforts to reform the acquisition system, wasteful practices still add billions of dollars to defense acquisition costs. Many new weapons cost more, are less capable than anticipated and experience schedule delays. Moreover, the need for some of these costly weapons is questionable, particularly since the collapse of the Soviet Union. These problems are typical of DOD's history of inadequate requirements determination for weapons systems; projecting unrealistic cost, schedule, and performance estimates; developing and producing weapons concurrently; and committing weapons systems to production before adequate testing has been completed.[35]

Defense contractors want to stay in business; this means winning DOD contracts. In competitive bidding, contracts are awarded to the lowest bidder. When contracts are not put out to bid because there is only a sole source, or because of a desire to keep firms in the business so there can be competition in the future, both the Pentagon and the contractors have an incentive to look good by coming in low. Once a service selects a contractor, there is little chance that the contractor will lose the job. Contracts are initially given for relatively low cost research and development. The firm that does the research and development almost always is assured of performing production as well (thus eliminating price competition during the production phase). Contractors, therefore, are willing, and the system demands, that the initial bid be unrealistically low. Contractors know or hope they can recoup research losses on production overhead. Consequently, contractors often give unrealistically low bids to get a project started thus placing the force of bureaucratic inertia on their side, a process called "buying in."

The services have incentives to play along with the "buy-in" game. They want to fund as many programs as possible, even though many receive less than optimal resources. It is more difficult to launch a program than to keep it going once it is started. It is also easier to launch an inexpensive program than an expensive one. In such circumstances, the services have strong incentives to accept the most optimistic cost estimates.

Costs can be underestimated any number of ways. An unrealistically low inflation rate may be used. Particular resource costs may not be fully accounted for. Additionally, necessary components may not be included in the estimate, either deliberately or because of changes in specifications or the addition of features.

---

[34]General Accounting Office, *Defense Contract Pricing*, December 1992, p. 7 (GAO/HR-93-8).

[35]Statement of Frank Conahan, *Defense Programs and Spending: Need for Reforms,* Testimony Before the Committee on the Budget, House of Representatives, April 27 1995, p. 4. (GAO/T-NSIAD/95-149).

The time horizon for defense budgeting also contributes to cost overruns. Since each defense program must receive annual appropriations (and most must receive annual authorizations), neither the Defense Department nor defense contractors can safely commit resources for more than one year. This short-run view of defense budgeting is further aggravated by congressional concern with reelection and the short time defense officials usually spend at any one job (about two years). "Because of the short-term focus of the congressional and defense officials, problem areas in the defense industry often get a 'quick-fix'—more fixed-price contracts, more incentive contracts . . . more reporting requirements—rather than the basic reforms needed for lasting improvements."[36]

A final factor that contributes to overruns is that military managers are trained primarily in field operations and not in the complex business of procurement and program management. Because the job is so difficult and the chances of failure are high, until recently promising officials avoided careers in this field. But since the passage of the Defense Acquisition Workforce Improvement Act (DAWIA), DOD has made a great effort to try to improve acquisition management expertise through increased education and training.[37]

The causes of cost overruns are well known without our knowing how to correct them. Taking old technology off the shelf is a lot cheaper but not necessarily more effective. It is not only costs that change but also technology; the desire to have the best leads to new specifications and retrofitting all along the line, which is very expensive. Dropping projects prematurely is as bad as carrying them on way past their time. Contractors do take advantage, but forcing them out of business leaves DOD without sufficient variety in the future. According to Rand, the corporations, too, suffer from uncertainty: "In virtually every program we surveyed, neither the total volume of demand for a system, nor the rate of that demand, matched what had been projected at the outset of the program."[38] What is most needed, that elusive yet vital quality called good judgment, is hard to find. What is most wanted from the political authorities, a steady hand, is hardest to obtain. A contribution to greater continuity in decision making in contracting is the Procurement Reform Act of 1994 that requires DOD to take into account contractor performance in awarding new contracts, a practice previously prohibited.

Waste

In past years there have been many charges of waste and mismanagement leveled against government. Some of the worst horror stories depicted the Defense Department as composed of bumbling bureaucrats being ripped off by dishonest contractors. Stories circulated about the Pentagon paying $91 for a 3-cent screw, $110 for a 4-cent diode, and $9,609 for a 12-cent Allen wrench. These stories may be true, though it is not easy for an outsider to tell.[39]

---

[36]Fox, "Revamping the Business of National Defense," p. 65.

[37]Communication from L. R. Jones.

[38]Andrew Mayer, "Erosion of the Defense Industrial Base at the Subcontractor Level," typescript, n.d., p. 4.

[39]Steve Kellman argues that many of the stories were exaggerated. The $91 screw and the $110 diode were not indicative of waste, he says, but of accounting procedures. Often contractors will allocate

Some waste can also be traced to the budget process. "Annual appropriations cycles often waste money, since weapons systems and spare parts, for instance, may have to be ordered in uneconomical quantities in order to stay within the year's budget."[40] It is in spare parts, not in setting priorities, that the DOD prefers to absorb cuts.

Despite the implications of reports on waste, the Defense Department does review equipment costs. When a contractor submits designs for spare parts for the original weapon, for example, a Defense Department contracting officer will review the designs and make suggestions about substituting common-use for custom-designed parts where appropriate. An independent evaluation by DOD value engineers is undertaken at a later stage to analyze whether custom-designed items are necessary. In the case of the $9,609 Allen wrench, the system worked. Value engineers in the DOD found that an ordinary wrench should be substituted for a proposed custom-designed one.[41] DOD Project managers are now encouraged to buy products "off the shelf" where available and appropriate.

This is not to say that waste does not occur. At the heart of the problem is the tendency for the Pentagon, motivated by congressional micro-management as well as bureaucratic tendency, to spell out detailed specifications (as is done for major procurements) for everyday items. It hopes to avoid blame by proceeding according to the rules. The need for a whistle resulted in 16 pages of military specifications, including the requirement that the item should "make an audible characteristic sound when blown by the mouth with medium or high pressure." There are similarly thorough specifications for taco shells and fruitcakes.[42]

Concern also has been expressed about misdirection of funding from higher- to lower-priority items. A sample of what a GAO study found includes: The army resurfaced tennis courts and installed swimming pool filters at a cost of $443,000, while fire alarms at the same installation that would have cost $163,000 were not funded; a navy boathouse was repaired and painted only to be demolished less than six months later; the air force used funds to refurbish officers' clubs and replace sprinkler systems on golf courses, even though this money could have been used for unfunded backlogs of runway repaving and roofing projects.[43]

My own amateur judgment is that the most serious waste occurs because of incessant program and product changes. Without a greater understanding of why there are so many "add-ons" or "enhancements"—keeping up with opponents, technological advances, discoveries of weakness along the production path, self-protection by managers, criticism from Congress, etc.—we will not get to the root of the matter.

---

overhead on an "item" basis rather than a "value" basis. For example, if there is an overhead total of $1 million to be allotted over 10,000 parts, some contractors will allocate $100 to each item regardless of its proportionate cost. Thus a $15,000 item will appear at a cost of $15,100 and a 4-cent item as $100.04 [Steve Kellman, "The Grace Commission: How Much Waste in Government?" *The Public Interest,* No. 78 (Winter 1985), p. 64]. Unfortunately, it is not certain that such procedures exist.

[40]Ibid., pp. 80–81.

[41]Ibid., p. 65.

[42]"In Wake of Foul-Ups, the Pentagon Is Pressured to Shop Around for Bargains on Everyday Goods," *Wall Street Journal,* October 3, 1986, p. 50.

[43]Report to the Congress, "Defense Budget: A Look at Budgetary Resources."

The sheer size of the defense budget makes mismanagement and waste more likely. For example, in 1991, the Department of Defense consolidated its business operations into the Defense Business Operations Fund (DBOF). The Fund took over nine existing industrial and stock funds as well as several other organizations. It was estimated that in 1995 the Fund would have revenues of about $77 billion, making it equivalent to one of the world's largest corporations. Clearly, this is no mom-and-pop-store operation. It provides such goods and services as overhaul of major equipment and sales of vital inventory items.[44] Yet, at the end of 1994, the Fund was estimated to have incurred about $1.7 billion in accumulated operating losses; accurate financial data on its annual $1 billion to $2 billion capital asset program was not available, nor apparently in accordance with the budget; and Fund financial reports were inaccurate, financial reports incomplete, and audit trails were inadequate.[45]

Every year the Department of Defense spends over $80 billion to research, develop, and procure weapons systems. This sum represents a huge amount in contracts, but it appears that accounting systems are not adequate to deal with them. In 1993, DOD overpaid contractors $1.3 billion more than it should have done. As of September 1993, the Pentagon was unable to match $19.1 billion worth of disbursements to specific requirements in acquisition contracts.[46] About a year later, GAO reported that "DOD's records contained at least $24.8 billion of problem disbursements as of June 1994. As of February 1995, the amount of problem disbursement transactions had increased to $33 billion."[47] In 1991, when a centralized Defense Finance and Accounting Service was initiated, there were 66 major financial systems and 162 major accounting systems in operation. Efforts to improve and modernize financial administration are being made under a Senior Financial Management Oversight Council, working with a chief financial officer and steering committee under the Chief Financial Officers Act.[48]

Inventories are another problem. The spotlight is on buying new things—but what is on the shelf already? Organizations pride themselves on keeping forces and equipment operational, which means ready availability of spare parts, fuel, and redundancy in general. But keeping stocks is expensive; equipment and supplies deteriorate; and in an era of limits, efficient organizations streamline their inventories so they do not tie up scarce capital unnecessarily.

---

[44]General Accounting Office, *Financial Management: DOD's Efforts to Improve Operations of the Defense Business Operations Fund.* Statement of David O. Nelleman before the Subcommittee on Military Readiness and Defense Infrastructure, U.S. Senate Committee on Armed Services, April 28 1994, p. 1; See also Patricia E. Byrnes, "Defense Business Operating Fund: Description and Implementation Issues," *Public Budgeting and Finance,* Vol. 13 (Winter 1993), pp. 29–44.

[45]Ibid., pp. 5–9. See also General Accounting Office, *Financial Management: Status of the Defense Business Operations Fund,* March 1994 (GAO/AIMD-94-80); General Accounting Office, *Defense Business Operations Fund: Management Issues Challenge Fund Implementation,* March 1995 (GAO/AIMD-95-79); Thompson and Jones, *Reinventing the Pentagon,* pp. 86–87. L. R. Jones states that many of these problems have since been corrected.

[46]Conahan, p. 9.

[47]Ibid.

[48]David C. Morrison, "Green-Eyeshade Blues," *National Journal,* December 10, 1994, pp. 2898–2901.

During the defense buildup in the 1980s, inventories in certain areas appear to have been rapidly increased. For example, the air force increased its inventory of aircraft parts by over 200 percent (from $9.2 billion in 1980 to $28 billion in 1988), while the Navy increased its aircraft parts inventory almost as much (from $4.6 billion in 1980 to $12.9 billion in 1987). Almost one third of this new inventory acquisition was for "unrequired stock."[49] Between 1980 and 1988, the navy's unrequired ship and submarine parts inventory tripled.[50] What unrequired inventory means is literally thousands of items—compressor rotor blades, engine case assemblies, duct segments, fuel control, and other spare parts—worth millions of dollars were lying around and probably would never be used.[51]

It is easy to find examples of waste and abuse in any large program. In the Defense Department, which signs 52,000 contract actions every working day, even if a 99.9 percent purity in contract actions were achieved, 15,000 actions would still be defective.[52]

DEFENSE VERSUS DOMESTIC BUDGETING

Before delving deeper into the intricacies of funding for the armed forces, it will be informative to compare defense budgeting with its domestic counterparts. Since pejorative comparisons are often made as if one or the other were not getting its due, we need to know more about how domestic relates to defense budgeting.

The defense budget has a highly symbolic value. The amount of spending for defense is believed by some observers to be an indicator to foreign countries, and to the home front, of American resolve to assert our national interests.[53] What the money is spent for, in this regard, is less important than how much is being spent: If budget levels are thought to affect the behavior of potential foreign threats, budget totals then become an instrument of foreign policy.

Defense differs from domestic budgeting in other crucial ways. One I have already described: The defense budget process does not begin with a ceiling (as it did in Truman and Eisenhower's time), but rather with estimates of all the military might that would be necessary to defend against the worst imaginable threat. This "no resource limit" approach began in the early 1960s under former Secretary of Defense Robert McNamara and President John F. Kennedy, on the grounds that whatever was required should be provided, and the approach appears to have con-

---

[49]General Accounting Office, *Defense Inventory: Growth in Air Force and Navy Unrequired Aircraft Parts*, March 1990, p. 15 (GAO/NSIAD-90-100).

[50]General Accounting Office, *Defense Inventory: Growth in Ship and Submarine Parts*, March 1990, p. 13 (GAO/NSIAD-90-11).

[51]General Accounting Office, *Defense Inventory: Growth in Air Force and Navy Unrequired Aircraft Parts*, pp. 16–22; General Accounting Office, *Defense Inventory: Changes in DOD's Inventory*, 1989–93, August 1994, pp. 4–5 (GAO/NSIAD-94-235).

[52]Report of the Secretary of Defense Caspar W. Weinberger to the Congress, Fiscal Year 1987, February 5, 1986.

[53]Kanter, *Defense Politics*, p. 5.

tinued.[54] The result of trying planning without budgeting, that is, without resource constraints, is that important decisions get put off until the last possible minute because every participant wants to know what the real restraints are like. While it is true that fiscal pressures do affect spending on defense, these constraints come close to the end, not the beginning of the process.

But since the 1990 Budget Enforcement Act, defense requests have been constrained by the expenditure caps. For the first three years there were separate caps for defense spending, and then defense and domestic discretionary expenditures were forced to compete under a single cap. The end of the Cold War also changed planning for defense, as the Soviet threat could no longer justify unrestricted demands for resources. In September 1993, the Clinton administration set out its defense program along the lines of a "Bottom-Up Review," a comprehensive assessment of defense strategy and the resources required to carry it out.[55] The guiding assumption was the capability of the United States to fight two major regional conflicts concurrently, as well as to support peacemaking activities. The subsequent budget projections called for reductions of $104 billion over the next five years, below the previous administration's baselines.[56]

A second difference is that defense, which represents less than one-quarter of the budget, makes up over half of the "relatively controllable" expenditures in the federal budget. But this is a gross comparison, based only on the proportion of funds passing through the annual appropriations process; it would be seriously misleading if it were used to suggest that all or most of defense spending is up for grabs at any one time.

Since the defense budget is considered "must pass legislation" and usually "veto proof," the temptation to attach unrelated legislation (called "riders") has grown as well. Moreover, as numbers of congressional players in defense rise—there is now a bipartisan Military Reform Caucus with over a hundred of its 133 members unrelated to a defense-oversight committee—it has become more difficult to tell what is, or is not, germane to national defense. The great increase in legislative staff is helping to make this interest more than cursory. "The downside," Gordon Adams, director of the Defense Budget Project in Washington added, "is that you do get this phenomenon of everybody looking for their issues and having the staff to exploit it: a combination of micro-management and flag-waving."[57]

A third and substantial difference between defense and domestic budgeting is procedural: Owing its origins to Charles Hitch, Robert Anthony, and Robert McNamara, the OMB has not played the same adversarial role as in regard to domestic programs. Leaving out entitlements, which do not go through the appropriations

---

[54]Meyers, *Strategic Budgeting*, p. 174; L. R. Jones, "Policy Development, Planning, and Resource Allocation in the Department of Defense," *Public Budgeting and Finance*, Vol. 11, No. 3, Fall 1991, p. 18.

[55]L. Aspin, *National Security in the Post-Cold War World*, (Washington, D.C.: Office of the Secretary of Defense, September 1993).

[56]Andrew F. Krepinevich, *The Bottom-Up Review: An Assessment* (Washington D.C.: Defense Budget Project, 1994), pp. 8–9.

[57]David C. Morrison, "Chaos on Capital Hill," *National Journal*, September 17, 1986, p. 2305.

process at all, federal agencies usually submit their requests to OMB in September. In recent years, these requests have been preceded by OMB "guidance," telling the agencies how much they might expect will be cut or how high they can go. The director's review panel at OMB makes its recommendation to the president and domestic agencies can appeal to him for a restoration of funds. Not so in defense.

Instead of providing an independent review, OMB works as a part of a DOD team to come up with a joint recommendation to the president.[58] Under presidents Kennedy and Johnson, it became a matter of tradition that the budget director would have to appeal budgetary decisions of the Secretary of Defense to the president—a direct reversal of the relationship between the other department heads and the budget director. Budget Director David Stockman tried to restore the traditional relationship—the onus is on agencies to carry appeals—but President Reagan supported his Secretary of Defense.[59] OMB scorekeepers on appropriations action send a letter detailing objections to each act on a domestic bill in subcommittee vote, full committee, etc. But on defense, one reported, "We just say 'it's too little; the Pentagon will send the details later.'" The OMB role became even weaker under the Reagan presidency—staff left because their role was short-circuited. It may be that growing congressional cuts and criticism of defense programs are rooted in part in OMB's abandonment of its adversary position.

There is one area in which everyone knows that defense differs from the domestic spending: Secret activities appear (or don't appear) in the budget process either as generally appropriated funds with undisclosed purposes (confidential funds) or as completely covert funds where everything, including the appropriations, is kept secret (secret funds). Sometimes the activities funded by secret or confidential funds are called "black programs." Secret funds have been with us since the early days of our republic.[60] In 1811, Congress secretly provided President Madison with $100,000 to take temporary possession of some territory south of Georgia out of fear that the land would pass from Spain to another foreign power. During World War II, $1.6 billion was secretly provided to fund the development of the atomic bomb.[61]

Billions of secret funds are expended on weapons systems. While there is little doubt among legislators that "black" budget programs are necessary for national security, Congress has become increasingly concerned with the significant rise of such requests from an estimated $5.5 billion in fiscal 1981 to a commonly accepted figure of $28 billion in 1994.[62] What concerns Congress is that the Defense Department has a tendency, according to the House Armed Services Committee's ranking Republican, William Dickinson (R-Ala.), "to put things into the

[58]L.R. Jones, "Policy Development, Planning, and Resource Allocation in the Department of Defense," p. 20. See also Gordon Adams, *The Role of Defense Budgets in Civil Military Relations* (Washington, D.C.: Defense Budget Project, 1992), p. 14.

[59]David Stockman, *The Triumph of Politics* (New York: Harper & Row, 1986).

[60]Louis Fisher, *Constitutional Conflicts between Congress and the President* (Princeton: Princeton University Press, 1985), pp. 244–47.

[61]Louis Fisher, *Presidential Spending Power* (Princeton: Princeton University Press, 1975), p. 214.

[62]David Morrison, *National Journal,* April 1, 1987, p. 867.

black unnecessarily or to prolong them in the black world unnecessarily, probably because it is easiest to do work without somebody looking over your shoulder."[63] As Roy Meyers a House Armed Services staffer, remarked, "There is overwhelming evidence that programs were classified black to protect them from budgetary controls, for even advocates for defense spending publicly voiced this belief." He concluded: "The best example of stealth technology is where the Air Force hid the money."[64]

Acknowledging the occasional need for secrecy, annual appropriations acts for defense, following the provisions of 10, United States Code 140, give authority to the services to use their operations and maintenance money for Emergency and Extraordinary (E&E) expenses. These come in two categories: One for extending official courtesies to guests of the United States (hardly an emergency), and the other "when the use of normal funding channels would compromise the security of operations, jeopardize the safety of personnel and sources involved, or result in losing an investigative or intelligence opportunity."[65] The amounts are tiny, coming to about $25 million a year.[66] Their importance is that, subject to DOD regulation, they can be used for any purpose the Secretary of Defense or the service secretaries deem proper.

Can E&E funds be used to violate the law? Executive Order 12333 on United States Intelligence Activity asserts that the collection or information must be in accord with the Constitution and must not involve assassinations and unauthorized electronic eavesdropping. Otherwise, the field of legality—illegality is muddy. A GAO report states that

> We asked Defense officials whether E&E funds could be used in violation of law and found that their views varied. An OSD general counsel official would not say whether the funds could be used illegally, but told us that the purpose of the emergency and extraordinary authority was to make funds available for uses which would otherwise be unauthorized. An Army general counsel official advised us that he interpreted the OSD view to be that the funds could be used for any purpose unless specifically prohibited by statute. The official explained that if a statute does not specifically state that E&E funds cannot be used, then these funds could be used in contravention of that statute.[67]

Presumably, then, diverting funds from one purpose to another might be legal unless specifically prohibited in the authorizing statute. Should anyone get the idea that DOD can do anything it wants with appropriations, however, a brief study of internal reprogramming of funds should suggest otherwise.

---

[63]Ibid.

[64]Roy Meyers, *Strategic Budgeting*, p. 60.

[65]U.S. General Accounting Office, "Internal Controls: Defense's Use of Emergency and Extraordinary Funds," Report to the Chairman Legislation and National Security Subcommittee, Committee on Government Operations, House of Representatives, GAO/AFMD-86-44, June 1986, p. 2.

[66]Ibid. "E&E expenses in fiscal years 1984 and 1985 were about $24 million and $25 million respectively. In both fiscal years, approximately 86 percent of the E&E expenses were for confidential purposes."

[67]GAO, "Internal Controls," p. 4.

REPROGRAMMING

The stringency of congressional control is undoubtedly an indicator of distrust. Congress simultaneously wants defense to be done well and worries that appropriations may be excessive. Because defense is by far the largest purchaser of goods and services, Congress is also concerned with defense as a continuation of constituency policy. Where military bases are located, what DOD buys from whom, according to which criteria, subjects defense to all sorts of social, economic, and ultimately political judgments. Now that most domestic spending is in the form of payments to individuals (entitlements), the defense budget becomes a candidate for the "new pork barrel." Of course it is more than that—the debate over defense spending is still largely concerned with national security—but a lot of money still remains to aid localities, and many other worthies.

"Reprogramming," to use the GAO definition, "is the use of funds for purposes other than those originally contemplated at the time of appropriation."[68] In the five years from 1981 to 1986, requests to use defense funds already appropriated for other purposes came to some $29 billion or 2.7 percent of the total. A small proportion of a huge amount can still be pretty big.

Reprogramming is not the same as the *transfer of funds.* Transfers move money from one appropriations account to another; reprogramming moves money from one item to another within the same account. Transfers can be undertaken only with specific formal authority while reprogramming is based on informal understandings. Taking money from maintenance to give to personnel, for instance, is a transfer, while providing more money for certain items and less for others within the maintenance account constitutes reprogramming.

Always there are exceptions. When defense appropriations accounts are very large and very controversial, and when Congress has created statutory subdivisions—as with army missile procurement and navy shipbuilding and conversion—the rules for transfer apply. And while reprogramming ordinarily takes place at the request of the military services, Congress may decide to fund certain items by directing that they be taken from others, such as a pay raise subtracted from air force procurement. This tactic leaves the military unhappy but not as unhappy as if they had to determine where what are called "undistributed adjustments" will come from. For if Congress says to find the money within the defense budget but does not specify where, the services struggle over whose hide it will come from.

There are four types of reprogramming. Congressional Prior Approval Reprogramming occurs when it is known that the legislature is especially interested, when the DOD uses its general transfer authority (you can do it, apparently, but you have to ask), and when there is increased procurement for an item already approved. When the agreed-upon dollar amounts in the appropriation law are exceeded, or new programs or items are undertaken that would lead to continuing costs, congressional Notification Reprogrammings are supposed to take place. Both Prior Approval and Notification Reprogramming require approval by the

---

[68]GAO, "Budget Reprogramming: Department of Defense Process for Reprogramming Funds." Briefing Report to the Honorable David Pryor, United States Senate, GAO/NSIAD-86-164BR, July 1986, p. 1. The following description is drawn from this report.

Secretary or Assistant Secretary of Defense. Internal Reprogramming, which has to be approved by the DOD comptroller, involves accounting changes that reclassify dollar amounts between and within appropriations accounts. The purpose is to leave an audit trail so Congress can see what went where. Finally, Below-Threshold Reprogramming, as its name implies, does not require prior approval but can be handled within a service. Nevertheless, a semiannual report of cumulative changes in line-items goes to Congress so it can maintain its oversight responsibilities. In case of doubt, say a new program begun by a small amount, Congress expects advance notification by mail.

How large is large enough to require that Congress be notified? It depends. Criteria vary between $2 million to add a line item in procurement and $10 million to increase an existing procurement line item or a budget activity in military personnel.[69]

The objectives of reprogramming are to prevent DOD from undertaking new programs or items under the guise of old activities, while permitting flexibility where merited. Four congressional committees—the House and Senate appropriations subcommittees on defense and the Armed Services committees (secret matters bring in the two intelligence committees)—decide what is merited. Since all this oversight is carried on without a statutory basis, reprogramming requirements are not legally binding, but are rather, as GAO says, a matter of "keeping faith." Since all four committees must approve a request for Prior Approval, any one can turn it down. The result is negotiation and differentiation. The Subcommittee on Defense of the Senate Appropriations Committee turns Notification Reprogrammings into Prior Approval Reprogrammings by demanding that it give approval.

Reprogramming reviews are carried out a bit differently by the various committees. Upon receipt of a request for reprogramming, the staff of the Senate Armed Services Committee sends copies to the legislative assistants of all members and to the professional staff members. All professional staff must sign off. If, in ten days, no objection is received, a favorable response for submission to DOD is prepared. This draft response is then circulated to the committee general counsel and the party majority and minority staff directors for approval. A single senatorial objection is sufficient to deny reprogramming, though this could be overridden by a vote of the full committee. No such vote has yet been held.

The staff of the Senate Appropriations Subcommittee reviews the requests, shows them to the chair and ranking minority members and anyone else especially interested, and prepares a letter containing a decision. The staff may request a subcommittee vote in five to seven days. Though formal hearings are not usually held, reprogramming may be discussed at other hearings or at sessions where appropriations bills are being marked up prior to decision. Whether or not Congress is in session, the committee expects DOD to wait for a response letter before proceeding with reprogramming.

In the House Committee on Armed Services, Prior Approval Reprogramming is given a full-dress discussion during regular business meetings. Notifications of reprogramming are sent only to staff who take up objections with the chair. A letter of objection stops the reprogramming.

---

[69]Ibid., p. 10.

Following its receipt of reprogramming request forms, the Subcommittee on Defense of the House Appropriations Committee holds hearings at which the comptrollers of the services testify. Committee action is taken at markup sessions. The subcommittee is especially interested in anything it sees as new; it responds by phone or letter and has procedures for expediting decisions. Even internal reprogramming may be brought up if the staff or a member wishes to intervene.

DOD waits for a written affirmative response before proceeding with certain reprogramming actions. OMB, as in almost all budgetary matters, is involved in establishing the criteria for reprogramming and in approval of transfers. Most matters are routine, but, if dissatisfied, OMB can hold up a request.

With all these fingers in the budget pie, the question has naturally arisen as to whether the reprogramming process might be a wee bit too cumbersome. If managers in business were thought to require such close supervision, they would more likely be fired.[70] The unique aura of the governmental milieu comes across as committee staff uniformly respond that "cumbersome is desirable" because it assures that only high priority requests will be brought up.

The point of giving the reader such a heavy dose of procedure is that practices like these fill the lives of agency and congressional budgeters, who live, perforce, in each other's pockets. Trust is essential, for without it the wheels would turn ever so slowly. Should it happen that differences over policy were translated into distrust of motives, budgeting in defense would be like walking through tar.

DISSENSUS ON DEFENSE

Whether one listens to advocates of higher or lower spending, they all agree that the defense effort should be apportioned to estimates of the perceived threat from abroad. While there is some agreement, there is considerable disagreement over how much and exactly what the United States ought to do. The best argument in favor of spending on national defense remains the straightforward one: The nation will be better be able to defend itself. Unfortunately, without being able to try different types and amounts of defense, it is difficult to know whether more or less or different would have been better.

The pattern of defense budgeting has been one of peaks and valleys, that encourage Defense Department officials and defense advocates to get as much as they can as fast as they can as long as they can. Between World War II and the Reagan build up, the longest period of real annual increases for defense was three years. Between 1963 and 1969, the combination of a missile buildup and the Vietnam War led to a 23 percent (or $34.1 billion) increase in real purchasing power; between 1970 and 1979, due to a combination of the end of the war in Vietnam and concentration on domestic policy, defense spending declined by 25 percent (or $58 billion) in real terms. President Reagan entered office with two years of real military growth created by the Carter administration. He was able to extend that increase for four more years (a total of six consecutive years). By 1983, after four years of substantial increases, the defense budget had risen by $62 billion

---

[70]For more on micro-management by Congress, see Jones and Bixler, Chapters 1, 4, and 5.

since 1979.[71] The defense roller coaster was in full swing, but not for long. By 1985, it had reached its peak, and a decade later defense spending was estimated to have lost 35 percent of its purchasing power from the peak year.

Combined with efforts to diminish domestic spending and lower taxes, however, the strategy of maximizing defense dollars both reflected and deepened the dissensus on public policy. Domestic policy became defense policy in that slimming the former became the way to fatten the latter. Defense policy became domestic policy in that more for defense became less for domestic, mostly welfare programs. As defense was divorced from whatever was intrinsic to it, more for defense came to be viewed as an inegalitarian taking from the worst-off elements in the population. As the parties polarized over issues of equality, defense spending became more partisan and more ideological and became part and parcel of broader issues in which human resources were pitted against military hardware.

Erosion of the Base

Symptomatic of rising dissensus is the inability of governmental actors to agree on what constitutes a proper budgetary base. As Congress has made increasingly greater cuts in presidential requests, DOD has tried to choose the highest base from which to seek the president's standard request of 3 percent above inflation. Instead of choosing a low figure, usually what Congress actually provided the previous year, DOD has gone either for the prior year's presidential proposal or the amount in the resolution recommended by the Senate Budget Committee.

An example of controversy over the base will help illuminate what is at stake in this debate. The 1987 defense budget was originally built on an August 1985 resolution calling for no real increase for defense in fiscal 1986 (equaling $302.4 billion), followed by two years of 3 percent real growth. But with the adoption of the Balanced Budget Act, the baseline for 1986 was reduced to $286.1 billion. On February 4, 1986, Secretary Weinberger continued to argue for a $320.3 billion 1987 budget, suggesting that this request represented a 3 percent real increase over the base (now $286.1 billion). The secretary brushed aside a difference over the defense budget baseline by saying "We're not talking about 'actual.' This budget is 3 per cent real growth over what would have been zero this year."[72] Needless to say, this selective choice of a base was hotly disputed. Over the years, the White House staff discovered that the political price of adopting a higher base than Congress would use or approve was to reduce the acceptability of the president's proposed budget as a starting point for discussing spending.

The decline of real defense spending after the mid-1980s changed assumptions about the base, and increased dissensus about what that base should be. The caps for defense discretionary spending under the BEA pushed the baseline for defense budget authority below the rate of inflation. The demise of the Soviet Union at the end of 1991 took away the major rationale for maintaining Cold War

---

[71]Study by the Staff of the U.S. General Accounting Office, "Defense Spending and Its Relationship to the Federal Budget," GAO/OLRD-83-80, June 9, 1983, p. 5.

[72]David Morrison, "Old Pentagon Script," *National Journal*, February 8, 1986, pp. 320–21. For further examples, see Roy Meyers, *Strategic Budgeting*, pp. 130–31.

levels of defense spending. New efforts to define the base—Bush's base force and Clinton's bottom-up review—set levels of current and projected spending well below what these had previously been. The impact on actual outlays of these developments has been marked, but they have in no way resolved the issue of what the base should be, either now or in the future.

The 1990 summit agreement and Budget Enforcement Act set caps on defense discretionary spending for the following three years. One effect was to confuse the base figures even further. The caps related to budget authority *and* to outlays, so that there were two sets of figures: While constraints on budget authority eventually translate into reduced outlays, there is a distinct lag as earlier budget authority appears in current spending; conversely, resources apparently available within the budget authority cap may disappear because of the more stringent outlay caps.[73] "Defense discretionary" covers all but a few hundred million dollars in the defense budget, but includes not only DOD programs but also those of other agencies (primarily nuclear weapons programs of the Department of Energy).[74]

The defense caps for 1991 to 1993 pushed discretionary outlays each year to a lower level, from $317 billion in 1991 to $292 billion in 1993. In 1991, to comply with the caps, the Bush administration adopted a long range "Base Force" plan for a smaller military force.[75] If it were assumed that real defense spending would have continued at Cold War levels from 1990 to 1997, the savings from the "Base Force" plan would have amounted to over $400 billion.[76]

The biggest influence on spending was the end of the Cold War. In one interpretation, the $414 billion cumulative savings was a peace dividend, available for domestic purposes. If the base could be further reduced to $250 billion in 1997, there would be an even bigger dividend of an additional $213 billion, making a total savings of $627 billion, no small change. But did the peace dividend really exist? Or was it an imaginary number, dependent on an imaginary construct—a figure for baseline spending that could never have been actualized.

What really was the base for defense spending? In 1993, the "firewalls" between defense, domestic, and international discretionary spending were dismantled according to plan and replaced with a single cap. This cap would effectively freeze appropriations between 1995 and 1998. If inflation were assumed at 3 percent a year, discretionary programs would shrink in real terms by 10 percent over this period.[77] The base for defense would depend on its relationship with domestic discretionary spending: Any decision to preserve real domestic discretionary spending would require deeper cuts for defense below the rate of inflation.

---

[73]Congressional Budget Office, *The Economic and Budget Outlook: Fiscal Years 1995–1999* (Washington, D.C.: January 1994), p. 39.

[74]Congressional Budget Office, *The Economic and Budget Outlook: Fiscal Years 1993–1997* (Washington, D.C.: January 1992), p. 49.

[75]Ibid., p. 53.

[76]See William Kaufmann, *Assessing the Base Force: How Much Is Too Much?* (Washington, D.C.: Brookings Institution, 1992).

[77]Congressional Budget Office, *The Economic and Budget Outlook 1995–1999* (Washington, D.C.: January 1994), p. 37.

The Clinton administration reconsidered the whole question of the defense base in its "Bottom-Up Review" (BUR), which advocated further reductions from the Base Force structure, primarily to accord with a new benchmark, the capability of the United States to win two almost simultaneous major regional conflicts. The BUR furnished yet another base option for defense budgeting. Its assumptions were arguable.[78] For some, they were too restricted; for others, too much. One problem was a mismatch between the Clinton five-year-defense program (which assumed a further reduction of $104 billion from the Base Force estimates) and the BUR requirements. In the short term, there appeared to be a funding gap of anywhere between $13 billion to $47 billion over the five year period. Further calculations suggested a long-term annual funding gap of some $20 billion to $30 billion a year, making the BUR force structure "clearly not affordable over the long term."[79] Which of these estimates was correct depended on how the base was conceptualized and calculated.

The concept of an agreed base or starting point lends certainty and stability to budgeting. While budgets are growing, the base may be easy to ascertain, if not always to accept. When the process is in reverse, and budgets decline from year to year, the base becomes confused. Instead of one base, there are many: Actual spending; "real" spending; extrapolations of past spending adjusted for inflation; various plans for the future; spending limitations; ideas about "needs." The base is no longer an accepted beginning figure against which to measure policy proposals, but a bid for resources, adding to conflict rather than reducing it. Choice of base presages choice of argument. Multiple baselines produce multiple estimates of savings, but the instability is not restricted to totals. Reductions are not achieved smoothly or automatically: They require changes in priorities, which translate into specific and critical issues in the budget process.

Micro-Management

The congressional politics of defense budgeting changed, in the words of James Lindsay, from the "inside game" in the 1960s to the "outside game" in the 1980s. Defense deliberations in both the Armed Services Committees and the Defense Appropriations subcommittees were at one time dominated by senior congressional leaders. Representative Carl Vinson (D-Ga.) and his successor, Representative L. Mendel Rivers (D-S.C.), committee chairmen of the House Armed Services Committees through the 1960s, "ran the committees as their personal baronies."[80] The four standing committees had no formal jurisdiction; hearings and markups of the annual defense authorization bills were completed in full committee, which were controlled by Vinson and Rivers. While less autocratic than the chair of the House Armed Services Committee, Representative George

---

[78]See General Accounting Office, *Bottom-Up Review: Analysis of Key DOD Assumptions*, January 1995 (GA0/NSIAD-95-56).

[79]Krepinevich, *The Bottom Up Review*, p. 57; Congressional Budget Office, *Analysis of the Administration's Future Years Defense Program for 1995 through 1999* (Washington, D.C.: January 1995), p. 48.

[80]James M. Lindsay, "Congress and Defense Policy: 1961 to 1986," *Armed Forces & Society*, Vol. 13, No. 3 (Spring 1987), p. 377. The following discussion is drawn from this article.

Mahon (D-Tex.), chairman of the House Appropriations Defense subcommittee, dominated deliberations (along with the most senior members of the subcommittee). Similarly, in the Senate defense committees, "The norms of apprenticeship and deference to the committee chair were strong, and the chair possessed a wide range of formal powers to direct the committees operations."

In the 1970s, Congress saw a rise in influence of junior members of the defense committees and subcommittees. This more dispersed power can be attributed to several reforms adopted in the 1970s, including the Subcommittee Bill of Rights, which provided subcommittees with formal jurisdictions, budgets, authorization to hold hearings, staff selected by the subcommittee chair, and which stripped committee chairmen of their power to make subcommittee assignments. While power was wielded less autocratically during the 1970s, influence remained primarily within the defense committees. In the early 1970s, there was a rise in floor activity precipitated largely by congressional dissatisfaction with the conduct of the Vietnam War. This heightened interest in defense issues was reflected in criticisms of defense programs (particularly the Anti-Ballistic Missile) and major weapons systems (especially the C-5 transport plane). With the end of the war, though, this interest tapered off.

In the 1980s, the locus of defense discussion shifted from the committees to the much broader community of interested members. The rise of the House Democratic Caucus exemplified the new influence of outsiders. In May 1983, the caucus was able to force the House Democratic leadership to oppose the production of the MX missile. In 1984 the caucus forced the House Armed Services Committee to accept dozens of delegates to the House-Senate conference on the defense authorization bill in addition to the regular House-Senate conferees. This action was prompted by a fear among the Democratic leadership that the regular conferees would be unable to defend controversial amendments added by the House. The caucus was also able to replace Melvin Price with Les Aspin as chair of the House Armed Services Committee. Aspin, who was the seventh-ranking Democrat on the committee, was selected over five more senior (and more conservative) Democrats.

The defense committees also found their recommendations challenged more frequently on the floor. Decreased success on the floor, in turn, created a fear by committees that their legislation would be defeated unless crafted to anticipate the reactions of floor members.

Rivalry (called "turf wars") between the Armed Services and Defense Appropriations subcommittees, whose budget jurisdictions had become nearly equivalent, reached pandemic proportions. As one observer noted, "The Defense Appropriations Subcommittees are doing more legislating; the Armed Services Committees are doing more 'budgeteering.'"[81] Whereas only 3 percent of the defense budget was subject to annual legislative authorization in 1947, today 70 percent of it is so treated.[82] Whether this expansion of authorization is due to

---

[81]Robert J. Art, "Congress and the Defense Budget: Enhancing Policy Overnight," *Political Science Quarterly,* Vol. 100, No. 2 (Summer 1985), pp. 227–48; quote on 228.

[82]Les Aspin, "Congress vs. Department of Defense," in Thomas M. Franck, *The Tethered Presidency* (New York: New York University Press, 1981), p. 251; Rovner, *Defense Dollars and Sense,* p. 28.

ideological differences (Armed Services has been more favorable to higher spending than Appropriations in the House), disputes over arms control and how much should be devoted to conventional readiness versus new weapons, distrust of each other and the executive, or patronage and district benefits, the consequence has been growing uncertainty.

The politicization on defense issues is also evidenced in the proliferation of committees involved in defense. Ten Senate committees and 11 House committees have formal jurisdiction over one aspect or another of defense policy. And other committees without formal jurisdiction now hold hearings on particular defense matter.[83]

The three-tiered layers of consideration, from budget resolutions on totals to Armed Services on authorizations to appropriations subcommittees on budget authority, each of which has to occur in sequence, leads to compounding delays. The extension of annual authorization resulted in closer scrutiny of the budget by the Armed Services committees. This, in turn, required the appropriations subcommittees to examine a larger number of line items. The reaction by Congress against the "imperial presidency" and against Vietnam in the 1970s caused Congress to even more closely scrutinize the defense budget. And the expansion of congressional staff provided the committees with the capability to examine the budget in detail. As more members have become involved in decisions on a politically volatile defense budget, budgeting delays have compounded.

Indicative of this increased scrutiny, the total number of pages in appropriation committees' reports on the defense budget increased from 138 in 1968 to 593 in 1984. The Armed Services committees' reports increased from 80 pages in 1968 to 858 in 1984.[84] The length of the annual reports issued by both Armed Services committees and Defense Appropriations subcommittees rose from an average of 231 pages between 1961 and 1969 to 829 pages in the 1970s and then to 1,186 pages between 1980 and 1985.[85] Where in 1962 the Senate and House Armed Services committees held 17 hearings that produced 1,400 pages of testimony, in 1985 the separate hearings rose to 80 and the testimony amounted to 11,246 pages. The GAO reports that from 1982 to 1986, 1,420 hours were spent by 1,306 DOD witnesses at hearings before 84 committees and subcommittees.[86]

Because of the rise in committee activity and floor debate, Congress has become increasingly involved in revising defense budget details. In 1969 Congress made 180 changes to the defense authorization bill and 650 revisions to the appropriations bill. These numbers increased to 222 and 1,032, respectively, in 1975 and skyrocketed by 1985 to 1,145 authorization adjustments and 2,156 appropriations adjustments.[87] Out of 2,600 line-items in procurement for weapons and munitions alone in 1986, for example, the Armed Services committees made 1,000 changes in authorizations.

---

[83]Lindsay, "Congress and Defense Policy," p. 389.

[84]In Rovner, *Defense Dollars and Sense.*

[85]Lindsay, "Congress and Defense Policy," p. 373.

[86]Morrison, "Chaos on Capital Hill," p. 2302.

[87]Lindsay, "Congress and Defense Policy," p. 373. See also Jones and Bixler, *Mission Budgeting to Realign National Defense.*

The result has been a defense budget that has been passed on time for the fiscal year only three times in 15 years. On average, defense bills have been 80 days late after the start of the fiscal year.[88] The appropriations subcommittees recommend funds for programs never authorized and the Armed Services committees make funding changes at the line-item level.[89] With fiscal 1987 half over, disagreements between the committees left $6 billion in expenditures in limbo. There are so many changes in toto—over 1,800 in 1985 alone, together with 458 required studies—that it is difficult for defense officials to know where they are.[90] "If I am going to be responsible to make certain that I have done a good job trying to prioritize defense systems," Donald A. Hicks, then defense undersecretary for research and engineering, admonished the Senate Appropriations Subcommittee on Defense in 1985, "I can hardly be held responsible if in one-third of my programs I am told by Congress what to do, not to kill a program or to add this or subtract that."[91]

There are numerous instances of projects being forced on DOD in order to maintain local employment. Unlike the 1960s, when it could only be acquired by cultivating support of committee members (a lengthy and uncertain process), "pork" has now been democratized. The barrel has been placed out in the street. Now everyone, junior committee members as well as other legislators, has a chance to use defense to benefit their constituents. As the New York State delegation fought to maintain funds for the T-46 jet trainer, which the air force wanted to cancel because of poor performance, for instance, the ranking Republican on the House Armed Services Committee, William M. Dickinson of Alabama, told his colleagues off: "Many of the very people who voted to cut the defense budget Friday led the fight to stuff the T-46 into the budget Monday. The T-46 is a $3 billion program of airborne pork . . . a program that wasn't even included in the $320 billion budget request these same people call bloated."[92] Most members agree with Representative Jim Courter of New Jersey: "We can't reform the Pentagon until we've reformed ourselves."[93]

The complaint of the Packard Commission was that late in the calendar year, as DOD is trying to firm up its budget proposal for the coming year, the previous year's budget is still being debated. Whenever Congress acts on the past year, DOD, at the last minute, has to revamp its submission for the coming year.[94] "Unfailingly," Carlucci reports from personal experience, despite the joint DOD–OMB review, "after you have put the budget together, OMB will make a run on Christmas Day [the ghost of Stockman past?], and then you have to redo it overnight." Can this be true? Carlucci claims that there are as many as 900 late

[88]Morrison, "Chaos on Capital Hill," p. 2303.

[89]Ibid., pp. 2303–2306.

[90]Report to the President by the President's Blue Ribbon Commission on Defense Management, "National Security Planning and Budgeting," June 1986, pp. 15–16.

[91]Morrison, "Chaos on Capital Hill," p. 2303.

[92]Ibid., p. 2305.

[93]Ibid., p. 2302.

[94]President's Blue Ribbon Commission, "National Security Planning and Budgeting," p. 16.

line-item changes. "As late as December, based on issues raised by the OMB review," the Packard Commission revealed, "the President has directed changes to the Secretary's budget plan that have affected thousands of line items and that have required major revisions to the Five-Year Defense Program." Obviously, DOD does not have much time to calculate the consequences of these changes or to appeal for reconsideration (a "reclama") by the president. Since DOD, like other departments operating under OMB's quarterly apportionment rules, is not allowed to spend more than 20 percent of its funds in the last quarter, it has to do a lot of guessing on its huge (say, $90 billion) procurement budget. Afterwards, DOD has to go back to Congress if it wishes to reprogram its funds.[95] While the executive branch is changing the defense budget as it is being made, Congress, for added emphasis, is doing the same.

If, as Senator Stevens of Alaska said, "You're dealing with a government that's run by continuing resolution"[96] (resolutions to provide funding in the absence of regular appropriations measures), the political context of CRs is bound to affect a department whose budget passes through the appropriations process. CRs are used to pressure the president or other legislators into giving in on a matter in dispute. Thus CRs are often written for irregular periods, which may fit the rhythm of legislative bargaining but create additional uncertainty for administrators. Without a definite accounting period, DOD has to operate under the prior year's funding. "The timing and scope of these changes," the Packard Commission concluded, "prevent the DOD from making coherent linkages among the three defense budgets that it manages at any one time—the budget being executed, the budget under review by the Congress, and the budget that DOD is developing for the upcoming fiscal year."[97] Unfortunately, the close attention Congress pays to the military budget does not translate into discussions of the overall direction of military spending, a task that arguably would be a more fruitful use of congressional resources.

While members of Congress wish to influence the defense budget, they often do not want to take responsibility for specific decisions terminating programs. According to Representative Les Aspin, chair of the House Armed Services Committee, "Congress almost never cuts a major weapons procurement request from the Administration's defense budget. It usually approves those systems requested though not always the amount sought."[98] What accounts for the practice of stretching out procurement when everyone pays lip service to its undesirability?

Stretch-Outs

One reason for this practice of partial funding (and the corresponding unwillingness to eliminate a defense program) stems from the development of entrenched

---

[95]Frank Carlucci, "A Private Sector and National Perspective," The State of American Public Service, Occasional Papers, National Academy of Public Administration, sixth in a series of reports on American government, p. 7.

[96]Morrison, "Chaos on Capital Hill," p. 2302.

[97]President's Blue Ribbon Commission, "National Security Planning and Budgeting," p. 16.

[98]Art, "Restructuring the Military-Industrial Complex," pp. 429–30.

interests. Large defense contractors gather congressional support for purchasing their products by distributing production facilities and subcontracts over a wide geographic area, thereby maximizing the number of representatives having constituents with a direct economic interest in securing a contract for a weapons system. North American Rockwell exercised this strategy close to the absolute limit in producing the controversial B-1 bomber. Parts of the B-1 were made in 48 states and 400 congressional districts.[99] The services and DOD civilians attempt to cultivate political support by creating programs with large and dispersed constituencies. Presidents can cancel programs that would bust the budget or are no longer militarily useful due to changing conditions. President Jimmy Carter campaigned on a pledge to cancel the B-1 bomber, arguing it was too expensive, Soviet air defenses had grown too dangerous, and the cruise missile had rendered the B-1 obsolete. Despite a House and Senate controlled by his own party, Carter barely killed the program in the House with a majority of three votes.[100] Ronald Reagan picked it up.

Once a service, contractors, Congress, and labor groups have committed themselves to a program, it is difficult to stop procurement and deployment. Representative Michael Harrington, former member of the House Armed Services Committee, described this situation:

> By the time a weapons program reaches the stage at which it becomes a prominent issue of debate, the battle is lost. The defense department's near monopoly on relevant information together with the vested bureaucratic and economic interests which propel the high-budget high-prestige weapons programs conspire to give such programs an unstoppable momentum.[101]

Were this often-expressed view the only truth—programs get in but never out—the defense budget would be larger than the gross national product. The truth is programs are canceled or underfunded, leading to eventual abandonment or "stretching out." Thus, in its FY 1996 budget proposal, the Clinton administration sought to achieve reductions in its procurement budget by stretching out or deferring six major weapons programs.[102]

Other reasons help to explain this reluctance to eliminate defense programs. Members of Congress may not feel qualified and they may not wish to take the heat if whatever they advocate turns out badly or if something they eliminate turns out to have been necessary. They are well aware that, in the event of actual hostilities, public opinion may shift from thinking too much has been done for defense to not enough was done to give the fighting forces the best of everything, especially if opponents have something advanced that the United States lacks.

---

[99]Pascall, *Trillion Dollar Budget,* p. 104.

[100]Norman J. Ornstein and Shirley Elder, "The B-1 Bomber: Organizing at the Grassroots," in Eston White, *Studies in Defense* (Washington, D.C.: National Defense University Press, 1983), p. 46.

[101]Michael Harrington, "Building Arms Control into the National Security Process," *Arms Control Today* (February 1975), p. 4.

[102]Steven M. Kosiak, *Analysis of the Fiscal Year 1996 Defense Budget Request* (Washington, D.C.: Defense Budget Project, March 1995), p. 12.

Table 9.3   DEFENSE OUTLAY RATES BY APPROPRIATION TITLE

| | (percent of first-year budget authority) | | | | | |
| | Year | | | | | |
Appropriation Title	1st	2nd	3rd	4th	5th	6th*
Military personnel	97.79	1.49	0.05	0	0	0
Operation and maintenance	73.02	21.03	2.69	0	0	0
Procurement	14.64	31.32	26.69	13.35	6.73	0.42
Research, development test and evaluation	46.62	40.33	7.96	1.74	0	0
Military construction	12.91	36.09	25.96	10.35	7.71	2.61
Family housing	46.36	29.56	13.49	3.57	1.80	0.82

*Sixth-year spendout rates are not given for the current fiscal year in the *Financial Summary Tables*, though they are given for the preceding year. For fiscal 1987 procurement, military construction, and family housing, the sixth-year outlay rates are estimated assuming the same six-year total lapsed-funding percentage (cents on the dollar not spent) as exhibited by the six-year outlay rates beginning in fiscal 1986, which are given in the *Financial Summary Tables* for fiscal 1987.

Source: Department of Defense, *Financial Summary Tables, Fiscal Year 1987*, tab M. Not shown are outlay rates for special foreign currency program and Defense-wide contingencies. In Joshua M. Epstein, *The 1987 Defense Budge*t (Washington D.C.: The Brookings Institution, 1986), p. 5.

When Congress must make cuts, they are made along the path of least resistance. Traditionally, this means that when defense is cut the burden falls on the readiness and manpower accounts of the services. Manpower is the number of people employed by the services and readiness comprises repairs, maintenance of equipment, and the expenses needed to keep the service's equipment in working order. Both the services and Congress have incentives to cut (more accurately to "cap") these accounts first. Congress prefers manpower caps because the effects are not concentrated in any one district. Additionally, as Table 9.3 indicates, manpower and readiness cuts are "quick" money, resulting in an immediate decrease in outlays. Outlay rates for procurements, on the other hand, are distributed over several years, so an identical cut in procurement budget authority would result in a much smaller annual decrease in outlays. When Congress is looking for an immediate way to cut a budget, these fast spend-out accounts produce quick results. In the environment of defense budgeting, famine is expected to follow feast. When the famine hits, defense will most likely cut readiness and manpower, knowing that funds for these categories are easiest to restore and quicker to rebuild than major procurements. Manpower and readiness cuts thus spare procurement contracts. As a bonus to Congress and the military, manpower, and readiness cuts can be spread to preserve the force structure.

Congress also will often make cuts in general but not in particular or make additions without stating specifically what programs are to be reduced. DOD may be told to absorb part of the annual pay raise when that supplemental comes up late in the fiscal year. Budget requests may be cut with DOD being told to make up for them by "undistributed adjustments."[103] In the fiscal 1985 budget, for example,

---

[103]Joint DOD–GAO Working Group on PPBS, p. 73.

Congress cut the president's request by $20.5 billion, yet only half a billion, or 2 percent, involved termination of procurement or cancellation of programs. The rest was made up of stretching out procurement, reducing the level of effort, and accounting changes.[104] So what? "Large annual contracts may be deobligated and renegotiated monthly," the joint DOD–GAO Study Group observed, "resulting in higher costs and severe disruption to those programs involved. Delays in contract awards for combat readiness and other initiatives and delay or cancellation of combat training exercises are common."[105] Once weapons procurement or combat readiness is stretched out, moreover, the unit costs of these endeavors change, resulting in "reconsidering previously discarded alternatives that a stretch-out now makes cost effective."[106] Instability feeds on itself.

One hears complaints to the effect that only the military make decisions about weapons systems. As Les Aspin once said,

> The real battles over weapons and defense policy are not fought out in Congress, the public arena, but in the Pentagon itself. It is in the Puzzle Palace of the Potomac, as the career military dubs the Pentagon, that the decision is made as to whether a new helicopter takes precedence over a new tank. It is in that Disneyland East that the decision is taken whether investment for conventional warfare should take precedence over investment for strategic warfare.[107]

Hyperbole aside, the question arises as to who ought to initiate and promote weapons programs. Presumably, members of Congress and their staffs, fascinated as they are with individual weapons systems, lack the expertise and the time. While they cannot replace contracting officers, however, members can hamstring their authority.[108] The problem is that they want to do what they can't—choose weapons—and do not wish to do what they might—contribute to overall defense policy. "If they would just concentrate on new policy," Appropriations Subcommittee Chairman Ted Stevens said of the Armed Services Committees, "we would get along a lot better. They want not only to devise the programs, they want to say how many nuts we have that fit certain kinds of bolts [and dictate] that they only be made in one state."[109] In the end, if Congress cannot get its act together on defense, it may be unable to defend one of its sacred cows—the division between authorizing and appropriations committees.

Amid these competing certainties—spending is unstable; no, it is unstoppable—students of the procurement process have reached certain conclusions. They would like a variety of concepts and systems to be developed at an early stage when programs are easier to stop. With two or three prototypes in existence, and a vigorous and impartial testing program (hopefully, in place), choices would

---

[104]President's Blue Ribbon Commission, "National Security Planning and Budgeting," p. 16.

[105]Joint DOD–GAO Working Group on PPBS, p. 85.

[106]Ibid., p. 47.

[107]Aspin, "Congress vs. Department of Defense," p. 247.

[108]See the Packard Commission's section on "Determination of the Contracting Officer's Authority," President's Blue Ribbon Commission on Defense Management, June 1986, pp. 347–48.

[109]*National Journal*, September 27, 1986, pp. 2305–2306.

be more intelligent. Then, with that added assurance, procurement of sufficient quantities would be efficient. The trouble with the story is that it "front loads" the costs. Design and testing become separate and expensive items. Most of what is done is deliberately designed to be discarded. But Congress has thus far shown no disposition for such forward funding. Rejected prototypes are counted as failures. In these circumstances, DOD tries to hitch its wagon to rising weapons systems whose financial future depends on overselling from the very beginning because that is what Congress will support.

The United States is the only nation, so far as I know, that budgets for defense on an annual basis. This is said to be too short and too frequent. The annual appropriations and authorization process has been blamed for what the Senate leader on defense, Democratic Senator Sam Nunn of Georgia, often refers to as "the trivialization of Congress' responsibilities for oversight . . . and excessive micromanagement." I think this criticism puts the cart of stability before the horse of policy and hence political agreement. What Nunn desires, discussions of broad defense issues, presumes basic consensus about the amount of resources that should be committed to the military and the types of weapons systems that should be pursued.

If one has to choose between the old days when DOD had much freer rein (Pentagon witnesses routinely used to submit questions in advance at hearings until in 1969 "a committee member read both the prepared question and its answer"[110]) and the present adversarial climate, chaos is preferable to order. No doubt it would be better if skepticism were saved for larger questions of defense policy. If the political leadership cannot agree on the largest questions—the "how muches" and "what fors"—either DOD will get to choose by default or no one will be able to make intelligent choices.

Yet by the mid-1990s, by most measures, the decline in defense spending had become a given. But the results satisfied neither side. For some, expenditures remained far too high, and reductions were illusory in the face of no probable and substantial external threats. For others, the military was being starved of essential personnel, facilities, and weaponry, and becoming a "hollow force." At the end of 1994, the Republican Contract with America promised to "restore" national security funding, "to maintain our credibility around the world."[111]

DEFENSE RESTORATION?

Has the defense slowdown run its course? By 1995, no one seemed to be talking about a "peace dividend" any more. Instead the political and institutional forces that favored growth rather than cutback seemed to be reemerging. The international scene still contained no major threat. Since the Gulf War engagements had been minor, and if not altogether successful, their outcomes did not seem to be related to underfunding. But the terms of discourse had changed, and in 1995 the

---

[110]D. Ronald Fox, *Arming America: How the U.S. Buys Weapons* (Cambridge, Mass.: Harvard University Press, 1974), quoted in Morrison, "Chaos on Capital Hill," p. 2303.

[111]*Congressional Quarterly Weekly Reports,* November 12, 1994, p. 3218.

passage of a defense appropriations bill in Congress, which provided *more* than the president's request in a year of massive budget cutting and balanced budget rhetoric, was only the culmination of a variety of signals that things had changed.

The Clinton budget proposal for FY 1996 set the stage. It announced that the military services were now prepared for two conflicts of Gulf War size occurring almost simultaneously, i.e., the main goal of the BUR had been achieved. There had been, it continued "a bipartisan commitment to downsize and reshape the U.S. military. We are *near completion of this process,* which we have carried out in a steady, careful and sustained way."[112] The budget then emphasized not the cuts that had taken place, but three increases since March 1993—for "funding short-falls," for a pay increase in 1994, and for a new program, the Defense Funding Initiative announced in December 1994 which would add $25 billion for defense programs in the next six years. This addition would partially paper over the $49 billion shortfall, which the administration admitted, over the next five years in financing the BUR; the remainder would be dealt with by eliminating nearly $8 billion in modernization and dropping inflation estimates by $12 billion. But this move would not satisfy critics, such as CBO which believed a further $47 billion was necessary through fiscal 1999, or GAO which placed the shortfalls at over $100 billion more short of meeting long-term needs.[113] Of course, the gap could be treated not as one of financial shortfall, but of over-programming which could be dealt with, as in the past, by cutting back plans. The Clinton administration's request for $257.8 billion in budget authority for national defense represented about a 4.8 percent inflation-adjusted decrease from the previous year, and funding was planned to decline a total of nearly 10 percent over the following five years, to rise by about one percent a year after the turn of the century.[114] But the president's plan was countered by the commitment of the Republican majority to "restore defense."

Those who wished to increase defense spending faced essentially the same questions as those who wished to reduce it. How much is enough? And which areas should be augmented and which should be cut? The old "sky's the limit" approach, in which one could never have too much defense was no longer tenable. After the 1994 election prominent Republican defense specialists urged a multi-year plan of sustained defense increases to keep pace with inflation, billed as a constant dollar or "hard freeze."[115] This strategy would have cost nearly $100 billion more over the next five years than Clinton proposed to spend. But besides "defense hawks," there were also "deficit hawks" and "tax cut hawks."[116] More cogent arguments would be needed to prevail in these circumstances. Debates focused on three major issues—base closings, readiness, and modernization.

---

[112]United States Budget for Fiscal Year 1996, p. 122.

[113]David C. Morrison, "Defense Deadlock," *National Journal,* February 4, 1995, p. 276.

[114]Kosiak, *Analysis of the Fiscal Year 1996 Defense Budget Request,* p. 1.

[115]Pat Towell, "Deficit Dampens GOP's Hopes for a Budget Increase," *Congressional Quarterly Weekly Reports,* April 29, 1995, p. 1191.

[116]Art Pine, "GOP's Defense Plans Are at War with Budget Goals," *Los Angeles Times,* January 20, 1995, p. A19.

Base Closings

One of the most politically explosive issues in defense budget cutting has been the closing of military bases. Base closings throw thousands of people out of work and can depress local economies, so they will, obviously, be fought by those in Congress whose states and districts would be affected. Yet it is acknowledged that the United States has far more bases than it needs.[117] To counteract the effects of local interests, therefore, Congress had devised a special procedure. The 1990 Defense Base Closure and Realignment Act authorized base closures in 1991, 1993, and 1995, according to a set process. Services and defense agencies submitted their candidates for closure and realignment to the Secretary of Defense for his review, after which he submitted his recommendations to an independent Base Closure and Realignment Commission (BRAC). All bases had to be compared equally against selection criteria and the current force structure plan. These criteria, developed by DOD, included military value, return on investment (i.e., savings), and economic and environmental impacts. The BRAC could add, delete, or modify the Secretary's requirements, and then submitted its proposed list to the president, who could either accept or reject them. If he accepted them, the list was forwarded to Congress and became final unless Congress enacted a resolution rejecting the whole list.[118]

The three rounds of base closures in 1988, 1991, and 1993 had resulted in 70 full or partial closures of major bases and scores of others. They represented a reduction of 14 percent of major domestic bases, and a net present value savings over 20 years of over $17 billion, with annual recurring savings of $1.8 billion. The cumulative effect of the four rounds of base closings was expected to result in a total of about $6 billion in recurring annual savings. The 1995 round was expected to result in 33 closures of major bases, 26 major realignments, and 27 modifications of previous decisions, affecting 146 installations nationwide.[119] According to the Pentagon, eventual savings over 20 years could total $18.4 billion.[120]

Yet the base closings in 1995, approved by both president and Congress, represents a slowdown in defense budget cutting. The size of the cutbacks was much smaller than the 175 closures, realignments and unit eliminations in 1993. The 15 percent cumulative drop in the number of bases is much less than the estimated 40 percent reduction in inflation adjusted funding from 1985 to 1997 or the 33 percent reduction in force structure. "It is clear that we still have more bases than we need," admitted Defense Secretary William Perry.[121]

There were also charges that closed bases were never really closed down or were reopened with new names or purposes, though the Pentagon hotly contested

---

[117]Thompson and Jones, *Reinventing the Pentagon,* pp. 198–215.

[118]General Accounting Office, *Military Bases: Analysis of DOD's 1995 Process and Recommendations for Closure and Realignment,* Report to the Congress and the Chairman, Defense Base Closure and Realignment Commission (GAO/NSIAD-95-133), p. 19.

[119]Conahan, *Defense Programs and Spending,* p. 5.

[120]Donna Cassatta, "GOP Says Proposed Cuts Fail to Pass Muster," *Congressional Quarterly Weekly Report,* March 4, 1995, p. 694.

[121]Ibid.

the accusations.[122] In any case, both president and Congress appeared to be losing whatever enthusiasm they once had for the business: After all, it was estimated that this fourth round of base closures would result in direct and indirect job losses of nearly 100,000, for relatively paltry savings. Almost half of California's congressional delegation voted against the list on the grounds that their state was unfairly targeted,[123] while, for example, none of five air force depots were closed despite post–Cold War cuts in aircraft, and Pentagon analyses showing excess workers and equipment.[124] And, of course, hundreds of thousands of American military personnel are still stationed at bases in Japan, Korea, and Europe.

It also turned out that base closing was often, at least in the short run, not an easy way of saving money. Years of occupation by the military had often left an environmental mess which had to be cleaned up. In FY 1995, over $5 billion was spent to detoxify bases.

Readiness

Readiness is a powerful argument for increasing defense spending. After all, who wants to have an "unready" defense force? Past wars, particularly the Korean War, had revealed serious shortcomings in arms, equipment, and training resulting in needless and devastating deaths and injuries. The Cold War required levels of preparedness for high technology war at any time, and "readiness became *the* touchstone for defense planning."[125] By 1980, deficiencies in readiness—spare parts, munitions, personnel—provided the justification for the build-up of the Reagan years. Yet by the beginning of the Clinton presidency, there were charges of a "hollow force." These charges seemed supported immediately after the 1994 election, when the Chief of Staff went before TV cameras to make a bid for more funding, and the Pentagon disclosed that five of the army's twelve divisions had suffered a significant decline in military preparedness.[126]

Were things really that bad? After all, scarcely four years before, the United States military had successfully carried out the Desert Storm operation. Several experts had recently testified to an acceptable level of readiness, including the CBO and a Defense Science Board task force.[127] But a problem did exist because of the way Congress and DOD budget (or rather don't budget) for operations. Believe it or not, no money is actually set aside in the budget for the main business of the Pentagon—fighting wars. What happens, if the military actually embark on military operations, is that money is expended from O and M and training accounts, i.e., readiness, and is later made up when Congress passes a supplemental appropriation. So every time United States forces undertake peacekeeping efforts—Rwanda, Somalia, Haiti—a hole is left in the readiness of the armed forces.

[122]*Los Angeles Times,* October 11, 1994, p. A18.

[123]*Los Angeles Times,* September 9, 1995, p. A21.

[124]Cassatta, p. 694.

[125]David Morrison, "Ready for What?" *National Journal,* May 20, 1995, p. 1219.

[126]*Los Angeles Times,* November 16, 1994, p. A18.

[127]Morrison, "Ready for What?," p. 1220.

Presumably this arrangement helps tighten congressional control of defense policy. During the 1995 budget debates, efforts were made to gain advance funding for various anticipated peacekeeping operations—"readness preservation authority"—but these efforts were unsuccessful.[128]

In any case, the readiness debate was losing its salience. Readiness, in an era of limits, has to compete with other military goals. There was the issue of whether readiness now (near-term readiness) undermined long-term readiness. Richard Betts has commented ". . . it seems that a fixation on retaining readiness now is less attuned to potential worst cases than an approach that limits a concern with immediate readiness and bolsters future readiness."[129] With the Pentagon spending an estimated $90,000 per troop in 1995 (compared with $75,000 in 1980 and $87,000 in 1990), and a level of planned O & M expenditures only a little less than that spent under Bush, it was hard to sustain the unreadiness argument, although in fact the House did add $3 billion to Clinton's O & M request.[130] On to the more fruitful ground of future readiness, otherwise known as modernization.

Modernization

Modernization encompasses research and development into new weapons systems and actually developing and buying those systems. In FY 1985, $96.8 billion was allotted to procurement; for FY 1996, the president requested only $39.4 billion, a decline of 14 percent from the previous year. Research and development has fared somewhat better, dropping only 17 percent from the 1985 peak. The administration's request for $34.3 billion for FY 1996 represents a drop of 6 percent from the previous year.[131]

The case for modernization rests on military, economic, and political arguments. The military argument was that it was necessary to maintain technological superiority over the Soviet Union. Once that threat disappeared, however, this argument seemed more difficult to sustain. Why should vast resources continue to be pumped into unneeded weaponry? The economic rationale related to the dependency of whole regions of the United States on weapons manufacture. The political argument derived from the political ties of both parties with the defense industry in different states and localities, as well as genuine differences regarding the priority of military defense. As the debates over 1996 defense authorization and appropriation bills got under way, the major battles were over procurement. As always, the detail is overwhelming. But a few examples demonstrate how single decisions are forming the basis for future growth, and the tortuous lines of political division. At the time of writing, none of these stories is yet complete.

Shrinking Military Industrial Capacity   President Reagan's goal was to build a 600-ship navy. It was never realized and the navy's planned force has shrunk to

---

[128]David Morrison,"Let the Bickering Commence," *National Journal*, February 18, 1995, p. 427.

[129]Richard Betts, *Military Readiness: Concepts, Choices, Consequences* (Washington, D.C.: Brookings Institution, 1995).

[130]Morrison,"Ready for What?," p. 1222.

[131]Kosiak, pp. 10–11.

less than 350 ships, while its annual shipbuilding budget has been reduced from an average of $11 billion to only about $5 billion.[132] Since 1991 there has been no funding for submarines. The result was that the two major submarine building yards at Newport News Virginia and Electric Board in Connecticut and Rhode Island (both major employers in their states) were in danger of going out of business.

The Clinton administration therefore proposed building a third Sea Wolf submarine, at a cost of $1.5 billion at Electric Boat and also contracting with it to design and build two new, smaller and cheaper submarines. The Newport News company, it was believed, could continue in business because of its more diverse base of military and commercial contracts. The primary rationale was to maintain capacity in nuclear shipbuilding, allowing a hedge against disaster if one shipyard went under, and promote potential competition. Although the Sea Wolf would be superseded early in the next century, there was a current gap that allegedly needed to be bridged, to track the "super-quiet" Russian submarines. The proposal was backed by senior Pentagon leaders, organized labor, and Speaker Newt Gingrich.

But there was quite a lot wrong with this scenario. The Newport News company naturally protested against not being allowed to bid for the proposed new design. Many Republicans were against interfering with the free market to keep a specific company afloat. The military rationale seemed at very least questionable. And the $1.5 billion would go a long way toward financing other projects held dear by various members of Congress.

In the end, the Senate National Security Committee approved the third Sea Wolf, allowed the second new submarine to be built by Newport News, and added over $100 million to the project. The House authorization bill did not provide any funds, but in conference the Sea Wolf gained funding.

Policy Making Through Defense Appropriations   Appropriation of relatively small sums may have a disproportionate effect on policy making. Over $36 billion has been spent on ballistic missile defense systems ("Star Wars") since 1983, with questionable results. On taking office and as a result of the BUR, the Clinton administration drastically scaled back and reorganized the $40 billion Bush plan for missile defenses, but in the FY 1996 budget still planned to spend $16 billion over the next five years, with nearly $3 billion in 1996.[133]

To understand the controversy, it is necessary to go back to the 1972 Anti-Ballistic Missile (ABM) Treaty, which forbade the use of offensive weapons as defensive interceptors and limited such weapons to 100 anti-missile interceptors at a single site. The ABM Treaty is linked with the Strategic Arms Reduction Treaty (START I), which has just gone into effect, and START II which has been ratified

---

[132]Pat Towell, "Plan to Keep Shipyard Afloat Stokes Political Battle," *Congressional Quarterly Weekly Report,* May 20, 1995, p. 1435.

[133]Pat Towell, "Senate Bill Boosts ABM Effort," *Congressional Quarterly Weekly Report,* July 29, 1995, p. 2288.

by the United States, but not yet by Russia. These treaties would agree to reduce both sides' stockpiles of strategic warheads to about 3,500.[134]

Anti-ballistic missiles fall into two categories. The bulk of Clinton's FY 1996 request of nearly $3 billion was for "theater missiles," defenses against short-range missiles.[135] Since 1993, talks have been in progress with Russia to define and demarcate just what these are, and the extent to which they fall under the limitations of the ABM Treaty. This issue is in itself controversial, but the major area of dispute was the development of a "national" defense system designed to prevent a ballistic missile threat against the United States.

The Clinton FY 1996 budget request contained $370 million for the national anti-missile system, but there was strong Republican pressure to move ahead with a full-scale program. The House passed a bill for deployment of national missile defenses as soon as possible, and added over $760 billion to Clinton's request. The Clinton administration responded with a proposal for a $5 billion "emergency response system," but this fell short of the kind of "missile shield" defense hawks had in mind. In the Senate, both defense authorization and appropriations bills added $300 million to the Clinton request. The original version of the Senate authorization bill defined the distinction between theater and strategic missiles. It would require deployment of a multisite anti-missile defense system; and it would authorize $50 million for the Energy Department to conduct small test expositions of existing nuclear weapons to ensure they still worked.[136]

These provisions had serious policy implications. The administration's plan would begin deploying some theater missile defense weapons in 1998, but the national anti-missile program was limited to a "technology readiness program," indefinitely deferring deployment, but reducing lead time for development and deployment if a long-term ballistic missile threat were to emerge.

Proponents of the Senate plan argued that the expansion of national defenses was only intended to deter a limited number of missiles from a "rogue" nation, such as North Korea. The small nuclear explosions would only cause a small amount of nuclear fission. And they were concerned that the demarcation talks would subject some theater missile systems to treaty limits. But there could be serious international repercussions. The Senate plan would clearly contravene the ABM Treaty, and possibly threaten implementation of START I and ratification of START II, while preempting the demarcation talks with Russia. The nuclear tests would undermine efforts to negotiate a nuclear test ban treaty by the end of 1996. The relatively small budget issue represented a much larger policy issue—whether United States security rested on treaties or weaponry; whether the threat came from Russia or other countries; and whether there was really any threat at all.

After the president initially vetoed the defense authorization bill specifically because of its inclusion of funding for a national anti-missile program, a compromise was reached, which took out the requirement for deployment by 2001, but

---

[134]*Los Angeles Times,* June 16, 1995, p. A28.

[135]Kosiak, p. 14.

[136]Pat Towell and Donna Cassatta, "Senate Backs Nuclear Tests, Anti-Missile Program," *Congressional Quarterly Weekly Report,* August 5, 1995, p. 2380.

still left $3.5 billion for ballistic missile programs for FY 1996, over half a billion more than the administration requested. But in mid-February 1996, the administration announced cuts of $2.5 billion in these programs, slowing down development of long-range missiles in favor of short-range cruise missiles.[137]

The B2 Bomber Camel's Nose   The B2 strategic bomber is an advanced technological weapon that can evade enemy radar. Under the Bush administration, plans were made to cap the fleet at 20 aircraft at a cost of nearly $45 billion. The last four were authorized in 1993, and the Clinton administration's FY 1996 budget requested about $1 billion essentially to finish the program. It did not request any more.

How many B2 bombers does the United States need in the post–Cold War era? How many can it afford? What are the alternatives? These issues were never really debated in Congress in 1995. Defense hawks wanted another 20 B2 bombers; they did not get their way, and scarcely advanced their arguments. But they were successful in slipping the camel's nose under the tent through an appropriation of $493 million to fund radar and other components to keep the B2 production lines open.[138]

Defense hawks touted the exotic cutting edge technologies of the B2 bomber, but their real argument was the jobs the program would bring. There were supporters and opponents from both parties. Republican Budget Committee chair, John Kasich (R-Oh.) teamed up with Ron Dellums (D-Cal.) and attempted to cap the force at 20 planes in the House defense authorization bill. They were defeated not only by leaders of the House National Security Committee, but by bipartisan support for the bomber from Democrats in California, Texas, and other states which would stand to benefit from the jobs the program would provide.[139] Seventy-three Democrats voted against the amendment that would have blocked the program.

Opponents of the expansion questioned the need for more B2 bombers because of their high price and the break-up of the Soviet Union which was their primary target. The Senate did not include B2 funding in its appropriation, but the conference bill retained $493 of the $553 million for components to build future bombers that had been included in the House bill.

The Sea Wolf, ABM system, and B2 bomber are only three examples from the 1995 debates, which included consideration of additional funding for a variety of expensive weaponry such as the Comanche helicopter, the F22 fighter, BAT warheads, C17 cargo planes, as well as less dramatic upgradings and restocking of other items. The House–Senate conference approved a defense appropriations bill for $243 billion, nearly $7 billion more than the Clinton request. Within the bill, over $8 billion was for new spending for military personnel, weapons procurement, and research and development.[140] The president, while on a trip to Europe,

---

[137]*Los Angeles Times,* February 17, 1996, p. A6.

[138]Kosiak, p. 15.

[139]Pat Towell, "Secret Weapon: Old Time Arm-Twisting," *Congressional Quarterly Weekly Report,* June 17, 1995, p. 1756.

[140]*Wall Street Journal,* September 25, 1995, p. A2.

particularly related to sending a United States peacekeeping force to Bosnia, agreed to sign the bill "under protest." He initially vetoed and later signed the defense authorizations bill, although it authorized over $7 billion more than he had requested.

This was not the end of the story. It turned out that the military, from the Joint Chiefs of Staff to the commanders-in-chief, as well as the civilian defense leadership, were adamantly opposed to any additional B2 orders. The president agreed to spend the additional funds voted for the program in 1996, and requested an additional study, but nonetheless sided with the Pentagon. For the moment, at least, it seemed that the camel's nose ploy had failed. The DOD felt it could not afford the $30 billion required for an enhanced B2 fleet in the face of higher priorities and interservice rivalry, in which the Navy and Army saw themselves as paying the B2 bill by cuts in their own budgets.

Does this budget mark the turning of the tide for defense budgets? Have forces that have for some years been quiescent now reemerged? One answer is that although force structure had declined, defense budgets had not really diminished to the point that might have been expected given the end of the Cold War. The 30 percent decline over the past decade is measured in constant dollars, or "real" spending: Table 9.1 shows the unadjusted defense spending *above* the so-called 1985 peak. William Kaufmann has argued that force structure and overheads could be cut by half, resulting in annual outlays of only $180 billion.[141] Why did defense spending not drop to this level? Perhaps the reasons lie not only in the policy decisions, but also in the ways defense budget decisions are made.

[141]Thompson and Jones, *Reinventing the Pentagon*, p. 8.

Chapter
10

Reform

There's nothing wrong with the process, it's those who are in the process.

—Senator Phil Gramm

That process has gone all to hell.

—Representative Leon Panetta

I can't imagine anybody wanting to go back to a time when we had no budget process, to inform you as to what the situation is and . . . what the choices are.

—Representative Anthony Beilenson

Budgeting has become the major issue of American political life because it brings to a head questions about what kind of a government we will have and, therefore, what kind of a people we will be.

This chapter is about how people have tried to improve the process, and how the original norms of budgeting have evolved and been augmented. It is not always easy to remember that the budget itself constituted a reform. As the role of government changed, principles of budgeting have changed too, reflecting not, perhaps as we would expect, technical advances or the increased speed of modern life, but political transformations and the budgetary responses to political problems. Later changes and proposed reforms in budgetary arithmetic (how do you count?), time span, and decision-making criteria, were not neutral but political. The budget process still swings uneasily between centralization and decentralization, within both executive and legislature, and the tension and compromises they involve have important results for outcomes. Process reforms, seen as ways to solve political problems, continue to be advocated while thinking little of the changes they would probably bring about in the nature and level of revenues and spending. Is the process broken, or are we disappointed in the tenor of political life? Meanwhile quieter reforms in credit budgeting and financial management may have been important in improving control and transparency. The chapter ends with reconsideration of budgetary norms, and their place in a time of limits.

This seems like (and is) a lot. If, when readers think "reform," they also think about changes in "what kind of government" and "what kind of people," they will be on the right track.

NORMS OF BUDGETARY BEHAVIOR

There is no better way to understand what has happened to budgeting in our time than to consider the radical changes in the norms of desirable behavior that used to guide budgeters. Budgets emerged at the beginning of the nineteenth century as the result of reforms which replaced centuries of muddle and mismanagement with expenditure control based on norms of annularity, comprehensiveness, legislative appropriation, audit, and balance. While lip service is still paid to these norms, their assumptions—accepted limits on taxes and spending, predictability for a year, and departmental control of spending—no longer hold. Federal budgets today are evaluated against their long-term implications; they consist of many different kinds of spending; they are unbalanced, uncertain, and dependent on circumstances beyond their control.

The norm of balance established an equilibrium between spending and taxing. Strong feelings about the limits of taxation (modified at the margin by raising or lowering tax rates) established effective ceilings for government spending. Everyone concerned, consequently, had a pretty good idea of allowable spending for years to come. Bids by departments to increase their shares beyond the level of expected increases, if any, would be resisted by other departments and program advocates who knew that much more for some department meant much less for others. Spending thus was inhibited at the source; bids to "break the bank" were not put in because everyone knew that also meant breaking social solidarity among departments. The interests entrusted to the care of these spending departments would expect to suffer. Along with budget balance, then, went the widely shared assumption that requests for funds would be made in the context of fairly firm spending limits. Budgets would not merely bubble up from below but would be shaped by pressure from above, pressure that affected the perception of departments about what was reasonable to ask for as well as what they might get. This budget restraint reflected a political system dominated by "insiders," whose wishes to keep taxes low were matched by their ability to do so in a situation of highly unequal distribution of resources and power.

Balance as a desirable norm, however, began to be weakened by near-universal acceptance of Keynesian economic precepts: Don't balance the budget, dummy, balance the economy at some hypothetical equilibrium point that would bring full employment. But as faith in Keynesian economics receded, as "full" employment was reinterpreted as a variable and not a constant at a good deal less than full employment, and as "fine tuning" the economy gave way to consistent deficit spending, the idea of the budget as a means to maintaining economic growth, stable prices, and full employment also faded. A budget in the grip of economic uncertainty would itself be an expression of uncertainty, without clear criteria for decision making. For these drifting budgets, without agreements on the basic issues of the levels of taxing and spending, the norm of balance has eroded even further; it lacks operational guidance. One side wants higher taxing and spending; the other, the reverse. So both swear fealty to the idea of balance while clinging to their opposite preferences as to the level and distribution of taxing and spending.

The norm of comprehensiveness stipulated the ideal that all revenues go to the central Treasury and that all expenditures be made within a comprehensive set of accounts. Although there were some special funds, the vast bulk of revenue did go to the Treasury. Today no one needs to be told that direct loans, loan guarantees, tax preferences, off-budget corporations, regulations that increase costs in the private sector, open-ended entitlements, and other such devices have made a hash out of comprehensiveness.

Comprehensive accounting once meant accounting by departments; governmental expenditure, except for a special fund here and there, meant department expenditure. If you controlled departments, the understanding was, you controlled expenditure. Today, when spending by departments on goods and services in industrial democracies accounts for only a third of spending, the inescapable conclusion is that traditional norms do not cover the bulk of expenditure. Most money is spent to affect citizen behavior rather than to support direct government actions. Since most spending is done by individuals who receive payments or loads, and by subnational governments, the irrelevance of department control is clear.[1]

Control of spending has declined along with the norm of comprehensiveness because one cannot simultaneously maximize in opposing directions. Varying the level of spending to help modulate swings in the economy is not compatible with keeping departmental spending constant. The more interest a government has in influencing citizen behavior, say by encouraging use of medical facilities, the less such a government is able to control its own spending.

Nor can it be said, following the norm of comprehensiveness, that there is a house of budgeting whose conceptual rooms are comparable. Accounting is in a shambles: Money borrowed one way ends up entirely in the budget; another way, partially; and a third way, not at all. Because there is no common budgetary currency, it is not possible to reallocate resources from loans to tax preferences to entitlements to departmental spending to government corporations (not, at least, in the sense of being intended).

A phenomenon that used to be confined to poor countries—repetitive budgeting, remaking the budget several times a year[2]—has now become standard practice in relatively rich nations as well. Whether the budget is formally redrawn or not, its underlying premises, financial assumptions, and actual allocations are subject to rapid change measured in months rather than years. Because governments cannot control large proportions of their budgets, they lack the reserves to cope with short-run economic fluctuations. Therefore, they reconfigure allowable spending several times a year. Annularity, the one budgetary norm thought to be

---

[1]See the important paper by Allen Schick, "Off-Budget Expenditure: An Economic and Political Framework." Paper prepared for the Organisation for Economic Co-operation and Development, Paris, August 1981.

[2]Naomi Caiden and Aaron Wildavsky, *Planning and Budgeting in Poor Countries* (New York, 1974). Paperback edition by Transaction, Inc. (New Brunswick, N.J., 1980).

unassailable (because so simple and so uncontroversial), has been gravely weakened.

So what? Does it matter if some old-fashioned norms—derived from an era in which industrialization had hardly begun—have outlived their usefulness? Not necessarily, a prudent person would reply, providing such norms have been replaced by something better or, at least not noticeably worse. For, if one set of norms no longer applies and another is not yet in sight, budgeting is adrift, without rudder or compass. This means that the main governmental process for reconciling differences and setting directions—for consent and for steering—creates problems instead of solutions.

Why did the norms erode? The answer lies in changes in the scope and nature of public spending. Over half the budget came to consist of stable commitments in the form of various kinds of entitlements, and to these might be added multi-year contracts and interest payments. It has been some time since these were labeled "back door" spending, an indication of their acceptance and legitimation. In effect, government took on many of the risks of individuals, particularly those of old age, disability, destitution, and the instability and uncertainties of markets. From a strictly budgetary (as opposed to an economic or social perspective) point of view, this transfer of risk involved governments in massive transfers of resources and the assumption of high uncertainty. The swings in projections of budget deficits during the first half of the 1990s—between $350 billion and $162 billion—give some idea of the uncertainty now involved in budgeting. It is hardly surprising that annularity is less a serious decision-making principle than a pause for a single year in a steadily marching series of assumptions about where the budget is headed next.

The coexistence of entitlements and appropriations in the same budget affects not only predictability but comprehensiveness. Because the appropriations process was insufficiently elastic to accommodate pressures for spending, and annual decisions would impose unacceptable uncertainty, entitlement spending could escape appropriations control. Complete comprehensiveness was probably always something of an illusion—budgets tend to fragment as central controls are found too restrictive and uncertain. Loans and loan guarantees, off-budget entities, special funds, earmarked taxes, tax expenditures, or preferences in the tax code,[3] all impair the ideal of comprehensiveness. Regulations, too, are a form of spending, as private parties must bear the cost even though these amounts do not appear in agency budgets. Comparison of all these different kinds of expenditures becomes impossible.

The decline of comprehensiveness weakens budget control, as transactions take place outside the scope of the budget. There is, it seems, a constant centrifugal force operating on budgets, as efforts are made to escape their boundaries, and corresponding efforts are made to regain unity. The placing of social security off budget, and President Clinton's use of a special reserve to rescue the Mexican

---

[3] See John F. Witte, "Tax Philosophy and Income Equity," in Robert A. Solo and Charles Anderson, eds., *Value Judgment and Income Distribution* (New York: Praeger, 1981), pp. 340–78; and Ronald King, "Tax Expenditures and Systematic Public Policy." Paper prepared for delivery at the Annual Meeting of the American Political Science Association, Denver, Colorado, September 2–5, 1982.

peso after it appeared Congress would not agree, are recent examples of the former. Reform of credit programs and the bringing of several smaller agencies on budget during the 1980s, are examples of the latter. If the budget does not express the whole of government spending, the idea of balance too is less feasible—just what is it that is to be balanced?

The norms of annularity, comprehensiveness, and balance conjure up a time when the budget process "worked"—a time of gentlemanly accepted "limits," of budgetary stability and incremental change. There is some doubt whether or when this period of "classical" budgeting actually existed.[4] If and when it did, these norms represented budgetary values which might be set against other values—such as winning wars, greater individual security, less inequality of wealth, tasks beyond the capability of the private sector to accomplish. If a budget process based on the traditional budgetary norms would prevent the emergence of these values, then it would be transformed.

Yet no one, it seems, was really happy with the result: There was too much disagreement on how much spending there should be and on what, and on how much taxes should be and who should pay. There was a constant nagging refrain that the budget was out of control, though few could articulate just what this meant.

Central control makes most sense against a historical background of agreement, so that only small propositions of the budget remain in dispute. The old *Politics of the Budgetary Process* could focus on incremental differences because the base was largely agreed. When there is disagreement about the starting point as well as the desirable outcome of budgetary negotiation, incremental change is in trouble.

Another explanation for the demise of the traditional budget process lies in economic growth—its presence from the end of World War II until the mid-1970s and its lessening or absence thereafter. It is easy to reach agreements, the growth theory holds, when everyone is getting more. Incrementalism, Schick says, is based on the expectation of continued plenty. Now that prosperity has declined, incrementalism has gone with it.[5]

Doubtless, the decline of expected revenues does make things harder all the way around. Had the parties agreed, a slowdown in spending accompanied by an increase in taxation could have balanced the budget. But one side wanted to maintain spending levels and the other to cut income taxes. Budget imbalance means more than a gap between spending and revenue; imbalance also signifies that the major political parties are too far apart to agree on how the budget should be balanced—by tax increases or spending cuts. This is dissensus.

Which comes first, the change in budgetary norms, or the change in spending practices? Did the practices change the norms or vice versa? My view is that both change together. The purpose of norms is to justify practices. When there is a

---

[4]See critique in Roy T. Meyers, *Strategic Budgeting* (Ann Arbor, Mich.: University of Michigan Press, 1994), Chapter 1.

[5]Allen Schick, "The Politics of Budgeting: Can Incrementalism Survive in a Decremental Age?" Paper prepared for the 1982 Annual Meeting of the American Political Science Association, Denver, Colorado, September 2–5, 1982.

strong desire to change behavior, as in the New Deal America of the 1930s in regard to government spending, there is also a search for new norms to rationalize that conduct. It is not only that John Maynard Keynes found answers for America but also that influential Americans were actively looking for a theory to justify greater government spending—so they found him.[6] And later on, we observe that many new spigots were being opened in the 1960s and 1970s, spending that coincided with the civil rights and environmental movements, seeking enhanced equality and concern for ecology through governmental action. There is a struggle over theory as well as over practice; each influences the other so that one cannot say which came first but only that ideas and actions go together.

The importance of budgetary norms can be seen indirectly in new practices and proposals for reform that are meant to make up for what used to be. Budget resolutions, constitutional spending limits, and other budget methods, such as the presidential item veto, which we will discuss in this chapter, are all efforts to do by law what once was done by custom—namely, provide accepted premises under which conflict over the budget could be negotiated so as to resolve disagreements while still imparting stability to government. Once, the norms of balance, annularity, and comprehensiveness performed that task. Let us, by reviewing different proposals, appraise to what extent the genie of agreement can be put back into the bottle of budgeting.

FORMS OF BUDGETING[7]

So far as I know, existing forms of budgeting have never been compared systematically, characteristic for characteristic, with the leading alternatives.[8] By doing so, we can see better which characteristics of budgetary processes suit different purposes under a variety of conditions.

What purpose should any form of budgeting be expected to serve? Control over public money and accountability to public authority were among the earliest purposes. Predictability and planning—knowing what there will be to spend over time—were not far behind. From the beginning, relating expenditure to revenue was of prime importance. In our day we have added macro-economic management, intended to moderate inflation and unemployment. Spending is supposed to be varied to suit the economy. In time, the need for money came to be used as a lever to enhance the efficiency or effectiveness of policies. Here we have it: Budgeting is supposed to contribute to continuity (for planning), to change (for policy evaluation), to flexibility (for the economy), to rigidity (for limiting spending), and to openness (for accountability).

These different and (to some extent) opposed purposes contain a clue to the perennial dissatisfaction with budgeting. Obviously no single form can simultane-

---

[6]Felix Frankfurter, later a Justice of the Supreme Court, played such a role. See H. N. Hirsch, *The Enigma of Felix Frankfurter* (New York: Basic Books, 1981).

[7]This section is a revised version of "A Budget for All Seasons? Why the Traditional Budget Lasts," in *Public Administration Review*, No. 6 (November/December 1978), pp. 501–509.

[8]But, for a beginning, see Allen Schick, "The Road to PPB: The Stages of Budget Reform," in *Public Administration Review* (December 1966), pp. 243–58.

ously provide continuity and change, rigidity and flexibility. And no one should be surprised that those who concentrate on one purpose or the other should find budgeting unsatisfactory; or that, as purposes change, these criticisms should become constant.

The ability of a budgetary form to score high on one criterion may increase the likelihood of its scoring low on another. Planning requires predictability, and economic management requires reversibility. Thus, there may well be no ideal mode of budgeting. If so, this is the question: Do we compromise by choosing a budgetary process that does splendidly on one criterion but terribly on others? Or, do we opt for a process that satisfies all these demands even though it does not score brilliantly on any single one?

A public-sector budget is supposed to ensure accountability. By associating government publicly with certain expenditures, opponents can ask questions or contribute criticisms. Here the clarity of the budget presentation—linking expenditures to activities and to responsible officials—is crucial. As a purpose, accountability is closely followed by control: Are the authorized and appropriated funds being spend for the designated activities? Control (or its antonym "out of control") can be used in several senses: Are expenditures within the limits (1) stipulated or (2) desired? While a budget (or item) might be "out of control" to a critic who desires it to be different, in this nomenclature control is lacking only when limits are stipulated and exceeded.

Budgets may be mechanisms of efficiency—doing whatever is done at least cost, or getting the most out of a given level of expenditure—and/or of effectiveness—achieving certain results in public policy, such as improving child health or reducing crime. An efficient program may still be ineffective.

In modern times, budgeting also has become an instrument of economic management and of planning. With the advent of Keynesian economics, efforts have been made to vary the rate of spending so as to increase employment in slack times or to reduce inflation when prices are deemed to be rising too quickly. Here (leaving aside alternative tax policies) the ability to increase and decrease spending in the short run is of paramount importance. For budgeting to serve planning, however, predictability (not variability) is critical. The ability to maintain a course of behavior over time is essential.

Budgeting is not only an economic but also a political instrument. Since inability to implement decisions nullifies them, the ability to mobilize support is as important as making the right choice. So, too, is the capacity to figure out what to do, that is, to make choices. Thus the effect of budgeting on conflict and calculation—the capacity to make and support decisions—must also be considered. When conflict overwhelms calculation (that is, when there is dissensus), subterfuge, either to permit some sort of agreement or to carry on the struggle, may overwhelm the more desirable qualities of budgeting.

REFORM WITHOUT CONFLICT

A large part of the literature on budgeting in the United States is concerned with reform. The goals of proposed reforms are couched in similar language—economy, efficiency, improvement, or just better budgeting. The president, the Congress and its committees, administrative agencies, even the interested citizenry all stand to gain by some change in the way the budget is formulated, presented, or evaluated. For a long time there was little or no realization among the reformers that effective change in budgetary relationships must necessarily alter the out- comes of the budgetary process. Today this is widely recognized. Far from being a neutral matter of "better budgeting," proposed reforms inevitably contain impor- tant implications for the political system, that is, for the "who gets what" and the "who ought to get," and even the "who ought to decide what is worth getting" of governmental decisions. What are some of the major political implications of bud- getary reform? I begin with the noblest vision of reform: development of a norma- tive theory of budgeting (stating what ought to be) that would provide the basis for allocating funds among competing activities.

In 1940, in what is still the best discussion of the subject, V. O. Key lamented "The Lack of a Budgetary Theory." He called for a theory that would help answer the basic question of budgeting on the expenditure side: "On what basis shall it be decided to allocate X dollars to Activity A instead of Activity B?"[9] Although several attempts have been made to meet this challenge,[10] not one has come close to suc- ceeding—and for an excellent reason: The task, as posed, is impossible to fulfill.

For a normative theory of budgeting to be more than an exercise, to have any practical effect, it must actually guide the making of governmental decisions. Ex- penditures that are passed by Congress, enacted into law, and spent must in large measure conform to the theory, which is tantamount to prescribing that virtually all government activities be carried on accordingly.

The budget (for whatever the government does must be paid for from public funds) is the financial reflection of what the government does or intends to do. A theory that contains criteria for determining what ought to be in the budget, therefore, is nothing less than a theory stating what government ought to do. If we substitute the words "what the government ought to do" for the words "ought to be in the budget," it becomes clear that a normative theory of budgeting would be a comprehensive and specific political theory detailing what the government's ac- tivities ought to be at a particular time. Given that the budget represents the out- come of political struggle, a normative theory of budgeting suggests the elimination of any such conflict over the government's role in society. Such a the- ory, therefore, is utopian in the fullest sense of the word: Its creation and accep- tance would mean the end of politics.

By suppressing dissent, dictatorial regimes do enforce their normative theo- ries of budgeting on others. Presumably, we reject this solution to the problem of conflict in society and insist on democratic procedures. How then arrive at a the- ory of budgeting that is something more than one person's preferences?

Two crucial aspects of budgeting are "how much?" and "what for?" The prob- lem is not only "how shall budgetary benefits be maximized?" as if it made no dif-

---

[9]V. O. Key, Jr., "The Lack of a Budgetary Theory," *The American Political Science Review*, Vol. 34 (De- cember 1940), pp. 1137–44.

[10]Verne B. Lewis, "Toward a Theory of Budgeting," *Public Administration Review*, Vol. 12 (Winter 1952), pp. 42–54; "Symposium on Budget Theory," *Public Administration Review*, Vol. 10 (Winter 1950), pp. 20–31; Arthur Smithies, *The Budgetary Process in the United States* (New York: McGraw- Hill, 1955).

ference who received or paid for them, but also "who shall pay for and who shall receive how much in the way of budgetary benefits?" One may purport to solve the problem of budgeting by proposing a normative theory that specifies a method for maximizing returns for budgetary expenditures. If it is impossible to impose a set of preferred policies on others, however, this solution breaks down. It amounts to no more than saying that if you can persuade others to agree with you, then you will have achieved agreement. Yet such a state of universal agreement hardly has arisen.

Another approach is to treat society as a single organism with a consistent set of desires. Instead of revenue being raised and the budget being spent by and for many individuals who no doubt have varied preferences, these processes would be regarded, in effect, as if only a single individual were concerned. This approach sidesteps the central problem of social conflict, of the need somehow to aggregate different preferences so that a decision may emerge. (After all, the grave difficulties we experience in agreeing on annual budgets today are not a result of individual incapacity; any number of representatives and presidents could make a coherent budget; it is gaining the consent of others that is difficult.) How can we compare the worth of expenditures for irrigation to certain farmers with that of widening a highway to motorists, or weigh the desirability of aiding old people to pay medical bills against the degree of safety provided by an expanded defense program?

In the real world, the process Americans have developed for dealing with interpersonal comparisons in government is not economic but political. Conflicts are resolved (under agreed-upon rules) through the political system by translating different preferences into units called votes or into such types of authority as veto power. There need not be (and there is not) full agreement on goals or the preferential weights to be accorded to different goals. Participants directly threaten, compromise, and trade favors in regard to policies in which values are implicitly weighted, and then agree to register the results according to the rules for tallying votes.

Bargaining takes place among many dispersed centers of influence, and favors are swapped as in the case of logrolling public-works appropriations. Since no single group can impose its preferences upon others within the American political system, special coalitions are formed to support or oppose specific policies. In this system of fragmented power, support is sought at numerous centers of influence—congressional committees, congressional leadership, the president, the Office of Management and Budget, interdepartmental committees, departments, bureaus, private groups, on and on. Nowhere does a single authority have power to determine what is going to be in the budget.

THE POLITICS IN BUDGET REFORM

The seeming irrationalities of a political system that does not provide for formal consideration of the budget as a whole (except by the president, who cannot control the final result) have led to many attacks and proposals for reform. But such reforms are aimed at the wrong target. If the present budgetary process rightly or wrongly is deemed unsatisfactory, then one must alter in some respect the political system of which the budget is but an expression. It makes no sense to speak as if one could make drastic changes in budgeting without also altering the distribution of influence. This task, however, is inevitably so formidable that most reformers prefer to speak only of changing the budgetary process (as with the Congressional Budget and Control Act of 1974 or Gramm–Rudman–Hollings), as if by some subtle alchemy the intractable political element also could be transformed into a more malleable substance.

In actuality, it is the other way around. The budget is inextricably linked to the political system; by far the most significant way of influencing the budget, therefore, would be to introduce basic political changes. Give presidents powers enabling them to control the votes of their party in Congress; enable a small group of members to command a majority of votes on all occasions so they can push their program through (now that would be a budget committee!); then, you will have exerted a profound influence on the content of the budget.

Further, no significant change can be made in the budgetary process without also affecting the political process. There would be no point in tinkering with the budgetary machinery if, at the end, the pattern of outcomes was precisely the same as before. On the contrary, budget reform has little justification unless it results in different kinds of decisions and, when and if this has been accomplished, the play of political forces has necessarily been altered.

Since the budget represents conflicts over whose preferences shall prevail, moreover, one cannot speak of "better budgeting" without considering who benefits and who loses or by demonstrating that no one loses. Just as the supposedly objective criterion of "efficiency" has been shown to have normative implications,[11] so a "better budget" may well be a cloak for someone's hidden policy preferences. To propose that the president be given an item veto, for example, is an attempt to increase the influence of those particular interests that have superior access to the Chief Executive (rather than, say, to the Congress).

Unit of Measurement: Cash or Volume

Budgeting can be done not only in terms of cash but also in terms of volume. Instead of promising to pay so much over the next year or years, the commitment can be made in terms of operations to be performed or services to be provided. The usual way of guaranteeing a volume of activity is indexing the program against inflation so its purchasing power is kept constant. Why might someone want to budget in terms of volume (or in currency held constant as to purchasing power)? To aid planning: If public agencies know that they can count not on variable currency but rather on what that currency actually can buy (i.e., on a volume of activity), they can plan ahead as far as the budget runs. Indeed, if one wishes to make decisions now instead of at future periods, so as to help assure consistency over time, then estimates based on stability in the unit of effort (so many applications processed or such a level of services provided) are the very way to go about it.

---

[11]Dwight Waldo, *The Administrative State* (New York: Ronald Press, 1948); Herbert A. Simon, "The Criterion of Efficiency," in *Administrative Behavior,* 2nd ed. (New York: Macmillian, 1957), pp. 172–97.

So long as purchasing power remains constant, the distinction between budgeting in cash or by volume makes no difference. But should the value of money fluctuate (and, in our time, this has meant inflation), the public budget must expand available funds so as to provide the designated volume of activity. Budgeters then lose control of money because they have to supply whatever is needed. Given large and unexpected changes in prices, the size of budget in cash terms obviously would fluctuate wildly. But it is equally obvious that no government could permit itself to be so far out of control. Hence, the very type of stable environment that budgeting by volume is designed to achieve turns out to be its major unarticulated premise.

Given an irreducible amount of uncertainty in the system, not every element can be stabilized at the same time. Who, then, will enjoy stability? And who will bear the costs of change? The private sector and the central budget office pay the price for budgeting by volume. What budgeting by volume says, in effect, is that the public sector will be protected against inflation by getting its agreed level of services before other needs are met. The real resources necessary to make up the gap between projected and current prices must come from the private sector in the form of taxation or borrowing. In other words, for the public sector, volume budgeting is a form of indexing against inflation.

By the mid-1990s, the idea of volume budgeting had been firmly institutionalized in baseline budgeting. Budget decisions are increasingly discussed in terms of a future baseline: This year's budget for an agency might be above what it received in the previous year, but if it were below the baseline, it would count as a cut. As baselines are projected into the future, the cuts in terms of constant dollars can become alarming. Yet baselines are indispensable in forecasting the future; witness the scheme to balance the budget by the year 2002, which depends on the accuracy of baselines for anticipated revenues and expenditures. In contrast, appropriations debates in 1995 were conducted almost entirely in terms of cuts from the previous year's budget. If conceived in terms of baselines, which would have automatically added a percentage for inflation, the cuts would have been considered greater, and even agencies whose budgets were frozen or received a slight increase, would be counted as having received a cut.

Time Span: Months, One Year, Many Years

Multiyear budgeting, that is, viewing resource allocation in a long-term perspective, has long been proposed as a reform to enhance rational choice. Considering one year at a time, it has been argued, leads to short-sightedness (only next year's expenditures are reviewed), overspending (because huge future disbursements are hidden), conservatism (incremental changes do not open up larger future vistas), and parochialism (programs tend to be viewed in isolation rather than by comparison to future costs in relation to expected revenue). Extending the budget time span to two, three, or even five years, it is argued, would enable long-range planning to overtake short-term reaction, and to substitute financial planning for merely muddling through. The old tactic of the camel's nose—beginning with small expenditures while hiding larger ones that will arise later on—is rendered more difficult. Moreover, the practice of stepped-up spending to use up resources before the end of the budgetary year would decline in frequency.

One of the reforms suggested by the National Performance Review in its 1993 Report *From Red Tape to Results: Creating a Government That Works Better and Costs Less* (Gore Report) was a biennial budget, and previously quite detailed bills had been put forward to implement the idea.[12] A two-year budget would not change much. There is no reason to believe it would facilitate agreement or encourage better understanding, but it might be approved as a sort of budget officers' humane act. Instead of working 80 hours a week every year, participants in budgeting might get a breather every other year. Being less tired, they just might decide more wisely. In any event, no great harm is likely to be done and a bit of good might be accomplished.

A multiyear budget would work well for certain parts of the budget, like military procurements, which take years to complete. But benefit, salary, and operating expense categories are ill-suited to long-term budgeting. The size of these items is significantly influenced by external factors, such as inflation, that are difficult to predict. The problem of prediction appears more formidable when it is recalled that preparation of the budget begins almost a year before the budget is implemented. A two-year budget cycle, consequently, would have to forecast economic changes almost three years into the future. The result may be that budgeters would "spend more time tinkering with the assumptions over the 33-month period and, even assuming good faith, making some decisions on longer-term assumptions that would have to be altered even more dramatically later on."[13]

Much depends, to be sure, on how many budgetary commitments last. The seemingly arcane question of whether budgeting should be done on a cash or volume basis has assumed importance because of the increasing habit of multiyear budget agreements and the latest plan to balance the budget over the next seven years. The longer the term of the budget, the more significant becomes inflation. To the extent that price changes are automatically absorbed into budgets (volume budgeting), a certain amount of activity is guaranteed. But to the extent that agencies thus must absorb inflation, the real scope of activity will decline. Multiyear budgeting in cash terms, without indexing, diminishes the relative size of the public sector and leaves the private sector larger. Not always up front in discussing the time span of the budget, but very important, is the debate over the relative shares of the public and private sectors—which sector will be asked to absorb inflation and which will be allowed to expand into the other.

A similar issue of relative shares is created within government by proposals to budget in some sectors for several years, and in others, for only one year. Entitlements, for example, can be perpetual. To operate in different time spans poses the question of which sectors of policy are to be exposed to the vicissitudes of life in the short term and which are to be protected from them. Like any other device, multiyear budgeting is not neutral but distributes indulgences differently among

---

[12]See Naomi Caiden, "The New Rules of the Budget Game," *Public Administration Review*, Vol. 44, No. 2 (March–April 1984), pp. 109–117.

[13]Symposium on Budget Balance, p. IV–30.

the affected interests. Although being treated as an entitlement, until basic legislation changes, is no guarantee of future success, it is better for beneficiaries. But entitlements, if they grow large, are not necessarily better for government because they reduce legislative discretion.

Another potential downside to multiyear budgeting is the increased permanence of programs. Just as some programs may have a more difficult time getting into the budget, so "hard in" often implies an even "harder out." Once an expenditure gets included in a multiyear projection, it is likely to remain because it has become part of an interrelated set of proposals that might be expensive to disrupt. Thus control in a single year may have to be sacrificed to the maintenance of limits over the multiyear period. And, should there be a call for cuts, promised reductions in future years (which are always "iffy") are easily traded for maintenance of spending in the all-important present.

Suppose, however, that it were deemed desirable to reduce some expenditures significantly in order to increase others. Due to the built-in pressure of continuing commitments, what could be done in a single year is extremely limited. But making arrangements over a 2–5 year period would permit larger changes in spending to be affected in a more orderly way. This is true; other things, however—prices, priorities, politics—seldom remain equal. At a time when maintaining the annual budget has become problematical, so that the budget may have to be remade several times a year, lengthening the cycle possibly will just compound uncertainty. As Robert Hartman put it, "There is no absolutely right way to devise a long-run budget strategy."[14]

Calculation: Incremental or Comprehensive

Just as the annual budget on a cash basis is integral to the traditional process, so also is the budgetary base; normally, only small increases or decreases to the existing base are considered in any one period. If such budgetary practices may be described as incremental, the main alternative to the traditional budget is one that emphasizes comprehensive calculation. The main modern forms of the latter are planning, programming, and budgeting (PPB) and zero-base budgeting (ZBB).

Think of PPB as embodying horizontal comprehensiveness—comparing alternative expenditure packages to decide which of them best contributes to large programmatic objectives. ZBB, by contrast, might be thought of as manifesting vertical comprehensiveness: Every year alternative expenditures from base zero are considered, with all governmental activities or objectives being treated as discrete entities. In short, PPB compares programs, while ZBB compares alternative funding levels for the same program.

The strength of PPB lies in its emphasis on policy analysis to increase effectiveness: Programs are evaluated, found wanting, and presumably replaced by alternatives designed to produce superior results. Unfortunately, PPB engenders a conflict between error recognition and error correction. For an error to be altered, it must be relatively easy to correct; but PPB makes this hard. The "sys-

---

[14]Robert A. Hartman, "Multiyear Budget Planning," in Joseph A. Pechman, ed., *Setting National Priorities: The 1979 Budget* (Washington, D.C.: The Brookings Institution, 1978), p. 312.

tems" in PPB are characterized by their proponents as highly differentiated and tightly linked. The rationale for program budgeting lies in its connectedness: Like groups are grouped together. Program structures are meant to replace the confused concatenations of line-items with clearly differentiated, nonoverlapping boundaries—that is, only one set of programs to a structure. Hence a change in one element or structure necessarily reverberates throughout every element in the same system.

Budgeting by programs, precisely because money flows to objectives, makes it difficult to abandon objectives without also abandoning the very organization that gets its money for those activities. The cutting edge of dealing with competition among programs lies in postulating a range of policy objectives small enough to be encompassed and large enough to overlap so that there can be choices (tradeoffs) among them. Instead, PPB tends to generate a tendency either toward only a few generalized objectives (so anything and everything can fit under them), or such a multitude of objectives that each organizational unit has its own home and does not have to compete with any other.[15] Participants learn how to play any game.

The ideal ahistorical information system is zero-base budgeting. The past, as reflected in the budgetary base, is explicitly rejected: There is no yesterday; nothing will be taken for granted; everything at every period is subject to searching scrutiny. As a result, calculations become unmanageable.

To say that a budgetary process is ahistorical is to conclude that the sources of error multiply while the chances of correcting mistakes decrease: If history is abolished, nothing is ever settled. Old quarrels resurface as new conflicts. Both calculation and conflict increase exponentially, the former complicating selection and the latter obstructing error correction. As mistrust grows with conflict, willingness to admit (and hence to correct) error diminishes. Doing without history is a little like abolishing memory—momentarily convenient, perhaps, but ultimately embarrassing.

Nowhere does a true zero-based budget practice exist. Everywhere the "zero" is ignored and the base gets larger, amounting, in the end, to 80 to 90 percent of the prior year; this, of course, is a reversion to incremental budgeting. What is worse, ZBB cannot give expression to the main reason for most activities, namely, to support some other activity. By building the budget entirely from the bottom up, the justification for expenditures is divorced from their connections to other activities and purposes. This does not make sense.[16] It does explain why ZBB has declined in use. But why do people keep resurrecting it? Because ZBB holds out the hope of liberation from restraints of the past, as if they could be willed away.

ZBB and PPB share an emphasis on the virtue of objective. Program budgeting seeks to relate longer to smaller objectives among different programs, and zero-base budgeting promises to do the same within a single program. The policy implications of these budgeting methods, which distinguish them from existing

---

[15]See Jeanne Nienaber and Aaron Wildavsky, *The Budgeting and Evaluation of Federal Recreation Programs, or Money Doesn't Grow on Trees* (New York: Basic Books, 1973).

[16]See Thomas H. Hammond and Jack H. Knott, *A Zero-Based Look at Zero-Base Budgeting* (New Brunswick, N.J.: Transaction, 1979).

approaches, derive from their overwhelming, shared concern with ranking objectives. Thinking about objectives is one thing, however; making budget categories out of them is quite another. Of course, if one wants the objectives of today to be the objectives of tomorrow, if one wants no change, then it is a brilliant idea to build the budget around objectives. Conversely, if one wishes to alter existing objectives radically, it may be appropriate to highlight the struggle over them. But if one desires flexibility (sometimes known as learning from experience), it must be possible to change objectives without simultaneously destroying the organization by withdrawing financial support.

Both PPB and ZBB are expressions of a view in which ranking objectives is rendered tantamount to reason. Alas! An efficient mode of presenting results in research papers—find objectives, order them, choose the highest valued—has been confused with proper processes of social inquiry. For purposes of resource allocation, which is what budgeting is about, it is irrational to rank objectives without considering resources. The question cannot be "What do you want?"—as if there were no limits—but should be "What do you want compared to what you can get?" After all, an agency with a billion dollars would not only do more than it would with a million but might well wish to do something quite different. Resources affect objectives as well as vice versa. Budgeting should not separate what reason tells us belongs together.

There is a critical difference between the financial form in which the budget is voted in the legislature and the different ways of thinking about budgeting. It is possible to analyze expenditures in terms of programs, over long periods of time, and in many other ways, without requiring that the form of analysis be the same as the form of appropriation. All this can be summarized: The more neutral the form of presenting appropriations, the easier to translate other changes—in program, direction, organizational structure—into the desired amount without increasing the rigidity in categories, and thus erecting barriers to future changes.

The forms of budgeting that once occupied center stage (PPB, ZBB, and similar reforms) have lost their allure, but the impetus toward a more analytical focus for budgeting has not diminished. In 1993, the Government Performance and Results Act was passed with the aims of improving federal program effectiveness and public accountability, improving public service delivery, providing more objective information to Congress on the achievement of statutory objectives and on the relative efficiency and effectiveness of programs and spending, and to improve internal management. By systematically holding federal agencies accountable for achieving program results, the Act would "improve the confidence of the American people in the capability of the Federal Government."[17] Emphasis was on the setting of program goals, measuring performance against them, and reporting on progress. Following a series of pilot projects, agencies would submit five-year strategic plans to OMB. These plans would include mission statements, general goals and objectives (including outcome goals), a description of how they are to be achieved, and how performance goals would be related to the general objectives, a description of key factors beyond the agency's control that could significantly affect attainment of those objectives, and a description of program evaluations used

---

[17]Government Performance and Results Act, p. 1.

to revise the goals. From 1999, each agency will also be required to submit an annual performance plan, covering each program activity in its budget. The plan should establish performance goals in an objective, quantifiable, and measurable form; describe the processes and resources necessary to meet them; establish performance indicators to measure outputs, service levels, and outcomes for each program activity; provide a basis for comparing goals and results; and describe the means to be used to verify and validate measured values. Provision was made for alternative procedures where quantifiable goals were not appropriate. Each agency would also be required to submit an annual program performance report to the president and Congress, comparing program indicators with performance over the previous three years and giving reasons why goals were not achieved.

These provisions were accompanied by others allowing greater managerial flexibility. After 1999, the performance plans might include proposals to waive administrative procedural requirements and controls including staffing levels, remuneration levels, and transfers, subject to approval by OMB. The waiver proposal would have to include a quantified assessment of how the relaxed requirements would actually affect performance and the achievement of goals, and would have to specify that it would only be for a limited time.

These measures are similar to those taken in recent years in a number of industrialized countries, emphasizing managerial discretion and flexibility together with responsibility for attaining specified performance goals. The problem, as with previous reform attempts, is to link information on performance with decisions on budget allocations. In today's highly charged political environment, the weight likely to be given to such information is somewhat doubtful. The direction of these and similar reforms raises once again the issues of centralization and decentralization.[18]

Centralization and Decentralization

The provisions of the Government Performance and Results Act parallel those of the recommendations of the National Performance Review, which also stressed performance based budgeting and greater flexibility. It also sought to streamline a process that traditionally had been a bottom-up process, which focused on the needs of agencies, but put very little emphasis on performance and results. According to Allen Schick, there was relatively little policy guidance from the president and OMB at the beginning of the process, and the emphasis on detail and inputs was intensified by the fragmentation of the budget among the committees of Congress. Centralized intervention in the budget process tended to come at the end, rather than the beginning, when the president and OMB resolved outstanding matters, and options previously left open were closed.[19]

---

[18]See United States General Accounting Office, *Managing for Results: Experiences Abroad Suggest Insights for Federal Management Reforms*, May 1995 (GAO/GGD-95-120); also Allen Schick, *The Federal Budget: Politics, Policy, Process* (Washington, D.C.: Brookings Institution, 1995), p. 187 for a schedule of the Act.

[19]Ibid, p. 55.

The NPR envisaged more of a top-down process, in which instructions at the beginning would guide the process. In 1994, therefore, OMB issued ceilings on agency requests, although at the end, the president still intervened to finalize budget requests with department heads, an unprecedented degree of intervention. The turmoil of 1995 probably ruled out the kind of streamlined process envisaged by the NPR, but meanwhile OMB had been reconsidering its own role and organization.

As a result of a searching self-examination under the title OMB 2000, it was concluded that in order to carry out the "reinventing government" agenda of reducing the workforce by over quarter of a million employees, streamlining the bureaucracy, and measuring performance, OMB's oversight role needed to integrate budget analysis, management review and policy development. New resource management offices would divide up the area of the budget. Their staff would be policy analysts, who would make recommendations on existing and new policy implementation, provide information to Congress on the resource requirements of policy proposals, and ensure management initiatives were implemented. At the same time, the instructions and schedules for agency budget preparation would be revised to require an integrated management and budget process, including performance measures.

To try to integrate budget policy, cross-cutting themes would be identified early in the budget process and communicated to agencies so they could be addressed, and the president's budget organized around them. Ad hoc staff teams would conduct multiyear budget planning, try to foresee future problems, and undertake program analyses. OMB would expect to improve its working relationship with the agencies by greater cooperation and information sharing. Strategic thinking would be enhanced by budget review of the areas of jurisdiction of the committees and subcommittees of Congress to gain a better understanding of policy tradeoffs likely to occur. These reforms may herald a more centralized analytical kind of process, but it is too early for their assessment.

LIMITS

The idea of budgeting from above—either by limiting revenue and requiring expenditure to fit within it, or limiting spending and forbidding revenue to exceed that level—would revolutionize resource mobilization and resource allocation. Budgeting by addition would no longer be possible; adding requests together would not work because exceeding a prearranged total would be ruled out. More for one program or agency, consequently, would mean less for another. Budgeting by subtraction—tradeoffs among good things that could not all be funded—would usher in a new budgetary order.

Attempts to gain passage of a constitutional amendment to enforce a balanced budget go back to at least 1936, and the movement has gained momentum in the last few years. Since 1990, four versions of the amendment have been proposed, but each has been defeated in Congress. In order to amend the constitution, it is necessary to gain agreement of two-thirds majority in each chamber of Congress and ratification of three fourths of the state legislatures. Alternatively, two thirds of the states may petition a constitutional convention.

The Republican "Contract with America" contained a proposal for a constitutional balanced budget amendment, in which the president must present a budget to Congress in which total outlays were no greater than total receipts. Excess spending or increases in taxes would require a three-fifths majority in each house, and the amount of the national public debt would be capped, with increase in the limit only possible with a three-fifths majority of Congress. The amendment could be waived only in the event of a declaration of war or an imminent and serious threat to national security.[20]

This amendment did not specify the level at which the budget should be balanced, but it would have effectively pushed down and frozen spending because of the probable inability to gain super-majorities for tax increases or debt. This version of a balanced budget amendment differs from a more elastic proposal in which government expenditures would be related to the level of economic growth and allowed to rise each year by a specified percentage of GDP.

The political result of such a limitation, according to its advocates, would be to increase cooperation in society and conflict within government. As things stand, so the limitation's supporters contend, program advocates within government, by increasing their total share of national income, have every incentive to raise their spending while reducing their internal differences. Why fight among their public selves if private persons will pay? Thus conflict is transferred from government to society.

Once limits are enacted, however, the amendment's advocates believe, the direction of incentives would be reversed: There would be increasing cooperation in society and rising conflict in government. Citizens in society would have a common interest whereas the sectors of policy—housing, welfare, environment, defense—would be plunged into conflict. Organizations interested in income redistribution to favor poorer people would come to understand that the greater the increase in real national income, the more there would be for government to spend on their purposes. Instead of acting as if it didn't matter where the money came from, such groups would have to consider how they might contribute to enhanced productivity. Management and labor, majorities and minorities, would be thinking about common objectives, about how to get more out of one another rather than about how to take more from the other.

But the idea of a limitation of this kind has never reached Congress, whereas the simpler balanced budget amendment seems to have an irresistible appeal despite many quite sensible arguments against it. Balancing the budget at all costs ignores the stabilization function of the budget and would actually require cuts as revenues ebbed in a recession. As Robert Eisner has pointed out,

> Each additional point of unemployment is associated with at least $50 billion of additional deficit, as revenues shrink and outlays grow. If unemployment were to rise from the current 5.4% to, say, the 7.6% of June 1992, the deficit could be expected to rise by more than $110 billion. What would be law then tell us to do? Tell taxpayers to try harder? Stop some "entitlement" checks . . . Or pray?[21]

---

[20]Sandra J. Nixon, "Budget Amendments: An Idea . . . That Never Goes Out of Style," *Congressional Quarterly Weekly Report,* January 14 1995, p. 143.

[21]Robert Eisner, "We Don't Need Balanced Budgets," *Wall Street Journal,* January 11, 1995.

While it has become fashionable to denigrate the capability of the federal government in fiscal policy to guide the economy, it is still generally conceded that the federal budget has an inbuilt counter-cyclical tendency which acts to ameliorate and stabilize recessions. According to Laura Tyson, Chair of the Council of Economic Advisers, it is doubtful whether the Federal Reserve could shoulder the entire burden of economic stabilization through interest rate changes. She believes that monetary policy affects the economy indirectly and only with notoriously long time lags, and there are limits to how low interest rates can be pushed to stimulate the economy.[22]

Another objection is the inevitable entry of litigation into budget matters. There would also be a number of implications for the character of contemporary budgeting. For one thing, there would have to be grave concern about exceeding allowed totals. Hence money would have to be kept back in the form of large contingency funds. For another, entitlements could not be guaranteed at full value; if the total were about to be breached, payments might have to be reduced, say from 100 to 97 percent of the guarantee. The amendment, that is, would modify open-ended promises to citizens—you will get yours no matter what—with only the promise (by their collective expression, the government) that beneficiaries would get something close to what they expected.

THE LINE-ITEM VETO

With the 1988 election coming up, facing the unpleasant task of explaining away historically unprecedented deficits, unwilling to talk of raising taxes, and unable to reduce domestic spending—it was understandable that Republicans spoke favorably of the line-item veto. So long as the Democrats resisted, blame for continuing deficits could be placed on them. And focusing entirely on the immediate future, Republicans could indulge themselves in fantasies of their leader cutting and slashing, slashing and cutting, until big government was vetoed out root and branch. But that is all it was—a fantasy.

Experience in state governments has been cited to support the efficacy of the item veto. The argument for the item veto rests on a combination of alleged cuts made by states, together with a version of the marginal fallacy. On the surface it does appear that under certain governors in some states, such as Ronald Reagan in California, the item veto eliminated 1 or 2 percent of spending, which, if cumulated over a number of years, adds up to significant reductions. I say "alleged" savings because it is well known that legislators pad their requests in anticipation of vetoes.

Apparently, it is possible to interweave items so that they are not separable, thereby nullifying the intent of the item veto. At least, Roy D. Morey, writing about Arizona, says that "A major reason why the governor has not used the item veto more frequently is that the legislature has deliberately constructed appropriation bills in such a way as to stymie its use."[23] It appears that the item veto was

---

[22]Laura D'Andrea Tyson, "It's a Recipe for Economic Chaos," *Washington Post*, February 7, 1995.

[23]Roy D. Morey, "The Executive Veto in Arizona: Its Use and Limitations," *The Western Political Quarterly*, Vol. 19, No. 3 (September 1966), quote on p. 512.

more powerful in Pennsylvania where governors have used it a good deal. But this conclusion must be modified by interaction effects: "When a legislator, even though opposed in principle to an appropriations, is reasonably certain that the governor will slice it down to more moderate size," M. Nelson McGeary states in his study of Pennsylvania, "he is tempted to bolster himself politically by voting large sums of money to a popular cause."[24] Where there is no item veto, as in North Carolina, Coleman B. Ransome, Jr., reports that "the legislature seems to have developed some sense of responsibility; there can be no buckpassing of undesirable legislation to the governor with the knowledge that he will veto the bill in question and thus take the burden from the legislature."[25]

A fatal impediment to a federal line-item veto shows up in the detailed and separable character of state budgets, which makes it relatively easy for most governors to select out the parts they wish to reject. At the federal level, however, budget items are far larger and more aggregated. Thus there would normally be no way for a president to veto individual public works projects, since the budget lists only general totals, while individual projects are found in committee reports. Hence the president would have to veto all public works spending and not just the projects to which he objected.[26]

It takes little imagination to realize that presidents far different from Ronald Reagan or George Bush are going to occupy the White House. Would a Mario Cuomo or an Edward Kennedy (to mention just two well-known liberal Democrats) use the item veto to increase defense and decrease domestic spending, or might not it be just the other way around? Might not a president interested in increasing domestic spending hold defense spending ransom to achieve that very purpose?

Even granting proponents the best of their possible worlds—their president in the White House ready to throttle the expenditure machine does not rescue the item veto from the charge of inappropriateness. Presidents do not usually wish to cut defense, which amounts to around 21 percent of the budget. Without the item veto, President Reagan helped reduce small, means-tested entitlements; and his ability and/or unwillingness to cut the large universal entitlements, especially social security, in view of the political price, would, in any event, have remained unaffected by the item veto. Nor is this all. Together these social welfare programs amount to about 52 percent of the budget. Allowing approximately 15 percent (and rising!) for interest on the debt, this leaves little more than a small number (12 percent) on which to try the item veto.

Even there, in the midst of what is left of general government, there is much that will prove resistant to the item veto. There is misadventure. Rejecting smaller items may increase support for overriding vetoes on larger ones. There is politics.

---

[24]M. Nelson McGeary, "The Governor's Veto in Pennsylvania," *American Political Science Review*, Vol. 41, No. 5 (October 1974), p. 943.

[25]Coleman B. Ransome, Jr., *The American Governorship* (Westport, Conn.: Greenwood Press, 1982), p. 159.

[26]See Louis Fisher, "The Item Veto: The Risks of Emulating the States." Prepared for delivery at the 1985 Annual Meeting of the American Political Science Association, New Orleans, August 29–31, 1985.

Perhaps the president's people think he will use the item veto to eliminate or reduce politically important expenditures on which there has long been a negative professional consensus, for example, agricultural and maritime subsidies, way-below-market prices for grazing rights on federal land, water for irrigation in the west, all sorts of river and harbor projects, and the like. In any event, though there are, as always, tempting targets for elimination, there is not enough to make a big difference in that 12 percent of the federal budget which in part has already been severely pruned.

There is misconception. The item veto cannot quell the widespread will to spend. What it does is convey an image of presidents valiantly trying to stem the tide of spending but, for want of this one weapon, being overwhelmed by hordes of congressional spenders. There is no truth in this. Presidents have been in the forefront of spending. In this respect, think not only of Democrat Lyndon Johnson but of Republican Richard Nixon, in whose administration, and in service to his vaunted flexibility, huge increases took place in social security, loan guarantees, and other prospending developments too numerous to mention.

The general case against the sufficiency of the item veto is overwhelming. Line up the world leaders favoring public expenditure as a proportion of GNP among democracies: In all of these countries, cabinets have the power to determine the entire spending budget, item by item. These governments do not need an item veto because nothing gets into the budget without their approval. Why, then, do the budgets grow? Part of the reason (in some but by no means all of these spending leaders) is that most have coalition governments or corporatist arrangements in which the cost of consent is side payments to partners, thus increasing the size of the budget. To the extent that the United States shares this characteristic of divided government—either because the presidency and all or part of Congress are held by different parties or because, though ostensibly of the same party, their policy preferences differ—there is no reason to believe the item veto will do what total formal control of the budget cannot.

It is not that most of these governments do not have periodic budget-cutting drives, but that these campaigns are never (that's right, never) successful.[27] Hence the essential nature of the problem is clarified: governmental self-control. Governments must (1) want to reduce spending and (2) have an effective technology for doing so. The item veto does not qualify as an effective instrument of spending control because it locks the Treasury doors after the spending bids have already been proposed.

According to Lord Bryce, the item veto is one of those practices that "is desired by enlightened opinion."[28] The executive would be strengthened (doubly so in Bryce's day, since at the end of the nineteenth century the executive budget was not yet a reality) and responsibility more clearly identified and located in a cen-

---

[27]See Daniel L. Tarschys, "Curbing Public Expenditures: A Survey of Current Trends." Paper prepared for the Joint Activity on Public Management Improvement of the Organization for Economic Co-operation and Development, Paris (Technical Co-Operation Service), April 1982.

[28]House Resolution No. 1879, 49th Congress, 1st Session, 3. Quoted in John F. Wolf, "The Item Veto in the American Constitutional System," *Georgetown Law Journal*, Vol. 25 (1936), p. 113.

tralized place. Indeed, the origin of the item veto in the United States lies in the Constitution of the Confederate States. The rationale there and then was avowedly to bring in some of the advantages of the British way. As we know, this hypothesis was never put to the test because the political system in which it was embedded was overthrown.

In the context of the separation of powers, the effects of a line-item veto might be counterproductive. The president would be seen as responsible for legislation (i.e., the bits he did not veto) instead of Congress. Congress would have an incentive to be more irresponsible, relying on the president to veto the more extreme or unsound parts of legislation. Where deals were made in Congress, the president would also become an active player, choosing which parts of measures to favor. Thus a measure designed to reduce spending and increase responsibility for budgetary totals probably would have exactly the opposite effects—increasing irresponsibility as well as the size of the budget.

All these arguments notwithstanding, in 1995 Congress came nearer to passage of a line item veto than ever before, even though the Republican congressional majority, for the time being at least, would be augmenting the power of a Democratic president. However, since a true line-item veto would require an amendment to the Constitution, House and Senate passed different bills to try to provide the equivalent, but at the time of writing, a conference to gain agreement on the issue has not been held.

The line-item veto was a popular measure: Seventy-one Democrats joined 223 Republicans to pass the House version, and bipartisan support was also evident in the Senate where a different version passed by 69–29. The Senate bill was simpler, as it would break up each piece of taxing and spending legislation into sections, which the president could approve or veto separately. The House bill took an expedited rescissions approach, in which the president would sign a bill, and could then within the next ten calendar days (except Sundays) after the bill had passed Congress, go back and eliminate tax or spending items. Then Congress would have 20 days to act before these rescissions took effect, but could defeat them only with a two-thirds majority. Thus any president with support of one third of Congress could prevail in disputes over selected items.[29] The deep freeze into which the line item veto fell for five months indicates not only the differences in approach between the two Houses, but also perhaps some second thoughts about providing the president with such power within the narrow window to make his choices prevail over those of Congress. On the other hand, the narrowness of the window may blunt the measure's potential.

The line-item veto, like a constitutional balanced budget amendment, falls into the category of "grand reforms," and it is possible that neither will ever gain sufficient agreement for passage, simply because no one can really work out what their effects would be. Other kinds of reform are more modest in their claims, seeking on their face merely to provide clearer and more useful information for all concerned in budgeting, not excepting the citizen. But since no change in bud-

[29]David Rogers, "House Votes Line-Item Veto for President but Measure Is Facing Trouble in Senate," *Wall Street Journal*, February 7, 1995, p. A5.

geting is neutral in its effects, their impacts may be more lasting, though their passage came about without sound and fury, and they do not partake in the fashionableness of the newer managerial approaches.

CREDIT REFORM

Earlier we discussed concern about loans and loan guarantees. In 1990, the Federal Credit Reform Act changed the basis for accounting for credit transactions in the budget. Previously the federal budget accounted for all credit transactions on a cash basis, which recognized transactions only as money was paid out or received.[30] Not only did this practice give a misleading idea of total credit (because of netting out of off-setting repayments), but it also failed to take into account the real costs of credit, and biased decisions in favor of loan guarantees which appeared as costless—unless and until default took place.[31]

The aim was for policy makers to be able to compare credit programs with others in making budgetary decisions. The objectives of the Act were to measure more accurately the cost of federal credit programs; to reveal their costs in a way comparable to other programs; to encourage delivery of benefits in the most appropriate form; and to improve allocation of resources. The Act required that subsidy costs should be calculated, expressed in terms of net present value, and included in outlays at the time the credit transaction was made. It also established new sets of accounts for separating the subsidized costs and the non-subsidized cash flows. Implementation and oversight are in the hands of OMB, which is required to track, control, record, classify, and account for all credit transactions.

In 1994, the federal government was still the largest credit institution in the United States, with over $5.8 trillion in outstanding direct loans, loan guarantees, and insurance. (See Table 10.1.) If government sponsored enterprise credit were included, the total reached $7.3 trillion, and if deposit insurance were also counted, the federal government assisted directly or indirectly over 35 percent of private domestic borrowing in the United States. Outstanding credit is expected to rise at an accelerated pace over the next five years.[32] Subsidy costs of loans and loan guarantees on budget are expected to rise anywhere from $27 billion to $59 billion, or about an increase of one-third above last year's amount. Recording the subsidy costs provides Congress with a tool to control this form of expenditure, because cutting the amount of the loan subsidy cuts the amount that may be loaned.

---

[30]Congressional Budget Office, *Budgeting for Administrative Costs under Credit Reform,* January 1992, p. ix.

[31]For further information on the shaping of federal credit reform, see James M. Bickley, "The Bush Administration's Proposal for Credit Reform," *Public Budgeting and Finance,* Vol. 11, No. 1, Spring 1991, pp. 50–65; Thomas J. Cuny, "Federal Credit Reform," *Public Budgeting and Finance,* Vol. 11, No. 2, Summer 1991, pp. 19–32; and David B. Pariser, "Implementing Federal Credit Reform: Challenges Facing Public Sector Financial Managers," *Public Budgeting and Finance,* Vol. 12, No. 4, Winter 1992, pp. 19–34.

[32]United States Budget, FY 1996, Analytical Perspectives, p. 121.

Table 10.1 SUMMARY OF OUTSTANDING FEDERAL AND FEDERALLY ASSISTED CREDIT

| | | (in billions of dollars) | |
Year	Direct loans	Guaranteed loans	Government-sponsored enterprise loans	Total
1974	61	180	44	286
1984	233	394	301	927
1991	160	723	1105	1988
1992	156	704	1225	2085
1993	151	693	1105	1949
1994	151	699	1502	2352

Note: For earlier totals, see Table 4.1.

Source: Budgets of the United States Government, 1974–1996.

FINANCIAL MANAGEMENT

Frank Hodsoll, on becoming chief financial officer for the federal government, recalls his shock on taking office "to discover that many programs didn't know the results of their outlays, the location and value of their inventories, the wear and tear on their buildings, the aging of their receivables, and the souring of their loan and guarantee portfolios."[33] Without effective financial management, all the budgeting strategies, policies, skills, and expertise would fall short of their objectives. Financial management is necessary to know whether money allocated has been used for the purposes intended, and whether monies have been duly collected, as well as provide information about commitments, savings, tradeoffs, policy and program outcomes, and savings.

The field of financial management is a broad one, and well beyond the scope of this book. An idea of its reach may be gleaned from recent criticisms by Price Waterhouse of one small area: the House of Representatives. Their findings documented overspending of members' allowances due to "a convoluted budget process, weak controls over spending and overcommitments to purchase goods and services, and poor financial information." There was no system for tracking leased assets on their terms and costs and poor information about equipment. Controls over computer security, payments to vendors, disbursements for all kinds of payments from travel to catering, and personnel records were weak.[34]

The 1990 Chief Financial Officers Act was designed to address weaknesses in federal financial management that had been documented for some time.[35] It aimed to strengthen financial operations by two main measures. First, chief financial officers have been appointed in 23 departments and agencies, and OMB has oversight of financial management through a chief financial officer for the whole

---

[33]Frank Hodsoll, "Facing the Facts of the CFO Act," *Public Budgeting and Finance,* Vol. 12, No. 4, Winter 1992, p. 72.

[34]"Mismanagers' Journal," *Wall Street Journal,* July 20, 1995, p. A12.

[35]For background to the Act, see L. R. Jones and Jerry L. McCaffery, *Public Budgeting and Finance,* Vol. 12, No. 4, Winter 1992, pp. 75–86.

of the federal government. In this way, a structure was put in place specifically to establish, implement, and monitor financial management policies for the system as a whole. In the agencies, the chief financial officers report to agency heads, oversee all financial management activities, develop integrated agency and financial management and accounting systems, and take responsibility for financial management personnel, as well as monitoring the financial execution of the budget. The intent is to consolidate accounting, budgeting and other financial functions under the CFO, and five-year plans were required to show how this would be done.

Second, agencies are required to produce annual audited financial statements and management reports by FY 1997. These reports will include a statement of financial position, a statement of operations, a cash flow statement, and a statement of reconciliation to the budget. Further efforts to improve accounting concepts and standards are being made on an ongoing basis by the Federal Accounting Standards Advisory Board.[36]

OVERLOADING BUDGETING

In the period of classical budgeting, there was an effective, albeit informal, ceiling beyond which spending could not go. Nowadays there are basic disagreements about the size and composition of the public sector. Bringing back the good old ways implies something that can no longer be achieved, namely, summoning up agreement on the underlying beliefs that once made them work.

Indeed, budget resolutions, automatic spending reductions to achieve balance, item vetoes, balanced budget amendments, and offsets are all formal substitutes for what used to be done informally. If (and when) congressional majorities do wish to control spending, we have seen that spending ceilings safeguarded by requiring that additions be balanced by subtractions (or by new revenues) work powerfully well. There's a way if there's a will. Suppose, however, that not one, but several wills are incompatible? Then perhaps the contemporary budgetary stalemate may be seen not as an aberration but as a sign of continuing dissensus. What, then, can be hoped for from budgeting?

The budgetary process is an arena in which the struggle for power over public policy is worked out. Budgeting is a forum for the exercise of political power, not a substitute for that power. By itself, budgeting cannot form majorities and enforce their will. While the rules for voting on spending and taxing may make agreement marginally easier or harder, they cannot close unbridgeable gaps. It is more reasonable to suppose that general political processes shape budgeting than that budgeting determines political alignments.

---

[36]See Robert Bramlett and Frank Rexford, "The Federal Accounting Standards Advisory Board: A View of Its Role One Year Later," *Public Budgeting and Finance*, Vol. 12, No. 4, Winter 1992, pp. 87–101.

Chapter
11

The Deficit

W hy do students of budgeting and of American politics need to understand the deficit? Two reasons are paramount: One is that the federal deficit has become part of the language of budgeting; to understand what is said and done about budgeting, therefore, it is necessary to understand the deficit. The other and perhaps more important reason is that the deficit has become the leading issue of our time. As Joseph White and I put it,

> Political time is counted not in years but in issues; a political era is defined by the concerns that dominate debate and action, so that about other issues we ask: How does that affect? . . . The budget has been to our era what civil rights, communism, the depression, industrialization, and slavery were at other times. Nor does the day of the budget show signs of ending. . . . Year after year the key question has been, What will the president and Congress do about the deficit?[1]

I deliberately do not refer to the impact of the deficit on the economy because the importance of that impact is part of the controversy.

Where did the deficit come from? What were its causes and what are its consequences? Are its consequences so bad as to require a drastic solution? Who or what was to blame for the creation of an annual $200 billion (or without Social Security surpluses but with the savings and loan bailout, $300 billion) deficit? And what size should the deficit be?

WHO DONE IT?[2]

In February 1983 the Congressional Budget Office (CBO) projected $200 billion deficits far into the future. It explained that "to a great extent" the 1983 and 1984

> deficits are attributable to the economic recession, which has reduced federal revenues and increased federal outlays for unemployment compensation and other in-

---

[1]Joseph White and Aaron Wildavsky, *The Deficit and the Public Interest* (Berkeley: University of California Press, 1990), pp. xv–xvi.

[2]Except for the last section, this chapter is a revised version of work done with Joseph White, *The Deficit and the Public Interest* (Berkeley: University of California Press, 1990); and "How to Fix the Deficit–Really," *The Public Interest*, No. 94 (Winter 1989), pp. 3–24.

come maintenance programs. But even as these cyclical crises wither as economic recovery proceeds, the proposed deficits remain . . . high. . . . This indicates a long-term mismatch between federal spending and taxing.[3]

This long-term mismatch was what economists called the "structural deficit." This structural deficit amounted to 3.6 percent of GNP difference between income and outgo, consisting of a rise in outlays of 1 percent of GNP, and a drop in revenues of 2.6 percent. By this standard, the major source of the deficit problem was the reduction in revenues, though there was also a lack of spending restraint.

Any analysis was flawed, however, if it assumed that 1981's 20.9 percent of GNP was a politically acceptable base level for federal taxes. The pattern of the 1970s was to let inflation increase the tax burden and then have a tax cut. In 1978, revenues had been 19.1 percent of GNP, but bracket creep, payroll tax increases for social security, the windfall-profits tax on oil, and the effects (from 1977 to 1979) of a progressive income tax on increasing real incomes had increased the tax burden.

The trend in federal government tax burdens from 1961 to 1981 showed that taxes, including higher income taxes, were a lot higher than had been customary. The 1981 tax burden was higher than most people or politicians desired.[4] While it is clear that Carter was willing to use bracket creep to narrow the deficit, most observers in Washington in 1980 assumed there would be a tax cut in the early 1980s no matter who got elected.

If a normal level of revenues is roughly 19 percent of GNP, not roughly 21 percent, then the long-term budget problem was not simply an artifact of the Reagan tax cuts. We must, therefore, turn our attention to the outlay side.

1. In 1979—a pretty good year for the economy—outlays at 20.8 percent of GNP were 1.2 percent of GNP above revenues.
2. Spending growth from 1979–1985, roughly 2.4 percent of GNP, can be entirely explained by increases in defense, social security, medicare, and debt interest. The real growth in social spending was entirely a product of the bad economy, which disguised the significant reductions made in domestic discretionary programs and in means-tested entitlements during this period.[5]
3. During the same period, social security got into trouble. Its difficulty stemmed from the recession's effect on GNP, and from stagflation in the last half of the 1970s. The recession slowed production, and thus revenue collection, while not slowing the growth in program recipients or the delayed effects of their COLAs (cost of living adjustments). Stagflation

---

[3]Congressional Budget Office, "Reducing the Deficit: Spending and Revenue Options," A Report to the Senate and House Committees on the Budget—Part III, February 1983, p. 1.

[4]Gregory B. Mills and John L. Palmer, *The Deficit Dilemma* (Washington, D.C.: Urban Institute, 1983) pp. 8–10, give a short summary of the tax increases. See also Allen Schick, *The Federal Budget: Politics, Policy, Process* (Washington, D.C.: Brookings Institution, 1995), p. 4.

[5]For extensive discussion, see Jack A. Meyer, "Budget Cuts in the Reagan Administration: A Question of Fairness," in D. Lee Bauden, ed. *The Social Contract Revisited* (Washington, D.C.: Urban Institute, 1984), pp. 33–64.

caused benefits, linked to prices, to grow faster than either the economy or contributions to the social security fund, which increased more slowly than wages. These combined effects threw the social security system into crisis as payments to recipients grew faster than collections from workers. Medicare, meanwhile, grew mainly because of the tremendous cost inflation in the medical business, a trend with which Congress had been wrestling for years.[6] Given underlying demographic trends (more old people), only an optimist could predict even a stabilization of this medicare increase.

4. Net interest costs increased drastically because the government had to borrow more as deficits increased; then borrowing and interest began to feed on themselves, generating higher deficits, more borrowing, and, it was argued, higher interest rates. The economy's troubles—inflation and then unemployment, creating first an insistence by lenders for higher rates and then a great need to borrow to make up for lower incomes—were the major cause of the government's interest-rate problems.

5. The defense buildup began under the Democrats; not until 1983 did the Reagan budgets significantly increase outlays.[7] Still, a substantial part of the increase in the "structural deficit" was due to Reagan administration plans to raise defense spending.

These upward trends in entitlements, in interest costs, and in defense suggest that given the behavior of the economy, any president and any Congress would have faced a serious deficit problem by 1983. They suggest also that only part of the problem was avoidable.

Spending grew because of past decisions made about entitlements for the elderly: They grew because the eligible population grew—people were living longer, and more and more of them were fully vested in the social security system; there were also big, multiple legislated hikes in social security in the 1969–1972 period with the support of Republican President Richard Nixon. In 1962, the Old Age and Disability funds had 16.8 million beneficiaries; in 1972, 25.2 million; in 1982, 31.9 million.[8] Spending grew in medicare because virtually nobody anticipated the costs of coverage; Congress began struggling with medical inflation soon after the program began. Costs grew, finally, because politicians kept benefits in line with rising prosperity (but out of line with contributions by recipients), eager to please a powerful group of voters and confident that continuing economic growth would enable current workers to pay the bill. The last big increase in social security coverage in 1972 tells both sides of the story: Democrats and Republicans competed to woo the elderly; the resulting increase "was financed largely by a change in actuarial assumptions" that politicians had little reason to reject.[9] But

---

[6]See CBO, "Reducing the Deficit," pp. 98–99.

[7]See CBO, "The Economic and Budget Outlook," p. 153.

[8]Committee on Ways and Means, U.S. House of Representatives, *Background Material and Data on Programs Within the Jurisdiction of the Committee on Ways and Means,* Committee Print, 99th Congress, 1st Session, 99-2, February 22, 1985 (U.S. Government Printing Office), pp. 55–56.

[9]Martha Derthick, *Policymaking for Social Security* (Washington, D.C.: Brookings Institution, 1979) p. 357.

the economy did not behave as expected, and almost everybody was asking the wrong question.

With the first OPEC oil shock in 1973, the economy went into a "quiet depression,"[10] and social security got into deep trouble. Revenues for the trust fund would not cover the outlays. Social security had to be "rescued" twice. Whether social security's taxes could fund the system's expenses was important. But throughout the program's history, no one asked a second question: *If social security taxes increased, would those be new taxes or replace old ones?* (Tax aficionados speak of "fiscal cannibalism" where one tax eats up another.) Government raised the social security payroll tax from 3.1 percent of GNP in 1962 to 6.6 percent in 1982.[11] And it was scheduled by legislation to go higher. When these new taxes took effect, the government usually cut other taxes to compensate. This strategy worked because either the economy grew so strongly that other programs could live with a smaller share, or because spending (and thus revenues) was diverted from the shrinking defense budget to domestic (mostly welfare) programs. But it never had to make that choice—higher taxes on social security in addition to or in subtraction from income and other taxes—in advance. The repetition of what appears to be a truism—social security is self-financing—by Ronald Reagan, his congressional opponents, and spokesmen for the elderly, though true as far as it goes, left the profoundly mistaken impression that by far the biggest domestic program did not affect the rest of government. Nonsense. Individuals and businesses feel taxation from all sources, so government eventually had to face the consequences of social security expansion either in deficits, higher taxes, or lower spending later on other things.

Here's the catch: Maybe the government *could not* have chosen in advance. No one could foresee the size of future problems; perhaps they would be small, for economic growth heals many ills. Perhaps it was for people in the future to choose whether they wanted higher taxes or fewer programs, or even (gasp!) higher deficits. Even if politicians in 1962 had decided that other programs would have to be cut by the same amount by 1972, for instance, how could they have done so? All right, one might say: If you can't plan, don't make the commitment. Don't have a national retirement plan, or policies with long-term, increasing costs. Toss out civil service pensions and medicare while you're at it. But that inaction would be intolerable. People in real life make long-term commitments like buying a house (even with an adjustable-rate mortgage). They marry, have children, plan to send them to college; they will figure out later what to sacrifice to that end. The government, with heavy public support, committed itself to social security. There is little evidence that people, on the whole, dispute that commitment or its necessity. Some problems come with the territory.

Is there, then, no room for choice? Yes, there is; one can always exercise prudence. Increases in payments to recipients, for example, could have been smaller. Many provisions, such as early retirement, could have been less generous. When bad times come, the nation must decide who will bear the costs of change. But

---

[10]The term is Frank Levy's. See his *Dollars and Dreams: The Changing American Income Distribution* (New York: Russell Sage Foundation, 1987).

[11]CBO, "The Economic and Budget Outlook," p. 162.

choice is politically circumscribed by the difficulty of breaking promises on which millions have planned their lives. Because old commitments did not match the new economy, huge deficits would have occurred even without Ronald Reagan—unless you think taxes were going well above the level that helped defeat Jimmy Carter. The Democrats' response would have been that they would have cut taxes by less than Reagan did and accelerate defense less. If true, that would have made a modest difference.

A reasonable conclusion would be that all who govern now and in the past half century share some of the blame for the deficit, some more than others, but few guiltless. Hardly anyone anticipated the relatively poor economic performance of the 1970s. Much of this slowdown may be due to international oil increases or to vast numbers of new entrants (especially women) into the labor market or the emergence of new economic powers on the world scene or too high taxes or insufficient demand or too little saving, some of which government could affect and much of which it could not.[12]

It has been alleged that Reagan engineered the large deficit in order to keep down domestic spending. Not so.[13] He hoped that his policies would be successful; that is, the nation would avoid a recession and lower tax rates would bring in higher revenues. Once faced with a big deficit, however, he did choose to accept it rather than raise income taxes substantially.

THE DEFICIT PANIC

The most obvious result of both President Reagan's choices and the policies he inherited, however, was the deficit panic of the 1980s. The deficit became the dominant policy problem, an issue that shaped consideration of all other issues. It was blamed for every economic ill, from inflation to unemployment to high interest rates to the large trade imbalance, from the strong dollar to the weak dollar. Strife over the deficit spilled over from policy into procedure, hogging the congressional agenda, encouraging paralyzing legislation, such as Gramm–Rudman, frustrating legislators, and stalemating the government. Otherwise, it was benign.

All political factions, hamstrung by the deficit, increased the pressure on themselves by using the deficit to attack each other. Liberals, blocked from responding to their definition of social needs by a lack of money, claimed prosperity under Ronald Reagan was bought on the credit card, to be charged to our grandchildren. Conservatives blamed ills like high taxes on the legacy of liberal overspending. Centrists, hating the deficit for its own sake as a sign of the government's inability to control itself, accused everyone, including themselves, of cowering before "special interests." Moderates, exemplified by people like Pete Peterson, former head of Lehman Brothers investment house and former Secretary of Commerce, excoriated the existing political system for failing to balance

---

[12]See Frank Levy, *Dollars and Dreams* (Russell Sage Foundation, 1987), for a splendid analysis of how demographic changes affect spending outcomes.

[13]This judgment is based on numerous interviews and a perusal of virtually all of the documentary record. See White and Wildavsky, *The Deficit and the Public Interest*.

the budget. Whereas the economic conservatives want liberty and growth and the egalitarian liberals want equality and growth, these social conservatives want balanced growth. Their Cassandra cries are heard on radio, television, newspapers, magazines, wherever people listen. And they invoke the public interest over and over as if there was only a single interest and they were the only ones who knew exactly what it was.

Propagated by so many factions for so many different reasons, the anti-deficit clamor has persisted for so long that it has taken on a life of its own. The deficit has become a self-fulfilling crisis. The deficit is a difficulty, I contend, but it is not a disaster next to which all else is insignificant.

When the deficit panic began in 1980, it was supposedly due to the deficit's inflationary effect. Jimmy Carter was excoriated for a proposed deficit of $15.6 billion! When the deficit burgeoned and inflation shrank, however, the panic did not decline accordingly. As Herbert Stein expressed the common syllogism, budget deficits cause bad things, so whatever bad things were happening to us were blamed on deficits. The evolution of its supposed evils, from inflation to recession to strong dollar to weak dollar, and more, suggests that the massive disapproval of deficits has been supported by no consistent logic of cause and effect. The cause is constant but the supposed effects keep changing.

Economic arguments about the deficit have been inconsistent. By economic arguments I mean those made in the public sphere of policy debate. When *Time* and *Newsweek* do a cover article on the deficit, or report that a market crash requires deficit reduction, it is part of the process of political debate that shapes notions of how to manage the economy. Since that debate is a process of persuasion, even otherwise trustworthy economists sometimes shade their arguments for effect in order to push the policy they desire. Excessive condemnation of the deficit has proceeded, in part, from such experts putting matters too strongly for fear of otherwise being ignored by politicians, or in order to counter the minority of economists who dismiss the deficit's importance. Where the press presents majority economic wisdom, the schools of economists make arguments that fit into wider politico-economic agendas.

Skepticism on the effects of deficits is well-expressed in Guess and Koford's study of OECD countries:

> The U.S. results, taken by themselves, imply that deficits do not cause, but are themselves caused by inflation and reduced national product. If the United States continues to enjoy rapid economic growth and reduced inflation, we expect that the budget deficits should shrink from current projections. However, the broader seventeen-country results show that any definite relationship is difficult to pinpoint. We conclude that the macroeconomic harmfulness of budget deficits has not been shown, certainly for deficits within historical experience."[14]

Although the deficit need not cause inflation or recession, a weak dollar or a strong dollar, reasons for concern remain. The deficit feeds the interest costs of the federal government. More and more of the federal dollar goes to debt service.

---

[14]George Guess and Kenneth Koford, "Inflation, Recession and the Federal Budget Deficit (or, Blaming Economic Problems on a Statistical Mirage)," *Policy Sciences*, Vol. 17 (1984), pp. 385–402; quote on p. 400.

From an economically conservative point of view, this may be desirable. From an economically liberal view, this restriction is doubly undesirable: Debt creates economic opportunities for the well-off and limits new social programs for poor people. Net interest payments roughly equaled the size of the deficit in fiscal year 1988. Many Democrats have been concerned that the deficit crowds out social program initiatives, now and in the future. Giving up programs now, however, for programs they might not get later is sure to seem to them like a bad bargain. Their ideal is higher revenues without reductions in their favored domestic programs.

A second argument says the budget must be balanced, or more, so as to increase national savings. Productivity has grown slowly; more productivity requires more investment; investment requires more savings; the United States saves less than its major competitors, particularly Japan; government deficits, by definition, reduce national savings; since our growth was too slow even before the era of big deficits, we therefore have to raise saving above the level of that time. Therefore, the federal government needs to bring its budget into balance or even surplus.

This savings argument has become the major reason academic economists object to the deficit. Savings, surely, is a Good Thing (though at other times it has appeared too much of a Good Thing), but I have a few questions. If investment is so strongly related to productivity growth, why did growth decrease steadily through the 1970s, while investment remained steady? Growth is a long-term problem, not a short-term crisis: Why is it to be treated as requiring immediate drastic changes in the entire federal government rather than a slow movement toward less consumption and more investment throughout our economy? That would require attention to the composition of outlays, the type of taxes, and many other complicated matters. Would it be morally right for government to force individuals to save more? The counterargument goes that it is precisely because we seem unable to shift the long-term pattern of individual saving that the net dissaving of the federal government (that is, the deficit) becomes so important. Could a fall-off in savings be due to other factors, such as changes in the life cycle (e.g., baby boomers spending more on education, housing, and children, therefore temporarily saving less)? Could it be that Americans only appear to be saving less because equity in mortgages and a significant part of pensions are not counted as savings?

It bothers some people to discover foreigners are taking up the slack and investing more in the United States. I consider that an act of confidence. Now if there were capital flight, that would be a reason to worry. Why does it matter to us where the money comes from? In the nineteenth century, a great deal of development in the United States took place with foreign money. Why shouldn't they share our risks?

Even if all other things are not quite equal, I would like the nation's investment to increase. That is a very long-term concern; it makes little difference whether the budget reaches some desired state in five or eight or ten years. The savings argument therefore does not justify a demand that the federal budget be balanced soon. It does argue for lower deficits, while telling us little about how much lower, how quickly.

The argument that the deficit must be reduced to guarantee market confidence is ubiquitous. Yet it presumes falsely that we can both know and influence what the financial markets "expect." Certainly we cannot assume that markets think (if they do) like an economist. For example, the dollar's steady increase in Reagan's first term cannot simply be ascribed to high U.S. interest rates. The United States was running high trade deficits, exchanging paper for goods, which ought to produce a countervailing trend for the paper (the dollar) to depreciate. If large budget and trade deficits increase the value of a currency, the dollar should be riding high, which it is not. Perhaps investors put their money where they trust the government. They fled the franc when socialist François Mitterand was elected president of France, then bought dollars when America was governed by the hypercapitalist Reagan. This may be rational, but has nothing to do with inflation, interest rates, or other measurable variables.

Nobody knows why markets, whether in stocks or bonds or currencies or hog bellies, go in any particular direction, at any time. If they did, they would be rich. There are tendencies and explanations that look obvious in retrospect, but markets are panicky, neurotic, swayed by a million forces we don't understand, and thus unpredictable. And they don't behave the way their "experts" claim.

Market gurus told the politicians in 1980 that a $15 billion deficit would create hyperinflation; then when the government ran deficits of more than that per month, the markets threw a massive party (the stock market boom), but kept claiming the deficit was terrible. Would you have much confidence in such experts' judgment?

Economists are hardly alone in thinking politicians have not done enough about the deficit. In giving talks on the deficit, I ask the audience whether they believe Congress and the president have done a little, a fair amount, or a lot to reduce the deficit. In every instance an overwhelming proportion signifies that the politicians have done very little. The audience mistakes the apparent lack of progress in reducing the deficit, especially to balance the budget, for failure to take corrective action. Not true.

As Rodney Dangerfield gets no respect, politicians neither get nor give themselves credit. From 1982 on, Congress has gored a series of special interests, ranging from doctors to defense contractors. You don't take on the AMA (freezing physician payments on medicare), or Wall Street (many of the provisions of the 1984 tax bill), or the armed services and arms makers (cutting defense in the past six years), unless you really care about the deficit. Through 1986, according to the most careful analysis of policy changes, the politicians had reduced the fiscal year 1986 deficit by an estimated $162 billion, or 3.9 percent of gross national product, from what it would have been if past policies had been left in place.[15] Why, then, did these efforts not show up in absolutely smaller deficits?

Perhaps these analyses give Congress a bit too much credit. Policy in 1981 included a projected defense buildup of 7 percent real growth per year. You can save a lot of money by scaling down such an increase; it hurts less than cutting from what people already have. Yet the defense buildup was stopped because moderate Republicans and conservative Democrats who supported it in 1980 and

[15]Joseph J. Minarik and Rudolph G. Penner, "Fiscal Choices," in Isabel V. Sawhill, ed., *Challenge to Leadership* (Washington, D.C.: Urban Institute, 1988), pp. 279–316; John Palmer did his calculations for "Should We Worry About the Deficit?" by John Palmer and Stephanie Gould, *The Washington Monthly*, May 1986, pp. 43–46.

1981 decided that reducing the deficit was more important. (No one then imagined that the cold war would be won, thus allowing even bigger cuts in 1990.) Nevertheless, despite persistent and positive congressional efforts, the deficit did not decline.

Unfortunately for our politicians, the deficit problem was too big, always bigger than it seemed. Going back through summaries of each year's efforts, we can see Congress swimming upstream. Each year's policy change was balanced by revisions in the economic assumptions, namely, worse than projected, so the deficit kept ending up around $200 billion. Since they were not getting anywhere, politicians came to believe they were not doing anything.

Dealing with the huge budget shortfall was made even more difficult by political dissensus. Many of us can think of ways to reduce the deficit substantially. So could any legislator. Yet the problem of budgeting is not for any one of us to create a budget alone but to do it together. Assembling a majority behind any scheme is difficult, because anything substantial we do will change the size, shape, and role in society of our government. You might say that the participants in budgeting agree on everything except how much revenue should be raised and who should pay, how much should be spent and on which programs. The budget is about the future shape of government and society, not just balance; balance at low or high levels of spending would make a difference for our future.

Politicians could not balance the budget because the policy costs of doing so would have been huge. Before the costs of the savings and loan bailout ballooned, making the task obviously impossible, Joseph White and I asked what kind of deficit reduction in the first year of a new government, elected in 1988, would give a balanced budget, as Gramm–Rudman promised, by fiscal year 1992? Allowing for complexities of implementation, we estimated that the new government could meet the Gramm–Rudman target if it changed policy by $100 billion on taking office. How much is that in policy terms?

One hundred billion dollars roughly equals the U.S. navy. Not a smaller navy but no navy. One hundred billion dollars is larger than medicaid, the Department of Education, National Institutes of Health (including cancer and AIDS research), Department of Justice, Department of State, and Federal Highway Administration combined. That is the scale of policy change—no navy or any six domestic departments of your choice—required to eliminate the deficit through spending cuts.

How could we have found over $100 billion from taxes? Individual income taxes would have to be raised by 21 percent, almost completely reversing the 1981 tax cut. Or we could have raised individual income taxes by 10 percent, corporate taxes by 20 percent, and doubled excise taxes. Even the most dedicated fan of the public sector can imagine the political difficulty of such tax hikes. Instead one might try a "balanced" package, say raising income taxes by 10 percent, cutting the navy 20 percent (pick a fleet!), and abolishing medicaid. That sounds no easier.

Even more narrow options for deficit reduction had difficulties: Small does not mean harmless. For example, determining eligibility or benefit levels for Aid to Dependent Children and food stamps by counting as income payments under the Low-Income Home Energy Assistance program (LIHEAP) would have saved $225 million in FY90. It would eliminate duplication as well as a situation in which some recipients of LIHEAP are better off monetarily than nonrecipients who actually earn more. But the change would penalize families whose energy bills are particularly high, exactly the large families the program is supposed to help. What are they to do, shower in the dark? Move south?

These examples should put common calls for "tough choices" in perspective. Choices are tough because the consequences either way are unpalatable. Often people hide these choices by talking about cutting the deficit in stages: $30 billion one year, $20 billion the next year, and so on. It may well be desirable to cut spending incrementally. But that does not change the huge amounts of reductions required to approach a balanced budget. Cutting in stages doesn't change the policy stakes. Indeed, what you would have to do if you did it all at once is the smallest measure of the stakes, for that approach would maximize the savings from lower interest payments. There is no "free lunch" of harmless deficit reductions. Politicians who do not want to slash medicaid or education or infrastructure or defense or raise income taxes by more than they have ever been raised in peacetime are not showing a lack of courage; they are making a reasonable choice about the national interest.

Budgeting is a process of discovering and enforcing preferences. The most basic difficulty is matching preferences about programs and totals. In the 1980s, panic about the deficit led both elites and the public to claim a breakdown of governance, for the total, the deficit, was too big. Yet it is fair to argue that, facing tough choices, Congress and the president have bargained responsibly, balancing the costs and benefits of both lower deficits and the policy choices to get there. The macroeconomic logic of balancing the budget is, at best, confused; balancing the budget would have serious policy costs. These costs are not simply "politics" or "special interests." Social Security is in the special interest of the elderly; the navy is in the special interest of the people who serve in and sell to it. They are also policies that define the nation; a nation that at least tries to guarantee to all citizens a financially decent old age, and one that is served by cutting such programs to eliminate the deficit is an open question. Politics is about debating such questions, not assuming they have only one answer.

Looking at the deficit as a policy problem like any other, the following conclusions seem reasonable:

1. There is no economic necessity to balance the budget. Mainstream economics provides no reason why deficits of 2–3 percent of GNP should cause panic, and smaller deficits, say 1 percent of GNP, are surely acceptable.[16]
2. The deficit persists not because of a lack of political "courage" but because politicians and the public judge, correctly, that serious efforts to reduce it—whether tax hikes or cuts in domestic or defense spending—themselves have serious consequences for the general welfare.

---

[16]See James Savage, "Deficits and the Economy: The Case of the Clinton Administration and Interest Rates," in Naomi Caiden and Joseph White, eds., *Budgeting, Policy, Politics: An Appreciation of Aaron Wildavsky* (New Brunswick N.J.: Transaction Publishers, 1995), p. 97.

If citizens were to look at the federal government's actual accomplishments in holding down the size of the deficit, they might be optimistic about further progress. Were these same citizens to look at the ideological divisions over how to reduce the deficit, they might well be more pessimistic. There were grounds in the 1990 legislation—to cut the deficit and alter once more the process of budgeting—for both feelings. As congressional Democrats in 1991 wanted to meet the recession with increased spending, they discovered that the new legislation prevented them from doing so. What will happen when the general public discovers they are being forced to save by artificially inflating the size of the deficit is anybody's guess. This part of the deficit story comes next.

BALANCED BUDGET HYSTERIA

During the first half of the 1990s, deficit panic turned into balanced budget hysteria. Hysteria is a state of alarm, not fully justified by the situation, in which emotion takes over from rationality. In conditions of political hysteria, facts are not calmly assessed, consequences are not calculated, and public sentiments may be exploited for unrelated agendas.

This chapter earlier concluded that the federal deficit was not an overwhelming problem, and that any good achieved by balancing the budget would be outweighed by its consequences. By mid-decade, budget balance was upheld as a supreme political goal, to be achieved whatever the cost, and hitherto unthinkable program reductions suddenly became credible. What had happened to enshrine budget balance as the conventional wisdom at a time when the deficit was going *down,* and the economy and productivity were, by many indicators, improving? Why were politicians contemplating radical and obviously unpopular reductions in federal expenditures, when experience indicated that those who had taken this path of virtue in the past had been punished, not rewarded, for their rectitude? Why was a link between budget balance and economic prosperity so easily accepted without examining evidence whether such linkage really existed? Why was there so little consideration in advance of what budget balance would actually entail? How did budget balance become the primary policy goal, when so many other agendas demanded satisfaction?

In times of rapid change and uncertainty, simplistic solutions, particularly if backed by authoritative opinions and doomsday scenarios, may have an irresistible appeal. The argument for a balanced budget is seductive in its simplicity and virtue. It appears that a balanced budget will usher in a golden age of prosperity, free our children from crippling debt, and place government on a sustainable and effective path.

To claim that the federal budget is without problems would be misleading. To claim that merely balancing revenues and expenditures would solve them would be even more misleading. For every plan to balance a budget incorporates an agenda or program. In expressing support for a balanced budget, voters are expressing a preference not only for that goal, but also for a whole series of choices. Simply wanting a balanced budget may not necessarily imply support for any specific proposal. But where such a program exists, a balanced budget, with its intuitive appeal, may be only a symbol or surrogate for a much deeper and broader political agenda.

Sentiments in favor of a balanced budget are not new, but these have rarely spelled out how balance would be achieved. The spearhead of the budget balancing campaign of the mid-1990s carried an ideological thrust in a specific political direction. Balancing the budget was to be the vehicle for an agenda whose principal element was the radical reversal of the role of the federal government. The instrumental nature of budget balance was further underlined by the simultaneous proposal for tax reductions which would clearly make the task more difficult as well as favor the wealthier section of the population. This section traces the rise of balanced budget hysteria, and how it has been used to further an agenda of radical reversal.

The Rise of Balanced Budget Hysteria

In April 1994, a group of experts on the federal budget gathered at the University of Virginia to discuss the current budgetary situation. Although the deficit naturally figured prominently in their discussions, there was virtually no hint of the imminence of radical and concerted action to balance the budget.[17] Yet warning signals had been apparent for some time. Nearly two years earlier, the Comptroller General of the United States had testified on the necessity of prompt action to balance the budget, preferably by 2001, or to create a budget surplus by 2005. He predicted "an explosion of federal spending" related to demographic trends and the continuation of current policies, projecting deficits of as much as 20 percent of GDP by 2020 if no action were taken. He explicitly linked deficits with economic trends: "Deficits by themselves do not create crises, but they do erode the savings needed for private investment and economic growth."[18]

These two themes—alarm at growing deficits and their responsibility for economic malaise—easily became accepted wisdom. The deficit was not a central concern of Bill Clinton's electoral campaign. He was more interested in economic stimulus through infrastructure financing and investment tax credits, and human resource development, but he felt the pressure for deficit reduction. In his State of the Union address, Clinton declared that while there was nothing intrinsically good about deficit reduction alone, it was necessary to reverse the trend toward a government which was unable to act because the burden of debt servicing prevented development of programs to help people.[19] Backed by the deficit hawks in his administration, though with less than wholehearted support from the Democratic party, Clinton acted accordingly. As his economic stimulus program went down to defeat in Congress, deficit reduction became the major policy initiative in his first budget. But his 1993 narrow victory for nearly half a trillion in deficit re-

---

[17]James Savage, ed., "Symposium: President Clinton's Budget and Fiscal Policy: An Evaluation Two Budgets Later," *Public Budgeting and Finance*, Vol. 14, No. 3, Fall 1994, pp. 3–40.

[18]Statement of Charles A. Bowsher, "Budget Policy: Long-Term Implications of the Deficit," Testimony before the Subcommittee on Deficits, Debt Management and International Debt of the Senate Finance Committee, June 5 1992, p. 1. (GAO/T-OCG-92-4).

[19]*Congressional Quarterly Weekly Report*, November 14, 1992, p. 3631.

duction over five years was already being overshadowed by much more radical calls for action.

In the 1992 presidential election, independent Ross Perot had gained only 19 percent of the vote, but it was a critical 19 percent, which in the future might tip the balance between the parties. Perot had tapped a vein of dissatisfaction of "business as usual" in American politics, and of people who wanted straightforward answers to over-complicated and obfuscated issues such as the federal budget deficit. Budget balance was a central feature of the Perot campaign, and it was quickly taken up by think tanks, such as the Heritage Foundation. The founding of the Concorde Coalition by Paul Tsongas (previously a contender for the Democratic presidential nomination) and Walter Rudman (of Gramm–Rudman–Hollings) marked the beginning of a concerted campaign for an agenda in which budget balance would provide the driving power for cutting federal domestic expenditures, returning power to the states, dismantling business and environmental regulations, cutting taxes, and reforming welfare programs. The movement culminated in the Contract with America, whose first provision was "to restore fiscal responsibility to an out-of-control Congress, requiring them to live under the same budget constraints as families and businesses." The Contract would "require the federal budget to be balanced by 2002 or seven years after enactment, whichever is later."[20]

The Republican victory in the November 1994 elections was widely interpreted as a mandate for the Contract program, although polls showed only about a quarter of the electorate had even heard of it let alone read it.[21] But the polls also showed that a majority of Americans felt that balancing the budget was an important, and maybe the most important, thing to do. Why?

In times of confusion and rapid transformation, people feel threatened by changes they do not understand and often do not like. The federal deficit seemed a symbol of all that was wrong, and something had to be done. The title of Peter Peterson's book, *Facing Up: How to Rescue the Economy from Crushing Debt and Restore the American Dream,* captured the mood of the times.[22] But how big a threat to our happiness was the federal deficit, if at all?

How Big Were the Deficits?

The baseline deficit is what will happen if no policy changes are made. Throughout 1991, baseline deficit projections were adjusted upwards, and by January 1992, CBO was forecasting unprecedented deficits of $352 billion for FY 1992 and $327 billion for FY 1993.[23] The administration's estimate for FY 1992 was even higher at $400 billion, although its mid-session review revised its projection

---

[20]*Congressional Quarterly Weekly Report,* November 12, 1994, p. 3216.

[21]"Results of the 1994 Congressional Elections," *Government in America Newsletter,* HarperCollins, Spring 1995, p. 4.

[22]Peter Peterson, *Facing Up: How to Rescue the Economy from Crushing Debt and Rescue the American Dream* (New York: Simon and Schuster, 1993).

[23]Roy Meyers, "Federal Budgeting and Finance in 1991: The Future Is Now," *Public Budgeting and Finance,* Vol. 12, No. 2, Summer 1992, pp. 4–5; Congressional Budget Office, *The Economic and Budget Outlook: Fiscal Years 1993–1997,* 1992, p. xv.

to $333.5 billion.[24] By the time President Clinton took office in January 1993, the immediate outlook was gloomy. For FY 1992, the deficit had set a record at $290 billion, and for FY 1993, deficits were projected well over $300 billion. Only slight decline in later years was forecast, and the medium-term outlook was not encouraging as the deficit was forecast to reach over $350 billion.

These projections were not fulfilled. Table 6.2 details changing deficit projections by CBO over time. It shows that actual deficits were much less than those projected. The economy played a part in this dramatic decline, as did President Clinton's FY 1993 budget measures. Critics could still point to long-term projections which showed rising deficits toward the turn of the century, if nothing were done. The Comptroller and Auditor General, for example, reiterated that "Left unchecked through 2025, growing deficits would result in collapsing investment, a declining capital stock, and, inevitably, a declining economy."[25] Armageddon, it seemed, was just around the corner. How dire was the situation really?

Budget deficits of over $100 billion sound awful, but taken as a percentage of the economy the figure is not as daunting. Between 1992 and 1995, the deficit declined from over 4 percent of GDP to 2.7 percent, projected to drop to 2 percent by 2000. By the beginning of 1994, according to OECD figures, the United States deficit was the smallest of the G7 economies. Using a somewhat different measure, the general-government budget deficit, which included central, state, and local governments and social security funds, OECD economists calculated that the deficit figure would fall to 2.7 percent of GDP in 1994 from a peak of 4.5 percent in 1992, and would narrow further to 2.1 percent in 1995. These figures compared with 1994 figures of 3 percent for Japan, 4 percent for Germany, and about 6 percent for Britain and France.[26] Clinton's 1996 budget endorsed the position that budget deficits of 3 percent or less were sustainable, setting deficits at about 2 percent for the rest of the century. Further, the doomsday scenario rested on the assumption "if nothing were done"; it was unlikely that nothing would be done, and little reason to believe that the budget, if not balanced, was out of control, and an immediate and future threat to economic well-being, as the conventional wisdom had rapidly come to accept.

The Balanced Budget Agenda

The Contract with America provided no specifics on how to balance the budget. A much blunter message was expressed in a fiscal manifesto set out by the Heritage Foundation, which claimed credit for key elements of the Republican program. In "Rolling Back Government: A Budget Plan to Rebuild America," budget balancing was the motive force for a radical overhaul of federal government policy in accordance with a coherent philosophy, reflecting faith in market economics and individual choice.[27]

---

[24]Richard Doyle and Jerry McCaffery, "The Budget Enforcement Act in 1992: Necessary But Not Sufficient," *Public Budgeting and Finance,* Vol. 13, No. 2, Summer 1993, pp. 29, 36.

[25]United States General Accounting Office, *The Deficit and the Economy: An Update of Long-Term Simulations,* April 1995 (GAO/AIMD/OCE-95-119), p. 41.

[26]*The Economist,* February 12, 1994, p. 73.

[27]*Los Angeles Times,* April 28, 1995, p. A17.

Tax cuts to encourage savings and investment were central to the strategy, since economic growth was held to depend on the ability of companies and individuals to accumulate and invest capital, which they could only do if sufficient disposable income were left in their hands. Moreover, since the economy was assumed to work most efficiently if left to itself, where choices were made purely in accordance with "enlightened self-interest" and the "invisible hand" of the marketplace, lower taxes would lead to economic decisions being made more in accordance with individual, rational choices. Conversely, but according to the same logic, subsidies of all kinds, constituting "corporate welfare" should also be eliminated. It was equally important that lowered revenues would force cutbacks in federal programs.

It was also axiomatic that the federal government was involved in a large number of activities in which, by strict economic criteria, it should not be. For many years, economists had attempted to distinguish the proper boundaries for provision of services by governments. The narrow category of "pure public goods" they came up with (characterized by nonrivalness and nonexclusion) had been somewhat broadened by the idea of "externalities," but taken to its logical conclusion, the theory justified a government role which went little beyond provision of defense and public order. Privatization was seen as a viable alternative to the federal government in dozens of activities, again reflecting the preference for individual choice, and individual payment for services received. According to this philosophy it would be possible to eliminate whole federal departments, and to abolish a range of federal programs such as transportation, education, scientific research, and commercial activities.

The third element was devolution. Again in accordance with the principle of choice, it was held that decentralized decision making would produce better results than centralized uniform policies. Specifically, load shedding to the states would encourage greater variety and experimentation, more responsibility, and policies more in accord with what the "people" in each state wanted. Such devolution should be distinguished from the existing policies of delegation in which states and localities were mere agents to carry out federal instructions. Devolution would take place within the limitation of the new unfunded mandates legislation which prevented the federal government from imposing money costing demands (mandates) on the states without compensation. Instead, states would receive block grants which they would be free to use as they sought fit. Again, an expected consequence of this policy would be lower expenditures by the federal government, which would be freed from the burden of funding a large number of entitlements to individuals.

These three elements—tax and subsidy cuts, privatization, and devolution—formed the triad on which budgetary strategy would be based. To these should be added the buttressing of defense and anticrime policies, as well as various ideological items such as deregulation.

"If wishes were horses," says the old proverb, "then beggars would ride." The horse of budget balance was carrying a good deal of baggage. How would it cope when it came up against the realities of American politics? Was it actually possible to balance the budget *and* carry through the above agenda?

As the race horse of budget balance slowed in the 1995 budget process, it came to resemble more a carthorse dragging along a much less coherent load.

Ideological items were piled on top of those with real budgetary significance; programs were slashed or retained according to political, rather than economic criteria; and in an effort to make budget balance feasible, it was necessary to add in the major categories of medicare and medicaid. But the direction of the route was not in doubt: As the means for budget balance became more and more restricted (no tax increases; no change in social security; more untouchable areas of the budget), what remained was essentially those programs which served the weakest members of society. In Chapter 12, we will follow the course of this politics of radical reversal, but before we do so, we need briefly to consider the ramifications of the agenda for budget balance.

To bring revenues and expenditures into more even balance is not an unworthy goal. Policies to implement reduced deficits only turn into hysteria where an insistence on budget balance is buttressed by doubtful arguments, used to carry through a questionable set of policies, and pursued without serious consideration of its consequences. The program for a balanced budget was not neutral: It was a specific policy for reducing the fiscal and social policy roles of the federal government.

Many questions remained unanswered. What would happen to federal fiscal policy? What would be the effect on employment? How would the those elements of society who could not compete in the market place—children, low wage earners, the disabled—be cared for? Where economic stability was linked to an unemployment rate of 6 percent of the workforce, what provision would be made for those unemployed, and what would happen if this threshold were to drift even higher? What would happen to income distribution in a situation where real incomes of most working people had been stagnant or declining for a number of years? How would states and local governments cope with increased burdens as the federal government further restricted its role? Would tax cuts at federal level translate into increases at state and local levels? Would devolution mean greater inequality? Could the nonprofit sector fill the gap left by elimination or reduction of social programs? To these, and similar questions, the 1995 budget debate provided few answers.

Chapter *12*

The Politics of Radical Reversal

W hy was 1995 different from all other years? At the end of 1994, the Republican party gained majorities in both houses of Congress, with a program to balance the budget, boost defense, and diminish the role of the federal government. Nothing so remarkable about that, you might say. Although Democrats had controlled Congress for over forty years, party succession in democratic countries is to be expected. The Republican agenda seemed to differ little from the conservative program of Ronald Reagan when *he* came into office in 1981. Yet 1995 *was* different. While the program might be the same, the fervor and determination with which it was advanced were not. And while the formal institutions and processes of Congress were no different from before, the new majority set out to use the budget of a single year as the primary vehicle for accomplishing radical and irreversible change for many years to come.

THE POLITICS OF RADICAL REVERSAL

The Republican agenda might be seen in a number of ways. For some it was merely the latest phase of a cyclical movement which swung in one period in favor of government action and in another, against. For others, it was part of a more generalized attack on the public sector, made up in equal parts of distaste for bureaucracy and regulation, and resentment of taxation against a background of sluggish economic growth and stagnant incomes. Many, including bright young economists, saw the dismantling of government controls, reduction of taxation, and the liberalization of the economy as the key to future prosperity and a reinvention of the way in which the public's business was conducted. Still others regarded the Republican program as the beginning of a moral crusade to regain lost values and reassert individual responsibility (even though these might sometimes be in conflict). Yet another element saw the Republican victory as the opportunity for pressing pro-business policies. From the opposite perspective, the package of tax cuts, program cuts, and entitlement cuts would balance the budget on the backs of the poor, take a punitive approach to social problems, reverse measures protecting the environment, and restore the distribution of income that existed prior to the depression.

Much of the Republican agenda was expressed in the House Republicans' manifesto, the *Contract with America*.[1] It stressed a balanced budget, including a constitutional amendment to ensure that it happened, as well as a presidential line-item veto. It outlined measures to change welfare, cut taxes, boost defense, crack down on crime, reinforce parental responsibility, carry out certain legal reforms, and impose term limits on members of Congress. The jumble of often quite specific proposals of the Contract represented a broader program, which used the rhetoric of a balanced budget to promote much more fundamental change. The devolution to state governments of primary responsibility for large areas of governmental activity would mark the ending of the federal initiative and commitment in social matters which had begun with the depression. Its significance lay not only in the changed constitutional balance but in the lesser financial capacity and political will of the states to fund social policy, and the disparities among them. Devolution, tax cuts, and program cuts would enhance the private sector in relation to the public sector and strengthen market forces. They would reduce the role of government in providing a social safety net, redistributing income, offsetting dysfunctions of the economy, and providing goods and services not forthcoming from the market. These core ideas, augmented with other agendas, and translated into various policy arenas, constituted the package to which the Republican majority committed itself to put into action.

Who were the Republicans? Republican members of Congress represented over 36 million voters; they had attracted over 9 million more votes than they had in 1990. They won more House votes than Democrats in every region, completely reversing the position from 1992. The change was particularly notable in the South, where Republicans outvoted Democrats in every state except Mississippi.

The popular vote was reflected in Congress. Before the election there were 256 Democrats and 178 Republicans in the House, and 56 Democrats and 44 Republicans in the Senate. After the election, there were 230 Republicans and 204 Democrats in the House, and 53 Republicans and 47 Democrats in the Senate. The change was accentuated by turnover. The House had 87 new members, 73 Republicans and 14 Democrats. The Senate had 11 new members, all Republicans. More than half the current members in the House were elected in 1990 or later, and so were 29 of the 100 Senators, representing a generational transformation.[2] As time went by, the Republican members would be augmented by Democratic defections, but not enough to change the general balance.

The shock troops of the Republican majority were the younger, single-minded, hard-edged members of the House. Imbued with the rightness of their cause, they felt the end justified the means, and their majority not only entitled them to push through their agenda, but also represented a mandate from the American people.

The Republican strategy was to use the budget process of a single year to set in motion and commit the nation to its program. To do so, the Republicans would

---

[1]*Congressional Quarterly Weekly Report*, November 12, 1994, pp. 3216–3219.

[2]*Los Angeles Times*, February 14, 1995, p. A6.

need to rewrite the budget equation. They wanted to cut taxes, increase defense, *and* balance the budget. Even with favorable economic assumptions, these objectives could not be achieved within the present terms. Cuts in domestic discretionary spending would not be enough. It would be necessary to confront the fast growing entitlement programs—an item not on the original agenda.

The discipline and cohesion of the Republican majority enabled them to rewrite the budget equation in the budget resolution and reconciliation instructions. Polarization seemed complete and the level of rhetoric and vituperation reached new heights. It appeared that only the countervailing power of the presidency could block the radical agenda of the congressional majority. By the end of the year, the politics of radical reversal seemed to have turned into a raw power conflict determined by majority dominance, opportunistic leverage, threats, and deadlock.

While the surface fervor continued unabated, however, political and institutional realities worked toward compromise and middle ground between the two sides. The details of authorizations, appropriations, and reconciliation blurred the clean lines of ideological division. In the approach to the next election, neither side wished to be seen as beyond reason, intransigent, or responsible for breakdown.

As the long saga of the budget unwound during the year, the basic assumptions which had governed previous budget policy gradually changed. Debate came to focus not on *whether* there should be cuts, but on how much; not *whether* budget balance was desirable, but how it should be achieved; not *whether* taxes should be reduced, but which ones; not *whether* social provision should be diminished, but how reforms should be carried out. There was still much room for disagreement, but the terms of the discussion had shifted. Events outstrip my pen, and the eventual outcome is still in doubt, so that prediction is hazardous. It may very well be that in striving for too much, the Republicans overreached themselves, and instead of definitively changing the future, they will have ended with their program in tatters. But whatever might emerge from the struggle, the center appears to have moved, whether permanently or not, remains to be seen. Why did this happen?

The Republican majority were not totally united on all the issues. The most troublesome were those which on their face were not really related to the budget at all, such as abortion and the environment, but proved significant issues in the budget debates. Members also varied in the degree of their radicalism, and the extent to which they wished to depart from the status quo, and especially to sign on to proposals originating on the far right. The standards of economic purity and moral rectitude might take second place to regional or constituency considerations, or to a genuine sense of what was politically possible or decently equitable. There were also legitimate questions of who or what the Republican majority actually stood for. Little evidence of whole-hearted embrace of the Contract existed, and Senate Republicans had not endorsed it. And as the Republican program evolved, became more specific, and broadened to include entitlements, polls showed increasing public uneasiness with legislative proposals.

Neither were the Democrats completely united in their opposition. The Democratic party was split between social liberals who wanted to increase social spending to deal with social ills, and fiscal conservatives who wished to cut spending and reduce the deficit. "Old style," "liberal" Democrats leaned toward economic nationalism, opposing broad trade agreements such as NAFTA, demanding greater sharing of profits and power by corporations, linking social problems to underlying economic injustice, and maintaining or expanding existing federal policies on welfare, income redistribution and crime. The "new" Democrats advocated strategies to adapt to economic globalization, opening overseas markets, and retraining American workers, while rethinking liberal approaches on crime, welfare, and family breakdown to emphasize greater individual responsibility.[3] Each of these positions offered potential allies for the Republicans, the former supporting growing isolationism and protection, and the latter working for modification of social programs. While most votes were along party lines, both individuals and significant blocks of Democrats repeatedly voted for Republican measures, and there were a few outright defections. One block of Democrats, the Coalition, consistently sought a middle ground, and by the end of the year had attracted further support. As "Blue Dogs," they emerged as a significant force in the movement toward compromise in the deadlocks on continuing resolutions and the reconciliation bill.

As budget legislation moved through Congress, the president had to make difficult choices. If he opposed the Republican agenda in its entirety, he might be seen as unreasonable and obstructive. To cooperate completely would risk losing his own party and undercut initiatives he had endorsed in the past. He could veto, but could not be sure if he could sustain his veto in Congress, although the Republican majority was less than two-thirds in either House.

Gradually the president adopted a centrist strategy, which incorporated many of the elements of the Republican agenda—a balanced budget; increased defense expenditures; cuts in medicare and increases in premiums; a "middle class" tax cut; welfare reform; acceptance of rejections of his spending proposals. Increasingly, differences were being defined by amounts rather than principles. The gulf still existed: On the Republican side, the zealots insisted their program was not negotiable—program cuts, entitlement cuts, balanced budget, and tax cuts. And as the polls indicated the growing unpopularity of that program, the president strengthened his stance as protector of social programs, the middle class, and the environment. But the gulf itself was not quite as wide as it once seemed.

In any case, the budget process discourages radical positions. It diffuses power and sets up numerous opportunities for the advance or defense of numerous agendas. Budget committees, authorizing committees, appropriations committees and their subcommittees, and tax committees demand not one majority, but multiple majorities on multiple issues. And the committees are only one part of a story which involves House and Senate, conference deliberations and floor votes. Institutional fragmentation strengthens partial perspectives against the whole, pits moderate against radical, and encourages regional and economic interests. To attempt radical change is to run the gauntlet of a process which repeatedly tests every issue, and requires every fight to take place again and again.

The budget drama plays out before an audience of public opinion. Each side has to weigh its objectives against the perception of its ability to govern responsi-

---

[3]John Brummett, *Highwire: The Education of Bill Clinton* (New York: Hyperion, 1994), pp. 92–93.

bly in the eyes of the voters. In its reluctance to assume the blame for the ultimate disaster—no budget at all—each side has to consider what it is willing to compromise and on what it is worth taking a stand. Right from the beginning of the process, the participants responded to their perceptions of public acceptability, exemplified in the debates on the balanced budget constitutional amendment and the rescissions bill.

PROLOGUE: CONSTITUTIONAL AMENDMENT AND RESCISSION

The constitutional amendment to balance the budget and the rescissions bill, debated at the very beginning of the congressional session, were very different measures. The constitutional amendment was largely symbolic and was defeated, while the rescissions bill was a very specific and substantive measure and was successful. But each measure in its way prefigured the themes of the budget debate to come: the power and limitations of the majority, and redefinition of the common ground between the parties.

The details of the constitutional amendment have been described in Chapter 10. Both the overwhelming support for the amendment in the House from both parties (the vote was 300 to 125) and the narrow loss in the Senate underlined a measure of common ground. In fact, the amendment would probably have received the necessary two-thirds majority in the Senate had it not been for the issue of social security. The unwillingness of the Republican leadership to provide sufficient safeguards to protect social security from any future budget balancing exercise cost the votes of several supporters. From this point on social security was absent from the budget debates. And, as an echo and foretaste of business as usual, the proposal contained a specific exemption for the Tennessee Valley Authority, inserted on the initiative of (guess who?) the Republican Senator from Tennessee.

The rescissions bill made clearer the divisions between the parties and the ability of the majority to get its way. What, you may ask, is a rescissions bill? Tucked away toward the end of the President's Budget for FY 1996 was Table S-11, Summary of Supplemental and Rescission Proposals.[4] It listed additions and subtractions for the current year's (FY 1995) budget authority for selected agencies, netting out to just over $8 billion. There were no accompanying explanations, but the list included emergency supplementals for international aid (to eliminate Jordan's debts following the Jordan-Israel peace treaty), defense (partly to cover the Haiti peacekeeping expedition), and more disaster aid (particularly for California earthquake assistance).

Supplemental bills were not unusual, and President Reagan had successfully gained rescissions from the current year's budget in 1981. But this supplemental was turned around to enable the Republican majority to transform it into a rescissions bill of its own, and to propose $17 billion worth of cuts to the current year's budget. In a stunning display of majority power, the House bill cut a wide range of

---

[4]United States Budget, *Fiscal Year 1996*, p. 207.

social and environmental programs and added amendments to prevent abortion funding under medicaid, increase timber harvesting on federal land, and block certain air pollution rules.[5]

The Senate Appropriations Committee almost unanimously rejected some of the most controversial provisions, such as cutting the federal home heating subsidy, and modified others, for example, restoring some of the funds for the president's education and youth programs and the Corporation for Public Broadcasting. The full Senate added more rescissions and compensated the committee restorations with cuts in airport improvements, HUD reserves, and administrative savings, defeated a variety of nongermane amendments, and sent nearly $16 billion in savings to conference.

Conferees agreed to deep cuts including housing (deeper than the original proposals), summer jobs programs, home heating subsidies, national service, and public broadcasting. They also cut airport improvement grants (but these would not have been spent anyway), water treatment plants, and a variety of park, forest, and energy projects, foreign aid, and agriculture. They rescinded most of the Senate federal buildings and highway projects cuts, traditional pork barrel categories. Some of the more controversial amendments were also jettisoned.

The rescissions bill passed Congress more or less on party lines. The president, affronted by the conference's additional cuts in education and youth programs as well as community development banks and WIC, vetoed it.[6] After some compromises, he signed it six weeks later. It still included cuts in job training, low income housing and energy assistance, education, energy research, foreign aid, and national parks.[7]

This guerrilla raid on the budget exemplified the budget debates to come. It illustrated the primary dividing line between the parties—Democrats for social spending and Republicans against—but it also demonstrated the potential for compromise, as Democrats traded their support for some concessions, in effect redefining the center. Thus, David Obey, ranking Democrat on the House Appropriations Committee, remarked "The Senate demonstrated that you do not have to go to the extremes the House went to in cutting programs for children and the elderly."[8]

The bill also demonstrated the extent to which the majority party was able to use leverage to achieve its program, and the potential for deadlock in the system. The Republicans used "must pass" legislation to force confrontation with the president, and the president used a veto threat to try to gain changes. On both sides these tactics would be employed repeatedly during the budget process. A division between House and Senate was apparent, as the Senate, while remaining committed to general principle, defined its own somewhat less radical and confrontational approach. Finally, the bill took over five months to pass, during which, detailed provisions were inserted, removed, reinserted, and modified in a mind-numbing

---

[5]*Congressional Quarterly Weekly Report,* March 4, 1995, p. 676 and March 18, 1995, p. 797.

[6]Ibid., May 20, 1995.

[7]Ibid., July 22, 1995, p. 2157.

[8]Ibid., May 6, 1995, p. 1231.

journey toward its conclusion. By the time the bill was finally signed in July, it was only a sideshow to the budget debates which had been in full swing for some time.

BUDGETS AND COUNTERBUDGETS: REWRITING THE BUDGETARY EQUATION

1995 was a year of many budgets. At the beginning there was the president's budget, quickly set aside by the resolution and reconciliation instructions of the congressional Republicans, which became the authoritative framework for the details of the budget. Belatedly, the president offered another budget framework in response. Each side tried to rewrite the budget equation and each contributed toward a new consensus, although this was far from complete. Later, appropriations bills and the reconciliation bill would constitute yet more budgets, to be followed by continuing resolutions and yet another presidential proposal. (The chart on p. 310 provides a guide to the process.) Let us begin with the efforts to shape the budget framework, and see how they both polarized the parties and yet brought them together.

In the "old" budget equation, mandatory expenditures were allowed to grow more or less unchecked; discretionary expenditures were virtually frozen at 1993 levels by the caps, with changes in priorities funded either from juggling domestic discretionary programs or using defense to finance domestic initiatives; and the deficit was slowly diminishing as the result of the spending caps, tax increases, and a more favorable economy. This position was no longer viable.

The Budget and the Economy

By the mid-1990s, an accepted wisdom seemed to have emerged on budget assumptions. Briefly, they echoed the Federal Reserve's recipe for economic stability: moderate economic growth (about 2.5 percent); low inflation (about 3 percent); steady interest rates; and unemployment about 6 percent. As long as these predictions of the future were blessed by the CBO, they would be accepted and could safely be built into the federal budget. Both the president's budget and the congressional resolution adopted similar figures, and at this point there was little discussion of them.[9]

Obviously, an economic downturn would change the figures, but even assuming stable conditions, translating assumptions into forecasts was a tricky business. For example, for the current year, the president's experts set the deficit at $193 billion, while the CBO experts believed it would be $14 billion lower.[10] For the following year, the experts switched places: The administration deficit projection was $200 billion, while the CBO forecast was $211 billion! For the year 2000, CBO projected the deficit $80 billion higher than the administration.

The prospect of budget balance opened up a whole new speculative area regarding the effects of a balanced (or balancing) budget on the economy and recip-

---

[9]Congressional Budget Office, *An Analysis of the President's Budgetary Proposals for FY 1996*, April 1995, p. 9; George Hager, "The Arduous Budget Talks of 1990 May Offer a Map to the Road Ahead," *Congressional Quarterly Weekly Report*, January 3, 1995, p. 1565.

[10]Ibid., p. 4.

TOTAL 12.1   BALANCING THE BUDGET OVER SEVEN YEARS

House and Senate versions of the Resolution Compared with
the Final Congressional Resolution and the President's Plan
(in billions of dollars)

	HOUSE	SENATE	PRESIDENT	CONGRESS
Deficit reduction	1.04 trillion	958	520*	894[†]
Savings from				
lower interest	256	184	155	(170)
Tax cuts	353	0	105	245
		($174 conditional)		
Medicare savings	288	256	128	270
Medicaid savings	187	175	54	182
			(offset by $24.3 expansion)	
Defense increases	67.8	0	3	58
Non-defense				
discretionary savings	192[†]	190[†]	197	190[†]
Other mandatory savings	219	209	38	175

* The Clinton proposal balanced the budget over $10 years, requiring $1.1 trillion. The comparisons are for seven years.

[†] Measured against the 1995 enacted level (not the inflation adjusted baseline).

Source: Figures were revised several times. The figures in this table are taken from *Congressional Quarterly Weekly Report*, July 1, 1995, p. 1905, and do not add because of conceptual inconsistencies.

rocal effects on the budget. What about "dynamic scoring"? Let's count tax cuts as a revenue increase instead of a decrease, because the increased economic activity that would presumably take place would of course increase revenues. After no less a critic than the chairman of the Federal Reserve Board voiced disapproval, little more was heard of this one. Along similar lines, the CBO "found" a $170 billion windfall in presumed savings from a presumed drop in interest rates and economic growth over seven years,[11] and the House and Senate resolutions and the president's plan discovered even more. (See Table 12.1) Such a "fiscal dividend" would clearly improve the possibilities for balancing the budget, if it really did materialize.[12]

Balancing Revenues and Expenditures

The president did not attempt to balance his budget, but instead stabilized it at about $200 billion to the end of the century, when it would stand at just over 2 percent of GDP, an enviable figure for many European countries and the lowest level since 1979.[13] In contrast, Congress set out a path to balance the budget by the year 2002. To make things harder, the House included over $350 billion in tax cuts and a large increase for defense. In the Senate resolution, where the ardor of

[11]Congressional Budget Office, *The Economic and Budget Outlook: An Update*, August 1995, p. 34.

[12]Jeff Shear, "Why Treasury May Need a Bigger Vault," *National Journal*, May 27, 1995, p. 1286.

[13]United States Budget, *Fiscal Year 1996*, Table 2–1, p. 40.

tax cut advocates was met with caution, a new procedure was established: A tax cut would only be allowed if reconciliation instructions were consistent with the resolution to ensure a balanced budget by 2002.[14] The final resolution included $245 billion in tax cuts, after certification from CBO was duly obtained.

The budget resolution, which was followed by reconciliation instructions, invoked an extraordinary amount in deficit reduction, $894 billion measured against a freeze in 1995 spending levels, and about $1.25 trillion against the CBO estimated deficit baseline. It also made the task more difficult by adding in over $300 billion in tax cuts and defense increases.

The debates and votes on the resolution sharply divided the parties. The Republicans took a lofty tone. In the House, the Majority Whip, Tom DeLay, pronounced "Today we make a historic decision. We can protect the status quo or we can make a courageous stand for America."[15] In an impassioned speech, Budget Committee Chairman John Kasich said "What our vision is for the twenty-first century is a vision of taking power and money and control and influence from this city and giving it back to men and women all across this country."[16] In response, Minority Leader Richard Gephardt denounced the plan as a heartless attack on the poor and elderly, and Senator Edward Kennedy said the resolution was a "direct attack on senior citizens, children, families and veterans."[17]

But the middle ground was already slipping away. Even in the midst of his attack, Gephardt said "All of us believe our budget must be brought into balance. It's a question of how you do it."[18] At least two Democratic budget balancing alternative plans were put forward, attracting some Democratic, but no Republican, support. Finally the president jumped into the fray, ignoring his original budget, with a new plan to balance the budget in ten years, requiring $1.1 trillion in deficit reduction, and including over $100 billion in tax cuts (see Table 12.1). Although not all the Democratic party endorsed the position, budget balance and tax cuts were now an integral part of the budget equation.

Mandatory and Discretionary Spending

The decisions on budget balance and tax cuts drove further decisions on mandatory spending. The president's budget had allowed entitlements to rise, constrained only by previous cuts. But now it would be necessary to cut them to attain the new totals. As part of the new consensus, social security remained untouched; other entitlements would meet two thirds of the needed deficit reduction. The congressional resolution, the compromise between House and Senate plans, cut the rates of medicare ($247 billion in cuts) and medicaid ($182 billion) spending by more than half over the next seven years. Cuts in antipoverty programs (includ-

[14]The provision is reproduced in Congressional Budget Office, *The Economic and Budget Outlook: An Update*, August 1995, p. 40.

[15]Janet Hook, "House Adopts GOP Plan to Balance Budget by 2002," *Los Angeles Times*, May 19, 1995, p. A17.

[16]Ibid., p. A1.

[17]*Los Angeles Times*, June 30, 1995, p. A28.

[18]Ibid., May 19, 1995, p. A17.

ing AFDC, food programs, supplemental social insurance, and the earned income tax credit) were scheduled to yield over $100 billion in savings. A further $75 billion would be cut from federal retirement, farm subsidies, unemployment benefits, and student loans (see Chapter 8). Details would follow in the reconciliation bill. Meanwhile, the Clinton plan, too, announced entitlement cuts. Once again, the center had moved.

Defense and Domestic Spending

The president's budget had continued the trend in defense spending, cutting defense by 3.8 percent as part of a plan to reduce military spending until 1998, when it would start to rise again. But the House had other ideas, and while the Senate was content with the president's allocation, the resolution increased military spending by about $35 billion over seven years, although this would constrain spending to 17 percent below the baseline.[19] In response, the president added $25 billion to his figure (See Chapter 9). Yet again, the sides were coming closer.

Domestic Discretionary Spending

The president's budget worked within the totals imposed by the caps, making marginal adjustments in favor of his priorities of education, research and training, the environment, and anticrime programs. It cut international aid, agriculture, and transportation, and proposed more "reinventing government" reorganizations and consolidations. In contrast, the resolution proposed about $190 billion in cuts in nondefense discretionary payments, nearly half the total, compared with enacted 1995 levels. If measured against a baseline allowing for inflation, the cut would be about $390 billion, or 30 percent.[20]

Both House and Senate made specific recommendations. The House proposed eliminating the departments of Commerce, Education and Energy, another 13 agencies, 69 boards, commissions, and authorities, and 284 federal programs, while the Senate would also recommend abolishing the Commerce Department and eliminate over 100 federal programs. The president responded with a proposal for domestic spending cuts of $197 billion against the baseline, to be achieved by across the board cuts. The ground once more had moved.

The conference report on the resolution also imposed new caps on discretionary spending from FY 1996 through FY 2002, separating defense and nondefense spending through 1998. The caps would only be enforceable in the Senate, and only for FY 1996. Any appropriations bill whose totals exceeded these targets would be barred from Senate floor consideration by a point of order which could only be overridden by a 60 vote majority.[21] (See Table 12.2.)

---

[19]Congressional Budget Office, *An Update*, p. 37.

[20]George Hager, "Today's Appropriators Preside Over a Shrinking Empire," *Congressional Quarterly Weekly Report*, May 20, 1995, p. 1365.

[21]George Hager, "Furor over First Spending Bills Promises a Stormy Summer," *Congressional Quarterly Weekly Report*, July 15, 1995, p. 2044.

Table 12.2   NEW DISCRETIONARY SPENDING CAPS IN THE CONGRESSIONAL
BUDGET RESOLUTION

	1996	1997	1998	1999	2000	2001	2002
Defense							
Budget Authority	265.4	268.0	269.7	—	—	—	—
Outlays	264.0	265.7	264.5	—	—	—	—
Non-defense							
Budget Authority	219.7	214.5	221.0	—	—	—	—
Outlays	267.7	254.6	248.1	—	—	—	—
Total discretionary							
Budget Authority	485.1	482.4	490.7	482.2	489.4	496.6	498.8
Outlays	531.8	520.3	512.6	510.5	514.2	516.4	515.1

Source: Fiscal 1996 Budget Resolution (H Con Res 67—HRept 104-5), Congressional Quarterly Weekly Report, July 15, 1995, p. 2044.

Substance versus Rhetoric

Why was it that an objective previously regarded as unattainable suddenly appeared feasible? Could Congress really look such large cuts in the eye and not blink? As CBO put it, with characteristic understatement, "Balancing the budget over the next seven years will require many hard decisions about taxing and spending policies."[22]

The resolution and reconciliation instructions, passed almost entirely on party lines, were only the first step. The "hard decisions" would have to be taken in the complexities of the budget process, which framed the issues and revisited them again and again (see page 310). Would congressional Republicans continue to vote together on the substantive expenditure cuts, especially where extraneous issues were brought into the vote? Could they successfully present social program cuts in terms of the need to balance the budget, the devolution of government, and the spirit of necessary sacrifice for a greater common goal? Or would these issues be seen as rich versus poor, big business versus working people, profits versus the general interest, and benefits for some at the expense of burdens for others? Would ideological commitment triumph over business as usual?

INCREMENTALISM IN MIRROR IMAGE: APPROPRIATIONS

The politics of subtraction in 1995 was not the simple reversal of incrementalism, but rather its mirror image. The appropriations committees were charged with cutting domestic discretionary spending, which made up 17 percent of the budget by some $10 billion below the 1995 level to meet the 1996 targets.[23] Cutting, not increasing, the base in this way, meant losers not winners, raising the potential for conflict. Partisanship replaced consensus; debates focused on policy and ideology;

[22]Congressional Budget Office, The Economic and Budget Outlook: An Update, August 1995, p. 37.

[23]George Hager, "Furor over First Spending Bills Promises Stormy Summer," p. 2041.

The Budget Process

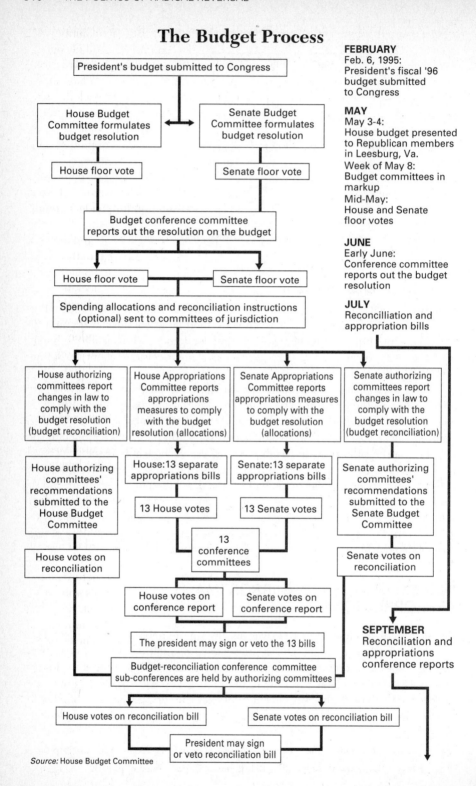

President's budget submitted to Congress

House Budget Committee formulates budget resolution ⟷ Senate Budget Committee formulates budget resolution

House floor vote

Senate floor vote

Budget conference committee reports out the resolution on the budget

House floor vote — Senate floor vote

Spending allocations and reconciliation instructions (optional) sent to committees of jurisdiction

House authorizing committees report changes in law to comply with the budget resolution (budget reconciliation)

House Appropriations Committee reports appropriations measures to comply with the budget resolution (allocations)

Senate Appropriations Committee reports appropriations measures to comply with the budget resolution (allocations)

Senate authorizing committees report changes in law to comply with the budget resolution (budget reconciliation)

House authorizing committees' recommendations submitted to the House Budget Committee

House:13 separate appropriations bills

Senate:13 separate appropriations bills

Senate authorizing committees' recommendations submitted to the Senate Budget Committee

13 House votes

13 Senate votes

House votes on reconciliation

13 conference committees

Senate votes on reconciliation

House votes on conference report

Senate votes on conference report

The president may sign or veto the 13 bills

Budget-reconciliation conference committee sub-conferences are held by authorizing committees

House votes on reconciliation bill

Senate votes on reconciliation bill

President may sign or veto reconciliation bill

Source: House Budget Committee

FEBRUARY
Feb. 6, 1995: President's fiscal '96 budget submitted to Congress

MAY
May 3-4: House budget presented to Republican members in Leesburg, Va.
Week of May 8: Budget committees in markup
Mid-May: House and Senate floor votes

JUNE
Early June: Conference committee reports out the budget resolution

JULY
Reconcilliation and appropriation bills

SEPTEMBER
Reconciliation and appropriations conference reports

and pressure from the leadership strove to enforce totals. But the majorities were not always cohesive, and the multiple, repetitive decision process still encouraged bargaining, modifications of hard-line positions, and more varied agendas.

The appropriations committees were critical to the success of a large part of the Republican agenda not only to balance the budget but to roll back the activities of the federal government, particularly in view of the slow progress of the legislative program. The Speaker had appointed the House Appropriations chair and demanded letters of loyalty from the top Republicans on the committee.[24] In a closed-door meeting with the Appropriations chair and subcommittee chair, Gingrich reminded them "You are going to be in the forefront of the revolution. You have the toughest jobs in the House. If you don't want to do it, tell me."[25] First in the rescissions bill and later in the congressional resolution, the budget committees provided not only overall totals, but also detail about the cuts they wanted.

But the appropriations committees had their own prerogatives, and their own way of doing business. Traditionally, they subordinated partisanship to the work of producing appropriations bills, working "congenially to advance spending they mutually agreed on and [resisting] partisan agendas, whether Democratic or Republican."[26] Bipartisan, pragmatic, and quiet, their style contrasted with House Speaker Gingrich's partisan, media-savvy, and abrasive attitude.[27] Theirs was a culture of building and trading favors, and also of a determined independence. "[The budget] becomes real when our bills pass," said House Appropriations Committee chairman, Robert Livingston. Another subcommittee chairman declared "I don't think we care about the cuts he [Gingrich] wants. . . . He may have to live with the cuts we give him."[28]

Appropriations committees also differed from budget committees in their concerns. The budget committees had set out a seven-year plan; the appropriations committees were concerned about next year's budget, a traditional, year-at-a-time approach to budgeting. The budget committees viewed the budget as a whole and in large blocks; the appropriations committees, because of the way their jurisdictions were defined, had to trade one interest against another, below tight limits. More for the space program would mean less for housing programs and urban development. Anticrime measures had to compete head-on with economic development.[29] Support of one program automatically involved members in cutting others, quite the reverse of the traditional vote trading process.

Ideology and older interests played out their agendas in the rhetoric of budget cutting, changing priorities, and festooning appropriations bills with riders. Complex coalitions and pork barrel politics set prices for agreement. Some programs were targeted for elimination and others for preservation, unrelated to their budgetary impact. Attempts were made to swallow whole agencies. And in

---

[24]David Rogers, "Budget Round II," *Wall Street Journal,* May 19, 1995, p. A4.

[25]*Washington Post,* August 13, 1995, p. A6.

[26]*Congressional Quarterly Weekly Report,* March 4, 1995, p. 677.

[27]Rogers, p. 1.

[28]Ibid.

[29]Ibid., p. A4.

social and environmental policy areas, a slash-and-burn strategy attempted to implement, through the budget, the politics of radical reversal. The scope and detail of the debates defies easy summary. What follows is a brief description of the sometimes changed, sometimes perennial, and often inconsistent, way of doing business.

Complex Coalitions

The case of agriculture illustrates how the juxtaposition of different interests and the multiple steps of the budget process complicated decision making, blurred lines of jurisdiction among the committees, and brought together strange bedfellows in complex coalitions. The agriculture appropriations bill contained two elements of contention: nutrition programs (making up two-thirds) and subsidies to farmers. As entitlements, these were also under the jurisdiction of the agriculture committees, which in 1995 had to reauthorize the farm bill after five years. In the past, rural conservatives in support of farm subsidies and urban liberals in support of nutrition programs joined together on the House Appropriations Subcommittee to support the status quo. The Republican attack on food stamps and nutrition programs might encourage urban liberals to vote against farm programs to preserve programs for the poor.

The message to all concerned at the beginning was loud and clear: Cut the budget, and in particular, cut and even eventually eliminate the system of price supports and subsidies to farmers. House and Senate leadership, conservative think tanks, free market conservatives, environmentalists, food manufacturers, consumer advocates, and even the chairman of the Senate Agriculture Committee, endorsed this position. They argued that agriculture would gain from increased competition, improved market conditions, and increased crop diversification; that the subsidies were "corporate welfare;" that they drove up commodity prices and undercut American exports; and that they supported undesirable environmental practices and represented "staggering waste."

But the Republicans were by no means unanimous in their hostility to farm programs. Although rural congressional districts formed a minority (only 76–100, depending on who did the counting, out of 435 House seats), they were in the Midwest and South where farmers depended heavily on subsidies. Many of these seats had been won in the last election by relatively narrow margins, and in the 1985 election, loss of the Senate Republican majority had been attributed to the loss of those seats following reauthorization of the farm bill. Freshmen Republicans and others, including Senate Majority Leader Dole and Senate Minority Leader Daschle, argued that farm programs stimulated the economy and guaranteed inexpensive food. Support programs worked well, and their sudden elimination would lead to devastation of rural America as well as undermining current agricultural stability and a large export industry. In any case, farm subsidies had fallen over the past decade from $26 billion to about $10 billion. All governments subsidize agriculture, and removing of subsidies and price supports would result in a flood of subsidized commodities entering the country to threaten the livelihood of the farmers and all those dependent on the food industry, directly and indirectly, for employment.

The Clinton administration, while supporting more crop variety, program reform, and some program cuts, also generally supported farm interests and opposed radical change: Agriculture Secretary Glickman saw himself as an "advocate for agriculture."[30] Farm lobby groups were active on the Hill and had made substantial contributions to 1994 candidates.

After initial skirmishing on the agriculture committees and budget committees that left subsidy programs more or less intact, the focus shifted to the House Appropriations agriculture subcommittee. With the Republicans split on the issue of subsidies versus budget cutting, it was necessary to maintain bipartisan support for the bill. The nutrition programs retained their position with only minor cuts. Subsidies were reduced, but through a favorable market situation, not expenditure cuts. The brunt of the cuts fell on agricultural research and extension projects, rural development, conservation, and export programs.

The House Appropriations Committee approved the bill and rejected amendments to end tobacco subsidies, cut the peanut program, and eliminate subsidies for wealthy farmers. Debate centered not on the funding choices, but on the administration proposal for tougher food inspections which was postponed. When the bill came to the floor of the House, efforts to cap the number of participants in the WIC program and to bar use of funds for tobacco crop insurance failed.

The Senate Appropriations Committee, with an eye to presidential priorities, softened the cuts in rural housing and development programs. To do so, it had to find savings in other programs, infringing on the authorizing committees' territory. This move was not unusual, but in 1995 it was resorted to more frequently and illustrates the complex trading among different agendas. For example, the business supported export promotion program was capped at $800 million, though not eliminated (but in a blow to the minks, the Committee struck out a House provision that would have barred use of export promotion funds for the Mink Export Development Council). A $41 million disaster aid provision for cotton farmers, which had been inserted by Republican Thad Cochran of Mississippi and funded by an acreage freeze on the Conservation Reserve Program, was also a target for Democrats seeking to restore rural housing financing.[31]

The haggling continued until the bill finally emerged from conference nearly $6 billion below the FY 1995 figure, but the major conflict over subsidies and nutrition programs was deferred to the Agriculture Committees and the reconciliation bill. The debates illustrate the difficulties of cutting budgets and pursuing ideologies in the face of conflicted politics. The resilience of local interests was attested to by the survival of pork.

The Survival of Pork

The survival of special research grants at the same time that university research was being sacrificed to the budget axe in the agriculture appropriations subcom-

---

[30]*Wall Street Journal,* March 22, 1995, p. A8; *Congressional Quarterly Weekly Report,* May 13, 1995, p. 1316; *Congressional Quarterly Weekly Report,* June 24, 1995.

[31]David Rogers, "Senate Panel Softens House-Passed Cuts in Rural Programs to Try to Avoid Veto," *Wall Street Journal,* September 15, 1995, p. A18.

mittee exemplifies the survival of the age-sanctioned practice of pork: the placing of projects in members' districts. Allen Schick has sensibly pointed out that the actual amount of such earmarking in the budget is quite small, and that even complete elimination of pork would not make much of a contribution to budget balance.[32] Perhaps this is just as well, since it was not difficult to find examples of pork even in today's straitened circumstances, despite the pledge of the House Appropriations Committee: "We're not going to just stop projects in Democrats' districts. We're going to stop projects across the board. We're going to slow down the pork barrel. There's no doubt about it."[33]

Examples abound. For instance, the House Appropriations Committee cut the allocation for the Army Corps of Engineers 6 percent below 1995 spending, but still included almost $20 million in funding for about 20 new construction projects, including three in the subcommittee chairman's home state of Indiana.[34] In the transportation appropriations subcommittee's mark up, no money was allowed for highway "demonstration" projects, a traditional pork barrel category, but the bill contained mass transit funds for high occupancy vehicle lane designations in Utah; hundreds of millions of dollars for previously authorized projects in the 1991 surface transportation law; and subsidies for rural airports.[35] The Senate Appropriations Committee also wrote in an exemption from the cap on highway construction to the tune of $23 million for roads in Indian reservations, at the request of Pete Domenici, the chairman of the Budget Committee and Senator from New Mexico.[36]

The House Appropriations Committee preserved the Appalachian Regional Commission against the recommendation of the House Budget Committee, as well as the Botanic Garden, a facility supported by Chairman Livingston's wife. But the Botanic Garden was later killed in the Senate.[37] The final version of the energy bill added $55 million to the administration's proposal for water projects, "including several written into the legislation on behalf of senior Republicans in both chambers."[38]

And so it went on: federal courthouses here,[39] a food services institute there,[40] a physical fitness center at a naval shipyard in Washington,[41] a controversial dam in

---

[32]Allen Schick, *The Federal Budget: Politics, Policy, Process* (Washington D.C.: Brookings Institution, 1995), p. 141.

[33]Jackie Koszczuk, "Lord of the Long Knives," *Congressional Quarterly Weekly Report,* May 20, 1995, p. 1366.

[34]*Congressional Quarterly Weekly Report,* June 24, 1995, p. 1833.

[35]Ibid., p. 1831.

[36]Ibid., August 5, 1995, p. 2357.

[37]Ibid., July 22, 1995, p. 2143.

[38]David Rogers, "Congress Approves $37.45 Billion Bill for Transportation," *Wall Street Journal,* November 1, 1995, p. A3.

[39]*Congressional Quarterly Weekly Report,* July 29, 1995, p. 2258.

[40]*Wall Street Journal,* September 21, 1995, p. A11.

[41]*Congressional Quarterly Weekly Report,* July 8, 1995, pp. 1990–1.

Northern California.[42] As the appropriations process continued, it was clear that appropriators were "still ready and willing and able to finance projects that benefit members or districts."[43]

Why does pork survive in an era of tight fiscal limits? For the same reasons it always has. Additionally, the Republican leadership was often reluctant to control the details of spending as long as the totals were met, and were aware of their need to gather votes where they could and to maintain the momentum of the appropriations process. Ideological purity gave way to pragmatism, and many Republicans, including Speaker Gingrich, supported federal government participation in infrastructure. As a freshman member of the House Appropriations Committee, George Nethercutt, put it (presumably with a straight face), "I don't think we can assume just because a special project is funded, that project is not meritorious."[44]

Balancing Acts

Because totally disparate functions and agencies may be grouped together in a single appropriation, when the appropriations committees divided up the total allowances of the budget resolution among their subcommittees to shape the appropriations bills, programs jostled one another. For example, a vote for stepped up law enforcement translated into less for foreign aid and commerce in the appropriations bill for Commerce, Justice, and State. Some programs were hurt simply because they were grouped together with others of higher priority.[45]

In the transportation appropriations bill, funding had to be balanced among highways, airports, and mass transit. In the House version of the bill, total spending would be nearly $1 billion less than in 1995, but programs would not be cut evenly. The winners would be the federal aid highway program and the airport improvement program, each of which would receive increases from the cuts in mass transit and Amtrak (which would lose one quarter of its subsidies). In the Senate, however, the appropriations committee cut budget authority about 10 percent more than the House, and approved a freeze on spending on highway construction, cutting deeply into airport construction, Amtrak, and mass transit operating subsidies, which were slashed by nearly half with the biggest cuts coming in cities over 200,000 in population.[46]

Economy and Ideology

Budget cutting was not the only agenda. The appropriations process provided multiple opportunities to assert political positions that really had little to do with money issues. With time short, appropriations seemed a fast track way to gain leg-

---

[42]Marc Reisner, "Concrete for America? Count Him In!," *New York Times,* August 20, 1995, p. E3.

[43]*Congressional Quarterly Weekly Report,* July 8, 1995, p. 1190.

[44]Ibid., p. 1991.

[45]Ibid., July 29, 1995, p. 2272.

[46]Ibid., August 5, 1995.

islative changes, normally the province of the authorizing committees, and became a major vehicle for legislative action. Mused Allen Schick, "The paradox of 1995 is that in some ways, the Appropriations committees are weaker in money matters and stronger in legislative matters, which is exactly the opposite of what it's supposed to be."[47] The following are only a few of myriad examples that might be cited.

The issues were contentious. The House bill funding the Environmental Protection Agency prevented the agency from enforcing regulations affecting wetlands protection, automobile emissions inspections, and drinking water standards. Money for enforcement of statutes, such as the Clean Air Act and Clean Water Act, would be withheld until Congress had voted to reauthorize them.[48] But the riders were ultimately defeated in the House by a coalition of Democrats and 65 moderate Republicans, largely from the Northeast and Midwest, although 29 Democrats voted to retain them.[49] The bill still emerged from conference with riders including allowing logging in the Tongass National Forest, and allowing selling of mining rights on federal land for as little as $250 an acre.[50]

There were many other riders attacking environmental policies, including a moratorium on listing new wildlife and plants under the Endangered Species Act, and reversing a ban on issuing low-cost "patents" allowing mining claims on federal lands.[51]

Many of the riders were highly provocative and were eventually dropped. They included a prohibition on the federal government doing business with companies that replaced striking workers with permanent employees;[52] reversal of the ban on offshore drilling for oil and gas;[53] prohibition of organizations receiving federal funds engaging in lobbying and other political activities;[54] and a prohibition on federal contracts being awarded on the basis of reverse discrimination.[55]

The issues ranged up and down the whole gamut of federal government activities. The Senate Appropriations Committee acted to block a new Agriculture Department rule to ban labeling of frozen poultry as "fresh," a move upheld on the Senate floor.[56] The Committee also responded to pressures by roofing and house-

---

[47]George Hager, "As They Cut, Appropriators Add a Stiff Dose of Policy," *Congressional Quarterly Weekly Report,* July 29, 1995, p. 2247.

[48]*New York Times,* July 19, 1995, p. A10; *Los Angeles Times,* July 29, 1995.

[49]James Gerstenzang, "House, Reversing Itself, Drops Bid to Limit EPA Powers," *Los Angeles Times,* November 13, 1995, pp. A1, A23.

[50]50 James Gerstenzang, "White House Threatens Veto of Environmental Measures," *Los Angeles Times,* September 23, 1995, p. A3.

[51]*Congressional Quarterly Weekly Reports,* June 24, 1995.

[52]*New York Times,* September 29, 1995.

[53]*Congressional Quarterly Weekly Report,* June 24, 1995.

[54]David Wessel and Jackie Calmes, "No Progress Made on Shutdown," *Wall Street Journal,* November 16, 1995, p. A22; Jennifer Corbett, "House Votes to Curb Activity of Non-Profit Groups," *Los Angeles Times,* September 5, 1995, p. A20.

[55]*Congressional Quarterly Weekly Report,* July 22, 1995, p. 2144.

[56]*Wall Street Journal,* September 15, 1995, p. A 18; *Wall Street Journal,* September 20, 1995, p. A6.

building industries to limit enforcement of new OSHA safety rules,[57] and there was language written into the bill to change its direction from rule enforcement to voluntary compliance.[58] The House version of the appropriations bill for Commerce, Justice and State contained provisions blocking funds to normalize relations with Vietnam and to support peacekeeping operations involving United States troops operating under foreign command.[59]

The biggest ideological fights were over abortion, an issue which crossed party lines and appeared in several appropriations bills. For example, the House and Senate versions of the Treasury, Postal appropriations bill included restoration of a ban on abortions for women enrolled in taxpayer subsidized federal employee health care plans, though the Senate version contained exceptions for rape, incest, or a woman's health.[60] The House Appropriations bill for Labor Health and Human Services included dozens of amendments, which were freely admitted as paybacks to the Christian Coalition and other antiabortion groups. Republicans joined Democrats to defeat efforts to transfer funding for Title X, the administration's main family-planning program, to locally controlled programs with no mandate for family planning. But a provision was approved to bar the use of federal medicaid funds to pay for abortion in case of rape or incest: 52 Republicans voted against the provision, and 40 Democrats for it.[61]

An interesting situation arose in the House consideration of the transportation appropriations bill. The House Appropriations Committee, which had passed a measure to repeal labor protection provisions over Democratic opposition, asked for a rule from the Rules Committee to protect its action from procedural challenges on the House floor. The rule would also have protected 15 unauthorized mass transit projects included in the bill. The chairman of the House Transportation and Infrastructure Committee was so outraged by the attempt to circumvent his committee on this latter issue that he joined the Democrats in asking the House Rules Committee not to allow the waiver. When the Rules Committee complied, the House Republican leadership forced the two committee chairs into a compromise, which required the House to pass an authorization for the disputed transit projects, but which also protected the repeal of the labor protection provisions. But all this maneuvering came to nothing as an unexpected bipartisan coalition, in which 44 Republicans joined with a unanimous Democratic vote, defeated the repeal on the floor of the House, claiming that it would cause thousands of blue-collar transit workers to lose collective bargaining rights. All of which goes to show that the Republican leadership could not always count on getting its own way, and that surprises still do happen.[62]

---

[57]*Wall Street Journal*, September 15, 1995, p. A18.

[58]*Los Angeles Times*, July 29, 1995.

[59]*Congressional Quarterly Weekly Report*, July 29, 1995, p. 2272.

[60]Andrew Taylor, "Treasury-Postal Bill Passes After Abortion Debate," *Congressional Quarterly Weekly Report,* September 12, 1995, p. 2439.

[61]*New York Times*, August 4, 1995, pp. A1 and A24.

[62]*Congressional Quarterly Weekly Report*, July 22, 1995, p. 2170; *Congressional Quarterly Weekly Report*, July 29, 1995.

Targeting Programs

Further fissures were opened in party unity through efforts to eliminate or save specific programs. In many cases the amount of funding involved was relatively small, so the motivation for cutting was not primarily economy, while programs might be saved even where the party leadership was in favor of termination.

For example, the Corporation for Public Broadcasting had already lost funding in the rescissions bill. It was attacked by a solid Republican coalition composed of fiscal conservatives (who wanted to save money), free market advocates (who saw it as a program for the rich and wished to privatize it), and ideological conservatives (against its alleged liberal programming bias). Against this position were arguments that it was not a program for the rich, that the federal contribution was only 14 percent of expenditures and represented seed money, and that it would not be possible to fill the federal funding gap.[63] An attempt to eliminate the agency failed on the floor of the House, because some Republicans supported it, but funding was cut by nearly a quarter.[64]

The National Endowments for Arts and Humanities were also targets. The House Appropriations Committee voted for a three-year phase out of the agencies, giving rise to contentious debates on the floor of the House: New York Republicans actually supported further funding of the NEA, but right-wing Republicans attempted to gain its immediate demise. In the end, the House voted to abolish NEA in two years and NEH in three years, and to cut spending by 40 percent.[65]

Many other examples may be related of programs targeted for elimination. Sometimes this occurred in a roundabout way. For example, the East Mojave National Park had been created in 1992 amidst considerable controversy, as it had previously been administered by the Bureau of Land Management as a multiuse area. The Interior appropriations subcommittee voted the National Park Service $1 for its administration, effectively giving it back to the BLM, and freezing its budget to about one third of its request.[66] About two dozen energy conservation programs were targeted for extinction, as well as the Strategic Petroleum Reserve, the Yucca Mountain high-level nuclear waste depository, the Institute of American Indian and Alaska Native Culture and Arts Development, the Advisory Council on Historic Preservation, and the Congressional Office for Technology Assessment.

The survival of the space station also illustrates the complex dynamics of program rescue. Despite a bipartisan effort to cancel the space station by freshmen members, the House Science Committee reauthorized the program for seven years. It appeared that opposition had been augmented by Democrats, who actually supported the station but wanted an increase in funding for the space agency (NASA) in the Veterans Affairs–Housing and Urban Development (VA–HUD) appropriations bill, in opposition to the cut proposed by the House Budget Com-

---

[63]*Los Angeles Times,* January 31, 1995, p. A10.

[64]*New York Times,* August 4, 1995.

[65]*Los Angeles Times,* July 19, 1995.

[66]*Los Angeles Times,* September 23, 1995, p. A3.

mittee. In the end, NASA sustained only a modest cut compared to the Budget Committees' recommendation, and funding was retained for the space station.

Sometimes the recommendations of the budget committees were modified or overturned by determined subcommittee chairs or bipartisan coalitions, whose choices in turn might be upset by supporters or detractors of specific programs on the floor of the House or Senate. For example, President Clinton had requested $62 million for domestic violence programs in the Department of Health and Human Services, but the draft appropriations bill in the House funded them at $400,000. However, the House Commerce, Justice and State appropriations subcommittee agreed to transfer $40 million in crime trust funds to the Labor, Health and Human Services and Education subcommittee, which then voted $73 million for the program. Similarly, many House Republicans and most Democrats sustained funding for the Economic Development Administration, slated for elimination in the House budget resolution.[67] On the other hand, the Corporation for National and Community Service, a priority of the president, was terminated.[68]

The appropriators also targeted programs with a weak constituency, like the gas turbine modular helium reactor. The rationale was cogently argued by David Minge, a Democrat from Minnesota—"I ask my colleagues: Do you think your constituents would approve of throwing more money into a black hole of waste? I think not." But when it came to another big project, the advanced light water reactor backed by powerful large companies, or the advanced spallation neutron source facility, no coalition in favor of termination appeared.[69]

Sometimes a regional program would attract bipartisan support to avoid the budget axe. A broad coalition of Republicans and Democrats, including many from states in the region, voted against abolishing the Appalachian Regional Commission, although its funding was cut in half, and the Tennessee Valley Authority also survived with funding cut by about a third. In general, fiscal conservatives were unable to muster coalitions in favor of radical budget cutting against shifting interests favoring a variety of water and energy projects.[70]

Swallowing Whole Departments

Republican party rhetoric and the budget resolutions set their sights not only on specific programs, but also on whole departments, such as the Departments of Commerce, Education and Energy. This proved harder than it first appeared.

For example, the initiative of Republican freshmen to eliminate the Energy Department was backed by the Republican leadership. Said John Kasich, House Budget Committee chair, "We don't want this department at the end of the day."[71]

---

[67]*Congressional Quarterly Weekly Report*, July 22, 1995, p. 2196.

[68]Ibid., July 15, 1995, p. 2069.

[69]Ibid., p. 2052.

[70]Allan Freedman, "Department Likely to Survive as Focus Moves to Cutbacks," *Congressional Quarterly Weekly Report*, June 10, 1995, p. 1633.

[71]*Congressional Quarterly Weekly Report*, June 17, 1995, p. 1736; *Congressional Quarterly Weekly Report*, July 15, 1995.

But the Department also represented an array of programs, dealt with by a variety of committees, which could not simply be eliminated or placed elsewhere overnight. The House Government Reform and Oversight Committee was reluctant to move in the face of an already crowded agenda. The House Science Subcommittee on Energy and Environment approved authorization for research and development programs, focusing on cutting, not eliminating the Department. The Energy and Water Development Appropriations Subcommittee followed its lead, concentrating on reorienting priorities within the Department and cutting the overall appropriation. Similarly, the Commerce Department involved the jurisdictions of no fewer than eleven authorizing committees.[72] But the Department's funding did not emerge unscathed.

Slash and Burn Budgeting?

What did all the sound and fury signify? Was it true, as Democrats contended that federal programs were gutted by the actions of 1995, and as Republicans contended, that 1995 was an epochal year in changing the entire direction of the federal government? Or was Herbert Stein nearer the mark when he said that really all that divided the two sides were relatively minor money matters?[73]

Despite skillful work by the Speaker in urging through the Republican program, involving greater centralization than had been seen in the House for decades, the sheer range of issues and disputes over them, hindered speedy passage.[74] In the Senate, where the Republican majority was much smaller, the pace was even slower. In both houses, passage of appropriations bills was delayed by disputes, often over policy rather than money, and disagreements between the House and Senate further delayed matters. By the beginning of the fiscal year, only two bills had been sent to the president, and while ten others had passed both House and Senate, conferences and final votes were still outstanding.

A quick review of those appropriations bills that had passed both House and Senate revealed three main points. First, the totals were, with certain exceptions, usually below or near the previous year's appropriation. The cuts did not usually seem enormous, but the base was last year's appropriation, not a baseline that allowed for inflation. Second, most appropriations were several billion below the president's request, which had usually (though not always) asked for an increase. Third, the aggregate cuts for each appropriations bill concealed far greater cuts for parts of the bills. These proposed cuts represented the thrust of the Republican agenda for appropriations in the House, and directly countered presidential priorities, resulting in threats of presidential veto.

Three bills in particular were the target of large cuts. The Veterans Affairs–Housing and Urban Development (VA–HUD) spending bill was particu-

---

[72]Donna Cassata, "Freshmen 'Have to Get' Commerce," *Congressional Quarterly Weekly Reports*, June 29 1995, p. 2273. See also Ben Wildavsky, "On the Block," *National Journal*, July 22, 1995, pp. 1880–1884.

[73]Interview with Herbert Stein on *The News Hour with Jim Lehrer*, November 22, 1995.

[74]See Michael Weisskopf and David Maraniss, "In a Moment of Crisis, the Speaker Persuades," *Washington Post*, September 13, 1995, p. A8.

larly contentious, since it contained funding for the Environmental Protection Agency (EPA), housing programs and the president's national service program. The House version of the bill cut EPA funding by over a third. The superfund program and water infrastructure revolving fund would each be cut by a third; the safe drinking water revolving fund would receive no funding at all; and the regulatory budget and other programs would lose about one-fifth. It is very doubtful that the agency could operate at the same level if these cuts were carried out.[75] When the bill reached the Senate, some of the EPA funding was restored, and the legislative riders deleted, but superfund funding was cut even further, and money for the revolving funds and research and development deleted altogether. In House–Senate negotiations, the agency's enforcement budget was still cut by 22 percent.[76] The final version was vetoed by the president.

The House bill cut the appropriation for the Department of Housing and Urban Development by one quarter. Several programs were cut by as much as a half or a third, but funds were increased for housing voucher and family subsidies.[77] Although moderate Republicans restored some funding (e.g., preventing rent increases in public housing), and the HUD secretary was able to blunt the cuts by other savings, the proposed HUD appropriation was still down by about one-fifth from the 1995 level. Funding for the Federal Emergency Management Agency was reduced by nearly half; the president's national service program and an economic development initiative were swept away; but the National Science Foundation, veterans programs, and the space station were cut minimally, though their budgets would still be less than those for the previous year.[78] The president vetoed the bill at the end of December 1995.

Conflict dragged on over Interior appropriations. Compromise between House and Senate resulted in an overall cut of about 10 percent from the previous year, with cuts fairly evenly spread except for energy conservation, land acquisition by the National Park Service, Indian education programs, and the National Endowments for the Arts and Humanities. But the bill, which contained a variety of riders relating to mining royalties, logging in the Tongass National Forest, the Mojave Desert, and the Endangered Species Act, was rejected in the House in a surprise vote when 48 Republicans voted with the Senate majority, and the bill was recommitted to conference. This bill was also vetoed.

Major issues were at stake in the Labor, Health and Human Services and Education bill, and the House leadership stressed its importance. Democrats had little success in attempting to reshape the bill which cut discretionary spending roughly 10 percent from 1995 levels. Nearly 200 programs would be cut or eliminated. Targets included OSHA, whose budget was cut by a quarter and its enforcement powers limited; low-income energy assistance; education programs

[75]*Congressional Quarterly Weekly Report,* August 5, 1995, p. 2366.

[76]David Rogers, "Congressional Republicans Use Spending Bills as Bargaining Chips over the Budget," *Wall Street Journal,* November 17, 1995, p. A16.

[77]*Congressional Quarterly Weekly Report,* July 29, 1995, p. 2270.

[78]David Rogers, "Congressional Republicans Use Spending Bills as Bargaining Chips in Battle over the Budget," *Wall Street Journal,* November 17 1995, p. A16.

Table 12.3   STATUS OF APPROPRIATIONS BILLS AT THE END OF NOVEMBER 1995

	(in billions of dollars)	
	Fiscal 1996 Spending	Percentage Change from Fiscal 1995
Signed into law		
Energy and water	19.3	−5.6
Agriculture	13.3	−0.5
Transportation	12.5	−8.9
Treasury	11.3	−3.0
Military construction	11.2	+26.5
Legislature	2.1	−10.2
Passed: on Clinton's desk		
Defense	243.0[c]	Unchanged
Pending: Clinton accepts level		
Natural resources	12.2	−9.9
Foreign aid	12.1	−11.1
D.C.	0.7	Unchanged
Pending: level in controversy		
Labor, health, education	62.8[a]	−10.3
HUD/VA/other agencies	61.3	−13.0
Commerce, Justice, State	23.1[b]	+ 0.6

[a]Senate level: House is $1.8 billion lower
[b]Senate level: House is $600 million higher
[c]Clinton accepted bill in December

Source: Wall Street Journal, November 27, 1995, p. A 1.

such as Goals 2000 and summer youth employment; and the NLRB (about one-third cut).[79] Eighteen Republicans voted against the bill and six Democrats voted for it.

Some of these cuts (Goals 2000; compensatory education; safe and drug-free schools) received some partial replacement in the Senate Appropriations Subcommittee debate.[80] But the House debate was blurred by the riders concerned with use of federal funds for abortion, and although many moderate Republicans wavered in their support for the bill, they rallied to urgent appeals by the leadership to maintain the momentum toward budget balance. At the end of 1995, the bill had still not passed Congress.

By the beginning of the fiscal year, only two appropriations bills had been signed by the president. At the end of November, four more had been signed and the level of funding had been accepted on three others. With the exception of military construction, reductions in appropriations averaged 5 percent below 1995 levels. (See Table 12.3.)

[79]Congressional Quarterly Weekly Report, October 7, 1995, p. 3071.

[80]David Rogers, "Gap Between House, Senate Republicans Reflects Conflict within the Party Itself," Wall Street Journal, September 14, 1995, p. A20.

The overall figures masked much deeper cuts in certain programs, which the president sometimes accepted, perhaps for concessions in other areas. For example, in agriculture, rural development aid was cut by 10 percent and rural housing preservation grants by half. In transportation, a shift in priorities was represented by the 43 percent cut in operating assistance for mass transit and a 25 percent cut in Amtrak subsidy, while highway construction funds (a traditional pork barrel category) were increased. The Treasury bill cut enforcement funding for the IRS by $300 billion out of a $4.4 billion budget, and also restrained antiabortion language. The energy and water bill retained many local projects, but cut solar and fission research. Whether large or small, these and similar cuts represented changes in priorities, and cuts in programs and services. And domestic appropriations in future years would have to shrink even further if the president approved the extension of the domestic spending caps attached to the reconciliation bill passed by Congress.[81] But at the end of the fiscal year, attention focused on the lack of appropriations for most of the federal government, necessitating a continuing resolution.

CONFRONTATION: CONTINUING RESOLUTIONS AND THE DEBT LIMIT

Continuing resolutions, because Congress had not passed some or all of the appropriations bills by the beginning of the fiscal year were not unusual. Even interruptions in federal government operations were not so exceptional—there had been nine since 1981, though none since 1990. The crisis of 1995 was different because of its length (a first shutdown was for six days, and the second for nineteen), and because Congress tried to use the leverage of the essential continuing resolution, and its approval of a raise in the debt limit, to gain advance commitment by the president to important elements in its forthcoming reconciliation bill. The reconciliation bill would contain the entitlement and taxation proposals on which a future balanced budget depended, as well as a number of other measures. It was a key part of the Republican program.

Congress and the president had agreed with little problem to a continuing resolution to keep government running until mid-November, even though the temporary funding it enacted was below the levels so far agreed to in appropriations bills still going through Congress.[82] But by mid-November, the president had signed only the bills for agriculture and military construction, and vetoed the appropriation for the legislative branch (on the grounds it would be unfair to vote funds for Congress while denying them to other federal employees). Of the ten bills outstanding, Clinton had threatened to veto at least five, as well as the recon-

---

[81]Janet Hook, "Republicans Win Early Budget Battles," *Los Angeles Times,* November 26, 1995, p. A28.

[82]David Rogers, "GOP Proposes Stopgap Spending Bill Imposing a Deeper Cut than Its Budget," *Wall Street Journal,* September 21, 1995.

ciliation bill. Meanwhile, the federal government had reached the debt limit ($4.9 trillion), requiring Congress to raise it.

The sense of crisis had been building for a month. At the beginning of September, Treasury Secretary Rubin had warned that "even the appearance that the government will default on its debts would roil the financial markets and cause severe economic problems." Unless the limit was raised before the end of October, the government would be unable to borrow money to pay its debts. The Republicans were unimpressed, suggesting the government could function on a cash flow basis, and called on President Clinton to prevent a crisis by balancing the budget over seven years.[83]

A month later, the Treasury began to cut back its short-term borrowing and again called on Congress to raise the debt limit. White House Chief of Staff Panetta reiterated the president's determination to veto any balanced budget bill that contained unacceptable spending, including a debt limit increase, and blamed congressional Republicans for creating an "atmosphere of instability."[84] There was a brief interlude when it appeared Speaker Gingrich was willing to increase the debt ceiling temporarily, but in apparent deference to radical elements, backed down.[85]

Attitudes hardened as a showdown neared. On November 13, the continuing resolution would expire, and on November 15 the Treasury Department would owe nearly $25 billion in interest payments. As Congress prepared a new continuing resolution and bill to raise the debt limit with conditions attached, a senior Treasury Department official remarked "The bus is near the edge of the cliff."[86] The twin possibilities of simultaneous federal government shutdown and financial default seemed imminent.

What were the issues? The immediate concerns were the conditions set out by Congress to resolve the short-term spending and borrowing crisis and their unacceptability to the president. Some of the most objectionable clauses (abolition of the Commerce Department; ban on lobbying by organizations receiving federal money) had been removed during the debates in Congress. What remained was a short-term spending bill, which sharply cut funding and eliminated a scheduled medicare premium reduction, and a temporary raising of the debt ceiling until December 12 when it would drop to below the existing level. The debt limit bill would also prevent the Treasury from using cash from trust funds to avoid the limit, and confirm Congress's intent to raise it again until legislation eliminating the deficit in 2002 was signed. Both bills would commit the president to balancing the budget by 2002; would require federal agencies to weigh the projected costs

---

[83]Jack Nelson, "Rubin Urges Congress to Raise Debt Ceiling," Los Angeles Times, September 8, 1995, p. A33.

[84]Jonathan Peterson, "Treasury to Scale Back on Borrowing to Avert Debt Crisis," Los Angeles Times, October 18, 1995, pp. A1, A21.

[85]Wall Street Journal, October 19, 1995, pp. A23, A13.

[86]Jonathan Peterson, "Default Scenario Looms Larger as Budget War Rages," Los Angeles Times, November 9, 1995, p. A26.

of regulations against their expected benefits and allow Congress to kill new regulations; and would limit appeals by death row prisoners.[87]

The Republican strategy was to use the leverage of the two measures to force the president to pass the reconciliation bill. They wanted to deliver on the promises they had made on election to Congress and to balance the budget in seven years. If the president acceded to their demands, they would have triumphed, and if he did not, they would be able to blame him for the consequent breakdown. Declared Majority Leader Robert Dole, "If the government shuts down, his fingerprints are going to be all over it."[88]

The administration for their side labeled the Republican tactics "a form of terrorism."[89] Buoyed by recent polls which showed public opinion swinging in his favor, the president reiterated his intention to veto the bills, on the grounds that they were attempts to impose policy and should be legislated separately. The president, having so far taken a mostly passive role in the budget débate, now needed to show he would "stand firm," and to "draw a line in the sand," even if this involved the possibility of a stopgap bill right through to the election in November 1996. In this stalemate, a senior White House official said, "Voters would ultimately see him as the leader who saved Medicare from excessive spending curtailment, preserved the environment, and headed off tax cuts that give too much to the rich."[90] At a meeting with the congressional leadership on November 1, both administration and Republicans appeared to realize the limitations on compromise on both sides and the necessity for each to work out proposals acceptable to their own parties.

It was in the interest of both sides to come to an agreement. It was also in their interest to show how hard it was and to magnify the crisis—the Republican leadership to impress on the party's radical wing that they risked gaining nothing if they did not give in on something, and the president to impress on the Democratic liberal wing that certain concessions were necessary if anything was to be preserved at all. Both sides had to impress the voters that they were the responsible party of government, and so could not afford blame for a prolonged shutdown. "They will blame all of us," said Speaker Gingrich.[91] But each side saw its electoral appeal differently, and an imminent disaster as demonstrating its serious commitment to the cause. Thus Senate Budget Committee Chairman Pete Domenici: "The issue is whether we're going to get a real balanced budget—after all the ef--

[87]Eric Pianin and Ann Devroy, "Clinton and GOP Push Fiscal Standoff to Brink," *Washington Post,* November 11, 1995, p. A1.

[88]Helen Dewar and John E. Young, "Political Stakes Are High as Each Side Cries Foul in Budget Showdown," *Washington Post,* November 10, 1995, p. A10.

[89]Paul Richter and Jonathan Peterson, "Federal Shutdown Nears Despite GOP Budget Action," *Los Angeles Times,* November 10, 1995, p. A32; Eric Pianin and Ann Devroy, "Clinton and GOP Push Fiscal Stand Off to Brink," *Washington Post,* November 11, 1995, p. A1.

[90]Jack Nelson, "Clinton Draws Line in the Sand on Budget," *Los Angeles Times,* November 10, 1995, p. A34.

[91]Janet Hook, "Showdown: High Stakes Game for Both Parties," *Los Angeles Times,* November 14, 1995, p. A14.

fort we've put into it—or not."[92] And the president: "I've worked hard for 25 years on these issues [education, welfare, health care reform and other social issues]. I care deeply about them. I don't care if I go to 5 percent in the polls. I think your bill is bad for America and I'm not going to sign it."[93]

The president vetoed the continuing resolution and the debt limit bill. The federal government closed down, except for essential activities, and the Treasury Secretary carried out a maneuver to "disinvest" in two federal trust funds as a technical way to lower federal debt and allow fresh borrowing under the debt limit so that the federal government would not default.[94]

The negotiations were at an impasse. The president denounced the Republicans for using "the threat of a government shutdown to force America to accept their cuts in education and technology and the environment." The continuing resolution would have required "a level of cuts in Medicare and Medicaid, in education, in the environment and a tax increase on working people, all of which I find highly objectionable."[95] For their part, Republicans contended that Clinton distorted their proposed budget cuts and blamed him for precipitating the crisis by not making a realistic effort to balance the budget.[96]

Given the rhetoric on both sides, the end to the impasse came relatively quickly and enabled both sides to claim advantage. Congress passed a new version of the continuing resolution, allowing normal government operation with only one condition—that the president should agree to balance the budget in seven years, using CBO assumptions, while dropping the medicare premium increase. Again the president promised to veto it, but the tide was running against both parties. The Republicans' position in the polls was lagging, and in Congress nearly 50 House Democrats and 7 Senate Democrats voted for the latest version of the continuing resolution.

The final compromise achieved both sides' bottom lines. It stated that Congress and the president "shall enact" a balanced budget by the year 2002, based on the projections of the CBO "following a thorough consultation and review with OMB and other government and private experts." One up for the Republicans. On the other hand, the agreement stipulated that the balanced budget must "protect future generations, ensure Medicare solvency, reform welfare and provide ad-

---

[92]Ibid., p. A15.

[93]Edward Chen, "Sharp Edges and Blunt Talk as Two Sides Meet," *Los Angeles Times,* November 15, 1995, p. A16.

[94]What the Secretary did was to cancel $61.3 billion in securities held by two federal retirement funds, thus freeing the government to sell more debt to the public without violating the limit. This action would carry the government through to the end of December, and other options could carry it through to mid-February or March 1996. Alan Murray, "Debt Limit Crisis Is Not Over Yet," *Wall Street Journal,* November 27, 1995, A1.

[95]Jerry Gray, "Feuding Goes On as GOP Presents Its Budget Plan," *New York Times,* November 17, 1995, p. A14.

[96]Paul Richter and Janet Hook, "800,000 Federal Workers Idled in Budget Impasse," *Los Angeles Times,* November 15, 1995, p. A1.

equate funding for Medicaid, education, agriculture, national defense, veterans and the environment." Further, "the balanced budget shall adopt tax policies to help working families and to stimulate future growth.[97] One up for the Democrats. House Speaker Gingrich hailed the accord as

> one of the great historic achievements in modern America. And I think every family is going to have a better Thanksgiving because we really are now looking out for the children of America, and we really are providing them a chance to have a future in which they're not going to be crushed by debt and taxation and high interest rates.[98]

But the president appeared to have reserved his right to block any budget plan that did not meet his priorities: "The real winners tonight are the American people because now we can have an open honest discussion about how best to balance the budget. . . . Nothing will be agreed to unless all elements are agreed to."[99]

The question of whose deficit projections would be used was critical. In July, the administration had updated its forecasts; its figures for economic growth and inflation diverged slightly from those of CBO. The CBO March forecast, relied on by Congress, had seen real growth at 2.3 percent, while the new administration figure was 2.5 percent, the CBO figure for inflation was 3.1 percent, and the administration figure was 3.2 percent. Together with other assumptions about the growth of profits, and calculations of the Consumer Price Index and GDP Inflator which measure inflation, the differences were responsible for a discrepancy of over $400 billion in deficit projection![100]

The Republicans made a great deal of the need for "honest numbers," but as Felix Rohatyn has pointed out, seven years is a long time, and projections are notoriously uncertain. There was no process established to keep the movement toward the balanced budget on track.[101] And President Clinton's big "concession" to agree to balance the budget in seven years seemed less impressive, as Herbert Stein skeptically remarked, in the light of virtually every president's pledge to balance the budget.[102] The agreement to use revised projections satisfied both sides for the moment and maintained the pretence that absolutely accurate forecasts really did exist. Meanwhile the major conflict over the reconciliation bill assumed urgency.

---

[97]Alan Miller, "Budget Deal Reached to End Government Shutdown," *Los Angeles Times,* November 20, 1995, p. A6.

[98]John Broder and James Gerstenzang, "Accord Doesn't Signal the End of Budget Fight," *Los Angeles Times,* November 20, 1995, p. A6.

[99]Todd S. Purdum, "President and GOP Agree to End Federal Shutdown and Negotiate a Budget," *New York Times,* November 20, 1995, p. A1.

[100]David Wessel, "The Art of Tweaking: White House's Altered Forecast on Economy Underlies Capitol Hill Budget Deal," *Wall Street Journal,* November 3, 1995, p. A16.

[101]Felix Rohatyn, "The Budget: Whom Can You Believe," *New York Review of Books,* August 10, 1995, pp. 48–9. See also Robert Eisner, "The Deficit Is Budget Battle's Red Herring," *Wall Street Journal,* November 28, 1995, p. A13.

[102]Interview with Herbert Stein, *The News Hour with Jim Lehrer,* November 22, 1995.

Much then seemed to have been left unresolved. Nothing had been decided on the debt limit, which had come to be seen as symbolic by the far right.[103] The president still vowed to veto the reconciliation bill, and the outstanding appropriations bills were problematic. The president signed four more bills immediately after the agreement, despite disagreement with some of their contents. Meanwhile, the major conflict over the reconciliation bill assumed urgency.

RECONCILIATION AND INTRANSIGENCE

The reconciliation bill packaged together the work which had been carried out for months by the various committees of Congress to rewrite legislation on revenues and entitlements. (It also included a variety of measures which had been attached because this seemed a good way to get them passed, e.g., opening up the Arctic Wildlife Reserve to oil development.) The aim was to pass measures that would conform to the spending and savings limits set out in the reconciliation instructions attached to the congressional resolution. The resulting bill, over 1,700 pages long, was subject to only 20 hours of debate in each House, and required a single vote—yes or no. Separate versions were passed by House and Senate, reconciled in conference, and an agreed measure finally passed in each House, almost entirely along party lines. The president immediately stated he would veto it. Polarization seemed complete.

The reconciliation bill was seen as the key to budget balance. But the primary goal of budget balance was brought into question by the Republican insistence on a tax cut of $245 billion, which of course made the task much harder. Among other proposals, the tax cuts included child tax credits, reductions in the capital gains tax, reduction in the rate of corporate tax, and creation of new forms of Individual Retirement Accounts. They also included several allowances for post-secondary education, adoption, and elderly care, as well as several business-friendly tax concessions, such as continuation of ethanol subsidies,[104] windfall tax savings for thrift institutions,[105] and extension of the business research credit.[106] These tax cuts were offset by $33 billion in increased revenues from restricting the eligibility criteria for the Earned Income Tax Credit, which had reduced taxes for the working poor. *The Economist*, not usually noted for its charitable approach, characterized the tax measures as "unnecessary, badly targeted and over-favorable to the rich."[107]

---

[103]It was doubtful that it would be possible to continue to use the civil service retirement fund to enable the federal government to borrow the $160 billion it would need up to the November 1996 election, even though the fund held over $300 billion. It appeared that legally access was limited to the amount of one year retirement benefits in any one year. Alan Murray, "Debt Limit Crisis Is Not Over Yet," *Wall Street Journal*, November 27, 1995, p. A1.

[104]James Bovard, "Dole, Gingrich and the Big Ethanol Boondoggle," *Wall Street Journal*, November 2, 1995, p. A14.

[105]John R. Wilke, "Thrifts May Reap Windfall with Budget Bill Measure," *Wall Street Journal*, November 27, 1995, pp. A4, A6.

[106]Christina Duff, "Friendly Footwork in Congress Spells Special Tax Breaks for Some Businesses," *Wall Street Journal*, November 27, 1995, p. A5.

[107]"Right Size, Wrong Contents," *The Economist*, November 11, 1995, p. 16.

The other side of the equation was spending cuts. The reconciliation bill set out new caps which would reduce domestic discretionary expenditures to 30 percent below the baseline. But the major thrust was to reshape the entitlements. Much of the debate on specific issues in health and welfare entitlements has been covered in Chapter 8. At this point we examine the major divisions between the parties.

The scale of change in the entitlements programs was unprecedented. They encompassed over half a trillion dollars in cuts from medicare, medicaid, welfare, agricultural subsidies, and student loans, as well as smaller programs. The cut in medicare of $270 billion was well in excess of the $130 billion the administration estimated as sufficient to secure the viability of the trust funds, and the legislation involved substantial restructuring of the program. Whether these changes would actually produce the savings targeted was unclear, but if they did not, a "look back" clause would impose further cuts. Medicaid, cut by $163 billion, ceased to be an entitlement, and the federal commitment was replaced by lump sum grants to the states. The $82 billion cut in programs loosely grouped together as welfare also ended federal entitlement status, and involved reductions in cash welfare, food stamps, nutrition aid, and supplemental security income for the disabled. The proposal turned over the programs to the states and allowed them to deny cash benefits to unmarried mothers under 18 and those who had more children while on welfare. Agricultural subsidies were replaced by capped and shrinking payments to farmers, and other changes added up to $13 billion in savings. The student loan program was cut by an estimated $5 billion, and an entire program was eliminated.[108]

The reconciliation bill, on one reading, represented in the words of Martin Olav Sabo, a House Democrat from Minnesota, "two very different visions of America's future. I call on my colleagues to reject a vision of America that seeks to reward those who have already prospered in our economy while imposing burdens on those who have not." Added Representative John Dingell, the dean of the House, "This is one of the worst pieces of legislation I've seen in my 40 years in Congress."[109] Understandably, Republicans saw things differently.

The division between the sides was underscored by the choice of more stringent proposals over more moderate ones: larger cuts from food stamps ($37 billion instead of the Senate proposal for $28 billion); rejection of more lenient Senate work requirements for welfare and cut in child care provision; erasing Senate retention of elderly nursing home standards and commitment to aid all disabled poor under medicaid; deeper cuts in services to legal immigrants.[110]

For his part, the president had said, "I am not prepared to discuss the destruction of Medicare and Medicaid, the gutting of our commitment to education, the ravaging of our environment, or raising taxes on working people."[111] In re-

---

[108]*Wall Street Journal*, November 17, 1995, p. A4.

[109]Jackie Calmes and Christopher Georges, "Senate, House Close to Votes on Budget, Taxes," *Wall Street Journal*, October 27, 1995, p. A2.

[110]Christopher Georges, "Budget Bill Dismisses Moderates' Input," *Wall Street Journal*, November 20, 1995, p. A14.

[111]Hilary Stout, "Clinton, After His Veto, Will Have Tricky Job of Trying to Strike a Budget Deal on His Terms," *Wall Street Journal*, October 30, 1995, p. A20.

sponse to a request from the Republicans for specific proposals, at the end of November, the administration set out nine principles: high-quality medical care for
the elderly under medicare, adequate funding for medicaid, tax fairness, maintenance of real funding in education, sustain progress in environmental protection,
provide adequate resources to move people from welfare to work, preserve the
strength of America's farms, provide enough military spending to meet the nation's needs, and continue providing veterans with the benefits to which they are
entitled.[112]

UNFINISHED BUSINESS

Developments during the two and a half months between the end of the first shutdown of government in mid-November, and the passage of a continuing resolution
at the end of January to fund the government until mid-March both emphasized
the polarization of the dispute between the sides and the extent of agreement between them. The euphoria of the November agreement did not last long, as cracks
inevitably appeared in the papered over disagreements. The president's declared
agenda was to protect health, social, environmental, and education programs,
even within a balanced budget framework. The Republicans were determined to
ensure a balanced budget in the next seven years, to reverse the role of the federal
government, and to implement large tax cuts. The result was deadlock: a 19-day
federal government shutdown; congressional refusal to raise the debt limit; and
presidential vetoes of appropriations bills, the reconciliation bill, and a new welfare reform bill.

Neither side was to sustain its position completely. The president repeatedly
revised his figures. The Republicans discovered that closing the federal government, though within the grand tradition of refusing supply to an intransigent executive, extorted too high a political price, and revised their strategy to provide a
series of continuing resolutions for partial government funding. They also made
some concessions on tax reductions and expenditure cuts. Even the debt limit, the
apparent ultimate and invincible weapon to force budget choices on the executive,
might turn out to be the equivalent of a nuclear warhead whose fallout would destroy victor and vanquished alike.

The budget seemed to have evaporated into a few appropriations and piecemeal continuing resolutions. Neither side appeared to see electoral advantage in
agreement on a funding plan, at least for the coming year, although the main indicators were not so far apart. Both sides seemed to have lost. The Republicans, by
refusing to compromise, had failed to realize their dream of a balanced budget,
tax cuts, and determination of the course of budgetary policy for the next seven
years. The president, by acceding to demands for a balanced budget, large expenditure cuts, and tax reductions, had adopted much of the Republican program.
But the Republican loss was not the president's gain, since funding by continuing
resolution in fact meant funding well below existing levels. How did all this happen?

---

[112]*Los Angeles Times,* November 25, 1995, p. A25.

In early December 1995, budget talks collapsed and the president vetoed the reconciliation bill, providing a 50-page fact sheet on the reasons why. However, he did offer a new budget proposal, his third in 1995. This proposal balanced the budget in seven years and incorporated about $140 billion more savings than his previous plan in June 1995. About a quarter ($36 billion) came from recalculation of the Consumer Price Index, and almost as much from sale of assets, notably auction of space on the broadcasting spectrum. Medicare, medicaid, and tax reductions would be unchanged from the June proposal, but an additional $15 billion would be taken from welfare spending and a further $64 billion from unspecified cuts in domestic discretionary programs, about 5 percent below current levels or 20 percent from the baseline.

The Republicans rejected the plan and found further justification in the new CBO forecast a few days later. The CBO projected that there would be an additional $135 billion in deficit reduction over the next seven years, but that the president's latest proposal would result in a $115 billion deficit in 2002, and over the whole period savings would fall short by $350 billion. The Republicans reconfigured some of the major indicators of their budget, and talks resumed to try to avert a new federal government shutdown on December 15. Congress passed three appropriations bills (Interior; Veterans Affairs, Housing and Urban Development; and Commerce, Justice and State) which the president promptly vetoed. The budget talks collapsed; the Republicans contending that the president refused to present a new "good faith" plan to conform to CBO figures, and the president insisting he was being pressured to make unacceptable cuts in the health programs.

This time the federal shutdown lasted 19 days and involved furloughs of 260,000 to 280,000 federal employees, compared with 800,000 in November, since only six appropriations bills were now still in contention. Although many government services continued, such as issue of social security checks and medicare payments, protection of public health and safety, and the post office, the crisis was more severe. Within a week, Congress approved a stopgap law to fund temporary benefits for veterans and welfare recipients. But the effects of the shutdown were still noticeable as passports and visas were unobtainable, federally funded unemployment offices closed, tourists found national parks, museums, and monuments closed, and funds for programs as diverse as Head Start, FEMA, medicaid, courts, and services to the elderly began to run out. Regulatory functions relating to immigrants, the environment and health were impeded. As federal employees went unpaid, the ripple effects spread, and public opinion grew more adverse to the Republicans and more favorable to the president.

The stakes for both sides were high, and each blamed the other for the shutdown. The continued popularity of the seven-year balanced budget was attested by a largely symbolic vote in the House of Representatives (December 19), won by 351 votes to 40, with 133 Democrats voting for it. But neither side seemed prepared to budge on what it saw as advantage. In addition to vetoing the three appropriations bills, the president vetoed the defense authorization bill, and when the House passed a welfare reform bill, he said he would veto that also. Various plans to end the shutdown were blocked by Republicans who believed that, in Speaker Gingrich's words, "giving up on balancing the budget would be a tragedy

Table 12.4   KEY FEATURES OF BUDGET PROPOSALS

| | January 10, 1996 | |
	President's proposal	Republican proposal
Medicare savings	125	168
Medicaid savings	59	85
Welfare and Earned Income Tax Credit Cut	53	75
Tax reductions	87	177
Cuts in domestic discretionary programs	295	349

Source: Los Angeles Times, January 19, 1996, p. A4.

that would haunt us for the rest of our lives."[113] Even though the leadership might be willing to compromise, many of the rank and file saw the budget fight as the moral equivalent of war, and believed they could win if only they stood firm.

By the beginning of January 1996, it seemed clear that the Republican strategy to shut down government to force the president's hand had failed. It only made them appear extreme and willing to use over quarter of a million federal employees as pawns. The tactic to use the debt ceiling as leverage had also been foiled by Treasury Secretary Rubin's tactics, and although the position would be dire by the beginning of March if nothing were done, blame for the consequences of a federal default was a daunting prospect.

The Republican leadership, therefore, changed course. The House, which had earlier rejected a short-term continuing resolution passed by the Senate, now acceded to leadership proposals for a new strategy of selective funding. The president, after initial hesitation, agreed to a continuing resolution to fund the government until January 26, 1996, on condition he submit a new balanced budget proposal using congressional figures. Congress also passed a "targeted appropriation," restoring funds for the rest of the fiscal year for 17 high-profile agencies, including law enforcement, medicare, medicaid, National Institutes for Health, Centers for Disease Control, black lung benefits, and some Native American programs. This strategy allowed Congress to pick and choose and, in effect, make policy through continuing resolution. Thus they fully funded a deaf school in Washington but not Head Start; federal mortgages for single-family homes but not housing subsidies for the poor; meals on wheels but not elderly transportation programs.

Meanwhile, the two sides had actually moved closer together. On January 7, the president endorsed a Senate Democratic plan, which would achieve a total of $605 billion in savings by 2002, and which was certified as resulting in a balanced budget by CBO. But although the dollar amounts were closer, neither side wanted to appear to have given in. (See Table 12.4.) Negotiations broke off on January 9, 1996, and only briefly resumed on January 17. The outlook for an agreement appeared bleak.

---

[113]Los Angeles Times, December 19, 1995, p. A16.

A week later, agreement was reached on another continuing resolution to fund the government until mid-March of 1996. A few concessions were made by each side. Democrats accepted program cuts in education, abolition of the Office of Technical Assistance and Bureau of Mines, and Republicans modified some abortion restrictions and returned funding to the president's national service and police initiatives. Other measures included in the bill were a ban on embryo research, limits on programs for international population control, and prohibition of "excessive" travel by Cabinet secretaries! Congress and the president also agreed on the terms of the previously vetoed defense authorization bill, which had shed its move to create an antimissile defense, but retained abortion restrictions.

The continuing resolution was labeled the Balanced Budget Downpayment Act. It was accompanied by a Republican offer to end formal budget talks with the president and instead enact those spending and tax cuts already agreed to as an amendment to a measure to raise the debt limit. The offer represented a truce in the budget battle, but would enact only a minuscule portion of the deficit reductions envisaged in the original Republican program. But it would solve the debt limit problem, avoid any further government closure, and enable both sides to devote their energies to the 1996 election campaign. At the time of writing, its fate is unknown. Republican freshmen, with little to see for their efforts, still vow to pursue their program, and a bipartisan group is still exploring the possibility of agreement.

Yet, it would be misleading to regard the budget battles of 1995 as totally without effect. While the radical Republicans did not gain their professed goals (at least so far), they changed the terms of the debate. While the president may have gained the central ground, this is not the same center as it was a year ago. Much of the Republican agenda—cuts in entitlement and domestic discretionary programs and tax reductions—was adopted by the president, and even those issues which remain contentious, such as welfare reform or the environment, are being debated in a different way. In his State of the Union address, the president's statement that the era of big government was over, qualified though it was, signaled a change in assumptions and a shift in the central ground.

In a more concrete way also, Republicans gained advantage. They were able to use the continuing resolutions to restrain federal spending and make policy. The first continuing resolution (September 30 to November 13) set spending at the average level of House and Senate appropriations bills where they had both acted, and at the lower of either house's level or the previous year's spending, whichever was lower. Where neither house had acted, spending would be at 90 percent of the previous year's level. The later continuing resolutions (November 19–20 to December 15; January 5 to January 26; and January 26 to March 15) set similar levels: except where an item in the Clinton budget had been refused funding by Congress, spending would be set at 75 percent of the previous year's funding. The last continuing resolution also funded certain programs for the remainder of the fiscal year, and had the effect of funding the three appropriations bills vetoed by the president at the level Congress had set.[114] On the other hand,

---

[114]Louis Fisher, "Government by Continuing Resolution: Smaller Is Inevitable," *Los Angeles Times,* January 28, 1996, p. E3.

unless some agreement were reached on the reconciliation bill, no tax or entitlement changes would take place. At the time of writing, there was still great uncertainty regarding the need for a further continuing resolution and action on the debt limit.

The year 1995 was extraordinary in its dramatic departures from previous budget practice. It reflected not only the immediate political situation, but a more general crisis and response, also evident in other industrialized countries. In Europe, the requirements of the Maastricht Treaty creating a European Monetary Union demanded a reduction of national government deficits to 3 percent of GDP and government debt to 60 percent of GDP, goals clearly unrealizable in many countries. To meet them, it would be necessary to modify or even dismantle the welfare state. The prolonged and serious strike in France at the end of 1995 indicated public reaction to measures to slash public expenditures and retract pension and health benefits. Moreover, demands to cut the role of government were being made in the face of high unemployment, growing crime, large-scale immigration, environmental degradation, and the diffuse impacts of the difficulties of the "transitional economies" of Russia and Eastern Europe.

Beyond the pressing current issues lay compelling demographic trends. In several countries, it was estimated that persons over 65 would constitute over one quarter of the population early in the twenty-first century. At issue was the sustaining of the health and pension benefits of the elderly, while maintaining and improving the standard of living (through private and collection provisions) of the working population and their children. The politics of radical reversal was pitting old against young in a zero sum game.

In the United States, the budget battles of 1995 framed these issues in terms of individualism and reliance on the market against government intervention in the general interest and coping with social problems. But, as we have seen, the lines were not clear cut. Other disputes centered on the division between rich and poor, on business advantage through public largesse, on arguments about moral rectitude and standards of behavior, as well as the conflict between children and the elderly.

How did the budget process cope with these conflicts? Perhaps the process really did work the way it was intended. The fragmentation of congressional procedures and sharing of power between executive and legislature prevented any single group from forcing through a highly contentious and far-reaching program, and required compromise to maintain the working of the system. The budget process reflected the pluralist nature of American politics in which issues splintered along a series of fault lines, rather than a single ideological front. The Republicans overreached themselves, and by attempting too much they ended with no budget at all.

From a different perspective, the budget process was an impediment to the legitimate realization of the will of the majority, which reflected the desires of the American people. The Republican leadership (particularly the Speaker of the House) coordinated and streamlined a coherent program and shepherded it through Congress in an unprecedented display of power and persuasion. In a parliamentary system, where the executive is drawn from and dependent on a legislative majority, its policies would have become law. But the existence of an independent executive forced the congressional majority into confrontation, a confrontation they were unable to win through crude tactics of refusal of supply.

In fact, the American system of shared powers deals uneasily with absolute, unshakable positions. Either side may insist on its prerogative and maintain its cause is so right that it can in no way be modified. Congress may legitimately hold government hostage, preventing it from expending funds or borrowing, as a weapon in the holy war for a balanced budget, tax cuts, and radical change. The president may legitimately veto appropriations bills. But the price of obstinacy is often deadlock, with political consequences that may be unsustainable.

To pretend that this is the way the federal budget process should work is a mockery. In 1995, illusion and reality became so confused that public pronouncements required deconstruction to make any sense at all. The illusion—a balanced budget within a certain number of years based on competing figures which might or might not turn out correct—drove the reality—cuts in discretionary and mandatory spending which would have serious repercussions for large numbers of individuals.

Institutions, too, have suffered. Instead of one president's budget, we had at least four. Appropriations bills were delayed beyond any reasonable period after the beginning of the fiscal year. Continuing resolutions were used to sidestep the budget and force policy, both on levels of funding and substantive issues. Reconciliation was used to include highly controversial policy changes with extremely curtailed debate. The use of the debt limit as leverage, on the one hand, and tactics to evade it, on the other, are simply not a sensible way to conduct government. Government shutdowns were costly, inconvenienced citizens, and hurt public servants' morale. The Congressional Budget Office, a respected source of objective information, was treated as a political football. Duress substituted for reasoned argument as an apparently acceptable way of determining budget policy.

What if there were no budget at all for FY 1996? Would it matter? Was 1995 an aberration, the result of a particular set of circumstances? Will voters in the 1996 presidential and congressional elections reject the Republican radicals? Or have the budget conflicts of this year changed the terms of discourse permanently? Do they reflect a change in the central assumptions governing political life? Or is this year just the beginning of a prolonged period of turbulence reflecting deeper societal tensions? Can the budget process still provide a meaningful framework for determining policies and priorities? As always, more questions than answers.

Glossary*

appropriated entitlements Budget authority provided in annual appropriations, although payment must be made to all eligible people who apply. Examples of appropriated entitlements are medicaid, Supplemental Security Income, Aid to Families with Dependent Children, and veterans compensation.

appropriation An act of Congress that permits federal agencies to incur obligations and to make payments out of the Treasury for specified purposes. Appropriations are one form of budget authority.

appropriation act A statute that provides funds for federal programs. An appropriation act generally follows enactment of authorizing legislation unless the authorizing legislation itself provides the budget authority.

authorization (authorizing legislation) Substantive legislation enacted by Congress that sets up or continues legal operation of a federal program or agency either indefinitely or for a specific period of time or sanctions a particular type of obligation or expenditure within a program. Authorizing legislation is usually a prerequisite for subsequent appropriations or other kinds of budget authority to be contained in appropriation acts. Such legislation may limit the amount of budget authority to be provided subsequently or may authorize the appropriation of "such sums as may be necessary." Budget authority may be provided in the authorization (see Backdoor authority) which eliminates the need for subsequent appropriations or requires only an appropriation to liquidate contract authority or reduce outstanding debt.

backdoor authority Budget authority provided in legislation outside the appropriations process. The most common forms of backdoor authority are authority to borrow (borrowing authority), contract authority, and entitlements. In some cases (e.g., interest on the public debt), a permanent appropriation is provided that becomes available without current actions by the Congress.

backdoor spending Authority of federal agencies to spend money through the Treasury rather than going through the appropriations process.

borrowing authority Statutory authority (substantive or appropriation) that permits a federal agency to incur obligations and to make payments for specified purposes out of borrowed monies. Section 401 of the Congressional Budget Act of 1974 limits new borrowing authority (except for certain instances) to such extent or in such amounts as are provided in appropriation acts.

budget amendment A formal request submitted to the Congress by the president, after his formal budget transmittal but prior to completion of appropriation action by the Congress, that revises previous requests, such as the amount of budget authority.

budget authority Authority provided by law to enter into obligations that will result in immediate or future outlays involving federal government funds. Budget authority

---

*Most of the definitions of these terms are taken verbatim or adapted from *A Glossary of Terms Used in the Federal Budget Process and Related Accounting, Economic, and Tax Terms,* U.S. General Accounting Office, March 1981, 3rd ed., PAD-81-27. Terms of more recent origin have been defined by Dean Hammer.

does not include authority to insure or guarantee the repayment of indebtedness incurred by another person or government. The basic forms of budget authority are appropriations, authority to borrow, and contract authority. Budget authority may be classified by the period of availability (one-year, multiyear, no-year), by the timing of congressional action (current or permanent), or by the manner of determining the amount available (definite or indefinite).

capital budget A divided budget with investment in capital assets excluded from calculation of the budget surplus or deficit. A capital budget provides for separating financing of capital or investment expenditures from current or operating expenditures.

concurrent resolution on the budget Under the Congressional Budget Act of 1974, a resolution passed by both houses of Congress, but not requiring the signature of the president, which sets forth, reaffirms, or revises the congressional budget for the United States government for a fiscal year. There were two such resolutions required preceding each fiscal year. The first required concurrent resolution, due by May 15, established the congressional budget. The second required concurrent resolution, due by September 15, reaffirmed or revised it. Other concurrent resolutions for a fiscal year could be adopted at any time following the first required concurrent resolution for that fiscal year.

The Balanced Budget Act of 1985 revised this process. Only one annual budget resolution is required, with action by both houses scheduled to be completed by April 15. The resolution now contains figures for the five succeeding fiscal years.

continuing resolution Legislation enacted by the Congress to provide budget authority for specific ongoing activities in cases where the regular fiscal year appropriations for such activities have not been enacted by the beginning of the fiscal year. The continuing resolution usually specifies a maximum rate at which the agency may incur obligations, based on the rate of the prior year, the president's budget request, or an appropriation bill passed by either or both houses of the Congress.

contract authority A form of budget authority under which contracts or other obligations may be entered into in advance of an appropriation or in excess of amounts otherwise available in a revolving fund. Contract authority must be funded by a subsequent appropriation or the use of revolving fund collections to liquidate the obligations. Appropriations to liquidate contract authority are not classified as budget authority since they are not available for obligation. Section 401 of the Congressional Budget Act of 1974 limits new contract authority, with few exceptions, to such extent or in such amounts as are provided in appropriation acts.

current policy budget Projections of the estimated budget authority and outlays for the upcoming fiscal year to operate federal programs at the level implied by enacted appropriations and authorizations of the current fiscal year without policy changes, but adjusted for inflation, changes in the numbers and kinds of beneficiaries, and in some instances to reflect the continuation of certain programs scheduled to terminate.

current services estimates Estimated budget authority and outlays for the upcoming fiscal year based on continuation of existing levels of service, that is, assuming that all programs and activities will be carried on at the same level as in the fiscal year in progress and without policy changes in such programs and activities. These estimates of budget authority and outlays, accompanied by the underlying economic and programmatic assumptions on which they are based (such as the rate of inflation, the rate of real economic growth, the unemployment rate, program caseloads, and pay increases), are transmitted by the president to the Congress when the budget is submitted.

deferral of budget authority Any action or inaction by an officer or employee of the United States government that temporarily withholds, delays, or effectively precludes the obligation or expenditure of budget authority, including authority to obligate by contract in advance of appropriations as specifically authorized by law and including the establishment of reserves under the Antideficiency Act as amended by the Impoundment Control Act. The president must provide a special message to Congress reporting a proposed deferral of budget authority. Deferrals may not extend beyond the end of the fiscal year in which the message reporting the deferral is transmitted. Deferrals can be overturned only by Congress passing a law, which the president must sign.

entitlements Legislation that requires the payment of benefits to any person or unit of government that meets the eligibility requirements established by such law. Authorizations for entitlements constitute a binding obligation on the part of the federal government, and eligible recipients have legal recourse if the obligation is not fulfilled.

expenditures See OUTLAYS.

fazio rule House procedure whereby appropriation subcommittees cannot be subject to points of order under Section 602(a) for total spending if their spending proposals are within their allocations for discretionary (not mandatory) budget authority from the Appropriations Committee's 602(b) process.

fiscal policy Federal government policies with respect to taxes, spending, and debt management, intended to promote the nation's macro-economic goals, particularly with respect to employment, gross national product, price level stability, and equilibrium in balance of payments. The budget process is a major vehicle for determining and implementing federal fiscal policy. The other major component of federal economic policy is monetary policy.

fiscal year Any yearly accounting period, without regard to its relationship to a calendar year. The fiscal year for the federal government begins on October 1 and ends on September 30. The fiscal year is designated by the calendar year in which it ends (e.g., fiscal year 1992 is the fiscal year ending September 30, 1992).

impoundment Any action or inaction by an officer or employee of the U.S. government that precludes the obligation or expenditure of budget authority provided by Congress. Two kinds of impoundment are rescission and deferral.

loan guarantee A loan guarantee is an agreement by which the government pledges to pay part or all of the loan principal and interest to a lender or holder of a security, in the event of default by a third-party borrower. The subsidy costs of new loan guarantees are now counted in the budget.

multiyear budgeting A budget planning process designed to make sure that the long-range consequences of budget decisions are identified and reflected in the budget totals.

obligational authority The sum of budget authority provided for a given fiscal year, balance of amounts brought forward from prior years that remain available for obligation, and amounts authorized to be credited to a specific fund or account during that year, including transfers between funds or accounts.

off-budget outlays Outlays of off-budget federal entities whose transactions have been excluded from the budget totals under provisions of law, even though these outlays are part of total government spending.

offsets Requirement that an appropriation subcommittee's spending that exceeds the amount allocated to it by the Budget Resolution under Section 602(b) be matched by a reduction in other outlays and/or an increase in revenues equivalent to the amount of spending being added. Offsets may also apply to making up decreases in revenue proposed in tax legislation.

offsetting receipts All collections deposited into receipt accounts that are offset against budget authority and outlays rather than reflected as budget receipts in computing budget totals. Under current budgetary usage, cash collections not deposited into receipt accounts (such as revolving fund receipts and reimbursements) are deducted from outlays at the account level. These transactions are offsetting collections but are not classified as "offsetting receipts."

outlays The amount of checks issued, interest accrued on most public debt, or other payments, net of refunds and reimbursements. Total budget outlays consist of the sum of the outlays from appropriations and funds included in the unified budget, less offsetting receipts. The outlays of off-budget federal entities are excluded from the unified budget under provisions of law, even though these outlays are part of total government spending.

paygo A process for keeping expenditures within major elements of the budget by requiring that additions to outlays above amounts set by budget resolutions or in law be made up by new sources of revenue or by reductions elsewhere within (and only within) that category. See also OFFSETS.

permanent appropriations Authority to spend provided in authorizing legislation without the need for subsequent annual appropriations. Examples include medicare, social security, and interest on the public debt.

planning program budgeting system (PPBS) A budgetary process that initially sets out goals (the planning phase), develops and approves programs for reaching these objectives (the programming phase), and prices and allocates inputs required for reaching these objectives (the budgetary phase).

president's budget A proposed budget for a particular fiscal year transmitted to the Congress by the president in accordance with the Budget and Accounting Act of 1921, as amended.

reconciliation process A process used by Congress to reconcile amounts determined by tax, spending, and debt legislation for a given fiscal year with the ceilings enacted in the required concurrent resolution on the budget for that year. Section 310 of the Congressional Budget Act of 1974 as amended provides that the required concurrent resolution on the budget, which sets binding totals for the budget, may direct committees to determine and recommend changes to laws, bills, and resolutions, as required to conform with the binding totals for budget authority, revenues, and the public debt. Such changes are incorporated into either a reconciliation resolution or a reconciliation bill.

reprogramming Utilization of funds in an appropriation account for purposes other than those contemplated at the time of the appropriation. Reprogramming is generally preceded by consultation between federal agencies and the appropriate congressional committees. It involves formal notification and, in some instances, opportunity for disapproval by congressional committees.

rescission A bill or joint resolution that cancels, in whole or in part, budget authority previously granted by Congress. Rescissions proposed by the president must be transmitted in a special message to Congress. Under Section 1012 of the Congressional Budget and Impoundment Control Act of 1974, unless both houses of Congress complete action on a rescission bill within 45 days of continuous session after receipt of the proposal, the budget authority must be made available for obligation.

sequestration Under the Balanced Budget Act of 1985, the withholding of budget authority, according to an established formula, up to the amount required to be cut to meet the deficit target.

supplemental appropriation An act appropriating funds in addition to those in an annual appropriation act. Supplemental appropriations provide additional budget authority beyond original estimates for programs or activities (including new programs authorized after the date of the original appropriation act).

transfer of funds When specifically authorized in law, all or part of the budget authority in one account may be transferred to another account.

trust fund Funds collected and used by the federal government for carrying out specific purposes and programs according to terms of a trust agreement or statute, such as the social security trust fund.

unified budget The current form of the budget of the federal government (beginning with the 1969 budget) in which receipts and outlays from federal funds and trust funds are consolidated. When these fund groups are consolidated to display budget totals, transactions that are outlays of one fund group for payment to the other fund group (i.e., interfund transactions) are deducted to avoid double-counting. Transactions of off-budget federal entities are not included in the unified budget.

zero-base budgeting Zero-base budgeting for analysis of alternative methods of operation at various levels of effort, including the possibility that the activity in question will not be funded at all.

Guide To Acronyms

AFDC	Aid to Families with Dependent Children	**HBC**	House Budget Committee
BEA	Budget Enforcement Act of 1990 (Title XIII)	**JCS**	Joint Chiefs of Staff
		JSPD	Joint Services Planning Document
BOB	Bureau of the Budget	**LIHEAP**	Low-Income Home Energy Assistance Program
CBO	Congressional Budget Office		
CCC	Commodity Credit Corporation	**MDA**	maximum deficit amount
CEA	Council of Economic Advisers	**NASA**	National Aeronautics and Space Administration
CETA	Comprehensive Employee Training Administration		
		NEC	National Economic Commission
COLAs	cost-of-living adjustments	**OBRA**	Omnibus Budget Reconciliation Act of 1990
CR	continuing resolution		
CRS	Congressional Research Service	**OECD**	Organization for Economic Co-Operation and Development
DOD	Department of Defense		
DRB	Defense Resources Board	**OMB**	Office of Management and Budget
E&E	Emergency and Extraordinary		
EOP	Executive Office of the President	**OSD**	Office of the Secretary of Defense
EPA	Environmental Protection Agency	**OSHA**	Occupational Health and Safety Administration
FAA	Federal Aviation Administration	**PDMs**	program decision memoranda
FFB	Federal Financing Bank	**POMs**	program objective memoranda
GAO	Government Accounting Office	**PPB**	planning, programming, and budgeting
GATT	General Agreement on Tariffs and Trade		
		RFC	Reconstruction Finance Corporation
GNP	gross national product		
GRH	Gramm–Rudman–Hollings Deficit Reduction Act	**RIF**	reduction in force
		SBC	Senate Budget Committee
GSEs	government-sponsored enterprises	**WIC**	Women, Infants, and Children
		ZBB	zero-base budgeting

Bibliography

Adams, Gordon. *The Politics of Defense Contracting: The Iron Triangle.* New Brunswick, N.J.: Transaction Press, 1982.

Art, Robert J. "Congress and the Defense Budget: Enhancing Policy Oversight." *Political Science Quarterly,* Vol. 100, No. 2 (Summer 1985), pp. 227–48.

Asbell, Bernard. *The Senate Nobody Knows.* Garden City, N.Y.: Doubleday, 1978.

Aspin, Les. "Congress vs. Department of Defense." In Thomas M. Franck, ed. *The Tethered Presidency.* New York: New York University, 1981.

Berman, Larry. *The Office of Management and Budget and the Presidency.* Princeton, N.J.: Princeton University Press, 1979.

Bickley, James M. "The Federal Financing Bank: Assessments of Its Effectiveness and Budgetary Status." *Public Budgeting and Finance,* Vol. 5, No. 4 (Winter 1985), pp. 51–63.

Birnbaum, Jeffrey H., and Alan S. Murray. *Showdown at Gucci Gulch: Lawmakers, Lobbyists, and the Unlikely Triumph of Tax Reform.* New York: Random House, 1987.

Bolles, Albert S. A *Financial History of the United States, 1774–89.* New York: Appleton, 1879.

———. *The Financial History of the United States from 1861 to 1885.* New York: Appleton, 1886.

Borcherding, Thomas, "A Hundred Years of Public Spending, 1870–1970." In Thomas Borcherding, ed. *Budgets and Bureaucrats: The Sources of Government Growth.* Durham, N.C.: Duke University Press, 1977.

Borg, Sten G., and Francis G. Castles. "The Influence of the Political Right on Public Income Maintenance Expenditure and Equality." *Political Studies,* Vol. XXIX (December 1981), pp. 604–21.

Bovbjerg, Randall R., and John Holahan. *Medicaid in the Reagan Era: Federal Policy and State Choices.* Washington, D.C.: Urban Institute, 1982.

Bramlett, Robert W. "The Federal Accounting Standards Advisory Board." *Public Budgeting and Finance,* Vol. 11 (Winter 1991), pp. 11–19.

Braybrooke, David, and Charles E. Lindblom. *A Strategy of Decision.* New York: Free Press, 1963.

Bruner, Jerome S., Jacqueline J. Goodnow, and George A. Austin. *A Study of Thinking.* New York: Wiley, 1956.

Buchanan, James M., and Richard E. Wagner. *Democracy in Deficit: The Political Legacy of Keynes.* New York: Academic Press, 1977.

———. *Fiscal Responsibility in Constitutional Democracy.* Leiden and Boston: Martinus Nijhoff Social Sciences Division, 1978.

Buck, A. E. "The Development of the Budget Idea in the United States." *Annals of the American Academy of Political and Social Science,* Vol. LXIII (May 1924).

———. *Public Budgeting.* New York: Harper, 1929.

345

Bullock, Charles. "The Finances of the United States from 1775–1789 with Special Reference to the Budget." In Frederick Turner, ed. *Bulletin of the University of Wisconsin, Vol. 1, 1894–1896.* Madison: University of Wisconsin Press, 1897.

Burkhead, Jesse. *Government Budgeting.* New York: Wiley, 1956.

Caiden, Naomi. "After the Earthquake: The President's Budget for FY 1996." *Public Budgeting and Finance,* Vol. 15 (Summer 1995), pp. 3–17.

———. "The Myth of the Annual Budget." *Public Administration Review,* Vol. 42 (November/December 1982), pp. 516–23.

———. "The Politics of Subtraction." In Allen Schick, ed. *Making Economic Policy in Congress.* Washington, D.C.: American Enterprise Institute, 1984, pp. 100–103.

———. "The New Rules of the Federal Budget Game." *Public Administration Review,* March–April 1984, pp. 109–117.

———. "Paradox, Ambiguity and Enigma: The Strange Case of the Executive Budget and the United States Constitution." *Public Administration Review,* Vol. 47 (January–February 1987), pp. 84–92.

Caiden, Naomi, and Joseph White, eds. *Budgeting, Policy, Politics: An Appreciation of Aaron Wildavsky.* New Brunswick, N.J.: Transaction Publishers, 1995.

Caiden, Naomi, and Aaron Wildavsky. *Planning and Budgeting in Poor Countries.* New York: Wiley, 1974. Paperback edition by Transaction, Inc., New Brunswick, N.J., 1980.

Christensen, Jorgen Gronnegard. "Growth by Exception: Or the Vain Attempt to Impose Resource Scarcity on the Danish Public Sector." *Journal of Public Policy,* Vol. 2 (May 1982).

Cleveland, Frederick A. "Leadership and Criticism." *Proceedings of the Academy of Political Science,* Vol. 8 (1918–20).

Cleveland, Frederick A., and Arthur E. Buck. *The Budget and Responsible Government.* New York: Macmillan, 1920.

Cogan, John F. *The Budget Puzzle: Understanding Federal Spending.* Stanford, Ca.: Stanford University Press, 1994.

Collender, Stanley E. *The Guide to the Federal Budget: Fiscal 1987.* Washington, D.C.: The Urban Institute Press, 1986.

———. "A Primer on the New Budget Process" and "Political Winners and Losers Under GRH Number 3." *Federal Budget Report,* Vol. 9, No. 23 (November 12, 1990), pp. 1–12.

Cuny, Thomas J. "Federal Credit Reform." *Public Budgeting and Finance,* Vol. 11 (Summer 1991), pp. 19–32.

———. "The Pending Revolution in Federal Accounting Standards." *Public Budgeting and Finance,* Vol. 15 (Fall 1995), pp. 22–34.

Davis, Otto A., M. A. H. Dempster, and Aaron Wildavsky. "On the Process of Budgeting II: An Empirical Study of Congressional Appropriations." In R. F. Byrne, A. Charnes, W. W. Cooper, A. A. Davis, and Dorthy Gilford, eds. *Studies in Budgeting.* Amsterdam: North Holland, 1971, pp. 292–375.

———. "Toward a Predictive Theory of the Federal Budgetary Process." *The British Journal of Political Science,* Vol. 4, Part 4 (October 1974), pp. 419–52.

Dawes, Charles G. *The First Year of the Budget of the United States.* New York: Harper, 1923.

Dempster, M. A. H., and Aaron Wildavsky. "On Change: Or, There Is No Magic Size for an Increment." *Political Studies,* Vol. XXVII (September 1979), pp. 371–89.

Derickson, Alan. "The Origins of the Black Lung Insurgency." *Journal of Public Health Policy,* Vol. 4, No. 1 (March 1983).

Derthick, Martha. *Uncontrollable Spending for Social Services Grants.* Washington, D.C.: The Brookings Institution, 1975.

———. *Policymaking for Social Security.* Washington, D.C.: The Brookings Institution, 1979.

Dobell, Rod. "Pressing the Envelope: The Significance of the New, Top-Down System of Expenditure Management in Ottawa." *Public Options,* November/December 1981, pp. 13–18.

Dorfman, Joseph. *The Economic Mind in American Civilization 1918–1933.* New York: Viking Press, 1959.

Downs, Anthony. "Why the Government Is Too Small in a Democracy." *World Politics,* Vol. XII (July 1960), pp. 541–63.

Eisner, Robert. *How Real Is the Federal Deficit?* New York: Free Press, 1986.

Doyle, Richard, and Jerry L. McCaffery. "The Budget Enforcement Act in 1992: Necessary But Not Sufficient." *Public Budgeting and Finance,* Vol. 13 (Summer 1993), pp. 20–37.

Ellwood, John W., ed. *Reductions in U.S. Domestic Spending: How They Affect State and Local Governments.* New Brunswick, N.J.: Transaction Books, 1982.

———. "The Great Exception: The Congressional Budget Process in an Age of Decentralization." In Lawrence Dodd and Bruce Oppenheimer, eds. *Congress Reconsidered,* 3rd ed. Washington, D.C.: CQ Press, 1985.

Ellwood, John W., and James A. Thurber. "The New Congressional Budget Process: The Hows and Whys of House-Senate Differences." In Lawrence Dodd and Bruce Oppenheimer, eds. *Congress Reconsidered.* New York: Praeger, 1977, pp. 163–92.

Enthoven, Alain C., and Wayne K. Smith. *How Much Is Enough?* New York: Harper & Row, 1971.

Feldman, Paul, and James Jandrow. "Congressional Elections and Local Federal Spending." *American Journal of Political Science,* Vol. 28, No. 1 (February 1984), pp. 147–64.

Fenno, Richard F., Jr. "The House Appropriations Committee as a Political System: The Problem of Integration." *The American Political Science Review,* Vol. 56 (June 1962), pp. 310–24.

———. *The Power of the Purse: Appropriations Politics in Congress.* Boston: Little, Brown, 1966.

Ferejohn, John A. "Logrolling in an Institutional Context: A Case Study of Food Stamps Legislation." Working Papers in Political Science, P-5-85. Palo Alto, Calif.: Hoover Institute, 1985.

Fiorina, Morris. *Congress—Keystone of the Washington Establishment.* New Haven, Conn.: Yale University Press, 1977.

Fisher, Louis. *President and Congress.* New York: Free Press, 1972.

———. *Presidential Spending Power.* Princeton: Princeton University Press, 1975.

———. "The Authorization-Appropriation Process in Congress: Formal Rules and Informal Practices." *Catholic University Law Review,* Vol. 29, No. 5 (1979), pp. 52–105.

———. "In Dubious Battle? Congress and the Budget." *The Brookings Bulletin,* Vol. 17 (Spring 1981), pp. 6–10.

———. "The Budget Act of 1974: A Further Loss of Spending Control." In Thomas Wander et al., eds. *Congressional Budgeting.* Baltimore: Johns Hopkins University Press, 1984, pp. 170–89.

———. *Constitutional Conflicts Between Congress and the President.* Princeton: Princeton University Press, 1985.

Fisher, Louis, and Neal Devins. "How Successfully Can the States' Item Veto Be Transferred to the President?" *Georgetown Law Journal,* Vol. 75, No. 1 (October 1986), pp. 159–97.

Fitzpatrick, Edward Augustus. *Budget Making in a Democracy.* New York: Macmillan, 1918.

Forsythe, Dall W. *Taxation and Political Change in the Young Nation 1781–1833.* New York: Columbia University Press, 1977.

Fox, Ronald J. *Arming America: How the U.S. Buys Weapons.* Cambridge: Harvard University Press, 1974.

———. "Revamping the Business of National Defense." *Harvard Business Review,* Vol. 62, No. 5 (September/Octover 1985).

Gansler, Jacques S. "How to Improve the Acquisition of Weapons." In Robert J. Art et al., eds. *Reorganizing America's Defense.* Washington, D.C.: Pergamon Brassey, 1985.

Gilmour, Robert. "Central Legislative Clearance: A Revised Perspective." *Public Administration Review,* Vol. XXXI (March/April 1971), pp. 150–58.

Greenberg, D. "Renal Politics." *New England Journal of Medicine,* Vol. 298, No. 25 (June 22, 1978).

Greenfield, Margaret. *Medicare and Medicaid: The 1965 and 1967 Social Security Amendments.* Westport, Conn.: Greenwood, 1968.

Greenstein Robert, and Paul Leonard. *A New Direction: The Clinton Budget and Economic Spending Plan.* Washington, D.C.: Center on Budget and Policy Priorities, 1993.

Greider, William. "The Education of David Stockman." *The Atlantic Monthly,* December 1981, pp. 27–54.

Guess, George, and Kenneth Koford. "Inflation, Recession and the Federal Budget Deficit (or, Blaming Economic Problems on a Statistical Mirage)." *Policy Sciences,* Vol. 17 (1984), pp. 385–402.

Haas, Lawrence J. "New Rules of the Game." *National Journal,* November 17, 1990, pp. 2793–97.

Hammond, Thomas H., and Jack H. Knott. *A Zero-Based Look at Zero-Base Budgeting.* New Brunswick, N.J.: Transaction, 1979.

Hardin, Clifford M., and Arthur T. Denzau. "Closing the Back Door on Federal Spending: Better Management of Federal Credit." Formal Publication #64, September 1984, Center for the Study of American Business, Washington University, St. Louis, Missouri.

Harper, Edwin L., Fred A. Kramer, and Andrew M. Rouse. "Implementation and the Use of PPB in Sixteen Federal Agencies." *Public Administration Review,* Vol. XXIX (November/December 1969).

Harrington, Michael. "Building Arms Control into the National Security Process." *Arms Control Today,* February 1975.

Hartman, Robert W. "Multiyear Budget Planning." In Joseph A. Pechman, ed. *Setting National Priorities: The 1979 Budget.* Washington, D.C.: The Brookings Institution, 1978.

———. "Congress and Budget-Making," *Political Science Quarterly,* Vol. 97, No. 3 (Fall 1982), pp. 381–402.

———. "Making Budget Decisions." In Joseph A. Pechman, ed. *Setting National Priorities: The 1983 Budget.* Washington D.C.: The Brookings Institution, 1982.

———. "Budget Summit 1990: The Role of Economic and Budget Analysis." Paper prepared for the Association for Public Policy Analysis and Management Conference, October 18–20, 1990.

Heclo, Hugh. "Executive Budget Making." In Gregory B. Mills and John L. Palmer, eds. *Federal Budget Policy in the 1980s.* Washington D.C.: The Urban Institute, 1984.

Heclo, Hugh, and Aaron Wildavsky. *The Private Government of Public Money: Community and Policy inside British Political Administration,* 2nd ed. London: Macmillan, 1981.

Hibbs, Douglas A., Jr., and Christopher Dennis. "The Politics and Economics of Income Distribution Outcomes in the Postwar United States." Transcript, 1986.

Hitch, Charles. *Decision-Making for Defense.* Berkeley: University of California Press, 1970.

Huntington, Samuel P. *The Common Defense.* New York: Columbia University Press, 1961.

Hush, Lawrence W. "The Federal, and the State and Local Roles in Government Expenditures." *Public Budgeting and Finance,* Vol. 13 (Summer 1993), pp. 38–55.

Iglehart, J. K. "Funding the End-Stage Renal Disease Program." *The New England Journal of Medicine,* Vol. 306, No. 8 (February 25, 1982).

Ippolito, Dennis S. *Hidden Spending: The Politics of Federal Credit Programs.* Chapel Hill: University of North Carolina Press, 1984.

———. *Uncertain Legacies: Federal Budget Policy from Roosevelt through Reagan.* Charlottesville: University Press of Virginia, 1990.

Johnson, Bruce. "From Analyst to Negotiator: The OMB's New Role." *Journal of Policy Analysis and Management,* Vol. 3, No. 4 (1984).

———. "OMB and the Budget Examiner: Changes in the Reagan Era." *Public Budgeting and Finance,* Vol. 9 (Winter 1988), pp. 3–21.

———. "The OMB Budget Examiner and the Congressional Budget Process." *Public Budgeting and Finance,* Vol. 9 (Spring 1989), pp. 5–14.

Jones, Bryan D., Frank R. Baumgartner, and James L. True, "The Shape of Change: Punctuations and Stability in United States Budgeting, 1964–1994." The Center for Presidential Studies, Texas A & M University. Working Paper #42, November 1995.

Jones, L. R. "Policy Development, Planning, and Resource Allocation in the Department of Defense." *Public Budgeting and Finance,* Vol. 11 (Fall 1991), pp. 15–27.

Jones, L. R., and Glen Bixler. *Mission Budgeting to Realign National Defense.* Greenwich, Conn.: JAI Press, 1992.

Jones, L. R., and Jerry L. McCaffery. "Federal Financial Management Reform and the Chief Financial Officers Act." *Public Budgeting and Finance,* Vol. 12 (Winter 1992), pp. 75–86.

———. "Implementation of the Federal Chief Financial Officers Act." *Public Budgeting and Finance,* Vol. 13 (Spring 1993), pp. 68–76.

Kamlet, Mark S., and David C. Mowery. "The Budgetary Base in Federal Resource Allocation." *American Journal of Political Science,* Vol. 24, No. 4 (November 1980), pp. 806–21.

———. "Budgetary Side Payments and Government Growth: 1953–1968." *American Journal of Political Science,* Vol. 27, No. 4 (November 1983), pp. 636–64.

———. "Contradictions of Congressional Budget Reform: Problem of Congressional Emulation of Executive Branch." Typescript, 1984.

———. "The First Decade of the Congressional Budget Act: Legislative Imitation and Adaptation in Budgeting." *Policy Sciences,* Vol. 18, No. 4 (December 1985), pp. 313–34.

———. "Influences on Executive and Congressional Budgetary Priorities, 1953–1981." *American Political Science Review,* Vol. 81, No. 1 (March 1987), pp. 155–73.

Kamlet, Mark S., David C. Mowery, and Tsai-Tsu Su. "Whom Do You Trust? An Analysis of Executive and Congressional Economic Forecasts." *Journal of Policy Analysis and Management,* Vol. 6, No. 3 (1987), pp. 365–84.

Kanter, Arnold. *Defense Politics.* Chicago: University of Chicago Press, 1975.

Kasten, Richard, and Frank Sammartino. "Who Pays for Federal Deficit Reduction?" Paper prepared for the Association for Public Policy Analysis and Management Conference, October 18–20, 1990.

Kaufmann, William W. *A Reasonable Defense.* Washington D.C.: The Brookings Institution, 1986.

Keith, Robert, and Edward Davis. "Congress and Continuing Appropriations: New Variations on an Old Theme." *Public Budgeting and Finance,* Vol. 5 (Spring 1985).

Kellman, Steve. "The Grace Commission: How Much Waste in Government?" *The Public Interest,* No. 78 (Winter 1985).

Kerr, L. E. "Black Lung." *Journal of Public Health Policy,* Vol. 1, No. 1 (March 1980).

Kettl, Donald. *Deficit Politics: Public Budgeting in Its Institutional Context.* New York: Macmillan, 1992.

———. "The Great Budget Debate." *VIPPSNews,* Vanderbilt Institute for Public Studies, Vol. 4, No. 2 (Summer 1990), pp. 1–2.

Key, V. O., Jr. "The Lack of a Budgetary Theory." *The American Political Science Review,* Vol. 34 (December 1940), pp. 1137–44.

Kim, Sun Kil. "The Politics of a Congressional Budgetary Process Backdoor Spending." *Western Political Quarterly,* Vol. 21 (December 1968), pp. 606–23.

Kimmel, Lewis H. *Federal Budget and Fiscal Policy 1789–1958.* Washington D.C.: The Brookings Institution, 1959.

King, Ronald. "Tax Expenditures and Systematic Public Policy." Paper presented for delivery at the Annual Meeting of the American Political Science Association, Denver, Colorado, September 2–5, 1982.

Kliman, Albert J., and Louis Fisher. "Budget Reform Proposals in the NPR Report." *Public Budgeting and Finance,* Vol. 15 (Spring 1995), pp. 27–38.

Kogan, Richard. "The Budget Enforcement Act of 1990: A Technical Explanation." November 1, 1990, unpublished.

Korb, Lawrence. "The Budget Process in the Department of Defense 1947–77: The Strengths and Weaknesses of Three Systems." *Public Administration Review,* Vol. XXXVII (July/August 1977), pp. 334–36.

———. "The Process and Problems of Linking Policy and Force Structure through the Defense Budget Process." In Robert Harkavy and Edward Kolodziej, eds. *American Security Policy and Policy Making.* Lexington, Mass.: Lexington Books, 1980.

Kolata, G. B. "NMC Thrives Selling Dialysis." *Science,* Vol. 208 (April 25, 1980).

Kristensen, Ole P. "The Logic of Bureaucratic Decision-Making as a Cause of Governmental Growth." *European Journal of Political Research,* Vol. 8 (1980), pp. 249–64.

Larkey, P. D., C. Stolp, and M. Winer. "Theorizing about the Growth of Government: A Research Assessment." *Journal of Public Policy,* Vol. 1 (1981), pp. 157–220.

Lawton, Frederick J. "Legislative-Executive Relationships in Budgeting as Viewed by the Executive." *Public Administration Review,* Vol. 13 (Summer 1953), pp. 169–76.

Lekachman, Robert. *The Age of Keynes.* New York: McGraw-Hill, 1966.

LeLoup, Lance. "Discretion in National Budgeting: Controlling the Controllables." *Policy Analysis*, Vol. 4, No. 4 (Fall 1978), 455–75.

LeLoup, Lance, Barbara Luck Graham, and Stacey Barwick. "Deficit Politics and Constitutional Government: The Impact of Gramm–Rudman–Hollings." *Public Budgeting and Finance*, Vol. 7, No. 1 (Spring 1987), pp. 83–104.

Leonard, Herman B. *Checks Unbalanced: The Quiet Side of Public Spending*. New York: Basic Books, 1986.

Levine, Charles H., and Paul L. Posner. "The Centralizing Effects of Austerity on the Intergovernmental System." *Political Quarterly*, Vol. 96 (Spring 1981), pp. 67–85.

Levine, Charles H., and Irene Rubin, eds. *Fiscal Stress and Public Policy*. Beverly Hills: Sage Publications, 1980.

Levy, Frank. *Dollars and Dreams: The Changing American Income Distribution*. New York: Russell Sage Foundation, 1987.

Lewis, Verne B. "Toward a Theory of Budgeting." *Public Administration Review*, Vol. 12 (Winter 1952), pp. 42–54.

Lindblom, Charles E. "Decision-Making in Taxation and Expenditure." In *Public Finances: Needs, Sources and Utilization, National Bureau of Economic Research*. Princeton: Princeton University Press, 1961, pp. 295–336.

———. "The Science of 'Muddling Through.'" *Public Administration Review*, Vol. XIX (Spring 1959), pp. 79–88.

Lindsay, James M. "Congress and Defense Policy: 1961 to 1986." *Armed Forces & Society*, Vol. 13, No. 3 (Spring 1987).

Maas, Arthur. "In Accord with the Program of the President?" In Carl Friedrich and Kenneth Galbraith, eds. *Public Policy*, Vol. 4. Cambridge, Mass.: Graduate School of Public Administration, 1954, pp. 77–93.

MacDonald, Maurice. *Food Stamps and Income Maintenance*. New York: Academic Press, 1977.

McGeary, M. Nelson. "The Governor's Veto in Pennsylvania." *American Political Science Review*, Vol. 41, No. 5 (October 1947).

MacMahon, Arthur. "Congressional Oversight of Administration." *Political Science Quarterly*, Vol. LVIII (June and September 1943), pp. 161–90, 380–414.

———. "Woodrow Wilson: Political Leader and Administrator." In Earl Latham, ed. *The Philosophy and Policies of Woodrow Wilson*. Chicago: University of Chicago Press, 1958, pp. 100–22.

Manley, John F. "The Conservative Coalition in Congress." *American Behavioral Scientist*, Vol. 17, No. 2 (November/December 1973), pp. 223–48.

Mansfield, Harvey C., Jr. "The American Election: Entitlements Versus Opprtunity." *Government and Opposition*, Vol. 20, No. 1 (Winter 1985), pp. 3–17.

Marvick, L. Dwaine. *Congressional Appropriation Politics*. Ph.D. Dissertation, Columbia University, 1952.

Marx, Fritz Morstein. "The Bureau of the Budget: Its Evolution and Present Role." *American Political Science Review*, Vol. 39, No. 4 (August 1945), pp. 653–84.

———. "The Bureau of the Budget: Its Evolution and Present Role, II." *American Political Science Review*, Vol. 39 (October 1945), pp. 869–98.

Mayhew, David. *Congress: The Electoral Connection*. New Haven: Yale University Press, 1974.

Meyer, Jack A. "Budget Cuts in the Reagan Administration: A Question of Fairness." In D. Lee Bauden, ed. *The Social Contract Revisited.* Washington D.C.: Urban Institute, 1984, pp. 33–64.

Meyers, Roy T. *Strategic Budgeting.* Ann Arbor: University of Michigan Press, 1994.

Miles, Jerome A. "The Congressional Budget and Impoundment Control Act: A Departmental Budget Officer's View." *The Bureaucrat,* Vol. 5, No. 4 (January 1977).

Mills, Gregory B., and John L. Palmer. *The Deficit Dilemma.* Washington D.C.: Urban Institute, 1983.

Minarik, Joseph J., and Rudolph G. Penner. "Fiscal Choices." In Isabel V. Sawhill, ed. *Challenge to Leadership.* Washington D.C.: Urban Institute, 1988.

Morey, Roy D. "The Executive Veto in Arizona: Its Use and Limitations." *The Western Political Quarterly,* Vol. 19, No. 3 (September 1966).

Mosher, Frederick C. *Program Budgeting: Theory and Practice, with Particular Reference to the U.S. Department of the Army.* Chicago: Public Administration Service, 1954.

———. *The GAO: The Quest for Accountability in American Government.* Boulder, Colo.: Westview Press, 1979.

———. *A Tale of Two Agencies: A Comparative Analysis of the General Accounting Office and the Office of Management and Budget.* Baton Rouge: Louisiana State University Press, 1984.

Mowery, David S., Mark S. Kamlet, and John P. Crecine. "Presidential Management of Budgetary and Fiscal Policymaking." *Political Science Quarterly,* Vol. 95, No. 1 (Fall 1980), pp. 395–425.

Moynihan, Daniel P. *The Politics of a Guaranteed Income.* New York: Random House, 1973.

Myers, Margaret G. *A Financial History of the United States.* New York: Columbia University Press, 1970.

Myers, Robert J. *Medicare.* Bryn Mawr, Penn.: McCahan Foundation, 1970.

Naylor, E. E. *The Federal Budget System in Operation.* Washington D.C.: Hayworth Printing, 1941.

Nelson, Dalmas H. "The Omnibus Appropriations Act of 1950." *Journal of Politics,* Vol. XV (May 1953), pp. 274–88.

Neustadt, Richard. "Presidency and Legislation: The Growth of Central Clearance. *American Political Science Review,* Vol. 48 (September 1954), pp. 641–71.

———. "Presidency and Legislation: Planning the President's Program." *American Political Science Review,* Vol. XLIX (December 1955), pp. 980–1021.

Ney, R. T. "The ESRD Medicare Program—A Clarification." *Dialysis and Transplantation,* Vol. 10, No. 3 (March 1981).

Niskanen, William A. *Bureaucracy and Representative Government.* Chicago: University of Chicago Press, 1971.

———. "Deficits, Government Spending and Inflation: What Is the Evidence?" *Journal of Monetary Economics,* Vol. 4 (August 1978), pp. 591–602.

Oak, Dale P. "An Overview of Adjustments to the Budget Enforcement Act Discretionary Spending Caps." *Public Budgeting and Finance,* Vol. 15 (Fall 1995), pp. 35–55.

Ornstein, Norman J., and Shirley Elder. "The B-1 Bomber: Organizing at the Grassroots." In Eston White, ed. *Studies in Defense.* Washington D.C.: National Defense University Press, 1983.

Palmer, John, and Stephanie Gould. "Should We Worry About the Deficit?" *The Washington Monthly* (May 1986), pp. 43–46.

Pariser, David B. "Implementing Federal Credit Reform: Challenges Facing Public Sector Financial Managers." *Public Budgeting and Finance,* Vol. 12 (Winter 1992), pp. 19–34.

Pascall, Glenn. *The Trillion Dollar Budget.* Seattle: University of Washington Press, 1985.

Payne, James L. "Voters Aren't So Greedy After All." *Fortune,* August 18, 1986, pp. 91–92.

Penner, Rudolph G. "Forecasting Budget Totals: Why Can't We Get It Right?" In Michael J. Boskin and Aaron Wildavsky, eds. *The Federal Budget: Economics and Politics.* San Francisco: Institute for Contemporary Studies, 1982, pp. 89–110.

Perloff, Harvey Stephen. *Modern Budget Policies: A Study of the Budget Process in Present-Day Society.* Ph.D. Dissertation submitted to the Departments of Government and Economics, Harvard University, December 1, 1939.

Peters, Jean. "Reconciliation 1982: What Happened?" *PS,* Vol. 14, No. 4 (Fall 1981), pp. 732–36.

Phaup, Marvin. "Accounting for Federal Credit: A Better Way." *Public Budgeting and Finance,* Vol. 5, No. 3 (Autumn 1985), pp. 29–39.

Pocock, J. G. *The Political Works of James Harrington.* Cambridge, Mass.: Cambridge University Press, 1977.

Popick, Bernard. "The Social Security Disability Program. III. The Black Lung Benefits—an Administrative Case Study." *Journal of Occupational Medicine,* Vol. 13, No. 7 (July 1971).

Potter, Jim. *The American Economy between the World Wars.* New York: Wiley, 1974.

Pristave, R. J., and J. B. Riley. "HCFA Publishes Final ESRD Prospective Reimbursement Regulations." *Dialysis and Transplantation,* Vol. 12, No. 6 (June 1983).

Ransome, Coleman B., Jr. *The American Governorship.* Westport, Conn.: Greenwood Press, 1982.

Reischauer, Robert. "Mickey Mouse or Superman? The Congressional Budget Process during the Reagan Administration." Paper presented to APPAM, Philadelphia, October 20–22, 1983.

Rettig, R. A. "The Policy Debate on Patient Care for Victims of End-Stage Renal Disease." *Law and Contemporary Problems,* Vol. 40, No. 4 (Autumn 1976).

———. "End-Stage Renal Disease and the 'Cost' of Medical Technology." *In Medical Technical Technology: The Culprit behind Health Care Costs?* U.S. DHHS, 1979.

———. "The Politics of Health Cost Containment: ESRD." *Bulletin of New York Academy of Medicine,* Vol. 56, No. 1 (January/February 1980).

Rivlin, Alice M. "The Political Economy of Budget Choices: A View from Congress." Paper presented at AEA meeting, December 29, 1981.

———. "Reform of the Budget Process." *The American Economic Review,* Vol. 74, No. 2 (May 1984), pp. 133–37.

Rovner, Mark. *Defense Dollars and Sense.* Washington D.C.: Common Cause, 1983.

Rubin, Irene S. "Budgeting for Our Times: Target Base Budgeting." *Public Budgeting and Finance,* Vol. 11 (Fall 1991), pp. 5–14.

———. *Shrinking the Federal Government: The Effect of Cutbacks on Five Federal Agencies.* New York: Longman, 1985.

Ruddock, Andrew E. "A Critique of Various Study Documents." In Dan M. McGill, ed. *Financing the Civil Service Retirement.* Homewood, Ill.: Richard D. Irwin, 1979.

Sanders, Arthur. "Public Attitudes on Public Spending." Paper prepared for the 1984 Annual Meeting of the American Political Science Association, Washington D.C., August 30–September 2, 1984.

Savage, James (ed.) "Symposium: President Clinton's Budget and Fiscal Policy: An Evaluation Two Budgets Later." *Public Budgeting and Finance*, Vol. 14 (Fall 1994), pp. 3–40.

———. "Deficits and the Economy: The Case of the Clinton Administration and Interest Rates." In Naomi Caiden and Joseph White, eds. *Budgeting, Policy, Politics: An Appreciation of Aaron Wildavsky.* New Brunswick, N.J.: Transaction Publishers, 1995, pp. 93–110.

Shanks, J. Merrill, and Warren Miller. "Policy Direction and Performance Evaluation: Complementary Explanations of the Reagan Elections." Presented to the Annual Meeting of the American Political Science Association, New Orleans, August 29–September 1, 1985.

Schelling, Thomas C. *The Strategy of Conflict.* Cambridge: Harvard University Press, 1960.

Schick, Allen. *The Federal Budget: Politics, Policy, Process.* Washington, D.C.: Brookings Institution, 1995.

———. *Making Economic Policy in Congress.* Washington, D.C.: American Enterprise Institute, 1983.

———. "The Road to PPB: The Stages of Budget Reform." In *Public Administration Review*, December 1966, pp. 243–58.

———. "The Budget Bureau That Was: Thoughts on the Rise, Decline, and Future of a Presidential Agency." *Law and Contemporary Problems*, Vol. XXXV (Summer 1970), pp. 519–39.

———. "Budgetary Adaptations to Resource Scarcity." In Charles H. Levine and Irene Rubin, eds. *Fiscal Stress and Public Policy.* Beverly Hills: Sage Publications, 1980.

———. *Congress and Money.* Washington D.C.: Urban Institute, 1980.

———, ed. *Perspectives on Budgeting.* American Society for Public Administration, 1980.

———. "Controlling the Budget by Statute: An Imperfect but Workable Process." In Alvin Rabushka and William Craig Stubblebine, eds. *Constraining Federal Taxing and Spending.* Stanford, Calif.: Hoover Institution, 1982.

———. "Controlling the 'Uncontrollables': Budgeting for Health Care in an Age of Mega-Deficits." Paper prepared for AEI Pew Fellows Conference, November 1985.

———. "The Evolution of Congressional Budgeting." In Allen Schick, ed. *Crisis in the Budget Process.* Washington D.C.: American Enterprise Institute, 1986.

———. "From the Old Politics of Budgeting to the New." In Naomi Caiden and Joseph White, eds., *Budgeting, Policy, Politics: An Appreciation of Aaron Wildavsky.* New Brunswick, N.J.: Transaction Publishers, 1995, pp. 133–42.

———. *The Capacity to Budget.* Washington D.C.: Urban Institute, 1990.

Schier, Steven E. "Thinking about the Macroeconomy: The House and Senate Budget Committees in the 1980s." Paper presented for 1985 Annual Meeting of APSA, New Orleans, August 29–September 1, 1985.

Shultz, George P., and Kenneth W. Dam. *Economic Policy beyond the Headlines.* New York: W. W. Norton and Co., 1977.

Shultz, William J., and M. R. Caine. *Financial Development of the United States.* New York: Prentice-Hall, 1937.

Seligman, Edwin R. A. *The Income Tax.* New York: Macmillan, 1921.

Simon, Herbert A. "The Criterion of Efficiency." *In Administrative Behavior,* 2nd ed. New York, Macmillan, 1957.

——. *Models of Man.* New York: Wiley, 1957.

Simon, Herbert A., Donald Smithburg, and Victor Thompson. "The Struggle for Existence." *In Public Administration.* New York: Knopf, 1950, pp. 381–422.

Smithies, Arthur. *The Budgetary Process in the United States.* New York: McGraw-Hill, 1955.

Stein, Herbert. *The Fiscal Revolution in America.* Chicago: University of Chicago Press, 1969.

Stewart, Charles Haines, III. *The Politics of Structural Reform: Reforming Budgetary Structure in the House, 1865–1921.* Dissertation submitted to Stanford University, August 1985.

Stockman, David. "The Social Pork Barrel." *The Public Interest,* No. 39 (Spring 1975), pp. 3–30.

——. *The Triumph of Politics.* New York: Harper & Row, 1986.

Stone, Deborah. *The Disabled State.* Philadelphia: Temple University Press, 1984.

Straussman, Jeffrey D. "Spending More and Enjoying It Less." *Comparative Politics,* January 1981, pp. 235–51.

Tarschys, Daniel L. "The Growth of Public Expenditures: Nine Modes of Explanation." *Scandinavian Political Studies.* Vol. 10 (1975), pp. 9–31.

——. "Curbing Public Expenditures: Current Trends." *Journal of Public Policy,* Vol. 5 (1985), pp. 23–67.

Thompson, Fred, and L. R. Jones. *Reinventing the Pentagon: How the New Public Management Can Bring Institutional Renewal.* San Francisco: Jossey Bass, 1994.

Thompson, James D., and Arthur Tuden. "Strategies, Structures, and Processes of Organizational Decision." In J. D. Thompson, et al., eds. *Comparative Studies in Administration.* Pittsburgh: University of Pittsburgh Press, 1959.

Tobin, James. "The Future of Social Security: One Economist's Assessment." Working Paper #4, Project on the Federal Social Role, National Conference on Social Welfare, Washington D.C., 1985.

Tomer, John F. "Revenue Sharing and the Intrastate Fiscal Mismatch." *Public Finance Quarterly,* Vol. 5 (October 1977).

Van Gunsteren, Herman R. *The Quest for Control.* New York: Wiley, 1976.

Verba, Sidney, and Gary R. Orren. *Equality in America: The View from the Top.* Cambridge, Mass.: Harvard University Press, 1985.

Waldo, Dwight. *The Administrative State.* New York: Ronald Press, 1948.

Walker, Robert. "William A. Jump: The Staff Officer as a Personality." *Public Administration Review,* Vol. XIV (Autumn 1954), pp. 233–46.

Walker, Wallace Earl. *Changing Organizational Culture: Strategy, Structure, and Professionalism in the U.S. General Accounting Office.* Knoxville, University of Tennessee Press, 1986.

Weaver, R. Kent. "Controlling Entitlements." In John E. Chubb and Paul E. Peterson, eds. *The New Direction in American Politics.* Washington D.C.: The Brookings Institution, 1985.

Webber, Carolyn, and Aaron Wildavsky. *A History of Taxation and Expenditure in the Western World.* New York: Simon and Schuster, 1986.

Weicher, John C. *Entitlement Issues in the Domestic Budget.* Washington, D.C.: American Enterprise Institute, 1985.

White, Joseph. "(Almost) Nothing New Under the Sun: Why the Work of Budgeting Remains Incremental." In Naomi Caiden and Joseph White, eds. *Budgeting, Policy, Politics: An Appreciation of Aaron Wildavsky.* New Brunswick, N.J.: Transaction Publishers, 1995, pp. 111–32.

———. "What Budgeting Cannot Do: Lessons of Reagan's and Other Years." In Irene Rubin, ed. *New Directions in Budget Theory.* Albany: SUNY Press, 1988, pp. 165–202.

———. "Better News Than They Think." *San Diego Union,* October 7, 1990.

White, Joseph, and Aaron Wildavsky. *The Deficit and the Public Interest.* Berkeley: University of California Press, 1990.

———. "How to Fix the Deficit—Really." *The Public Interest,* No. 94 (Winter 1989), pp. 3–24.

White, Leonard D. *The Jeffersonians: A Study in Administration History, 1801–1829.* New York: Macmillan, 1951.

———. *The Jacksonians: A Study in Administrative History, 1829–1861.* New York: Macmillan, 1954.

———. *The Federalists: A Study in Administrative History.* New York: Macmillan, 1961.

Wildavsky, Aaron. *Dixon–Yates: A Study in Power Politics.* New Haven: Yale University Press, 1962.

———. *The Politics of the Budgetary Process.* Boston: Little, Brown, 1964; revised 4th ed., 1984.

———. "The Political Economy of Efficiency: Cost-Benefit Analysis, Systems Analysis, and Program Budgeting." *Public Administration Review,* Vol. 26, No. 4 (December 1966), pp. 292–310.

———. "Rescuing Policy Analysis from PPBS." *Public Administration Review,* Vol. 29, No. 2 (March/April 1969), pp. 189–202.

———. *The Budgeting and Evaluation of Federal Recreation Programs, or Money Doesn't Grow on Trees.* With Jeanne Nienaber. New York: Basic Books, 1973.

———. *Budgeting: A Comparative Theory of Budgetary Processes.* Boston: Little, Brown, 1975; revised 2nd ed., Transaction Publishers, 1986.

———. "Doing Better and Feeling Worse: The Political Pathology of Health Policy." *Daedalus,* Winter 1976, pp. 105–23.

———. "Ask Not What Budgeting Does to Society but What Society Does to Budgeting." Introduction to the second edition of *National Journal Reprints.* Washington D.C., 1977.

———. "A Budget for All Seasons? Why the Traditional Budget Lasts." *The Public Administration Review,* No. 6 (November/December 1978), pp. 501–509. Also in B. Geist, ed. *State Audit: Developments in Public Accountability.* London & Bassingstoke: Macmillan, 1981, pp. 253–68.

———. *Speaking Truth to Power.* Boston: Little, Brown, 1979.

———. *How to Limit Government Spending.* Los Angeles and Berkeley: University of California Press, 1980.

———. "Budgets as Compromises among Social Orders." In Michael J. Boskin and Aaron Wildavsky, eds. *The Federal Budget: Economics and Politics.* San Francisco, 1982, pp. 21–38.

————. "Modelling the U.S. Federal Spending Process: Overview and Implications." With Michael Dempster. In R. C. O. Matthews and G. B. Stafford, eds. *The Grants Economy and Collective Consumption.* London & Basingstoke: Macmillan, 1983, pp. 267–309.

————. "The Transformation of Budgetary Norms." *Australian Journal of Public Administration,* Vol. XLII, No. 4 (December 1983), pp. 421–32.

————. "The Unanticipated Consequences of the 1984 Presidential Election." *Tax Notes,* Vol. 24, No. 2 (July 9, 1984), pp. 193–200.

————. "Budgets as Social Orders." *Research in Urban Policy,* Vol. 1 (1985), pp. 183–97.

————. "A Cultural Theory of Expenditure Growth and (Un)Balanced Budgets." *Journal of Public Economics,* Vol. 28 (1985), pp. 349–57.

————. "Item Veto without a Global Spending Limit: Locking the Treasury after the Dollars Have Fled." *Notre Dame Journal of Law, Ethics and Public Policy,* Vol. 1, No. 2 (1985), pp. 165–76.

————. "The Logic of Public Sector Growth." In Jan-Erik Lane, ed. *State and Market.* London: Sage Publications, Ltd., 1985, pp. 231–70.

Willoughby, William Franklin. *The National Budget System with Suggestions for Its Improvement.* Baltimore: Johns Hopkins, 1927.

Wilmerding, Lucius W., Jr. *The Spending Power: A History of the Efforts of Congress to Control Expenditures.* New Haven: Yale University Press, 1943.

Wilson, Woodrow. *Congressional Government: A Study in American Politics.* Boston: Houghton Mifflin, 1895.

Witte, John F. "Tax Philosophy and Income Equality." In Robert A. Solo and Charles Anderson, eds. *Value Judgment and Income Distribution.* New York: Praeger, 1981, pp. 340–78.

————. *The Politics and Development of the Federal Income Tax.* Madison: University of Wisconsin Press, 1985.

Wolf, John F. "The Item Veto in the American Constitutional System." *Georgetown Law Journal,* Vol. 25 (1936).

Young, James Sterling. *The Washington Community, 1802–1828.* New York: Columbia University Press, 1966.

Credits

Index